The Anthropology of Globalization

Blackwell Readers in Anthropology

As anthropology moves beyond the limits of so-called area studies, there is an increasing need for texts that do the work of synthesizing the literature while challenging more traditional or subdisciplinary approaches to anthropology. This is the object of this exciting new series, *Blackwell Readers in Anthropology*.

Each volume in the series offers seminal readings on a chosen theme and provides the finest, most thought-provoking recent works in the given thematic area. Many of these volumes bring together for the first time a body of literature on a certain topic. The series thus both presents definitive collections and investigates the very ways in which anthropological inquiry has evolved and is evolving.

The Anthropology of Globalization

A Reader

Edited by

Jonathan Xavier Inda and Renato Rosaldo

Blackwell
Publishing

© 2002 by Blackwell Publishing Ltd

BLACKWELL PUBLISHING
350 Main Street, Malden, MA 02148-5020, USA
9600 Garsington Road, Oxford OX4 2DQ, UK
550 Swanston Street, Carlton, Victoria 3053, Australia

First published 2002 by Blackwell Publishing Ltd

7   2006

Library of Congress Cataloging-in-Publication Data

The anthropology of globalization: a reader/edited by Jonathan Xavier Inda and Renato Rosaldo.
     p. cm.—(Blackwell readers in anthropology; 1)
  ISBN 0-631-22232-4 (alk. paper) — ISBN 0-631-22233-2 (alk. paper)
  1. Anthropology. 2. Globalization. I. Inda, Jonathan Xavier. II. Rosaldo, Renato.
  III. Series.

GN27 .A673 2001
306—dc21   2001025966

ISBN-13: 978-0-631-22232-3 (hardback); ISBN-13: 978-0-631-22233-0 (paperback)

A catalogue record for this title is available from the British Library.

Set in 10 on 12 pt Sabon
by Kolam Information Services Pvt. Ltd, Pondicherry, India.
Printed and bound in the United Kingdom
by TJ International Ltd, Padstow, Cornwall

The publisher's policy is to use permanent paper from mills that operate a sustainable forestry policy, and which has been manufactured from pulp processed using acid-free and elementary chlorine-free practices. Furthermore, the publisher ensures that the text paper and cover board used have met acceptable environmental accreditation standards.

For further information on
Blackwell Publishing, visit our website:
www.blackwellpublishing.com

Contents

Contributors

Lila Abu-Lughod is Professor of Anthropology and Women's Studies at Columbia University.

Vincanne Adams is Associate Professor of Anthropology, History, and Social Medicine at the University of California, San Francisco.

Arjun Appadurai is Samuel N. Harper Professor of Anthropology and of South Asian Languages and Civilization at the University of Chicago.

Donald L. Donham is Professor of Anthropology at Emory University.

James Ferguson is Professor of Anthropology at the University of California, Irvine.

Carla Freeman is Assistant Professor of Anthropology and Women's Studies at Emory University.

Jonathan Friedman is Professor of Social Anthropology at the University of Lund, Sweden.

Joan Gross is Associate Professor of Anthropology at Oregon State University.

Akhil Gupta is Associate Professor of Cultural and Social Anthropology at Stanford University.

Ulf Hannerz is Professor of Social Anthropology at Stockholm University, Sweden.

Jonathan Xavier Inda is Assistant Professor of Chicano Studies at the University of California, Santa Barbara.

Brian Larkin is Assistant Professor of Anthropology at Barnard College.

Bill Maurer is Associate Professor of Anthropology at the University of California, Irvine.

David McMurray is Assistant Professor of Anthropology at Oregon State University.

Birgit Meyer is a senior lecturer at the Research Center "Religion and Society" at the University of Amsterdam.

Eric Michaels was an ethnographer and a theorist of visual arts, media, and broadcasting. He was a lecturer in media studies at Griffith University in Brisbane at the time of his death in 1988.

Aihwa Ong is Professor of Anthropology at the University of California, Berkeley.

Renato Rosaldo is Lucie Stern Professor in the Social Sciences at Stanford University.

Roger Rouse is Assistant Professor of Anthropology at the University of California, Davis.

Nancy Scheper-Hughes is Professor of Anthropology at the University of California, Berkeley.

Ted Swedenburg is Associate Professor of Anthropology at the University of Arkansas.

Anna Tsing is Professor of Anthropology at the University of California, Santa Cruz.

Mayfair Mei-hui Yang is Professor of Anthropology at the University of California, Santa Barbara.

Acknowledgments

We owe special thanks to Leo Chavez, Eve Darian-Smith, Jim Ferguson, Richard Flores, Bill Maurer, Aihwa Ong, Roger Rouse, and Kay B. Warren for their wonderful suggestions and helpful insights. We are also deeply grateful to our editor at Blackwell, Jane Huber, for her enthusiastic support of this project. Furthermore, we wish to express our appreciation to the authors whose work is included in this volume for their contributions to developing the anthropology of globalization. Finally, Jonathan would like to thank the Rockefeller Foundation and the Institute for Social, Behavioral, and Economic Research (ISBER) at UC Santa Barbara for funding this project; the faculty, staff, and students at UC San Diego's Center for the Study of Race and Ethnicity for their hospitality; and his research assistants, Arthur Elizarov and Michelle Madsen Camacho, for their help in preparing the manuscript. And Renato wishes to thank Mary Louise Pratt and his colleagues in the Department of Cultural and Social Anthropology at Stanford for their support.

2000 American Anthropological Association; Anna Tsing, "The Global Situation," *Cultural Anthropology* 15(3), Copyright © 2000 American Anthropological Association.

Africa 67(3) 1997, for Brian Larkin, "Indian Films and Nigerian Lovers: Media and the Creation of Parallel Modernities."

BLACKWELL PUBLISHERS, for Birgit Meyer, "Commodities and the Power of Prayer," *Development and Change* 29(4) 1998, Copyright © Institute of Social Studies.

Diaspora 1(1) Spring 1991, for Roger Rouse, "Mexican Migration and the Social Space of Postmodernism."

DUKE UNIVERSITY PRESS, for Ulf Hannerz, "Notes on the Global Ecumene," in *Public Culture* 1(2) Spring 1989, Copyright © 1989; Joan Gross, David McMurray, and Ted Swedenburg, "Arab Noise and Ramadan Nights: *Rai*, Rap and Franco-Maghrebi Identities," in *Displacement, Diaspora and Geographies of Identity*, ed. Smadar Lavie and Ted Swedenburg, Copyright © 1996 Duke University Press; Akhil Gupta and James Ferguson, "Beyond 'Culture': Space, Identity, and the Politics of Difference," in *Culture, Power, Place: Explorations in Critical Anthropology*, ed. Akhil Gupta and James Ferguson, Copyright © 1997 Duke University Press; Aihwa Ong, "The Pacific Shuttle: Family, Citizenship, and Capital Circuits," in *Flexible Citizenship: The Cultural Logics of Transnationality*, Copyright © 1999 Duke University Press.

PRINCETON UNIVERSITY PRESS, for Lila Abu-Lughod, "The Marriage of Feminism and Islamism in Egypt," in *Remaking Women: Feminism and Modernity in the Middle East*, ed. Lila Abu-Lughod, Princeton University Press, 1998.

SAGE PUBLICATIONS, for Jonathan Friedman, "Globalization and Localization," in *Cultural Identity and Global Process*, Sage Publications, 1994.

TAYLOR & FRANCIS, for Mayfair Mei-hui Yang, "Mass Media and Transnational Subjectivity in Shanghai," in *Ungrounded Empires: The Cultural Politics of Modern Chinese Transnationalism*, ed. Aihwa Ong and Donald M. Nonini, New York: Routledge, 1997.

UNIVERSITY OF CALIFORNIA PRESS, for James Ferguson, *Expectations of Modernity: Myths and Meanings of Urban Life on the Zambian Copperbelt*, Copyright © 1999 The Regents of the University of California.

UNIVERSITY OF CHICAGO PRESS, for Nancy Scheper-Hughes, "The Global Traffic in Human Organs," *Current Anthropology* 41(2) 2000.

UNIVERSITY OF MINNESOTA PRESS, for Eric Michaels, "Hollywood Iconography: A Warlpiri Reading," in *Bad Aboriginal Art: Tradition, Media and*

Technological Horizons, University of Minnesota Press, 1994; Arjun Appadurai, "Disjuncture and Difference in the Global Cultural Economy," in *Modernity at Large: Cultural Dimensions of Globalization*, University of Minnesota Press, 1996.

Introduction

A World in Motion

Jonathan Xavier Inda and Renato Rosaldo

Consider the following five snapshots.[1]

Snapshot One: In Barbados, on the data-entry floor of the Data Air off-shore information processing facility, more than 100 women sit at clustered computer stations, entering data from some 300,000 ticket stubs from one airline's 2,000 daily flights. One floor below, an equal number of women work as "approvers," entering data from medical claims sent for processing by one of the largest insurance companies in the United States. Their fingers fly and the frenetic clicking of keys fills a vast and chilly room as Walkman-clad women work eight-hour shifts at video display terminals, typing to the latest dub, calypso, or easy-listening station.

Snapshot Two: In France, North African women are gathered for a wedding in an Avignon *banlieue*. Most of the women are sitting on low cushions along the wall at one end of the rented room. Older women are decked out in long, empire-waisted, shiny polyester Algerian dresses and gold marriage belts. Some younger ones are similarly clad in "traditional" outfits, while others are sporting slacks or miniskirts plus accessories like geometric earrings or necklaces hung with miniature pastel-colored pacifiers. Some women flew in from Algeria especially for the wedding, while others traveled north from Marseilles or south from St. Etienne. *Rai* provides much of the sound track for the wedding festivities.

Snapshot Three: In Ghana, a fervent pentecostalist preacher warns the members of his church about the dangers imbued in western commodities.[2] He tells them of the following experience. One day he, the preacher, bought a pair of underpants at the local market. The day he started wearing them he began having sexual dreams in which he had intercourse with beautiful ladies, although in daily life he was alone. Only after some time did he realize that the underpants had caused the dreams; having thrown them away, he slept undisturbed by seductive women. The preacher concludes his story by offering a remedy to neutralize the danger inherent in goods: prayer. Only through prayer is it possible to prevent an object's destructive powers from damaging its owner's life.

Snapshot Four: Meanwhile, in northern Nigeria the sight of a 15 foot image of Sridevi, dancing erotically on the screens of the open-air cinemas, or the tall, angular figure of Amitabh Bachchan radiating charisma through the snowy, crackly reception of domestic television, have become powerful, resonant images in Hausa popular culture. Stickers of Indian films and stars decorate the taxis and buses of the north, posters of Indian films adorn the walls of tailors' shops and mechanics' garages, and love songs from Indian film songs are borrowed by religious singers who change the words to sing praises to the Prophet Mohammed.

Snapshot Five: And in Egypt, many secularist liberals, progressives, and "feminists" fear that women's rights are now under threat. They see signs of this in the growing popularity in the last two decades of the new forms of dress called Islamic or modest dress and the adoption in particular of the form of head covering called the *hijab*. The latter was institutionalized in the reversion to more conservative personal status laws and publicized in calls made in parliament, mosques, and the media for women's return to the home and their "traditional," "non-westernized" roles.

We begin with these snapshots because, at a general level, they illustrate nicely what is now commonly known, not least in anthropological circles, as globalization. This term refers (simply for now) to the intensification of global interconnectedness, suggesting a world full of movement and mixture, contact and linkages, and persistent cultural interaction and exchange. It speaks, in other words, to the complex mobilities and interconnections that characterize the globe today. The general picture these snapshots conjure is thus of an increasingly interconnected world. It is of a world where borders and boundaries have become increasingly porous, allowing more and more peoples and cultures to be cast into intense and immediate contact with each other.

We also commence with these snapshots because, at a more specific level, each highlights a particular mobility or cultural flow – respectively, of capital, people, commodities, images, and ideologies – through which the spaces of the globe are becoming increasingly intertwined. Take, for example, the case of Barbados. The scene of women deftly typing in the "open air" office of Data Air illustrates how, as technologies of communication and transportation have made capital more and more mobile, the search to reduce the costs of production has led corporations farther and farther afield, resulting in a rapid shift of labor-intensive industrial production and service work from the United States, Japan, and western Europe to new and highly dispersed low-wage sites around the globe. Places such as Barbados have thus become nodes in the rapidly developing and ever-densening network of capital interconnections that epitomize the modern world.

Or take the case of France. The women in the Avignon *banlieue* represent the extensive post-World War II movement of populations from the less affluent parts of the globe into the major urban centers of the "developed" and "developing" nations; the result being that peoples and cultures formerly located in different parts of the world now find themselves inhabiting the same physical terrains, and the spaces of the "West" find themselves homes to a host of diverse and sometimes incommensurable cultures. This intensification of global mobility and interconnectedness has turned places such as France into spaces of juxtaposition and mixture, spaces where disparate cultures converge, collide, and grapple with each other, often in conditions of radical inequality.

Or the case of Ghana. Here the preacher's exhortations about the dangers of western (predominantly North American, western European) commodities highlight the ambivalence of Ghanaians, and indeed of people around the world, to the increasing global standardization of cultural goods, tastes, and practices. From clothes, food, and music to architecture, film, and television, there is no denying that certain (western) styles and brands – Coca-Cola, McDonalds, Calvin Klein, Microsoft, Levis, Nike – have achieved global prominence, so much prominence, in fact, that they can be found practically anywhere in the world. As this flow of commodities continues apace, as it keeps accelerating across the globe, the cultural lines that connect the world become ever more dense and mass consumption increasingly becomes a primary mediator in the "encounter" between peoples and cultures from around the planet.

Then there is Nigeria. The popularity of Indian film here accentuates the increasing importance of the media in allowing Hausa viewers to partake, as they go about their everyday lives, in the imagined realities of other cultures. More specifically, the snapshot shows the way Indian films participate in the dialogic construction of Hausa popular culture, for they offer Hausa men and women an alternative world, not altogether unlike their own, from which they may envision new forms of fashion, beauty, love, and romance. Indian films thus present Hausa (and other non-western) viewers with a means of creatively engaging with forms of tradition different from their own but which do not emanate from the West, in effect highlighting how the circulation of media within and between non-western countries has become an increasingly important aspect of global cultural flows.

And finally Egypt. The fear expressed by secularist liberals about the fate of women's rights hints at the troubled relationship between feminism and cultural nationalism: a relationship in which "the woman question" excites political and ideological struggles framed in terms of cultural authenticity versus foreign influence. There is thus an important tension in Egypt (and elsewhere) about the proper role of women in society. It is a tension between those who seek to place women's emancipation, however defined, at the center of the formation of the nation and those who would call into question such a project as an alien western imposition. This snapshot can therefore be seen as an instance of the global circulation of western ideologies – most often made up of elements of the Enlightenment worldview such as freedom, welfare, rights, democracy, and sovereignty – and of the cultural interconnections and tensions that result as these ideologies are localized in various places around the world.

We begin with these pictures, then, because they provide us with a nice panoramic view of the world of globalization. It is a world of motion, of complex interconnections. Here capital traverses frontiers almost effortlessly, drawing more and more places into dense networks of financial interconnections; people readily (although certainly not freely and without difficulty) cut across national boundaries, turning countless territories into spaces where various cultures converge, clash, and struggle with each other; commodities drift briskly from one locality to another, becoming primary mediators in the encounter between culturally distant others; images flicker quickly from screen to screen, providing people with resources from which to fashion new ways of being in the world; and ideologies circulate rapidly through ever-expanding circuits, furnishing fodder for struggles couched in terms of cultural authenticity versus foreign influence. The pictures thus describe a world in which a myriad of processes, operating on a global scale, ceaselessly cut across national boundaries, integrating and connecting cultures and communities in new space-time combinations, and "making the world in reality and in experience more inter-connected" (Hall 1996: 619).[3] They speak of an intensely interconnected world – one where the rapid flows of capital, people, goods, images, and ideologies draw more and more of the globe into webs of interconnection, compressing our sense of time and space, and making the world feel smaller and distances shorter. This is the world of globalization.[4]

A few words of caution, however. There is no doubt that the world as a whole is experientially shrinking. Twentieth-century innovations in technology – particularly in transportation and communication – have made it easier and quicker for people and things to get around. It is not necessarily the case, though, that the world is shrinking for everyone and in all places (Allen and Hamnett 1995). The experience of globalization is a rather uneven process. For instance, while some people may possess the political and economic resources to trot across the world, many more have little or no access to transport and means of communication: the price of an airplane ticket or a phone call is just too high for them. And more generally, there are large expanses of the planet only tangentially tied into the webs of interconnection that encompass the globe. According to John Allen and Chris Hamnett, for example, whole areas of Africa "are quite literally off all kinds of maps – maps of telecommunications, maps of world trade and finance, maps of global tourism and the like" (1995: 2).[5] Such places thus have few circuits connecting them to anywhere, only routes of communication and transportation that pass over or through them. The point here, then, is that while the world may be full of complex mobilities and interconnections, there are also quite a number of people and places whose experience is marginal to or excluded from these movements and links. Indeed, not everyone and everyplace participates equally in the circuits of interconnection that traverse the globe. And this, too, is the world of globalization.

The purpose of this reader is to provide an introduction to this world of globalization, to this world of complex mobilities and (uneven) interconnections.[6] More specifically, it offers an anthropological take on such a world. The book is an exercise in the anthropology of globalization.[7] Of course, anthropologists are not the only ones interested in this issue. Since the late 1980s or so, globalization has become one of the most important academic topics. It is thus a central concern of quite a number of disciplines, from sociology and economics to media and literary studies. Anthropology, however, brings a unique perspective to bear on the topic. The tendency of much of the literature on globalization is to focus on the macro scope of the phenomenon, thinking of it principally in terms of very large-scale economic, political, or cultural processes. Anthropology, on the other hand, is most concerned with the articulation of the global and the local, that is, with how globalizing processes exist in the context of, and must come to terms with, the realities of particular societies, with their accumulated – that is to say historical – cultures and ways of life.[8] The anthropology of globalization, in other words, is concerned with the situated and conjunctural nature of globalization. It is preoccupied not just with mapping the shape taken by the particular flows of capital, people, goods, images, and ideologies that crisscross the globe, but also with the experiences of people living in specific localities when more and more of their everyday lives are contingent on globally extensive social processes (Foster 1999).[9] What anthropology offers that is often lacking in other disciplines is a concrete attentiveness to human agency, to the practices of everyday life, in short, to how subjects mediate the processes of globalization (Povinelli and Chauncey 1999). Thus to provide an anthropological introduction to globalization is to focus at once on the large-scale processes (or flows of subjects and objects) through which the world is becoming increasingly interconnected and on how subjects respond to these processes in culturally specific ways. This is precisely what this book does. The articles offered here map the world of globalization in a way that highlights human agency and imagination. They are a selection of the best critical anthropological work produced on globalization since the late 1980s or so. It is work that has both created and developed the anthropology of globalization.[10] The book therefore furnishes a blend of new writing and old, of the latest "cutting-edge" material and the best pioneering work.

In the rest of this introductory chapter, we present a more comprehensive view of globalization than offered above. First, we provide a more elaborate definition of globalization. We suggest that the term implies something more radical about the world than the mere fact of increasing global interconnectedness: it points to a basic reorganization of time and space. Given this more extensive definition, we then consider the cultural dynamics of globalization. This is the realm of global activity that has attracted the most anthropological attention. In the last section, we provide a brief overview of the reader and point to some of its limitations.

The Spaces and Times of Globalization

Earlier we defined "globalization" rather simply as the intensification of global interconnectedness. To be sure, this is in large part what globalization is all about. The world today is witnessing an intensification of circuits of economic, political, cultural, and ecological interdependence. This is a world in which the radical acceleration in the flows of capital, people, goods, images, and ideologies – subjects and objects, in short – across the face of the globe has brought even the most remote parts of the world in contact with metropolitan centers. However, globalization suggests something much more profound about the modern world than the simple fact of growing global interconnectedness. It implies a fundamental reordering of time and space. We would like to offer, then, a more theoretical take on globalization, one that draws from the work of the two authors who have best captured this profound reorganization of time and space: David Harvey and Anthony Giddens.[11]

Speeding it up

David Harvey (1989) conceptualizes globalization principally as a manifestation of the changing experience of time and space. He captures this change in the notion of "time-space compression," which refers to the manner in which the speeding up of economic and social processes has experientially shrunk the globe, so that distance and time no longer appear to be major constraints on the organization of human activity. In other words, the term points to how the pressures of technological and economic change have continually collapsed time and space, resulting in the anni-hilation of space by time: in the reorganization of time in such a way as to overcome the barriers of space. (one brief example of this collapse is the fact that, it is now possible for folks in London to experience the same thing, say a media event or a business transaction, at the same time as people in Thailand (Waters 1995).) For Harvey, then, globalization involves the "shrinking" of space and the shortening of time. It entails the speeding up of the pace of life, such that the time taken to do things, as well as the experiential distance between different locations in space, becomes progressively shorter. For him, in sum, globalization is intimately linked with the intensification and speeding up of time-space compression in economic and social life.

This process of time-space compression (and hence of globalization), Harvey argues, is not a gradual or continuous occurrence. Rather, it takes place in discrete phases of short and concentrated bursts. The world at any particular moment is not the product of a smooth linear compression of time and space, but the result of a more discontinuous historical unfolding. These eruptions of time-space compres-sion, Harvey notes, can be attributed to the periodic crises of overaccumulation that plague the capitalist system. Today's world, for instance, is in just such a phase, one that started during the early 1970s (Harvey 1989: 141–72). It began with a crisis of overaccumulation in the Fordist system of mass production of western economies. This system, based on Henry Ford's model of centralized mass-assembly production of standardized products, had become so successful and efficient that it began to overproduce, resulting in the massive lay-off of workers, and effectively reducing demand for products. Consumer markets thus became completely saturated. And since there were not enough consumers to buy these goods, corporate profits began to decline, which in turn precipitated a fall in government revenues. This meant the onset of fiscal problems for governments, who consequently found it increasingly difficult to sustain their commitment to their welfare programs. They attempted to solve the problem primarily by printing extra money, but this only set in motion a wave of uncontrollable inflation. This crisis jarred the Fordist system to such a degree that the model of mass production (which entailed rigid arrangements between the state, capitalists, and workers to maintain high levels of employment, investment, and consumption) became unraveled.

In its place, there has emerged a post-Fordist regime of flexible accumulation. This regime, according to Harvey, "rests on flexibility with respect to labor processes, labor markets, products, and patterns of consumption. It is characterized by the emergence of entirely new sectors of production, new ways of providing financial services, new markets, and, above all, greatly intensified rates of commercial, technological, and organizational innovation" (1989: 147). For example, labor markets have become flexible through the introduction of new forms of labor regulation – outsourcing, subcontracting, putting-out and "home work" strategies – and the hiring of large numbers of temporary, part-time, and seasonal workers; production arrangements have become malleable owing to a shift away from rigid centralized firms oriented towards mass production to small, decentralized firms oriented towards niche markets; and capital has become less anchored as a result of the deregulation of the global financial market. This flexibility is aimed at reducing the turnover time of capital: the amount of time necessary for money furnished to fund new production to be recovered with a profit through the sale of services and goods. In other words, the goal is to speed up the process of both production and consumption, for, as the old capitalist adage says, time is money, or rather time costs money. Thus one finds that practices such subcontracting and outsourcing, as well as other organizational shifts, coupled with new technologies of electronic control, have all decreased turnover times in many domains of production (e.g., clothing, electronics, automobiles, machine tools, and construction). Moreover, improved modes of communication and information, together with rationalizations in methods of distribution (e.g., inventory control, packaging, and market feedback), have made it possible for commodities to move around through the market system at a faster pace; twenty-four-hour-a-day financial services and markets have increased the mobility of capital; and the mobilization of fashion in niche markets has facilitated a speed-up in the pace of consumption in clothing, ornaments, and across a wide range of recreational activities and life-styles (e.g., pop music styles, leisure and sporting habits, and video and children's games). In this post-Fordist phase of capitalism, the regime of flexible accumulation reigns – whether in the realm of high finance, production systems, consumption, or labor markets – and the pace of economic and social life has generally accelerated.

The main implication of all this is that, for Harvey, we are currently caught in a particularly intense moment of time-space compression. The general speed-up in the turnover time of capital is rapidly shrinking the world. Time is quickly annihilating space. He puts this in the following terms:

The satellite communications systems deployed since the early 1970s have rendered the unit cost and time of communication invariant with respect to distance. It costs the same to communicate over 500 miles as it does over 5,000 via satellite. Air freight rates on commodities have likewise come down dramatically, while containerization has reduced the cost of bulk sea and road transport. It is now possible for a large multinational corporation like Texas Instruments to operate plants with simultaneous decision-making with respect to financial, market, input costs, quality control, and labor process conditions in more than fifty different locations across the globe. Mass television ownership coupled with satellite communication makes it possible to experience a rush of images from different spaces almost simultaneously, collapsing the world's spaces into a series of images on a television screen. The whole world can watch the Olympic Games, the World Cup, the fall of a dictator, a political summit, a deadly tragedy... while mass tourism, films made in spectacular locations, make a wide range of simulated or vicarious experiences of what the world contains available to many people. (Harvey 1989: 293)

The world today, in other words, is subject to the concurrent implosion of space and the speed-up of all facets of economic and social life. Yes, space is shrinking. The pace of life is speeding up. The time taken to do things is becoming progressively shorter. The world, in short, is witnessing the intensification of the compression of time and space. And so, as the world appears to shrink and distances seemingly diminish, as happenings in one place come to impact instantaneously on people and places miles away, "we have to learn how to cope with an overwhelming sense of *compression* of our spatial and temporal worlds" (Harvey 1989: 240; emphasis in original).

Stretching it out

Anthony Giddens, like Harvey, considers globalization to involve a profound reorganization of time and space in social and cultural life. However, while Harvey focuses on the general speed-up of economic and social processes, Giddens is more preoccupied with the stretching of social life across time and space. Giddens captures this preoccupation in the notion of "time-space distanciation," which refers to "the conditions under which time and space are organized so as to connect presence and absence" (1990: 14). The basic argument is that social life consists of two basic kinds of social interaction. The first entails face-to-face contact. Here people engage directly with each other as they go about their everyday lives in what are often closely bounded local spaces. The second form consists of more remote encounters, those made possible by transport and communications systems, those that people engage in across space and time. The first type of interaction tends to predominate in premodern societies. These are societies in which the "spatial dimensions of social life are, for most of the population, and in most respects, dominated by 'presence' – by localized activities" (p. 18). With the advent of modernity, however, the second sort of social intercourse becomes increasingly important. Modernity tears the spatial orbit of social life away from the confines of locality, "fostering relations between 'absent' others, locationally distant from any given situation of face-to-face interaction" (p. 18). In other words, it disembeds or lifts out social relations from local contexts of interaction and rearranges them across extensive spans of time-space. One important effect of this disembedding is to make place, "which refers to the physical settings of social activity as situated geographically," increasingly phantasmagoric (p. 18). This means that, in conditions of modernity, locales are haunted, so to speak, by that which is absent. They are constituted not just by what is immediately present but also by influences quite removed from them. Modern localities, then, are settings for distanciated relations – for relations at a distance, stretched out across time and space.

It is in terms of space-time distanciation that Giddens understands the process of globalization. For him, globalization broadens the scope of the disembedding process, so that "larger and larger numbers of people live in circumstances in which disembedded institutions, linking local practices with globalized social relations, organize major aspects of day-to-day life" (Giddens 1990: 79). Said otherwise, it intensifies the level of time-space distanciation and correspondingly stretches out the relations between local and distant social practices and events. Giddens thus defines globalization "as the intensification of worldwide social relations which link distant localities in such a way that local happenings are shaped by events occurring many miles away and vice versa" (p. 64), emphasizing how the emergence of instantaneous global communication and mass transportation, as well as the expansion of complex global systems of production and exchange, reduce the hold of local environments over people's lives. For example, the jobs of Chinese "Mattel" factory workers may be more dependent on the sale of Barbies in the United States than on the direct actions of local management. This does not mean, however, that place (or locale) has ceased to be significant in the organization of everyday life. It simply means that as social connections extend laterally across time and space, localities around the world become less dependent on circumstances of co-presence (on face-to-face interaction) and more on interactions across distance (on relations with absent others). For Giddens, then, globalization points to the interlocking of the local and the global; that is, it "concerns the intersection of presence and absence, the interlacing of social events and social relations 'at a distance' with local contextualities" (1991: 21). In short, globalization expresses basic aspects of space-time distanciation. It is fundamentally about the transformation of space and time.

The two perspectives sketched out above undoubtedly contain a number of significant differences.[12] For our purposes, however, we want to take them as complementary viewpoints. Together they highlight the basic, present-day spatial-temporal parameters of globalization. Drawing on the work of David Held et al. (1999: 15), we suggest that globalization consists of the following characteristic elements. First of all, given the development of worldwide modes of transport and communication, globalization implies a speeding up of the flows of capital, people, goods, images, and ideas across the world, thus pointing to a general increase in the pace of global interactions and processes. Second, it suggests an intensification of the links, modes of interaction, and flows that interconnect the world, meaning that ties across borders are not sporadic or haphazard but somewhat regularized. Third, globalization entails a stretching of social, cultural, political, and economic practices across frontiers so as to make possible action at a distance – that is, so that happenings, decisions, and practices in one area of the globe can come to have consequences for communities and cultures in remote locales of the globe. And finally, as a result of all this speeding up, intensification, and stretching, globalization also implies a heightened entanglement of the global and local such that, while everyone might continue to live local lives, their phenomenal worlds have to some extent become global as distant events come to have an impact on local spaces, and local developments come to have global repercussions.[13] All told, globalization can be seen as referring to those spatial-temporal processes, operating on a global scale, that rapidly cut across national boundaries, drawing more and more of the world into webs of interconnection, integrating and stretching cultures and communities across space and time, and compressing our spatial and temporal horizons. It points to a world in motion, to an interconnected world, to a shrinking world.

The Cultural Dynamics of Globalization

Given this general framework, let us now consider the cultural dynamics of globalization. This is the sphere of global activity that has received the most anthropological attention. This is not to say that anthropologists neglect or fail to consider other aspects of globalization, say, the economic or the political.[14] Indeed, they hardly could. For these are not completely separate realms of activity. What anthropologists tend to do, though, is interpret these other spheres through the prism of the cultural. Indeed, the cultural realm – the realm of meaning, one might say – most often takes conceptual priority. This prioritization is done, however, without necessarily positing the cultural dimension as the master sphere through which everything about globalization must be understood. Anthropologists realize that globalization is a complex, multifaceted process that operates simultaneously in diverse realms – the cultural, the economic, the political, the environmental, and so on – and can thus be embraced from numerous angles (see Nederveen Pieterse 1995). The cultural functions as just one such angle: as one of a number of important ways through which one can grasp the elephant of globalization (assuming, of course, that there is an elephant there to grasp). What does it mean, then, to speak of the cultural dynamics of globalization?

The de/territorialization of culture

Let us begin with the notion of culture itself. The concept has a long and complicated history. Raymond Williams (1976) describes it as one of the two or three most complex words in the English language. "Culture" can thus be a rather slippery idea. We would like to sidestep the problems of definition, however, and propose what might be considered a standard conceptualization of the term. We understand culture, for the purposes of this volume, "as the order of life in which human beings construct meaning through practices of symbolic representation" (Tomlinson 1999: 18). It is the sphere of existence in which people make their lives, individually and collectively, meaningful; and it encompasses both the practices through which meaning is generated and the material forms – popular culture, film, art, literature, and so forth – in which it is embodied.

In anthropology, the historical tendency has been to connect this realm of meaning construction, this realm of culture, very closely to the particularities of place (Clifford 1997; Malkki 1997). The idea of "a culture," for instance, which refers to a group of people – whether a nation, ethnicity, tribe, or so forth – who more or less use a system of shared meanings to interpret and make sense of the world, has traditionally been tied to the idea of a fixed territory. Akhil Gupta and James Ferguson elaborate on this in the following terms:

The distinctiveness of societies, nations, and cultures is predicated on a seemingly unproblematic division of space, on the fact that they occupy "naturally" discontinuous spaces....For example, the representation of the world as a collection of "countries," as on most world maps, sees it as an inherently fragmented space, divided by different colors into diverse national societies, each "rooted" in its proper place....It is so taken for granted that each country embodies its own distinctive culture and society that the terms "society" and "culture" are routinely simply appended to the names of nation-states, as when a tourist visits India to understand "Indian culture" and "Indian society" or Thailand to experience "Thai culture" or the United States to get a whiff of "American culture."

Of course, the geographical territories that cultures and societies are believed to map onto do not have to be nations. ...On a smaller scale perhaps are our disciplinary assumptions about the association of culturally unitary groups (tribes or peoples) with "their" territories: thus "the Nuer" live in "Nuerland" and so forth. The clearest illustration of this kind of thinking are the classic "ethnographic maps" that purported to display the spatial distribution of peoples, tribes, and cultures. (chapter 3 in this volume)

The inclination in anthropology, then, has been to assume an isomorphism between place and culture. Culture has been seen as something rooted in "soil." It has been thought of as a bounded entity that occupies a specific physical territory. The idea of culture has thus rested on the assumption of rupture, on the assumption of an intrinsic discontinuity between places as the loci of particular formations of meaning. It has traditionally pointed to a world of human differences conceptualized as a mosaic of cultures – with each culture, as a universe of shared meanings, radically set apart from every other. In short, as James Clifford has noted, "the idea of culture" has historically carried with it an "expectation of roots, of a stable, territorialized existence" (1988: 338).

Nowadays, though, it is impossible, or at least rather unreasonable, to think of culture strictly in such localized terms, to view it as the natural property of spatially circumscribed populations.[15] Globalization has radically pulled culture apart from place. It has visibly dislodged it from particular locales. The signs of this disembedding are everywhere. Just think back to the snapshots we discussed at the beginning of the essay. These are all essentially about the traffic in meaning. They are about the global mobility of cultural forms and products. Consider the scene of North African women in France, for example. It illustrates how people, or cultural subjects, nowadays readily traverse national boundaries, a process that brings cultures formerly located in different parts of the world into the same physical terrains, thus turning numerous places into spaces of cultural juxtaposition and mixture. Or take the case of commodities in Ghana. It shows how cultural objects – clothes, food, music, and so forth – circulate rapidly through ever-expanding networks, networks so extensive that certain styles or brands, such as Coca-Cola, McDonalds, and so forth, have achieved an almost ubiquitous presence in the world. Or contemplate the episode of mass media in Nigeria. This, too, is about cultural objects on the move. It highlights how images drift easily across the globe, allowing an increasing number of viewers to participate in the imagined realities of other cultures. This world of the snapshots is thus no "cultural mosaic, of separate pieces with hard, well-defined edges" (Hannerz 1992: 218). Rather, it is a world of culture in motion. It is a world where cultural subjects and objects – that is, meaningful forms such as capital, people, commodities, images, and ideas – have become unhinged from particular localities. The snapshots, in other words, suggest that culture is highly mobile. They point to how cultural interconnections increasingly stretch across the globe, eroding the "natural" connection or isomorphism between culture and place.

On one level, then, anthropologists have come to conceptualize culture as deterritorialized. The term is used to refer to this general weakening of the ties between culture and place, to the dislodging of cultural subjects and objects from particular or fixed locations in space and time. It points to how cultural processes readily transcend specific territorial boundaries. It designates a world of things fundamentally in motion. This should not be taken to mean, though, that anthropologists now think of culture as free-floating, without anchors. Indeed not. For anthropologists realize that the uprooting of culture is only half of the story of globalization. The other half is that the deterritorialization of culture is invariably the occasion for the reinsertion of culture in new time-space contexts. In other words, for anthropologists, cultural flows do not just float ethereally across the globe but are always reinscribed (however partially or fleetingly) in specific cultural environments. The signs of this reinscription, like the marks of deterritorialization, are everywhere evident. We need only turn, again, to our snapshots. The Algerian women *in* Avignon, for instance, are not aimless wanderers. The western commodities *in* Ghana are not meandering endlessly around the globe. And the Indian films *in* northern Nigeria are not flickering endlessly from screen to screen. They are all, instead, localized in very specific time-space contexts: that of France, Ghana, and Nigeria respectively. These snapshots are thus not simply of cultural subjects and objects in motion but also of their contingent localizations, of their reinsertion in particular cultural milieus. On another level, then, anthropologists have come to conceptualize culture as reterritorialized. The term refers to this process of reinscribing culture in new time-space contexts, of relocalizing it in specific cultural environments. It suggests that while the connection between culture and specific places may be weakening, it does not mean that culture has altogether lost its place. It just signifies that culture has been placed otherwise, such that it no longer necessarily belongs in or to a particular place. In short, it means that culture continues to have a territorialized existence, albeit a rather unstable one.

The point of all this is that, for anthropologists, globalized culture is never simply deterritorialized. It is also always reterritorialized. We are not dealing, in other words, with two separate processes. Rather, they occur simultaneously. It is a double movement, if you will. We would like to capture this double movement with the neologism de/territorialization. The term captures at once the lifting of cultural subjects and objects from fixed spatial locations and their relocalization in new cultural settings. It refers to processes that simultaneously transcend territorial boundaries and have territorial significance. The key to the meaning of this term is the slash. It allows us to separate "de" from "territorialization," thus calling attention to the fact that deterritorialization always contains territorialization within itself. For us, this means that the root of the word always to some extent undoes the action of the prefix, such that while the "de" may pull culture apart from place, the "territorialization" is always there to pull it back in one way or another. So there is no deterritorialization without some form of reterritorialization. There is no dislodging of everyday meanings from their moorings in particular localities without their simultaneous reinsertion in fresh environments. You can't have one process without the other. It is a matter of both at once. It is a matter of de/territorialization.

Cultural imperialism and the homogenization of the world

One of the important issues that the de/territorialization of culture raises concerns the organization of the flow of meaning in the world, or what might be called the cultural economy of globalization. It may very well be the case that culture is being dislodged from one locality and placed in another, thus generally weakening the ties of culture to particular sites. But this says nothing about the sort of culture that is being disembedded or about its origins and destinations. Does culture, for example, flow equally from and to all locations? Or does its dissemination involve some form of asymmetry? In other words, is there a power geometry to globalization and what might it be (see Massey 1994)?

A powerful answer to this set of questions comes from the discourse of cultural imperialism, a perspective that offers a highly critical stance towards the globalization of culture.[16] One of the central propositions of this discourse is that the de/territorialization of culture is not a benign matter.[17] For there is indeed a power geometry to the processes of globalization. It is one in which the traffic in culture moves primarily in one direction: sometimes it is seen to move from the First World (or West/center) to the Third World (or rest/periphery), other times more specifically from the United States to the rest of the world. In either case, given the asymmetries that putatively structure the flow of meaning, the discourse of cultural imperialism suggests that the processes of globalization involve the domination of certain cultures over others. In other words, this discourse understands the increased global movement of cultural goods primarily as a process of cultural imposition and dominance – of the imposition and dominance of western (predominantly American) culture over the remainder of the globe. The significance of this pattern of domination, from the point of view of this discourse, is that it is leading to the cultural homogenization of the world. The scenario that is often outlined is one in which, as global cultural influences continuously batter the sensibilities of the people of the periphery, "peripheral culture will step by step assimilate more and more of the imported meanings and forms, becoming gradually indistinguishable from the center" (Hannerz 1991: 122). The de/territorialization of culture is thus conceived as promoting a convergence of cultural styles inasmuch as western culture is being embraced in localities around the globe. It is seen, in other words, as leading to the increasing elimination of cultural difference in the world and hence to the crescent production of a world of sameness. The impact of western culture is perceived as simply too overwhelming.

This, then, in general terms, is how the discourse of cultural imperialism regards the globalization of culture. The discourse, however, can be broken down and explored a little further. It actually presents us with at least two specific, albeit interrelated, visions of global cultural uniformity (see Tomlinson 1999).[18] The first vision attributes the increasing synchronization of world culture to the ability of transnational capital, most often seen as American-dominated and mass-mediated, to distribute cultural goods around the globe. One version of this vision runs more or less as follows.[19] Since World War II, the global distribution of power points has shifted massively, such that the United States has become increasingly dominant, while European hegemony has diminished. A new empire, that of America, has thus come to replace the western European colonial system that had ensnared much of the world since the nineteenth century. This new imperial regime owes its ascendance to economic might, which germinates principally from the actions of US-based transnational corporations, and communications knowhow, which has permitted American business and military interests to largely monopolize the development of electronically based systems of communication. This monopoly has been so strong that the American broadcasting system, which is essentially a commercial system dependent on advertising revenue, has functioned as an archetype for the formation of broadcasting systems around the globe, particularly in the Third World. One problem with the dissemination and adoption of this commercial system of mass media is that it has opened up Third World countries to the large-scale importation of consumer-oriented foreign programs. The outcome has been an electronic invasion that promises to eradicate local traditions everywhere. Local culture, in other words, is meeting with submersion from the mass-produced emissions of commercial broadcasting. It is in danger of being drowned underneath a deluge of commercialized media products and other consumer goods pouring from America and a few other power points in the West. The Third World's adoption of a commercial system of broadcasting has thus been no innocent proposition. These countries have become strapped and buckled to an American-dominated global system of communication and commodity production that threatens to supplant traditional cultural values with the values of consumerism. The scenario often painted, then, is one in which the spread of American/western cultural goods is leading to the absorption of peripheral cultures into a homogenized global mono-culture of consumption. It is a vision of a world culturally synchronized to the rhythms of a mass-mediated global marketplace.

The second vision of global uniformity attributes the synchronization of the world to the spread of western culture more generally.[20] This means that globalization entails more than just the simple spread of American/western cultural goods, more than the development of a global taste for McDonalds, Levis, Coca-Cola, and the like. It actually involves, as John Tomlinson points out, "the installation worldwide of western versions of basic social-cultural reality: the West's epistemological and ontological theories, its values, ethical systems, approaches to rationality, technical-scientific worldview, political culture, and so on" (1997: 144). In other words, globalization entails the dissemination of all facets of the West's way of being: from musical forms, architecture, and modes of dress to eating habits, languages (specially English), philosophical ideas, and cultural values and dispositions – those concerning, for example, freedom, democracy, gender and sexuality, human rights, religion, science, and technology. And this is not just a post-World War II develop-ment either. Globalization is in fact "the continuation of a long historical process of western 'imperialist' expansion – embracing the colonial expansions of the sixteenth to the nineteenth centuries – and representing an historical pattern of increasing global cultural hegemony" (Tomlinson 1997: 143–4). This vision of cultural uni-formity implies that the world is gradually being made over in the image of the West. It indicates that cultural diversity is disappearing as non-western cultures are pro-gressively incorporated into a western-dominated homogenized culture. The rami-fication here is that western culture has been globalized to such an extent that the West has lost its "natural" connection to a specific geographical territory. The West is no longer an assemblage of cultural practices linked to a particular territorial foundation. It has been deterritorialized, uprooted from its historical birthplace. As such, the West no longer refers simply to Europe. It names instead a worldwide cultural formation.[21] It designates a machine of sorts, one producing planetary unification, one ushering in the worldwide standardization of life-styles. The West describes, in short, the cultural condition of the world. It is simply everywhere, dooming the world to uniformity.

To sum up, then, the discourse of cultural imperialism, taken as a whole, under-stands the experience of de/territorialization as the global dissemination of certain cultural practices, goods, styles, institutions, and so forth, the result being the increasing cultural homogenization of the world. It suggests that western culture, whether in the form of consumer goods or otherwise, has been lifted from its territorial grounding only to be replicated across the world, leaving a trail of uniformity behind it. Globalization thus becomes coterminous with Americanization or, more generally, with westernization. There is something to be said for this vision of the world. It presents a not entirely implausible scenario. The signs of global uniformity, at least on some level, are there. There is no denying that western cultural forms can be found everywhere (or almost so). Take clothes or food, for example: there are certain styles and brands – we earlier mentioned Coca-Cola, McDonalds, and so forth – that have become household names all over the world (even if not everyone can afford to buy them). Or take film and television: CNN, MTV, the Disney Channel are globally recognized icons; American television shows are usually the most watched in the world, *Dallas* and *Baywatch* being two more or less recent examples; and Hollywood films – *Titanic, Rambo, Star Wars* – and their stars – Leonardo DiCaprio, Sylvester Stallone, Harrison Ford – have extraordinary worldwide visibility. Or take the realm of ideas: notions of freedom, welfare, rights, democracy, sovereignty seem to be in everyone's vocabulary, indicating that the Enlightenment worldview has much of the world in its thrall. These examples are only the more obvious signs of cultural uniformity. We could point to many others. But we think the point is sufficiently made: there is an abundance of evidence suggesting that western cultural forms have a ubiquitous presence in the world. It would thus appear that there is no denying that the world is becoming to some extent homogenized, that it is becoming to some degree westernized. It is plain as day. All one has to do is look around.

A different picture of the world

From an anthropological perspective, however, the situation is not plain as day. All one has to do is look around – a little harder though. What one finds is that the picture the discourse of cultural imperialism draws of the world fails to adequately capture its complexities. The world, indeed, is a much more complicated place. It will be our job in what follows to explore just how much more complex the world actually is. The tack we will take is to focus on three fundamental problems with the discourse of cultural imperialism, a main goal being to cast doubt on the vision of the world as a homogenized or westernized entity. The first problem deals with the fashion in which alien cultural products are said to act upon their consumers in the Third World. An important assumption of the cultural imperialism discourse is "that TV programs which are made for a commercial television system will unavoidably express consumerist values, both in the programs themselves and in the advertising which constitutes the financial basis of the system; and that these representations will in turn create wants and foster consumerist motivations in their recipients, in such a way that these recipients become harnessed to a western-based system of commodity production and exchange" (Thompson 1995: 170–1). The main problem with this assumption is that it constructs Third World subjects as passive consumers of imported cultural goods. The discourse of cultural imperialism, in other words, relies on what is called the hypodermic model of media effects (Morley and Robins 1995: 126): a model that presupposes that media texts have direct cultural effects on those who view them. This basically means that cultural effects are imputed from an examination of the cultural forms themselves rather than from careful attention to the actual context of viewing. This is too simple a model of cultural reception. The process of reading cultural texts is actually a rather complicated affair, one that entails the active participation of the viewing subject in the construction of meaning (see Morley 1992). Third World consumers faced with an imported text, media or otherwise, will not simply or necessarily absorb its ideologies, values, and life-style positions. Rather, they will bring their own cultural dispositions to bear on such a text, interpreting it according to their own cultural codes (see Ang 1985; Liebes and Katz 1990). What takes place in the viewing encounter is that foreign cultural forms have a tendency to become customized.[22] They are interpreted, translated, and appropriated according to local conditions of reception.[23]

The classic example of this process of customization is Liebes and Katz's (1990) well-known study of the reception of *Dallas* in Israel (focusing on four different ethnic groups: Arabs, Russian Jews, Moroccan Jews, and kibbutz members), the United States, and Japan. The basic finding of the investigation was that viewers from diverse cultural backgrounds attributed very different meanings to the program. The various groups, for example, had different explanations for the motivations of the characters in *Dallas*:

the Americans and the kibbutz members invoke a sort of Freudian theory, perceiving individuals as governed by irrational drives and connecting these with childhood events. Thus, J. R.'s personality is thought to derive from his having been second to Bobby in his mother's favor. Interpretations of this kind, of course, relieve individuals of much moral responsibility. In contrast, a large proportion of the Russian statements invoke determinism of another form, as if people behaved in a particular way because their roles impelled them to; as if businessmen, for example, or women, were programmed by society. The Moroccans also blame society, but invoke a Hobbesian model in which individuals must fend for themselves in the jungle of the world. Only the Arabs – who focus not on motivation but on family interrelations and moral dilemmas – find the individual free and responsible enough to struggle against temptation and constraint. (Liebes and Katz 1990: 103)

Given the clear and systematic differences in the ways the various groups interpreted *Dallas*, Liebes and Katz conclude that the process of reception is not a straightforward imposition of meaning but a creative encounter between "the symbolic resources of the viewer and the symbolic offerings of the text" (p. 6). They suggest, in other words, that the reception of media products is an intricate cultural process that entails the active involvement of individuals in making sense of the images they consume.

Eric Michaels (chapter 13 in this volume) provides another important example of the customization of alien cultural forms. His work focuses, in part, on the reception of Hollywood videotapes among Warlpiri Aborigines in the western Central Desert of Australia. Michaels's most suggestive finding was that the Aboriginal peoples were not familiar with the genres and conventions of western narrative fiction. They were unable to distinguish, for example, romance from documentary, or to judge the truth value of Hollywood cinema. The reason for this is that in traditional Warlpiri culture all stories are true. Fiction simply does not exist as an epistemological form through which to make sense of the world. This situation produces, according to Michaels, quite extraordinary interpretations of Hollywood programs. He elaborates in the following manner:

Comparisons between Warlpiri story form and imported video fictions demonstrated that in many instances, content (what is supplied in the narrative) and context (what must be assumed) are so different from one system to the other that they might be said to be reversed. For example, Warlpiri narrative will provide detailed kinship relationships between all characters as well as establishing a kinship domain for each. When Hollywood videos fail to say where Rocky's grandmother is, or who's taking care of his sister-in-law, Warlpiri viewers discuss the matter and need to fill in what for them is missing content. By contrast, personal motivation is unusual in Aboriginal story; characters do things because the class (kin, animal, plant) of which they are members is known to behave this way. This produces interesting indigenous theories, for example, of national character to explain behavior in *Midnight Express* or *The A-Team*.

The point here is that for Warlpiri viewers Hollywood videos are not necessarily complete, authoritative texts. They are instead partial stories that require "a good deal of interpretive activity on the part of viewers to supply contents as well as contexts with which to make these stories meaningful." Michaels's conclusion, then, is that it is not possible to know in advance what the effects of particular television programs might be on traditional Aboriginal audiences. It is only in the actual context of viewing that meaning can be determined.

These two examples should not be taken to imply that foreign texts have no cultural influence at all. It is not our intention to romanticize the process of interpretation. It may be that consuming subjects are active makers of sense. But this does not mean they can therefore do whatever they want with the goods they consume. There are limits to how one can interpret a text.[24] All we mean to suggest is this: that the process of interpretation, and hence the influence that foreign programs have on their audiences, is rather more complicated than the discourse of cultural imperialism, with its hypodermic model, permits. Cultural materials just do not transfer in a unilinear manner (see Tomlinson 1999). They always entail interpretation, translation, and customization on the part of the receiving subject. In short, they can only be understood in the context of their complex reception and appropriation.

The implications of this way of conceptualizing the reception of imported products are rather profound. It gives us cause to rethink the idea that the world is being homogenized. The discourse of cultural imperialism argues that the spread of western cultural goods is leading to the incorporation of peripheral cultures into a synchronized global monoculture. The problem here, though, as Tomlinson points out, is that the cultural imperialism argument makes "unwarranted leaps of inference from the simple presence of cultural goods to the attribution of deeper cultural or ideological effects" (1997: 135). In other words, it simply assumes that the sheer presence of western forms has a self-evident cultural effect on Third World subjects. However, if it is the case (as we are arguing) that consumers do not necessarily absorb the ideologies, values, and life-style positions of the texts they consume, if it is true that subjects always bring their own cultural dispositions to bear on such texts, then the case for the homogenization of the world loses much of its force. The only way to really show that the world is being homogenized is to demonstrate not only the ubiquity of western cultural forms but also that the consumption of these goods is profoundly transforming the way people make sense of their lives. Indeed, the homogenization scenario only makes sense if it can be established that the consumers of foreign cultural products are internalizing the values allegedly contained in them, whatever these values might be. The point, then, is that the ubiquity of western cultural forms around the world cannot in and of itself be taken as evidence that the world is being homogenized. Homogenization entails much more than this: it entails the transformation of the way people fashion their phenomenal worlds (see Tomlinson 1999). This is not to say that there has been no cultural convergence at all in the world. It is to suggest, though, that as long as the process of customization is hard at work, the specter of homogenization will be kept somewhat at bay and the world will remain full of difference.

The second problem with the discourse of cultural imperialism's vision of the world has to do with the tendency to analyze globalization simply as a flow from the West to the rest. To be sure, there is substantial asymmetry in the flow of meaning in the world: the center mostly speaks, while the periphery principally listens (Hannerz 1992: 219). But this does not mean that the periphery does talk back at all. For indeed it does. Culture does move in the opposite direction, that is, from the rest to the West. There is no denying this. The signs of it are everywhere. Take the case of food, for example: there are certain cuisines – such as Indian, Chinese, Korean, Thai, and Mexican – that have become standard eating fare for many in the West. Or take the realm of religion: it is not just Christianity and Judaism that command the attention of the faithful but increasingly also "non-western" religions such as Islam and Buddhism. Or take music: the listening pleasures of those in the West now include not only rock-and-roll and R&B but also samba, salsa, reggae, *rai*, juju, and so forth. Or take, finally, the case of people, which undoubtedly represents the most visible sign of this reverse traffic in culture: since World War II, largely as the result of poverty, economic underdevelopment, civil war, and political unrest, millions of people from the less affluent parts of the world have been driven to seek a future in the major urban centers of the "developed" and "developing" nations.[25] The result is a monumental presence of Third World peoples in the metropolises of the West. One finds, for example, people from the Caribbean basin (Cubans, Dominicans, Haitians, Puerto Ricans, Jamaicans), Asia (Chinese, Cambodian, Indian, Korean, Pakistani, Japanese), and Latin America (Mexicans, Guatemalans, Colombians) in the US; from Algeria, Tunisia, and Morocco in France; from Turkey and North Africa in Germany; from Morocco and the Dominican Republic in Spain; from Indonesia and Suriname in the Netherlands; from Senegal and Albania in Italy; and from the Caribbean, India, Pakistan, and Bangladesh in the United Kingdom (Hall 1996). What has happened, as a result of all this reverse traffic in culture, is that the periphery has set itself up within the very heart of the West. As such, the encounter between the core and the periphery no longer takes place simply "out there." It now also comes to pass "here." The core has been peripheralized, as it were (see Sassen-Koob 1982).

A significant effect of this peripheralization of the core has been that the nation-states of the West have been somewhat unsettled. This unsettling – and we will shortly see what is meant by this – has a lot to do with the nature of contemporary population movements. The interesting thing about migrants nowadays is that, in general, when they move across national boundaries, they do not simply leave their "homelands" behind (see Basch et al. 1994).[26] Rather, they are able to forge and maintain distanciated social relations – relations at a distance, across time and space – that link together their home and host societies. In other words, migrants today often form what might be called diasporic attachments; this refers to this dual affinity or doubled connection that mobile subjects have to localities, to their involvement in webs of cultural, political, and economic ties that encompass multiple national terrains.[27] These are people who have become practiced exponents of cultural bifocality (Rouse, chapter 7 in this volume). Or, as Stuart Hall has put it,

They are people who belong to more than one world, speak more than one language (literally and metaphorically), inhabit more than one identity, have more than one home; who have learned to negotiate and translate *between* cultures, and who, because they are irrevocably the product of several interlocking histories and cultures, have learned to live with, and indeed to speak from, *difference*. They speak from the "in-between" of different cultures, always unsettling the assumptions of one culture from the perspective of another, and thus finding ways of being both *the same as* and at the same time *different from* the others amongst whom they live. (1995: 206; emphasis in original)

Contemporary migrants (or at least many of them) thus represent different ways of being someone in a shrinking world. They are mobile subjects who draw on diverse assemblages of meanings and locate themselves in different geographies simultaneously.

The classic anthropological example of this diasporic process is Roger Rouse's (chapter 7 in this volume) study of the movement of labor migrants from the rural Mexican town of Aguililla, located in the southwest corner of the state of Michoacán, to the North American community of Redwood City, found on the northern edge of California's celebrated Silicon Valley. One of Rouse's basic observations is that the social-spatial image of "community," identified as a "discriminable population with a single, bounded space – a territory or place," has historically been used to understand the experiences of Mexican migrants to the US as a relatively unproblematic one-way movement from one national space to another, that is, as a movement in which "migrants and their descendants experience a more or less gradual shift from one ordered arrangement to another, either fully converting to the dominant way of life or forging their own form of accommodation in an ordered synthesis of old and new." Mexican immigrants have thus conventionally been viewed as persons who uproot themselves, leave behind home, country, and community, and endure the painful process of incorporation into a new society and culture. Rouse argues, however, that since World War II the image of the territorially bounded community "has become increasingly unable to contain the postmodern complexities that it confronts." For Mexican migrants have developed socio-spatial arrangements that question the received ways of viewing migration and that thus call for alternative cartographies of social space. What has happened, to put it simply, is that the Aguilillan "migrants" who have settled in Redwood City have not severed their ties to "home" but have instead maintained connections so intense that Aguililla and Redwood City can no longer be conceived as separate communities:

Through the constant migration back and forth and the growing use of telephones, the residents of Aguililla tend to be reproducing their links with people that are two thousand miles away as actively as they maintain their relations with their immediate neighbors. Still more, and more generally, through the continuous circulation of people, money, commodities, and information, the diverse settlements have intermingled with such force that they are probably better understood as forming only one community dispersed in a variety of places. (Rouse 1988: 1–2; quoted in García Canclini 1995: 231–2)

Put otherwise, Aguilillan migrants have not abandoned one national space for another but have formed – through the continuous circulation of people, capital, goods, images, and ideas – a community that stretches across national boundaries. Rouse refers to this territorially unbound community as a transnational migrant circuit, emphasizing that it is here rather than in any particular locale that the lives of Aguilillans take place. Aguilillan migrants thus occupy no singular national space. They live their lives transnationally. They are cultural bifocals who belong simultaneously to more than one home and hence to no one home in particular. They are, in short, the fruit of several interlocking nations and cultures.

What all this indicates is that we are witnessing a world in which significant social relations and the parameters of community are no longer, if they ever were, simply confined within the limits of a single territorial national space. We are witnessing a world, in other words, that has become strewn with migrants who inhabit imagined communities of belonging that cut across and encompass multiple national terrains. The implications of this development for western nation-states, to get back to the question of unsettling, are rather profound. The nation-state, according to Arjun Appadurai, has historically functioned "as a compact and isomorphic organization of territory, ethnos [or people], and governmental apparatus" (1996: 42). This basically means that it has traditionally been constructed as a territorially circumscribed and culturally homogeneous political space. The main way the nation-state has achieved this cultural homogeneity is through systematically subjecting the individuals living within its spatial frame to a wide array of nationalizing technologies. These technologies of nationhood include the granting of citizenship rights; the development of rules on nationality; the invention of symbols of nationhood such as flags, ceremonials, the celebration of historical figures, and the observance of national holidays; the provision of social welfare policies, conscription, and public bureaucracies; and the building of roads, schools, hospitals and prisons (Axford 1995: 152–3). The nation-state, then, has historically operated with coercive practices designed to forge its subjects into a single homogeneous national community. And it has by and large been very effective at creating this uniform space of nationness, successfully nationalizing not only those folks born on its soil but also the many migrants who settle within its boundaries.[28] Nowadays, however, western nation-states are no longer able to adequately discipline and nationalize all the subjects under their domain. They cannot fully produce proper national subjects – subjects defined by residence in a common territory, a shared cultural heritage, and an undivided loyalty to a common government. A case in point: the many migrants who live their lives across national boundaries. These are people who, because they are intimately linked to more than one place and to no one place in particular, are able to escape, to some degree, the nationalizing apparatuses of the nation-state. These are people, that is, who cannot be fully subjected to the nationalizing or assimilating imperatives of one nation-state since their experience is not limited to that single space. The basic problem here is that these days the nation-state functions less and less as a self-contained, autonomous entity and more and more as a transit depot through which an ever-increasing number of migrants pass, thus making it almost impossible for the technologies of nationhood to do their job and delimit the contours of a singular national order.

The result of this inability to construct a monolithic national community, of the incapacity to turn migrants into proper national subjects, is that the nation-states of the West have become homes to a host of diverse and sometimes incommensurable cultures. They have been turned into meeting places for a broadening array of peoples and cultures. They have developed into sites of extraordinary cultural heterogeneity.[29] The significance of this unfolding is twofold. First of all, it means that the isomorphism of territory, ethnos, and legitimate sovereignty has to some extent been undone. The ethnos and the territory no longer neatly coincide. The nation-state is no longer the place of the ethnos. It has become instead the place of the ethni. Second, this unfolding also means that the cultural centeredness of the West has been somewhat called into question. For what can it mean to be English or American or French or, simply, western when these countries have become containers of African, Asian, and Latin American cultures? Contemplate, for instance, the following remarks from Jo-Jo, a young white reggae fan in Birmingham's ethnically diverse Balsall Health neighborhood:

There's no such thing as "England" any more ... welcome to India brothers! This is the Caribbean! ... Nigeria! ... There is no England, man. This is what is coming. Balsall Heath is the center of the melting pot, 'cos all I ever see when I go out is half-Arab, half-Pakistani, half-Jamaican, half-Scottish, half-Irish. I know 'cos I am [half-Scottish/half-Irish] ... who am I? ... Tell me who I belong to? They criticize me, the good old England. Alright, where do I belong? You know I was brought up with blacks, Pakistanis, Africans, Asians, everything, you name it ... who do I belong to? ... I'm just a broad person. The earth is mine ... you know we was not born in Jamaica ... we was not born in "England." We were born here, man. (Hebdige 1987: 158–9, quoted in chapter 3, this volume)

Jo-Jo perhaps overstates the case a bit. There are many people who continue to define England as a homogenous national space and wish to keep its culture intact, unified within, and with strongly marked borders dividing it from others (Hall 1995). But certainly the idea of a culturally stable and unitary England no longer has the hold it once had. And the same could be said of France, the US, and most other First World nations, whose spaces have similarly become zones of heterogeneity. In a world of motion, the nation-states of the West have indeed been unsettled as antiquated efforts to map the world as an assemblage of homogeneous culture areas or homelands are "bewildered by a dazzling array of postcolonial simulacra, doublings and redoublings, as India and Pakistan seem to reappear in postcolonial simulation in London, prerevolution Teheran rises from the ashes in Los Angeles, and a thousand similar cultural dramas are played out in urban and rural settings all across the globe" (Gupta and Ferguson, chapter 3 in this volume). In a world of complex mobilities, in short, the normative character of the western nation-state has been called into question.[30]

Three general points spring from this discussion of reverse cultural flows. The first is that the process of globalization is much too complex to be thought of merely as a westernizing affair. For it involves not just the circulation of western subjects and objects but also the dissemination of non-western cultural forms. Globalization, in other words, cannot be conceived solely as a matter of one-way, western imperialism. It must be understood instead as a process of mutual, if uneven, infiltration: with the West permeating the rest and vice versa. The second, and related, point is that the process of globalization cannot be thought of merely as a homogenizing affair. For it is also, on some level, about heterogenization. It is about the differentiation of the world. Or, more precisely, it is about the differentiation of the West. The idea here is simply that a primary effect of the peripheralization of the core, or of the reverse traffic in culture, has been to turn the spaces of the West into dense sites of cultural heterogeneity. The final point is that as a result of all this back and forth movement, from the West to the rest and vice versa, the familiar lines between "here" and "there," center and periphery, and West and non-West have to some extent become blurred. That is to say, insofar as the Third World is in the First and the First World is in the Third, it has become difficult to specify with any certitude where one entity begins and the other one ends (see Gupta and Ferguson, this volume). Where, for example, does one draw the boundaries of Mexico when so many of "its people" live in the US? Or where does one draw the boundaries of the US when "its capital" has such a strong presence in Mexico? This is not to say that these geo-political categories have ceased to be useful. Indeed not. But they have become more difficult to map considering that we live in a world of "crisscrossed economies" and "intersecting systems of meaning" (Rouse, chapter 7 in this volume). In the end, globalization cannot be thought of simply as a westernizing affair, nor can it be viewed solely as a homogenizing one. It must be read instead as a complex process that brings the West to rest and the rest to the West. It must be understood, in short, as a process of mutual imbrication.

The third, and last, problem with the cultural imperialism scenario is that it neglects those circuits of culture that circumvent the West – those which serve primarily to link the countries of the periphery with one another. These circuits can sometimes be more important and influential in shaping local milieus than those that connect the First World to the Third. So it is a major mistake to exclude them from the analysis of globalization. The signs of this peripheral traffic in culture are many. Consider the itineraries of capital: in China, to note just one case, the most important streams of finance come not from the West but from the Chinese communities of Taiwan, Hong Kong, and Southeast Asia (Yang, chapter 14 in this volume). Or take the flow of commodities: in the northeastern Indian settlement of Rangluwa, for example, the foreign commodities the populace consumes – clothing, cosmetics, and so forth – are more often than not from China rather than from the West (Borooah 2000). Or consider the movement of people: one can find populations from India in South Africa, Fiji, Guyana, and Trinidad and Tobago; from China in Malaysia, Thailand, Indonesia, the Philippines, Mexico, and El Salvador; from Afghanistan in the Islamic Republics of Iran and Pakistan; and from Egypt, Pakistan, Eritrea, India, and the Philippines in Saudi Arabia and other Arab Gulf countries (see Malkki 1997; Margold 1995). This, of course, is only to cite a few examples. Or take, finally, the case of the mass media, undoubtedly one of the most visible signs of the peripheral flow of culture: the India film industry, for example, serves not only the Indian subcontinent but also Indonesia, Malaysia, and areas of Africa; Mexican and Brazilian soap operas are popular not just in Latin America but in Russia as well; and Hong Kong supplies films not simply for mainland China, Taiwan, and the Chinese diaspora but also for other parts of the Third World. Such are the manifestations of the peripheral flow of culture. What they suggest, above all, is that the global cultural encounter takes place not just between the West and the rest but also within the periphery itself. It also takes place between the countries of the Third World.

There are two significant implications of this peripheral flow of culture. The first is that, for some countries of the periphery, the specter of Americanization or westernization may be less worrisome than, say, the prospects of Indianization, Indonesianization, or Vietnamization (Appadurai, chapter 2 in this volume). This is the case for Sri Lanka, Irian Jaya, and Cambodia respectively. For some Third World countries, then, the worry is not so much about western domination as it is about the enormous cultural power of other non-western nations. One important analysis of this cultural dynamic is Mayfair Yang's study (chapter 14 in this volume) of mass media and transnational subjectivity in Shanghai. Yang's central argument is that, for China (or, more specifically, for the Chinese state), the fear of western cultural domination is of minor concern in comparison to the consternation over the subversive influence of overseas Chinese communities. To be sure, she notes, American film and television have made some inroads into China but the far more invasive influence has been Hong Kong and Taiwan popular culture:

One most vivid indication of this cultural invasion can be found in the pop songs that young people listen to and the popularity of karaoke singing. There is something mesmerizing about the repetition of endless stories of love and disappointment. Hong Kong and Taiwan popular culture has gained a firm foothold in the mainland . . . with visiting singers giving concerts to packed halls filled with adoring fans paying high prices for tickets. Sixteen- and seventeen-year-old girls want to embrace and kneel in the footsteps of such male idols as Tong Ange and Tang Yongling. The longing to be a star oneself can be temporarily satisfied using the imported karaoke audiovisual systems now found in karaoke bars and in many work units, schools, and restaurants. Music stores have sprung up to sell this music on cassettes. Hong Kong songs are sung in Cantonese by young Shanghainese whose point of comparison these days is not Beijing but Hong Kong.

The importance of this Hong Kong and Taiwanese cultural invasion, according to Yang, is that it has exposed Shanghainese subjects to overseas Chinese culture and thus made it possible for them to construct news ways of being Chinese – ways not prescribed by the apparatuses of the centralized state. This cultural invasion, in other words, has enabled Chinese national subjects to fashion identity spaces that "spill out over the constrictive molds of a fixed, state-spatialized Chinese identity and homogeneous national culture". One can see, then, how the introduction of Hong Kong and Taiwan popular culture into mainland China might give the Chinese state cause to worry. It is a development that has disrupted the ability of the state to form proper national subjects – subjects whose allegiance and orientation is strictly to the state and the nation it embodies. This is not to suggest, though, that the Chinese state has completely lost its subject-making capacity. This is hardly the case. But it is to suggest that the Chinese state is no longer the sole arbiter of the identity of its subjects: it now has to compete for their minds and allegiances with a host of "foreign" entities. The upshot of all this is that for

China, as well as for many other countries of the periphery, the West is not the only, or even the major, cultural power they have to contend with. Just as worrisome are the many cultural forces within the Third World itself. Just as distressing are the cultural powers of the periphery.

The second implication is that, in some cases, the peripheral flow of culture is not perceived as a threat but welcomed as a resource that allows people to participate, on an ongoing basis, in the imagined realities of other cultures. One notable examination of this cultural dynamic is Brian Larkin's study (chapter 15 in this volume) of Indian films among the Hausa of northern Nigeria. Larkin's basic argument is that Indian films allow Hausa viewers to imaginatively engage with a cultural tradition different from their own and thus to envision new styles of fashion, beauty, love, and romance. The crucial thing about these films, as well as about the styles they inspire, according to Larkin, is that they emanate not from the West but from another Third World country. As such, they are not associated, in the minds of Nigerians, with a cultural imperialist power.[31] This makes their incorporation into Hausa culture much more readily acceptable. Larkin puts this in the following terms:

For Hausa viewers, Indian films offer images of a parallel modernity to the West, one intimately concerned with the changing basis of social life, but rooted in conservative cultural values. Characters in Indian films struggle over whether they should speak Hindi or borrow from English, whether they should marry the person they love or wed the person their parents choose. In these and many other decisions like them the narrative tensions of Indian films raise, consider and resolve minor and major anxieties within contemporary Indian society, anxieties that are relevant to Hausa viewers. Moreover, when Hausa youth rework Indian films within their own culture by adopting Indian fashions (such as the headscarves or jewellery of Indian actresses), by copying the music styles for religious purposes, or by using the filmic world of Indian sexual relations to probe the limitations within their own cultural world, they can do so without engaging with the heavy ideological load of "becoming western."

Larkin's basic argument, in other words, is that Indian films provide Hausa viewers with a meaningful cultural alternative to the aesthetic productions of the West, an alternative that allows them to explore modern forms of existence not linked to the history of western cultural imperialism. Indian films furnish them with a way to fashion new selves without having to take on the West and its ideological baggage. What this example highlights is that peripheral flows of culture figure prominently in generating interconnections between different peoples and cultures – interconnections that allow individuals to construct new ways of being in the world. As such, the traffic in culture within the Third World does not necessarily have to be about cultural domination. It can also be just about allowing people to creatively partake in the imagined realities of different cultures.

The basic point that emerges from all this is that the discourse of cultural imperialism's vision of the West overrunning the Third World, once again, cannot capture what is taking place in the world today. The idea here is that while the circuits that connect the West to the Third World are undoubtedly the prime movers of the global traffic in culture, they are by no means the only important forces around. There are also quite a few circuits that circumvent the West altogether, circuits that serve mainly to interconnect the countries of the periphery with each other. And these can be just as powerful in shaping the local environments of the periphery as any that go through the First World. This means that the West is not necessarily the only or primary foreign influence on many Third World countries. It indicates that the global cultural encounter takes place not just between the core and the periphery but also within the non-western world itself. As such, globalization cannot be thought of simply as a westernizing or homogenizing matter. It must be understood instead as an intricate process that brings not just the West to the rest or the rest to the West but also one part of the periphery to another. It has to be grasped as a much more complex, crisscrossing global affair.[32]

A dislocated world

The argument we have been making is that the discourse of cultural imperialism understands the increased global traffic in culture principally as a process of cultural imposition and dominance: of the imposition and dominance of western culture over the rest of the world. Moreover, we have noted that this pattern of domination is perceived as bringing about the increasing cultural homogenization of the world. The scenario that is often sketched is one in which western cultural practices, institutions, goods, and styles are being lifted from their territorial grounding and replicated across the world; the result being that the cultures of the periphery are being pounded out of existence. The de/territorialization of culture, in other words, is envisioned as leading to the elimination of cultural difference in the world as western culture is increasingly embraced in localities around the globe. It is seen as promoting the production of a world of sameness. We have also suggested, however, that from an anthropological perspective this westernization/homogenization scenario fails to adequately capture what is going on in the world. One basic problem with this take on globalization is that the traffic in culture is conceptualized as simply moving in one direction: from the West to the rest. To be sure, this center to periphery flow is a crucial component of the global cultural economy. But it is not the only thing that globalization is about. Globalization is actually a much more complex process, one that also involves substantial movements of culture from the periphery to the core as well as within the periphery itself. Another basic problem is that western cultural texts are perceived as having a self-evident cultural effect on Third World subjects, the effect being to westernize them. But this is an erroneous perception. The peoples of the periphery do not simply or necessarily absorb the ideologies, values, and life-style positions putatively embedded in the foreign cultural goods they consume. More often than not they actually customize these imported forms, interpreting them according to local conditions of reception. From an anthropological perspective, then, the process of globalization, we have suggested, is much too complex to be thought of merely as a westernizing affair, one that is leading to the obliteration of cultural difference in the world. We have argued that globalization is not in any simple way battering the cultures of the periphery out of existence and bringing forth a world of sameness.

What all of this implies is that the world can no longer be viewed simply as a matter of one-way, western cultural imperialism. It cannot be conceptualized just in terms of core–periphery relations. The world is just too complex a place. What we need, then, is a more nuanced view of the globe than that provided by the discourse of cultural imperialism. We need a different image of the world than the core–periphery model. The image we would like to put forth is that of dislocation. We propose, in other words, to view the world as a dislocated cultural space. The term "dislocation" is borrowed from Ernesto Laclau (1990), who uses it to refer to structures whose center has been displaced – displaced in such a way as to be supplemented not by another center but by a plurality of them. The main structures Laclau has in mind are modern societies or nation-states. But we think that the world as a whole can be conceptualized in similar terms. For the world, like the nation-state, has no single cultural power center from which everything radiates. The West may have historically played this role. But this is no longer the case. The West has been displaced and now has to compete with a plurality of power centers around the world. This is not to suggest, though, that the West has ceased to be the major player in the global cultural economy. It certainly has not. But it does mean that it no longer occupies an unchallenged position of dominance in the world. The world can thus be said to be dislocated to the extent that there is not just one global cultural power center but a plurality of them, even if the West stands out among these. In other words, the world can be thought of as a dislocated cultural space insofar as global cultural power has ceased to be concentrated in the West and become somewhat diffused. It can be considered dislocated, in short, to the degree that the traffic in culture or the flow of meaning does not just originate in the West but also in places all over the globe. To think in terms of dislocation is to view the world not in terms of a monolithic core–periphery model but as a complexly interconnected cultural space, one full of crisscrossing flows and intersecting systems of meaning. It is, in sum, to view the world (and hence globalization) not as a western project but as a global one.

The Organization of the Reader

Such is the complex world of globalization. The aim of this reader, as noted earlier, is to provide an anthropological introduction to this world. The articles gathered here are a selection of the most sophisticated anthropological work on globalization published in English since the late 1980s. We have organized this rich material into six thematic parts (each of which carries a short introduction of its own, along with suggestions for further reading). The first part, "Thinking the Global," brings together general theoretical efforts to map the global condition. The articles suggest, much like this introduction, that the picture of globalization as a homogenizing, one-way flow of culture from the West to the rest does not adequately capture the complex realities of the contemporary world. The rest of the sections move away from this broad mapping of globalization to track the trajectories of specific global cultural flows. Part II, "Itinerant Capital," focuses on the mobility of capital, concentrating on its articulations with local cultural formations. Part III, "Mobile Subjects," is concerned with the movement of people, focusing primarily on the extensive post-World War II migrations from the countries of the periphery to the major urban centers of the "developed" and "developing" world.[33] Part IV,

"Roving Commodities," tracks the global flow of commodities, concentrating on the way the consumption of goods often mediates the "encounter" between peoples and cultures from around the world. The fifth part, "Traveling Media," deals with the meanderings of the mass media, highlighting the increasingly important role they play in the quotidian realities of people from all over the globe. And the sixth part, "Nomadic Ideologies," explores the circulation of western ideologies and discourses, focusing on how these narratives both constrict the lives of and create new subject positions for the peoples of the periphery.

The volume as a whole, then, aims to capture the complexities of the globalization process. It is concerned with tracking the paths taken by the numerous cultural flows – of capital, people, goods, images, and ideologies – that traverse the globe, as well as with exploring the local experiences of people as their everyday lives become increasingly contingent on globally stretched out social relations. The volume, in other words, simultaneously focuses on the macro processes through which the globe is becoming increasingly interconnected and on the manner subjects mediate these processes in culturally specific ways. It focuses, in short, on the conjunctural and situated character of globalization.

To conclude, we would like to call attention to some of the realities that have shaped the construction of this book. The anthropology of globalization is an exciting and rapidly growing field. We would have liked to capture all of this excitement and growth. Unfortunately, the limitation on space and the realities of budgets necessarily made such a task impossible. The volume therefore contains a number of important gaps. There is no intellectual justification for these exclusions other than the need to erect artificial limits. Let us point to some of the most obvious of these gaps. First, a number of important global phenomena are absent from the volume. They include transnational social movements, global religious communities, global cities, and transnational pollution. Second, the volume is also missing the work of what might be called precursor theorists. Here we are thinking of the writings of Eric Wolf, Sidney Mintz, June Nash, and Michael Taussig on the political economy of culture. This is work that does not explicitly deal with globalization but that paved the way for current anthropological theorizations of the global. Third, while the geographical reach of the book is fairly broad, there are a few areas of the world glaringly missing, including Eastern Europe and Russia. Fourth, we would have liked to pay more attention to issues of gender, race, and sexuality, but the need to broadly map the processes of globalization made this task unfeasible. Nevertheless, a number of the articles do touch on these issues (see Abu-Lughod; Adams; Donham; Freeman; Gross, McMurray, and Swedenburg; Larkin; Ong; and Yang). And fifth, we would have liked to include more work dealing with the effects of globalization on the First World. But since most disciplines that deal with globalization tend to focus on the West, we felt this volume should be localized mainly in the Third World. This way the book serves as a corrective to much of the literature on globalization. Such are the omissions of this book, or at least some of them. No doubt there are others. We hope the reader will forgive us for these exclusions and enjoy the material that *is* included here.

NOTES

1 These snapshots are modified quotations taken from various articles included in this volume. See, respectively, ch. 4, Freeman; ch. 9, Gross, McMurray, and Swedenburg; ch. 11, Meyer; ch. 15, Larkin; ch. 18, Abu-Lughod. The quotation marks have been intentionally left off.

2 In this book, we use the term "western" or "the West" principally as a shorthand for the United States and Western Europe, as well as for the cultural products and practices of these countries.

3 See Robertson 1992 for a genealogy of the concept of globalization.

4 We should note here that globalization is not a wholly new phenomenon. The world has for many centuries been an interconnected space (Abu-Lughod 1989; Wallestein 1974; Wolf 1982). Arjun Appadurai (ch. 2 in this volume), for instance, traces this interconnectedness back to the late fifteenth and early sixteenth centuries, when the West's encounter with the rest of the world created an overlapping set of ecumenes in which congeries of conquest, money, migration, and commerce began to form durable cross-cultural bonds. However, the problems of distance and the confines of technology have generally restricted the interactions of the past, so that it has been very difficult (that is, only at great cost and with great effort) to sustain dealings between culturally and spatially separate groups. So it is really only over the course of the past century, with the advent of modern technology – particularly with the innovations in transportation and communication, such as the introduction or improvement of airplanes, telephones, computers and video – that we have entered into a more profound condition of neighborliness, one that encompasses, to varying degrees, even those traditionally most remote from one another. Twentieth-century improvements in technology, then, have made possible interactions of a new magnitude and intensity. Developments in rail and air transport, for example, propel more people faster and longer distances than ever before. High-speed trains dash across the landscape at remarkable speeds, while supersonic jets shrink the extensive landmasses and oceans of the world. And if one prefers not to (or for whatever reason cannot) travel to other regions of the world, people and places reach us in the form of food, clothes, music, television images, and the like; and all kinds of technologies, from the telephone to the internet, enable us to be in touch with people half-way across the world, almost "as if they were present" (Allen and Hamnett 1995: 1). We thus find ourselves in a world that has become smaller over time, one in which borders and boundaries have become more porous than ever, allowing more people and cultures to be cast into "intense and immediate contact with each other," to be brought "closer" together, as it were (Morley and Robins 1995: 115).

5 James Ferguson (ch. 6 in this volume) thus argues that globalization should not be seen simply as a phenomenon of pure connection. It should also be understood in terms of disconnection.

6 We put "uneven" in parenthesis because, while we recognize that the experience of people and places that are marginalized from global processes is important, the book (as well as the rest of this introduction) places more emphasis on the experience of those that are part of planet-wide webs of interconnection. The reason for this focus is that the anthropological literature that deals explicitly with globalization tends to focus on the experience of the latter.

7 The book is also to some extent concerned with related concepts such as transnationalism. Michael Kearney articulates the difference between transnationalism and globalization as follows: "Transnationalism overlaps globalization but typically has a more limited purview. Whereas global processes are largely decentered from specific national territories and take place in a global space, transnational processes are anchored in and transcend one or more

nation-states. Thus transnationalism is the term of choice when referring, for example, to the migration of nationals across the borders of one or of more nations" (1995: 548). See Hannerz 1996 and Ong 1999 for other articulations of the difference between globalization and transnationalism.

8 To be fair, anthropologists are not the only ones concerned with the articulation of the global and the local. But such discussions in other disciplines tend to stay at a theoretical level. There is hardly ever any concrete engagement with the local. Anthony Giddens, for example, views globalization as concerning "the intersection of presence and absence, the interlacing of social events and social relations 'at a distance' with local contextualities" (1991: 21). However, his analysis doesn't go much beyond this. There is no concrete engagement with these local contextualities.

9 See Anna Tsing's concluding article in this volume for a problematization of the common distinction between the "global" and the "local," as well as for a critique of the rhetoric of circulation and flows as the ruling image for global interconnections.

10 The concern of this book is primarily with anthropological work that explicitly focuses on globalization (and related concepts such as transnationalism and diaspora). It does not include, for example, the work of early twentieth-century diffusionists or the writings of 1960s and 1970s political economists of culture. While such work no doubt deals with what we now call global processes, it does not focus on globalization *per se*. Discussions of globalization don't begin in earnest until the late 1980s or so.

11 The work of Waters 1995 and McGrew 1996 has been very helpful in conceptualizing this section.

12 One important difference is that while Harvey sees capitalism as the main driving engine of globalization, Giddens views global processes as operating along four dimensions: capitalism; the inter-state system; militarism; and industrialism.

13 We should note here, as Anthony McGrew points out, that these time/space changes "are not uniformly experienced across the globe. Some regions of the globe are more deeply implicated in global processes than others, and some are more deeply integrated into the global order than others. Within nation-states, some communities (e.g. financial ones) are tightly enmeshed in global networks, while others (e.g. the urban homeless) are totally excluded (although not entirely unaffected) by them. And, even within the same street, some households are more deeply embedded in global processes than others" (1996: 479–80).

14 Globalization as a whole must be understood in terms of simultaneous, complexly related processes in the realms of economy, politics, culture, technology, and so forth. See Held et al. 1999 for one attempt to provide an overall take.

15 To be sure, culture has always been more mobile and less fixed than the classical anthropological approach implies (see Gupta and Ferguson, ch. 3 in this volume). National, regional, and village boundaries have never enclosed culture in the manner that classical anthropological depictions have often indicated. What the intensification of global interconnectedness means, then, is just that the fiction that such boundaries contain cultures and thoroughly regulate cultural exchange can no longer be maintained.

16 The discourse of cultural imperialism is not as popular in academic circles as it was during the 1970s and 1980s (Tomlinson 1999). Nevertheless, it remains an important critical position for understanding the process of globalization. We find this discourse a useful starting point for discussing the cultural dynamics of globalization because it highlights the global asymmetries in the flow of meaning. Such asymmetries continue to be an important part of the world of globalization.

17 The discourse of cultural imperialism is actually a heterogeneous ensemble of complicated, ambiguous, and contradictory ideas. Here, however, our main concern is to identify some of the central tenets that run through the discourse. We thus necessarily gloss over its tensions and contradictions. See Tomlinson 1991 for a more nuanced view of this discourse.

18 The work of John Tomlinson (1997, 1999) significantly influenced the following discussion of the two visions of global uniformity that follows.

19 This scenario is drawn from one of the most important exponents of this view: the American media critic Herbert Schiller. He articulates this view most powerfully in his 1969 classic *Mass Communications and American Empire*.

20 This second vision of global cultural uniformity is drawn more or less from Latouche 1996.

21 This doesn't mean that the West as a geographical entity has ceased to exist. What has happened, to be more precise, is that "the West" as a cultural formation has been pulled apart from "the West" as a geographic entity. The West, in other words, has been de/territorialized.

22 Other names for this process of interpreting foreign cultural forms according to local conditions of reception are indigenization (Appadurai, ch. 2 in this volume), transculturation (Lull 2000), and creolization (Hannerz 1992). We prefer the term "customization" because it is less ideologically loaded than terms such as indigenization, which carry connotations of being rooted in the soil. See Malkki 1997 for a discussion of the problems with metaphors of rootedness.

23 The discussion of customization that follows focuses on the reception of film and television texts. However, this notion is also useful for talking about how people consume commodities (see Friedman, ch. 10, and Meyer, ch. 11, in this volume) and for how they interpret foreign ideologies (see Donham, ch. 17 in this volume).

24 Morley and Robins, for example, point out that television "programs are usually made in such a way as to 'prefer' one reading over another and to invite the viewer to 'take' the message in some particular way, even if such a 'reading' can never be guaranteed" (1995: 127).

25 It is important to point out here that, as a result of this movement of populations, there has been a rise in mass-media flows from the Third World to the First (see Naficy 1993). These mass-media flows cater principally to immigrant populations.

26 The classic literature on immigration has constructed a picture of migrants as beings who leave behind home and country to endure the painful process of incorporation into a new society and culture. Recent scholarship suggests, however, that this picture is not quite accurate, for immigrants have always, to varying degrees and in different ways, maintained networks of interconnection (Glick Schiller et al. 1995). This is not to say that there are no differences between migrants today and those of the past. One main difference is that, given the introduction of modern technologies of transport and communication (telephone, television, airplanes, fax machines, and so forth), it is now a lot easier for immigrants to maintain networks of interconnection. Today's interconnections are thus more dense and intense.

27 The term "diaspora" has a long and complicated history. Unfortunately, we do not have the space to deal with this history here. Suffice it to say that the term has traditionally been used to refer to the Jewish experience of forced exile from Palestine. And nowadays it is commonly employed to designate the experience of forced dispersal more generally (as in the case of Africans) and to speak of those migrant populations that maintain ties with their countries of origin. See Safran 1991 for a discussion of diasporas in modern society.

28 We say "by and large" because nation-states vary (and have historically varied) in their ability to penetrate the nooks and crannies of the everyday lives of the people under their domain. In other words, they are not always (and have not always been) successful in defining and containing the lives of their citizens.

29 This heterogenization of the spaces of the West has not come without its problems, however. There has actually been great resistance in both Europe and the US to this heterogenization. Verena Stolcke (1995), for example, argues that over the past decade or so Europe has witnessed the rise of a political rhetoric of exclusion in which Third

World immigrants and their descendants have been constructed as posing a threat to the nation because they are culturally different. Numerous strategies have thus been developed to nationalize, repatriate, and marginalize these populations. See also Gross et al. ch. 9 in this volume.

30 This is not to imply that the nation-state has become obsolete. Indeed not. The nation-state continues to operate today with great effectiveness. Aihwa Ong, for example, suggests that "the nation-state – along with its juridical-legislative systems, bureaucratic apparatuses, economic entities, modes of governmentality, and war-making capacities – continues to define, discipline, control, and regulate all kinds of populations, whether in movement or in residence" (1999: 15). All we mean to suggest, then, is that while the nation-state might continue to exist, its normative character is not going unchallenged.

31 This is not to say that other countries do not view India as a cultural imperialist power. But this is not the case, for the most part, in Nigeria.

32 If we had the space, we would complicate this picture even further by taking into account the numerous flows of culture that take place within the West itself. See Morley and Robins 1995 for a discussion of mass-media flows and Klimt 2000 for a discussion of population movements.

33 The movement of people is, of course, more complex than this. It involves more than just the flow of populations from the Third World to the First. There are also substantial movements of people from the First World to the Third, most notably tourists (see Ebron 1999), and within both the Third and First Worlds (see Klimt 2000; Malkki 1997; Margold 1995). Unfortunately, we do not have room in the reader to cover this complexity.

REFERENCES

Abu-Lughod, Janet L.
   1989 *Before European Hegemony: The World System AD 1250–1350*. New York: Oxford University Press.
Allen, John and Chris Hamnett
   1995 Introduction. In *A Shrinking World? Global Unevenness and Inequality*. John Allen and Chris Hamnett, eds. Pp. 1–10. New York: Oxford University Press.
Ang, Ien
   1985 *Watching Dallas: Soap Opera and the Melodramatic Imagination*. London: Methuen.
Appadurai, Arjun
   1996 Sovereignty without Territoriality: Notes for a Postnational Geography. In *The Geography of Identity*. Patricia Yaeger, ed. Pp. 40–58. Ann Arbor: University of Michigan Press.
Axford, Barrie
   1995 *The Global System: Economics, Politics, and Culture*. New York: St. Martin's Press.
Basch, Linda, Nina Glick Schiller, and Cristina Szanton Blanc
   1994 *Nations Unbound: Transnational Projects, Postcolonial Predicaments, and Deterritorialized Nation-States*. Langhorne, PA: Gordon and Breach.
Borooah, Romy
   2000 Transformations in Trade and the Constitution of Gender and Rank in Northeast India. *American Ethnologist* 27(2): 371–99.

Clifford, James
  1988 *The Predicament of Culture.* Cambridge, MA: Harvard University Press.
  1997 *Routes: Travel and Translation in the Late Twentieth Century.* Cambridge, MA: Harvard University Press.
Ebron, Paulla A.
  1999 Tourists as Pilgrims: Commercial Fashioning of Transatlantic Politics. *American Ethnologist* 26(4): 910–32.
Foster, Robert J.
  1999 Melanesianist Anthropology in the Era of Globalization. *The Contemporary Pacific* 11(1): 140–58.
García Canclini, Néstor
  1995 *Hybrid Cultures: Strategies for Entering and Leaving Modernity.* Minneapolis: University of Minneapolis Press.
Giddens, Anthony
  1990 *The Consequences of Modernity.* Stanford: Stanford University Press.
  1991 *Modernity and Self-Identity.* Cambridge: Polity Press.
Glick Schiller, Nina, Linda Basch, and Cristina Szanton Blanc
  1995 From Immigrant to Transmigrant: Theorizing Transnational Migration. *Anthropological Quarterly* 68(1): 48–63.
Hall, Stuart
  1995 New Cultures for Old. In *A Place in the World? Places, Cultures, and Globalization.* Doreen Massey and Pat Jess, eds. Pp. 175–213. New York: Oxford University Press.
  1996 The Question of Cultural Identity. In *Modernity: An Introduction to Modern Societies.* Stuart Hall, David Held, Don Hubert, and Kenneth Thompson, eds. Pp. 595–634. Cambridge, MA: Blackwell Publishers.
Hannerz, Ulf
  1991 Scenarios for Peripheral Cultures. In *Culture, Globalization, and the World-System: Contemporary Conditions for the Representation of Identity.* Anthony D. King, ed. Pp. 107–28. Binghamton: Department of Art and Art History, State University of New York at Binghamton.
  1992 *Cultural Complexity: Studies in the Social Organization of Meaning.* New York: Columbia University Press.
  1996 *Transnational Connections: Culture, People, Places.* London: Routledge.
Harvey, David
  1989 *The Condition of Postmodernity.* Oxford: Blackwell Publishers.
Hebdige, Dick
  1987 *Cut 'n' Mix: Culture, Identity, and Caribbean Music.* London: Methuen.
Held, David, Anthony McGrew, David Goldblatt, and Jonathan Perraton
  1999 *Global Transformations: Politics, Economics, and Culture.* Cambridge: Polity Press.
Kearney, Michael
  1995 The Local and the Global: The Anthropology of Globalization and Transnationalism. *Annual Review of Anthropology* 24: 547–65.
Klimt, Andrea
  2000 Enacting National Selves: Authenticity, Adventure, and Disaffection in the Portuguese Diaspora. *Identities* 6(4): 513–50.
Laclau, Ernesto
  1990 *New Reflections on the Revolution of Our Time.* London: Verso.
Latouche, Serge
  1996 *The Westernization of the World: The Significance, Scope and Limits of the Drive towards Global Uniformity.* Cambridge: Polity Press.

Liebes, Tamar and Elihu Katz
   1990   *The Export of Meaning: Cross-cultural Readings of* Dallas. New York: Oxford
   University Press.
Lull, James
   2000   *Media, Communication, Culture: A Global Approach*. 2nd edn. Cambridge: Polity
   Press.
Malkki, Liisa H.
   1997   National Geographic: The Rooting of Peoples and the Territorialization of National
   Identity among Scholars and Refugees. In *Culture, Power, Place: Explorations in Critical
   Anthropology*. Akhil Gupta and James Ferguson, eds. Pp. 52–74. Durham, NC: Duke
   University Press.
Margold, Jane A.
   1995   Narratives of Masculinity and Transnational Migration: Filipino Workers in the
   Middle East. In *Bewitching Women, Pious Men: Gender and Body Politics in Southeast
   Asia*. Aihwa Ong and Michael G. Peletz, eds. Pp. 274–98. Berkeley: University of
   California Press.
Massey, Doreen
   1994   *Space, Place, and Gender*. Minneapolis: University of Minnesota Press.
McGrew, Anthony
   1996   A Global Society? In *Modernity: An Introduction to Modern Societies*. Stuart Hall,
   David Held, Don Hubert, and Kenneth Thompson, eds. Pp. 466–503. Cambridge, MA:
   Blackwell Publishers.
Morley, David
   1992   *Television, Audiences, and Cultural Studies*. London: Routledge.
Morley, David and Kevin Robins
   1995   *Spaces of Identity: Global Media, Electronic Landscapes, and Cultural Boundaries*.
   London: Routledge.
Naficy, Hamid
   1993   *The Making of Exile Cultures: Iranian Television in Los Angeles*. Minneapolis:
   University of Minnesota Press.
Nederveen Pieterse, Jan
   1995   Globalization as Hybridization. In *Global Modernities*. Mike Featherstone, Scott
   Lash, and Roland Robertson, eds. Pp. 45–68. London: Sage Publications.
Ong, Aihwa
   1999   *Flexible Citizenship: The Cultural Logics of Transnationality*. Durham, NC: Duke
   University Press.
Povinelli, Elizabeth A. and George Chauncey
   1999   Thinking Sexuality Transnationally: An Introduction. *GLQ: A Journal of Lesbian
   and Gay Studies* 5(4): 439–50.
Robertson, Roland
   1992   *Globalization: Social Theory and Global Culture*. London: Sage Publications.
Rouse, Roger
   1988   Mexicano, Chicano, Pocho: La Migración Mexicana y el Espacio Social del
   Posmodernismo. *Página Uno*, supplement to *Unomásuno*, December 31: 1–2.
Safran, William
   1991   Diasporas in Modern Societies: Myths of Homeland and Return. *Diaspora* 1(1):
   83–99.
Sassen-Koob, Saskia
   1982   Recomposition and Peripheralization at the Core. *Contemporary Marxism* 5:
   88–100.

Schiller, Herbert I.
  1969   *Mass Communications and American Empire*. New York: Augustus M. Kelly.
Stolcke, Verena
  1995   Talking Culture: New Boundaries, New Rhetorics of Exclusion in Europe. *Current Anthropology* 36(1): 1–24.
Thompson, John B.
  1995   *The Media and Modernity: A Social Theory of the Media*. Stanford: Stanford University Press.
Tomlinson, John
  1991   *Cultural Imperialism*. Baltimore, MD: Johns Hopkins University Press.
  1997   Internationalism, Globalization, and Cultural Imperialism. In *Media and Cultural Regulation*. Kenneth Thompson, ed. Pp. 117–62. London: Sage Publications.
  1999   *Globalization and Culture*. Chicago: University of Chicago Press.
Wallerstein, Immanuel
  1974   *The Modern World System*, vol. 1. New York: Academic Press.
Waters, Malcolm
  1995   *Globalization*. London: Routledge.
Williams, Raymond
  1976   *Keywords*. New York: Oxford University Press.
Wolf, Eric R.
  1982   *Europe and the People without History*. Berkeley: University of California Press.

Part I

Thinking the Global

This first part of our reader presents several general theoretical efforts to map the global condition. These articles suggest, much as we did in our introduction, that the picture of globalization as a homogenizing, one-way flow of culture from the West to the rest does not adequately capture the complex realities of the contemporary world. Hannerz's chapter, for example, points out that while the circuits that connect the West to the rest of the world are no doubt the chief conduits of the global traffic in culture, they are certainly not the only important circuits around. One also has to contend with those that bring the culture of the periphery to the center as well as with the ones that interconnect the countries of the Third World with one another. Appadurai's piece suggests that the global cultural economy is a complex, overlapping, and disjunctive order, one best understood in terms of the relationship among five dimensions of global cultural flows: ethnoscapes (the moving landscape of people), mediascapes (the distribution of the electronic capabilities to disseminate information), technoscapes (the global configuration of technology), financescapes (the disposition of global capital), and ideoscapes (a chain of ideas composed of elements of the Enlightenment worldview). Finally, the article by Gupta and Ferguson is concerned with exploring the production of difference in a world of culturally, politically, and economically intertwined and interdependent spaces. The aim of these chapters is thus to present a nuanced view of the globe, one that highlights the multiple routes of culture and the fact that globalization is not in any simple way producing a world of sameness.

SUGGESTIONS FOR FURTHER READING

Appadurai, Arjun
  1996   *Modernity at Large: Cultural Dimensions of Globalization*. Minneapolis: University of Minnesota Press.

Appadurai, Arjun, ed.
  2000   Globalization. Theme issue. *Public Culture* 12(1).
Clifford, James
  1997   *Routes: Travel and Translation in the Late Twentieth Century.* Cambridge, MA: Harvard University Press.
Friedman, Jonathan
  1994   *Cultural Identity and Global Process.* London: Sage Publications.
  1999   The Hybridization of Roots and the Abhorrence of the Bush. In *Spaces of Culture: City, Nation, World.* Mike Featherstone and Scott Lash, eds. Pp. 230–56. London: Sage Publications.
García Canclini, Néstor
  1995   *Hybrid Cultures: Strategies for Entering and Leaving Modernity.* Minneapolis: University of Minneapolis Press.
Gupta, Akhil, and James Ferguson, eds.
  1997   *Culture, Power, Place: Explorations in Critical Anthropology.* Durham, NC: Duke University Press.
Hannerz, Ulf
  1992   *Cultural Complexity: Studies in the Social Organization of Meaning.* New York: Columbia University Press.
  1996   *Transnational Connections: Culture, People, Places.* New York: Routledge.
Jameson, Fredric, and Masao Miyoshi, eds.
  1998   *The Cultures of Globalization.* Durham, NC: Duke University Press.
Meyer, Birgit, and Peter Geschiere, eds.
  1999   *Globalization and Identity: Dialectics of Flow and Closure.* Oxford: Blackwell Publishers.
Miller, Daniel, ed.
  1995   *Worlds Apart: Modernity through the Prism of the Local.* London: Routledge.
Ong, Aihwa
  1999   *Flexible Citizenship: The Cultural Logics of Transnationality.* Durham, NC: Duke University Press.
Rouse, Roger
  1995   Thinking through Transnationalism: Notes on the Cultural Politics of Class Relations in the Contemporary United States. *Public Culture* 7(2): 353–402.
Tomlinson, John
  1999   *Globalization and Culture.* Chicago: University of Chicago Press.
Wilson, Rob, and Wimal Dissanayake, eds.
  1996   *Global/Local: Cultural Production and the Transnational Imaginary.* Durham, NC: Duke University Press.

1

Notes on the Global Ecumene

Ulf Hannerz

Cultural interrelatedness increasingly reaches across the world. More than ever, there is now a global ecumene.[1] To grasp this fact, in its wide range of manifest-ations and implications, is the largest task now confronting a macro-anthropology of culture. These notes are devoted to two of the issues involved: they identify the nature of center–periphery relationships in cultural terms, and scrutinize the notion that the world is becoming culturally homogenized.

Culture and Center–Periphery Relationships

Until the 1960s or so, acknowledgements of the fact that 'we are all in the same world' were mostly pieties, with uncertain political and intellectual implications. Since then, in the social sciences, the globalizing tendency has usually involved a view of asymmetry; key conceptual pairs have been center (or core) and periphery, metropolis and satellite.[2] Asymmetries are present in the global social organization of meaning as well. But what kind of asymmetries are they? How closely aligned are the asymmetries of culture with those of economy, politics, or military might? How do center–periphery relationships in the world affect structures of meaning and cultural expression?

In political and military terms, the world [during much] of the twentieth century [had] two superpowers, and whatever freedom of movement other countries [exer-cised], whether great or small, it [tended] ultimately to be constrained by this arrangement. In economic terms, the century has by and large seen the United States in a dominant position, with a number of lesser powers grouped around it, varyingly in ascent or decline. In cultural terms, are there other powers than these?

From *Public Culture* 1(2): 66–75. Copyright © 1989, Duke University Press.

The question at least has two sides (which may be to simplify matters). There is that cultural production in the periphery which is somehow in response to the political and economic dominance of the center. Here the world system as defined in political and/or economic terms is obviously given cultural recognition of a sort. On the other hand, there is the issue of cultural diffusion. What defines the center–periphery relationship here are above all asymmetries of input and scale. When the center speaks, the periphery listens, and on the whole does not talk back.

In this case, the cultural centers of the world are not by definition identical with political and economic centers. Are they in practice? Let us consider this in gross terms, as an issue of the overall cultural influence of nations. It can be argued that the center–periphery relationships of culture are not, at least at any particular point in time, a mere reflection of political and economic power. In the American case, the congruence is undeniable. The general cultural influence of the Soviet Union in the world [in the decades of its greatest strength], on the other hand, [remained] modest compared with its political and military power. Among the lesser powers, Britain and France may at present be stronger as cultural than as economic and political centers; this is perhaps debatable. Japan, on the whole, keeps a low cultural profile in the world, despite its economic success. Most of what it exports does not seem to be identifiably marked by Japaneseness.

If the global pattern of center–periphery relationships in culture thus has some degree of separateness, it is easy to see in some instances what is behind a greater cultural influence. To a degree the present cultural influence of Britain and France reflects the fact that the old-style colonial powers could more or less monopolize the center–periphery cultural flow to their domains. In large parts of the world this still makes London or Paris not just *a* center but *the* center. In old settler colonies, historical ties are yet closer, as links of kinship and ancestry also connect the periphery to a specific center. In Australia, when critics refer to 'the cultural cringe', it is the deference to things English they still have in mind. Language is obviously also a factor which may convert political power into cultural influence, and then conserve the latter. As people go on speaking English, French and Portuguese in postcolonial lands, in postcolonial times, old center–periphery relationships get a prolonged lease on life. If all this means that the center–periphery relationships of culture tend to exhibit some lag relative to present and emergent structures of political and economic power, it might also mean that Japan could yet come into greater cultural influence in the world.

One might speculate that people also make different assumptions, in a metacultural fashion, about the nature of the relationship between themselves and their culture. By and large, Americans may not expect that the meanings and the cultural forms they invent are only for themselves; possibly because they have seen at home over the years that practically anybody can become an American. The French may see their culture as a gift to the world. There is a *mission civilisatrice*. The Japanese, on the other hand – so it is said – find it a strange notion that anyone can 'become Japanese', and they put Japanese culture on exhibit, in the framework of organized international contacts, as a way of displaying irreducible distinctiveness rather than in order to make it spread. (Notably, many of those who engage in introducing aspects of Japanese culture to the world are alien culture brokers.[3])

Staying with the conception of cultural centers as places where culture is invented and from which it is diffused, however, one cannot be satisfied with only the very generalized picture of the relative standing of a handful of countries as wholes. Too much is missing, and too much is assumed. Countries do not always exercise their influence at the same level across the gamut of cultural expressions. American influence is at present very diverse, but perhaps most conspicuous in science, technology and popular culture; French influence on world culture is rather of the high culture variety, and in fields like upmarket food and fashion; there is widespread interest in the organization and culture of Japanese corporations. In such more specialized ways, places like the Vatican and the Shia holy city of Qom also organize parts of the world into center–periphery relationships of culture, for certain purposes. As far as asymmetries of cultural flow are concerned, there is likewise the notable instance of the Indian film industry, offering entertainment for large parts of the Third World.

In this context one should also keep in mind that particularly in such fields as science and technology, the spread of knowledge between nations can be actively prevented, for reasons of economic, political and military advantage. Indeed, there are signs that large-scale restrictive management of knowledge is on the increase.[4] Often it is primarily a part of competitive relationships between centers, but it constrains the cultural flow between center and periphery as well, maintaining the advantage of the former.

It is another characteristic of the structure of center–periphery relationships that it has many tiers. Some countries have a strong influence in their regions, due to a well-developed cultural apparatus – Mexico in Latin America, for example, and Egypt in the Arab world. A shared language and cultural tradition can be important in this way, at the same time as a sizeable domestic market for cultural products can give one country an advantageous position in having something to export to the rest of the region. Such regional centers may base their production on meanings and forms wholly internal to the region, or they may operate as cultural brokers, translating influences from first-tier centers into something more adapted to regional conditions.

World cultural flow, it appears, has a much more intricate organization of diversity than is allowed in a picture of a center–periphery structure with just a handful of all-purpose centers. A further issue, obviously, if one tries to arrive at a kind of present-day global cultural flow chart, is to what extent the peripheries indeed talk back; which would in large part be a question of the cultural influence of the Third World on the Occident.

Reggae music, swamis, and Latin American novels exemplify the kind of counter-currents that may first enter one's mind; culture coming fully developed, as it were, from periphery to center, and at the same time culture which the periphery can give away, and keep at the same time. There are indeed instances like these. Yet judging by them alone, however much more desirable one would find it to be able to speak of world culture in terms of equal exchange, the conclusion can at present hardly be avoided that asymmetry rules.

But then there are also other kinds of cultural transfers from periphery to center, which in themselves exemplify asymmetry in other manners. One involves particular embodiments of meaning; objects of art, ritual or other significance, which may not be readily replaceable at the periphery, but which are at one time or other exported, due to the superior economic and political power of the center, and absorbed by its museums or other collections. Here one may see indeed a tangible impoverishment of the cultures of the periphery – often especially in terms of immediate access to the best in one's cultural heritage, as what is removed is what the center defines as capital-C culture of the periphery. This is now a field of controversy, with the representatives of the periphery insisting upon the moral right to demand the decommoditization and repatriation of artifacts to their own countries.[5]

There is likewise the kind of periphery-to-center transfer in which people like anthropologists can come to play a part. Much knowledge concerning the periphery is more available in the center than in the periphery itself, and especially to the specialists on the periphery from the center, because of the greater capacity of the center to organize and analyze knowledge in certain ways. The center may extract the raw materials for this knowledge, so to speak, from the periphery, but as such, it may at the same time remain there, for again, informants and others need not give up the knowledge that they give away. But the process of refining the materials often only occurs in the knowledge institutions of the center, and it is not at all certain that the final product gets back to the periphery. Sometimes, this kind of center–periphery asymmetry is labeled academic imperialism; as we see, it entails a flow in the opposite direction of that usually thought of as cultural imperialism.

Anyway, all this is in gross terms, as a way of beginning to look at cultural management at the most inclusive level. In fact, one does not get very far by talking about the influence of nations, for nations as such, as corporate actors, have only a limited part in the global cultural flow. They may appear in guises such as the USIA, the Fulbright Commission, the British Council, and the Alliance Française, and interact in their own terms in organizations such as UNESCO. Much of the traffic in culture in the world, however, is transnational rather than international. It ignores, subverts and devalues rather than celebrates national boundaries. When we talk about American influence or French influence or Mexican influence, we throw together a great many kinds of asymmetrical relationships, perhaps with a number of symmetrical ones for good measure. A more precise realization of how contemporary world culture is constituted can only result when we take them apart again.

Some Questions about Alarmism

The forecast that the center–periphery flow of culture will lead to the disappearance of cultural differences in the world is encountered fairly frequently these days. "One conclusion still seems unanimously shared," claims a prominent media researcher; "the impressive variety of the world's cultural systems is waning due to a process of 'cultural synchronization' that is without historical precedent" (Hamelink 1983: 3). Horror tales are told: "The incredibly rich local musical tradition of many Third World countries is rapidly disappearing under the onslaught of dawn-to-dusk American pop music." "For starving children in the Brazilian city of Recife, to have a Barbie doll seems more important than food." The prime mover behind this pan-human replication of uniformity is late western capitalism, equipped with media technology, forever luring more communities into dependency on the fringes of an expanding world-wide consumer society. The transnational cultural apparatus is an instrument of hegemony.

The alarmist view of the threat of global cultural homogenization cannot be dismissed out of hand. Yet some questions should be raised which may cast some general light on the problem of the efficacy of the transnational cultural apparatus.

One question is whether the transnational influences must really be seen as wholly deleterious. Current conceptions of cultural imperialism exemplify on the largest imaginable scale the curious fact that according to the economics of culture, to receive may be to lose. In that way, they are a useful antidote to old 'white man's burden' notions of the gifts of culture from center to periphery as unadulterated benefaction. But perhaps a closer examination allows us to see more shades in the picture. In the areas of scholarship and intellectual life in general, we hardly take a conflict for granted between the transnational flow of culture and local cultural creativity the way we do with popular culture. Without a certain openness to impulses from the outside world, we would even expect science, art and literature to become impoverished. Obviously, for example, Nigerian literary life could hardly exist were it not for the importation of literacy and a range of literary forms. But there would not have been a Nigerian Nobel Prize winner in literature in 1986 if Wole Soyinka had not creatively drawn on both a cosmopolitan literary expertise and an imagination rooted in a Nigerian mythology, and turned them into something unique.

Nevertheless, the transnational diffusion of popular culture tends to be described, among intellectuals and policymakers at least, rather unremittingly in terms of its destructive and distracting powers. And this is as true in debate in the Third World (or on behalf of the Third World, among interested outsiders) as in a country like Sweden which, if finer distinctions are to be made, would probably be described as part of the semi-periphery (but hardly, on the other hand, of the semi-center) as far as transnational cultural flow is concerned.

Why, then, are we so quick to assume that in this field the relationship between local and imported culture can only be one of competition? Established assumptions about cultural purity and authenticity probably come to the surface here. We imagine that local products are threatened with extinction through the importation of 'cheap foreign junk'. In such references one may detect some hypocrisy, insofar as they imply that all local products are of great intellectual or esthetic merit, never merely cheap local junk. But we also ignore the possibility that the formal symbol systems of popular culture and the media, and the skills in handling the symbol systems, can be transferred between cultures. As long as there is room for local cultural production as well, this may in itself be helped in its development by the availability of a wider range of models. And at least to the extent that the Nigerian example is anything to go by, it seems to be a dubious assumption that there will never be such room for local production, or that it cannot be created. (But I will have a little more to say about the particular Nigerian conditions below.)

It may be objected that such notions of cultural enrichment are not to the point, that even if what is imported is seen as equipment, models and stimuli, it is still destructive insofar as it irreversibly changes local culture. Whatever modifications these imports undergo, however much they are integrated with indigenous culture, they may impose alien formats on it. When literacy comes in, whatever modes of thought may be linked to pure orality are likely to be corrupted.[6] A Nigerian sitcom is still a sitcom. The very shape of popular culture as a social organizational phenomenon, with its great asymmetry in the relationship between performers and audience, might threaten older and more participatory arrangements of cultural expression.

Again this is a serious argument. But there is perhaps only a thin line between a defense of authenticity and an antiquarianism which often turns out to be vicarious. Nigeria, for example, could hardly in this postcolonial era go back completely to its precolonial cultural heritage, for pure tradition and its collective form of expression would not serve the contemporary structures of the country and could not match the everyday experiences and desires of many Nigerians today. A popular culture, and a media technology, are now as much necessities in large parts of the Third World as they are in the Occident, and the more realistic hope for continued cultural diversity in the world, with some linkage to local heritage, would rather seem to be for a diversity in motion, one of coexistence as well as creative interaction between the transnational and the indigenous.

Another problem with alarmism tends to be the quality of the evidence for it. Quite frequently it is anecdotal – "I switched on the television set in my hotel room in Lagos (or Manila, or Tel Aviv, or Geneva), and found that *Dallas* was on." In a more sophisticated version, it may be pointed out that on one Third World television channel or other, some high percentage of the programming is imported.

To be more completely persuasive, however, arguments about the impact of the transnational cultural flow would have to say something about how the people respond to it. The mere fact that Third World television stations buy a lot of imported programs, for example, often has more to do with the fact that they are cheap than that audiences are necessarily enthralled with them. We may have little idea about how many television sets are on, when they are shown, and much less what is the quality of attention to them.

At least as problematic is the sense that people make of the transnational cultural flow. Even when we refer to it as a 'flow of meaning', we must keep in mind the uncertainties built into the communicative process. If one cannot be too sure of perfect understanding even in a face-to-face interaction in a local context with much cultural redundancy, the difficulties (or the opportunities for innovative interpretations, if one wants to see it another way) multiply where there is largely a one-way cultural flow, between people whose perspectives have been shaped in very different contexts, in places very distant from one another. The meaning of the transnational cultural flow is thus in the eye of the beholder; what he sees we generally know little about.[7]

One intricate issue here is the relationship between different symbolic modes and the global diversity of culture. Do some symbolic forms, in some modes, travel better than others? We know well enough where the barriers of incomprehension are between languages. How is the transnational spread of popular culture affected by varying sensibilities with respect to other modes, particularly the musical and gestural? One may rather facilely explain the popularity of Indian and Hong Kong movies over much of the Third World by referring to the fact that they are cheap (which appeals to distributors) and action-packed (which appeals to somewhat unsophisticated audiences). But the latter point may hide as much as it reveals.

What kind, or degree, of precision is there in the audience appreciation of the symbolic forms of another country?[8]

It seems also that the consequences of transnational cultural flow must be understood as they unfold over time. The murderous threat of cultural imperialism is often rhetorically depicted as involving the high-tech culture of the metropolis, with powerful organizational backing, facing a defenseless, small-scale folk culture. Such encounters do perhaps occur. Yet at other times and in other places this is a very ahistorical view. In Nigeria, in the case of popular music but probably with reference to other popular culture forms as well, it seems important that the process by which external borrowings have been absorbed has some time depth. Metropolitan popular music, its genres and its instruments, have filtered into the West African coast societies gradually over the last century, introduced to begin with by modest means. There has been time, then, to absorb such influences, and in turn modify the modifications, and to fit the new popular culture to the evolving national social structure, its audiences and its situations. And this is the local scene which now meets the transnational cultural industries of the late twentieth century.

One can think of two rough scenarios of the long-term effects of transnational cultural flows. I would like to call them the scenarios of saturation and maturation. The former would suggest that as the transnational cultural apparatus unendingly pounds on the sensibilities of the peoples of the periphery, local culture will cumulatively assimilate more and more of the imported meanings and forms, becoming gradually indistinguishable from them. At any one time, what is considered local culture is a little more like transnational imports than what went before it as local culture. This may not sound altogether implausible. The maturation scenario, on the other hand, is based on the possibility that with time, imported cultural items which were at first to some degree in their unaltered, wholly alien forms would with time come to be taken apart, tampered and tinkered with, as people would evolve their own way of using them in a manner more in line with a culture of fundamentally local character.

The two scenarios describe opposing trajectories, but in real life they may well appear interwoven with one another. On the whole, the history of Nigerian popular music seems to have much in common with the maturation scenario. And one can see reasons why this should be so: developed native musical traditions; an early involvement with foreign cultural imports at a time when the pressure of the transnational cultural apparatus was modest, thus allowing time to adapt; a sizeable market for the local product. Yet this is not to say that the Nigerian market cannot continuously make some room for new music from abroad as well.

The nature of the market is the factor of some importance, not least when one can see the transnational cultural flow as a flow of commodities. Often the importation of culture seems to presume a market which is, as it were, middling poor. Again, when for example Nigerian television stations, and other stations more or less on the periphery, buy programming from the center, the reason is that they cannot afford to produce their own. On the other hand, they are not poor enough not to be able to import. But the more or less peripheral places can differ in these respects, and can differ also with regard to different kinds of cultural commodities, and can differ over time. Nigeria, the most populous country in Africa, at times quite affluent due to its oil exports, is better equipped than most to engage in cultural import substitution and build up its own internal cultural apparatus. It is also one of those countries which may find some market for its own cultural commodities in its wider region, and eventually to some extent reach a wider market yet. It has some potential for becoming a center of sorts in its own right. Smaller national markets may be more dependent on the importation of popular cultural goods from either regional or global centers.

On the other hand, if cultural commodities will only flow transnationally to places where markets exist, there may be places too poor to hold much promise in this regard. As the countries of the periphery are often vulnerable to changes in the relationship of local economies to that of the world, moreover, markets may shift dramatically over time. Small town people who bought imported popular fashions in the marketplace yesterday are perhaps no longer able to do so today; they have other reasons for the import substitution. Quite possibly, if the hold of the center on the economies of the peripheries is such as to weaken them, at one time or over time, that very fact may also limit its own cultural power over them.

NOTES

1 Kopytoff (1987: 10) defines the ecumene as a "region of persistent cultural interaction and exchange." Kroeber (1948: 423), recalling that the Greeks in antiquity used this term for "the inhabited world," comments that it "has a modern utility as a convenient designation of the total area reached by traceable diffusion influences from the main higher centers of Eurasia at which most new culture had up to then been produced". Again, a world culture ordered by center–periphery relationships.
2 The core–periphery conceptual pair (at times with semi-periphery thrown in to form a trio) is favored by Wallerstein 1974; the metropolis–satellite contrast may remain most strongly associated with Frank (e.g., 1967); Shils, although writing from a very different perspective, may have done more than anybody else to put the center–periphery pair into circulation (e.g., 1975). For a slightly earlier attempt, see Moore 1966.
3 A comment by Amar Nath Pandeya at a meeting of Asian academics is to the point: "We in India receive information on Japanese society and science via America, and Americans' image of Japan is given to us as if it were what Japan really is. Japan exports cars and machines, but not culture or science; Japanese scholars and academic circles are not responsive to international needs. What we want to know is not the American people's view of Japan, but the Japanese people's view of Japan" (Abdel-Malek and Pandeya 1981: 12).
4 See, for example, contributions to the volume edited by Gibbons and Wittrock (1985).
5 See discussion of such issues in McBryde 1985.
6 See for example Rodgers's (1984) analysis of the impact of literacy on Batak thinking about kinship.
7 A classic instance from anthropology is the Tiv reinterpretation of *Hamlet*, as recounted by Laura Bohannan (1966). A news item on *Dallas*, the television serial, in the *International Herald Tribune* tells a similar story (Friedman 1986). A team of communication researchers at Hebrew University in Jerusalem conducted a study of how Israelis of different national origins decoded American television programs generally, and *Dallas* specifically. The most striking finding was that the groups came up with quite divergent interpretations of the program. Recent Russian immigrants were suspicious of the show and paid attention to the

credit to find out who was the power behind it. One of them said, "they want us to think the rich are unhappy so we average people will feel more content." They also looked in a more deterministic way at the activities of the characters – JR did what he did because he had to, as a businessman. The Moroccan Jews as well as the Israeli Arabs saw the show as some sort of depiction of reality, but a reality they were uncomfortable with. The Arabs did not want to watch *Dallas* in mixed company, and when it had shown Sue Ellen leaving her husband JR to go and live with her lover, this group of viewers apparently unconsciously censored the occurrence and reported that she had returned to her father. The kibbutz Israelis were most like Americans in the response, according to this study. They related to it playfully, as a source of fantasy.

8 Worth (1981: 72) touches upon such problems in his discussion of film anthropology, as he asks how cinematic understandings are distributed. Do "film language" communities have anything to do with language communities; do they relate to the distribution of cognitive styles? Sperber's (1985) "epidemiological" concern with the differential cognitive contagiousness of representations may also be related to transnational cultural flows in different symbolic modes.

REFERENCES

Abdel-Malek, Anour, and Amar Nath Pandeya (eds.) 1981. *Intellectual Creativity in Endogenous Culture*, Tokyo: The United Nations University.

Bohannan, Laura. 1966. "Shakespeare in the Bush," *Natural History*, 75(7): 28–33.

Frank, Andre Gunder. 1967. *Capitalism and Underdevelopment in Latin America*, New York: Monthly Review Press.

Friedman, Thomas L. 1986. "Israeli Cultural Groups View 'Dallas' but See a Different Show," *International Herald Tribune*, April 3.

Gibbons, Michael, and Bjorn Wittrock (eds.) 1985. *Science as a Commodity*, Harlow, Essex: Longman.

Hamelink, Cees T. 1983. *Cultural Autonomy in Global Communications*, New York: Longman.

Kopytoff, Igor. 1987. "The Internal African Frontier: The Making of African Political Culture," in *The African Frontier*, Bloomington: Indiana University Press.

Kroeber, A. L. 1948. *Anthropology*, New York: Harcourt, Brace.

McBryde, Isabel (ed.) 1985. *Who Owns the Past?*, Melbourne: Oxford University Press.

Moore, Wilbert E. 1966. "Global Sociology: The World as a Singular System," *American Journal of Sociology*, 71: 475–82.

Rodgers, Susan. 1984. "Orality, Literacy, and Batak Concepts of Marriage Alliance," *Journal of Anthropological Research*, 40: 433–50.

Shils, Edward. 1975. *Center and Periphery*, Chicago: University of Chicago Press.

Sperber, Dan. 1985. "Anthropology and Psychology: Towards an Epidemiology of Representations," *Man*, 20: 73–89.

Wallerstein, Immanuel. 1974. *The Modern World-System*, New York: Academic Press.

Worth, Sol. 1981. *Studying Visual Communication*, Philadelphia: University of Pennsylvania.

2

Disjuncture and Difference in the Global Cultural Economy

Arjun Appadurai

It takes only the merest acquaintance with the facts of the modern world to note that it is now an interactive system in a sense that is strikingly new. Historians and sociologists, especially those concerned with translocal processes (Hodgson 1974) and the world systems associated with capitalism (Abu-Lughod 1989; Braudel 1981–4; Curtin 1984; Wallerstein 1974; Wolf 1982), have long been aware that the world has been a congeries of large-scale interactions for many centuries. Yet today's world involves interactions of a new order and intensity. Cultural transactions between social groups in the past have generally been restricted, sometimes by the facts of geography and ecology, and at other times by active resistance to interactions with the Other (as in China for much of its history and in Japan before the Meiji Restoration). Where there have been sustained cultural transactions across large parts of the globe, they have usually involved the long-distance journey of commodities (and of the merchants most concerned with them) and of travelers and explorers of every type (Helms 1988; Schafer 1963). The two main forces for sustained cultural interaction before this century have been warfare (and the large-scale political systems sometimes generated by it) and religions of conversion, which have sometimes, as in the case of Islam, taken warfare as one of the legitimate instruments of their expansion. Thus, between travelers and merchants, pilgrims and conquerors, the world has seen much long-distance (and long-term) cultural traffic. This much seems self-evident.

But few will deny that given the problems of time, distance, and limited technologies for the command of resources across vast spaces, cultural dealings between socially and spatially separated groups have, until the past few centuries, been bridged at great cost and sustained over time only with great effort. The forces of cultural gravity seemed always to pull away from the formation of large-scale

From *Modernity at Large: Cultural Dimensions of Globalization*, pp. 27–47. Minneapolis: University of Minnesota Press, 1996.

ecumenes, whether religious, commercial, or political, toward smaller-scale accretions of intimacy and interest.

Sometime in the past few centuries, the nature of this gravitational field seems to have changed. Partly because of the spirit of the expansion of western maritime interests after 1500, and partly because of the relatively autonomous developments of large and aggressive social formations in the Americas (such as the Aztecs and the Incas), in Eurasia (such as the Mongols and their descendants, the Mughals and Ottomans), in island Southeast Asia (such as the Buginese), and in the kingdoms of precolonial Africa (such as Dahomey), an overlapping set of ecumenes began to emerge, in which congeries of money, commerce, conquest, and migration began to create durable cross-societal bonds. This process was accelerated by the technology transfers and innovations of the late eighteenth and nineteenth centuries (e.g., Bayly 1989), which created complex colonial orders centered on European capitals and spread throughout the non-European world. This intricate and overlapping set of Eurocolonial worlds (first Spanish and Portuguese, later principally English, French, and Dutch) set the basis for a permanent traffic in ideas of peoplehood and selfhood, which created the imagined communities (Anderson 1983) of recent nationalisms throughout the world.

With what Benedict Anderson has called "print capitalism," a new power was unleashed in the world, the power of mass literacy and its attendant large-scale production of projects of ethnic affinity that were remarkably free of the need for face-to-face communication or even of indirect communication between persons and groups. The act of reading things together set the stage for movements based on a paradox – the paradox of constructed primordialism. There is, of course, a great deal else that is involved in the story of colonialism and its dialectically generated nationalisms (Chatterjee 1986), but the issue of constructed ethnicities is surely a crucial strand in this tale.

But the revolution of print capitalism and the cultural affinities and dialogues unleashed by it were only modest precursors to the world we live in now. For in the past century, there has been a technological explosion, largely in the domain of transportation and information, that makes the interactions of a print-dominated world seem as hard-won and as easily erased as the print revolution made earlier forms of cultural traffic appear. For with the advent of the steamship, the automobile, the airplane, the camera, the computer, and the telephone, we have entered into an altogether new condition of neighborliness, even with those most distant from ourselves. Marshall McLuhan, among others, sought to theorize about this world as a "global village," but theories such as McLuhan's appear to have overestimated the communitarian implications of the new media order (McLuhan and Powers 1989). We are now aware that with media, each time we are tempted to speak of the global village, we must be reminded that media create communities with "no sense of place" (Meyrowitz 1985). The world we live in now seems rhizomic (Deleuze and Guattari 1987), even schizophrenic, calling for theories of rootlessness, alienation, and psychological distance between individuals and groups on the one hand, and fantasies (or nightmares) of electronic propinquity on the other. Here, we are close to the central problematic of cultural processes in today's world.

Thus, the curiosity that recently drove Pico Iyer to Asia (1988) is in some ways the product of a confusion between some ineffable McDonaldization of the world and the much subtler play of indigenous trajectories of desire and fear with global flows of people and things. Indeed, Iyer's own impressions are testimony to the fact that, if *a* global cultural system is emerging, it is filled with ironies and resistances, sometimes camouflaged as passivity and a bottomless appetite in the Asian world for things western.

Iyer's own account of the uncanny Philippine affinity for American popular music is rich testimony to the global culture of the hyperreal, for somehow Philippine renditions of American popular songs are both more widespread in the Philippines, and more disturbingly faithful to their originals, than they are in the United States today. An entire nation seems to have learned to mimic Kenny Rogers and the Lennon sisters, like a vast Asian Motown chorus. But *Americanization* is certainly a pallid term to apply to such a situation, for not only are there more Filipinos singing perfect renditions of some American songs (often from the American past) than there are Americans doing so, there is also, of course, the fact that the rest of their lives is not in complete synchrony with the referential world that first gave birth to these songs.

In a further globalizing twist on what Fredric Jameson has recently called "nostalgia for the present" (1989), these Filipinos look back to a world they have never lost. This is one of the central ironies of the politics of global cultural flows, especially in the arena of entertainment and leisure. It plays havoc with the hegemony of Eurochronology. American nostalgia feeds on Filipino desire represented as a hypercompetent reproduction. Here, we have nostalgia without memory. The paradox, of course, has its explanations, and they are historical; unpacked, they lay bare the story of the American missionization and political rape of the Philippines, one result of which has been the creation of a nation of make-believe Americans, who tolerated for so long a leading lady who played the piano while the slums of Manila expanded and decayed. Perhaps the most radical postmodernists would argue that this is hardly surprising because in the peculiar chronicities of late capitalism, pastiche and nostalgia are central modes of image production and reception. Americans themselves are hardly in the present anymore as they stumble into the megatechnologies of the twenty-first century garbed in the film-noir scenarios of sixties' chills, fifties' diners, forties' clothing, thirties' houses, twenties' dances, and so on ad infinitum.

As far as the United States is concerned, one might suggest that the issue is no longer one of nostalgia but of a social *imaginaire* built largely around reruns. Jameson was bold to link the politics of nostalgia to the postmodern commodity sensibility, and surely he was right (1983). The drug wars in Colombia recapitulate the tropical sweat of Vietnam, with Ollie North and his succession of masks – Jimmy Stewart concealing John Wayne concealing Spiro Agnew and all of them transmogrifying into Sylvester Stallone, who wins in Afghanistan – thus simultaneously fulfilling the secret American envy of Soviet imperialism and the rerun (this time with a happy ending) of the Vietnam War. The Rolling Stones, in their fifties, gyrate before eighteen-year-olds who do not appear to need the machinery of nostalgia to be sold on their parents' heroes. Paul McCartney is selling the Beatles to a new audience by hitching his oblique nostalgia to their desire for the new that smacks of the old. *Dragnet* is back in nineties drag, and so is *Adam-12*, not to speak of *Batman* and *Mission Impossible*, all dressed up technologically but remarkably faithful to the atmospherics of their originals.

The past is now not a land to return to in a simple politics of memory. It has become a synchronic warehouse of cultural scenarios, a kind of temporal central casting, to which recourse can be taken as appropriate, depending on the movie to be made, the scene to be enacted, the hostages to be rescued. All this is par for the course, if you follow Jean Baudrillard or Jean-François Lyotard into a world of signs wholly unmoored from their social signifiers (all the world's a Disneyland). But I would like to suggest that the apparent increasing substitutability of whole periods and postures for one another, in the cultural styles of advanced capitalism, is tied to larger global forces, which have done much to show Americans that the past is usually another country. If your present is their future (as in much modernization theory and in many self-satisfied tourist fantasies), and their future is your past (as in the case of the Filipino virtuosos of American popular music), then your own past can be made to appear as simply a normalized modality of your present. Thus, although some anthropologists may continue to relegate their Others to temporal spaces that they do not themselves occupy (Fabian 1983), postindustrial cultural productions have entered a postnostalgic phase.

The crucial point, however, is that the United States is no longer the puppeteer of a world system of images but is only one node of a complex transnational construction of imaginary landscapes. The world we live in today is characterized by a new role for the imagination in social life. To grasp this new role, we need to bring together the old idea of images, especially mechanically produced images (in the Frankfurt School sense); the idea of the imagined community (in Anderson's sense); and the French idea of the imaginary (*imaginaire*) as a constructed landscape of collective aspirations, which is no more and no less real than the collective representations of Émile Durkheim, now mediated through the complex prism of modern media.

The image, the imagined, the imaginary – these are all terms that direct us to something critical and new in global cultural processes: *the imagination as a social practice*. No longer mere fantasy (opium for the masses whose real work is else-where), no longer simple escape (from a world defined principally by more concrete purposes and structures), no longer elite pastime (thus not relevant to the lives of ordinary people), and no longer mere contemplation (irrelevant for new forms of desire and subjectivity), the imagination has become an organized field of social practices, a form of work (in the sense of both labor and culturally organized practice), and a form of negotiation between sites of agency (individuals) and globally defined fields of possibility. This unleashing of the imagination links the play of pastiche (in some settings) to the terror and coercion of states and their competitors. The imagination is now central to all forms of agency, is itself a social fact, and is the key component of the new global order. But to make this claim meaningful, we must address some other issues.

Homogenization and Heterogenization

The central problem of today's global interactions is the tension between cultural homogenization and cultural heterogenization. A vast array of empirical facts could be brought to bear on the side of the homogenization argument, and much of it has come from the left end of the spectrum of media studies (Hamelink 1983; Mattelart

1983; Schiller 1976), and some from other perspectives (Gans 1985; Iyer 1988). Most often, the homogenization argument subspeciates into either an argument about Americanization or an argument about commoditization, and very often the two arguments are closely linked. What these arguments fail to consider is that at least as rapidly as forces from various metropolises are brought into new societies they tend to become indigenized in one or another way: this is true of music and housing styles as much as it is true of science and terrorism, spectacles and constitutions. The dynamics of such indigenization have just begun to be explored systemically (Barber 1987; Feld 1988; Hannerz 1987, 1989; Ivy 1988; Nicoll 1989; Yoshimoto 1989), and much more needs to be done. But it is worth noticing that for the people of Irian Jaya, Indonesianization may be more worrisome than Americanization, as Japanization may be for Koreans, Indianization for Sri Lankans, Vietnamization for the Cambodians, and Russianization for the people of Soviet Armenia and the Baltic republics. Such a list of alternative fears to Americanization could be greatly expanded, but it is not a shapeless inventory: for polities of smaller scale, there is always a fear of cultural absorption by polities of larger scale, especially those that are nearby. One man's imagined community is another man's political prison.

This scalar dynamic, which has widespread global manifestations, is also tied to the relationship between nations and states, to which I shall return later. For the moment let us note that the simplification of these many forces (and fears) of homogenization can also be exploited by nation-states in relation to their own minorities, by posing global commoditization (or capitalism, or some other such external enemy) as more real than the threat of its own hegemonic strategies.

The new global cultural economy has to be seen as a complex, overlapping, disjunctive order that cannot any longer be understood in terms of existing center–periphery models (even those that might account for multiple centers and peripheries). Nor is it susceptible to simple models of push and pull (in terms of migration theory), or of surpluses and deficits (as in traditional models of balance of trade), or of consumers and producers (as in most neo-Marxist theories of development). Even the most complex and flexible theories of global development that have come out of the Marxist tradition (Amin 1980; Mandel 1978; Wallerstein 1974; Wolf 1982) are inadequately quirky and have failed to come to terms with what Scott Lash and John Urry have called disorganized capitalism (1987). The complexity of the current global economy has to do with certain fundamental disjunctures between economy, culture, and politics that we have only begun to theorize.[1]

I propose that an elementary framework for exploring such disjunctures is to look at the relationship among five dimensions of global cultural flows that can be termed (a) *ethnoscapes*, (b) *mediascapes*, (c) *technoscapes*, (d) *financescapes*, and (e) *ideoscapes*.[2] The suffix *-scape* allows us to point to the fluid, irregular shapes of these landscapes, shapes that characterize international capital as deeply as they do international clothing styles. These terms with the common suffix *-scape* also indicate that these are not objectively given relations that look the same from every angle of vision but, rather, that they are deeply perspectival constructs, inflected by the historical, linguistic, and political situatedness of different sorts of actors: nation-states, multinationals, diasporic communities, as well as subnational groupings and movements (whether religious, political, or economic), and even intimate face-to-face groups, such as villages, neighborhoods, and families. Indeed, the individual actor is the last locus of this perspectival set of landscapes, for these landscapes are eventually navigated by agents who both experience and constitute larger formations, in part from their own sense of what these landscapes offer.

These landscapes thus are the building blocks of what (extending Benedict Anderson) I would like to call *imagined worlds*, that is, the multiple worlds that are constituted by the historically situated imaginations of persons and groups spread around the globe (see Appadurai 1996: ch. 1). An important fact of the world we live in today is that many persons on the globe live in such imagined worlds (and not just in imagined communities) and thus are able to contest and sometimes even subvert the imagined worlds of the official mind and of the entrepreneurial mentality that surround them.

By *ethnoscape*, I mean the landscape of persons who constitute the shifting world in which we live: tourists, immigrants, refugees, exiles, guest workers, and other moving groups and individuals constitute an essential feature of the world and appear to affect the politics of (and between) nations to a hitherto unprecedented degree. This is not to say that there are no relatively stable communities and networks of kinship, friendship, work, and leisure, as well as of birth, residence, and other filial forms. But it is to say that the warp of these stabilities is everywhere shot through with the woof of human motion, as more persons and groups deal with the realities of having to move or the fantasies of wanting to move. What is more, both these realities and fantasies now function on larger scales, as men and women from villages in India think not just of moving to Poona or Madras but of moving to Dubai and Houston, and refugees from Sri Lanka find themselves in South India as well as in Switzerland, just as the Hmong are driven to London as well as to Philadelphia. And as international capital shifts its needs, as production and technology generate different needs, as nation-states shift their policies on refugee populations, these moving groups can never afford to let their imaginations rest too long, even if they wish to.

By *technoscape*, I mean the global configuration, also ever fluid, of technology and the fact that technology, both high and low, both mechanical and informational, now moves at high speeds across various kinds of previously impervious boundaries. Many countries now are the roots of multinational enterprise: a huge steel complex in Libya may involve interests from India, China, Russia, and Japan, providing different components of new technological configurations. The odd distribution of technologies, and thus the peculiarities of these technoscapes, are increasingly driven not by any obvious economies of scale, of political control, or of market rationality but by increasingly complex relationships among money flows, political possibilities, and the availability of both un- and highly skilled labor. So, while India exports waiters and chauffeurs to Dubai and Sharjah, it also exports software engineers to the United States – indentured briefly to Tata-Burroughs or the World Bank, then laundered through the State Department to become wealthy resident aliens, who are in turn objects of seductive messages to invest their money and know-how in federal and state projects in India.

The global economy can still be described in terms of traditional indicators (as the World Bank continues to do) and studied in terms of traditional comparisons (as in Project Link at the University of Pennsylvania), but the complicated technoscapes (and the shifting ethnoscapes) that underlie these indicators and comparisons are further out of the reach of the queen of social sciences than ever before. How is one to make a meaningful comparison of wages in Japan and the United States or of real-estate costs in New York and Tokyo, without taking sophisticated account of the very complex fiscal and investment flows that link the two economies through a global grid of currency speculation and capital transfer?

Thus it is useful to speak as well of *financescapes*, as the disposition of global capital is now a more mysterious, rapid, and difficult landscape to follow than ever before, as currency markets, national stock exchanges, and commodity speculations move megamonies through national turnstiles at blinding speed, with vast, absolute implications for small differences in percentage points and time units. But the critical point is that the global relationship among ethnoscapes, technoscapes, and finan-cescapes is deeply disjunctive and profoundly unpredictable because each of these landscapes is subject to its own constraints and incentives (some political, some informational, and some technoenvironmental), at the same time as each acts as a constraint and a parameter for movements in the others. Thus, even an elementary model of global political economy must take into account the deeply disjunctive relationships among human movement, technological flow, and financial transfers.

Further refracting these disjunctures (which hardly form a simple, mechanical global infrastructure in any case) are what I call *mediascapes* and *ideoscapes*, which are closely related landscapes of images. *Mediascapes* refer both to the distribution of the electronic capabilities to produce and disseminate information (newspapers, magazines, television stations, and film-production studios), which are now avail-able to a growing number of private and public interests throughout the world, and to the images of the world created by these media. These images involve many complicated inflections, depending on their mode (documentary or entertainment), their hardware (electronic or preelectronic), their audiences (local, national, or transnational), and the interests of those who own and control them. What is most important about these mediascapes is that they provide (especially in their television, film, and cassette forms) large and complex repertoires of images, narra-tives, and ethnoscapes to viewers throughout the world, in which the world of commodities and the world of news and politics are profoundly mixed. What this means is that many audiences around the world experience the media themselves as a complicated and interconnected repertoire of print, celluloid, electronic screens, and billboards. The lines between the realistic and the fictional landscapes they see are blurred, so that the farther away these audiences are from the direct experiences of metropolitan life, the more likely they are to construct imagined worlds that are chimerical, aesthetic, even fantastic objects, particularly if assessed by the criteria of some other perspective, some other imagined world.

Mediascapes, whether produced by private or state interests, tend to be image-centered, narrative-based accounts of strips of reality, and what they offer to those who experience and transform them is a series of elements (such as characters, plots, and textual forms) out of which scripts can be formed of imagined lives, their own as well as those of others living in other places. These scripts can and do get disaggre-gated into complex sets of metaphors by which people live (Lakoff and Johnson 1980) as they help to constitute narratives of the Other and protonarratives of possible lives, fantasies that could become prolegomena to the desire for acquisition and movement.

Ideoscapes are also concatenations of images, but they are often directly political and frequently have to do with the ideologies of states and the counterideologies of movements explicitly oriented to capturing state power or a piece of it. These ideoscapes are composed of elements of the Englightenment worldview, which consists of a chain of ideas, terms, and images, including *freedom, welfare, rights, sovereignty, representation*, and the master term *democracy*. The master narrative of the Enlightenment (and its many variants in Britain, France, and the United States) was constructed with a certain internal logic and presupposed a certain relationship between reading, representation, and the public sphere. (For the dynamics of this process in the early history of the United States, see Warner 1990.) But the diaspora of these terms and images across the world, especially since the nineteenth century, has loosened the internal coherence that held them together in a Euro-American master narrative and provided instead a loosely structured synopticon of politics, in which different nation-states, as part of their evolution, have organized their political cultures around different keywords (e.g., Williams 1976).

As a result of the differential diaspora of these keywords, the political narratives that govern communication between elites and followers in different parts of the world involve problems of both a semantic and pragmatic nature: semantic to the extent that words (and their lexical equivalents) require careful translation from context to context in their global movements, and pragmatic to the extent that the use of these words by political actors and their audiences may be subject to very different sets of contextual conventions that mediate their translation into public politics. Such conventions are not only matters of the nature of political rhetoric: for example, what does the aging Chinese leadership mean when it refers to the dangers of hooliganism? What does the South Korean leadership mean when it speaks of discipline as the key to democratic industrial growth?

These conventions also involve the far more subtle question of what sets of communicative genres are valued in what way (newspapers versus cinema, for example) and what sorts of pragmatic genre conventions govern the collective readings of different kinds of text. So, while an Indian audience may be attentive to the resonances of a political speech in terms of some keywords and phrases reminiscent of Hindi cinema, a Korean audience may respond to the subtle codings of Buddhist or neo-Confucian rhetoric encoded in a political document. The very relationship of reading to hearing and seeing may vary in important ways that determine the morphology of these different ideoscapes as they shape themselves in different national and transnational contexts. This globally variable synaesthesia has hardly even been noted, but it demands urgent analysis. Thus *democracy* has clearly become a master term, with powerful echoes from Haiti and Poland to the former Soviet Union and China, but it sits at the center of a variety of ideoscapes, composed of distinctive pragmatic configurations of rough translations of other central terms from the vocabulary of the Enlightenment. This creates ever new terminological kaleidoscopes, as states (and the groups that seek to capture them) seek to pacify populations whose own ethnoscapes are in motion and whose mediascapes may create severe problems for the ideoscapes with which they are presented. The fluidity of ideoscapes is complicated in particular by the growing diasporas (both voluntary and involuntary) of intellectuals who continuously inject new meaning-streams into the discourse of democracy in different parts of the world.

This extended terminological discussion of the five terms I have coined sets the basis for a tentative formulation about the conditions under which current global flows occur: they occur in and through the growing disjunctures among ethnoscapes, technoscapes, financescapes, mediascapes, and ideoscapes. This formulation, the core of my model of global cultural flow, needs some explanation. First, people, machinery, money, images, and ideas now follow increasingly nonisomorphic paths; of course, at all periods in human history, there have been some disjunctures in the flows of these things, but the sheer speed, scale, and volume of each of these flows are now so great that the disjunctures have become central to the politics of global culture. The Japanese are notoriously hospitable to ideas and are stereotyped as inclined to export (all) and import (some) goods, but they are also notoriously closed to immigration, like the Swiss, the Swedes, and the Saudis. Yet the Swiss and the Saudis accept populations of guest workers, thus creating labor diasporas of Turks, Italians, and other circum-Mediterranean groups. Some such guest-worker groups maintain continuous contact with their home nations, like the Turks, but others, like high-level South Asian migrants, tend to desire lives in their new homes, raising anew the problem of reproduction in a deterritorialized context.

Deterritorialization, in general, is one of the central forces of the modern world because it brings laboring populations into the lower-class sectors and spaces of relatively wealthy societies, while sometimes creating exaggerated and intensified senses of criticism or attachment to politics in the home state. Deterritorialization, whether of Hindus, Sikhs, Palestinians, or Ukrainians, is now at the core of a variety of global fundamentalisms, including Islamic and Hindu fundamentalism. In the Hindu case, for example, it is clear that the overseas movement of Indians has been exploited by a variety of interests both within and outside India to create a complicated network of finances and religious identifications, by which the problem of cultural reproduction for Hindus abroad has become tied to the politics of Hindu fundamentalism at home.

At the same time, deterritorialization creates new markets for film companies, art impresarios, and travel agencies, which thrive on the need of the deterritorialized population for contact with its homeland. Naturally, these invented homelands, which constitute the mediascapes of deterritorialized groups, can often become sufficiently fantastic and one-sided that they provide the material for new ideoscapes in which ethnic conflicts can begin to erupt. The creation of Khalistan, an invented homeland of the deterritorialized Sikh population of England, Canada, and the United States, is one example of the bloody potential in such mediascapes as they interact with the internal colonialisms of the nation-state (e.g., Hechter 1975). The West Bank, Namibia, and Eritrea are other theaters for the enactment of the bloody negotiation between existing nation-states and various deterritorialized groupings.

It is in the fertile ground of deterritorialization, in which money, commodities, and persons are involved in ceaselessly chasing each other around the world, that the mediascapes and ideoscapes of the modern world find their fractured and fragmented counterpart. For the ideas and images produced by mass media often are only partial guides to the goods and experiences that deterritorialized populations transfer to one another. In Mira Nair's brilliant film *India Cabaret*, we see the multiple loops of this fractured deterritorialization as young women, barely competent in Bombay's metropolitan glitz, come to seek their fortunes as cabaret dancers and prostitutes in Bombay, entertaining men in clubs with dance formats derived wholly from the prurient dance sequences of Hindi films. These scenes in turn cater to ideas about western and foreign women and their looseness, while they provide tawdry career alibis for these women. Some of these women come from Kerala, where cabaret clubs and the pornographic film industry have blossomed, partly in response to the purses and tastes of Keralites returned from the Middle East, where their diasporic lives away from women distort their very sense of what the relations between men and women might be. These tragedies of displacement could certainly be replayed in a more detailed analysis of the relations between the Japanese and German sex tours to Thailand and the tragedies of the sex trade in Bangkok, and in other similar loops that tie together fantasies about the Other, the conveniences and seductions of travel, the economics of global trade, and the brutal mobility fantasies that dominate gender politics in many parts of Asia and the world at large.

While far more could be said about the cultural politics of deterritorialization and the larger sociology of displacement that it expresses, it is appropriate at this juncture to bring in the role of the nation-state in the disjunctive global economy of culture today. The relationship between states and nations is everywhere an embattled one. It is possible to say that in many societies the nation and the state have become one another's projects. That is, while nations (or more properly groups with ideas about nationhood) seek to capture or co-opt states and state power, states simultaneously seek to capture and monopolize ideas about nationhood (Baruah 1986; Chatterjee 1986; Nandy 1989). In general, separatist transnational movements, including those that have included terror in their methods, exemplify nations in search of states. Sikhs, Tamil Sri Lankans, Basques, Moros, Quebecois – each of these represents imagined communities that seek to create states of their own or carve pieces out of existing states. States, on the other hand, are everywhere seeking to monopolize the moral resources of community, either by flatly claiming perfect coevality between nation and state, or by systematically museumizing and representing all the groups within them in a variety of heritage politics that seems remarkably uniform throughout the world (Handler 1988; Herzfeld 1982; McQueen 1988).

Here, national and international mediascapes are exploited by nation-states to pacify separatists or even the potential fissiparousness of all ideas of difference. Typically, contemporary nation-states do this by exercising taxonomic control over difference, by creating various kinds of international spectacle to domesticate difference, and by seducing small groups with the fantasy of self-display on some sort of global or cosmopolitan stage. One important new feature of global cultural politics, tied to the disjunctive relationships among the various landscapes discussed earlier, is that state and nation are at each other's throats, and the hyphen that links them is now less an icon of conjuncture than an index of disjuncture. This disjunctive relationship between nation and state has two levels: at the level of any given nation-state, it means that there is a battle of the imagination, with state and nation seeking to cannibalize one another. Here is the seedbed of brutal separatisms – majoritarianisms that seem to have appeared from nowhere and microidentities that have become political projects within the nation-state. At another level, this disjunctive relationship is deeply entangled with the global disjunctures discussed throughout this chapter: ideas of nationhood appear to be steadily increasing in scale and regularly crossing existing state boundaries, sometimes, as with the Kurds, because previous identities stretched across vast national spaces or, as with the Tamils in Sri Lanka, the dormant threads of a transnational diaspora have been activated to ignite the micropolitics of a nation-state.

In discussing the cultural politics that have subverted the hyphen that links the nation to the state, it is especially important not to forget the mooring of such politics in the irregularities that now characterize disorganized capital (Kothari 1989; Lash and Urry 1987). Because labor, finance, and technology are now so widely separated, the volatilities that underlie movements for nationhood (as large as transnational Islam on the one hand, or as small as the movement of the Gurkhas for a separate state in Northeast India) grind against the vulnerabilities that characterize the relationships between states. States find themselves pressed to stay open by the forces of media, technology, and travel that have fueled consumerism throughout the world and have increased the craving, even in the non-western world, for new commodities and spectacles. On the other hand, these very cravings can become caught up in new ethnoscapes, mediascapes, and, eventually, ideoscapes, such as democracy in China, that the state cannot tolerate as threats to its own control over ideas of nationhood and peoplehood. States throughout the world are under siege, especially where contests over the ideoscapes of democracy are fierce and fundamental, and where there are radical disjunctures between ideoscapes and technoscapes (as in the case of very small countries that lack contemporary technologies of production and information); or between ideoscapes and financescapes (as in countries such as Mexico or Brazil, where international lending influences national politics to a very large degree); or between ideoscapes and ethnoscapes (as in Beirut, where diasporic, local, and translocal filiations are suicidally at battle); or between ideoscapes and mediascapes (as in many countries in the Middle East and Asia) where the lifestyles represented on both national and international TV and cinema completely overwhelm and undermine the rhetoric of national politics. In the Indian case, the myth of the law-breaking hero has emerged to mediate this naked struggle between the pieties and realities of Indian politics, which has grown increasingly brutalized and corrupt (Vachani 1989).

The transnational movement of the martial arts, particularly through Asia, as mediated by the Hollywood and Hong Kong film industries (Zarilli 1995) is a rich illustration of the ways in which long-standing martial arts traditions, reformulated to meet the fantasies of contemporary (sometimes lumpen) youth populations, create new cultures of masculinity and violence, which are in turn the fuel for increased violence in national and international politics. Such violence is in turn the spur to an increasingly rapid and amoral arms trade that penetrates the entire world. The worldwide spread of the AK-47 and the Uzi, in films, in corporate and state security, in terror, and in police and military activity, is a reminder that apparently simple technical uniformities often conceal an increasingly complex set of loops, linking images of violence to aspirations for community in some imagined world.

Returning then to the ethnoscapes with which I began, the central paradox of ethnic politics in today's world is that primordia (whether of language or skin color or neighborhood or kinship) have become globalized. That is, sentiments, whose greatest force is in their ability to ignite intimacy into a political state and turn locality into a staging ground for identity, have become spread over vast and irregular spaces as groups move yet stay linked to one another through sophisticated media capabilities. This is not to deny that such primordia are often the product of invented traditions (Hobsbawm and Ranger 1983) or retrospective affiliations, but to emphasize that because of the disjunctive and unstable interplay of commerce, media, national policies, and consumer fantasies, ethnicity, once a genie contained in the bottle of some sort of locality (however large), has now become a global force, forever slipping in and through the cracks between states and borders.

But the relationship between the cultural and economic levels of this new set of global disjunctures is not a simple one-way street in which the terms of global cultural politics are set wholly by, or confined wholly within, the vicissitudes of international flows of technology, labor, and finance, demanding only a modest modification of existing neo-Marxist models of uneven development and state formation. There is a deeper change, itself driven by the disjunctures among all the landscapes I have discussed and constituted by their continuously fluid and uncertain interplay, that concerns the relationship between production and consumption in today's global economy. Here, I begin with Marx's famous (and often mined) view of the fetishism of the commodity and suggest that this fetishism has been replaced in the world at large (now seeing the world as one large, interactive system, composed of many complex subsystems) by two mutually supportive descendants, the first of which I call production fetishism and the second, the fetishism of the consumer.

By *production fetishism* I mean an illusion created by contemporary transnational production loci that masks translocal capital, transnational earning flows, global management, and often faraway workers (engaged in various kinds of high-tech putting-out operations) in the idiom and spectacle of local (sometimes even worker) control, national productivity, and territorial sovereignty. To the extent that various kinds of free-trade zones have become the models for production at large, especially of high-tech commodities, production has itself become a fetish, obscuring not social relations as such but the relations of production, which are increasingly transnational. The locality (both in the sense of the local factory or site of production and in the extended sense of the nation-state) becomes a fetish that disguises the globally dispersed forces that actually drive the production process. This generates alienation (in Marx's sense) twice intensified, for its social sense is now compounded by a complicated spatial dynamic that is increasingly global.

As for the *fetishism of the consumer*, I mean to indicate here that the consumer has been transformed through commodity flows (and the mediascapes, especially of advertising, that accompany them) into a sign, both in Baudrillard's sense of a simulacrum that only asymptotically approaches the form of a real social agent, and in the sense of a mask for the real seat of agency, which is not the consumer but the producer and the many forces that constitute production. Global advertising is the key technology for the worldwide dissemination of a plethora of creative and culturally well-chosen ideas of consumer agency. These images of agency are increasingly distortions of a world of merchandising so subtle that the consumer is consistently helped to believe that he or she is an actor, where in fact he or she is at best a chooser.

The globalization of culture is not the same as its homogenization, but globalization involves the use of a variety of instruments of homogenization (armaments, advertising techniques, language hegemonies, and clothing styles) that are absorbed into local political and cultural economies, only to be repatriated as heterogeneous dialogues of national sovereignty, free enterprise, and fundamentalism in which the state plays an increasingly delicate role: too much openness to global flows, and the nation-state is threatened by revolt, as in the China syndrome; too little, and the state exits the international stage, as Burma, Albania, and North Korea in various ways have done. In general, the state has become the arbitrageur of this *repatriation of difference* (in the form of goods, signs, slogans, and styles). But this repatriation or export of the designs and commodities of difference continuously exacerbates the internal politics of majoritarianism and homogenization, which is most frequently played out in debates over heritage.

Thus the central feature of global culture today is the politics of the mutual effort of sameness and difference to cannibalize one another and thereby proclaim their successful hijacking of the twin Enlightenment ideas of the triumphantly universal and the resiliently particular. This mutual cannibalization shows its ugly face in riots, refugee flows, state-sponsored torture, and ethnocide (with or without state support). Its brighter side is in the expansion of many individual horizons of hope and fantasy, in the global spread of oral rehydration therapy and other low-tech instruments of well-being, in the susceptibility even of South Africa to the force of global opinion, in the inability of the Polish state to repress its own working classes, and in the growth of a wide range of progressive, transnational alliances. Examples of both sorts could be multiplied. The critical point is that both sides of the coin of global cultural process today are products of the infinitely varied mutual contest of sameness and difference on a stage characterized by radical disjunctures between different sorts of global flows and the uncertain landscapes created in and through these disjunctures.

The Work of Reproduction in an Age of Mechanical Art

I have inverted the key terms of the title of Walter Benjamin's famous essay (1969) to return this rather high-flying discussion to a more manageable level. There is a classic human problem that will not disappear however much global cultural processes might change their dynamics, and this is the problem today typically discussed under the rubric of reproduction (and traditionally referred to in terms of the transmission of culture). In either case, the question is, how do small groups, especially families, the classical loci of socialization, deal with these new global realities as they seek to reproduce themselves and, in so doing, by accident reproduce cultural forms themselves? In traditional anthropological terms, this could be phrased as the problem of enculturation in a period of rapid culture change. So the problem is hardly novel. But it does take on some novel dimensions under the global conditions discussed so far in this chapter.

First, the sort of transgenerational stability of knowledge that was presupposed in most theories of enculturation (or, in slightly broader terms, of socialization) can no longer be assumed. As families move to new locations, or as children move before older generations, or as grown sons and daughters return from time spent in strange parts of the world, family relationships can become volatile; new commodity patterns are negotiated, debts and obligations are recalibrated, and rumors and fantasies about the new setting are maneuvered into existing repertoires of knowledge and practice. Often, global labor diasporas involve immense strains on marriages in general and on women in particular, as marriages become the meeting points of historical patterns of socialization and new ideas of proper behavior. Generations easily divide, as ideas about property, propriety, and collective obligation wither under the siege of distance and time. Most important, the work of cultural reproduction in new settings is profoundly complicated by the politics of representing a family as normal (particularly for the young) to neighbours and peers in the new locale. All this is, of course, not new to the cultural study of immigration.

What is new is that this is a world in which both points of departure and points of arrival are in cultural flux, and thus the search for steady points of reference, as critical life choices are made, can be very difficult. It is in this atmosphere that the invention of tradition (and of ethnicity, kinship, and other identity markers) can become slippery, as the search for certainties is regularly frustrated by the fluidities of transnational communication. As group pasts become increasingly parts of museums, exhibits, and collections, both in national and transnational spectacles, culture becomes less what Pierre Bourdieu would have called a habitus (a tacit realm of reproducible practices and dispositions) and more an arena for conscious choice, justification, and representation, the latter often to multiple and spatially dislocated audiences.

The task of cultural reproduction, even in its most intimate arenas, such as husband–wife and parent–child relations, becomes both politicized and exposed to the traumas of deterritorialization as family members pool and negotiate their mutual understandings and aspirations in sometimes fractured spatial arrangements. At larger levels, such as community, neighborhood, and territory, this politicization is often the emotional fuel for more explicitly violent politics of identity, just as these larger politics sometimes penetrate and ignite domestic politics. When, for example, two offspring in a household split with their father on a key matter of political identification in a transnational setting, preexisting localized norms carry little force. Thus a son who has joined the Hezbollah group in Lebanon may no longer get along with parents or siblings who are affiliated with Amal or some other branch of Shi'i ethnic political identity in Lebanon. Women in particular bear the brunt of this sort of friction, for they become pawns in the heritage politics of the household and are often subject to the abuse and violence of men who are themselves torn about the relation between heritage and opportunity in shifting spatial and political formations.

The pains of cultural reproduction in a disjunctive global world are, of course, not eased by the effects of mechanical art (or mass media), for these media afford powerful resources for counternodes of identity that youth can project against parental wishes or desires. At larger levels of organization, there can be many forms of cultural politics within displaced populations (whether of refugees or of voluntary immigrants), all of which are inflected in important ways by media (and the mediascapes and ideoscapes they offer). A central link between the fragilities of cultural reproduction and the role of the mass media in today's world is the politics of gender and violence. As fantasies of gendered violence dominate the B-grade film industries that blanket the world, they both reflect and refine gendered violence at home and in the streets, as young men (in particular) are swayed by the macho politics of self-assertion in contexts where they are frequently denied real agency, and women are forced to enter the labor force in new ways on the one hand, and continue the maintenance of familial heritage on the other. Thus the honor of women becomes not just an armature of stable (if inhuman) systems of cultural reproduction but a new arena for the formation of sexual identity and family politics, as men and women face new pressures at work and new fantasies of leisure.

Because both work and leisure have lost none of their gendered qualities in this new global order but have acquired ever subtler fetishized representations, the honor of women becomes increasingly a surrogate for the identity of embattled communities of males, while their women in reality have to negotiate increasingly harsh conditions of work at home and in the nondomestic workplace. In short, deterritorialized communities and displaced populations, however much they may enjoy the fruits of new kinds of earning and new dispositions of capital and technology, have to play out the desires and fantasies of these new ethnoscapes, while striving to reproduce the family-as-microcosm of culture. As the shapes of cultures grow less bounded and tacit, more fluid and politicized, the work of cultural reproduction becomes a daily hazard. Far more could, and should, be said about the work of reproduction in an age of mechanical art: the preceding discussion is meant to indicate the contours of the problems that a new, globally informed theory of cultural reproduction will have to face.

Shape and Process in Global Cultural Formations

The deliberations of the arguments that I have made so far constitute the bare bones of an approach to a general theory of global cultural processes. Focusing on disjunctures, I have employed a set of terms (*ethnoscape, financescape, technoscape, mediascape,* and *ideoscape*) to stress different streams or flows along which cultural material may be seen to be moving across national boundaries. I have also sought to exemplify the ways in which these various flows (or landscapes, from the stabilizing perspectives of any given imagined world) are in fundamental disjuncture with respect to one another. What further steps can we take toward a general theory of global cultural processes based on these proposals?

The first is to note that our very models of cultural shape will have to alter, as configurations of people, place, and heritage lose all semblance of isomorphism. Recent work in anthropology has done much to free us of the shackles of highly localized, boundary-oriented, holistic, primordialist images of cultural form and substance (Hannerz 1989; Marcus and Fischer 1986; Thornton 1988). But not very much has been put in their place, except somewhat larger if less mechanical versions of these images, as in Eric Wolf's work on the relationship of Europe to the rest of the world (1982). What I would like to propose is that we begin to think of the configuration of cultural forms in today's world as fundamentally fractal, that is, as possessing no Euclidean boundaries, structures, or regularities. Second, I would suggest that these cultural forms, which we should strive to represent as fully fractal, are also overlapping in ways that have been discussed only in pure mathematics (in set theory, for example) and in biology (in the language of polythetic classifications).

Thus we need to combine a fractal metaphor for the shape of cultures (in the plural) with a polythetic account of their overlaps and resemblances. Without this latter step, we shall remain mired in comparative work that relies on the clear separation of the entities to be compared before serious comparison can begin. How are we to compare fractally shaped cultural forms that are also polythetically overlapping in their coverage of terrestrial space?

Finally, in order for the theory of global cultural interactions predicated on disjunctive flows to have any force greater than that of a mechanical metaphor, it will have to move into something like a human version of the theory that some scientists are calling chaos theory. That is, we will need to ask not how these complex, overlapping, fractal shapes constitute a simple, stable (even if large-scale) system, but to ask what its dynamics are: Why do ethnic riots occur when and where they do? Why do states wither at greater rates in some places and times than in others? Why do some countries flout conventions of international debt repayment with so much less apparent worry than others? How are international arms flows driving ethnic battles and genocides? Why are some states exiting the global stage while others are clamoring to get in? Why do key events occur at a certain point in a certain place rather than in others? These are, of course, the great traditional questions of causality, contingency, and prediction in the human sciences, but in a world of disjunctive global flows, it is perhaps important to start asking them in a way that relies on images of flow and uncertainty, hence *chaos*, rather than on older images of order, stability, and systematicness. Otherwise, we will have gone far toward a theory of global cultural systems but thrown out process in the bargain. And that would make these notes part of a journey toward the kind of illusion of order that we can no longer afford to impose on a world that is so transparently volatile.

Whatever the directions in which we can push these macrometaphors (fractals, polythetic classifications, and chaos), we need to ask one other old-fashioned question out of the Marxist paradigm: is there some pre-given order to the relative determining force of these global flows? Because I have postulated the dynamics of global cultural systems as driven by the relationships among flows of persons, technologies, finance, information, and ideology, can we speak of some structural-causal order linking these flows by analogy to the role of the economic order in one version of the Marxist paradigm? Can we speak of some of these flows as being, for a priori structural or historical reasons, always prior to and formative of other flows? My own hypothesis, which can only be tentative at this point, is that the relationship of these various flows to one another as they constellate into particular events and social forms will be radically context-dependent. Thus, while labor flows and their loops with financial flows between Kerala and the Middle East may account for the shape of media flows and ideoscapes in Kerala, the reverse may be true of Silicon Valley in California, where intense specialization in a single techno-logical sector (computers) and particular flows of capital may well profoundly determine the shape that ethnoscapes, ideoscapes, and mediascapes may take.

This does not mean that the causal–historical relationship among these various flows is random or meaninglessly contingent but that our current theories of cultural chaos are insufficiently developed to be even parsimonious models at this point, much less to be predictive theories, the golden fleeces of one kind of social science.

What I have sought to provide in this chapter is a reasonably economical technical vocabulary and a rudimentary model of disjunctive flows, from which something like a decent global analysis might emerge. Without some such analysis, it will be difficult to construct what John Hinkson calls a "social theory of postmodernity" that is adequately global (1990:84).

NOTES

1 One major exception is Fredric Jameson, whose work on the relationship between post-modernism and late capitalism has in many ways inspired this essay. The debate between Jameson and Aijaz Ahmad in *Social Text*, however, shows that the creation of a globalizing Marxist narrative in cultural matters is difficult territory indeed (Ahmad 1987; Jameson 1986). My own effort in this context is to begin a restructuring of the Marxist narrative (by stressing lags and disjunctures) that many Marxists might find abhorrent. Such a restruc-turing has to avoid the dangers of obliterating difference within the Third World, eliding the social referent (as some French postmodernists seem inclined to do), and retaining the narrative authority of the Marxist tradition, in favor of greater attention to global frag-mentation, uncertainty, and difference.
2 The idea of *ethnoscape* is more fully engaged in Appadurai 1996, ch. 3.

REFERENCES

Abu-Lughod, J. L. (1989) *Before European Hegemony: The World System AD 1250–1350.* New York: Oxford University Press.

Ahmad, A. (1987) Jameson's Rhetoric of Otherness and the "National Allegory," *Social Text* 17: 3–25.

Amin, S. (1980) *Class and Nation: Historically and in the Current Crisis.* New York and London: Monthly Review Press.

Anderson, B. (1983) *Imagined Communities: Reflections on the Origin and Spread of Nationalism.* London: Verso.

Appadurai, A. (1996) *Modernity at Large: Cultural Dimensions of Globalization.* Minnea-polis: University of Minnesota Press.

Barber, K. (1987) Popular Arts in Africa, *African Studies Review* 30(3) (September): 1–78.

Baruah, S. (1986) Immigration, Ethnic Conflict and Political Turmoil, Assam 1979–1985, *Asian Survey* 26(11) (November): 1184–206.

Bayly, C. A. (1989) *Imperial Meridian: The British Empire and the World, 1780–1830.* London and New York: Longman.

Benjamin, W. (1969) The Work of Art in the Age of Mechanical Reproduction [1936]. In H. Arendt (ed.) *Illuminations.* H. Zohn (trans.). New York: Schocken Books.

Braudel, F. (1981–4) *Civilization and Capitalism, 15th–18th Century* (3 vols.) London: Collins.

Chatterjee, P. (1986) *Nationalist Thought and the Colonial World: A Derivative Discourse?* London: Zed Books.

Curtin, P. (1984) *Cross-Cultural Trade in World History.* Cambridge: Cambridge University Press.

Deleuze, G., and F. Guattari (1987) *A Thousand Plateaus: Capitalism and Schizophrenia*. B. Massumi (trans.). Minneapolis: University of Minnesota Press.

Fabian, J. (1983) *Time and the Other: How Anthropology Makes Its Object*. New York: Columbia University Press.

Feld, S. (1988) Notes on World Beat, *Public Culture* 1(1): 31–7.

Gans, E. (1985) *The End of Culture: Toward a Generative Anthropology*. Berkeley: University of California Press.

Hamelink, C. (1983) *Cultural Autonomy in Global Communications*. New York: Longman.

Handler, R. (1988) *Nationalism and the Politics of Culture in Quebec*. Madison: University of Wisconsin Press.

Hannerz, U. (1987) The World in Creolization, *Africa* 57(4): 546–59.

——. (1989) Notes on the Global Ecumene, *Public Culture* 1(2) (Spring): 66–75.

Hechter, M. (1975) *Internal Colonialism: The Celtic Fringe in British National Development, 1536–1966*. Berkeley: University of California Press.

Helms, M. W. (1988) *Ulysses' Sail: An Ethnographic Odyssey of Power, Knowledge, and Geographical Distance*. Princeton, NJ: Princeton University Press.

Herzfeld, M. (1982) *Ours Once More: Folklore, Ideology and the Making of Modern Greece*. Austin: University of Texas Press.

Hinkson, J. (1990) Postmodernism and Structural Change, *Public Culture* 2(2) (Spring): 82–101.

Hobsbawm, E., and T. Ranger (eds.) (1983) *The Invention of Tradition*. New York: Cambridge University Press.

Hodgson, M. (1974) *The Venture of Islam, Conscience and History in a World Civilization* (3 vols). Chicago: University of Chicago Press.

Ivy, M. (1988) Tradition and Difference in the Japanese Mass Media, *Public Culture* 1(1): 21–9.

Iyer, P. (1988) *Video Night in Kathmandu*. New York: Knopf.

Jameson, F. (1983) Postmodernism and Consumer Society. In H. Foster (ed.) *The Anti-Aesthetic: Essays on Postmodern Culture*. Port Townsend, WA: Bay Press.

——. (1986) Third World Literature in the Era of Multi-National Capitalism, *Social Text* 15 (Fall): 65–88.

——. (1989) Nostalgia for the Present, *South Atlantic Quarterly* 88(2) (Spring): 517–37.

Kothari, R. (1989) *State against Democracy: In Search of Humane Governance*. New York: New Horizons.

Lakoff, G., and M. Johnson (1980) *Metaphors We Live By*. Chicago and London: University of Chicago Press.

Lash, S., and J. Urry (1987) *The End of Organized Capitalism*. Madison: University of Wisconsin Press.

Mandel, E. (1978) *Late Capitalism*. London: Verso.

Marcus, G., and M. Fischer (1986) *Anthropology as Cultural Critique: An Experimental Moment in the Human Sciences*. Chicago: University of Chicago Press.

Mattelart, A. (1983) *Transnationals and the Third World: The Struggle for Culture*. South Hadley, MA: Bergin and Garvey.

McLuhan, M., and B. R. Powers (1989) *The Global Village: Transformations in World, Life and Media in the 21st Century*. New York: Oxford University Press.

McQueen, H. (1988) The Australian Stamp: Image, Design and Ideology, *Arena* 84 (Spring): 78–96.

Meyrowitz, J. (1985) *No Sense of Place: The Impact of Electronic Media on Social Behavior*. New York: Oxford University Press.

Nandy, A. (1989) The Political Culture of the Indian State, *Daedalus* 118(4): 1–26.

Nicoll, F. (1989) My Trip to Alice, *Criticism, Heresy and Interpretation* 3: 21–32.

Schafer, E. (1963) *Golden Peaches of Samarkand: A Study of T'ang Exotics*. Berkeley: University of California Press.

Schiller, H. (1976) *Communication and Cultural Domination*. White Plains, NY: International Arts and Sciences.

Thornton, R. (1988) The Rhetoric of Ethnographic Holism, *Cultural Anthropology* 3(3) (August): 285–303.

Vachani, L. (1989) Narrative, Pleasure and Ideology in the Hindi Film: An Analysis of the Outsider Formula. MA thesis, Annenberg School of Communication, University of Pennsylvania.

Wallerstein, I. (1974) *The Modern World System* (2 vols.) New York and London: Academic Press.

Warner, M. (1990) *The Letters of the Republic: Publication and the Public Sphere in Eighteenth-Century America*. Cambridge, MA: Harvard University Press.

Williams, R. (1976) *Keywords*. New York: Oxford University Press.

Wolf, E. (1982) *Europe and the People without History*. Berkeley: University of California Press.

Yoshimoto, M. (1989) The Postmodern and Mass Images in Japan, *Public Culture* 1(2): 8–25.

Zarilli, P. (1995) Repositioning the Body: An Indian Martial Art and its Pan-Asian Publics. In C. A. Breckenridge (ed.) *Consuming Modernity: Public Culture in a South Asian World*. Minneapolis: University of Minnesota Press.

3

Beyond "Culture": Space, Identity, and the Politics of Difference

Akhil Gupta and James Ferguson

For a subject whose central rite of passage is fieldwork, whose romance has rested on its exploration of the remote ("the *most* other of others," Hannerz 1986), whose critical function is seen to lie in its juxtaposition of radically different ways of being (located "elsewhere") with that of the anthropologists' own, usually western culture, there has been surprisingly little self-consciousness about the issue of space in anthropological theory. (Some notable exceptions are Appadurai 1986, 1988; Hannerz 1987; Rosaldo 1988, 1989). This essay aims at a critical exploration of the way received ideas about space and place have shaped and continue to shape anthropological common sense. In particular, we wish to explore how the renewed interest in theorizing space in postmodernist and feminist theory (for example, in Anzaldúa 1987; Baudrillard 1988; Deleuze and Guattari 1987; Foucault 1980; Jameson 1984; Kaplan 1987; Martin and Mohanty 1986) – embodied in such notions as surveillance, panopticism, simulacra, deterritorialization, postmodern hyperspace, borderlands, and marginality – forces us to reevaluate such central analytic concepts in anthropology as that of "culture" and, by extension, the idea of "cultural difference."

Representations of space in the social sciences are remarkably dependent on images of break, rupture, and disjunction. The distinctiveness of societies, nations, and cultures is predicated on a seemingly unproblematic division of space, on the fact that they occupy "naturally" discontinuous spaces. The premise of discontinuity forms the starting point from which to theorize contact, conflict, and contradiction between cultures and societies. For example, the representation of the world as a collection of "countries," as on most world maps, sees it as an inherently fragmented

From *Culture, Power, Place: Explorations in Critical Anthropology*, ed. Akhil Gupta and James Ferguson, p. 33–51. Durham, NC: Duke University Press. Copyright © 1997, Duke University Press.

space, divided by different colors into diverse national societies, each "rooted" in its proper place (compare Malkki 1997). It is so taken for granted that each country embodies its own distinctive culture and society that the terms "society" and "culture" are routinely simply appended to the names of nation-states, as when a tourist visits India to understand "Indian culture" and "Indian society" or Thailand to experience "Thai culture" or the United States to get a whiff of "American culture."

Of course, the geographical territories that cultures and societies are believed to map onto do not have to be nations. We do, for example, have ideas about culture areas that overlap several nation-states, or of multicultural nations. On a smaller scale perhaps are our disciplinary assumptions about the association of culturally unitary groups (tribes or peoples) with "their" territories: thus "the Nuer" live in "Nuerland" and so forth. The clearest illustration of this kind of thinking are the classic "ethnographic maps" that purported to display the spatial distribution of peoples, tribes, and cultures. But in all these cases, space itself becomes a kind of neutral grid on which cultural difference, historical memory, and societal organization is inscribed. It is in this way that space functions as a central organizing principle in the social sciences at the same time that it disappears from analytical purview.

This assumed isomorphism of space, place, and culture results in some significant problems. First, there is the issue of those who inhabit the border, that "narrow strip along steep edges" (Anzaldúa 1987: 3) of national boundaries. The fiction of cultures as discrete, objectlike phenomena occupying discrete spaces becomes implausible for those who inhabit the borderlands. Related to border inhabitants are those who live a life of border crossings – migrant workers, nomads, and members of the transnational business and professional elite. What is "the culture" of farm workers who spend half a year in Mexico and half in the United States? Finally, there are those who cross borders more or less permanently – immigrants, refugees, exiles, and expatriates. In their case, the disjuncture of place and culture is especially clear: Khmer refugees in the United States take "Khmer culture" with them in the same complicated way that Indian immigrants in England transport "Indian culture" to their new homeland.

A second set of problems raised by the implicit mapping of cultures onto places is to account for cultural differences *within* a locality. "Multiculturalism" is both a feeble recognition of the fact that cultures have lost their moorings in definite places and an attempt to subsume this plurality of cultures within the framework of a national identity. Similarly, the idea of "subcultures" attempts to preserve the idea of distinct "cultures" while acknowledging the relation of different cultures to a dominant culture within the same geographical and territorial space. Conventional accounts of ethnicity, even when used to describe cultural differences in settings where people from different regions live side by side, rely on an unproblematic link between identity and place.[1] While such concepts are suggestive because they endeavor to stretch the naturalized association of culture with place, they fail to interrogate this assumption in a truly fundamental manner. We need to ask how to deal with cultural difference, while abandoning received ideas of (localized) culture.

Third, there is the important question of postcoloniality. To which places do the hybrid cultures of postcoloniality belong? Does the colonial encounter create a "new culture" in both the colonized and colonizing country, or does it destabilize the notion that nations and cultures are isomorphic? As discussed below, postcoloniality further problematizes the relationship between space and culture.

Last and most important, challenging the ruptured landscape of independent nations and autonomous cultures raises the question of understanding social change and cultural transformation as situated within interconnected spaces. The presumption that spaces are autonomous has enabled the power of topography successfully to conceal the topography of power. The inherently fragmented space assumed in the definition of anthropology as the study of cultures (in the plural) may have been one of the reasons behind the long-standing failure to write anthropology's history as the biography of imperialism. For if one begins with the premise that spaces have *always* been hierarchically interconnected, instead of naturally disconnected, then cultural and social change becomes not a matter of cultural contact and articulation but one of rethinking difference *through* connection.

To illustrate, let us examine one powerful model of cultural change that attempts to relate dialectically the local to larger spatial arenas: articulation. Articulation models, whether they come from Marxist structuralism or "moral economy," posit a primeval state of autonomy (usually labeled "precapitalist") that is then violated by global capitalism. The result is that both local and larger spatial arenas are transformed, the local more than the global to be sure, but not necessarily in a predetermined direction. This notion of articulation allows one to explore the richly unintended consequences of, say, colonial capitalism, with which loss occurs alongside invention. Yet, by taking a preexisting, localized "community" as a given starting point, it fails to examine sufficiently the processes (such as the structures of feeling that pervade the imagining of community) that go into the construction of space as place or locality in the first instance. In other words, instead of assuming the autonomy of the primeval community, we need to examine how it was formed *as a community* out of the interconnected space that always already existed. Colonialism then represents the displacement of one form of interconnection by another. This is not to deny that colonialism or an expanding capitalism does indeed have profoundly dislocating effects on existing societies. But by always foregrounding the spatial distribution of hierarchical power relations, we can better understand the processes whereby a space achieves a distinctive *identity* as a place. Keeping in mind that notions of locality or community refer both to a demarcated physical space and to clusters of interaction, we can see that the identity of a place emerges by the intersection of its specific involvement in a system of hierarchically organized spaces with its cultural construction as a community or locality.

It is for this reason that what Fredric Jameson (1984) has dubbed "postmodern hyperspace" has so fundamentally challenged the convenient fiction that mapped cultures onto places and peoples. In the capitalist West, a Fordist regime of accumulation, emphasizing extremely large production facilities, a relatively stable work force, and the welfare state combined to create urban "communities" whose outlines were most clearly visible in company towns (Davis 1986; Harvey 1989; Mandel 1975). The counterpart of this in the international arena was that multinational corporations, under the leadership of the United States, steadily exploited the raw materials, primary goods, and cheap labor of the independent nation-states of the postcolonial "Third World." Multilateral agencies and powerful western states preached and, where necessary, militarily enforced the "laws" of the market to encourage the international flow of capital, whereas national immigration policies ensured that there would be no free (that is, anarchic, disruptive) flow of labor to the high-wage islands in the capitalist core. Fordist patterns of accumulation have now been replaced by a regime of flexible accumulation – characterized by small-batch production, rapid shifts in product lines, extremely fast movements of capital to exploit the smallest differentials in labor and raw material costs – built on a more sophisticated communications and information network and better means of trans-porting goods and people. At the same time, the industrial production of culture, entertainment, and leisure that first achieved something approaching global distri-bution during the Fordist era led, paradoxically, to the invention of new forms of cultural difference and new forms of imagining community. Something like a trans-national public sphere has certainly rendered any strictly bounded sense of commu-nity or locality obsolete. At the same time, it has enabled the creation of forms of solidarity and identity that do not rest on an appropriation of space where contiguity and face-to-face contact are paramount. In the pulverized space of postmodernity, space has not become irrelevant: it has been *re*territorialized in a way that does not conform to the experience of space that characterized the era of high modernity. It is this reterritorialization of space that forces us to reconceptualize fundamentally the politics of community, solidarity, identity, and cultural difference.

Imagined Communities, Imagined Places

People have undoubtedly always been more mobile and identities less fixed than the static and typologizing approaches of classical anthropology would suggest. But today, the rapidly expanding and quickening mobility of people combines with the refusal of cultural products and practices to "stay put" to give a profound sense of a loss of territorial roots, of an erosion of the cultural distinctiveness of places, and of ferment in anthropological theory. The apparent deterritorialization of identity that accompanies such processes has made James Clifford's question (1988: 275) a key one for recent anthropological inquiry: "What does it mean, at the end of the twentieth century, to speak . . . of a 'native land'? What processes rather than essences are involved in present experiences of cultural identity?"

Such questions are, of course, not completely new, but issues of collective identity do seem to take on a special character today, when more and more of us live in what Edward Said (1979: 18) has called "a generalized condition of homelessness," a world where identities are increasingly coming to be, if not wholly deterritorialized, at least differently territorialized. Refugees, migrants, displaced and stateless peoples – these are perhaps the first to live out these realities in their most complete form, but the problem is more general. In a world of diaspora, transnational culture flows, and mass movements of populations, old-fashioned attempts to map the globe as a set of culture regions or homelands are bewildered by a dazzling array of postcolonial simulacra, doublings and redoublings, as India and Pakistan seem to reappear in postcolonial simulation in London, prerevolution Teheran rises from the ashes in Los Angeles, and a thousand similar cultural dramas are played out in urban and rural settings all across the globe. In this culture-play of diaspora, familiar lines between "here" and "there," center and periphery, colony and metropole become blurred.

Where "here" and "there" become blurred in this way, the cultural certainties and fixities of the metropole are upset as surely, if not in the same way, as are those of the colonized periphery. In this sense, it is not only the displaced who experience a displacement (compare Bhabha 1989: 66). For even people remaining in familiar and ancestral places find the nature of their relation to place ineluctably changed and the illusion of a natural and essential connection between the place and the culture broken. "Englishness," for instance, in contemporary, internationalized England is just as complicated and nearly as deterritorialized a notion as Palestinian-ness or Armenian-ness, for "England" ("the real England") refers less to a bounded place than to an imagined state of being or a moral location. Consider, for instance, the following quote from a young white reggae fan in the ethnically chaotic neighborhood of Balsall Heath in Birmingham:

There's no such thing as "England" any more... welcome to India brothers! This is the Caribbean!... Nigeria!... There is no England, man. This is what is coming. Balsall Heath is the center of the melting pot, 'cos all I ever see when I go out is half-Arab, half-Pakistani, half-Jamaican, half-Scottish, half-Irish. I know 'cos I am [half-Scottish/half-Irish]... who am I?... Tell me who I belong to? They criticize me, the good old England. Alright, where do I belong? You know, I was brought up with blacks, Pakistanis, Africans, Asians, everything, you name it... who do I belong to?... I'm just a broad person. The earth is mine... you know we was not born in Jamaica... we was not born in "England." We were born here, man. It's our right. That's the way I see it. That's the way I deal with it. (Hebdige 1987: 158–9)

The broad-minded acceptance of cosmopolitanism that seems to be implied here is perhaps more the exception than the rule, but there can be little doubt that the explosion of a culturally stable and unitary "England" into the cut-and-mix "here" of contemporary Balsall Heath is an example of a phenomenon that is real and spreading. It is clear that the erosion of such supposedly natural connections between peoples and places has not led to the modernist specter of global cultural homogenization (see Clifford 1988). But "cultures" and "peoples," however persistent they may be, cease to be plausibly identifiable as spots on the map.

But the irony of these times is that as actual places and localities become ever more blurred and indeterminate, *ideas* of culturally and ethnically distinct places become perhaps even more salient. It is here that it becomes most visible how imagined communities (Anderson 1983) come to be attached to imagined places, as displaced peoples cluster around remembered or imagined homelands, places, or communities in a world that seems increasingly to deny such firm territorialized anchors in their actuality. In such a world, it becomes ever more important to train an anthropological eye on processes of construction of place and homeland by mobile and displaced people.

Remembered places have, of course, often served as symbolic anchors of community for dispersed people. This has long been true of immigrants, who use memory of place to construct their new lived world imaginatively. "Homeland" in this way remains one of the most powerful unifying symbols for mobile and displaced peoples, though the relation to homeland may be very differently constructed in different settings. Moreover, even in more completely deterritorialized times and settings – settings not only where "home" is distant but also where the very notion of "home" as a durably fixed place is in doubt – aspects of our lives remain highly "localized" in a social sense. We need to give up naïve ideas of communities as literal entities (compare Cohen 1985) but remain sensitive to the profound "bifocality" that characterizes locally lived existences in a globally interconnected world and to the powerful role of place in the "near view" of lived experience (Peters 1997).

The partial erosion of spatially bounded social worlds and the growing role of the imagination of places from a distance, however, themselves must be situated within the highly spatialized terms of a global capitalist economy. The special challenge here is to use a focus on the way space is imagined (but not *imaginary*) as a way to explore the mechanisms through which such conceptual processes of place making meet the changing global economic and political conditions of lived spaces – the relation, we could say, between place and space. For important tensions may arise when places that have been imagined at a distance must become lived spaces. Places, after all, are always imagined in the context of political-economic determinations that have a logic of their own. Territoriality is thus reinscribed at just the point it threatens to be erased.

The idea that space is made meaningful is, of course, a familiar one to anthropologists; indeed, there is hardly an older or better established anthropological truth. East or west, inside or outside, left or right, mound or floodplain – from at least the time of Durkheim, anthropologists have known that the experience of space is always socially constructed. The more urgent task would seem to be to politicize this uncontestable observation. With meaning-making understood as a practice, how are spatial meanings established? Who has the power to make places of spaces? Who contests this? What is at stake?

Such questions are particularly important where the meaningful association of places and peoples is concerned. As Malkki (1997) shows, two naturalisms must be challenged here. The first is what we will call the ethnological habit of taking the association of a culturally unitary group (the "tribe" or "people") and "its" territory as natural, which we discussed in the previous section. A second and closely related naturalism is what we will call the national habit of taking the association of citizens of states and their territories as natural. Here the exemplary image is of the conventional world map of nation-states, through which schoolchildren are taught such deceptively simple-sounding beliefs as that France is where the French live, America is where the Americans live, and so on. Even a casual observer knows that not only Americans live in America, and it is clear that the very question of what is a "real American" is largely up for grabs. But even anthropologists still talk of "American culture" with no clear understanding of what such a phrase might mean, because we assume a natural association of a culture ("American culture"), a people ("Americans"), and a place ("the United States of America"). Both the ethnological and the national naturalisms present associations of people and place as solid, commonsensical, and agreed on, when they are in fact contested, uncertain, and in flux.

Much more-recent work in anthropology and related fields has focused on the process through which such reified and naturalized national representations are constructed and maintained by states and national elites (see, for instance, Anderson 1983; Handler 1988; Herzfeld 1987; Hobsbawm and Ranger 1983; Kapferer 1988; and Wright 1985). Such analyses of nationalism leave no doubt that states play a crucial role in the popular politics of place making and in the creation of naturalized links between places and peoples. But it is important to note that state ideologies are far from being the only point at which the imagination of place is politicized. Oppositional images of place have, of course, been extremely important in anticolonial nationalist movements, as well as in campaigns for self-determination and sovereignty on the part of contested nations such as the Hutu (Malkki 1997), the Eritreans, the Armenians, or the Palestinians (Bisharat 1997). Such instances may serve as a useful reminder, in the light of nationalism's often reactionary connotations in the western world, of how often notions of home and "own place" have been empowering in anti-imperial contexts.

Indeed, future observers of twentieth-century revolutions will probably be struck by the difficulty of formulating large-scale political movements *without* reference to national homelands. Whether we are speaking of the nonaligned movement (Gupta 1997) or the proletarian internationalist movement, what stands out is the extraordinary difficulty in attempting to rally people around such nonnational collectivities. Indeed, class-based internationalism's tendencies to nationalism (as in the history of the Second International or that of the USSR) and to utopianism imagined in local rather than universal terms (as in William Morris's *News from Nowhere* (1970), where "nowhere" (*utopia*) turns out to be a specifically English "somewhere") show with special clarity the importance of attaching causes to places and the ubiquity of place making in collective political mobilization.

Such place making, however, need not be national in scale. One example of this is the way idealized notions of "the country" have been used in urban settings to construct critiques of industrial capitalism (compare, for Britain, Raymond Williams 1973, with, for Zambia, Ferguson 1997). Another case is the reworking of ideas of "home" and "community" by such feminists as Biddy Martin and Chandra Talpade Mohanty (1986) and Caren Kaplan (1987). Yet it must be noted that such popular politics of place can as easily be conservative as progressive. Often enough, as in the contemporary United States, the association of place with memory, loss, and nostalgia plays directly into the hands of reactionary popular movements. This is true not only of explicitly national images long associated with the right but also of imagined locales and nostalgic settings such as "small-town America" or "the frontier," which often play into and complement antifeminist idealizations of "the home" and "family."[2]

Space, Politics, and Anthropological Representation

Changing our conceptions of the relation between space and cultural difference offers a new perspective on recent debates surrounding issues of anthropological representation and writing. The new attention to representational practices has already led to more sophisticated understandings of processes of objectification and the construction of otherness in anthropological writing. With this said, however, it also seems to us that more recent notions of "cultural critique" (Marcus and Fischer 1986) depend on a spatialized understanding of cultural difference that needs to be problematized.

The foundation of cultural critique – a dialogic relation with an "other" culture that yields a critical viewpoint on "our own culture" – assumes an already existing world of many different, distinct "cultures" and an unproblematic distinction between "our own society" and an "other" society. As George E. Marcus and Michael M. J. Fischer put it, the purpose of cultural critique is "to generate critical questions from one society to probe the other"; the goal is "to apply both the substantive results and the epistemological lessons learned from ethnography abroad to a renewal of the critical function of anthropology as it is pursued in ethnographic projects at home" (1986: 117, 112).

Marcus and Fischer are sensitive to the fact that cultural difference is present "here at home" too and that "the other" need not be exotic or far away to be other. But the fundamental conception of cultural critique as a relation between "different societies" ends up, perhaps against the authors' intentions, spatializing cultural difference in familiar ways, as ethnography becomes a link between an unproblematized "home" and "abroad." The anthropological relation is not simply with people who are different but with "a different society," "a different culture," and thus, inevitably, a relation between "here" and "there." In all this, the terms of the opposition ("here" and "there," "us" and "them," "our own" and "other" societies) are taken as received: the problem for anthropologists is to use our encounter with "them," "there," to construct a critique of "our own society," "here."

A number of problems exist with this way of conceptualizing the anthropological project. Perhaps the most obvious is the question of the identity of the "we" that keeps coming up in phrases such as "ourselves" and "our own society." Who is this "we"? If the answer is, as we fear, "the West," then we must ask precisely who is to be included and who excluded from this club. Nor is the problem solved simply by substituting "the ethnographer's own society" for "our own society." For ethnographers as for other natives, the postcolonial world is an interconnected social space; for many anthropologists – and perhaps especially for displaced Third World scholars – the identity of "one's own society" is an open question.

A second problem with the way cultural difference has been conceptualized within the "cultural critique" project is that, once excluded from that privileged domain "our own society," "the other" is subtly nativized – placed in a separate frame of analysis and "spatially incarcerated" (Appadurai 1988) in that "other place" that is proper to an "other culture." Cultural critique assumes an original separation, bridged at the initiation of the anthropological field-worker. The problematic is one of "contact," communication not within a shared social and economic world but "across cultures" and "between societies."

As an alternative to this way of thinking about cultural difference, we want to problematize the unity of the "us" and the otherness of the "other" and question the radical separation between the two that makes the opposition possible in the first place. We are interested less in establishing a dialogic relation between geographically distinct societies than in exploring the processes of *production* of difference in a world of culturally, socially, and economically interconnected and interdependent spaces. The difference is fundamental and can be illustrated by a brief examination of one text that has been highly praised within the "cultural critique" movement.

Marjorie Shostak's *Nisa: The Life and Words of a !Kung Woman* (1981) has been very widely admired for its innovative use of life history and has been hailed as a noteworthy example of polyphonic experimentation in ethnographic writing (Clifford 1986, 1988: 42; Marcus and Fischer 1986: 58–9; Pratt 1986). But with respect to the issues we have discussed here, *Nisa* is a very conventional and deeply flawed work. The individual, Nisa, is granted a degree of singularity, but she is used principally as the token of a type: "the !Kung." The San-speaking !Kung of Bots-wana (the "Bushmen" of old) are presented as a distinct, "other," and apparently primordial "people." Shostak treats the Dobe !Kung as essentially survivals of a prior evolutionary age: they are "one of the last remaining traditional gatherer-hunter societies," racially distinct, traditional, and isolated (1981: 4). Their experi-ence of "culture change" is "still quite recent and subtle" and their traditional value system "mostly intact" (p. 6). "Contact" with "other groups" of agricultural and pastoral peoples has occurred, according to Shostak, only since the 1920s, and only since the 1960s has the isolation of the !Kung really broken down, raising for the first time the issue of "change," "adaptation," and "culture contact" (p. 346).

The space the !Kung inhabit, the Kalahari Desert, is clearly radically different and separate from our own. Again and again the narrative returns to the theme of isolation: in a harsh ecological setting, a way of life thousands of years old has been preserved only through its extraordinary spatial separateness. The anthropo-logical task, as Shostak conceives it, is to cross this spatial divide, to enter into this land that time forgot, a land (as Edwin Wilmsen (1989: 10) notes) with antiquity but no history, to listen to the voices of women which might reveal "what their lives had been like for generations, possibly even for thousands of years" (Shostak 1981: 6).

The exoticization implicit in this portrait, in which the !Kung appear almost as living on another planet, has drawn surprisingly little criticism from theorists of ethnography. Mary Louise Pratt has rightly pointed out the "blazing contradiction" between the portrait of primal beings untouched by history and the genocidal history of the white "Bushman conquest" (1986: 48). As she says, "What picture of the !Kung would one draw if instead of defining them as survivors of the stone age and a delicate and complex adaptation to the Kalahari desert, one looked at them as survivors of capitalist expansion, and a delicate and complex adaptation to three centuries of violence and intimidation?" (p. 49). But even Pratt retains the notion of "the !Kung" as a preexisting ontological entity – "survivors," not products (still less, producers) of history. "They" are victims, having suffered the deadly process of "contact" with "us."

A very different and much more illuminating way of conceptualizing cultural difference in the region may be found in Wilmsen's devastating critique of the anthro-pological cult of the "Bushman" (1989). Wilmsen shows how, in constant interaction with a wider network of social relations, the difference that Shostak takes as a starting point came to be produced in the first place – how, one might say, "the Bushmen" came to be Bushmen. He demonstrates that San-speaking people have been in continuous interaction with other groups for as long as we have evidence for; that political and economic relations linked the supposedly isolated Kalahari with a regional political economy both in the colonial and precolonial eras; that San-speaking people have often held cattle and that no strict separation of pastoralists and foragers can be maintained. He argues powerfully that the Zhu (!Kung) have never been a classless society and that if they give such an impression, "it is because they are incorporated as an underclass in a wider social formation that includes Batswana, Ovaherero, and others" (1989: 270). Moreover, he shows that the "Bush-man/San" label has been in existence for barely half a century, the category having been produced through the "retribalization" of the colonial period (p. 280), and that "the cultural conservatism uniformly attributed to these people by almost all anthropologists who have worked with them until recently, is a consequence – not a cause – of the way they have been integrated into the modern capitalist economies of Botswana and Namibia" (p. 12).

With respect to space, Wilmsen is unequivocal: "It is not possible to speak of the Kalahari's isolation, protected by its own vast distances. To those inside, the outside – whatever 'outside' there may have been at any moment – was always present. The appearance of isolation and its reality of dispossessed poverty are recent products of a process that unfolded over two centuries and culminated in the last moments of the colonial era" (p. 157). The process of the production of cultural difference, Wilmsen demonstrates, occurs in continuous, connected space, traversed by economic and political relations of inequality. Where Shostak takes difference as given and concentrates on listening "across cultures," Wilmsen performs the more radical operation of interrogating the "otherness" of the other, situating the production of cultural difference within the historical processes of a socially and spatially interconnected world.

What is needed, then, is more than a ready ear and a deft editorial hand to capture and orchestrate the voices of "others"; what is needed is a willingness to interrogate, politically and historically, the apparent "given" of a world in the first place divided into "ourselves" and "others." A first step on this road is to move beyond naturalized conceptions of spatialized "cultures" and to explore instead the production of difference within common, shared, and connected spaces – "the San," for instance, not as "a people," "native" to the desert, but as a historically constituted and depropertied category systematically relegated to the desert.

The move we are calling for, most generally, is away from seeing cultural difference as the correlate of a world of "peoples" whose separate histories wait to be bridged by the anthropologist and toward seeing it as a product of a shared historical process that differentiates the world as it connects it. For the proponents of "cultural critique," difference is taken as starting point, not as end product. Given a world of "different societies," they ask, how can we use experience in one to comment on another? But if we question a pregiven world of separate and discrete "people and cultures" and see instead a difference-producing set of relations, we turn from a project of juxtaposing preexisting differences to one of exploring the construction of differences in historical process.

In this perspective, power does not enter the anthropological picture only at the moment of representation, for the cultural distinctiveness that the anthropologist attempts to represent has always already been produced within a field of power relations. Thus a politics of otherness exists that is not reducible to a politics of representation. Textual strategies can call attention to the politics of representation, but the issue of otherness itself is not really addressed by the devices of polyphonic textual construction or collaboration with informant-writers, as such writers as Clifford and Vincent Crapanzano (1980) sometimes seem to suggest.

In addition to (not instead of!) textual experimentation, then, there is a need to address the issue of "the West" and its "others" in a way that acknowledges the extratextual roots of the problem. For example, the area of immigration and immigration law is one practical area where the politics of space and the politics of otherness link up very directly. Indeed, if the separateness of separate places is not a natural given but an anthropological problem, it is remarkable how little anthropologists have had to say about the contemporary political issues connected with immigration in the United States.[3] If we accept a world of originally separate and culturally distinct places, then the question of immigration policy is just a question of how hard we should try to maintain this original order. In this perspective, immigration prohibitions are a relatively minor matter. Indeed, operating with a spatially naturalized understanding of cultural difference, uncontrolled immigration may even appear as a danger to anthropology, threatening to blur or erase the cultural distinctiveness of places that is our stock-in-trade. If, on the other hand, it is acknowledged that cultural difference is produced and maintained in a field of power relations in a world always already spatially interconnected, then the restriction of immigration becomes visible as one of the main means through which the disempowered are kept that way.

The enforced "difference" of places becomes, in this perspective, part and parcel of a global system of domination. The anthropological task of denaturalizing cultural and spatial divisions at this point links up with the political task of combating a very literal "spatial incarceration of the native" (Appadurai 1988) within economic spaces zoned, as it were, for poverty. In this sense, changing the way we think about the relations of culture, power, and space opens the possibility of changing more than our texts. There is room, for instance, for a great deal more anthropological involvement, both theoretical and practical, with the politics of the United States/Mexico border, with the political and organizing rights of immigrant workers, and with the appropriation of anthropological concepts of "culture" and "difference" into the repressive ideological apparatus of immigration law and the popular perceptions of "foreigners" and "aliens."

A certain unity of place and people has long been assumed in the anthropological concept of culture. But anthropological representations and immigration laws notwithstanding, "the native" is "spatially incarcerated" only in part. The ability of people to confound the established spatial orders, either through physical movement or through their own conceptual and political acts of reimagination, means that space and place can never be "given" and that the process of their sociopolitical construction must always be considered. An anthropology whose objects are no longer conceived as automatically and naturally anchored in space will need to pay particular attention to the way spaces and places are made, imagined, contested, and enforced. In this sense, it is no paradox to say that questions of space and place are, in this deterritorialized age, more central to anthropological representation than ever.

In suggesting the requestioning of the spatial assumptions implicit in the most fundamental and seemingly innocuous concepts in the social sciences such as "culture," "society," "community," and "nation," we do not presume to lay out a detailed blueprint for an alternative conceptual apparatus. We do, however, wish to point out some promising directions for the future.

One extremely rich vein has been tapped by those attempting to theorize interstitiality and hybridity: in the postcolonial situation (Bhabha 1989; Hannerz 1987; Rushdie 1989); for people living on cultural and national borders (Anzaldúa 1987; Rosaldo 1987, 1988, 1989); for refugees and displaced peoples (Ghosh 1989;

Malkki 1995a, 1995b, 1997); and in the case of migrants and workers (Leonard 1992, 1997). The "syncretic, adaptive politics and culture" of hybridity, Homi K. Bhabha points out (1989: 64), raises questions about "the imperialist and colonialist notions of purity as much as it question[s] the nationalist notions." It remains to be seen what kinds of politics are enabled by such a theorization of hybridity and to what extent it can do away with all claims to authenticity, to all forms of essentialism, strategic or otherwise (see especially Radhakrishnan 1987). Bhabha points to the troublesome connection between claims to purity and utopian teleology in describing how he came to the realization that "the only place in the world to speak from was at a point whereby contradiction, antagonism, the hybridities of cultural influence, the boundaries of nations, were not sublated into some utopian sense of liberation or return. The place to speak from was through those incommensurable contradictions within which people survive, are politically active, and change" (1989: 67). The borderlands make up just such a place of incommensurable contradictions. The term does not indicate a fixed topographical site between two other fixed locales (nations, societies, cultures) but an interstitial zone of displacement and deterritorialization that shapes the identity of the hybridized subject. Rather than dismissing them as insignificant, as marginal zones, thin slivers of land between stable places, we want to contend that the notion of borderlands is a more adequate conceptualization of the "normal" locale of the postmodern subject.

Another promising direction that takes us beyond culture as a spatially localized phenomenon is provided by the analysis of what is variously called "mass media," "public culture," and the "culture industry." (Especially influential here has been the journal *Public Culture*.) Existing symbiotically with the commodity form, profoundly influencing even the remotest people that anthropologists have made such a fetish of studying, mass media pose the clearest challenge to orthodox notions of culture. National, regional, and village boundaries have, of course, never contained culture in the way that the anthropological representations have often implied. But the existence of a transnational public sphere means that the fiction that such boundaries enclose cultures and regulate cultural exchange can no longer be sustained.

The production and the distribution of mass culture – films, television and radio programs, newspapers and wire services, recorded music, books, live concerts – are largely controlled by those notoriously placeless organizations: multinational corporations. The "public sphere" is therefore hardly "public" with respect to control over the representations that are circulated in it. Recent work in cultural studies has emphasized the dangers of reducing the reception of multinational cultural production to the passive act of consumption, leaving no room for the active creation by agents of disjunctures and dislocations between the flow of industrial commodities and cultural products. We worry at least as much, however, about the opposite danger of *celebrating* the inventiveness of those "consumers" of the culture industry (especially on the periphery) who fashion something quite different out of products marketed to them, reinterpreting and remaking them, sometimes quite radically and sometimes in a direction that promotes resistance rather than conformity. The danger here is the temptation to use scattered examples of the cultural flows dribbling from the "periphery" to the chief centers of the culture industry as a way of dismissing the "grand narrative" of capitalism (especially the "totalizing" narrative of late capitalism) and thus of evading the powerful political issues associated with western global hegemony.

The reconceptualization of space implicit in theories of interstitiality and public culture has led to efforts to conceptualize cultural difference without invoking the orthodox idea of "culture." This is as yet a largely unexplored and underdeveloped area. We do, clearly, find the clustering of cultural practices that do not "belong" to a particular "people" or to a definite place. Jameson (1984) has attempted to capture the distinctiveness of these practices in the notion of a "cultural dominant," whereas Ferguson (1999) proposes an idea of "cultural style" that searches for a logic of surface practices without necessarily mapping such practices onto a "total way of life" encompassing values, beliefs, attitudes, and so on, as in the usual concept of culture. We need to explore what Bhabha calls "the uncanny of cultural difference": "Cultural difference becomes a problem not when you can point to the Hottentot Venus, or to the punk whose hair is six feet up in the air; it does not have that kind of fixable visibility. It is as the strangeness of the familiar that it becomes more problematic, both politically and conceptually... when the problem of cultural difference is ourselves-as-others, others-as-ourselves, that borderline" (1989: 72).

Why focus on that borderline? We have argued that deterritorialization has destabilized the fixity of "ourselves" and "others." But it has not thereby created subjects who are free-floating monads, despite what is sometimes implied by those eager to celebrate the freedom and playfulness of the postmodern condition. As Martin and Mohanty (1986: 194) point out, indeterminacy too has its political limits, which follow from the denial of the critic's own location in multiple fields of power. Instead of stopping with the notion of deterritorialization, the pulverization of the space of high modernity, we need to theorize how space is being *re*territorialized in the contemporary world. We need to account sociologically for the fact that the "distance" between the rich in Bombay and those in London may be much shorter than that between different classes in "the same" city. Physical location and physical territory, for so long the *only* grid on which cultural difference could be mapped, need to be replaced by multiple grids that enable us to see that connection and contiguity – more general, the representation of territory – vary considerably by factors such as class, gender, race, and sexuality and are differentially available to those in different locations in the field of power.

NOTES

This paper was originally published in *Cultural Anthropology* 7(1) (1992): 6–23.

1 This is obviously not true of the "new ethnicity" literature, texts such as Anzaldúa 1987 and Radhakrishnan 1987.
2 See also Jennifer Robertson (1988, 1991) on the politics of nostalgia and "native place making" in Japan.
3 We are, of course, aware that a considerable amount of more recent work in anthropology has centered on immigration. But we think that too much of this work remains at the level of describing and documenting patterns and trends of migration, often with a policy science focus. Such work is undoubtedly important, and often strategically effective in the formal

political arena. Yet there remains the challenge of taking up the specifically *cultural* issues surrounding the mapping of otherness onto space, as we have suggested is necessary. One area where at least some anthropologists have taken such issues seriously is that of Mexican immigration to the United States; see, for instance, Alvarez 1987; Bustamente 1987; Chavez 1991; Kearney 1986, 1991; Kearney and Nagengast 1989; and Rouse 1991. Another example is Borneman 1986, which is noteworthy for showing the specific links between immigration law and homophobia – between nationalism and sexuality – in the case of the Cuban "Marielito" immigrants to the United States.

REFERENCES

Alvarez, Robert R., Jr. 1987. *Familia: Migration and Adaptation in Baja and Alta California, 1800–1975.* Berkeley: University of California Press.

Anderson, Benedict. 1983. *Imagined Communities: Reflections on the Origin and Spread of Nationalism.* London: Verso.

Anzaldúa, Gloria, 1987. *Borderlands/La Frontera: The New Mestiza.* San Francisco: Spinsters/Aunt Lute.

Appadurai, Arjun. 1986. "Theory in Anthropology: Center and Periphery." *Comparative Studies in Society and History* 28(1): 356–61.

——. 1988. "Putting Hierarchy in its Place." *Cultural Anthropology* 3(1): 36–49.

Baudrillard, Jean. 1988. *Jean Baudrillard: Selected Writings*, ed. Mark Poster. Stanford, CA: Stanford University Press.

Bhabha, Homi K. 1989. "Location, Intervention, Incommensurability: A Conversation with Homi Bhabha." *Emergences* 1(1): 63–88.

Bisharat, George E. 1997. "Exile to Compatriot: Transformations in the Social Identity of Palestinian Refugees in the West Bank." In *Culture, Power, Place: Explorations in Critical Anthropology*, ed. Akhil Gupta and James Ferguson, pp. 203–33. Durham, NC: Duke University Press.

Borneman, John. 1986. "Emigrés as Bullets/Immigration as Penetration; Perceptions of the Marielitos." *Journal of Popular Culture* 20(3): 73–92.

Bustamente, Jorge. 1987. "Mexican Immigration: A Domestic Issue or an International Reality." In *Hispanic Migration and the United States: A Study in Politics*, ed. Gaston Fernandez, Beverly Nagel, and Leon Narvaez. Bristol, IN: Wyndham Hall.

Chavez, Leo. 1991. "Outside the Imagined Community: Undocumented Settlers and Experiences of Incorporation." *American Ethnologist* 18(2): 257–78.

Clifford, James, 1986. "On Ethnographic Allegory." In *Writing Culture: The Poetics and Politics of Ethnography*, ed. James Clifford and George E. Marcus, pp. 98–121. Berkeley: University of California Press.

——. 1988. *The Predicament of Culture: Twentieth-Century Ethnography, Literature, and Art.* Cambridge, MA: Harvard University Press.

Cohen, Anthony. 1985. *The Symbolic Construction of Community.* New York: Tavistock.

Crapanzano, Vincent. 1980. *Tuhami, Portrait of a Moroccan.* Chicago: University of Chicago Press.

Davis, Mike. 1986. "The Political Economy of Late-Imperial America." In *Prisoners of the American Dream: Politics and Economy in the History of the US Working Class.* New York: Verso.

Deleuze, Gilles, and Félix Guattari. 1987. *A Thousand Plateaus: Capitalism and Schizophrenia.* Minneapolis: University of Minnesota Press.

Ferguson, James. 1997. "The Country and the City on the Copperbelt." In *Culture, Power, Place: Explorations in Critical Anthropology*, ed. Akhil Gupta and James Ferguson, pp. 137–54. Durham, NC: Duke University Press.

——. 1999. *Expectations of Modernity: Myths and Meanings of Urban Life on the Zambian Copperbelt*. Berkeley: University of California Press.

Foucault, Michel. 1980. *Power/Knowledge: Selected Interviews and Other Writings, 1972–1977*, ed. Colin Gordon. New York: Pantheon.

Ghosh, Amitav. 1989. *The Shadow Lines*. New York: Viking.

Gupta, Akhil. 1997. "The Song of the Nonaligned World: Transnational Identities and the Reinscription of Space in Late Capitalism." In *Culture, Power, Place: Explorations in Critical Anthropology*, ed. Akhil Gupta and James Ferguson, pp. 179–99. Durham, NC: Duke University Press.

Handler, Richard. 1988. *Nationalism and the Politics of Culture in Quebec*. Madison: University of Wisconsin Press.

Hannerz, Ulf. 1986. "Small Is Beautiful?" *Comparative Studies in Society and History* 28(2): 362–7.

——. 1987. "The World in Creolization." *Africa* 57(4): 546–59.

Harvey, David. 1989. *The Condition of Postmodernity: An Enquiry into the Origins of Cultural Change*. Cambridge, MA: Blackwell Publishers.

Hebdige, Dick. 1987. *Cut 'n' Mix: Culture, Identity, and Caribbean Music*. London: Methuen.

Hertzfeld, Michael. 1987. *Anthropology through the Looking-Glass: Critical Ethnography in the Margins of Europe*. New York: Cambridge University Press.

Hobsbawm, Eric, and Terence Ranger, eds. 1983. *The Invention of Tradition*. New York: Cambridge University Press.

Jameson, Fredric. 1984. "Postmodernism, or the Cultural Logic of Late Capitalism." *New Left Review* 146: 53–92.

Kapferer, Bruce. 1988. *Legends of People, Myths of State: Violence, Intolerance, and Political Culture in Sri Lanka and Australia*. Washington, DC: Smithsonian Institution Press.

Kaplan, Caren. 1987. "Deterritorializations: The Rewriting of Home and Exile in Western Feminist Discourse." *Cultural Critique* 6: 187–98.

Kearney, Michael. 1986. "From the Invisible Hand to Visible Feet: Anthropological Studies of Migration and Development." *Annual Review of Anthropology* 15: 331–61.

——. 1991. "Borders and Boundaries of State and Self at the End of Empire." *Journal of Historical Sociology* 4(1): 52–74.

Kearney, Michael, and Carol Nagengast. 1989. "Anthropological Perspectives on Transnational Communities in Rural California." Working Paper no. 3, Working Group on Farm Labor and Rural Poverty. Davis, CA: California Institute for Rural Studies.

Leonard, Karen. 1992. *Making Ethnic Choices: California's Punjabi Mexican Americans*. Philadelphia: Temple University Press.

——. 1997. "Finding One's Own Place: Asian Landscapes Re-visioned in Rural California." In *Culture, Power, Place: Explorations in Critical Anthropology*, ed. Akhil Gupta and James Ferguson, pp. 118–36. Durham, NC: Duke University Press.

Malkki, Liisa. 1995a. *Purity and Exile: Violence, Memory, and National Cosmology among Hutu Refugees in Tanzania*. Chicago: University of Chicago Press.

——. 1995b. "Refugees and Exile: From 'Refugee Studies' to the National Order of Things." *Annual Review of Anthropology* 24: 495–523.

——. 1997. "National Geographic: The Rooting of Peoples and the Territorialization of National Identity among Scholars and Refugees." In *Culture, Power, Place: Explorations in Critical Anthropology*, ed. Akhil Gupta and James Ferguson, pp. 52–74. Durham, NC: Duke University Press.

Mandel, Ernest. 1975. *Late Capitalism*, trans. Joris de Bres. New York: Verso.

Marcus, George E., and Michael M.J. Fischer. 1986. *Anthropology as Cultural Critique: An Experimental Moment in the Human Sciences*. Chicago: University of Chicago Press.

Martin, Biddy, and Chandra Talpade Mohanty. 1986. "Feminist Politics: What's Home Got to Do with It?" In *Feminist Studies/Critical Studies*, ed. Teresa de Lauretis, pp. 191–212. Bloomington: Indiana University Press.

Morris, William. 1970. *News from Nowhere* [1891]. London: Routledge and Kegan Paul.

Peters, John Durham. 1997. "Seeing Bifocally: Media, Place, Culture." In *Culture, Power, Place: Explorations in Critical Anthropology*, ed. Akhil Gupta and James Ferguson, pp. 75–92. Durham, NC: Duke University Press.

Pratt, Mary Louise. 1986. "Fieldwork in Common Places." In *Writing Culture: The Poetics and Poltics of Ethnography*, ed. James Clifford and George E. Marcus, pp. 27–50. Berkeley: University of California Press.

Radhakrishnan, Rajagopalan. 1987. "Ethnic Identity and Post-Structuralist Difference." *Cultural Critique* 6: 199–220.

Robertson, Jennifer. 1988. "Furusato Japan: The Culture and Politics of Nostalgia." *Politics, Culture, and Society* 1(4): 494–518.

——. 1991. *Native and Newcomer: Making and Remaking a Japanese City*. Berkeley: University of California Press.

Rosaldo, Renato. 1987. "Politics, Patriarchs, and Laughter." *Cultural Critique* 6: 65–86.

——. 1988. "Ideology, Place, and People without Culture." *Cultural Anthropology* 3(1): 77–87.

——. 1989. *Culture and Truth: The Remaking of Social Analysis*. Boston: Beacon.

Rouse, Roger. 1991. "Mexican Migration and the Social Space of Postmodernism." *Diaspora* 1(1): 8–23.

Rushdie, Salman. 1989. *The Satanic Verses*. New York: Viking.

Said, Edward W. 1979. "Zionism from the Standpoint of Its Victims." *Social Text* 1: 7–58.

Shostak, Marjorie. 1981. *Nisa: The Life and Works of a !Kung Woman*. Cambridge, MA: Harvard University Press.

Williams, Raymond. 1973. *The Country and the City*. New York: Oxford University Press.

Wilmsen, Edwin N. 1989. *Land Filled with Flies: A Political Economy of the Kalahari*. Chicago: University of Chicago Press.

Wright, Patrick. 1985. *On Living in an Old Country: The National Past in Contemporary Britain*. London: Verso.

Part II

Itinerant Capital

The remaining chapters in this volume represent a move away from the broad mapping of globalization presented in Part I in order to track the trajectories of specific global cultural flows.

This portion of the reader focuses on the mobility of capital, concentrating on its articulations with local cultural formations. Freeman's essay illustrates how the search to reduce the costs of production has led corporations to shift labor-intensive industrial production and service work from the United States, Japan, and western Europe to highly dispersed low-wage sites around the globe. More specifically, it focuses on how female workers in Barbados have negotiated their incorporation into these foreign-owned off-shore companies. Maurer's chapter uses the example of the British Virgin Islands to turn the anthropological gaze toward different junctures of the received story of the birth, death, and re-birth of the phoenix of international finance. And Ferguson's piece suggests that the globalization of capital should not be understood simply as a process of pure connection; for places such as Zambia have been disconnected and excluded in many ways from the mainstream of the global economy.

SUGGESTIONS FOR FURTHER READING

Alvarez, Robert R., Jr.
   1998   La Maroma, or Chile, Credit and Chance: An Ethnographic Case of Global Finance and Middlemen Entrepreneurs. *Human Organization* 57(1): 63–73.
Brodkin, Karen
   2000   Global Capitalism: What's Race Got to Do with It? *American Ethnologist* 27(2): 237–56.

Comaroff, Jean and John L. Comaroff, eds.
  2000   Millennial Capitalism and the Culture of Neoliberalism. Theme issue. *Public Culture* 12(2).
Frank, Andre Gunder
  1998   *ReOrient: Global Economy in the Asian Age.* Berkeley: University of California Press.
Freeman, Carla
  2000   *High Tech and High Heels in the Global Economy: Women, Work, and Pink-Collar Identities in the Caribbean.* Durham, NC: Duke University Press.
Gibson-Graham, J. K.
  1996/7   Querying Globalization. *Rethinking Marxism* 9(1): 1–27.
Maurer, Bill
  1995   Complex Subjects: Offshore Finance, Complexity Theory, and the Dispersion of the Modern. *Socialist Review* 25(3–4): 113–45.
Miller, Daniel
  1997   *Capitalism: An Ethnographic Approach.* Oxford: Berg.
Mills, Mary Beth
  1999   *Thai Women in the Global Labor Force: Consuming Desires, Contested Selves.* New Brunswick, NJ: Rutgers University Press.
Ong, Aihwa
  1987   *Spirits of Resistance and Capitalist Discipline: Factory Women in Malaysia.* Albany: State University of New York Press.
Povinelli, Elizabeth A.
  2000   Consuming *Geist*: Popontology and the Spirit of Capital in Indigenous Australia. *Public Culture* 12(2): 501–28.
Sassen, Saskia
  1996   *Losing Control? Sovereignty in an Age of Globalization.* New York: Columbia University Press.
Sawyer, Suzana
  1998   Phantom Citizenship and the Prosthetics of Corporate Capital: "Maria Aquinda et al. versus Texaco, Inc. USA." In *Crossing Currents: Continuity and Change in Latin America.* Michael B. Whiteford and Scott Whiteford, eds. Pp. 474–8. Upper Saddle River, NJ: Prentice-Hall.
Tsing, Anna
  2000   Inside the Economy of Appearances. *Public Culture* 12(1): 115–44.
Yang, Mayfair Mei-hui
  2000   Putting Global Capitalism in its Place: Economic Hybridity, Bataille, and Ritual Expenditure. *Current Anthropology* 41(4): 477–509.

4

Designing Women: Corporate Discipline and Barbados's Off-shore Pink-collar Sector

Carla Freeman

The Off-Shore Office as Scene for Research

The bright yellow awning-shaded tables of Chefette are crowded with young Bajan women animated in their lunchtime conversation; their colorful and fashionable dress turns the heads of passersby. Within moments, the fast-food tables empty, and the high-heeled workers of Data Air[1] escape the midday Caribbean sun, hurrying back to the air-conditioned hum of the "open office." These women represent vast changes in labor patterns and technology in the international arena. Their lives have suddenly become intertwined with service workers in such disparate places as Ireland, the Dominican Republic, Jamaica, Mauritius, and the United States, as the information age signals the virtual collapse of national boundaries and as labor and capital become increasingly internationalized. On the data-entry floor of this off-shore information processing facility, more than 100 women sit at clustered computer stations, entering data from some 300,000 ticket stubs from one airline's 2,000 daily flights. One floor below, an equal number of women work as "approvers," entering data from medical claims sent for processing by one of the largest insurance companies in the United States. This expanding company alone hires close to 1,000 Barbadian workers – almost all of whom are young women. Their fingers fly and the frenetic clicking of keys fills a vast and chilly room as Walkman-clad women work eight-hour shifts at video display terminals – constantly monitored for productivity and accuracy – typing to the latest dub, calypso, or easy-listening station. The muffled clatter of keys creates a sort of white noise, and the green glow of a sea of computer screens lends a sort of Orwellian aura to the tropical setting outside.

From *Cultural Anthropology* 8(2): 169–86. Copyright © 1993, American Anthropological Association.

Data Air and Multitext Corporation are both foreign-owned off-shore companies, one owned by an American and the other by a British multinational. Both set up shop in Barbados in the mid-1980s, and with the exception of the English general manager of Multitext, they are managed almost entirely by Bajans. The move from the American Southwest to Barbados has saved Data Air's parent company roughly 35 percent on its data-entry costs, in addition to the profits made from its expansion into insurance claims processing for one of America's largest firms. From the Barbadian standpoint, this company provides close to a thousand jobs, and its Bajan general manager anticipates that a recent expansion will generate significant foreign exchange, desperately needed as the country now faces newly introduced IMF structural adjustment measures.

Located under the general umbrella of manufacturing, and marking the latest version of high-tech rationalization of the labor process, the expansion of this new off-shore industry represents a massive and international commodification of information – in forms ranging from academic texts to airline tickets, consumer warranty cards, pornographic novels, specialized scientific articles, and literary classics. Data in various forms are currently either flown back and forth between "core" and "periphery" for overnight transactions or sent over fiber optic telephone lines for almost immediate return. New satellite technology facilitates fast and relatively inexpensive transmission of information between "offices" all over the world. In many ways, the shift of information-based work off-shore looks much like a newer, spruced-up version of the export processing model à la Arthur Lewis and Puerto Rico's Operation Bootstrap. In addition to management-level incentives and the arrangements made between local government and foreign industry, these information-based enterprises closely model their traditional manufacturing counterparts, and what looks like clerical work (generally considered white-collar "head" work) begins more closely to resemble low-skilled, highly rationalized assembly-line work in corporate garb.

A number of recent studies have addressed the ways in which the global economy, with its vast movements of capital, labor, and changing technology, is radically reshaping people's (and particularly women's) lives (e.g., Abraham-Van der Mark 1983; Beneria and Roldan 1987; Bolles 1983; Kelly 1987; Mies 1986; Nash and Fernandez-Kelly 1983; Ong 1987; Safa 1981; Sassen 1988; Ward 1990). Within the global orderings, traditional notions of boundaries and space have suddenly given way, which capital, labor, and relations of production and consumption that used to be structured along geographic lines are conflating as borders vanish altogether. This discussion moves between personal narratives of working women's lives and corporate doctrines and ideologies about gender and work in the context of both Barbados's economic development strategy and a burgeoning and globalized information age.

Although international movements of people, goods, culture, and ideologies are certainly not new historical phenomena in the West Indies, the current character and scale of these processes *are* arguably distinct. As these newly incorporated pink-collar workers so clearly reveal, "natives" (and this is particularly evident within the Caribbean) travel between "first" and "third" worlds in increasing numbers, and in their lives in Barbados, imported "first world" artifacts and ideologies (disseminated through the media, advertising, music, et cetera) abound. There are internationalized relations of production in which not only does the information to be "processed" zoom instantly between countries, but so, in a sense, do the processors themselves. This enormous mobility manifests itself at various levels within the labor process. In the case of Data Air, the airline tickets being processed are fitting emblems of the overall collapse of space and distance in this new information age. As part of the company incentive plan, employees are rewarded for exceptional production rates with "thank you cards" in the form of travel vouchers that can be exchanged for trips to other Caribbean islands, Canada, or the United States. In turn, such voyages reveal these women's further entrenchment in the international economy as they purchase clothes, jewelry, and household goods from abroad, both for their own consumption and for marketing back home in an active and diverse informal sector.

The critical labor process school, which followed in the tradition of Harry Braverman's *Labor and Monopoly Capitalism* (1974), argues that the radical restructuring of work currently occurring in the clerical arena is part of a generalized process whereby work is fragmented and deskilled as a necessary part of capitalism's "forward march...that will ultimately degrade all but the most skilled labor" (Baran and Teegarden 1987: 202). In the context of office work, however, it becomes increasingly clear that these processes take on a distinct character, and that we are witnessing the forging of a very particular, newly gendered working class. A number of recent feminist analyses have gone beyond early critical labor process frameworks to look at the particular ways in which restructurings of labor and capital and technological change have had gender-specific implications. These studies, along with recent research about women's massive recruitment into the "global assembly line," can help us better situate the experiences of Barbadian off-shore office workers.

The assumption is often made that clerical jobs constitute middle-class "mental" or "nonmanual" work. However, the contemporary range of new "office" contexts (with a one-to-one boss:secretary ratio at one extreme and vast data-processing pools at the other) forces us to look more closely at the organization of the labor process and to differentiate between types of office work, revising the oversimplified link between "clerical" and "middle class." Moreover, if we accept the importance of the distinction between manual and nonmanual work (versus manual and mental), then, as Braverman implies, clerical work in the form of high-volume information processing – with its low skill level, low pay, and repetitive, fragmented nature – more closely resembles factory work than traditional office work. The nature and spatial organization of clerical work has changed dramatically from its traditional boss–secretary arrangement. Alongside the development of the off-shore office has been the emergence of home-based clerical work in the United States, where women seeking autonomy, flexibility, and a better balance of work and family responsibilities perform a "double day" while simultaneously absorbing overhead costs and forgoing the benefits offered to full-time office staff. These parallel forms of information-based work make an interesting counterpoint to controversial presumptions about "available pools of labor" and their distinctly feminized makeup. Some feminist analyses of automation in the workplace argue that, although increased computerization of offices has led to a decline in some areas of boss–secretary exploitation, it simultaneously gives rise to other forms of control and oppression

(Barker and Downing 1980). Rosemary Pringle (1989) argues that the decline in status of clerical work in the 1950s and 1960s marked changes in the structure of femininity. "Rather than being 'proletarianized,' clerical workers lost some of their status as 'ladies' and were thrown into the mass category of 'girls.'" This happened, she says, through a process of "sexualization rather than through loss of control over the 'means of production'" (p. 193). In the case of clerical workers in vast word-processing pools and off-shore data-entry houses, I would argue that *both* processes are taking place together, creating a class of newly proletarianized and distinctly feminine subjects. The notion of "pink-collar" workers here implies these simultaneous feminization and proletarianization processes.

Woman as "Better Suited": Reinvention of a Familiar Myth

One development officer who specializes in the arena of off-shore information processing in Barbados put forth a familiar explanation for why women workers are preferred for this work. The preference, he said, is not a matter of deliberate selection, but due, rather, to the nature of the production process itself, as well as to the educational and cultural climate.

Women tend to do light assembly work which involves sitting and manipulating fine objects. Some persons claim that men don't have that good coordination....I don't know how true that is, but...some people claim that. I think it might more be a matter of aptitude—and aptitude is probably cultivated by your society and so on. A man is seen in movies and in real life doing things, moving and so on. A man is never seen sitting...sitting especially on a line manipulating fine things. And he may not have had the practice, because in terms of practice, women have had practice manipulating needles and doing fine intricate things, embroidery or cake icing, or being more delicate. And also they have smaller hands, so if you're going to manipulate fine things the physical structure may have some impact. Whatever the reason is, it so happens that women tend to do data entry, garments, electronic assembly, and men tend to do heavier type work. As for the reasons, I wouldn't try to imagine.

Like many other managers and government representatives, this development office resorts both to the biological rationale that women's passive, patient, and dexterous nature makes them best suited for sedentary, monotonous, and meticulous work, and to the liberal position of choice – that women do these jobs because they have the requisite skills and because they exercise individual free will. He vacillates between the "nature" and "culture" rationales for the selection of women, but in the final analysis he implies that these patterns are natural, matter-of-fact, and not up for challenge. From management through rank-and-file data-entry clerks, many with whom I spoke echo similar "commonsense" essentialist explanations: women perform these jobs because they are simply "better suited" for the work. One of the few male employees in a non-typing job at Data Air explained, "I never really thought about one of the keying jobs. I probably think my fingers are too big for the keyboard. To me, a lady would handle that a lot more better than a gentleman...'cause...the touch a lady has, it would be much more comfortable to her. And I personally am the type of guy that likes to be moving around – active – I mean lifting things and that kind of thing." More often than not, female keyers themselves stated simply that women know how to type, and that because these jobs require typing, men do not bother to apply. In Barbados, as in many other places, girls take typing in school, not boys. So, the logic behind "why women?" appears self-evident – since typing is the main requirement for data processing, only girls and women tend to apply for the jobs. A certain tautology pervades this logic and obviously ignores deeper levels of cultural ideologies surrounding gender-based occupational categories. In light of the usual argument, it is noteworthy that in the sister plant of Data Air located in the Dominican Republic, the work force (performing virtually identical jobs) is roughly half male and half female, a majority of whom hold postsecondary technical degrees.

A Data Air personnel assistant, who was conducting interviews to fill the current demand for 190 new insurance claims approvers, revealed an interesting twist not only to the question of why women are recruited, but specifically why young (and often single) mothers are recruited. She commented that the six women she had interviewed one day ranged in age from 18 to 22, and *all* had children. Although she sympathetically "wondered how they manage it all," she expressed the view that "in the long run they make the best workers.... They have better family values and a greater sense of responsibility" than many of the others, who are "too flashy" and "in there just for their paychecks." The implication here is that because these women bear the primary responsibility for their children, they work harder and exhibit greater commitment to their jobs. Interestingly, this assumption was strongly contra-dicted by an American manager of Multitext who argued that, although he had heard (and frankly had counted on the fact) that Barbadian women make good workers because they bear the bulk of the responsibility for their children, he sensed that the matriarchal and extended family instead provides young people with a "guaranteed safety net," thereby obviating precisely the autonomy and sense of responsibility on which he had banked.

A recent increase in crime, the emergence of gang violence, and widespread "indiscipline" among the youth of the country have led to numerous public outcries and a general fear that the traditionally conservative and peaceful social fabric of Barbadian life is quickly being worn thin. Most notable is a lament over the demise both of The Family, the primary locus of social life and economic resourcefulness, and of Christian morality. A number of contradictory arguments and accusations are made in the local press in a scramble to explain these recent and disturbing social changes. On the one hand, working women are blamed for neglecting their maternal obligations; on the other, the diminished role played by grandmothers and other extended female kin, who once bore great responsibility for socialization, is also acknowledged. Women are widely believed to be the natural and necessary minders of children across racial and class groups. From the standpoint of young employed women, the continued formal employment of their mothers and other female rela-tions, and a tendency to idealize marriage and the formation of nuclear families, pose serious implications for the historical precedence of family-based child care and shared domestic responsibilities offered by the traditional extended household (Powell 1986; Senior 1991).

In the context of the data-entry industry, two contradictory profiles of "ideal" workers underlie management's conceptualization of, and rationalizations for, hir-ing women workers. They reveal international corporate notions about women as workers, as well as long-held stereotypes about West Indian women as strong and independent matriarchs. The young single woman continues to be perceived as the quintessential off-shore worker. Family metaphors that incorporate her as a "daughter" portray her as a first-time worker, enjoying the freedom and independence that comes from earning a wage, and as a contributing but nonessential earner in her own household.[2] At the same time, "older" women with children (regardless of their household composition), whose wage-earning roles cast them as the backbone of their families, constitute an alternative stereotype. As the manager makes clear, the expectation is that "older" women will make up a particularly committed and responsible work force and thus ensure high-quality production. Indeed, these women are viewed as a distinct worker "generation" and are often referred to as the "old guard" – those who came to work for Data Air when the company opened its doors in 1983 and continue to constitute a committed work force nine years later. One member of the old guard described the distinctions between generations: they have different views regarding salaries, and the older women identify more with the growth of the company:

Now I'm 25. When I came here I was 18. . . . I was one of the youngest in my department. . . . Down here, although the age difference is only about 5–7 years apart, I think it is very noticeable. When I came here I was working for BDS$187.50 (US$93.75 biweekly). That is one figure I will never forget. How many of these people do you think are going to work for that? What they are making now is considerably more than what I was making then, but they don't think it's enough. I know people that even resign from here and just went home and sat down because they didn't think that coming in here and working for that salary made it worthwhile . . . they don't really stick it out. . . . I think that generation now are different . . . they don't take the same hassles that we have in our day. They're less tolerant. Most of these people in here was born in the '70s and I was born in the '60s. I think if you want you could call it a generation gap . . . they haven't seen this company transformed and maybe they don't feel a part of it, but we that were here saw the progress.

Contrary to the usual trend in export-processing industries around the globe, the old guard of Data Air represents a significant presence not only in numbers, but also in creating an alternative worker profile. In contrast to the more common tendency for women with children (or those who become pregnant) to be turned down or terminated from jobs, the old guard are often favored over younger "school leavers" in the Barbados-based data-entry industry.

Corporate Discipline in the Open Office

A number of elements distinguish the new information-processing enterprises from the off-shore assembly plants that preceded them, from the labor process itself to the ideologies that underlie the construction of an ideal feminine work force. Although the garment and electronic industries have also targeted young Third World women (Ong 1987), the particular methods of control and surveillance fostered by computer technology lend a new and multidimensional shape to the "corporate discipline" exercised in other off-shore factories. The video display terminal (VDT) is undoubtedly a manager's dream come true: every employee can be electronically observed without pause or error; her productivity can be measured for specific increments or longitudinally; and she need never be engaged in face-to-face contact. The computer thus becomes a tool that not only speeds specific job tasks, but that evaluates the worker as well.

Early industrialists devised numerous methods to regulate and direct bodies and bodily energies for productive labor. Foucault described these processes of industrial management as "laying the groundwork for a new kind of society, a 'disciplinary society,' one in which bodily discipline, regulation and surveillance are taken for granted" (as quoted in Zuboff 1988: 319). His analysis of the panopticon as a form of control can be applied to new labor contexts, thus allowing the intensely powerful and unrelenting eye of the computer to be seen as a reinvention of an old form of control. This old form was based on the 1787 architectural plan of Jeremy Bentham, the panopticon of which Foucault writes, which was designed to contain convicts and paupers and was used ultimately in prisons, asylums, and factories. The design included a "twelve sided polygon formed in iron and sheathed in glass in order to create the effect of . . . 'universal transparency' " (as quoted in Zuboff 1988: 320). As Foucault described it, "each individual, in his place, is securely confined to a cell from which he is seen from the front by the supervisor; but the side walls prevent him from coming into contact with his companions. He is seen but he does not see; he is the object of information, never a subject in communication" (Foucault 1979: 200).

The phenomenon of VDT workers in the information industry is, even in its clean and "cool" appearance, a haunting reminder of Bentham's eighteenth-century panopticon. The individual nature of the work process, whereby keyers are physically divided from one another at cellular stations, is coupled with a double layer of surveillance: the deep level of computer monitoring and the surface layer of human supervision. Managers' and supervisors' glass-enclosed offices surround the data-entry floor so that they can observe the overall hum of the shift, while workers, susceptible to their gaze, focus on the VDT screens. The information industry lends itself to a level of worker control and surveillance that far exceeds other forms of manufacturing industries in capitalizing on the power of the panopticon: the computer systems at which keyers work are capable of monitoring the workers' error rates, speed, and quantity of items processed. Lapses in keying, length and frequency of breaks, and worker productivity and discipline can be thus calculated and compared in precise and systematic ways.

As much as the computer facilitates this intense level of surveillance, technology *per se* cannot, however, be held singularly responsible for job deskilling and a newly configured corporate discipline. Focusing on hardware alone ignores the processes by which the technology is mediated through a host of other social practices (language, dress, et cetera). It is these processes that deserve greater attention within critical feminist labor studies. Technological transformations carry ideological, social, and economic implications that are distinctly gendered. Similarly, deskilling and new technologies cannot completely explain the greater preference for women within this or other labor-intensive industries. Such transformations are cleverly and integrally bound up in the forms of supervision as well as in the general expectation that clerical workers conform to so-called traditional female stereotypes (e.g., that they be pleasant, loyal, courteous, well groomed, and perhaps attractive, cheerful).

Although discipline and control have been central to sex-selectivity in the electronics and garment (manufacturing) industries, their role in the management of this new "clerical" enclave is even more pronounced and multifaceted – markedly in terms of dress. One corporate officer proudly proclaimed that the information-processing industry offers a work environment on a par with that of other offices and distinctly separate from manufacturing. "Women are expected to dress professionally here," he said. "This is not a production mentality like jeans and tee shirts." And, in fact, with a number of manufacturing industries located next to these data-entry facilities, many of the women themselves stated quite unequivocally that "you can tell by the way (a woman) looks" whether she is going to work at one of the garment factories or in data entry. Although they note little difference in the pay between the two, they clearly think that working in data entry was a step above the garment factories. Vividly illustrating this point was the expression of disbelief and even indignation on the part of several data processors when they learned of a fellow worker who quit her job as a keyer to work at a piece rate in a neighboring cigar factory.

Discussing the pros and cons of her job and the general atmosphere of this information enclave, buzzing with the sound of computer keys and "plenty of gossip," one young woman emphasized the importance of dress and appearance in maintaining the professional character of the workplace, as well as the ambivalence on the part of some of the workers about the true nature of the industry:

They had to talk to one or two people in there already about the way that they dress, but I never had to be spoken to like that. You should dress in a place like that not like if you're going to a party or a disco or going to town... [you should] dress as if you are working at an office...'cause some people don't really look at it as being an office....But if they were working in an office they would dress a certain way, so I think that if you think that way about working at an office, think that way about working at Multitext and dress to suit the occasion.

The corporate officer's emphasis on women's "professional" presentation as bound up in a particular worker "mentality" implies that the way one looks both reflects and shapes one's work ethic and productive capacity. The importance of this notion is expressed and absorbed in numerous ways. Such subtle additional job requirements as codes of dress and behavior, although obvious to the onlooker as setting workers apart from other industries, become invisible as forms of labor. In the arena of the "open office," dress and fashion become not only powerful metaphors of corporate discipline, but also a form of individual expression and pleasure. A few quotes from Data Air's employee-produced newsletter give a sense of the grave importance attributed to dressing and appearance and the complex way in which messages about dress are bound up in corporate ideals as well as in broader cultural values:

What you wear is really who you are and how you feel about yourself.

Clothing sends a message, a statement to others about you.

Clothing can whisper stability and high moral standards, or it can shout rebellion and discontent. It can serve as a form of identification.

Supervisors are concerned about the way you dress; for them it is more than an issue of personal taste. They want you to send the right message, one that projects you as a balanced, responsible person.

Ladies, before you select what to wear, you must decide whether the clothing is suitable for work. Materials that are so revealing should be reserved for the bedroom. Stop and think about the impression you are giving to onlookers; and it matters not whether you are on the night or day shift. You are dressing for work!

Deodorants! What you wear with what you wear! People won't notice how neatly and appropriately dressed you are if they're gasping for fresh air when you're in the same room!

Despite the fact that this service job is performed behind the scenes, in large, open production floors geographically remote and forever removed from face-to-face contact with its customers, off-shore data-entry operators are expected to present themselves as though they are indeed serving a client in a professional office place, face-to-face.

The enticing appeal of the clean, cool look of the "open office," the dress codes, and the slick-carpeted and air-conditioned work environment (much of which is demanded by the computer technology itself) go a long way in persuading the workers of the "professional" nature of their jobs. The contradictions between their factory wages and fancy titles, such as "material controller," "instructor specialist," and "assistant trainer," help heighten the ambiguities. Although women generally denied that their work experience in the data-processing industry had changed their images of themselves in any identifiable way, their clearly defined notions about how one should dress and behave at work – with a "professional" demeanor and appearance – stand in contrast with their descriptions of their previous work experiences and, to some extent, their class base. This "professional" identity is perceived as contradictory in their own minds and in the reality of the jobs they perform. For example, when comparing their present jobs in data entry to those in other industries (in terms of status, monetary reward, job mobility, and so forth), some women said that they could be making more money working as domestic or agricultural workers, and that their wages are comparable to those in a garment or electronics factory. Many of these women have actually had these jobs, but state that in the final analysis they would rather be in data entry because of the job setting and the "cool" look of the place. The manager-owner of one of the smaller, local data-entry operations explained the phenomenon as follows:

When you see a group of the young ladies, like the ones from Data Air, you can see that they're much better dressed than the ones from the assembly plant. That's my observation. They're probably not getting paid much better but their work environment is a cleaner one, a purer one, and they in fact live out that environment. . . . The Data Air office is very plush, so the young ladies working in there perceive that they are working in an office and they dress like it and they live like it. It's a very interesting phenomenon – it only got started when the data entry business got started – this new breed of office-type workers. They equate themselves with . . . clerical staff in an office and they carry themselves in that way.

Although, to greater or lesser degrees, women acknowledge exploitative production quotas, labor practices, and what one called the "we say and you do attitude," their pride associated with working in a "professional enterprise" (whether real or imagined) helps to quell some of these frustations and, in the face of rising unemployment and economic uncertainty, assists in maintaining very low attrition rates (2 percent). For example, although excessive discipline is one of the most often mentioned complaints about the job (along with pay and favoritism), it is also, in a peculiar way, cited as a contributing factor to the workplace professionalism so eagerly sought and identified with the "office" environment. One woman put the contradiction well, as she described, on the one hand, the company's obsessive concern for time and order – a half-hour lunch, constant monitoring, and "rules and regulations on everything under the sun" – and complained, on the other hand, that many of the "new girls don't understand the importance of a serious professional approach" to their jobs. They talk when they should be working and dress as though they're going out dancing or shopping in town, wearing "short short skirts and off-the-shoulder tops or rolled-up pant legs and flat shoes." Peer pressure in dress and demeanor both contradicts and plays into the hands of the corporate prescriptions: groups of workers may at one moment voice complaints to management about bathroom conditions or excessive overtime, and at the next moment tease and harass a fellow worker for her "inappropriate" clothes or her "unmannerly" work habits.

One young data worker and home needleworker, who bemoans the fact that she has to get up at 5:30 every morning and work overtime without fail each day, expressed no regret over leaving a more flexible (and profitable) arrangement where she worked part-time at the university law library and part-time as a seamstress at home. This by no means implies, as Lim claims (1985), that employment within these foreign, offshore high-tech companies liberates women from the constraints of a partiarchal tradition, or that it promotes greater economic autonomy among them. Rather, like multinationals in other parts of the world (Ong 1987), these high-tech enterprises have shrewdly tapped into a strong Barbadian concern with appearance and have turned this set of cultural values to the advantage of international capital by encouraging workers to identify with a well-defined corporate image. Corporate ideologies about femininity and work, and disciplinary measures that subtly enforce them, contribute to pink-collar workers' pride as "professional" workers. In other words, dress as a manifestation of corporate discipline becomes interwoven with the pervasive and conservative Barbadian ethic that places great emphasis on grooming and deportment.

A number of social critics have debated the fashion question – whether fashionable dress is a form of female oppression or self-expression and adult play. "Is it part of empty consumerism, or is it a site of struggle symbolized in dress codes? Does it muffle the self, or create it?" (Wilson 1990: 231). I would argue that dress becomes an arena in which local (class-based) and international corporate values are simultaneously contested and consented to. As Wilson convincingly states, the puritanical position that construes consumer culture as an opiate, "duping the masses into a state of false consciousness," fails to do justice to the complexities involved in women's decision-making and the psychological pleasures derived from fashion and dress. Women's experimentation with clothes reveals an aesthetic inventiveness that can be interpreted either as conformity to international corporate consumer culture or as enhancing their exploration of alternative subjectivities. Women of all ranks refer to their enjoyment and expenditure in clothes, as well as to the "pressure to dress hard" and the rampant gossip and teasing to which they are subject when their hairstyles and clothes fail to conform. One woman, who began as a supervisor for Data Air when the company opened and has since been promoted to shift manager, expressed her contradictory sense of the dress question in the following way:

Our policy is governed by a dress code.... We are not a factory. We call ourselves an "open office" and if you were working in an office, you wouldn't go in a jean skirt or jean pants or short skirts. You would dress as if you were an executive. That's what we expect our persons to do. Now when we realize that our people are not dressing the way we think they should, we speak with them; we have even gone as far as to ask persons to go back home and change because their attire was not properly suited for the work atmosphere. And we instill that in our people, so by practice and counseling, we have reached the stage where people recognize us for the way we look. They usually say we work for a lot of money [she laughs]. It's not that, but you're governed by a particular code you have to adhere to – *you are being watched*. And not only that but, because there are so many young persons, they usually talk about you if you don't look good. They say "how could you come in here looking like that?" and they want to keep the image up, and certainly as a manager, I wouldn't like to think that my people are coming in here and looking better than me [laughs again]. So you want to dress a certain way to be in line with them, because they do speak about you.

Even as a manager, she describes a sense of surveillance. In her position she is watched not only from above, but also from below, as she fears the scrutiny and criticism from younger fashion-conscious women on the production floor. Recently, and independently, work groups within these vast data-processing facilities have designed and commissioned needleworkers to make them uniforms – brightly colored skirt suits and dresses with distinctive scarves and pocket handkerchiefs to match. Although in some workplaces one might read the imposition of a uniform as a means of suppressing individuality and personal choice, in this case, women derive a sense of pride and shared identification from the uniform that they have fashioned themselves. For them, the uniform is a symbol of professional status comparable to airline workers and bank tellers, and presents an economical way of adhering to the style protocol.

Naming through titles, and image-making in general, can become an element of corporate control. Along with more conscious and direct measures (work quotas, overtime demands, incentive policies, time restrictions, et cetera), forms of image making are often so subtly bound up in a sort of internationalized mainstream feminine stereotype that it becomes hard to differentiate between corporate discipline – with its concomitant imposition of particular gender ideologies, culturally specific notions of women's work and femininity – and women's own changing, and perhaps contradictory, subjectivities. Whereas the Malaysian factory women in Aihwa Ong's work (1987) are reputed in their local contexts to be "loose" and "modern" for having adopted western-style clothes, the Barbadian women are often reputed to look well-off, and even showy, their dress obscuring the reality of their low-skilled, low-paid, tedious work. Following Ong, we might ask how, if at all, the "traditional" or stereotypic notion of the West Indian woman as matriarch, with varying but marked degrees of independence (Barrow 1986), and other ideologies are incorporated into women's new roles as workers at these new industries. Or, conversely, how is the ideology of western individualism and feminine docility reinscribed in the Caribbean context as a way of constructing its "ideal" female work force? These apparently contradictory notions become simultaneously inter-twined in the corporate arena of the off-shore office.

In the tradition of Esther Boserup (1970), Linda Lim (1985) asserts that as women become incorporated into multinational factories as wage workers, as part of a community of other women and through exposure to the bright lights and modern-ity of urban free-trade zones, they gain independence. Wittingly or not, she echoes the promotional materials of many multinational corporations and business opti-mists selling their hardware or off-shore enterprises to Third World governments. Although these factors, may, in fact, represent an element of the incorporation experience (and one that the women themselves often note), it is important also to recognize that the use of such rationales by foreign companies, local governments, and even popular cultural texts may entail clever ideological manipulation on the part of corporate capital that masks much of the reality of the work performed. The relative prestige associated with being one of "the Data Air family," however, along with the promise of independence (amorphous as it may be) and the fact that jobs are increasingly hard to come by in the context of newly implemented structural adjustment measures, seem to effectively convince many of the young women that they are fortunate to be where they are. One should look further, perhaps.

Many of the women testified that their motivations for working in the industry clearly extended beyond basic economic necessity. Some remarked on the import-ance of "getting out" and being among friends in addition to earning a wage and contributing to a household economy. Others alluded to the pride they feel in holding down a regular job, getting dressed up, and being "a working woman." Significantly, these other aspects of the work experience tend to be downplayed in the development literature about women's incorporation into these industries, whereas they are highlighted by development officers and industry managers. One might conclude, therefore, that this discourse is part of a deception or a ploy to distract the workers from the reality of their meager wages and the limits of their jobs. I would argue, however, that this conclusion precludes a more subtle analysis of the women's working experience and the contradictions between their "real" and "perceived" motivations and responses. In a similar vein, Sharon Stichter described textile workers in Egypt and Morocco who justified their employment purely in economic terms, as religious and social mores would otherwise dictate against their working for wages (1990: 55–6). In Barbados, and in the Caribbean in general, women's engagement in wage work has a long and extensive history, and female independence is considered high relative to other parts of the developing world (Barrow 1986). There is little need, therefore, for women to justify their desire for employment in the data-entry industry. Not one woman of the 85 women I inter-viewed indicated that her job created disdain or turbulence within her family. Most reported, instead, that their families were pleased about their work both because of the contribution it would make to the household economy and, more generally, because of the sense of responsibility associated with a full-time job and the prestige still surrounding any work involving a computer. No one described being either pressured to take a job in data entry or prohibited from doing so by a father or husband, as has been noted by others in Mexico, Malaysia, and so on (Beneria and Roldan 1987; Ong 1987).

This is not to say that many data processors do not express grave frustrations and see their jobs as "boring," "dead-end," and "stressful." Rather, the women's messages are complex and often contradictory. Some say that sitting in front of a computer for eight hours every day is "easy" or "cool" compared to other jobs that "have you on your feet all day" (e.g., shop assistant or garment assembly worker). Others, however, describe being "chained" to the machine. They express enormous frustration and annoyance at being treated like "school girls" with rules and regulations, and time constraints they must obey. They resent being surrounded by so many other "girls," where "every day is the same," and, perhaps worst of all, "with nowhere to go from there." At both Data Air and Multitext Corporation, incidents of computer-based theft or sabotage reveal ingenuity on the part of the workers as well as an unexpected sort of mastery over a fragmented and apparently sealed system. In each case, individual keyers figured out ways of "tricking the computer" by copying disks or hitting particular keys in such a way as to achieve exceptional speed and accuracy reports and effectively double their paychecks in the process. When the scandals were uncovered, management at both companies was forced to "tighten security" either by reorganizing the distribution of work to ensure greater control or, in the more extreme case, by making an enormous capital investment in an entirely new computer system. As in many other industries, and even under the exceedingly close supervision and control of the computer, workers have discovered high-tech loopholes that, if even for a short time and in the form of theft, enable them to gain an element of control over their labor.

Woman's Body: Site/Sight of Corporate Discipline and Style

I have alluded to a sort of "corporate style" that underlies the relations of production in the off-shore information-processing industry, and that plays a significant role in the constitution of the Barbadian off-shore data processor in ways that set her apart from other enclave workers (e.g., garment and electronics workers). Elements of ergonomic design that turn a factory shell into an "open office," along with an identifiable fashion statement on the part of employees from management down to rank-and-file production workers, become bound up in the overall labor process through a notion of corporate "style." Corporate image makers deploy this style through a variety of means, the most obvious being an official dress code that prescribes a "smart, professional" look. Corporate style molds discipline as well as ideologies. The image reinforces several contradictory messages and subjectivities for the workers themselves. When asked to account for the reputation of Data Air workers as exceptionally well dressed, some (including supervisors and managers) noted the pressure they feel to keep up with the fashion of the young workers on the floor. Many said that Bajan women simply love to dress. Therefore, even though they acknowledge the company's strict dress code, they may locate the distinguishing mark of the "Data Air girls" in themselves – their own cultural practices and sets of values. It is thus difficult to determine if and where the lines should be drawn between corporate control, worker consent and complicity in presenting themselves as the company prescribes, and broader cultural mores regarding dress and fashion.

The "well-dressed" reputation of the Bajan processors is accompanied by the assumption – expressed by a wide array of people outside the industry who witnessed the parade of young women workers en route to or from work – that they must be making good salaries to be able to afford such extensive and expensive-looking wardrobes. Thus, the notion of "professional style" is a powerful expression of a particular corporate ideology and discipline that runs through the labor process as well. Not only does it create a work force that looks distinct from other manufacturing industries, but it also helps shape the women's notions of themselves and the jobs they do. They dress "professionally" because there is a stated dress code and because peer pressure runs deep. Simultaneously, their dress persuades them that they work in a professional place and do a professional job. Along with the other aspects of decor and ergonomic design – the framed floral prints in the offices, the muted colors of the walls and carpeting, the high-tech look of the computer work stations with their swivel chairs and divided desk spaces, the soft lighting and air conditioning – the women's presentation of themselves as professional workers set this off-shore industry strikingly apart from others whose labor processes are remarkably similar. If, on the one hand, dress becomes a form of discipline by which the company can insist upon a certain look, which presumably translates into a certain work ethic, on the other hand, many women willingly consent to this demand, claiming it as part of their own cultural identity and individual expression.

In a recent article, Bolles and D'Amico-Samuels remark that, "like all people, folk in the Caribbean are often caught between conflicting notions of what they want, and are also responding to economic conditions beyond their immediate control" (1989: 175). In the context of what appear to be contradictory impulses, responses, and subjectivities on the part of the Barbadian data processors, this reminder is well taken. Women are being employed in low-skilled, low-paid jobs, which, despite the comfort of their air-conditioned environments and the status and appearance of being well-off as signified by their dress, entail monotonous and frequently stress-inducing work that presents little in the way of transferable skills or opportunity for advancement. Some of these women acknowledge these constraints in clear and direct terms, expressing a strong desire to find better jobs or go back to school. Others, however, seem essentially content with their data-processing jobs. Whether because of the "friendly atmosphere" and "nice working conditions," or because of the simple fact that, with or without prior work experience, jobs in Barbados are hard to find, many women clearly like their jobs and express great loyalty toward their employers. Several women repeated lines resonating from Data Air's corporate "mission": "We're like one big family," "We're all in it together," and "We [the company] will continue to grow as long as we keep our production high and do good quality work." Despite the fact that they work for a foreign company and have witnessed (and/or personally experienced) the sudden flight of similar off-shore companies (notably INTEL, an electronics assembly plant that closed its doors in 1985, but also garment factories that have shut down), most seem to have a surprising degree of faith in the company's commitment to them and to Barbados. Most women assumed that because people will always fly on airplanes and always get sick (therefore using tickets and submitting insurance claims forms), Data Air should always be in business, and as long as they work hard and do their jobs to the company's satisfaction, they assured themselves there should be no reason to worry. Again, as Bolles and D'Amico-Samuels put it, "work, no matter how dead-end, has meaning in terms of how a woman attempts to meet her familial responsibilities, and is also an essential part of her self-image and her conception of womanhood" (1989: 175).

The fact that women consent to corporate guidelines does not necessarily imply that they are simply and effectively duped by some sort of monolithic corporate construction of a feminine worker; rather, it emphasizes the complex and contradictory nature of their positions as workers and women. As revealed in the development officer's quotation above, the focus on women's "inherent" sense of responsibility, manual dexterity, patience, and so on, conceals very real measures of control within the workplace and reinforces, at the same time, a sexual division of labor that consistently places women in low-skilled, low-paid, dead-end jobs (Fernandez-Kelly 1989: 27).

Advances in computer technology itself are well underway, and it is only a matter of time (and a brief one at that) before the shape of data-entry jobs and the locus of information-based work are again radically altered. High-volume, low-skilled data-entry work will continue to exist as enclave industries off-shore, only until electronic scanning devices (or Optical Character Readers) are improved for accuracy and produced at lower costs. Barbadian workers are already in a wage bracket that increasingly prohibits them from competing for this low-end work with their lower-waged neighbors in Jamaica, the Dominican Republic, St. Lucia, Dominica, and St. Vincent. Although its English-speaking work force and proximity to the United States made Barbados attractive to companies years ago, strikingly high accuracy rates and comparatively low wages in Asia and Central and South America, as well as rapidly expanding satellite facilities, are making these drawing cards less enticing. As automated technologies replace the need for a vast data-entry arena off-shore, it seems clear that some companies will again shift operations closer to their North American or European home offices. Increasing numbers of companies are thus poised to move into more "up-market," off-shore computer-based arenas (e.g., software design, computer graphics, data-based research, animated video production services, computer-aided design (CAD)), such that developing countries are again forced to scramble to come to terms with the labor and technological demands that will enable them to vie for these potentially lucrative contracts. Although it is yet unclear how Barbados will respond to these impending changes, it seems clear that these shifts promise higher-skilled jobs for more-educated people and pose important questions in light of the gender-based incorporation patterns of those industries that preceded them. As the work becomes increasingly skilled, will the work force become less and less a female domain? Will we witness a reversal of the feminization of information processing as it ceases to entail only the rudimentary entering of data and moves into higher level, truly "white-collar" work? Predictions of this sort were made in Singapore's "second stage" of export-oriented manufacturing, which similarly emphasized higher-skilled, higher-value-added industries. Barbados might very well be following close behind in its scramble for high-tech development.

NOTES

Acknowledgements: This article is drawn from research conducted between 1989 and 1991, focusing on the expansion of off-shore information-processing industries in Barbados and the implications of this new high-tech sector for new strategies of economic development and within the lives of its young women workers. The research has been generously funded through grants from IIE/Fulbright, NSF dissertation fellowships, the Wenner-Gren Foundation for Anthropological Research and the OAS. An earlier version of this article was presented to the 15th Annual Conference of the Caribbean Studies Association, Trinidad and Tobago, May 22–6, 1990.

1 The names of companies and individuals have been changed.
2 This profile is consistent with off-shore workers in numerous industries around the world, and similar tactics of patronage and the factory as "family" metaphor are cited by others as well (Ong 1987).

REFERENCES

Abraham-Van der Mark, Eve E.
   1983   The Impact of Industrialization on Women: A Caribbean Case. In *Women, Men and the International Division of Labor.* June Nash and Maria Patricia Fernandez-Kelly, eds. Albany: SUNY Press.
Baran, Barbara, and Suzanne Teegarden
   1987   Women's Labor in the Office of the Future: A Case Study of the Insurance Industry. In *Women, Households and the Economy.* Lourdes Beneria and Catherine R. Stimpson, eds. New Brunswick, NJ: Rutgers University Press.
Barker, Jane, and Hazel Downing
   1980   Word Processing and the Transformation of the Patriarchal Relations of Control in the Office. *Capital and Class* 10: 64–99.
Barrow, Christine
   1986   Autonomy, Equality and Women in Barbados. Paper presented at the 11th Annual Caribbean Studies Association Meeting, Caracas, Venezuela.
Beneria, Lourdes, and Martha Roldan
   1987   *The Crossroads of Gender: Industrial Homework, Subcontracting and Household Dynamics in Mexico City.* Chicago: University of Chicago Press.
Bolles, A. Lynn
   1983   Kitchens Hit By Priorities: Employed Working-Class Jamaican Women Confront the IMF. In *Women, Men and the International Division of Labor.* June Nash and Maria Patricia Fernandez-Kelly, eds. Albany: SUNY Press.
Bolles, A. Lynn, and Deborah D'Amico-Samuels
   1989   Anthropological Scholarship on Gender in the English-Speaking Caribbean. In *Gender and Anthropology: Critical Reviews and Research and Training.* Sandra Morgen, ed. Washington, DC: American Anthropological Association.
Boserup, Esther
   1970   *Women's Role in Economic Development.* New York: St. Martin's Press.
Braverman, Harry
   1974   *Labor and Monopoly Capitalism.* New York: Monthly Review Press.

Fernandez-Kelly, Maria Patricia
    1989   Broadening of Purview: Gender and International Economic Development. Paper presented at the International Conference on Women and Development, State University of New York, Albany.
Foucault, Michel
    1979   *Discipline and Punish: The Birth of the Prison.* New York: Vintage Books.
Kelly, Deidre
    1987   *Hard Work, Hard Choices: A Survey of Women in St. Lucia's Export-Oriented Electronics Factories.* Institute of Social and Economic Research, Occasional Paper No. 20. Cave Hill, Barbados: University of the West Indies.
Lim, Linda
    1985   *Women Workers in the Multinational Enterprises in Developing Countries.* Geneva: International Labor Organization.
Mies, Maria
    1986   *Patriarchy and Accumulation on a World Scale: Women in the International Division of Labour.* London: Zed Books.
Nash, June, and Maria Patricia Fernandez-Kelly, eds.
    1983   *Women, Men and the International Division of Labor.* Albany: SUNY Press.
Ong, Aihwa
    1987   *Spirits of Resistance and Capitalist Discipline: Factory Women in Malaysia.* Albany: SUNY Press.
Powell, Dorian
    1986   Caribbean Women and their Response to Familial Experiences. *Social and Economic Studies* (35)2: 83–130.
Pringle, Rosemary
    1989   *Secretaries Talk: Sexuality, Power and Work.* New York: Verso.
Safa, Helen I.
    1981   Runaway Shops and Female Employment: The Search for Cheap Labor. *Signs* 6: 418–23.
Sassen, Saskia
    1988   *The Mobility of Labor and Capital: A Study in International Investment and Labor Flow.* Cambridge: Cambridge University Press.
Senior, Olive
    1991   *Working Miracles: Women's Lives in the English-Speaking Caribbean.* Cave Hill, Barbados: Institute for Social and Economic Research, University of the West Indies.
Stichter, Sharon
    1990   Women, Employment and the Family. In *Women, Employment, and the Family in the International Division of Labor.* Philadelphia: Temple University Press.
Ward, Kathryn, ed.
    1990   *Women Workers and Global Restructuring.* Ithaca, NY: ILR Press.
Wilson, Elizabeth
    1990   The Postmodern Chameleon. *New Left Review* 180 (March/April): 187–90.
Zuboff, Shoshana
    1988   *In the Age of the Smart Machine: The Future of Work and Power.* New York: Basic Books.

5

A Fish Story: Rethinking Globalization on Virgin Gorda, British Virgin Islands

Bill Maurer

First Diapause

The piscine order Cyprinodontiforms is a large order of fish comprised of over 450 species. Representatives of it are found on every continent except Australia and Antarctica, and they are generally small, from two to four inches long. Popularly known as "killifish," from the Dutch for "fish of the creek," they are renowned among tropical fish hobbyists for their bright colors. Many inhabit seasonal streams and ponds, murky bodies of water that dry up at regular intervals. Successive "generations survive as embryos wrapped in their egg-sacs, buried in the damp muddy bottom" (Riehl and Baensch 1997: 520). They are thus relatively unusual among vertebrates in that their embryos enter "stages of developmental arrest (diapause) when subjected to adverse environmental conditions" (Murphy and Collier 1997: 790). Diapause is correlated with a peculiar embryonic development in which the cells that would, in most other vertebrate embryos, "coalesce and proceed through embryogenesis...instead become amoeboid and disperse over the surface of the egg in the space between" an enveloping cell layer and the yolk sac (Murphy and Collier 1997: 797). Given the right conditions, the amoeboid cells reaggregate and continue to develop. Killifish eggs can go through three diapauses before embryogenesis must begin.[1]

From *American Ethnologist* 27(3): 670–701. Copyright© 2000, American Anthropologiocal Association.

Moving Targets of Globalization

Discussions about globalization are founded on assumptions about movement: that movement generates change, that movement is self-evident, and that increasing mobility characterizes the present (Appadurai 1996; Hannerz 1996). Some critics note that capital, goods, labor, and ideas have been moving from place to place ever since the rise of capitalism, if not before, through trade routes and ancient empires (e.g., Abu-Lughod 1989; Friedman 1995). Within political science, international political economy (IPE) scholars, while not dipping quite so far back into history, argue that the sorts of economic relationships that cultural critics point to as harbingers of a new era – flexible financing, foreign direct investment, floating exchange rates, paper trading and securitization, and all the other ancillary features of contemporary global finance (e.g., Cerny 1994; Helleiner 1994a; Kapstein 1994; Kindleberger 1987; Strange 1986; cf. Harvey 1989) – also characterized the heyday of nineteenth-century industrial capitalism, only to wither away after the world wars. In the late twentieth century, as one IPE reviewer puts it, the "phoenix" of international finance, a dead duck after World War II, has "risen" again (Cohen 1996). Feeding on creatures of the swamp like killifish, this phoenix is only one of many ethereal and sublime wonders that I will introduce in my forays after capital mobility.[2]

While many anthropologists have studied the effects of trade and finance on peasant societies, workers on the global assembly line, or small communities in the United States and elsewhere (e.g., Guyer 1995; Ong 1987; Pred and Watts 1992; Rouse 1991; Sassen 1988), most are at a loss to describe the character of capital movements or interrogate the potential transformative power of financial flows, except for occasional nods to "the end of Bretton Woods," referring to post-World War II international financial architectures and their dismantlings since the 1970s. Appadurai has called for the study of "financescapes" (1990), and other scholars have touched on the "consumption" side of new financial services by looking at the lives of elites (Marcus 1992). Within anthropology, there is also a rich vein of scholarship on globalization and the shop floors and fields of late capitalist production (Fernandez-Kelly 1983; Kearney 1995; Lugo 1990; Ong 1987; Yelvington 1995). Yet anthropology has been surprisingly silent on what money means, or even what money is, in globalized financescapes, perhaps because it is difficult to out-think dominant imaginings of virtual money and quicksilver capital.[3]

In trying to understand capital mobility in my own fieldsite, the British Virgin Islands, a tax haven the economy of which depends on massive flows of money into and out of the territory (see Maurer 1995a, 1995c, 1997a), I have been drawn to the IPE literature in political science because it seems to carry the specificity about capital movements that anthropological assessments often lack. I also question my attraction since the IPE literature leads to as many problems as possibilities. An orthodox Marxist approach to the world economy might find resonances with recent work in IPE, which views global finance as a "resurgence," and not a new phenomenon (e.g., Helleiner 1994a; Kapstein 1994; Kindleberger 1987). Indeed, the world described by contemporary IPE scholars sounds very much like that described by Hilferding (1981), Lenin (1989), and Luxemburg (1951), writing in the aftermath of the nineteenth-century era of free trade imperialism. It was a time of financial speculation, technological advance (especially in transport and communications), and vast transnational movements. Rosa Luxemburg, writing of the financialization of the world economy in the 1910s, makes arguments and uses rhetoric similar to those of Charles Kindleberger, an IPE authority, writing of the "resurgence of global finance" in the 1980s and 1990s.

[The] operations of capital, at first sight, seem to reach the height of madness. One loan followed hard on the other, the interests on old loans was defrayed by new loans, and capital borrowed from the British and French paid for the large orders placed with British and French industrial capital. While the whole of Europe sighed and shrugged its shoulders at [Egypt's] crazy economy, European capital was in fact doing business in Egypt on a unique and fantastic scale – an incredible modern version of the biblical legend about the fat kine which remains unparalleled in capitalist history. (Luxemburg 1951: 434)

The last decades have seen the development of ... currency swaps, interest swaps, repos – a device for selling a security with a contract to buy it back later at a set price to gain short-term liquidity – a bewildering panoply of options and futures contracts on government bonds, interest rates, stock-market indexes and the like, packages loans in which mortgages, automobile installment paper and credit-card debt are grouped and participants in the total sold, ... etc. etc. (Kindleberger 1987: 65)[4]

Both find madness and bewilderment in their efforts to pin down finance capital. In this, they walk in the shadow of Marx himself, who, in his famous pronouncement, likened finance to fantastic magic. "Primitive accumulation proceeded without the advance of even a shilling," he wrote. "As with the stroke of an enchanter's wand, [debt] endows unproductive money with the power of creation and thus turns it into capital, without forcing it to expose itself to the troubles and risks inseparable from its employment in industry or even in usury" (1977: 917, 919).[5]

I am intrigued by the magic and madness animating these influential accounts of capital mobility. As Rod Giblett argues, the formula that "all that is solid melts into air" under the "etherealizing project of modernity," borrows the chemical metaphor of sublimation – the transformation from a solid to a gaseous state (rising with the phoenix from the ashes, to the heights of madness perhaps) – without considering its obverse, desublimation – the transformation from solid to sticky, oozing liquid (Giblett 1996: 25). Sublimation is haunted, Giblett maintains, by its uncanny other; "slime is the secret of the sublime" (Sofoulis 1988, in Giblett 1996: 27). Is it possible to reframe the dizzying heights conjured by the enchanter's wand, the virtual objects of quicksilver capital zipping around the globe in networked circuits, as the amoeboid cells in a killifish embryo, sliding and sloshing, oozing in the muck? Is it possible, following J. K. Gibson-Graham (1996), to deny the image of contemporary capitalism as hard, penetrating, and all-encompassing – and as the only remaining alternative for political economic order, heralding the "end of history" (Fukuyama 1992) – and write instead a story about an open, porous, seeping, and dripping body of global capitalism, a tale that interrupts the continuity of the narrative of the rising phoenix? This would be a different story from the familiar one about the clean lines and fast networks of neoliberal efficiency. Less like a fiber optic network; more like a lava lamp.

Globalization is a keyword in countless recent publications and conference discussions. Conference-goers will frequently hear bold, confident statements to the effect that all this globalization talk is nonsense; it merely echoes the ideology of the new capitalist classes; it denies the history of other world-encompassing economic systems; after all, Lenin (1989) said it best – the last stage of capitalism is the global, imperial stage. While wary at every turn of the seductive language of new "globalist" elites and worried about being taken as merely recapitulating their triumphal tales of globalization,[6] I argue that the "there's nothing new under the sun" perspective is fundamentally flawed.[7] It assumes that the nature of the movement described by authors from Marx to Kindleberger is identical and that the objects being moved are comparable. It does so by foreclosing the possibility of viewing the different capitalist morphologies, and their leakages and eruptions, so grotesquely vivisected by Gibson-Graham (1996). In short, it leaves unasked the anthropological questions that most need answering: what counts as capital and what counts as movement? How do certain practices and processes constitute capital such that it can move? How do they also structure its movements so they can have the effects that globalization literature ascribes to them? How do they sublimate the messiness of capital formations into neat objects of property and neat narratives of progress? And what assumptions about historicity and historical development are built into dominant understanding of capital and its peregrinations?

Absence at the Core: The Copper Mine

In this article, I use the case of the British Virgin Islands in the eastern Caribbean to turn the anthropological gaze toward different moments of the received narrative of the birth, death, and re-birth of the phoenix of international finance. Using historical material from the free trade era of the British Empire, the period of the "death of the phoenix" of global finance in the postwar years, and the current free trade regime, I sketch out how specific social formations in these moments encouraged specific notions of finance, sovereignty, citizenship, and governance, which in turn informed the movements that empowered free trade (or protectionism) in these different social formations, as well as the objects and other entities being moved.[8]

My selection of these three historical periods derives from two factors. First, these are the central periods in historical accounts of the development of financial globalization. In these historical narratives, the postwar years are cast as an aberrant retrogression into a neo-Romantic time of protectionism, localism, and nationalism, interrupting the natural evolution of a world capitalist system that began, for many, with the conquest of the New World. They are key signposts on the timeline of capitalist development.[9] Second, these are the only time periods for which I have any significant data for the case at hand, the copper mine on Virgin Gorda. Though my fieldwork centered on the legislative and popular debates about citizenship, land, and finance, in conducting archival research and in indexing the minutes of the Legislative Council for the British Virgin Islands (BVI) Public Library, I came across occasional references to the copper mine, and, in interviews I conducted with former members of the Legislative Council, I always brought up the case of the copper mine simply because I was fascinated to hear what they would say about this odd little site on a remote corner of Virgin Gorda. As will become clear in the sections that follow, what I heard in these interviews were tales about political factions and contending interests – more about politics and less about the mine itself. And, as will also become clear, those contending interests endure in the political and social life of the BVI today.[10]

To discuss mobility of objects of capital, I am focusing on an object that does not seem to move at all – indeed, something that is not even "there": the mine is a hole, an absence, a missing object. Yet the mine has been part of different circulations in different historical moments. I argue that the copper mine in the late nineteenth century was a qualitatively different object from the copper mines of the middle and late twentieth century. Different sets of discourses around citizenship, finance, and nation congealed in the objects called the copper mine in different historical moments, granting the mine(s) temporary ontological stability and a certain temporal materiality. It is not merely a case of an object taking on different meanings in different eras; rather, the object itself gained its object-status in different ways during these eras. It was constructed by investors, legislators, and citizens through a constellation of beliefs and practices such that it was literally transformed. Different circulatory logics constituted the mine as an object. But, as I will show, these logics cannot be placed into neatly bounded historical stages to trace the development of a capitalism culminating in the financial globalization of the present.[11]

The sections of this article are intercut with reflections on the odd little killifish, allowing me, in the conclusion, to build a theoretical critique of narratives of historical progress that often enframe capital mobility. Dominant notions of capital – like those of kinship and evolution – rest on developmental sequences: stories about origins, continuities of consanguinity, and teleologies of historical progress. The critique of the study of kinship led anthropologists to question the notions of person, relation, and movement on which their "kinship thinking" rested. I hope to encourage a similar critical stance toward often-implicit anthropological "capital thinking." Circulating capital is like circulating connubium in that both are analytically bankrupt concepts that reveal more about the worlds anthropologists inhabit and take for granted than any underlying truths about the worlds we study.

No documentary evidence exists on the very early history of the site of the Virgin Gorda copper mine. Local stories hold that copper ore was first extracted by the Spanish in the mid-1600s. Remnants of an early horizontal mine tunnel exist in the seaside of Mine Hill, near sea level. These traces of earlier mining were discovered in 1725 (Dookhan 1975: 27). Today, the ruined mine is a seldom-visited tourist attraction. One approaches the site of the mine via a gravel road up Mine Hill, on the dry, rugged southeast side of Virgin Gorda. When I took my parents there, I had to ask them to get out of the rented jeep I was driving and help push it out of a rough spot in the road. All one can really see today is a ruined chimney and a slag heap. BVIslanders in their forties and fifties remember going to Mine Hill in their youth to look for molybdenum to play with, a soft mineral that (while poisonous) can be used like a pencil to make marks on paper or stone. Visiting tourists today are likely to find themselves all alone when they visit the site.

Second Diapause

Killifish are unique not merely because of their developmental diapauses. Unlike other small, colorful fish, they can rarely be bought at the local aquarium store. This is not because they are rare or difficult to collect or breed in captivity. Rather, it is because collection, breeding, and distribution of killifish is controlled through regional networks of killifish associations. The American Killifish Association maintains records of aquarists who breed killifish so that individuals wishing to acquire them may do so. Participating in the networks of fish trading, however, requires membership in the Association, which entitles a person to the bi-monthly *Journal of the American Killifish Association* and the monthly *Business Newsletter*. Members can acquire fish or, more often, eggs, by turning to the "Fish and Egg Listing," the real meat of the *Business Newsletter*. In accordance with Association policy, prices are nominal and are supposed to reflect the costs of harvesting and packaging the eggs or raising the fish to near-adulthood. The fishes' arrested development permits easy shipment through the mail in plastic containers filled with mud or peat-moss. According to Association literature, "fish exchanges" constitute "the most exciting and interesting phase of contact between the members of the hobby" (Markis and Langton 1990: 55). Through them, the Association fosters what it calls "fellowship" among its members. Fish and eggs, then, are not, strictly speaking, commodities, but rather a special kind of gift.

Listings in the *Business Newsletter* identify the fish by species name, often with a modifier indicating the geographic point of origin of the stock from which the eggs or their ancestors have come. Occasionally, the *Newsletter* contains columns discussing a member's recent voyage to a collection site. The *Journal* also contains such narratives, often lengthier, including GPS-derived coordinates of the collection sites, maps, detailed notes on water quality, temperature, weather at the time of collection, and so on. The fish are almost always identified and traded with reference to their geographic and temporal origins. The Association Code of Ethics requires that, wherever known, those originary coordinates be specified for all exchanges.[12]

British Free Trade and the Virgin Islands Mining Company, 1838–1914

The tale I am about to relate could be told in terms of parliamentary factions, contending interests, or a struggle for control with a foreordained outcome. One could craft a simple parable, a morality play involving the forces of free trade and the forces of protection. The problem with doing so is that the characters of such a play will resist the closure that their concretization into allegorical figures of fable would require. Historians may write their narratives like parables, inserting historical personae into predefined scripts, and, occasionally, I find myself falling back into them as well. But the story is not an allegory.

While a case could be made that the abolition of slavery in the West Indian colonies from 1834 to 1838 was the first blow to protectionism in the British Empire, historians usually trace the rise of free trade imperialism to the repeal of the Corn Laws in 1846 (Green 1976; Knorr 1963; Semmel 1970). The Corn Laws had attempted to foster post-enclosure British agriculture by placing high tariffs on imported grain. The free trade political economists argued that by inflating the price of grain at home, the Corn Laws necessarily led to the immiseration of the poor. This was of great concern to industrialists who feared that the market for their goods would dry up as working people had less and less to spend on manufactured items. The idea that export of manufactured goods to the colonies could pick up the difference had some persuasive force, but the repeal of the Corn Laws was primarily effected by the argument that removing tariffs and allowing the importation of cheap grain would ultimately put more money in the pockets of the working classes, who would then purchase more manufactured goods, thus increasing industrialization, creating more industrial jobs for the recently landless, raising the standard of living for all Britons.[13]

The repeal of the Corn Laws initiated a chain of other legislative actions aimed at liberalizing trade, including the repeal of the Navigation Acts in 1850. Here, however, I focus on the Sugar Duties Act, another piece of free trade legislation passed in 1846 that had a tremendous impact on the West Indies. After emancipation, West Indian sugar prices increased, and British merchants argued that they should be able to import sugar from other sources, whether free or slave grown. They successfully carried the movement for free trade in sugar. The Sugar Duties Act opened British markets to non-West Indian sugar and placed plantation owners in the colonies, who only a decade before had faced emancipation of the slave labor force, in a serious bind. Specifically, the Act equalized duties on sugar from slave and non-slave territories, with a gradual elimination of the protective tariff for colonial sugar to be completed by 1851 (Craton and Walvin 1970: 223). During the debates over this Act, the West India interests emerged as the "defenders of free labour engaged in a fateful competition with the forces of slavery" (Green 1976: 231). As James Matthew Higgins, a prominent defender of the West Indian interest, put it in 1848, "We ruin our colonies because slavery is so horrible, and buy our sugar at Brazil because slavery is so cheap" (in Green 1976: 233).

But the West India interest did not put forth a consistently protectionist position; it also argued for the abolition of the Navigation Acts so that West Indian estate owners would have access to free labor on the African coast and so that they could use the freight carriers of their choice instead of being limited to British ones (Green 1976: 234). The coordinates of late twentieth-century political economy fail to map the complexity and specificity of West India interests' "protectionism." It is not just a case of a group of people holding contradictory or inconsistent views. Rather, contemporary analytical categories and historiographic desires are inconsistent with a historical moment commonly introduced in a teleological narrative of historical development from protectionism to free trade in nineteenth-century empire.

As a result of the increasing competition from slave-grown sugar, and of the 1847 economic depression, 48 West Indian merchant houses in Liverpool and London went bankrupt (Craton and Walvin 1970: 223). Land values collapsed, banks stopped issuing credit to colonial sugar estates, colonial governments lost revenue, and workers rioted. In Trinidad and British Guiana, indentured labor systems, which brought in large numbers of South Asian and Chinese workers, helped preserve the sugar industry, but elsewhere the industry suffered. Parliament's response was to delay the end of the imperial sugar preference from 1851 to 1854 and to pass the Encumbered Estates Act in 1854. This act was "designed to facilitate the sale of properties laden with complicated debts" (Green 1976: 255). According to one historian, such sales tended to "concentrate West Indian property in the hands of metropolitan merchant houses, completing a trend which had begun in the eighteenth century" (Green 1976: 256). In the BVI and other smaller territories, however, the Encumbered Estates Act enabled free people of color to purchase land for the first time (Dookhan 1975: 135). A mythology about the Encumbered Estates Act has grown up in the BVI stemming from this time, when many ancestors of contemporary BVIslanders first purchased land that would later be passed on as "family land" for generations (see Maurer 1997b). The received historical narrative (a story of protectionism, free trade, and completed trends) fails to capture the specificity of historical practices and unintended effects of different constellations of power for different sites and actors, like the BVI and the titleholder to family land.

Indeed, the free trade era was crucial in the creation of Caribbean "peasantries" as a new form of colonial subject. Estate laborers purchased or squatted on abandoned estates and marketed their surplus (see Berleant-Schiller 1995; Lowes 1995; Maurer 1997c; Mintz 1974; Williams 1944). They also began to assert themselves as subjects of the Crown, with an entitlement to British identity (Maurer 1997a: 45–6). In addition, the free trade era contributed to a reconfiguring of colonial rule that had as much to do with governing a free peasantry as dealing with an ever-declining revenue base (Trouillot 1989). The British government drastically reduced the colonial bureaucracy throughout the region, dissolving legislatures and centralizing colonial authority in the larger islands and, for the Leewards, in Antigua (Rogers 1970; see also Green 1976: 260). Along with restructured governance and new peasantries, the free trade West Indies in the middle to late nineteenth century witnessed new speculative schemes put forward by metropolitan businessmen who sought investment opportunities after the partial collapse of sugar. It is in this context that I must place the first Virgin Gorda copper mine.

A Speculative Investment

The first copper mine was established in 1838 by Virgin Islands Mining Company of Liverpool. It extracted 90 tons of copper in 1841, using local laborers, but went bankrupt in 1842 (Dookhan 1975: 112). The mine reopened in 1859 and removed ore continuously until 1867, the year of a devastating hurricane (Dookhan 1975: 141). In the early 1860s, copper extracted from the mine constituted the Virgin Islands' *only* export to Britain, valued at £16,244 between 1860 and 1862 (Dookhan 1975: 139). Mining machinery from Britain constituted the colony's *only* British imports from 1859 to 1861 (Dookhan 1975: 141).[14]

Miners extracted ore from two vertical shafts extending about three hundred feet below sea level; the operation required constant pumping to evacuate the water that seeped into the shafts, and this, in turn, required a steam-driven pump that had to be fed coal from Puerto Rico. The ore was transported by coal-powered steamships directly from the difficult-to-access, rocky coast near Mine Hill, rather than being carried overland to the port of Spanish Town on the other side of the central ridge.

Like other foreign mining operations, the Virgin Gorda venture suffered from huge transport costs because of the rising price of coal (Toomey 1985: 126–37).

But what forces had led Liverpudlian businessmen to turn to Virgin Gorda in the first place? The answers lie in the impact of free trade on the copper industry in Britain and in another tale of unintended consequences, twisted trajectories, and fits and starts. British smelting interests in Swansea, the center of smelting activity up until the late 1840s, maintained dominance in the copper industry with the assistance of a system of copper duties that inflated the cost of foreign ore (mainly from South America) and enabled Swansea smelters to keep the price of Cornish ore low. The smelters quite effectively pitted ore suppliers against each other, using a system of public bidding and behind-the-scenes collusion to keep the price of ore down. In 1840, the prices of British, foreign, and colonial ore reached their lowest point in the century. Many foreign and colonial mining operations, like that on Virgin Gorda, failed.

But at mid-century, demand for copper skyrocketed because of the new electric industries, most notably, the submarine cable industry (Culver and Reinhart 1989: 725).[15] In spite of the copper duties, the increased demand encouraged new speculative mining operations in the colonies and elsewhere. In addition to the increased demand for copper, the copper industry itself underwent a radical change between the 1840s and 1860s because of the entry of Liverpudlian businessmen. They were in an ideal position to exploit ore sources abroad since Liverpool had been the center of early nineteenth-century slave trading, and later, merchant trading with the Americas. Many West Indian merchant houses were based in Liverpool. The entrance of Liverpool businessmen into the copper industry represented a redirection of capital away from West Indian plantations and toward West Indian and South American copper. The Virgin Gorda mine that operated from 1838 to 1842 represents one such redirection, opening, as it did, at the end of the "apprentice" period for newly freed Caribbean peoples and the beginning of the West Indies' new political economic era.

The old smelters managed to keep the price of ore low and charged high for smelted copper. The difference in price between ore and smelted copper peaked in 1840. Miners sought means to improve their ore prices, including smelting their own ores or "sending ores for sale to Liverpool instead of Swansea" (Valenzuela 1990: 663). Mining interests formed their own smelting company in 1841, called the English Copper Company, and managed to achieve a 13.6 percent share of British copper smelting by 1844. They also helped inflate the price of ore while lowering the price of smelted copper (Valenzuela 1990: 665). The established smelters responded by forming their own Smelting Association, based on quota purchases, and by arguing forcefully for the continuation of the copper duties on foreign ore.

New entrants into smelting obtained copper ore through a system of private contracting with foreign and colonial suppliers. For instance, one of the major shareholders in the P. Grenfell and Sons smelting company was also one of the original proprietors of the Cobre mines in Chile (Valenzuela 1990: 661). Similarly, the Williams, Foster, and Co. smelting company had a close connection with British Copper Co., a mining company in Cuba (Valenzuela 1990: 662). The Llanelly Copper Co., another new smelter, made an arrangement with John Bibby and Sons of Liverpool to buy ores in Chile and Peru with the "option of purchasing the ores on equal terms to what would be given for them at Swansea or by other smelting companies" (Valenzuela 1990: 662). By the late 1830s, about a fifth of the copper ore coming into Britain that was sold through private contract instead of public bidding came from Cuba, through the sort of operation that Bibby had with Llanelly (Valenzuela 1990: 663).

The definitive blow to the established smelters in Swansea came in 1848 with the repeal of the 1842 Copper Duties Act. The arguments for protection had come from Swansea smelters worried about competition from Liverpool smelters who were, as one commentator put it in the *Mining Journal* in 1848, "supplied with rich foreign ores" (Valenzuela 1990: 675). In a rhetorical move identical to that made by the old West India interests protesting the Sugar Duties Act, Swansea smelters claimed that the labor force abroad "consisted principally of slaves" and that Cornish miners would suffer from free trade (Valenzuela 1990: 677). Liverpool smelters, themselves partially representative of the old West India sugar interests who had opposed free trade in sugar, now vociferously argued for free trade in copper (Valenzuela 1990: 681). They claimed that the duties had hurt smelting in Britain by encouraging the development of smelting near foreign mines, especially in Chile (Valenzuela 1990: 682; 1992; 1996). As a result of the end of the copper duties, copper production outside of Britain and its colonies took off in the 1850s.

From the end of the copper duties to the 1860s, mining operations abroad became profitable investments. As a result, the number of smelting companies in Britain grew from ten to seventeen. The new smelters, independently of Swansea, "pushed up the price of copper ore through their demand and reduced the difference between the prices of copper and copper ore" (Valenzuela 1990: 669). This, therefore, was a period of expansion of mining operations abroad, less oriented toward Swansea and more oriented toward the new establishments in Liverpool. These new establishments engaged in the same sort of private contracting and direct investment that the Llanellys had done in the 1830s (Toomey 1985: 74–5). Non-Cornish mining operations flourished in the colonies and elsewhere and the United Kingdom lost its dominance in the world copper industry.[16] The development of smelting in Chile, Montana, and Michigan in the mid- to late nineteenth century struck a further blow to UK dominance. This is the period of the reopening and continuous operation of the Virgin Gorda copper mine, from 1859 to 1867.

These non-British mining operations suffered a setback in 1867, however – and not because of a West Indian hurricane. The war between Spain and Chile from 1865 to 1867 resulted in an "ore famine," since export of Chilean ore was suspended during this time. The disruption in Chile led to a "collapse of the financial and commercial support for the mining industry" among the speculative Liverpool and London investors (Toomey 1985: 64), and despite the shortage of ore, prices fell drastically causing many mines to cease production.

In 1867, the copper mine on Virgin Gorda closed. The owners sold off all the machinery and salvageable equipment from the mine, leaving boarded-up shafts, slag heaps, and the shells of a chimney and boiler house. Over the years, residents of Spanish Town began hauling their garbage over the ridge to the site of the abandoned copper mine. From a speculative investment gone bust, the mine became a dumpsite and remained so until the end of World War II, the coming of local legislative autonomy, and the beginning of a new model of economy, polity, and development.

So, what was the copper mine during the period of British free trade? It was a speculative investment by a group of Liverpool businessmen hoping to use their foreign and colonial connections forged, in part, during the slave trade, to profit from a shortage of copper and lowered import duties at the expense of Cornish and Welsh mining interests. It was also, in a sense, an ancillary operation of mining outfits in Cuba, which had emerged as an important copper exporter during this period, sending ore to Liverpool and not Swansea. The copper mine ceased to be a profitable venture when the mining industry's superstructure collapsed during the war between Spain and Chile.

The tale here is not simply one of savvy businessmen pursuing self-interest and redirecting resources and political positions with the changing winds of trade. The copper mine also represented a complex constellation of notions of citizenship, finance, governance, and commodity movement. Debates around free trade emphasized the difference between slave and free labor, whether in sugar or in mining, in the colonies or in Cuba and Brazil. Virgin Islanders were made colonial subjects at the same time that Cornish workers became "free laborers," both for the protectionist West India sugar interests and the protectionist Swansea smelters. The rhetoric of "free labor" emerged to counterbalance free trade. But not without considerable messiness and ambiguity. The free trade Liverpool smelting interests consisted of the same businessmen as the earlier, "protectionist" West India interests. Liverpool West India interests *opposed* free trade in sugar because they said it would put slave-grown sugar on British tables and harm the newly-freed West Indian laborers. Liverpool smelters *supported* free trade in copper because it promoted foreign commercial connections they had already established in the slave era and because not doing so would risk losing Britain's dominance of the smelting industry. For both the pro- and anti-free trade interests, the debate itself was a nationalist project – a protectionist project, ultimately geared toward ensuring the dominance of Empire in a new system of free trade imperialism, using the free laborer as a point of reference, and equating, or at least bringing on par, the West Indian peasant and the Cornish miner.

Third Diapause

Why keep killifish? Merely to enjoy their colors and unusual habits? The American Killifish Code of Ethics contains explicit recommendations – more on the order of moral injunctions. One keeps killifish because one is interested in their proper stewardship, in keeping a "population strong and viable through many generations to come" (Kelley 1999: 2). Good stewardship entails responsibilities. Most killifish can interbreed with individuals of other species – a point to which I will return later – but the Association strongly discourages hybridization. As stated by the AKA, "It is [our] policy... to discourage hybridization except for scientific and research purposes. The organization believes that the fishes should remain as they are in nature and that hobbyists should not intentionally change color patterns, form, or identity. Every member of the AKA is urged to maintain this policy" (Markis and Langton 1990: 48).

In the biblical Parable of the Talents (Matt. 25), a master entrusted his wealth to three servants before departing on a journey. To the first servant, he gave five talents; to the second, two; and to the third, one. The first two "traded" (Matt. 25: 16, 17) with the talents in business enterprises and thereby doubled their master's money. But the third "went and dug in the ground and hid his master's money" (Matt. 25: 18), like a killifish buries its eggs. Upon returning from his travels, the master praised the first two for investing his money so well and allowed them to "enter into [his] joy" (Matt. 25: 21, 23). The master condemned the third servant, however, excoriating him for not investing his money "with the bankers" so that the master could "have received what was [his] own with interest" (Matt. 25: 27). He took the talent away from the poor servant and gave it to the richest, and rendering the third servant abject; he "cast [him] into the outer darkness" where men "weep and gnash their teeth" (Matt. 25: 30).

Scholars and the faithful usually interpret this parable as a tale of good stewardship – in order to avoid the awkward exegesis that would result from viewing it in strictly economic terms, as a story about the benefits of usurious gain. In the currently dominant exegesis, it is a tale of orderly increase through good resource management. Stewardship over killifish entails an orderly increase, as well, structured by careful isolation of species that might interbreed and produce hybrids. Protecting and preserving the natural resource of the killifish means protecting and preserving the distinct species as they are found in nature. This insures that another kind of development will not enter an arrested stage – the individual species themselves will not enter a diapause, but will continue, uninterrupted, unto the last days. Realizing one's goal of maintaining a viable population of killifish means realizing the future of the species itself.

(Not) Building the Road to Mine Hill: Legislative Debates in the 1950s

Copper was not mined from the Virgin Gorda site again. After World War II, and a successful movement for legislative autonomy in the BVI, however, a copper mine congealed anew through a series of debates in the local Legislative Council, as this new body sought to find its purpose in the postwar and postimperial Caribbean. After achieving legislative autonomy, British Virgin Islander elites, like their counterparts in the Caribbean and much of the Third World, embarked on import substitution industrialization schemes. Development discourse dominated legislative discussion (see Escobar 1995; Ferguson 1990). Import substitution schemes competed in the 1950s with another emerging vision of development, based on tourism instead of industry. The tourism-based model of economic development eventually triumphed in the 1960s and 1970s, but only after Fidel Castro's successful revolution in Cuba led US tourism investors to seek out other beaches.

Legislative Council business during its first decade was almost exclusively about development, and, specifically, the development of the kind of infrastructure a modern, industrial nation was supposed to possess. Discussion of roads, jetties, radiotelephones, airfields, cattle dips, cement mixers, piles of sand and gravel, and applicants for "pioneer industry" licenses dominated legislative debate in the 1950s. The other major theme in these debates was the role of the legislature and government. In addition to granting itself the privileges associated with governing bodies of other modern nation-states (like honorific titles, special chairs, a seal, and ceremony), the British Virgin Islands' Legislative Council also successfully lobbied the British Foreign and Commonwealth Office for direct grants of British financial assistance ("grants-in-aid") for specific government projects (see Maurer 1997d:

84–7). These included the construction of an agricultural station and an airstrip (British Virgin Islands Legislative Council [hereafter BVILC] Minutes June 25, 1957; September 26, 1957; November 7, 1957). The new government also granted itself some of the powers previously reserved for the old colonial legislature based in Antigua, specifically, the power to declare holidays and the power to acquire land from private individuals. Legislators justified land acquisitions as essential to the furthering of development (BVILC Minutes January 29, 1957).

One feature of the new development discourse in the BVI was increased attention to the islands' natural resources. The period witnessed a number of resource-development schemes that to me seem bizarre – like the attempt to grow mahogany trees on the top of Sage Mountain, which necessitated deforesting the mountain only to replant it with a non-native species that cannot grow well in a dry climate at a high elevation. The wood turned out to be of poor quality, and so the spindly trees were later seeded with epiphytes and orchids to create a "rain forest" for touristic consumption (BVILC Minutes September 19, 1955 and November 17, 1960; interviews with J. R. O'Neal, 1992–3). Of interest here, however, were efforts to reactivate the copper mine, or, rather, to construct a mine anew.

A Natural Resource

In 1955, the Legislative Council invited a Canadian company (which left no records of its presence in the BVI) to determine the commercial potential of the site. It is significant that the Canadian company was mentioned in the same legislative session during which council members discussed a newly constructed slipper factory, a radiotelephones project, jetty construction, and the Beef Island airstrip project, which had been sent on to the Secretary of State for the Colonies for approval and a grant-in-aid. Interestingly, in the same session, the council members reiterated their desire to stand outside of the proposed "Federation of the West Indies" (BVILC Minutes September 19, 1955). The lawmakers were simultaneously exploring their "natural resources," "developing" their economy, and, in a complex move, affirming their "national" distinctiveness and autonomy while at the same time maintaining their colonial status and position under the Crown (see Maurer 1997d: 76–87 for further discussion of this process).

From 1955 to 1958, the Legislative Council was a flurry of activity around the potential of a copper mine to produce real benefits to national development. In 1957, the council members attempted to appropriate land at Mine Hill, at US $100 an acre, in order to construct a road to the abandoned mine site. Three people laid claim to the land that the government sought to acquire. The first offer was made to the three landowners in August, 1957; by late September, only one of the landowners had responded to the council members' proposition and assented to it; the other two had not responded (BVILC Minutes September 26, 1957).

While the status of the land around Mine Hill was unsettled, the Legislative Council kept itself quite busy with new legislation to prepare for the eventual riches a mine would bring. In 1958, it passed a Minerals (Vesting) Act in order

to vest all minerals in the Colony as defined in the Interpretation Clause in the Crown and to prohibit the prospecting for or mining of minerals except under a licence granted by the

Governor in Council and in accordance with the terms and conditions specified therein. In the case of a prospecting licence the terms of exploitation may be agreed with the exploited and set out in the licence. In the case of a mining licence royalties shall be payable in accordance with rules made by the Governor in Council. (BVILC Minutes January 16, 1958)

The Act sought to consolidate national properties in the literal sense. Resources would be vested in the Crown and placed under the authority of the Crown-appointed Governor. But the Governor could only act "in Council," under the direction and with the assent of the local legislature (which, ironically, is written into the Act as "the exploited"). This is a case of the BVI legislature's curious quasi-nationalist stance toward its own colonial jurisdiction, a stance that defies clean categorization as "nationalist" or "colonialist," as "sovereign" or "dependent."

Unlike nearly all other pieces of legislation that were brought before the Legislative Council in the 1950s, the Act did not pass on its first reading. Usually, development-oriented bills passed unanimously. Here, however, the Legislative Council split evenly, between members appointed by the Governor (joined by one elected member) and those elected by the people (BVILC Minutes January 16, 1958). In interviews with me, former members of the Legislative Council frequently characterized the conflicts that developed in the early days of legislative autonomy as conflicts between the "tea room boys" and the "barefoot boys" – quite a statement on the sublime and the dirty. The tea room boys consisted of the appointed members of the Legislative Council and one elected member, all of whom were seen as beholden to the old colonial administrative apparatus based in Antigua because of their connections to the Governor. Indeed, many had been educated by serving as clerks to colonial administrators. While they vociferously defended colonial status, they also were at the forefront of the drive for legislative autonomy. The barefoot boys were elected representatives from the countryside (with one exception). Like the tea room boys, they also defended colonialism but tended to strike a more populist tone as defenders of the people against the colonial Governor. While I cannot do justice to this here (but see Maurer 1997d, chs. 1, 2), the barefoot boys had a complex relationship with the English old guard, who, in many cases, actually supported the barefoot boys in local elections and worked behind the scenes to put them in office. English colonials did so to create a counterweight to the tea room boys, whose constituency of elite Road Town and Anegadian merchants, they believed, would some day stage a movement for political independence.

In the case at hand, the barefoot boys objected to the proposed government land appropriation. In other similar land appropriation cases, they would usually voice concerns but not block purchases and, often behind-the-scenes, they would try to ensure that landowners got a good deal.[17] In interviews, a former tea room boy commented that the actions of the barefoot boys never made sense to him because they were ultimately "for colonialism," too, and nurtured cozy relationships with the Governor. Barefoot boys told me that they viewed land acquisitions as a colonialist imposition on their nation, since it was the Governor in Council, the Queen's representative, who technically had the power to appropriate land and grant licenses for mining operations. Nevertheless, the former tea room boy maintained, the Governor in Council was under the constitutional requirement to act "in Council" and not on his own. What was at stake in these debates, however illogical they seemed to the tea room boys, was a definition of democracy and a construction of the people of the BVI, whose will could be represented by the legislature. Barefoot boys opposed land appropriations and minerals vesting ordinances as a strategic and symbolic move to assert a national identity, while maintaining colonial status. It was a move to constitute a people, not a move to challenge a political order.

Meanwhile, the two landowners at Mine Hill who had not responded to the council members' offer to purchase land threatened to sue the lawmakers for trespass. Apparently, several members of the Legislative Council had taken a trip to the site of the mine and walked over private property to get there (BVILC Minutes February 4, 1958), a point also confirmed in my interviews with members of the early Legislative Councils. The case was eventually settled out of court, and by 1959 the Legislative Council could order construction to begin on the road to Mine Hill. But the road was never finished, and in 1959, Laurence Rockefeller broke ground at Little Dix Bay on Virgin Gorda, definitively placing the Virgin Islands on the luxury tourism map. As a potential site for resource extraction and industrial investment, the mine was not mentioned again in the Legislative Council Minutes until 1973.

The copper mine of the 1950s was something of an *objet-manqué*. It never really happened; nevertheless, it figured centrally in legislators' attempts to develop their nation in accordance with a vision of progress and identity linked to specific forms of governance. Those forms of governance entailed a tricky balance between affirming the BVI as a part of the United Kingdom and Colonies, on the one hand, and aspiring to a place among the "family of nations" (Malkki 1992), on the other. Becoming a nation required symbols of autonomy such as flags and natural resources. It also required a government with powers like the ability to acquire land and the ability to be sued. In the vote over the minerals vesting bill, the forces of democracy blocked the goals of national development by reading national interests as colonial interests – an easy mistake, since they were one and the same. There is perhaps no clearer embodiment of the complex articulation of identity between colonial and national interests than in the financial relationships in which a system of grants from the colonial office bankrolled the development of the nation. These were both different "movements" and different "monies" than those of the nineteenth century, and they helped create a different object – or non-object, as the case may be – at the end of the road to Mine Hill.

Embryogenesis

End-Times Money Management: Protecting Your Resources Without Losing Your Soul presents the parable of the talents for a millennial Christian readership. Its author, Gary Moore (1999), emphatically opposes converting all of one's assets into gold and burying the bullion in the back yard. Instead, being a good steward means using one's talents to bring increase. Invest and keep on investing, in spite of the doomsayers. To do otherwise would be to bury the master's coin in the mud, desublimate gold into slime, deny exegesis and futurity in a vain effort to second-guess God's timetable for the Apocalypse.

Besides viewing the text as a parable of good stewardship, scholars and believers read the Parable of the Talents as an exhortation to interpret. The increase in the master's money becomes the textual supplementation of exegesis. It is no accident that Derrida uses the term *usure* for the metaphor of metaphoric exegesis that defers signifier onto signifier onto signifier in an endless increase that belies absence at the core. Usure supplements a text to cover over its lack of the transcendental signified (Derrida 1982: 209). Yet usure is both multiplication and exhaustion as it also signifies usage, as in rubbing out, drying up, and crumbling away (Derrida 1982: 210). When "read through the grid of multiplication of talents as exegetic activity," the monetary term signifies the "gloss to be added" to the text (Fitz 1975: 561).[18] The parable itself encodes the exegetical function as well. The five talents correspond to the Five Tablets or the Pentateuch, which, through the faith of the Apostles and the Jews who accept Jesus as Christ, double the Law with Faith. The second servant corresponds to the Gentiles, who received two talents – the Old and New Testaments – and affirm their faith doubly, "in their heart" and "by their mouth." The final tablet corresponds to the Truth of the Gospel, which Man, the third servant, in his foolishness, hides in the earth (see Kolve 1972: 323–4). Without faith or exegesis, unto the earth, the mud, will he too return.

This digression is necessary, for what it says about history is as relevant to the copper mine as it is to the killifish. History is usury, whether it is the history that charts clear trajectories of free trade, protectionism, and neoliberalism through solid locations and straight lines of capital mobility or the history that diagrams phylogenetic relationships among killifish in order to deduce and predict origins and project futures. History "exceeds itself" (Young 1990: 66), as it is produced through a process of supplementation to mask the "absence," and the abject, "at the center of its origin" (Young 1990: 66). Covering over the openings through which other meanings might ooze or drip, history asserts itself in its exegesis. So long as the free trade tale is retold, so long as the killifish eggs circulate with clear markers as to their supposed spatio-temporal origins and the fish are not allowed to hybridize,[19] all is well, and history "occlud[es] . . . its own conditions of historicity" (Young 1990: 67). Everything is kept nice and clean.

The Copper Mine and Tourism, 1973–96

When the copper mine entered legislative debate again in 1973, it emerged not as a natural resource but as a "national" resource for constructing a national identity and a national history. It took shape through particular understandings of time, history, nation, and governance that differ from those that constituted the mine in earlier eras. It also relied on different notions and objects of movement. Specifically, the copper mine came forth through the movement of a new subject, "the tourist," who, more than spending money or tanning on beaches, above all "looks," and with looks, casts moral judgments worth reputation and money. The BVI at the end of the twentieth century is a place constituted by such moral judgments, reputations, and moneys. As the territory comes to market itself as a tax haven, a site for the temporary housing of finance – something made possible, incidentally, by those old copper telecommunications cables of the late nineteenth century[20] – it increasingly relies on its image, and its leaders and citizens do their best to bolster that image.

By the mid to late 1970s, the BVI had become a successful tourist destination. It had also become a destination for poor immigrants from other Caribbean islands who came to work in construction and service jobs created by the tourist boom. Later, when the legislature put into place the administrative requirements for offshore finance, more immigrants came to the islands and built the buildings that house the offices and computers that move the money.

I have written elsewhere about the nexus of offshore finance and new exclusionary immigration and citizenship policies (see Maurer 1995a, 1995b, 1995c, 1997a, 1997d; see also Roberts 1994). The movements of money of offshore finance are different in kind from those of the earlier free trade era discussed above. The money that moved in the nineteenth century was in the form of investment capital and securitized properties in speculative enterprises like the first copper mine. It was directed by a clearly identifiable set of corporate actors and governments, toward fairly identifiable ends. It was still "paper entrepreneurialism" since, like the railroad schemes analyzed by Rosa Luxemburg (1951: 419–23), it was based on debts and expectations of future profits. But that paper enterpreneurialism was different from what is now going on in the BVI and other offshore financial service centers. People involved in offshore finance understand the movements and monies involved as de-linked from states and nations; they are using jurisdictions like the BVI to get around the administrative apparatus of "the state," conceptualized as a monolith and a regulator (Maurer 1998a). They are also, often, de-linking money and investment from productive enterprise – unlike the speculative investors in foreign and colonial copper schemes in the nineteenth century, the investors who now set their sights on the BVI are not doing so with the intention of actually producing anything. Rather, they are making money by moving it. *Investment* here is perhaps a misnomer, since the investment in offshore finance is an investment in the principles and practices of fluid capital itself, not the solid objects or tangible properties.[21]

The moneys invested have changed, as well (see Galbraith 1995; Hart 1986: 640; Weatherford 1997). Speculative nineteenth-century investment rested on credit relationships tied to gold, the final arbiter of international exchange. National development in the 1950s rested on faith in world reserve currencies, mainly the US dollar but also the British pound. In the BVI, as already noted, credit extended for national development came in the form of grants-in-aid directly from the British government. But what of the money of offshore finance? It is a pure sign, perhaps, backed not by a reserve currency or by a metal, but by other forms of specie in a near-infinite (if not truly infinite) deferral of value onto outstanding debts. This money lacks an origin or "any intrinsic iconic value which supposedly precedes the money signs defined in relation to it" (Rotman 1987: 96). One could therefore view it as imaginary, quicksilver, sublime, virtual money.[22] My goal in this article, however, is to get in the way of that view by wiping some slime on the lens before the snapshot can be taken.

Touristic Histories

The apparent lack of origin of offshore money does not take away from the necessary work of building a history in order to create a successful tourist site *and* offshore financial services center. In October of 1973, the Legislative Council discussed a proposal to make the copper mine more attractive as a tourist site. As one legislator proclaimed, the copper mine "is of historic significance in that it is the only known copper mine in the territory of the British Virgin Islands." This legislator called for the mine to be cleaned up "in order to make it more presentable for the people of the British Virgin Islands and visitors from outside." He went on:

when a tourist had seen a postcard of the copper mine, in the United States and Puerto Rico, and then visited Virgin Gorda and saw the copper mine with a big sign in front of it, marked "City Dump" what would pass through his mind? . . . When tourists looked and saw millions of cans and flies, at the copper mine, [I] wonder what would happen to tourism. (BVILC Minutes October 18, 1973)

Another commented that, while "relocating dumps [is] not an easy task," perhaps it should be done. He continued, "Locating the dump site at the copper mine did not seem important at the time [it was done], but it was now important because of [the mine's] historical significance" (BVILC Minutes October 18, 1973). The mine thus had no "historical significance" in advance of the tourist's gaze. Tourism created significance and necessitated the sublime fantasy of history. In the 1970s, this tourist gaze – or, rather, BVIslander imaginings of it – constituted the mine as a new object. It was an object that would become significant to the movements of money that the offshore finance business later directed toward the BVI.

During the debate on the dump, the Chief Minister, while stating that "we should try to keep the territory as clean as possible" and "cleanliness is next to Godliness" argued that he could not support the motion because it made no provision for constructing a new dumpsite. When the measure was put to a vote, the legislators were evenly divided; the Chief Minister's government members opposed it and the opposition members supported it. Here, however, the barefoot boys supported the measure to clean up the dumpsite, and the tea room boys opposed it. Some of the same individuals who earlier had voted *against* building the road to Mine Hill in the name of democracy supported the motion to relocate the people's dumpsite, while those who earlier supported the road now opposed relocating the dump. As in the vote in the 1950s, the non-unanimity was quite unusual. The Speaker of the House used his tie-breaking powers in this instance and cast his vote with the opposition, and the measure to clean up the dumpsite was carried.

I would not expect these individuals or constituencies to remain consistent over the years. But by the 1970s, after the arrival of large numbers of immigrants, the barefoot boys tended to oppose the extension of political rights to immigrants and their children, and the tea room boys (with some prominent exceptions) tended to support immigrants' rights. Immigrants' supporters cast the issue as one of fairness and democracy. Immigrants' opponents cast the issue as one of national survival. In conjunction with luxury tourism and offshore finance, *national survival* had a very particular valence. It meant the survival of an image of the nation that would attract tourists and investors. That image, the object of the tourist's and investor's gaze, was an image of "Britain" that demands attractive historical sites.

Today, tourism promotional material makes a point of stressing the copper mine's "Cornish" roots – roots, as demonstrated above, completely contrary to the mine's first conjuring in Liverpudlian businessmen's heads. As one piece of tourist literature states:

The copper mine, which is located on Virgin Gorda's desolate southwest tip was mined by Cornish miners between 1838 and 1867, and perhaps even earlier by the Spanish. The windswept area and stone buildings are reminiscent of Cornwall mines. Today the remains of the chimney, boiler house, cistern and mine shafts can be seen. (BVI Tourist Board 1996: 8, and incidentally, no, they cannot.)

Even the landscape somehow spiritually suggests Cornwall and thus a Britain that the British Virgin Islands never was. The discourse constitutes the land itself through a notion like the fiction of "family resemblance" of western kinship thinking (Schneider 1984), as self-evidently present in its evocation of another, imagined, place.

But a fine place it is for the world of offshore finance. Cornwall has a distinct resonance with a simpler, nineteenth-century time of hearty miners doing honest work and helping to build an empire through their effort and toil, benevolent businessmen leading industry to the far reaches of the globe, and imperial humanity revealing its own wonders to itself through the movement of goods, ideas, people, and money. Cornwall, in short, conjures Empire. And Empire gets investors to put their money in the *British* Virgin Islands (Maurer 1997a). The constitution of the copper mine as a piece of Cornwall in the Caribbean works together with the self-conscious promotion of the BVI as a piece of Britain in the Caribbean by officials and business leaders keen to market the territory to potential investors. It lends the territory a history, a time-depth beyond the past fifty years and back to the "ancient times" of "England's mountains green."

Where nineteenth-century colonial officials were concerned with the status of their newly created peasant subjects, and where these peasant subjects claimed membership in Empire as British subjects, late twentieth-century BVI leaders want to market their jurisdiction, the identity of which is crucial to all government actions. Such actions include not only preparing promotional material, but crafting exclusionary citizenship and immigration laws so that people legally "deemed not to belong" to the BVI are denied political participation and voice (see Maurer 1995b). They also include writing laws, not to regulate finance, but to facilitate it. Only thus can the BVI be raised to the sublime heights of the virtual economies of offshore finance.

Eruption

Killifish bubble up in the literature on evolutionary classification because of their wide geographical range. Is their current geographic spread a result of a series of diasporas? Or can they be found on widely separated continents and islands because of a vicariance event? Vicariance biogeography postulates relationships among species based on presumed or real geological transformations, in which barriers rupture populations of a species, resulting in their eventual divergence (Whittaker 1998: 41). The killifish endemic to the West Indies is a case in point: did the fish arrive via the sea, carried by currents on the open ocean, or, in a contorted continental chronicle of shifting plates moved by the molten magma where the metals form, did earth and sea seethe and froth between them? The literature supports the vicariance hypothesis in part because of the embryological criterion for biological classification (Murphy and Collier 1996, 1997).[23]

In drawing their conclusions about the vicariance hypothesis for killifish speciation and geographical range, biologists are compelled to rely on phenetic classification and paraphyletic groupings – classifications and groupings based on phenotype and not necessarily on phylogenetic connection (Murphy and Collier 1996, 1997; see also Ridley 1986). Paraphyletic groupings are based on relations of resemblance, not strict genealogy. They trouble the neat and orderly "tree" of species relationships.

"We're tired of trees," write Deleuze and Guattari. "We should stop believing in trees, roots, and radicles. They've made us suffer too much. All of arborescent culture is founded on them, from biology to linguistics" (1987: 15). Killifish, having evolved through vicariance events "by subterranean stems and flows," spreading "like a patch of oil" (Deleuze and Guattari 1987: 7), trouble the evolutionary tree. "The tree is filiation, but the rhizome is alliance, uniquely alliance. The tree imposes the very 'to be,' but the fabric of the rhizome is the conjunction 'and...and ...and...'" (Deleuze and Guattari 1987: 25). In other words, the killifish does not colonize in diaspora; it is not a clean seed carried on the ocean current or even in the international post. Rather, it oozes through the muck, even as the earth and seas move around it. You can put it in a Tupperware container, but what you have is still a carton of mud.

Deleuze and Guattari suggest "modes of effectivity and action which...scatter thoughts and images into different linkages or new alignments without necessarily destroying their materiality" (Grosz 1995: 127). Employing such a mode of analytical action allows me to link killifish to copper mines in an assemblage of objects that is not predetermined by any narrative of capitalist progress or the unfolding of the end of history in the manner of Fukuyama's pure market-space (1992). Rather, Deleuze and Guattari might call the conjoining of killifish and copper mines a metallurgical assemblage. "Metallurgy," they write, "in itself constitutes a flow necessarily confluent with nomadism" (1987: 404). Hidden and buried in the earth, metal courses through congealed veins of rhizomatic connection. Mines are dangerous for arborescent culture – they can undermine its roots – since "every mine is a line of flight in communication" with other geo-organic spaces (Deleuze and Guattari 1987: 412).[24] Miners burrow into the dirt to extract the ore, but, like the killifish, they have something in common with that third servant in the Parable of the Talents, who buried his coin in the earth and was cast out into the bowels of hell, ashes to ashes, muck to muck.

Moving Objects of Kinship and Capital

The critique of arborescent logics propounded by Deleuze and Guattari, and made flesh in the killifish, leads me to re-cast the problem of globalization literature in terms of the anthropological critique of the study of kinship and its assumptions about origins, movements, and genealogical trees. In his path-breaking critique of the anthropological study of kinship, Schneider (1984) argues that anthropologists had sought to explain kinship systems in different societies without first under-standing the metaphysical assumptions that went into their own construction of "kinship" itself. These assumptions were about both the persons related by kinship and the notion of relationship implied in the anthropological construct of kinship systems. In discovering kinship wherever they looked, anthropologists blinded themselves to alternative modes of relationship, affiliation of personhood, and identity not captured by their own kinship thinking.

Similarly, when critics of globalization look for either disjunctures or continuities in processes of capital mobility, they miss the construction of both capital and mobility in their own analyses and in the practices of the persons who create the phenomena they study.[25] Neglecting the practices that create the objects and pro-cesses of mobility leads analysts to miss alternative constructions that seriously challenge neat and teleological narratives of globalization. Just as the notions of relationship and person animating western kinship may be incommensurable with – or, at least, very difficult to translate into – other systems, so the constructs animat-ing different moments of the global economy may not be so similar to each other as they seem. Rather than searching for disjunctures or continuities with past world economies in order to make claims about their similarities or differences to present economies, perhaps critics of globalization should look for different configurations of meaning and power that render the global movements of different eras difficult to translate. We simply cannot compare the effects of finance on, say, sovereignty in nineteenth-century free trade and twentieth-century free trade because the nature of finance and sovereignty cannot be taken for granted analytically, nor can the notions of causality that are embodied in a search for impacts. Neither, for that matter, can we take as given the objects on which such impacts are achieved.[26]

My contribution comes out of a concern with the unexamined assumptions of the globalization and IPE literatures, which I have found helpful to my anthropological pursuits. While the IPE literature in political science contains the kind of specificity on the nature of global finance that the anthropology literature often lacks, it also effects interesting metaphysical sleights-of-hand in its accounts of capital mobility. Listen to a leading IPE scholar define financial globalization:

Global finance is assumed to encompass all types of cross-border portfolio-type transactions – borrowing and lending, trading of currencies or other financial claims, and the provision of commercial banking or other financial services. It also includes capital flows associated with foreign direct investment.... Financial globalization...refers to the broad integration of national markets associated with both innovation and deregulation in the postwar era and is manifested by increasing movements of capital across national frontiers. The more alter-native assets are closely regarded as substitutes for one another, the higher the degree of capital mobility. (Cohen 1996: 269)

This definition depends on the ultimate convertibility and fungibility of different forms of property as the cornerstone of capital mobility. But what are the processes that make the objects of property at issue able to be converted into one another, or able to be converted at all?

Capital mobility recalls a classic problem in the anthropological theory of kinship. Edward Tylor and others after him were perplexed by the system of marriage exchanges termed "circulating connubium" by van Wouden (Tylor 1889; van Wouden 1968; see also Fox 1980; Rutherford 1998) in which men seemed to exchange their sisters with other men for the purpose of marriage. Lévi-Strauss claimed to "solve" the problem, positing a parsimonious hypothesis that rooted the purported universality of the incest taboo in classical economics. He wrote:

Generalized exchange establishes a system of operations conducted "on credit." A surrenders a daughter or a sister to B, who surrenders one to C, who, in turn, will surrender one to A.... Consequently, generalized exchange always contains an element of trust.... There must be the confidence that the cycle will close again, and that after a period of time a woman will eventually be received in compensation for the woman initially surrendered. The belief is the basis of trust, and confidence opens up credit. In the final analysis, the whole system exists only because the group adopting it is prepared, in the broadest meaning of the term, *to speculate*. (1969: 265, emphasis in original)

As feminists have argued, Lévi-Strauss took for granted the following suppositions: that the value of any woman is identical to the value of any other woman; that the value of any woman inheres in the woman and is not a product of the exchange; and that women can be objectified as pieces of property (Collier 1988: 227; Rubin 1975). On what does that equivalency, inherent value, and objectification rest? Jane Collier writes,

Levi-Strauss [sic] alludes only to women's sexual attractiveness and to their performance of necessary tasks in societies where labor is divided by sex (Lévi-Strauss 1969 [1949]: 37–41). But the question is not what are women good for? Women – and men – do useful work and are sexually desirable....Rather, we should ask why, given their...attractiveness and usefulness, men and women do not just get together and live happily ever after. (1988: 227)

They do not, because men have rights in women that women do not enjoy in men or in other women. The question becomes, then, why do men come to have those rights in their female kin (Collier 1988: 227)? As Collier summarizes, Lévi-Strauss "takes for granted what is most perplexing: that people can have rights to objects or objectified others in the first place" (Collier 1988: 227).

Another assumption of Lévi-Strauss's analysis is that persons precede relationships. Marilyn Strathern and Michelle Rosaldo have gone to great lengths to demonstrate how the western liberal logic that posits individuals first and social relationships second simply does not hold for people who imagine themselves as constituted through their relationships with past and present others (Rosaldo 1983, 1984; Strathern 1988; see also Leenhardt 1979). Similarly, in his 1947 ethnography, Maurice Leenhardt remarks that a Melanesian "knows himself only by the relationships he maintains with others. He exists only insofar as he acts his role in the course of his relationships" (1979: 153). Leenhardt depicts the person of New Caledonia as a series of lines (a——b) representing relationships, radiating out from a central space, which he characterized as "empty":

Their social reality is not in their body but in this empty place where they have their names and which corresponds to a relationship.... But no name can cover the whole person. The Canaque [Caledonian] is obliged to have a different name for every domain which involves his person in various relationships and participations. In all this, he is unaware of himself; he is the empty space enclosed by the circle of *a*'s. (1979: 154, 156; quoted in Strathern 1988: 269; emphasis in original)

Strathern argues that Leenhardt's only mistake was to worry over that empty space at the center. She writes:

His mistake was to conceive of a center at all. The center is where twentieth-century Western imagination puts the self, the personality, the ego. For the "person" in this latter day Western view is an agent, a subject, the author of thought and action, and thus "at the center" of relationships. (1988: 269)

Literature on globalization begins from a similar unstated assumption: the objects of property come first; their movements, second. The case of the copper mine clearly illustrates the problem with this approach. The mine, like the "empty space enclosed by a circle of *a*'s," is a hole, an absence. It is thus like the transcendental referents of historical narratives of progress, covered over by usurious supplementation of exegesis and the reproduction effected by historical and monetary interest in the mine as an object of capital circulation. Historical interest in capital, for instance, is governed by a desire to tell and re-tell a story of the necessary loosening of the fetters constraining its movements, reproducing the narrative of quicksilver capital's triumph. Monetary interest, in turn, depends on historical interest – history-as-usury provides the exegesis that makes monetary usury possible, for the latter will only accrue to those entities of capital with clear trajectories of development that garner faith in their future progress. Kinship and capital are different moments in the same discursive field – or, with killifish eggs, in the same discursive swamp. They are linked by the notions of reproduction that sustain their fictions of clear origins, orderly progressions, and neat relationships of relatedness.[27]

It should come as no surprise that these notions of reproduction, from Lévi-Strauss to capital mobility, depend upon a series of sublimations, as well as devalued objects constructed so as to require their sublimation. The sublimation of these objects creates value. (1) The sublimation of the category *woman*: constructed as an open, messy, nonindividuated body, *woman* is controlled (by men) and made valuable (to men) by being made available for continuous circulation. (2) The sublimation of hybrids of all forms: hybrids are implicit in arborescent logics of kinship and evolution that call them forth even as they deny them the purity that brings value. (3) The sublimation of ambiguously speciated (and sexed)[28] creatures like killifish: species and sex are of key importance to biology, but it must go to great lengths to find them while it gains its value by enforcing them. (4) The sublimation of swamps, muck, mine-shafts and other not-quite-landmasses: wetlands and sub-terranean veins are constructed as creepy, abhorrent sites that blur land and water, and the geological and the organic; yet capitalism needs them as spaces to drain out, dig up, fill in, and work on in order to demonstrate progress.[29] (5) The sublimation of ambiguous formations of capital: specie does not follow from one form to the next, and cannot be converted like base metal to gold (or quicksilver), but it must nevertheless be fit into a natural, orderly progression culminating in universal commodification and pure abstract value.

Thus, in both kinship and capital (and killifish) the problem is one of ontology and teleology.[30] The critique of the study of kinship, as carried forward by Schneider's students Yanagisako and Delaney (1995), begins by questioning the ontology of bodies and reproduction and arguing that there is nothing given about biological facts – no transcendental or biological center of origin at the heart of kinship systems. Built into this is an argument about teleology: that there is no transcendental origin means there can be no unfolding of a trajectory of kinship or relatedness given in advance (Delaney 1986, 1991; Yanagisako 1985); both pasts and futures are transformed in figurations of kin. Similarly, my point about capital mobility is that the ontologies of moving objects of capitalism are never given in advance of relationships that produce and reproduce them, relationships that also interrupt teleologies of capital's advance, from its initial "penetration" to its "triumph" at the "end of history" (Derrida 1994; Fukuyama 1992).

The critique of arborescent metaphysics effected by Deleuze and Guattari (1987), simultaneously a critique of ontology, highlights the contingent articulations that create objects of property, that underwrite different forms of capital, and that permit different valences and vectors of movement. Rather like the persons of Strathern's Melanesian ethnography, the moving objects of capital need to be seen in terms of the relationships of power and meaning that call them forth in different historical moments. Those moments, in turn, cannot be linked in a developmental or teleological sequence. In other words, the notions of time, value, and agency built into triumphal tales of capitalist production and reproduction cannot be taken for granted. Only then can the phoenix of international finance be denied its soaring flights and sent back to the soot and slime where it belongs, with the killifish.

Recapitulation

Consider the mine of Empire that made slaves into subjects but in so doing had to deny their very hybridity and the impossibility of their becoming British no matter how much they might be disciplined and molded by the colonial state apparatus. Similarly, the copper mine could never be Cornwall, but rather served as Cornwall's dark shadow, its Other, depriving the Cornish mines of the central significance to imperial consolidation and introducing Latin American speculations troubling the clean constitution of the imperium.

The mine at mid-twentieth century, this object-that-was-not, was part of a hard, modern capitalism seeking development through exploitation of natural resources taken right from the very soil of the nation. This was to be pure sublimation and extraction of ore, to enable the British Virgin Islands to reach the lofty heights of the "family of nations" (Malkki 1992). But it failed utterly, exposing the lack at the center of such schemes, the absence at the origin of teleology; the mine remained a garbage dump.

Now, as the quicksilver capital of flexible financing requires shadowy offshores in which to park assets temporarily in their flights around the globe, the BVI is busily cleaning itself up – and removing the dumpsite. It offers transparent accounts without the taint of scandal and transparent histories with clear spatio-temporal origin points, like the Cornwall of the nineteenth century, histories considerably sanitized for the consumption of international investor. Of course, once you take away the rubbish heap, nothing is really there. The copper mine may be billed as a tourist attraction, but few tourists are actually attracted to it. All you see is slag. The mine serves as symbol only to allay investors' fears about the sort of place in which they are thinking about burying their talents.

With apologies to Marx, then: what is a killifish? A fish of the family Cyprino-dontiform. The one explanation is as good as the other. A killifish is a killifish. It becomes an *Aphyosemion aureum* only in certain relations. Torn from these relationships it is no more an *Aphyosemion aureum* than gold in itself is money, or sugar is the price of sugar (from Marx 1977: 28).

In the exchange of eggs, a supplement gets added to the killifish that allows it to develop into a species. The stewardship of the American Killifish Association provides not only increase – new killifish. Rather, that stewardship conjures the species. Forbidding the interbreeding of fish from different points of origin traces and reifies the collector's discovery in a remote locale. Circulating eggs – like circulating capital – is not just about keeping the boundaries between those locales separate and distinct, but, more, rendering those locates into unique singular points, and projecting those points into future genealogies that extend forward forever, to the end-time, and backward, to the Creation. Presumably, if you were to go back in time, and to the precise geographic coordinates indicated by a narrative of discovery, the fish you would find would be the same as the progeny of the egg-exchanges. Except that in nature killifish do not observe the AKA Code of Ethics.

The killifish is a creature of the slime. We are fooled by its brilliant colors, just as we are fooled by gold, or copper's shine, or the quicksilver used to separate them from their ores. We are fooled, too, by quicksilver capital, seemingly zipping around the globe, current in a copper cable or light in a fiber optic line, pure essence, transcendental sublime heralding the end of history.[31] But the line does not trace a developmental sequence, but rather diapause, desublimation, covered over by the false fixity of arborescent logics of specie and the sublime fantasy of history.

NOTES

Acknowledgments: I would like to thank the School of Social Sciences, the Department of Anthropology, and Global Peace and Conflict Studies at the University of California, Irvine, for their financial support and teaching release time while I was writing this article. Research in the British Virgin Islands was supported by NSF Grant SES–9208273, Law and Social Sciences Program, a MacArthur Foundation Dissertation Research Fellowship, the Center for International Security and Arms Control, and the Department of Anthropology at Stanford University. Different versions of it have been delivered at the American Anthropological Association meetings in Washington, DC (November 1997), and before the Departments of Anthropology at the University of California, Irvine, and at the University of Chicago (both in the spring of 1999). I would like to thank those audiences for their forbearance, and particularly Karen Leonard, Elizabeth Povinelli, and Nadia Abu El-Haj for the invitations to present my work. My colleagues at UCI have been very supportive of my work, and I would like to thank them for their intellectual generosity, and, for particular comments on this article, I would like to thank Duran Bell, Mike Burton, Teresa Calderia, Tom Douglas, Susan Greenhalgh, Jennifer Heung, Liisa Malkki, Richard Perry, and Tamara Teghillo. Various colleagues also provided support and intellectual guidance during the revision process: Robin Balliger, Mindie Lazarus-Black, Deborah Heath, Saba Mahmood, Sally Merry, Donald Moore, Diane M. Nelson, Hugh Raffles, Lisa Rofel, Anna Tsing, and Barbara Yngvesson. I would also like to thank the graduate students in the UCI reading group on "Alternative Modernities" in the Winter of 1998 for discussions that helped me reframe the article at a crucial juncture, particularly Megan Crowley and Rhonda Higdon-Loving. The five anonymous *AE* reviewers provided sharp and constructive commentary on this article; I only hope I have done justice to their valuable criticisms. Finally, I am in debt well beyond my ability to repay to three individuals: Jim Ferguson gave me a good kick early on and continued to prod me as this article was taking shape; Susan Coutin read several versions of this article and provided incredibly useful (and critical) comments that enabled me finally to finish; and Tom Boellstorff graciously read and re-read paragraphs and sections as I wrote and re-wrote them. I hope they will agree to raise my credit limit in the future. All errors or inconsistencies are my responsibility alone.

1 Killifish are akin to that fabulous Mexican monster, the axolotl, an aquatic salamander that was the subject of much debate among European encyclopedists and naturalists well into the nineteenth century (Bartra 1992). Throughout its life, this beast remains in its aquatic, larval state, in a state of arrested development – except, it seems, when transported to Europe. When the third Napoleon momentarily captured Mexico in 1863, the invaders shipped a number of axolotls to Europe where they could be observed live there for the first time. "In September 1865 the first generation of European creoles was born" (Bartra 1992: 100). These creoles, to everyone's "amazement and joy" (p. 100), left the larval state of their gilled parents and metamorphosed into terrestrial animals. The axolotl's transformation in Europe demonstrated the New World's own developmental arrest. For only as a European could the axolotl reach its necessary telos; only then could it be counted among the natural beasts placed by God in the Garden, and only in that unambiguous state could it march to the herald of the Great Trumpet at the Apocalypse. Roger Bartra, in his book of axolotli-dad, argues that the axolotl, against the modern triumphal tale of metamorphosis and telos, "defaces the beautiful landscape of evolution and progress" (p. 117). This article, offered in the same spirit – or, I should say, in the same slime – is inhabited by mythical beasts and is presented in the shadow of the end-times.

2 The more one looks for them, the more one finds other references to this mythical bird in relation to global finance. One recent example is in Laurent Jacque's article on the Thai financial crisis of 1997, the concluding heading of which asks, "Will the Thai phoenix rise again?" (1999: 97).

3 This is especially noteworthy given classic anthropological studies of money in "primitive" societies (e.g., Bohannan 1959, Taussig 1980). See Guyer 1995 and Parry and Bloch 1989 for reviews of recent work in the anthropology of money, as well as Hart 1986. Geographers have done better; see Leyshon and Thrift 1997 and Thrift 1996 for examples and reviews of literature. The expression *quicksilver capital*, incidentally, comes from the title of an alarmist book on capital mobility (McKenzie and Lee 1991).

4 These quotations could also be placed alongside a snippet from David Harvey, to form an even more compelling narrative of continuity organized around magic and madness:

This "bewildering" world of high finance encloses an equally bewildering variety of cross cutting activities, in which banks borrow massively short-term from other banks, insurance companies and pension funds assemble such vast pools of investment funds as to function as dominant "market markers," while industrial, merchant, and landed capital become so integrated into financial operations and structures that it becomes increasingly difficult to tell where commercial and industrial interests begin and where strictly financial interests end. (1989: 161)

As will be evident in my argument, I am most interested in the bewilderment conjured by the enchanter's wand.

5 Other recent ascriptions of insanity to contemporary and historical financial operations include Kindleberger's *Manias, Panics, and Crashes* (1989) and Strange's *Mad Money* (1998). Kindleberger uses great metaphors, too – financial crises are "hardy perennials" that "propagate" across national boundaries, and so forth (e.g., 1989: 3, 129).

6 Geographers have been writing brilliant analyses of these rhetorics and images (see McHaffie 1997). I am also indebted to various unpublished manuscripts by Susan Roberts in the Geography Department at the University of Kentucky.

7 I will not address works that argue, in part, that it is the analysts who have changed, more than the objective conditions, or at least structuring logics, of modern capitalism (Friedman 1995; Lash and Urry 1994).

8 The terms *finance, sovereignty, citizenship,* or *governance* cannot be taken to be stable entities, however, whose meanings scholars interrogate or whose constellations they examine in different moments. They are rather native categories that denote different entities and assemblages in different times. Michel Foucault's (1991) notion of "governmentality" helps me find an analytical language for exploring the interrelationships among these different native categories. *Governmentality* refers to modern systems of the governance of populations and polities together with the arts of individual self-regulation that any system of modern governance requires. I take governmentality as a constellation of power-effects, which are the "objects" that rebound upon each other and operate within their own causal chains; different relationships of power, and different strategies, produce different objects and thus different sets of "variables" held together in causal and functional time (see Barry, Osborne, and Rose 1996; Burchel, Gordon, and Miller 1991).

9 See, for example, Cohen 1996 and McMichael 1996, two very different authors with very different agendas who rely on the same historical sequencing of capitalist development.

10 A word about the Legislative Council Minutes: these are typewritten documents kept in the BVI Public Library, organized by year. They often contain verbatim transcripts of everything said in a Legislative Council session, along with draft text of bills and executive orders, and occasional editorial asides by the clerk of the council. With Janet Nibbs-Blyden, I compiled an index to these documents during my main period of fieldwork in the BVI. As I discuss in my book, the Legislative Council occupies a central place in local imaginings of the BVI "nation" (Maurer 1997d: 227–56), mainly because it has been the only truly autonomous local branch of government under the BVI's peculiar colonial relationship with the United Kingdom. I used Legislative Council Minutes as jumping-off points for interviews with former legislators and other BVI citizens – they provided me a crash course in BVI political history while I was in the field as well as a rich source of textual data on ways of speaking and thinking about political and cultural life, in particular moments of BVI history. I kept my eyes open for interesting disjunctures and slips in the minutes – places where individuals reversed positions on certain issues, places where the normally formal discourse of a Legislative Council session slipped into patois, places where personal issues and disagreements (and scandals) among legislators or in the community erupted into Council meetings. In a territory with such a small population (currently around 17,000 people), Council debates often took on the character of public

airings of dirty laundry. As such, former legislators and other citizens were only too eager to talk about them.

11 My thanks to Susan Coutin for pointing out the glaring absence in an earlier draft of this article that necessitated multiple reworkings of this paragraph.

12 American Killifish Association (AKA) Code of Ethics, Art. 2. Available at: http://www. aka.org/AKA/COETHICS.html, accessed April 4, 2000.

13 I can only briefly review here the change in British colonial policy in the mid-nineteenth century, from an old order of mercantile protectionism with its complicated system of tariffs and navigation restrictions, to the period of "free trade imperialism" (Semmel 1970). Thomas Malthus was one of the early critics of the industrial system and its connection to imperial expansion; he felt that England's agriculture was suffering and sought to slow down industrialization gone wild with the promise of markets abroad in the colonies (1967). Malthus was opposed by the classical political economists, whose theories began to take hold and whose revisioning of the "dismal science" led to messianic calls for the liberalization of the economy and an empire based on the principles of free trade. Many of these looked back to Adam Smith's *Wealth of Nations* (1976) for inspiration and found there a treatise for the abolition of restrictive trade policies that had seemed more concerned with establishing power than realizing profit. In fact, however, Smith's book is a complicated charter for a trade empire of mercantilism mixed with freer trade (see Semmel 1970: 24–30); Smith supported the Navigation Acts, for instance. Yet what parliamentary leaders picked up from Smith was his vision of a system based on the nominal independence of colonies interlinked in a free trade empire.

14 It bears pointing out that, at the time, Virgin Gorda was a backwater of a backwater colony. The population of the whole colony of the Virgin Islands hovered between five and six thousand between 1840 and 1860; of that, about two hundred were white (Dookhan 1975: 129). Most residents were subsistence farmers and fishermen.

15 By 1861, there were 11,000 miles of cable crisscrossing the globe; by 1880, there were 97,600 miles. 21,750 miles had been laid on the UK mainland in 1860 and required 91,000 miles of wire; by the end of the century, 424,300 tons of copper were being consumed each year, 300,000 of which went into the new electric industries (Toomey 1985: 41).

16 UK copper production fell from 60 percent of world production in 1840 to 13 percent in 1860 (Valenzuela 1990: 657).

17 This, in turn, contributed to a rising politics of graft and patronage in the territory, which intersected with discourses of equality and democracy (see Maurer 1997d: 97–9).

18 Fitz is referring here to the exegetical function of the term *usura* in the *Lais* of Marie de France, itself an exegesis of the Parable of the Talents.

19 And so long as the axolotl can be proven to metamorphose through its transposition into Europe (see n.1).

20 I explore the contingent interconnections of nineteenth- and twentieth-century Caribbean telecommunications cables in another article (Maurer 1997c).

21 In another article, I explore contrasts in the ideology and practice of securitized interests in property over the past couple of centuries (Maurer 1999). What bears emphasizing here is that offshore investors are interested in maintaining a system of flexible financing rather than building productive enterprise in the old-fashioned industrial sense of the term. I will not engage here in the debate about the status of industrial and financial capital, except to note that both are ultimately equally fictitious. See Spivak 1995 for a useful discussion of industrial capital, the money circuit, and reproduction, via Marx and Derrida.

22 In addition to the sources cited in this paragraph, refer to Brantlinger 1996, Goux 1990, Michaels 1987, and Vernon 1984 on the representational politics of monetary transformation, particularly around the turn-of-the-century debates over the gold standard and understandings of credit.

23 The embryological criterion for classification – using embryological characteristics to postulate phylogeny – has been somewhat controversial in taxonomic circles. A good introductory text explains the problem, using our friend from note 1, the axolotl, to make the case. "The tadpole characters in the adult axolotl are derived from a newt-like ancestral adult stage. But if we classified a fish, a newt, and an axolotl by means of the embryological criterion and their tadpolean characters, the axolotl would turn out as the sister species of the fish. In fact it is the sister of the newt" (Ridley 1986: 68).

24 I would like to thank Jim Ferguson and Liisa Malkki for taking me (like a canary in a cage?) down Deleuze and Guattari's mine shafts.

25 For instance, one of my IPE "heros," Eric Helleiner, neglects the metaphysics of capital mobility in the following blanket statement about money's ease of movement in the contemporary era: "Because money can move so quickly and easily, its mastery can often have extremely disruptive effects for the less mobile peoples, industries, and communities that are required to adjust to its quicksilver and volatile flows" (1994b: 295). While I wholeheartedly agree with his claim about the disruptive effects of capital mobility, I am troubled by the lack of reflection on what constitutes capital and mobility in the first place. Like Gibson-Graham (1996), I am unwilling to grant capital a quicksilver quality without first questioning the metaphors of mobility themselves that seem to grant money its mastery.

26 See Beck 1993 and Ritter 1997 on difficult-to-translate articulations of notions like property, money, politics, and interest. Beck's analysis of Louis Brandeis demonstrates that Brandeis's work does not neatly fit into received categories of tradition and modernity, markets and administration, and state and economy and thus remains difficult for contemporary scholars to interpret. I have argued much the same for Keynes in Maurer 1998b.

27 I would like to thank Susan Coutin and Carol Greenhouse for providing comments that helped me to develop this and the next paragraph. Nicholson 1987 and Rubin 1975 have helped me think through the issues raised in these paragraphs.

28 A number of killifish evince hermaphrodism, as do many kinds of fish. The axolotl, too, is a creature of mysterious sex (see Bartra 1992).

29 This, incidentally, is what Giblett's (1996) marvelous book, *Postmodern Wetlands*, is all about. It was, again, Jim Ferguson who led me into this swamp.

30 One of the anonymous reviewers for *AE* provided very insightful comments that guided the argument here. Where that reviewer saw a contrast between the critique of kinship and the critique of capital – the former, based on ontology, the latter, on teleology – my thinking, guided by Deleuze and Guattari's attack on arborescent metaphysics and helped along by Malkki's resequencing of it (Malkki 1992, 1995), brings the two together.

31 In *Spectres of Marx*, Derrida draws a "black picture on a blackboard" to counter narratives of the end of history. Gibson-Graham remarks, "In the nature of an image on a blackboard is its provisionality, the fact that it probably won't be there tomorrow" (1996: 241). Like the copper mine and the killifish, the image on the blackboard is contingent, the lines created by calcium deposits from that other fabulous rhizomatic assemblage, the coral reef.

REFERENCES

Abu-Lughod, Janet
   1989 *Before European Hegemony: The World-System AD 1250–1350*. New York: Oxford University Press.

Apparudai, Arjun
1990 Disjuncture and Difference in the Global Cultural Economy. *Public Culture* 2(2): 1–24.
1996 *Modernity at Large: Cultural Dimensions of Globalization*. Minneapolis: University of Minnesota Press.
Barry, Andrew, Thomas Osborne, and Nikolas Rose, eds.
1996 *Foucault and Political Reason: Liberalism, Neo-Liberalism and Rationalities of Government*. London: UCL Press.
Bartra, Roger
1992 *The Cage of Melancholy: Identity and Metamorphosis in the Mexican Character*. New Brunswick, NJ: Rutgers University Press.
Beck, Gerald
1993 *Alternative Tracks*. Baltimore, MD: Johns Hopkins University Press.
Berleant-Schiller, Riva
1995 From Labour to Peasantry in Montserrat after the End of Slavery. In *Small Islands, Large Questions: Society, Culture, and Resistance in the Post-Emancipation Caribbean*. Karen Fog Olwig, ed. Pp. 53–72. London: Cass.
Bohannan, Paul
1959 The Impact of Money on an African Subsistence Economy. *Journal of Economic History* 19(4): 491–503.
Brantlinger, Patrick
1996 *Fictions of State: Culture and Credit in Britain, 1694–1994*. Ithaca, NY: Cornell University Press.
British Virgin Islands Legislative Council Minutes
1950–92 Housed in the Caribbean Studies Unit, British Virgin Islands Public Library, Road Town, Tortola, BVI, and indexed in Bill Maurer and Janice Nibbs, "Index to the British Virgin Islands Legislative Council Documents 1950–1992," BVI Public Library, 1993.
British Virgin Islands Tourist Board
1996 *The British Virgin Islands*. Road Town, Tortola, British Virgin Islands, promotional brochure.
Burchell, Graham, Colin Gordon, and Peter Miller, eds.
1991 *The Foucault Effect: Studies in Governmentality*. London: Harvester Wheatsheaf.
Cerny, Philip
1994 The Dynamics of Financial Globalization: Technology, Market Structure, and Policy Response. *Policy Sciences* 27(4): 319–42.
Cohen, Benjamin
1996 Phoenix Risen: The Resurrection of Global Finance. *World Politics* 48(2): 268–96.
Collier, Jane F.
1988 *Marriage and Inequality in Classless Societies*. Stanford, CA: Stanford University Press.
Craton, Michael, and James Walvin
1970 *A Jamaican Plantation: The History of Worthy Park, 1670–1970*. Toronto: University of Toronto Press.
Culver, William, and Cornel Reinhart
1989 Capitalist Dreams: Chile's Response to Nineteenth-century World Copper Competition. *Comparative Studies in Society and History* 31(4): 722–44.
Delaney, Carol
1986 The Meaning of Paternity and the Virgin Birth Debate. *Man* N.S. 21(3): 494–513.
1991 *The Seed and the Soil: Gender and Cosmology in Turkish Village Society*. Berkeley: University of California Press.

Deleuze, Gilles, and Félix Guattari
    1987   *A Thousand Plateaus: Capitalism and Schizophrenia*. Brian Massumi, trans. Min-
            neapolis: University of Minnesota Press.
Derrida, Jacques
    1982   *Margins: of Philosophy*. Alas Bass, trans. Chicago: University of Chicago Press.
    1994   *Spectres of Marx: The State of the Debt, the Work of Mourning, and the New
            International*. Peggy Kamuf, trans. New York: Routledge.
Dookhan, Isaac
    1975   *A History of the British Virgin Islands, 1672–1970*. Epping, England: Caribbean
            Universities Press/Bowker.
Escobar, Arturo
    1995   *Encountering Development: The Making and Unmaking of the Third World*. Prin-
            ceton, NJ: Princeton University Press.
Ferguson, James
    1990   *The Anti-Politics Machine: "Development," Depoliticization and Bureaucratic
            Power in Lesotho*. Cambridge: Cambridge University Press.
Fernandez-Kelly, Maria Patricia
    1983   *For We Are Sold, I and My People*. Albany: SUNY Press.
Fitz, Brewster
    1975   The Prologue to the *Lais* of Marie de France and the Parable of the Talents: Gloss
            and Monetary Metaphor. *MLN* 90: 558–96.
Foucault, Michel
    1991   Governmentality. In *The Foucault Effect: Studies in Governmentality*. Graham
            Burchell, Colin Gordon, and Peter Miller, eds. Pp. 87–104. London: Harvester Wheat-
            sheaf.
Fox, James, ed.
    1980   *The Flow of Life: Essays on Eastern Indonesia*. Cambridge, MA: Harvard Univer-
            sity Press.
Friedman, Jonathan
    1995   Global System, Globalization and the Parameters of Modernity. In *Global Moder-
            nities*. Mike Featherstone, Scott Lash, and Roland Robertson, eds. Pp. 69–90. London:
            Sage Publications.
Fukuyama, Francis
    1992   *The End of History and the Last Man*. New York: Free Press.
Galbraith, John Kenneth
    1995   *Money: Whence it Came, Where it Went*, rev. edn. Boston: Houghton Mifflin.
Giblett, Rod
    1996   *Postmodern Wetlands: Culture, History, Ecology*. Edinburgh: Edinburgh University
            Press.
Gibson-Graham, J. K.
    1996   *The End of Capitalism (As We Knew It): A Feminist Critique of Political Economy*.
            Oxford: Blackwell Publishers.
Goux, Jean-Joseph
    1990   *Symbolic Economies: Marx and Freud*. Jennifer Curtis Gage, trans. Ithaca, NY:
            Cornell University Press.
Green, William
    1976   *British Slave Emancipation: The Sugar Colonies and the Great Experiment, 1830–
            1865*. Oxford: Oxford University Press.
Grosz, Elizabeth
    1995   *Space, Time and Perversion: Essays on the Politics of Bodies*. New York: Routledge.

Guyer, Jane, ed.
  1995   Money Matters: Instability, Values and Social Payments in the Modern History of West African Communities. Portsmouth, NH: Heinemann.
Hannerz, Ulf
  1996   Transnational Connections: Culture, People, Places. New York: Routledge.
Hart, Keith
  1986   Heads or Tails? Two Sides of the Coin. Man N.S. 21(4): 637–56.
Harvey, David
  1989   The Condition of Postmodernity. Baltimore, MD: Johns Hopkins University Press.
Helleiner, Eric
  1994a   States and the Re-Emergence of Global Finance: From Bretton Woods to the 1990s. Ithaca, NY: Cornell University Press.
  1994b   The World of Money: The Political Economy of International Capital Mobility. Policy Sciences 27(4): 295–8.
Hilferding, Rudolf
  1981 [1923]   Finance Capital: A Study of the Latest Phase of Capitalist Development. London: Routledge and Kegan Paul.
Jacque, Laurent
  1999   The Asian Financial Crisis: Lessons from Thailand. The Fletcher Forum of World Affairs 23(1): 87–99.
Kapstein, Ethan
  1994   Governing the Global Economy: International Finance and the State. Cambridge, MA: Harvard University Press.
Kearney, Michael
  1995   The Local and the Global: The Anthropology of Globalization and Transnationalism. Annual Review of Anthropology 24: 547–65.
Kelley, Brent
  1999   Editorial. Journal of the American Killifish Association 32(1): 2.
Kindleberger, Charles
  1987   International Capital Movements. New York: Cambridge University Press.
  1989   Manias, Panics, and Crashes: A History of Financial Crises, 2nd rev. edn. New York: Basic Books.
Knorr, Klaus Eugen
  1963   British Colonial Theories, 1570–1850. London: Frank Cass.
Kolve, V. A.
  1972   Everyman and the Parable of the Talents. In Medieval English Drama. Jerome Taylor and Alan Nelson, eds. Pp. 316–40. Chicago: University of Chicago Press.
Lash, Scott, and John Urry
  1994   Economies of Signs and Space. London: Sage Publications.
Leenhardt, Maurice
  1979   Do Kamo: Person and Myth in the Melanesian World. Chicago: University of Chicago Press.
Lenin, Vladimir
  1989 [1916]   Imperialism: The Highest Stage of Capitalism. New York: International Publishers.
Lévi-Strauss, Claude
  1969 [1949]   The Elementary Structures of Kinship. Boston: Beacon Press.
Leyshon, Andrew, and Nigel Thrift
  1997   Money/Space: Geographies of Monetary Transformation. London: Routledge.

Lowes, Susan
  1995   "They Couldn't Mash Ants": The Decline of the White and Non-White Elites in Antigua, 1834–1900. In *Small Islands, Large Questions: Society, Culture, and Resistance in the Post-Emancipation Caribbean*. Karen Fog Olwig, ed. Pp. 31–52. London: Frank Cass.
Lugo, Alejandro
  1990   Cultural Production and Reproduction in Ciudad Juared, Mexico: Tropes at Play among Maquiladora Workers. *Cultural Anthropology* 5(2): 173–96.
Luxemburg, Rosa
  1951 [1914]   *The Accumulation of Capital*. London: Routledge and Kegan Paul.
Malkki, Liisa
  1992   National Geographic: The Rooting of Peoples and the Territorialization of National Identity among Scholars and Refugees. *Cultural Anthropology* 7(1): 22–44.
  1995   *Purity and Exile: Violence, Memory, and National Cosmology among Hutu Refugees in Tanzania*. Chicago: University of Chicago Press.
Malthus, Thomas
  1967 [1803]   *An Essay on the Principle of Population*. New York: Dutton.
Marcus, George
  1992   *Lives in Trust: The Fortunes of Dynastic Families in Late 20th Century America*. Boulder, CO: Westview.
Markis, Alan, and Roger Langton
  1990   *The American Killifish Association's Beginner's Guide*. American Killifish Association.
Marx, Karl
  1977 [1861]   *Capital*, vol. I. New York: Vintage Books.
Maurer, Bill
  1995a   Complex Subjects: Offshore Finance, Complexity Theory, and the Dispersion of the Modern. *Socialist Review* 25(3–4): 113–45.
  1995b   Orderly Families for the New Economic Order: Belonging and Citizenship in the British Virgin Islands. *Identities* 2(1–2): 149–71.
  1995c   Writing Law, Making a "Nation:" History, Modernity, and Paradoxes of Self-Rule in the British Virgin Islands. *Law and Society Review* 29(2): 255–86.
  1997a   Creolization Redux: The Plural Society Thesis and Offshore Financial Services in the British Caribbean. *New West Indian Guide* 71(3–4): 249–64.
  1997b   Fractions of Blood on Fragments of Soil: Capitalism, the Commons, and Kinship in the Caribbean. *Plantation Society in the Americas* 4(2–3): 159–71.
  1997c   Islands in the Net: Telecommunications and Corporate Rhetoric in the Offshore Caribbean. Paper presented at the Western Humanities Conference, Riverside, CA, October 18.
  1997d   *Recharting the Caribbean: Land, Law and Citizenship in the British Virgin Islands*. Ann Arbor: University of Michigan Press.
  1998a   Cyberspatial Sovereignties: Offshore Finance, Digital Cash, and the Limits of Liberalism. *Indiana Journal of Global Legal Studies* 5(2): 493–519.
  1998b   Redecorating the International Economy: Keynes, Grant, and the Queering of Bretton Woods. Paper presented at the Center for Lesbian and Gay Studies Conference, CUNY, April 24.
  1999   Forget Locke? From Proprietor to Risk-Bearer in New Logics of Finance. *Public Culture* 11(2): 365–85.
McHaffie, Patrick
  1997   Decoding the Globe: Globalism, Advertising, and Corporate Practice. *Environment and Planning D: Society and Space* 15: 73–86.

McKenzie, Richard, and Dwight Lee
  1991   *Quicksilver Capital: How the Rapid Movement of Money is Changing the World.*
  New York: Free Press.
McMichael, Philip
  1996   Globalization: Myths and Realities. *Rural Sociology* 61(1): 25–55.
Michaels, Walter Benn
  1987   *The Gold Standard and the Logic of Naturalism: American Literature at the Turn of
  the Century.* Berkeley: University of California Press.
Mintz, Sidney
  1974   *Caribbean Transformations.* New York: Columbia University Press.
Moore, Gary
  1999   *End-Times Money Management: Protecting Your Resources Without Losing Your
  Soul.* Grand Rapids, MI: Zondervan Publishing House.
Murphy, W. J., and G. E. Collier
  1996   Phylogenetic Relationships within the Aplocheiloid Fish Genus Rivulus (Cyprino-
  dontiformes, Rivulidae): Implications for Caribbean and Central American Biogeography. *Molecular Biology and Evolution* 13(5): 642–9.
  1997   A Molecular Phylogeny for Aplocheiloid Fishes (Atherinomorpha, Cyprinodonti-
  formes): The Role of Vicariance and the Origins of Annualism. *Molecular Biology and
  Evolution* 14(8): 790–9.
Nicholson, Linda
  1987   Feminism and Marx: Integrating Kinship with the Economic. In *Feminism as
  Critique.* Seyla Benhabib and Drucilla Cornell, eds. Pp. 16–30. Minneapolis: University
  of Minnesota Press.
Ong, Aihwa
  1987   *Spirits of Resistance and Capitalist Discipline: Factory Women in Malaysia.* Albany:
  SUNY Press.
Parry, Jonathan, and Maurice Bloch, eds.
  1989   *Money and the Morality of Exchange.* New York: Cambridge University Press.
Pred, Allan, and Michael Watts
  1992   *Reworking Modernity: Capitalisms and Symbolic Discontent.* New Brunswick, NJ:
  Rutgers University Press.
Ridley, Mark
  1986   *Evolution and Classification: The Reformation of Cladism.* London: Longman.
Riehl, Rudiger, and Hans A. Baensch
  1997   *Baensch's Aquarium Atlas,* vol. 1, 2nd edn. Morris Plains, NJ: Tetra Press.
Ritter, Gretchen
  1997   *Goldbugs and Greenbacks: The Antimonopoly Tradition and the Politics of Finance
  in America, 1865–1896.* Cambridge: Cambridge University Press.
Roberts, Susan
  1994   Fictitious Capital, Fictitious Spaces: The Geography of Offshore Financial Flows. In
  Money, Power and Space. Stuart Corbridge, Ron Martin, and Nigel Thrift, eds. Pp. 91–
  115. Oxford: Blackwell Publishers.
Rogers, Howard Aston
  1970   The Fall of the Old Representative System in the Leeward and Windward Islands,
  1854–1877. Ph.D. dissertation, Department of History, University of Southern California.
Rosaldo, Michelle
  1983   The Shame of Headhunters and the Autonomy of Self. *Ethos* 11(3): 135–51.
  1984   Toward an Anthropology of Self and Feeling. In *Culture Theory: Essays on Mind,
  Self and Emotion.* Richard Schweder and Robert LeVine, eds. Pp. 137–57. Cambridge:
  Cambridge University Press.

Rotman, Bryan
    1987   *Signifying Nothing: The Semiotics of Zero.* Stanford, CA: Stanford University Press.
Rouse, Roger
    1991   Mexican Migration and the Social Space of Postmodernism. *Diaspora* 1(1): 8–23.
Rubin, Gayle
    1975   The Traffic in Women. In *Toward an Anthropology of Women.* Rayna Reiter, ed.
           Pp. 157–210. New York: Monthly Review Press.
Rutherford, Danilyn
    1998   Love, Violence, and Foreign Wealth: Kinship and History in Biak, Irian Jaya.
           Journal of the Royal Anthropological Institute N.S. 4(2): 255–81.
Sassen, Saskia
    1988   *The Mobility of Labor and Capital: A Study in International Investment and Labor
           Flows.* Cambridge: Cambridge University Press.
Schneider, David
    1984   *A Critique of the Study of Kinship.* Ann Arbor: University of Michigan Press.
Semmel, Bernard
    1970   *The Rise of Free Trade Imperialism.* Cambridge: Cambridge University Press.
Smith, Adam
    1976 [1776]   *An Inquiry into the Origins and Causes of the Wealth of Nations.* London:
           Clarendon Press.
Spivak, Gayatri
    1995   Ghostwriting. *Diacritics* 25(2): 65–84.
Strange, Susan
    1986   *Casino Capitalism.* Oxford: Basil Blackwell.
    1998   *Mad Money: When Markets Outgrow Governments.* Ann Arbor: University of
           Michigan Press.
Strathern, Marilyn
    1988   *The Gender of the Gift.* Berkeley: University of California Press.
Taussig, Michael
    1980   *The Devil and Commodity Fetishism in South America.* Chapel Hill: University of
           North Carolina Press.
Thrift, Nigel
    1996   *Spatial Formations.* London: Sage Publications.
Toomey, Robert R.
    1985   *Vivian and Sons, 1809–1924: A Study of the Firm in Copper and Related Industries.*
           New York: Garland.
Trouillot, Michel-Rolph
    1989   Discourses of Rule and the Acknowledgment of the Peasantry in Dominica, W. I.,
           1838–1928. *American Ethnologist* 16(4): 704–18.
Tylor, Edward Burnett
    1889   On a Method of Investigating the Development of Institutions: Applied to the Laws
           of Marriage and Descent. *Journal of the Royal Anthropological Institute of Great Britain
           and Northern Ireland* 18: 245–72.
Valenzuela, Luis
    1990   Challenges to the British Copper Smelting Industry in the World Market, 1840–
           1860. *Journal of European Economic History* 19(3): 657–86.
    1992   The Chilean Copper Smelting Industry in the Mid-nineteenth Century: Phases of
           Expansion and Stagnation, 1834–58. *Journal of Latin American Studies* 24(3): 507–50.
    1996   The Copper Smelting Company "Urmeneta y Errazuriz" of Chile: An Economic
           Profile, 1860–1880. *Americas* 53(2): 235–71.

van Wouden, F. A. E.
  1968 *Types of Social Structure in Eastern Indonesia*. Rodney Needham, trans. The Hague: Nijhoff.
Vernon, John
  1984 *Money and Fiction: Literary Realism in the Nineteenth and Early Twentieth Centuries*. Ithaca, NY: Cornell University Press.
Weatherford, Jack
  1997 *The History of Money*. New York: Three Rivers Press.
Whittaker, Robert J.
  1998 *Island Biogeography: Ecology, Evolution and Conservation*. Oxford: Oxford University Press.
Williams, Eric
  1944 *Capitalism and Slavery*. Chapel Hill: University of North Carolina Press.
Yanagisako, Sylvia
  1985 *Transforming the Past: Kinship and Tradition among Japanese Americans*. Stanford, CA: Stanford University Press.
Yanagisako, Sylvia, and Carol Delaney
  1995 Naturalizing Power. In *Naturalizing Power: Essays in Feminist Cultural Analysis*. Sylvia Yanagisako and Carol Delaney, eds. Pp. 1–22. New York: Routledge.
Yelvington, Kevin
  1995 *Producing Power: Ethnicity, Gender and Class in a Caribbean Workplace*. Philadelphia: Temple University Press.
Young, Robert
  1990 *White Mythologies: Writing History and the West*. New York: Routledge.

6

Global Disconnect: Abjection and the Aftermath of Modernism

James Ferguson

Introduction

In a recently completed book, *Expectations of Modernity* (1999), I explore how mineworkers in the town of Kitwe on the Zambian Copperbelt have dealt with a long period of economic adversity. The book deals with a range of ethnographic questions: changing forms of labor migration; new patterns of urban-to-rural mobility; the dynamics of household formation and dissolution; the relation of urban cultural forms to the micro-political-economic relations linking urban workers to their rural kin and allies. In all of these domains, I have been less interested in constructing a developmental sequence of social and cultural forms than in exploring their temporal coexistence; less interested in a succession of "typical" forms over time than in an understanding of the whole spread (what Stephen Jay Gould (1996) calls the "full house") of diverse modes of getting by that may exist at any one moment, and how that spread is affected by political-economic shifts over time.

In arguing for nonlinear, variation-centered models of social transformation (aiming to reconstruct what Gould (1996) calls the "bush" of actual variation rather than an ideal tree or ladder of succeeding "typical forms"), I have been concerned to demonstrate the inadequacy of what I call the modernist metanarratives through which urban life in Africa has so often been understood. Here, my target is not only the explicit Eurocentrism that allowed the Rhodes–Livingstone Institute anthropologists to see the Copperbelt as the new Birmingham of an African Industrial

Revolution, but equally the still-ubiquitous use of a set of linear, directional concepts to frame scholarly understandings of urban Africa – what I call the "-izations": urbanization, modernization, proletarianization, commoditization, etc.

The period since the mid-1970s or so in Zambia poses a formidable challenge to such habitual ways of understanding the meaning of urban Africa. With declining terms of trade, increasingly worked-out mines, and the crushing burden of a debt crisis, Zambia's copper-based, urban industrial economy has seen a sustained and profound contraction. This has brought with it not only impoverishment and hardship, but also a strange flood of new "-izations." The "Industrial Revolution in Africa" seems to have been called off: industrialization has been replaced by "de-industrialization". The long-documented flow of migrants to the Copperbelt cities, too, is now running backwards, with urban-to-rural migration now outpacing rural-to-urban – a phenomenon for which the term "counterurbanization" has been coined. The apparently inevitable process of proletarianization, meanwhile, is now replaced by mass layoffs and "back to the land" exercises: the "unmaking," rather than the making, of a working class. And now, with the privatization of the state-held mining company, it seems that even "Zambianization" (the nationalist policy of replacing white management with qualified black Zambians) is being replaced by what is now being called "de-Zambianization," the rehiring of white, expatriate management.

A new generation of Zambians, then, has come of age in a world where the modernist certainties their parents grew up with have been turned upside down, a world where life expectancies and incomes shrink instead of grow, where children become less educated than their parents instead of more, where migrants move from urban centers to remote villages instead of vice versa. It is the modernization story through the looking glass, where modernity is the object of nostalgic reverie, and "backwardness" the anticipated (or dreaded) future.

In reflecting on this extraordinary turn of events, this paper will move between two levels. The first level is the lived experience of actual Zambian workers, who have seen the modernist story-line transformed, in their own lifetimes, from a marvelous promise to a cruel hoax. The second level is a set of global transformations that allow us to see the Zambian case as part of a much more general phenomenon, which I argue is nothing less than the collapse of the global modernist project that once seemed to define the future of what we used to call "the developing world." I have in mind here not only the collapse of the developmentalist vision of the world that saw the "new nations" of the Third World as western nation-states in embryo, and spoke breathlessly of the "coming of age" of "emerging" African nations that would one day soon – through the miracle of political and economic development – somehow resemble England and France. That was one side of the story. But the other was a vision of historical progress through a process of hooking citizens up into a national – and ultimately universal – grid of modernity. This paper will discuss specifically the "grid" of electrical service, and the idea of a universal participation in modernity via copper connectivity as a metaphor for this. But we might think as well here of health care, where the postwar modernist ideal of a universal grid (epitomized in such things as the campaigns for universal vaccination against polio or smallpox) can be contrasted against today's tendency to fragmentation and privatization (which gives us not the polio vaccine, but AIDS combo therapy: managing the disease for those who can pay, while the poor are bluntly notified that it is economically more rational for them to die). Or schooling, where the universal grid of public education is today under siege all over the world. Or public space and the rule of law, where walled communities and fortified private spaces increasingly undermine the social and political promise of a universalistic "public." (I note that recent figures show that private police in "the new South Africa" now outnumber public police by a factor of three to one.)

By reflecting on Zambia's recent experience of decline and – in modernist terms – "failure," I do not mean to suggest that this experience forms a template for an inevitable African future (or even an inevitable Zambian future). On the contrary, my analysis of recent Zambian history leads to an emphasis on non-linear trajectories and multiplicities of pathways; to say that Africa is going "down" today is as false and misleading as it was to say that it was going "up" in the 1960s. But there is no disputing that the social experience of "decline" (notwithstanding the variety of causes and contexts) is today of quite wide relevance across many areas of the African continent (and, indeed, in many other regions – e.g. Russia or Indonesia – where recent political-economic restructuring has had comparable effects). For that reason, an analysis of the political and theoretical significance of that social experience may perhaps be of some wider relevance.

As an ethnographic point of entry into the social experience of decline on the Copperbelt, consider the following brief anecdote. One afternoon in 1989, I was chatting with a young officer of the mineworkers' union, who was expressing his dismay at how difficult it had become to find neckties of decent quality. Soon, we were talking about the two main retail shopping districts in Kitwe, one located in what had once been in colonial days the "European" town center, the other in the former "location" reserved for "Africans." What struck me was that these two shopping districts were still called (as they had been in colonial days) "first class" and "second class," respectively. Why, I wondered, did people continue this usage? Wasn't this an embarrassing holdover of colonial thinking, and of the idea of "second-class" status for Africans? Well, my companion replied, nobody really thought of it that way; it was just what the areas were called. Then he thought for a moment, and continued. "Anyway," he blurted with a bitter, convulsive laugh, "now it's all 'second-class', isn't it?" I take this very particular way of experiencing one's own social world as having become "second class" as a point of departure for what follows.

Abjection and the New World Society

When Godfrey Wilson wrote his "Essay on the Economics of Detribalization in Northern Rhodesia" in 1941, he considered that the Africans of Northern Rhodesia had just entered into an economically and culturally interconnected "world society," a "huge world-wide community" within which they would soon find a place for themselves as something more than peasants and unskilled workers (Wilson 1941: 12–13). The "civilized" clothing and manners to which so many urban Africans attached such importance, he argued, amounted to a claim to full membership in that worldwide community. Indeed, Wilson suggested, it was for this very reason than many white settlers resented and feared the well-dressed African who politely doffed his hat in the street, preferring to see Africans in suitably humble rags. Fine formal evening wear, ballroom dancing, European-style handshaking – these, Wilson argued, were not inauthentic cultural mimicry but expressed "the Africans' claim to be respected by the Europeans and by one another as civilized, if humble, men, *members of the new world society*" (Wilson 1942: 19–20, emphasis added).[1]

That claim to a full membership in "the new world society," of course, was refused in a racist colonial society. The color bar explicitly distinguished between "first-class" whites, who held the privileges of such membership, and "second-class" natives, who did not (see Ferguson 1999, ch. 1). But nationalism promised to change all that, by overturning the colonial system and banishing forever the insulting idea that Zambians should be second-class citizens in their own land. The early years of Zambia's independence seemed on the verge of delivering on that promise. The color bar was indeed dismantled as educated black Zambians rose to unprecedented positions of power and responsibility; a booming economy and strong labor unions meanwhile helped even ordinary workers to enjoy a new level of comfort and prosperity. As an "emerging new nation," Zambia appeared poised to enter the world of the "first class." It would be like other modern nations right down to its state-of-the-art national airline. . . . With a rising standard of living, bustling urban centers, and such symbols of modern status as suits made in London and a national airline, membership in the "new world society" seemed finally to be at hand.

It was the faltering of the "Industrial Revolution" that changed all that. For no sooner had the "blitzkrieg" of industrialization turned the world upside down for millions of Central Africans than rapid industrial decline set in motion another, even more devastating blitz. The economic hardships this has entailed have been staggering (see Ferguson 1999, ch. 1). But equally important, if harder to measure, has been the sense of a loss of membership in that "world society" of which Wilson spoke. Zambia, in the good times, had been on the map, a country among others in the "modern world." It was, older mineworkers reminded me, a place regularly visited by internationally known musical acts conducting world tours. One man recalled an early 1960s concert by the American country-and-western star Jim Reeves, for instance, and asked me with great feeling why such American acts no longer came to Zambia. But it is not just country-and-western acts that have stopped coming to Zambia. In the 1970s, international airlines such as British Caledonian, UTA, Lufthansa, and Alitalia connected Lusaka via direct flights to Frankfurt, Rome, London, and other European centers; British Caledonian even offered a flight to Manchester. Zambia's own national airline, Zambia Airways, also flew an impressive fleet of planes, proudly piloted by black Zambian pilots, to international destinations both expected (London, Frankfurt, New York) and surprising (Belgrade, Bombay, Larnaca). But as the economic situation deteriorated, the European carriers one by one dropped Zambia from their routes. Finally, in 1996, it was announced that Zambia Airways itself would be liquidated. Like the "Industrial Revolution," it had all apparently been a big mistake. Efficiency required that it be shut down. Today, a thrice-weekly British Airways plane to London is the only flight leaving Zambia for a non-African destination.

For many Zambians, then, as these details suggest, recent history has been experienced not – as the modernization plot led one to expect – as a process of moving forward or joining up with the world but as a process that has pushed them out of the place in the world that they once occupied. The only term I have found to capture this sense of humiliating expulsion is abjection (which I adapt from Kristeva (1982); see also Borneman (1996)). *Abjection* refers to a process of being thrown aside, expelled, or discarded. But its literal meaning also implies not just being thrown out but being thrown *down* – thus expulsion, but also debasement and humiliation. This complex of meanings, sad to report, captures quite precisely the sense I found among the Copperbelt mineworkers – a sense that the promises of modernization had been betrayed, and that they were being thrown out of the circle of full humanity, thrown back into the ranks of the "second class," cast outward and downward into the world of rags and huts where the color bar had always told "Africans" they belonged.

With much talk today of globalization, of new forms of worldwide interconnection, and of yet another "emerging" "new world society," it is useful to consider briefly where Zambia fits in all of this, and what the story I have told here of decline and abjection might have to say about the nature of this "new world order." The meaning of the Zambian case, I suggest, is not simply that it illustrates a gloomy process of decline and disconnection that has had no place in many of the rosier accounts of the new global economy. Beyond simply illustrating the downside of global capitalism, what has happened in Zambia reveals something more fundamental about the mechanisms of membership, exclusion, and abjection upon which the contemporary system of spatialized global inequality depends.

When the color bar cut across colonial Africa, it fell with a special force upon the "westernized Africans": those polished, well-dressed, educated urbanites who blurred the lines between a "civilized," first-class white world, and a supposedly "primitive," second-class black one. It was they – the "not quite/not white" (Bhabha 1997) – whose uncanny presence destabilized and menaced the racial hierarchy of the colonial social order. And it was they who felt the sting not just of exclusion but of abjection: of being pushed back across a boundary that they had been led to believe they might successfully cross. In a similar way, when the juncture between Africa and the industrialized world that had been presented as a global stairway (leading from the "developing" world to the "developed") revealed itself instead as a wall (separating the "first world" from the "third"), it was the Copperbelt and places like it – proud examples of just how modern, urban, and prosperous an emerging Africa could be – that experienced this boundary-fixing process most acutely, as a kind of abjection. The experience of abjection here was not a matter of being merely *excluded* from a status to which one had never had a claim but of being *expelled*, cast out-and-down from that status by the formation of a new (or newly impermeable) boundary. It is an experience that has left in its wake both a profound feeling of loss as well as the gnawing sense of a continuing affective attachment to that which lies on the other side of the boundary. When Copperbelt workers of an older generation spoke to me with such feeling of having once, long ago, owned a fine tuxedo or attended a concert by the Ink Spots or eaten T-bone steak at a restaurant, they were registering a connection to the "first class" that they had lost many years before but still felt, like the phantom pains from a limb long ago amputated.

When the Copperbelt mineworkers expressed their sense of abjection from an imagined modern world "out there," then, they were not simply lamenting a lack of connection but articulating a specific experience of *disconnection*, just as they inevitably described their material poverty not simply as a lack but as a loss. When we think about the fact that Zambia is today disconnected and excluded in so many ways from the mainstream of the global economy, it is useful to remember that disconnection, like connection, implies a relation and not the absence of a relation. Dependency theorists once usefully distinguished between a state of being undeveloped (an original condition) and a state of being underdeveloped (the historical result of an active process of underdevelopment). In a parallel fashion, we might usefully distinguish between being unconnected (an original condition) and being disconnected (the historical result of an active process of disconnection). Just as being hung up on is not the same thing as never having had a phone, the economic and social disconnection that Zambians experience today is quite distinct from a simple lack of connection. Disconnection, like abjection, implies an active relation, and the state of having been disconnected requires to be understood as the product of specific *structures and processes of disconnection*. What the Zambian case shows about globalization, I will suggest, is just how important disconnection is to a "new world order" that insistently presents itself as a phenomenon of pure connection.

Global Redlining and the Neoliberal New World Order: Zambia is No Exception?

As Neil Smith has recently argued, in spite of aggressive "structural adjustment" and a rhetorical celebration of "free-market capitalism," "what is remarkable about the last two decades [in Africa] is its virtual systematic expulsion from capitalism" (1997: 180). Indeed, a recent 35-page feature in *The Economist* on "The Global Economy," made almost no reference to Africa at all, making only a passing note of the "threat" to rich countries that may be posed by "the 500m or so people, most of them in Africa, who risk being left out of the global boom." With private ventures in the continent falling by 25 percent in the 1980s, and even further in the 1990s, Africa "has been treated to a crash course in the most vicious aspects of free-market capitalism while being largely denied any of the benefits" (pp. 180, 181). Effectively "redlined" in global financial markets, and increasingly cut off from governmental aid flows as well, most of sub-Saharan Africa today functions as "a veritable ghetto of global capital" (p. 179) – a zone of economic abjection that also makes a convenient object lesson for Third-World governments in other regions that might, without the specter of "Africanization" hanging over them, be tempted to challenge capital's regime of "economic correctness" (Smith 1997; Ferguson 1995).

The very possibility of "redlining" on such a massive scale reveals that the much-vaunted "flexibility" of the new forms of global economy involves not simply new forms of connection but new forms of disconnection as well. With increasing international wage competition and pressure on state welfare provisions, as Smith (1997: 187) notes, "the global economy is ever more efficient at writing off redundant spaces of accumulation: the flexibility of investment and market options is matched by a wholly new flexibility in disinvestment and abandonment." It is precisely this "flexibility" that makes global "redlining" possible, and that makes

Zambia's recent deindustrialization just as integral a part of globalization as the appearance of Mexican car factories or Shanghai skyscrapers.

To speak of expulsion and abandonment here is not to suggest that Zambia is today somehow outside of the world capitalist system (and thus needs to be brought back into it). The mining industry, though shrunken, continues to dominate the Zambian economy, and may even (if the current plan for full privatization brings the new capital for exploration and development that its boosters promise) expand again in years to come; capitalists continue to profit from Zambia's copper. Other forms of capitalist production of course remain important as well. But the more fundamental point here is that the abjected, "redlined" spaces of decline and disinvestment in the contemporary global economy are as much a part of the geography of capitalism as the booming zones of enterprise and prosperity; they reveal less the outside of the system than its underbelly. Expulsion and abandonment (in Smith's terms), disconnection and abjection (in my own), occur within capitalism, not outside of it. They refer to processes through which global capitalism constitutes its categories of social and geographical membership and privilege by constructing and maintaining a category of absolute non-membership: a holding tank for those turned away at the "development" door; a residuum of the economically discarded, disallowed, and disconnected – to put it plainly, a global "second class."

In its "Industrial Revolution" era, it was copper that connected Zambia to the world. The world needed Zambia's copper, and it was copper that put the new nation on the economic world map, while bringing in the export earnings that financed everything from cars for urban workers to state prestige projects like Zambia Airways. But copper not only connected Zambia economically, it also provided a vivid symbol of a specifically modern form of world connection. The copper wire bars produced by Zambian refineries literally did connect the world, via telephone and power cables that were forming a rapidly ramifying net across the globe. From the Soviet rural electrification program, to the United States' model Tennessee Valley Authority project, to the new South Africa's township electricity programs, electrification has provided the twentieth century with perhaps its most vivid symbol of modernization and development. Fusing a powerful image of universal connection in a national grid with the classical Enlightenment motif of illumination of the darkness, electrification has been an irresistible piece of symbolism for the modernist state (expressed perhaps most vividly in Lenin's suggestion that the "backward" Soviet peasantry be uplifted by melting enough church bells into copper wire to permit the placing of a light bulb in every village (Coopersmith 1992: 154–5)).[2] It was no different in Zambia, where the electrification of the townships was a compelling symbol of inclusion, a sign that Africans, too, were to be hooked up with the "new world society."

Today, the Copperbelt mine townships are still wired for electricity. But the service is intermittent, as equipment often breaks down, and the copper power cables are from time to time stolen for sale as scrap. What is more, few township residents can afford to pay the monthly charges for the use of electricity, so electric appliances go unused as women huddle around charcoal fires preparing the daily meals and the townships' skies fill with gray smoke each morning.

Nowadays, global interconnection does not depend so much on copper. The development of fiber optics and satellite communications technology, for instance, means that there is today much less need for copper-wired telephone cables. This "advance" in global connectivity is actually one of the causes of Zambia's drastic economic marginalization; the world "out there" can increasingly connect itself without relying on Zambia's copper (Mikesell 1988: 40).[3] Ironically, then, the communication revolution that is generally thought of as "connecting the globe" is playing a small but significant part in disconnecting Zambia.

There is a fundamental point suggested in this small detail. That is that what we have come to call globalization is not simply a process that links together the world but also one that differentiates it. It creates new inequalities even as it brings into being new commonalities and lines of communication. And it creates new, up-to-date ways not only of connecting places but of bypassing and ignoring them.

Most Zambians, let us remember, have never made a telephone call in their lives. Indeed, two out of three human beings alive today can say the same, according to one estimate.[4] With new technologies, will telecommunications now become more equally distributed, or even truly universal? One wonders. According to one recent report, at least, cellular telephone technology promises not to "hook up" the African masses but rather to make obsolete the very idea that they need to be "hooked up": many of the poorest parts of the world, the article claims, may now *never* be wired for phone service (*The Economist* 1993). For cellular technology allows businesses and elites to ignore their limited and often malfunctioning national telephone systems and do their business via state-of-the-art satellite connectivity, bypassing altogether the idea of a universal copper grid providing service to all.

Wilson's "new world society," for all its faults, implied a promise of universality and even ultimate equality that is strikingly absent from the current visions of the "new world order." In the plotline of modernization, some countries were "behind," it is true, but they were all supposed to have the means to "catch up" in the end. And Zambia was no exception. "Second-class" countries could and (the story promised) surely would eventually rise to the ranks of the "first class." Today, this promise is still mouthed by the ideologists of development here and there. But it is without much conviction. More characteristic is *The Economist*'s casual casting aside of that troublesome 500 million "or so" who have inexplicably missed the bandwagon of global growth. In the neo-liberal "new world order," apparently, Zambia (along with most of the rest of Africa) *is* to be an exception.

Many of the people I spoke with on the Copperbelt understood this very well – understood that "Africa," in the new global dispensation, was becoming a category of abjection. I noticed that whenever people were trying to convey their problems – to describe their suffering, to appeal for help, to explain the humiliation of their circumstances – they described themselves not as Zambians but as Africans. On the one hand, the term evoked all the images associated with Africa in contemporary international media discourse: pictures of poverty, starvation, and war; refugees, chaos, and charity. On the other, of course, it evoked the old colonial usage of African as a stigmatized race category. Putting the two connotations together suggested (tragically, if accurately) a reimposition of the old, despised "second-class" status but within a new macro-political order. As one old man put it, at the end of a wrenching narration of his country's downward slide: "We are just poor Africans, now" (see also Ferguson 1997).

The End of Development

A number of recent critical analysts have heralded the end of the "age of development."[5] For Wolfgang Sachs, editor of the influential critical work *The Development Dictionary* (1992), the whole project of development today "stands like a ruin in the intellectual landscape," a disastrous failure now made "obsolete," "outdated by history" (1992: 1, 2). It is not only that development has failed to deliver the economic growth and sociocultural modernization that it promised; more fundamentally, the whole ideal of development can no longer carry any conviction. Economically, Sachs argues, the very idea of the whole planet consuming at First-World levels presents an ecological disaster if not an impossibility, while socially and culturally, development offers only a thinly veiled westernization, a colonizing global monoculture that must choke out the "traditional" world's wealth of diverse local modes of life. To the extent that Third-World people have themselves sought development, in this view, they have been misguided; the schemas of development have provided only "the cognitive base for [a] pathetic self-pity" (1992: 2), which has been self-defeating, and which must continue no longer.

Esteva argues in similar fashion that development has led Third-World peoples "to be enslaved to others' experience and dreams" (Esteva 1992: 7). When United States President Harry Truman labeled two billion people as "underdeveloped" in 1949,

they ceased being what they were, in all their diversity, and were transmogrified into an inverted mirror of others' reality: a mirror that belittles them and sends them off to the end of the queue, a mirror that defines their identity, which is really that of a heterogeneous and diverse majority, simply in the terms of a homogenizing and narrow minority. (Esteva 1992: 7)

According to Esteva, the world would be well advised to do without such a concept (which is in any case "doomed to extinction" (1992: 7)), and proceed to emulate the "marginals" at the fringes of the capitalist economy who are rejecting the "needs" imposed by the economic worldview of development and reinventing a world without scarcity (much like Sahlins' "original affluent society" of hunters and gatherers) (1992: 19–22).[6]

There is reason to be doubtful of such sweeping claims for the end of development. Most obviously, it is clear that ideas of development – often remarkably unreconstructed ones at that – hold great sway in many parts of the world today, perhaps especially in areas (notably, many parts of East and Southeast Asia) that have enjoyed recent rapid economic expansion (though the recent "crash" that has stricken many countries in the region may yet shake that developmentalist faith). More theoretically, one might well be suspicious of criticisms of inevitable linear teleologies and progressive successions of epochs that proceed by constructing their own inevitable linear teleologies and progressive successions of epochs, as so many contemporary "post-" and "end of..." narratives seem to do.[7] But it remains true that something has happened in recent years to the taken-for-granted faith in development as a universal prescription for poverty and inequality. For Africa, at least, as for some other parts of the world, there is a real break with the certainties and expectations that made a development era possible. The "rolling back" of the state, the abandonment of the goal of industrialization, the commitment to what are euphemistically called "market forces" and "private enterprise," and the shattering of expectations for economic convergence with the West, all come together to create a very real end, at least at the level of perceptions and expectations, of at least the grander versions of the development project in Africa.

Is this something to be celebrated? Critics like Sachs and Esteva give to this question an unequivocally affirmative answer. Development, they point out, has distorted people's understandings of their own histories, imposed Eurocentric values and ideals, and crowded out innumerable local ways of doing things. The sooner it disappears, they suggest, the better. There is much to recommend this view. Certainly, there is no reason why the people of former colonial territories should accept economic and cultural convergence with the West (whether it is owning a car, wearing suits made in London, or having a "modern family") as the ultimate measure of achievement or progress; the critics are quite right to attack the ethno-centrism of such an assumption, and to point out its historical contingency (see Escobar's excellent critique (1995)). Moreover, the ecological and human degradation created by what have been termed "overdeveloped" societies is only too evident; it is not obvious that such societies constitute a model to be emulated. It is also possible to show, as I have attempted to do in my own previous work (Ferguson 1994), that the conceptual problematic of development has served, in concrete instances and through specifiable mechanisms, as what I have termed an "anti-politics machine," systematically misrecognizing and depoliticizing understandings of the lives and problems of people living in what has long since come to be known as the Third World.

But critics such as Sachs and Esteva sometimes seem to forget that the post-World War II conceptual apparatus of development did not create global inequality at a stroke but only provided a new means of organizing and legitimating an only-too-real inequality that was already very well established. It was not Truman's speech in 1949 that sent Africa and other colonial territories to the "back of the queue," as Esteva implies; conquest, colonial rule, and centuries of predatory violence and economic exploitation saw to it that they were already there. "Development" was laid on top of already-existing geopolitical hierarchies; it neither created north–south inequality nor undid it but instead provided a set of conceptual and organizational devices for managing it, legitimating it, and sometimes contesting and negotiating its terms (see Bose 1997; Cooper 1997; Cooper and Packard 1997; Gupta 1997, 1998). The subordinate position ascribed to the Third World in development discourse was therefore not a figment of the imagination or a mere Eurocentric illusion but reflected an intractable political-economic reality that could not, and cannot, be wished or relabeled away. Third-World people who have sometimes viewed themselves as located "at the end of the queue" are therefore not victims of a self-destructive mystification, and they hardly require to be scolded for "pathetic self-pity."

Nor is there any reason to link the forecast end of development with any general liberation or new autonomy, as many critics have tended to do. For if development did not inaugurate the inequalities it organized, neither can its demise be expected to make them suddenly disappear. Just as the end of one mode of organizing and legitimating a global hierarchy (colonialism) did not end inequality but reconfigured it, so does the (very partial) disintegration of another ("development") inaugurate not a new reign of freedom from scarcity and global hierarchy but a new modality of global inequality.

It is here, too, that we might register the ethnographic fact that the end of "the age of development" for Copperbelt workers (and, I suspect, for many others on the continent) has been experienced not as a liberation but as a betrayal. The "world society" that Godfrey Wilson anticipated has been taken out of play, and Zambians have been bluntly told that they are, and for the foreseeable future will remain, just so many "poor Africans." That the development story was a myth, and in some respects a trap, does not make the abrupt withdrawal of its promises any easier to take, or any less of a tragedy for those whose hopes and legitimate expectations have been shattered. If nothing else, "development" put the problem of global inequality on the table and named it as a problem; with the development story now declared "out of date," global inequality increasingly comes to appear not as a problem at all but simply as a naturalized fact.

In this context, simply celebrating the end of development is a response that is neither intellectually nor politically adequate. For without a continuing engagement with the problems of global inequality, there is a real danger that what Watts (1995) has termed "anti-development" critiques may aid and abet the current global abjection of Africa. The key questions in the present moment are less about the failures of Africa's developmentalist era than about what follows it. And here the celebration of social movements in a "postdevelopment era" has sometimes seemed to obscure the fact that the new political and economic institutions that govern the global political economy today are often even less democratic and more exploitative than those that preceded them. Not only international organizations such as the IMF, World Bank, and World Trade Organization, but also NGOs, social movements, and "civil society," today participate in new, transnational forms of governmentality that need to be subjected to the same sort of critical scrutiny that has been applied to "development" in the past (Ferguson 1995, forthcoming; cf. Watts 1995).

At a more conceptual level, if the modernist story of development has lost its credibility, the most pressing question would appear to be not whether we should lament or celebrate this fact but rather how we can reconfigure the intellectual field in such a way as to restore global inequality to its status as "problem" without reintroducing the teleologies and ethnocentrisms of the development metanarrative. What, in short, comes after "development" – both as an intellectual and cosmological framework for interpretation and explanation, and as a progressive political program for responding to its disastrous economic and social failures?

In seeking an answer to this question, we might do well to think seriously about the nonlinear loops and reversals that have characterized recent Zambian history. Much that was understood as backward and disappearing seems today to be most vital. Moore and Vaughan, for instance, have shown in their study of Zambia's Northern Province that the method of shifting cultivation known as *citemene*, long understood as the very essence of agricultural "backwardness," is alive and well in the 1990s, with most farmers continuing to incorporate it into their agricultural strategies – not as a way of trying to re-create the past but as a mode of coping with the overwhelming uncertainties of the present (Moore and Vaughan 1994: 234). Indeed, as a symbol of flexibility and diversification, they argue, the "old" *citemene* method appears especially well suited to the demands of both the present and the probable future.

I have made similar points in my book (Ferguson 1999). Urban/rural labor mobility, once seen as a sign of incomplete or stunted modernity and a failure to attain full proletarianization, today seems better adapted than ever to present and likely future conditions, while the supposed "main line" of permanent urbanization today appears as the anachronism (ch. 2). Likewise, in the domain of urban culture, it is a "old-fashioned" localism that prevails among today's Copperbelt mineworkers (ch. 3 and 4), while "up-to-date" cosmopolitanism is pressed to the wall (ch. 6). And the "modern" nuclear family that was supposed to represent the inevitable future of urban domesticity is, I have shown, a rare bird, too, surrounded as it is by a range of supposedly backward and pathological domestic strategies that appear better suited to contemporary conditions (ch. 7).

In the same spirit, we might wish to reappraise the place of the Copperbelt's long-denigrated "hangers-on": the unemployed, "useless" *lambwaza*. These are the heirs to the old Lamba "loafers":[8] originally, people of the Lamba ethnic group from the sparsely populated rural countryside surrounding the Copperbelt, ethnically stereotyped as lazy and idle (Siegel 1989). The Lamba habit of hanging about the compounds "unproductively" in the early days apparently earned them disdainful descriptions like the following (cited in Rhodesia 1956: 7): "a degraded people on a degraded soil, a race of 'hangers on,' inhabiting the midden of the mines, hawkers of minor produce, vice, and the virtue of their women."

Yet the *lambwaza* of today – hawkers and hangers-on from every ethnic group – would seem to be as "up to date" in their adaptation to contemporary urban conditions as anyone. To say this is not to join in the tendency I have criticized elsewhere (Ferguson 1999: 157–8) of unreservedly celebrating the "coping" abilities of the urban poor and the vitality of the so-called informal sector; such a move can too easily end up whitewashing or romanticizing poverty and unemployment. But neither are we justified in assuming that that this often stigmatized group constitutes a failed, marginal class peripheral to the "main line" of a stable working class. For the urban people in this large and diverse category (who appear to have in common only their dependence upon one or another sort of social and economic improvisation) are not simply failures or victims; if anything, they seem to represent an especially viable and durable urban alternative in times like these (cf. MacGaffey 1991; White 1990). Some, at least, seemed to be managing the hard times of the late 1980s more successfully than many who had "real jobs."[9]

In all of this, what emerges is a new respect for what Stephen Jay Gould (1996) would call the "full house" of different urban strategies – that copiously branching "bush" of coexisting variation – and a corresponding revaluation of forms of life that a more linear, progressive narration might consign to the past (see the discussion of Gould's (1996) variation-centered alternative to teleological evolutionary narratives in Ferguson 1999: 42–3). For the "dead ends" of the past keep coming back, just as the "main lines" that are supposed to lead to the future continually seem to disappoint. It is this that gives the Copperbelt's recent history its "recursive" quality (as Moore and Vaughan (1994) have remarked for Zambia's Northern Province), the sense of a continual reiteration of familiar themes, as old and supposedly bygone practices, patterns, and even policies sprout up again when least expected.[10]

A new way of conceptualizing urban life may be emerging in all of this, one that values multiplicity, variation, improvisation, and opportunism and distrusts fixed, unitary modes of practice and linear sequences of phases. For urban Zambians seem to have come, by their own paths, to an understanding at which scholars have recently arrived as well: the realization that global modernity is characterized not by a simple, Eurocentric uniformity but by coexisting and complex sociocultural alternatives (Appadurai 1996), and that the successful negotiation of it may hinge less on mastering a unitary set of "modern" social and cultural forms than on managing to negotiate a dense bush of contemporary variants in the art and struggle of living.

It may also be possible, it has occurred to me, to detect a fundamental mutation in the way that people are coming to talk about historical and economic change in the region. When I have heard Zambians in recent years talk about different parts of Africa, for instance, it seems to me that they no longer speak about this or that place as being ahead or behind, progressing well or too slowly. Instead, people are more likely to speak in terms of nonlinear fluctuations of "up" and "down" (as in "Mozambique is very bad right now, but I hear that Tanzania is coming back up" or "Congo has been down so long, it is bound to come back up soon"), or in terms of particular niches and opportunities that might provide a bit of space here or there. Such usages evoke less the March of Progress than an up-to-date weather report: good times and bad times come and go, the trick is to keep abreast and make the best of it. Postmodernist in a literal sense, this new style of understanding is driven by a pragmatic logic, the need to come to terms with a social world that can no longer be grasped in terms of the old scripts.

Scholars might learn from this example. One might well resist the idea that economic processes are really just like the weather: completely unresponsive to human purposes and beyond the control of human agency. To put matters thus would be to naturalize economic phenomena and to obscure the fact that they are always the products of human activity, always linked to political practices, and always subject to change (Ferguson 1995).[11] But the attempts of ordinary people to map the changes they have been living through in nonlinear, non-teleological ways, and to take seriously the full range of multiplicity and variation in social life, might yet have much to teach us. In political terms, certainly, there would seem to be a compelling need to find new ways of approaching "progressive" politics in an era when the term itself requires to be put in quotation marks. The linear teleologies on which virtually all conventional liberal and leftist political programs have rested simply will not take us very far in dealing with the sorts of challenges raised by the contemporary politics of global inequality, on the Copperbelt or elsewhere.

But to say that received ideas of progress require to be critically interrogated is not to render the pursuit of equality or social improvement antique or laughable. Beyond the celebrations of the postmodern or the end of development lie profoundly challenging issues: how can democratic and egalitarian political movements address the transnational social and economic processes that bypass the control of nation-states as they connect and enrich some regions and social classes, even while they disconnect, impoverish, and abject others (Escobar and Alvarez 1992; Ferguson, forthcoming; Gupta 1998)? How can the responsibility of First-World citizens, organizations, and governments to impoverished and disaster-stricken regions and people be reformulated in a way that avoids the well-known limitations of developmental and humanitarian modalities of power (Malkki 1995)? How can we acknowledge the historical and ethical obligations of connectedness, responsibility, and, indeed, guilt that link western wealth and security with African poverty and insecurity in an era when the modernist grid of universal copper connectivity has begun to disintegrate?

These formidable conceptual and political problems must be faced at the end of this modernist era, as much by those who lament its passing as by those who celebrate it. As the people of the Copperbelt know only too well, the upending of the project of modernity is not a playful intellectual choice but a shattering, compulsory socioeconomic event. While the intellectual consequences are profound for all, such an event affects Copperbelt workers far more directly than it does First-World scholars;[12] and viewed from the vantage point of the Copperbelt, it is about as playful as a train wreck. That the view from the Copperbelt is so different from that available from the academy gives it no automatic privilege; certainly no magic solutions to the daunting questions and problems listed here emerge from the experience of the men and women who saw the "Industrial Revolution" come and go within the span of a single lifetime. But at a time when First-World academics are wont to speak perhaps a little too confidently of globalization or postmodernity, and a little too happily about "the demise of metanarratives" or "the end of development," there may be something to be gained from contemplating a place where the globalization of the economy has been experienced as disconnection and abjection, and where the much-celebrated end of the universalizing project of modernity has meant an end to the prospect of African equality, and the re-establishment of a global color bar blocking access from the "first-class" world.

A return to modernist teleology, a new grand narrative that would trace the hopeful signs of an Africa once more "emerging" out of the gloomy ashes of Africa's "development" disaster is neither plausible nor desirable. The modernization narrative was always a myth, an illusion, often even a lie. We should all learn to do without it. But if the academic rejection of modernization and development is not simply to reproduce at another level the global disconnects of capital, migration, and information flows, we must replace it with other ways of conceiving the relations of historical connectedness and ethical and political responsibility that link Africa and the rest of the world. If the people who have, in good faith, lived out the agonizing, failed plotline of development and modernization are not to be simply disconnected and abjected from the new world order, it will be necessary to find new ways of thinking about both progress and responsibility in the aftermath of modernism.

NOTES

This paper grew out of a talk that presented some of the major conclusions of a previously published book, *Expectations of Modernity: Myths and Meanings of Urban Life on the Zambian Copperbelt* (University of California Press, 1999). I hope that the reader will forgive the occasionally oral style, and the fact that the argument refers to ethnographic material presented in the body of the monograph and not in the paper itself.

1 Hannerz (1996) has made a similar suggestion regarding the pursuit of international popular culture by black artists and intellectuals in the Sophiatown district of Johannesburg in the 1950s.

2 After a 1920 meeting, H. G. Wells reported that "Lenin, who like a good orthodox Marxist denounces all 'Utopias', has succumbed at last to a Utopia, the Utopia of the electricians" (Coopersmith 1992: 154).

3 I do not suggest that the reduction in the amount of copper used in communication technology is the major factor here; it is clearly but one among a number of factors leading to the decline of the copper industry in Zambia. I mention the association only as a way of pointing out some of the ironies associated with the apparently universal process of globalization.

4 The figure (obviously to be taken with a grain of salt, given the absence of direct evidence) appeared in *Harper's* (1997).

5 In addition to the authors discussed here, see Escobar's important study (1995), which also heralds a "post-development era," as well as the recent *The Post-Development Reader* (Rahnema 1997); see also Marglin and Marglin 1990 and Nandy 1988.

6 For the "original affluent society" essay, see Sahlins 1972. For a telling critique, see Wilmsen 1989.

7 Through such ironic reinscriptions of modernist teleology, the contemporary necessity of having to come to terms with the breakdown of modernism (i.e., post-*modernism* (an aftermath of modernism)) is routinely transmuted into a new evolutionary epoch (post-modernity, the next rung on the ladder) with its own "up-to-date" worldview ("*Postmodern*-ism," a suitable "latest thing" for the final chapter of the social theory textbook), and, indeed, its own triumphalist metanarrative of emergence.

8 Debra Spitulnik has suggested (personal communication) that the word *lambwaza* probably derives from the stem *Lamba*, in combination with the French *ois*, which is both a normal French word ending (as in *chinois*, *bourgeois*, etc.) and a French morpheme connoting idleness and laziness (as in *oiseux* (idle, pointless, useless) and *oisif* (idle, unemployed)). If this is correct, *lambwaza* would have an original meaning linked both to a specific ethnic group (the Lamba) and to a trait stereotypically associated with that group ("laziness"). In my fieldwork, however, I did not note any special relation between the Lambas and the term *lambwaza*, which referred to any unemployed youth "hanging around" the city.

9 I cannot say more about this interesting group, as I did not study them in any systematic way (perhaps because I, too, carried in my head assumptions about main lines and incidental peripheries).

10 Compare the deliberately "recursive" exposition, particularly in dealing with the legacies of the RLI, in Ferguson 1999.

11 Such a naturalization of the logic of a "complex system" occurs in the uses of "complexity theory" by economists, as shown in Maurer's critical review (1995).

12 I speak of First-World scholars here, because Zambian scholars, unfortunately, have experienced the economic crisis I have described here only too directly. One of the most vivid illustrations (at least for an academic) of the abjection and disconnection that I have tried to describe can be seen by visiting the University of Zambia library. Once a fine university library that could adequately support serious research in a range of fields, it resembled (at least when I last saw it) a kind of sad museum, with virtually no recent books or current periodical subscriptions at all. Salaries for university lecturers in Zambia, meanwhile, had by 1989 dropped so low that only by taking second and third jobs, and/or resorting to subsistence farming, were lecturers able to sustain themselves.

REFERENCES

Appadurai, Arjun
  1996 *Modernity at Large: Cultural Dimensions of Globalization.* Minneapolis: University of Minnesota Press.
Bhabha, Homi K.
  1997 Of Mimicry and Man: The Ambivalence of Colonial Discourse. In *Tensions of Empire: Colonial Cultures in a Bourgeois World.* Frederick Cooper and Ann Laura Stoler, eds. Berkeley: University of California Press.
Borneman, John
  1996 Until Death Do Us Part: Marriage/Death in Anthropological Discourse. *American Ethnologist* 23(2): 215–35.
Bose, Sugata
  1997 Instruments and Idioms of Colonial and National Development: India's Historical Experience in Comparative Perspective. In *International Development and the Social Sciences: Essays on the History and Politics of Knowledge.* Frederick Cooper and Randall Packard, eds. Berkeley: University of California Press.
Cooper, Frederick
  1997 Modernizing Bureaucrats, Backward Africans, and the Development Concept. In *International Development and the Social Sciences: Essays on the History and Politics of Knowledge.* Frederick Cooper and Randall Packard, eds. Berkeley: University of California Press.
Cooper, Frederick, and Randall Packard
  1997 Introduction. In *International Development and the Social Sciences: Essays on the History and Politics of Knowledge.* Frederick Cooper and Randall Packard, eds. Berkeley: University of California Press.
Coopersmith, Jonathan
  1992 *The Electrification of Russia, 1880–1926.* Ithaca, NY: Cornell University Press.
Economist, The
  1993 Telecommunications Survey. *The Economist* 329 (7834): 68ff. (supplement).
Escobar, Arturo
  1995 *Encountering Development: The Making and Unmaking of the Third World.* Princeton, NJ: Princeton University Press.
Escobar, Arturo, and Sonia Alvarez, eds.
  1992 *The Making of Social Movements in Latin America: Identity, Strategy, and Democracy.* Boulder, CO: Westview Press.
Esteva, Gustavo
  1992 Development. In *The Development Dictionary: A Guide to Knowledge as Power.* W. Sachs, ed. London: Zed Books.
Ferguson, James
  1994 *The Anti-politics Machine: "Development," Depoliticization, and Bureaucratic Power in Lesotho.* Minneapolis: University of Minnesota Press.
  1995 From African Socialism to Scientific Capitalism: Reflections on the Legitimation Crisis in IMF-ruled Africa. In *Debating Development Discourse: Institutional and Popular Perspectives.* D. B. Moore and G. J. Schmitz, eds. New York: St. Martin's Press.
  1997 The Country and the City on the Copperbelt. In *Culture, Power, Place: Explorations in Critical Anthropology.* Akhil Gupta and James Ferguson, eds. Durham, NC: Duke University Press.

1999 *Expectations of Modernity: Myths and Meanings of Urban Life on the Zambian Copperbelt*. Berkeley: University of California Press.

Forthcoming. Transnational Topographies of Power: Beyond "the State" and "Civil Society" in the Study of African Politics.

Gould, Stephen Jay

1996 *Full House: The Spread of Excellence from Plato to Darwin*. New York: Harmony Books.

Gupta, Akhil

1997 Agrarian Populism in the Development of a Modern Nation (India). In *International Development and the Social Sciences: Essays on the History and Politics of Knowledge*. Frederick Cooper and Randall Packard, eds. Berkeley: University of California Press.

1998 *Postcolonial Developments: Agriculture in the Making of Modern India*. Durham, NC: Duke University Press.

Hannerz, Ulf

1996 *Transnational Connections: Culture, People, Places*. New York: Routledge.

Harper's

1997 Harper's Index. *Harper's* 294 (1764): 15.

Kristeva, Julia

1982 *Powers of Horror: An Essay on Abjection*. New York: Columbia University Press.

MacGaffey, Janet

1991 *The Real Economy of Zaire: The Contribution of Smuggling and Other Unofficial Activities to National Wealth*. Philadelphia: University of Pennsylvania Press.

Malkki, Liisa H.

1995 Speechless Emissaries: Refugees, Humanitarianism, and Dehistoricization. *Cultural Anthropology* 11(3): 377–404.

Marglin, Frederique Apffel, and Stephen Marglin, eds.

1990 *Dominating Knowledge: Development, Culture, and Resistance*. New York: Oxford University Press.

Maurer, Bill

1995 Complex Subjects: Offshore Finance, Complexity Theory, and the Dispersion of the Modern. *Socialist Review* 25(3–4): 113–45.

Mikesell, Raymond F.

1988 *The Global Copper Industry: Problems and Prospects*. London: Croom Helm.

Moore, Henrietta L., and Megan Vaughan

1994 *Cutting Down Trees: Gender, Nutrition, and Agricultural Change in the Northern Province of Zambia, 1890–1990*. London: Heinemann.

Nandy, Ashis, ed.

1988 *Science, Hegemony, and Violence: A Requiem for Modernity*. Tokyo: United Nations University.

Rahnema, Majid, with Victoria Bawtree, eds.

1997 *The Post-Development Reader*. London: Zed Books.

Rhodesia, Government of Northern

1956 *Report of a Soil and Land-Use Survey: Copperbelt, Northern Rhodesia*. Lusaka: Department of Agriculture.

Sachs, Wolfgang, ed.

1992 *The Development Dictionary: A Guide to Knowledge as Power*. London: Zed Books.

Sahlins, Marshall

1972 *Stone Age Economics*. Chicago: Aldine Publishing Co.

Siegel, Brian V.

1989 The "Wild" and "Lazy" Lamba: Ethnic Stereotypes on the Central African Copperbelt. In *The Creation of Tribalism*. Leroy Vail, ed. Berkeley: University of California Press.

Smith, Neil
  1997   The Satanic Geographies of Globalization: Uneven Development in the 1990s.
    Public Culture 10(1): 169–89.
Watts, Michael
  1995   "A New Deal in Emotions": Theory and Practice and the Crisis of Development. In
    Power of Development. Jonathan Crush, ed. New York: Routledge.
White, Luise
  1990   *The Comforts of Home: Prostitution in Colonial Nairobi*. Chicago: University of
    Chicago Press.
Wilmsen, Edwin N.
  1989   *Land Filled with Flies: A Political Economy of the Kalahari*. Chicago: University of
    Chicago Press.
Wilson, Godfrey
  1941   *An Essay on the Economics of Detribalization in Northern Rhodesia (part 1)*.
    Rhodes–Livingstone Paper no. 5. Livingstone, Northern Rhodesia: Rhodes–Livingstone
    Institute.
  1942   *An Essay on the Economics of Detribalization in Northern Rhodesia (part 2)*.
    Rhodes–Livingstone Paper no. 6. Livingstone, Northern Rhodesia: Rhodes–Livingstone
    Institute.

Part III

Mobile Subjects

Part III of our reader is concerned with the movement of people, focusing primarily on the extensive post-World War II migrations from the countries of the periphery to the major urban centers of the "developed" and "developing" world. One of the basic arguments of these essays is that when migrants travel across national boundaries, they do not necessarily leave their homelands behind, but instead often forge cultural, political, and economic relations that link together their home and host societies. Rouse, for example, shows how Mexican migrants from Aguililla, Michoacán, who have settled in Redwood City, California, have not severed their ties to "home" but have instead maintained connections so intense that Aguililla and Redwood City can no longer be conceived as distinct communities. A related argument is that, as the boundaries of community have become less confined to the limits of a singular territorial national space, the nation-state has come to operate less as a self-contained unit and more as a way-station through which an increasing number of people shuttle. Ong's essay, for instance, discusses how mobile Chinese managers, technocrats, and professionals seek both to circumvent and to benefit from different nation-state regimes by selecting multiple sites for investments, work, and family relocation. And a third important argument of these essays is that the shuttling process has made it extremely difficult for the technologies of nationhood to fashion culturally monolithic national communities. The nation spaces of the West have thus been turned into sites of enormous cultural heterogeneity. Gross, McMurray, and Swedenburg articulate this argument best. Their piece focuses on how Franco-Maghrebis and their expressive culture have become crucially important to understanding contemporary French identity.

SUGGESTIONS FOR FURTHER READING

Basch, Linda, Nina Glick Schiller, and Cristina Szanton Blanc
  1994 *Nations Unbound: Transnational Projects, Postcolonial Predicaments, and Deterritorialized Nation-States*. Langhorne, PA: Gordon and Breach.
Brown, Jacqueline Nassy
  1998 Black Liverpool, Black America, and the Gendering of Diasporic Space. *Cultural Anthropology* 13(3): 291–325.
Carter, Donald Martin
  1997 *States of Grace: Senegalese in Italy and the New European Immigration*. Minneapolis: University of Minnesota Press.
Chavez, Leo R.
  1998 *Shadowed Lives: Undocumented Immigrants in American Society*, 2nd edn. Fort Worth, TX: Harcourt Brace College Publishers.
Daniel, E. Valentine, and John Chr. Knudsen, eds.
  1995 *Mistrusting Refugees*. Berkeley: University of California Press.
Ebron, Paulla A.
  1999 Tourists as Pilgrims: Commercial Fashioning of Transatlantic Politics. *American Ethnologist* 26(4): 910–32.
Gilroy, Paul
  1993 *The Black Atlantic: Modernity and Double Consciousness*. Cambridge, MA: Harvard University Press.
Louie, Andrea
  2000 Re-territorializing Transnationalism: Chinese Americans and the Chinese Motherland. *American Ethnologist* 27(3): 645–69.
MacCannell, Dean
  1992 *Empty Meeting Grounds: The Tourist Papers*. London: Routledge.
Malkki, Liisa H.
  1995 *Purity and Exile: Violence, Memory, and National Cosmology among Hutu Refugees in Tanzania*. Chicago: University of Chicago Press.
Margold, Jane A.
  1995 Narratives of Masculinity and Transnational Migration: Filipino Workers in the Middle East. In *Bewitching Women, Pious Men: Gender and Body Politics in Southeast Asia*. Aihwa Ong and Michael G. Peletz, eds. Pp. 274–98. Berkeley: University of California Press.
Ong, Aihwa, and Donald Nonini, eds.
  1997 *Ungrounded Empires: The Cultural Politics of Modern Chinese Transnationalism*. New York: Routledge.
Tambiah, Stanley J.
  2000 Transnational Movements, Diaspora, and Multiple Modernities. *Daedalus* 129(1): 163–94.
Van der Veer, Peter, ed.
  1995 *Nation and Migration: The Politics of Space in the South Asian Diaspora*. Philadelphia: University of Pennsylvania Press.
Werbner, Pnina
  1999 Global Pathways: Working Class Cosmopolitans and the Creation of Transnational Ethnic Worlds. *Social Anthropology* 7(1): 17–35.

7

Mexican Migration and the Social Space of Postmodernism

Roger Rouse

In a hidden sweatshop in downtown Los Angeles, Asian and Latino migrants produce automobile parts for a factory in Detroit. As the parts leave the production line, they are stamped "Made in Brazil."[1] In a small village in the heart of Mexico, a young woman at her father's wake wears a black T-shirt sent to her by a brother in the United States. The shirt bears a legend that some of the mourners understand but she does not. It reads, "Let's Have Fun Tonight!" And on the Tijuana–San Diego border, Guillermo Gómez-Peña, a writer originally from Mexico City, reflects on the time he has spent in what he calls "the gap between two worlds": "Today, eight years after my departure, when they ask me for my nationality or ethnic identity, I cannot answer with a single word, for my 'identity' now possesses multiple repertoires: I am Mexican but I am also Chicano and Latin American. On the border they call me 'chilango' or 'mexiquillo'; in the capital, 'pocho' or 'norteño,' and in Spain 'suda-ca.' . . . My companion Emily is Anglo-Italian but she speaks Spanish with an Argentinian accent. Together we wander through the ruined Babel that is our American postmodernity."[2]

1

We live in a confusing world, a world of crisscrossed economies, intersecting systems of meaning, and fragmented identities. Suddenly, the comforting modern imagery of nation-states and national languages, of coherent communities and consistent subjectivities, of dominant centers and distant margins no longer seems adequate. Certainly, in my own discipline of anthropology, there is a growing sense that our

From *Diaspora* 1(1) (Spring 1991): 8–23.

conventional means of representing both the worlds of those we study and the worlds that we ourselves inhabit have been strained beyond their limits by the changes that are taking place around us. Indeed, the very notion that ethnographers and their subjects exist in readily separable domains is increasingly being called into question.[3] But the problem is not confined to a single discipline, nor even to the academy at large. As Fredric Jameson has observed, the gradual unfolding of the global shift from colonialism and classic forms of dependency to a new transnational capitalism has meant that, during the last thirty years, we have all moved irrevocably into a new kind of social space, one which our modern sensibilities leave us unable to comprehend. With appropriate dramatic flair, he calls this new terrain "postmodern hyperspace."[4]

Jameson suggests that, in order to locate ourselves in this new space, we must make two moves. First, to understand why the crisis in spatial representation exists, we must identify as clearly as possible the broad politico-economic changes that have undermined the verisimilitude of existing images, and second, to understand where we are and where we can go from here, we must develop new images, new coordinates, a series of new and more effective maps. Jameson seeks to construct these alternative images through a critical reading of aesthetic forms such as novels, buildings, paintings, and films. But his focus seems unduly narrow. Given the ubiquity of the changes he describes and the profundity of their influence, the raw materials for a new cartography ought to be equally discoverable in the details of people's daily lives. And, from a radical perspective, the most significant materials surely lie in the circumstances and experiences of those working-class groups whose members have been most severely affected by the changing character of capitalist exploitation.[5]

In this article, I will develop these ideas by drawing on my work with rural Mexicans involved in migration to and from the United States. After outlining the images conventionally used to map the social terrain they inhabit, I will first build on their experiences to suggest new images better suited to charting their current circumstances and then indicate how these images may, in fact, be increasingly useful to us all as we try to map social landscapes found throughout Mexico and the United States.

2

Two socio-spatial images have dominated the modern discourse of the social sciences concerning the people of rural Mexico. I claim neither novelty nor insight for recognizing their influence. By underlining their importance and delineating their attendant assumptions, however, I hope to make it easier to understand both the nature of their limitations and the significance of the alternatives I shall propose.

The first image is one to which I shall attach the label "community."[6] The abstract expression of an idealized nation-state, it has been used concretely at numerous different levels, from the peasant village to the nation itself. It combines two main ideas.[7] First, it identifies a discriminable population with a single, bounded space – a territory or place. In so doing, it assumes that the social relationships in which community members participate will be much more intense within this space than beyond. It also assumes that members will treat the place of the community as the principal environment to which they adjust their actions and, correspondingly, that they will monitor local events much more closely than developments further afield. Second, the image implies a certain commonality and coherence, generally expressed either in the functionalist dream of an entity whose institutional parts fit together neatly to form an integrated whole or in the structural-functionalist vision of a shared way of life that exists not only in a multiplicity of similar actions but, more profoundly, in a single and internally consistent set of rules, values, or beliefs. From the perspective that these two ideas establish, the heterogeneities and complexities of the worlds we actually encounter are normally understood in terms of either super-ficial interactions between distinct communities or transitional moments in the movement from one form of integrity and order to another.

The second image is one that I shall label "center/periphery."[8] The abstract expression of an idealized imperial system, it too has been realized concretely at many different levels, from the rural town to the entire world system. This image involves three main ideas. First, it suggests that differences are organized concen-trically around a dominant core. Thus, power and wealth are greatest at the center and diminish gradually as one moves outwards through a series of surrounding zones, and different locations are associated with different ways of life according to the zone in which they are found. Second, the image implies a process of change in which the center exercises a privileged capacity to shape outcomes, whether it is extending its influence to the margins or molding people from the periphery who enter its terrain. And third, it suggests that fields ordered in this way are autonom-ous: each peripheral site is oriented to a single center and each center is independent of all others at the same level.

In many ways, these images are opposed. Formally, the idea of community tends to privilege homogeneity and stasis while the idea of center/periphery privileges variation and change. And, in practice, they have frequently been used against one another, community being the principal socio-spatial image invoked by moderniza-tion theory and center/periphery, of course, serving as a crucial counterimage for dependency theory and the world systems approach. But their opposition should not be exaggerated. In many works they have been used in tandem and, in fact, the key tension between modernization theory and its critics lies less in frictions over spatial imagery than in disagreements about the intentions of the center and the nature of its influence.[9] Indeed, even when the two images have been in conflict, they have supported one another negatively, each being treated as the only viable alternative to the other. Opposed, combined, or alternating, they have long dominated work on rural Mexico with the casual authority of the commonsensical.

Migration has always had the potential to challenge established spatial images. It highlights the social nature of space as something created and reproduced through collective human agency and, in so doing, reminds us that, within the limits imposed by power, existing spatial arrangements are always susceptible to change. In prac-tice, however, academics dealing with Mexican migration have rarely used it as the basis for a critical reappraisal of existing images. Instead, with a few notable exceptions, they have simply adapted the existing repertoire to make it fit the peculiarities of a mobile population. This is particularly apparent in the way they have used frameworks derived from the image of community to understand the experiences of the migrants themselves.

First, because migration is self-evidently a movement between places, it has commonly been treated as a movement from one set of social relationships to another. Thus, numerous studies have sought to gauge the changes that migrants have undergone by comparing the systems of family organization, kinship, and friendship dominant in their places of origin with those they have developed in the places to which they have moved.[10]

Second, as a movement between places, migration has also commonly been treated as a shift from one significant environment to another. Within a bipolar framework variously organized around oppositions between the rural and the urban, the traditional and the modern, and Mexico and the United States, many studies have examined how migrants take practices and attitudes adjusted to their original "niche" or setting and adapt them to the new locale in which they find themselves.[11]

And third, as a move between communities identified with distinct ways of life, migration has normally been seen as a process in which the migrants and their descendants experience a more or less gradual shift from one ordered arrangement to another, either fully converting to the dominant way of life or forging their own form of accommodation in an ordered synthesis of old and new. Such a perspective does recognize that contradictions can arise when people combine attitudes and practices associated with the place to which they have moved with others linked to their place of origin, but it has generally dealt with these in ways that sustain the primacy of order, treating them either as incongruities in form that disappear when viewed in terms of function or as temporary features peculiar to transitional situations. In the latter case, it has been particularly common to locate the contradictions within a widely used model of generational succession according to which the migrants themselves retain much of what they learned while growing up, they and their children balance traditional attitudes and practices maintained in intimate arenas such as the home and the ethnic neighborhood with others more appropriate to participation in the wider society, and a consistent sociocultural orientation appears only in the third generation.[12]

These ways of construing migration have faced a qualified challenge from accounts that treat it principally as a circular process in which people remain oriented to the places from which they have come. Under such circumstances, the patterns of social and cultural adjustment are clearly different.[13] But it is important to stress that the basic socio-spatial assumptions remain the same. As in accounts that emphasize a unidirectional shift, migrants are held to move between distinct, spatially demarcated communities and, in the long run, to be capable of maintaining an involvement in only one of them.

3

In recent years, however, this mobilization of modern socio-spatial images has become increasingly unable to contain the postmodern complexities that it confronts. Symptomatic of the unfolding shift to transnational capitalism, migration between rural Mexico and the United States since the Second World War, and especially since the mid-1960s, has been obliging us ever more insistently to develop an alternative cartography of social space. I can elaborate this argument most effectively by drawing on the case that I know best, the United States-bound migration that has been taking place since the early 1940s from the rural *municipio* of Aguililla in the southwest corner of the state of Michoacán.[14]

At first sight, Aguililla seems to be an isolated community dedicated to small-scale farming and manifestly part of the Mexican periphery. The *municipio* is located in the mountains that form the southern limit of the west-central region; its administrative center, also known as Aguililla, lies at the end of a poor dirt road, one of those points where the national transport system finally exhausts itself; the land has been used principally for the subsistence-oriented production of basic foodstuffs and the raising of livestock; and trade with the interior has been limited. It is the kind of place onto which urban dwellers find it easy to project their fantasies of difference and danger.

But appearances can be deceptive. Aguililla's growing involvement in transnational migration has profoundly changed both its economic orientation and its socio-spatial relationships. By the early 1980s, when I carried out fieldwork in the *municipio*, it had come to operate largely as a nursery and nursing home for wage-laborers in the United States. Almost every family had members who were or had been abroad; the local economy depended heavily on the influx of dollars; and many of the area's small farming operations continued only because they were sustained by migrant remittances. Concomitantly, the *municipio* has become part of a transnational network of settlements and, in so doing, has significantly modified its status as a marginal site within a purely national hierarchy of places. Over the years, migrants have established several outposts in the United States, by far the largest being the one they have formed amidst a rapidly growing Latino neighborhood in Redwood City, an urban area on the northern edge of California's famous Silicon Valley. There they now work principally in the service sector, as janitors, dishwashers, gardeners, hotel workers, house cleaners, and child minders – proletarian servants in the paragon of "postindustrial" society. Some Aguilillans have settled in Redwood City for long periods, but few abandon the *municipio* forever. Most people stay in the United States relatively briefly, almost all of those who stay longer continue to keep in touch with the people and places they have left behind, and even those who have been away for many years quite often return.

This pattern of migration must be understood as symptomatic of the way in which broad politico-economic developments involved in the unfolding of transnational capitalism have refracted themselves through the specificities of local circumstance. For many years, Aguilillans have placed a heavy emphasis on the capacity to create and maintain small-scale, family-run operations, ideally based in land, and, in relation to this goal, the broad developments have exerted contradictory pressures.

In the *municipio*, the nationwide diversion of capital to industry and commercial agriculture that has taken place since the 1940s has left the local economy without needed infrastructure, while the concentration of what government spending there has been in health and education has encouraged population growth and the broadening of people's horizons. As a result, it has become impossible for most Aguilillans to approach the realization of their goals solely through access to local resources. At the same time, however, the lack of large-scale land acquisitions in the *municipio* by commercially oriented owners, the periodic provision of small amounts of government aid to the area's farmers, and the enterpreneurial opportunities provided by the influx of dollars have all impeded full proletarianization. This, in turn, has meant that the old goals have not been abandoned and that migration has been seen principally as a way of raising outside funds to finance their local realization.[15]

Meanwhile, in the United States, the growing polarization of the labor market has created a mounting demand for Mexican workers to fill the bottom layers in agriculture, deskilled assembly, and, above all, services. Yet various factors have discouraged most Mexicans from staying permanently. In the case of Aguilillans, their cultural emphasis on creating and maintaining independent operations has led them to have deep-seated reservations about many aspects of life in the United States, prominent among them the obligation of proletarian workers to submit to the constant regulation of supervisors and the clock. In addition, the disappearance of many middle-level jobs and the attendant change in the shape of the labor market – from pyramid to hourglass – have made it increasingly difficult for people to see chances of upward mobility for themselves or, perhaps more significantly, for their children. And finally, the economy's steady downturn since the mid-1960s has markedly increased both the hostility and the legal restrictions that many of the migrants face.[16]

Influenced by these contradictory developments, Aguilillans have forged socio-spatial arrangements that seriously challenge the dominant ways of reading migration. First, it has become inadequate to see Aguilillan migration as a movement between distinct communities, understood as the loci of distinct sets of social relationships. Today, Aguilillans find that their most important kin and friends are as likely to be living hundreds or thousands of miles away as immediately around them. More significantly, they are often able to maintain these spatially extended relationships as actively and effectively as the ties that link them to their neighbors. In this regard, growing access to the telephone has been particularly significant, allowing people not just to keep in touch periodically but to contribute to decision-making and participate in familial events even from a considerable distance.

Indeed, through the continuous circulation of people, money, goods, and information, the various settlements have become so closely woven together that, in an important sense, they have come to constitute a single community spread across a variety of sites, something I refer to as a "transnational migrant circuit." Although the Aguilillan case undoubtedly has its local peculiarities, there is evidence that such arrangements are becoming increasingly important in the organization of Mexican migration to and from the United States.[17] Just as capitalists have responded to the new forms of economic internationalism by establishing transnational corporations, so workers have responded by creating transnational circuits.[18]

At the same time, as a result of these developments, it has become equally inadequate to see Aguilillan migration as a movement between distinct environments. Today, it is the circuit as a whole rather than any one locale that constitutes the principal setting in relation to which Aguilillans orchestrate their lives.[19] Those living in Aguililla, for example, are as much affected by events in Redwood City as by developments in the *municipio* itself, and the same is true in reverse. Consequently, people monitor what is happening in the other parts of the circuit as closely as they monitor what is going on immediately around them. Indeed, it is only by recognizing the transnational framework within which Aguilillans are operating that we can properly appreciate the logic of their actions. Thus, people in the United States may spend large amounts of time and money trying to obtain papers without ever seeking citizenship because it is as Mexican citizens with the right to "permanent residence" that they will be best equipped to move back and forth between the two countries. And they may send their children back to Mexico to complete their educations or to visit during school vacations at least in part because they want to endow them with the bilingual and bicultural skills necessary to operate effectively on both sides of the border.

Finally, it is mistaken to see Aguilillan experiences in terms of an inexorable move towards a new form of sociocultural order. Although transnational migration has brought distant worlds into immediate juxtaposition, their proximity has produced neither homogenization nor synthesis. Instead, Aguilillans have become involved in the chronic maintenance of two quite distinct ways of life. More importantly, the resulting contradictions have not come simply from the persistence of past forms amid contemporary adjustments or from involvement in distinct lifeworlds within the United States. Rather, they reflect the fact that Aguilillans see their current lives and future possibilities as involving simultaneous engagements in places associated with markedly different forms of experience. Moreover, the way in which at least some people are preparing their children to operate within a dichotomized setting spanning national borders suggests that current contradictions will not be resolved through a simple process of generational succession.

The different ways of life that Aguilillans balance can be understood partly by reference to spatially demarcated national or local cultures, but they should also be understood in terms of class. In numerous combinations, Aguilillans have come to link proletarian labor with a sustained attachment to the creation of small-scale, family-based operations; and even though these ways of making a living may be reconcilable economically, in cultural terms they are fundamentally distinct, involving quite different attitudes and practices concerning the use of time and space, the conduct of social relationships, and the orchestration of appearances.[20] Indeed, one of the main considerations preserving the polarized relationship between Aguililla and Redwood City has been the fact that the latter has offered Aguilillans so few opportunities to create independent operations while the former, partly through the continued influx of remittances, has remained a place in which such opportunities are still available.

Obliged to live within a transnational space and to make a living by combining quite different forms of class experience, Aguilillans have become skilled exponents of a cultural bifocality that defies reduction to a singular order. Indeed, in many respects, Aguilillans have come to inhabit a kind of border zone, especially if we follow Américo Paredes in recognizing that a border is "not simply a line on a map but, more fundamentally,... a sensitized area where two cultures or two political systems come face to face."[21] Socioeconomically, the relationship between Aguililla and Redwood City is strikingly similar to the relationship along the international border between twinned cities such as Ciudad Juárez and El Paso or Matamoros and Brownsville. They are mutually implicated in numerous ways, but the line between them never disappears. And culturally, life within the circuit corresponds closely to the situation that Gómez-Peña describes for the border linking Tijuana and San Diego: "In my fractured reality, but reality nonetheless, live two histories, languages, cosmogonies, artistic traditions, and political systems dramatically opposed – the border is the continuous confrontation of two or more referential codes."[22] For many years, the United States-Mexican border seemed like a peculiar space, a narrow strip quite different from what lay at the heart of the two countries. But this is no longer the case. Ties such as those between Aguililla and Redwood City, places two thousand miles apart, prompt us to ask how wide this border has become and how peculiar we should consider its characteristics.

4

Socio-spatial frames derived from the image of the community no longer serve to represent the local terrain that Aguilillans inhabit. It seems that images such as those of the circuit and the border zone may be more appropriate. But these claims do not apply solely to small-scale settlements. Partly as a result of the migration that Aguilillans exemplify, they are becoming increasingly relevant to social landscapes found throughout Mexico and the United States.

It is scarcely a revelation to suggest that Mexico's dependent status renders problematical any assumption of functional integration or the presence of a singular sociocultural order. However, the shift to transnational capitalism has both intensified and changed the nature of national disarticulation, particularly during the last thirty years. Foreign capital plays a more significant role in Mexico than ever before, and, more critically, thanks to the rising use of offshore plants that carry out only a part of the production process and the growing ease with which these plants can be transferred to other underdeveloped countries, the ties linking foreign capital to the rest of Mexican society are becoming progressively weaker. Moreover, as the massive flight of domestic capital during the 1980s illustrates only too well, the Mexican bourgeoisie is also orchestrating its actions increasingly within a transnational framework. At the same time, the growing institutionalization of migration to the United States through the medium of transnational circuits means that more of the Mexican population is oriented to developments outside the country and that this orientation is becoming steadily more pronounced. And finally, because of the expansion of a television system that carries numerous US programs, the mounting of satellite dishes that tune directly into US broadcasts, and the increasing exposure to US ways of life through migration, foreign cultural influences are becoming rapidly more pervasive. The black T-shirt with its English exhortation, defying any attempt to read the wake as the textual expression of a coherent local culture, is emblematic of a process pervading rural Mexico.

What is perhaps more striking is that a similar kind of disarticulation is beginning to appear in the United States, particularly in its major cities. The United States economy, long dominated by domestic capital, is now increasingly influenced by transnationally orchestrated foreign investment, especially from Britain, Canada, Germany, the Netherlands, and Japan.[23] As regards labor, although immigrant workers have been an important factor for many years, they are today arriving under circumstances that distance them much more fully from the rest of society. In particular, the declining availability of those middle-level jobs that once encouraged hope of upward mobility, the increased scapegoating and legal restrictions that have accompanied economic decline since the mid-1960s, and the related development of transnational circuits are all serving to subvert the older possibilities of assimilation to a single national order. And partly as a result, ways of life commonly identified with the Third World are becoming increasingly apparent in a country often treated as the apogee of First World advancement. Extreme poverty, residential overcrowding and homelessness, underground economies, new forms of domestic service, and sweatshops exist side by side with yuppie affluence, futuristic office blocks, and all the other accoutrements of high-tech postindustrialism.

Los Angeles is by no means typical, but the situation that had developed there by the mid-1980s offers a suggestive outline of emerging possibilities. In the downtown area, 75 percent of the buildings were owned wholly or in part by foreign capital, and as much as 90 percent of new multistory construction was being financed by investment from abroad.[24] In the larger conurbation, 40 percent of the population belonged to ethnic "minorities," many of them migrants from Asia and Latin America (estimates suggest that the figure will approach 60 percent by the year 2010).[25] And throughout the region, the growing contrasts between rich and poor and their increasingly apparent juxtaposition were prompting journalists to speculate about the "Brazilianization" of the city.[26] The hidden sweatshop in the heart of the metropolis, defying any attempt to claim a comfortable distance between Third World and First, calls attention to a trend that is gradually if unevenly affecting the whole of the country.[27]

Thus, in the United States as well as in Mexico, the *place* of the putative community – whether regional or national – is becoming little more than a *site* in which transnationally organized circuits of capital, labor, and communications intersect with one another and with local ways of life. In these circumstances, it becomes increasingly difficult to delimit a singular national identity and a continuous history, and the claims of politicians to speak authoritatively on behalf of this imagined community and its purported interests become increasingly hollow. But it is not just the image of the community which is compromised. The image of center and periphery is also coming under increasing strain. United States capital increasingly intersects with capital from other core countries not only in peripheral areas such as Mexico but also in the United States itself. The growing influence of foreign investment means that, in both countries, people must accommodate themselves to a capital that is increasingly heteroglot and culturally diverse. And the concentric distribution of differences in power, wealth, and ways of life is breaking down, in large part because the United States no longer works as effectively to transform those who enter its terrain. Alongside the more familiar tale of capitalist penetration in the periphery, we are beginning to witness what Renato Rosaldo has called "the implosion of the Third World into the first,"[28] or what Saskia Sassen-Koob calls "peripheralization at the core."

One of the results of these developments is that we are seeing a proliferation of border zones. The international border is widening and, at the same time, miniature borders are erupting throughout the two countries. In Mexico, the provisions granting special tariff dispensations to offshore production have stretched and distended the border for capital, especially now that the offshore plants, first established in the northern part of the country, are steadily moving southwards. At the same time, in the United States, the provisions regarding employer sanctions in the new immigration law have exploded the border for labor and relocated it in a multitude of fragments at the entrance to every workplace, while the recent amnesty has encouraged transnationally oriented migrants to extend their presence through-out the country. Moreover, the most readily dramatized juxtapositions of citizens and migrants are no longer confined to major urban sites such as downtown Los Angeles. They are also beginning to appear on the margins of suburbia as members of the native middle classes, scared by the real and imagined violence of these inner-city border zones, are developing residential enclaves in rural areas long inhabited by migrant farm workers.

Conditions in northern San Diego County illustrate the last of these trends in a particularly vivid way. Here, against the background of a burgeoning military-industrial economy, rapidly expanding middle-class suburbs have recently encroached on areas long filled with the ramshackle encampments of Latino migrants. In the words of the *Los Angeles Times*, the result has been a world where "squalid, plywood-and-cardboard hooches sit in the shadow of million-dollar mansions, where the BMW and Volvo sets rub elbows at the supermarket with dusty migrants fresh from the fields." Put more pithily by an academic familiar with the area, "What you have . . . is the first of the First World intermixing with the last of the Third World. It's Nicaragua versus Disneyland." Or, as one local suburban resident observed, "It's like we're living in the Third World here. It doesn't seem to me that this is part of the American Dream."[29]

But these collisions and complaints are not the only markers of a newly emerging border zone. One man in a local trailer park, offended by migrants taking water from his spigot, put barbed wire on the chain-link fence behind his trailer, installed a set of floodlights, and armed himself with a 12-gauge shotgun (see Bailey). Other residents have hunted migrants with paint-pellet guns and run them down with trucks. And, in November 1988, a local youth went one step further, shooting and killing two Latinos after confronting them near the camps. Asked to explain his actions, he said simply that he hated Mexicans (see Davidson; Mydans). This is Nicaragua versus Disneyland, then, not simply as Latino versus Anglo or Third World versus First but as the savage implosion of frontline violence within the sanitized dreamworlds of middle-class escape.

5

The forces shaping Aguilillans' lives are thus coming to affect everyone who inhabits the terrain encompassed by Mexico and the United States. Throughout this fractured territory, transnationalism, contradictions in development, and increasingly polar-ized economies are stretching images of community beyond their limits, bringing different ways of life into vivid, often violent juxtaposition, and encouraging the chronic reproduction of their incongruities. The impact of these changes clearly varies with the circumstances of the people they affect, but their reach is increasingly broad.

Under such circumstances, images such as the circuit and the border zone may help us understand not only the specificities of Aguilillan experience but social landscapes increasingly familiar to us all. If this is true, it adds weight to the idea that, in our attempts to orient ourselves amidst the complexities of postmodern hyperspace, we should look not only to art and literature but also to the lives of those "ordinary" people who inscribe their transient texts in the minutiae of daily experience. And this, in turn, suggests a pleasing irony with which to conclude, for it implies that, as in the case of Aguilillans and others like them, people long identified with an unworkable past may in fact be those from whom we have most to learn as we try to chart our way through the confusions of the present towards a future we can better understand and thus more readily transform.

NOTES

The first version of this paper was written in early 1988 while I was a visiting research fellow at the Center for US-Mexican Studies, University of California, San Diego. It draws on fieldwork carried out between 1982 and 1984 under a doctoral fellowship from the Inter-American Foundation. I am grateful to both organizations for their support. Many of the ideas contained in the paper were developed in a study group on postmodernism organized with colleagues from the center. My principal thanks – for comments, criticisms, and immensely pleasant company – go to the group's members: Josefina Alcazar, Alberto Aziz, Roger Bartra, Luin Goldring, Lidia Pico, Claudia Schatán, and Francisco Valdés. I have also benefited from Khachig Tölölyan's sensitive reading of the text.

1 See Lockwood and Leinberger, p. 35. The assertion of a false point of origin is apparently used so that the manufacturers can participate in foreign delivery contracts. See Soja, p. 217.
2 "Hoy, ocho años de mi partida, cuando me preguntan por mi nacionalidad o identidad étnica, no puedo responder con una palabra, pues mi 'identidad' ya posee repertorios múltiples: soy mexicano pero tambien soy chicano y latinoamericano. En la frontera me dicen 'chilango' o 'mexiquillo;' en la capital 'pocho' o 'norteño' y en España 'sudaca'... Mi compañera Emilia es angloitaliana pero habla español con acento argentino; y juntos caminamos entre los escombros de la torre de Babel de nuestra posmodernidad americana." Gómez-Peña (my translation used in the text).
3 See, for example, Clifford, p. 22; and Rosaldo, *Culture and Truth*, p. 217.
4 Jameson, p. 83. Like Jameson, I find it useful to follow Ernest Mandel in arguing for the emergence since the Second World War of a new phase in monopoly capitalism, but I prefer to label this phase "transnational" rather than "late" partly to avoid the implication of imminent transcendence and, more positively, to emphasize the crucial role played by the constant movement of capital, labor, and information across national borders.
5 See Davis, "Urban Renaissance"; and Lipsitz, esp. p. 161.
6 It is important to stress that I am concerned not with the various meanings of this particular term but instead with the image itself. The term serves merely as a convenient marker.
7 See Williams, pp. 65–6.
8 Williams, pp. 65–6.
9 The combination of these images is readily apparent in the classic works on rural social organization by Robert Redfield and Eric Wolf (*The Little Community and Peasant Society and Culture* and "Types of Latin American Peasantry"), both of whom draw heavily on Mexican materials, and can also be seen in Immanuel Wallerstein's tendency (in *The Capitalist World Economy*) to use nation-states as the constituent units of his world system, at least in the core.

10 This approach has been used in two related but different kinds of study. In work focusing on migration itself – especially on migration within Mexico – changes have commonly been gauged by comparing the forms of organization found in the points of destination with arrangements revealed by detailed research in the specific communities from which the migrants have come. See, for example, Butterworth; Kemper; and Lewis. In work on communities known to contain a significant number of migrants and descendants of migrants – and especially in work on Mexican and Chicano communities in the United States – it has been more common to compare forms of organization found in these communities with arrangements discovered secondhand through reading literature on the general areas or types of society from which the migrants have come. See, for example, Achor; Horowitz; Humphrey; Madsen; Rubel; and Thurston.

11 See, for example, Achor; Madsen; Rubel; Lomnitz; and Ugalde.

12 This approach has been manifest most commonly in work on migration to the United States, where the dominant tendency has been to challenge assumptions about full assimilation with analyses that stress the more or less gradual emergence of ethnic subcultures. See, for example, Achor; Horowitz; Madsen; and Rubel.

13 See, for example, Piore.

14 A more detailed account of the *municipio* and the history of its involvement in migration can be found in my "Mexican Migration." A *municipio* is a relatively small administrative unit occupying the rung immediately below the level of the state. In 1980, for example, the *municipio* of Aguililla, covering an area of roughly 630 square miles, was one of 113 such entities within the state of Michoacán. The term is difficult to gloss with any precision, however. "Municipality" is misleading because of its urban associations, while a gloss such as "county" runs the risk of suggesting something too large and too powerful. Given these difficulties, I use the term in its untranslated form.

15 For a fuller understanding of the broad processes affecting rural Mexico [since World War II] see Cockcroft; Hewitt de Alcántara.

16 For a fuller understanding of the changing character of the United States economy, particularly since the 1960s, see Sassen; and Davis, pp. 181–230.

17 Such evidence can be found most readily in a series of studies that have appeared [since the early 1980s] charting the emergence of what are generally described as "binational migrant networks." See, for example, Baca and Bryan; Kearney; Massey et al.; and Mines.

18 I use the term "transnational" in preference to "binational" partly to evoke as directly as possible the association between migrant forms of organization and transnational corporations. ("Transnational" is gradually replacing the more popular adjective "multinational," at least in academic discourse.) I also prefer it to "binational" because it allows for the possibility that a circuit might include sites in more than two countries. Specifically in the case of Aguilillans, there are indications that this may be coming about as migrants from particular places in Central America arrive in the Redwood City area and gradually attach themselves to the Aguilillan circuit. One of the advantages of such an attachment is that, if they need to leave the United States, they can go to Aguililla and call on social ties established there instead of having to make the longer, more expensive, and often more dangerous journey back to their own country. I use the term "circuit" in preference to "network" because it more effectively evokes the *circulation* of people, money, goods, and information, the pseudo-institutional nature of the arrangement (over purely individual ties), and the qualified importance of place (over purely social linkages). A fine analysis, sensitive to many of these issues, can be found in Kearney and Nagengast.

19 For an account of the ways in which places linked by migration can come to form a single "field of activity," see Roberts, esp. pp. 208–9.

20 These ideas are developed more fully in my "Mexican Migration" and "Men in Space."

21 Paredes, p. 68. See also Rosaldo, *Culture and Truth*, esp. pp. 196–217.

22 "En mi realidad fracturada, pero realidad al fin, cohabitan dos historias, lenguajes, cosmogonías, tradiciones artisticas y sistemas políticos drásticamente opuestos (la frontera es el enfrentamiento continuo de dos o más códigos referenciales)." Gómez-Peña, p. 3 (my translation used in the text). I do not mean to suggest by quoting Gómez-Peña that he and Aguilillans experience their particular border zones in exactly the same way. Clearly, people's experiences vary significantly according to their positions in local frameworks of power and as a function of the routes they have followed in reaching such positions.

23 See Sassen, esp. pp. 171–85.

24 Davis, "*Chinatown*, Part Two?," pp. 71–2; and Soja, p. 221.

25 Lockwood and Leinberger, p. 41. According to Soja (p. 215), more than two million Third World migrants settled in the Los Angeles area between the mid-1960s and the mid-1980s.

26 See Richman and Schwarz (quoted in Davis, "*Chinatown*, Part Two?," p. 77).

27 For a fuller picture of the changing political economy of Los Angeles, see Davis, "Urban Renaissance" and "*Chinatown*, Part Two?"; Sassen, pp. 126–70; and Soja, pp. 190–248. For reflections on these trends in other parts of the United States, see Franco; and Koptiuch.

28 Rosaldo, "Ideology," p. 85.

29 All three quotations come from Bailey and Reza.

REFERENCES

Achor, Shirley, *Mexican Americans in a Dallas Barrio*. Tucson: University of Arizona Press, 1978.

Baca, Reynaldo, and Dexter Bryan. "The 'Assimilation' of Unauthorized Mexican Workers: Another Social Science Fiction." *Hispanic Journal of Behavioral Sciences* 5 (1983): 1–20.

Bailey, Eric. "Tempers Flare Over Illegals in S.D. County." *Los Angeles Times*, 6 June 1988, San Diego County edn., p. 1.

Bailey, Eric, and H. G. Reza. "Illegals, Homeless Clash in S.D. County." *Los Angeles Times*, 5 June 1988, San Diego County edn., p. 36.

Butterworth, Douglas S. "A Study of the Urbanization Process Among Mixtec Migrants from Tilaltongo in Mexico City." *América Indígena* 22 (1962): 257–74.

Clifford, James, "Introduction: Partial Truths." In *Writing Culture: The Poetics and Politics of Ethnography*. Ed. Clifford and George E. Marcus. pp. 1–26. Berkeley: University of California Press, 1986.

Cockcroft, James. *Mexico: Class Formation, Capital Accumulation, and the State*. New York: Grove, 1983.

Davidson, Miriam. "Immigrant Bashing: The Mexican Border War." *The Nation* 12 (November 1990): 557–60.

Davis, Mike. "Urban Renaissance and the Spirit of Postmodernism." *New Left Review* 151 (1985): 106–13.

——. *Prisoners of the American Dream: Politics and Economy in the History of the U.S. Working Class*. London: Verso, 1986.

——. "*Chinatown*, Part Two? The 'Internationalization' of Downtown Los Angeles." *New Left Review* 164 (1987): 65–86.

Franco, Jean. "New York is a Third World City: Introduction." *Tabloid* 9 (1985): 12–13.

Gómez-Peña, Guillermo, "Wacha esa border, son." *La Jornada Semanal* (Mexico City) 25 October 1987, pp. 3–5.

Hewitt de Alcántara, Cynthia. *Modernizing Mexican Agriculture: Socioeconomic Implications of Technological Change, 1940–1970.* Geneva: UN Research Institute for Social Development, 1976.

Horowitz, Ruth. *Honor and the American Dream: Culture and Identity in a Chicano Community.* New Brunswick, NJ: Rutgers University Press, 1983.

Humphrey, Norman D. "The Changing Structure of the Detroit Mexican Family: An Index of Acculturation." *American Sociological Review* 9 (1944): 622–6.

Jameson, Fredric. "Postmodernism, or the Cultural Logic of Late Capitalism." *New Left Review* 146 (1984): 53–92.

Kearney, Michael. "From the Invisible Hand to Visible Feet: Anthropological Studies of Migration and Development." *Annual Review of Anthropology* 15 (1986): 331–61.

Kearney, Michael, and Carole Nagengast. *Anthropological Perspectives on Transnational Communities in Rural California.* Working Paper 3, Working Group on Farm Labor and Rural Poverty. Davis, CA: California Institute for Rural Studies, 1989.

Kemper, Robert V. *Migration and Adaptation: Tzintzuntzan Peasants in Mexico City.* Beverly Hills: Sage Publications, 1977.

Koptiuch, Kristin. "Third Worlding at Home." MS, 1989. Dept. of Anthropology, University of Texas, Austin.

Lewis, Oscar. "Urbanization Without Breakdown: A Case Study." *Scientific Monthly* 75 (1952): 31–41.

Lipsitz, George. "Cruising around the Hispanic Bloc: Postmodernism and Popular Music in Los Angeles." *Cultural Critique* 5 (1986–7): 157–77.

Lockwood, Charles, and Christopher B. Leinberger. "Los Angeles Comes of Age." *Atlantic Monthly* 261 (1988): 31–56.

Lomnitz, Larissa A. *Networks and Marginality: Life in a Mexican Shantytown.* Trans. Cinna Lomnitz. New York: Academic, 1977.

Madsen, William. *Mexican Americans of South Texas.* New York: Holt, 1964.

Massey, Douglas S., et al. *Return to Aztlán: The Social Process of International Migration from Western Mexico.* Berkeley: University of California Press, 1987.

Mines, Richard. *Developing a Community Tradition of Migration: A Field Study in Rural Zacatecas, Mexico, and in California Settlement Areas.* La Jolla, CA: Program in US–Mexican Studies, 1981.

Mydans, Seth. "Clash of Cultures Grows Amid American Dream." *New York Times,* 26 March 1990, A8.

Paredes, Américo. "The Problem of Identity in a Changing Culture: Popular Expressions of Culture Conflict along the Lower Río Grande Border." In *Views Across the Border: The United States and Mexico.* Ed. Stanley R. Ross. Pp. 68–94. Albuquerque: University of New Mexico Press, 1978.

Piore, Michael J. *Birds of Passage.* Cambridge: Cambridge University Press, 1979.

Redfield, Robert. *The Little Community and Peasant Society and Culture.* Chicago: University of Chicago Press, 1966.

Richman, Neal, and Ruth Schwarz. "Housing Homeless Families: Why L.A. Lags Behind." *Los Angeles Times,* 24 May 1987: Ed. sec., 1+.

Roberts, Bryan. "The Interrelationships of City and Provinces in Peru and Guatemala." *Latin American Urban Research* 4 (1974): 207–35.

Rosaldo, Renato. "Ideology, Place, and People Without Culture." *Cultural Anthropology* 3: 1 (1988): 77–87.

——. *Culture and Truth: The Remaking of Social Analysis.* Boston: Beacon, 1989.

Rouse, Roger. "Men in Space: Power and the Appropriation of Urban Form Among Mexican Migrants in the United States." MS, 1989. Dept. of Anthropology, University of Michigan, Ann Arbor.

——. "Mexican Migration to the United States: Family Relations in the Development of a Transnational Migrant Circuit." Dissertation, Stanford University, 1989.

Rubel, Arthur J. *Across the Tracks: Mexican-Americans in a Texas City.* Austin: University of Texas Press. 1966.

Sassen, Saskia. *The Mobility of Labor and Capital: A Study in International Investment and Labor Flow.* Cambridge: Cambridge University Press, 1988.

Sassen-Koob, Saskia. "Recomposition and Peripheralization at the Core." *Contemporary Marxism* 5 (Summer 1982): 88–100.

Soja, Edward W. *Postmodern Geographies: The Reassertion of Space in Critical Social Theory.* London: Verso, 1989.

Thurston, Richard G. *Urbanization and Sociocultural Change in a Mexican-American Enclave.* San Francisco: R. & E. Research Associates, 1974.

Ugalde, Antonio. *The Urbanization Process of a Poor Mexican Neighborhood.* Austin: Institute of Latin American Studies, University of Texas, 1974.

Wallerstein, Immanuel. *The Capitalist World Economy.* Cambridge: Cambridge University Press, 1979.

Williams, Raymond. *Keywords.* London: Fontana/Croom Helm, 1976.

Wolf, Eric. "Types of Latin American Peasantry: A Preliminary Discussion." *American Anthropologist* 57 (1955): 452–71.

8

The Pacific Shuttle: Family, Citizenship, and Capital Circuits

Aihwa Ong

Destabilizing Chineseness

During a recent late summer in the Ukraine, an angry mob dragging down a statue of Lenin reenacted the political collapse of the Soviet Union, while vendors selling Bolshevik trinkets reinvented the economy. David Chang, representing the Asia Bank in New York, was in town to snap up apartment houses and real estate before the dust settled. "Governments come and go," he said, "but business stays."[1]

In California, "the Silicon Valley way of divorce" among new Chinese immigrants has led to one failed marriage out of five. One "typical" Chinese couple – he is an engineer; she, an accountant – used to live in a half-million-dollar house with two well-schooled children. They invested in a second home and vacationed in Lake Tahoe. When the wife asked for a divorce, it was not because her husband had an affair, or at least not with another woman. "My husband works on his computer in the office during the day, comes home at 8 p.m., and continues to sit in front of his computer after dinner.... I am a 'computer widow' who is never asked how she is doing, nor what has happened to the family lately."[2]

In both of the above two stories, postmodern elements jostle for attention. These elements include *displacement* (Asians in western worlds), *fragmentation* (families broken up by emigration and divorce), *difference* (male and female subjectivities), and *impermanence* (in everyday arrangements). Were these reports about people other than Chinese, they would attract no more than a passing glance. But to me, such postmodern snapshots are a jarring reproach to academic descriptions of Chinese identity, family, and cultural practices.

From *Flexible Citizenship: The Cultural Logics of Transnationality*, pp. 110–36. Durham, NC: Duke University Press. Copyright © 1999, Duke University Press.

Much scholarship on Chinese subjects has been shaped by the orientalist concern with presenting the other as a timeless, unchanging culture. Recent attempts to revise the static image of Chineseness nevertheless still confine the analysis of ways of "being Chinese" within the clearly defined Chinese contexts of the nation-state and culture.[3] An essentializing notion of Chineseness continues to dog the scholarship because the Chinese past, nation, singular history, or some "cultural core" is taken to be the main and unchanging determinant of Chinese identity. Sometimes we forget that we are talking about one-quarter of the world's population. What is conveyed is the sense that people identifiable as "Chinese" exist in their own world, and even when they participate in global processes, they continue to remain culturally distinct. I suspect that the grand orientalist legacy continues to lurk in a field, dominated by historians, that is convinced of the singularity of this great inscrutable other. Younger scholars and feminists who seek to provide more complex, historically and geopolitically contingent accounts of Chinese cultural practices are often merely tolerated, if they are not marginalized for threatening to disrupt the stable tropes of high sinology. Perhaps not so ironically, as I have mentioned above, ambitious Asian politicians have made much political capital by borrowing academic representations of Chineseness for their own self-orientalizing projects.[4] Grand orientalist statements are dialectically linked to the petty orientalisms generated by transnational corporate and advertising media, which make pronouncements about oriental labor, skills, values, families, and mystery. The slogan for Singapore Airlines is "Singapore Girl, what a great way to fly."

But stories about capital, displacements, and hybridity explode the reigning notions about being Chinese. How do discrepant images reflect the changing social, economic, and political relations in which Chinese subjects are important participants? Today, overseas Chinese are key players in the booming economies of the Asia Pacific region. In what ways have their border-crossing activities and mobility within the circuits of global capitalism altered their cultural values and class strategies? This chapter explores how the flexible positioning of diasporan-Chinese subjects on the edge of political and capitalist empires affects their family relations, their self-representation, and the ways in which they negotiate the political and cultural rules of different countries on their itineraries. In contrast to Edward Said's depiction of the objects of orientalism as silent participants in western hegemonic projects,[5] I trace the agency of Asian subjects as they selectively engage orientalist discourses encountered on travels through the shifting cultural terrains of the global economy. Yet their countercultural production should not be interpreted as a simple reproduction of "the ways we are situated by the West" but as complex maneuvers that subvert reigning notions of the national self and the other in transnational arenas.

Perhaps more than other travelers and migrants, international managers and professionals have the material and symbolic resources to manipulate global schemes of cultural difference, racial hierarchy, and citizenship to their own advantage. Today, flexibility reigns in business, industry, labor, and the financial markets; all incorporate technologically enhanced innovations that affect the way people are differently imagined and regulated and the way they represent and conduct themselves transnationally.[6] But whereas international managers and professionals may be adept at strategies of economic accumulation and maneuvering, they do not operate in free-flowing circumstances but in environments that are controlled and shaped by nation-states and capital markets.

For instance, the form and meaning of citizenship have been transformed by global markets and floods of skilled and unskilled workers crossing borders. Although citizenship is conventionally thought of as based on political rights and participation within a sovereign state, globalization has made economic calculation a major element in diasporan subjects' choice of citizenship, as well as in the ways nation-states redefine immigration laws. I use the term *flexible citizenship* to refer especially to the strategies and effects of mobile managers, technocrats, and professionals seeking to both circumvent *and* benefit from different nation-state regimes by selecting different sites for investments, work, and family relocation. Such repositioning in relation to global markets, however, should not lead one to assume that the nation-state is losing control of its borders.[7] State regimes are constantly adjusting to the influx of different kinds of immigrants and to ways of engaging global capitalism that will benefit the country while minimizing the costs. For instance, nation-states constantly refine immigration laws to attract capital-bearing subjects while limiting the entry of unskilled laborers. From the perspective of immigrants such as well-heeled Hong Kongers, however, citizenship becomes an issue of handling the diverse rules, or "governmentality," of host societies where they may be economically correct in terms of human capital, but culturally incorrect in terms of ethnicity.[8]

To understand the tactical practices of this diasporan managerial class, we must locate them within and one step ahead of the various regimes of truth and power to which they, as traveling persons, are subject. Michel Foucault uses *regime* to refer to power/knowledge schemes that seek to normalize power relations.[9] By appealing to particular "truths" that have been developed about science, culture, and social life, these systems of power/knowledge define and regulate subjects and normalize their attitudes and behavior. The regimes that will be considered here are the regime of Chinese kinship and family, the regime of the nation-state, and the regime of the marketplace – all of which provide the institutional contexts and the webs of power within which Chinese subjects (re)locate and (re)align themselves as they traverse global space.

As Donald M. Nonini has argued, each kind of regime requires "the localization of disciplinary subjects," that is, it requires that persons be locatable and confinable to specific spaces and relations defined by the various regimes: the kinship network, the "nation," the marketplace.[10] In this sense, "flexible citizenship" also denotes the localizing strategies of subjects who, through a variety of familial and economic practices, seek to evade, deflect, and take advantage of political and economic conditions in different parts of the world. Thus, we cannot analytically delink the operations of family regimes from the regulations of the state and of capital. One can say, for example, that Chinese family discipline is in part shaped by the regulation of the state and by the rules of the global marketplace, but the convergence of Chinese family forms with flexible strategies of capital accumulation enables them to bypass or exploit citizenship rules – whatever the case may be – as they relocate capital and/or family members overseas. So while I talk about flexible citizenship, I am also talking about the different modalities of governmentality – as practiced by the nation-state, by the family, by capital – that intersect and have effects on each other, variously encoding and constraining flexibility in global (re)positioning. By analyzing different modalities of flexibility *and* governmentality under conditions of globalization, I identify contemporary forms that shape culture making and its products. First, how does the regime of diasporan Chinese kinship structure, deploy, and limit flexible practices?

Middling Modernity: Guanxi and Family Regimes in Diaspora

One form of elite-Chinese sensibility developed in the context of the late nineteenth century, when interregional commerce flourished under European colonialism in East and Southeast Asia. The entry of Chinese into mercantile capitalism ruptured the traditional links of filiation among Chinese subjects, Chinese families, and the Chinese social order. In nineteenth-century China, the Confucian concept of filial piety (*xiao*) governed the relations of superior and subordinate (father/son, husband/ wife, older/younger brothers). Because the family was considered a microcosm of the moral order, filial piety also figured in the relations of citizens to rulers.[11] But in nationalist discourse, elites striving to imagine a modern Chinese nation found that patriotism had little appeal in a climate of "semicolonialism," Japanese invasion, general lawlessness, and economic and social upheaval.[12] Republican China's founder, Sun Yat-sen, bemoaned the difficulty of extending loyalty to family into a loyalty to the new nation; he sadly compared the Chinese people to "a sheet of loose sand." European imperial domination and political humiliation did incite early modern anti-imperialist, antipatriarchal movements, especially among university students in Beijing. But among the commercial classes in the treaty ports, filial piety in the Confucian sense was narrowly focused on familial well-being and family interests, as well as on family firms outside China. Filial piety thereby became the substance for shaping other ways of being Chinese in the world.

A diasporan-Chinese modernity – in the "middling" sense of pragmatic everyday practices[13] – developed among emigrant Chinese in the colonial worlds of East and Southeast Asia. In city ports and colonial enclaves, Chinese subjects facing political mistreatment and intense competition for survival evolved an instrumentality in norms concerning labor organization, family practice, links between family and the wider economy, and dealings with political authorities.[14] London-trained anthropologist Fei Hsiao-tung was highly critical of the loss of Confucian ethics among this merchant class:

To such ports a special type of Chinese was attracted. They are known as compradors....They are half-cast in culture, bilingual in speech, morally unstable....Treaty ports... are a land where the acquisition of wealth is the sole motive, devoid of tradition and culture.

[Nevertheless] they occupy a strategic position in China's transition.... As their children grow up, they give them modern education and send them abroad to attend Western universities. From this group a new class is formed....But being reared in a cosmopolitan community, they are fundamentally hybrids. In them are manifest the comprador characteristic of social irresponsibility.[15]

The Chinese comprador class became notorious for the systematic ways its members amassed personal power and wealth at the expense of the new republic. By forming profitable links overseas, merchant and industrial families repositioned themselves as subjects of global trade rather than as loyal subjects of the Chinese motherland. Political and economic instabilities, and a weakly developed patriotism, encouraged merchant families to develop links to overseas colonial empires. This turning away from Confucian social ethics toward a family-centered notion of Confucianism found its greatest expression among overseas-Chinese communities that developed under western capitalism in Southeast Asia.

Modern Chinese transnationalism thus has roots in these historical circumstances of diaspora and European colonial capitalism; in the postcolonial era, Chinese family enterprises became fully integrated with the larger global economy. Chinese traders recruited labor gangs, organized construction and mining crews, built merchant houses, and also ran brothels, gambling houses, and opium dens – all activities that transgressed the localizing regimes of colonial powers – while at the same time, they became more firmly integrated within the colonial economies.[16] Their regional networks for labor and capital accumulation enabled Chinese traders to be the "wild men" who continually challenged political regimes and eluded their regulation.[17] As nationalism in China became channeled into party politics, many Chinese sojourners did express their patriotism by contributing funds to the leaders of the struggling republic. But in the colonies, paternal bonds and interpersonal relations structured networks for interregional trade and provided the institutional basis for a sense of a larger, diffused, "imagined" community of *huaqiao* [overseas Chinese].[18]

In the postcolonial era, most Southeast Asian states have remained suspicious of the political loyalty of their Chinese citizens, partly because of those citizens' economic domination and extensive overseas connections. Only Singapore and Taiwan, both of which possess a Chinese majority, have used Confucian education to inculcate state loyalty, which they maintain is analogous to filial piety. But in most countries, especially in Islam-dominated Malaysia and Indonesia, the discourse of nationalism draws on colonial models of race-based and multiethnic nationhood.[19] Thus, the cultural politics of being Chinese varies in different countries, but for many overseas Chinese, there is no obvious continuity between family interests and political loyalty (especially since most overseas Chinese have experienced anti-Chinese discrimination in their host countries). Outside of Taiwan and Singapore, there is a disengagement between Chinese cultural interests and national belonging in host countries identified with dominant ethnicities such as Vietnamese or Malay. For instance, in Malaysia, lower-class Chinese subjects often seek to evade the localizing mechanisms of the state that stigmatize them as "more Chinese" (i.e., less assimilated than upper-class Chinese) and hence subject to regulation as second-class citizens. This diffused sense of being diasporan Chinese has also been shaped by their flexible, mobile relations across political borders and by the kinship regime of truth and control.

Launching family businesses on the edge of empires, Chinese subjects depend on a careful cultivation of *guanxi* [interpersonal relations] and instrumentalist family practices. These habits, attitudes, and norms are not a simple continuation or legacy of some essentialized bundle of "traditional" Chinese traits. *Guanxi* networks in Southeast Asia are historically contingent; they are a kind of (post)colonial habitus, that is, they are the dispositions and practices that emphasize pragmatism, interpersonal dependence, bodily discipline, gender and age hierarchies, and other ethnic-specific modes of social production and reproduction in diaspora and under foreign rule.[20] Such overseas-Chinese habitus have ensured that the emigrant family has survived for generations while evading the discipline of the colonial (and later, the postcolonial) states, with their special regimes of othering Chineseness.

Produced and shaped under such conditions, the familial regimes of diasporan Chinese based on *guanxi* are not without their own violence and exploitation of workers, family members, kinsmen, and so on. In the early days of colonial capitalism, *guanxi* networks deployed Chinese emigrants in the "pig trade" (supplying coolies to labor camps throughout Asia), thus subjecting many to brutal control, lifelong indebtedness, poverty, and crime while enriching their patrons.[21] *Guanxi*, as a historically evolved regime of kinship and ethnic power, controls and often traps women and the poor while benefiting fraternal business associations and facilitating the accumulation of wealth for Chinese families in diaspora.

In everyday life, however, there is widespread misrecognition of *guanxi*'s violence, while its humanism is widely extolled by ordinary folk, businessmen, and cultural chauvinists alike. Such symbolic violence[22] – the erasure of collective complicity over relations of domination and exploitation – is also present in academic writings that unduly celebrate *guanxi* as the basis of the recent affluence of overseas Chinese.[23] Misrecognition of business *guanxi* as basically a structure of limits and inequality for the many and of flexibility and mobility for the few is part of the ritual euphemization of "Chinese values," especially among transnational Chinese and their spokesmen.[24]

Indeed, *guanxi* regimes and networks have proliferated within the institution of the subcontracting industry, the paradigmatic form of flexible industrialization throughout the Asia Pacific region. Many Chinese firms enter light manufacturing by subcontracting for global companies, producing consumer items such as jewelry, garments, and toys in "living-room factories."[25] In recent years, *guanxi* networks have been the channel for subcontracting arrangements between overseas-Chinese capital and enterprises in mainland China. A Sino-Thai tycoon, who is the largest investor in China, invokes *guanxi* to explain the growth of his conglomerate on the mainland. He compares his own business style to what he sees as the inflexibility of western firms: "American and European companies have adapted themselves to a very sophisticated legal-based society.... In China there is no law. There is no system. It is a government by individuals, by people."[26] Thus, the *guanxi* institution, as invoked and practiced, is a mix of instrumentalism (fostering flexibility and the mobility of capital and personnel across political borders) and humanism ("helping out" relatives and hometown folk on the mainland). Although *guanxi* connections may be mixed with patriotic sentiment, overseas-Chinese investors are also moved by opportunities for mobilizing cheap labor in China's vast capitalist frontier.[27] It is probably not possible to disentangle nostalgic sentiment toward the homeland from the irresistible pull of flexible accumulation, but the logic of *guanxi* points to sending capital to China while shipping the family overseas.

It may sound contradictory, but flexible citizenship is a result of familial strategies of regulation. Michel Foucault suggests that we think of modern power, in its "government" of population and the welfare of that population (biopolitics), as productive of relations, rituals, and truths.[28] I consider the rational, normative practices that regulate healthy, productive, and successful bodies within the family and their deployment in economic activities for economic well-being as family governmentality. The biopolitics of families, however, are always conditioned by wider political-economic circumstances.

The rise of Hong Kong as a global manufacturing center was secured after British colonial rule put down and domesticated trade unions and student activists during the 1960s, a state strategy that was common throughout Asia.[29] In subsequent decades, refugee families from all classes adapted through hard work, fierce competitiveness, and tight control over the family to improve overall family livelihood and wealth. Hong Kong social scientists use the term "utilitarian familialism" to describe the everyday norms and practices whereby Hong Kong families place family interests above all other individual and social concerns. One scholar observes that economic interdependency is the basic structuring principle – expressed as "all in the family" – a principle that mobilizes the immediate family and relatives in common interests.[30] An individual's sense of moral worth is based on endurance and diligence in income-making activities, compliance with parental wishes, and the making of sacrifices and the deferral of gratification, especially on the part of women and children. In her study of factory women, Janet Salaff found that daughters are instilled with a sense of debt to their parents, which they "repay" by shortening their schooling and earning wages that often go toward their brothers' higher education.[31] These writers seem to identify these family practices as something inherent in "Chinese culture"; they ignore the effects of state discipline and a highly competitive marketplace on refugee families. Such family regimes among the working classes have been responsible for the phenomenal growth of Hong Kong into a manufacturing giant. Among the upwardly mobile, biopolitical considerations inform family discipline in production and consumption. Besides acquiring the habitus of continual striving, children, especially sons, are expected to collect symbolic capital in the form of educational certificates and well-paying jobs that help raise the family class position and prestige. In imperial and republican China, the accumulation of degrees was an established way to rise from peasant to mandarin status or a way for merchants to rise socially in the eyes of officials.[32] In Hong Kong, the entrepreneur's rise to the highest status is determined solely by his wealth, regardless of how it has been accumulated, although he too may take on the trappings of mandarin learning.[33]

Familial regimes that regulate the roles of sons and daughters for the family well-being can also become discontinuous with or subvert the biopolitical agenda of the state. The British government's laissez-faire policy encouraged the population to pursue wealth with "flexibility and vigor" and, until the eve of the return of Hong Kong to Chinese rule, to express political freedom as a market phenomenon. This market-driven sense of citizenship was until recently viewed not as the right to demand full democratic representation but as the right to promote familial interests apart from the well-being of society.[34] Middling modernity thus places a premium on material goods and on an instrumental approach to social life, as indexed by the ownership of Mercedes-Benzes and market shares. There is a joke that professors spend more time playing the stock market than teaching. Risk taking and flexibility in the entrepreneurial sense induce an attenuated sense of citizenship. A young, single civil servant posted to San Francisco confided to me, "I don't think I need to associate myself with a particular country. I would rather not confine myself to a nationality defined by China or by the UK. I am a Hong Kong person. I grew up there, my family and friends are there, it's where I belong.... [But] I lack a sense of political belonging due to the British colonial system. But we have thrived on the system – in terms of the quality of life...roughly fair competition...in terms of moving up through the educational system...even though Hong Kong is not a democracy."[35] This person planned to get a British passport and try his luck wherever he could practice his talents. Like many savvy Hong Kongers, he was outwardly mobile, aligned more toward world market conditions than toward the moral meaning of citizenship in a particular nation. Such middling, disaffected modernism has been shaped within the politics of colonialism and the nation-states over a refugee and diasporan population, and yet these strategies are adept at subverting the political regimes of localization and control.

English Weather: National Character and Biopolitics

Since the 1960s, ethnic Chinese from Hong Kong and Southeast Asia have sought residential rights in western countries to escape political discrimination and anticipated upheavals that could disrupt business and threaten family security. But with the rising affluence of Asian countries and the relative decline of western economies, they may find that economic opportunities and political refuge are not both available in the same place – or even in the same region of the world. With the return of Hong Kong to mainland-Chinese rule, many Chinese professionals would like to continue working in Hong Kong and China but have parked their families in safe havens in Australia, Canada, the United States, and Great Britain. Many, however, have found that their search for overseas citizenship is constrained by the immigration policies of western countries that are equivocating over capital and ethnicity.

The contours of citizenship are represented by the passport – the regulatory instrument of residence, travel, and belonging. Citizenship requirements are the consequence of Foucauldian "biopolitics," in which the state regulates the conduct of subjects as a population (by age, ethnicity, occupation, and so on) and as individuals (sexual and reproductive behavior) so as to ensure security and prosperity for the nation as a whole. Under liberal democracy, biopolitical regulation (governmentality) helps construct and ensure the needs of the marketplace through a policy of acting and not acting on society.[36] For instance, in Hong Kong, the British liberal government has always alternated between government action and necessary inaction in the commercial realm to maintain the wide-open capitalist economy. The question of Hong Kong Chinese emigration to Great Britain, then, must be considered within the dialectics between liberal governmentality and transnational capitalism.

As the residents of a remnant of the British empire, Hong Kongers were designated British Dependent Territory Citizens (BDTC), with limitless rights of travel but no right to reside in Great Britain. After the reimposition of mainland-Chinese rule, these same residents came to be called British Nationals (Overseas) (BNO), with their conditions of domicile and travel unchanged. Hong Kong Chinese are thus normalized as an overseas population that is in, but not of, the empire; their partial citizenship rests on differences of territoriality, coloniality, and (unmentioned) British origins.

British immigration policy is on the threshold of structurally determining the relationship between class and race so that phenotypical variations in skin color can be transformed into social stratifications based on the assumed capital and labor potential of different groups of immigrants. Postwar immigration laws institutionalized racial difference through the progressive exclusion of "colored" immigrants from the Commonwealth.[37] In the early 1960s, under public pressure to restrict colored immigrants (who were said to overwhelm housing and state benefits), the Conservative government withdrew the right of colored UK passport holders to enter Britain. A few years later, the same government granted the right of entry and settlement to several million "white" people from South Africa. This action was defended by a government white paper that maintained that expanded Commonwealth immigration creates social tensions; the immigrant presence had to be resolved if "the evil of racial strife" was to be avoided.[38] Although the language of immigration law was not explicitly racist, the distinction between whites and coloreds from the Commonwealth and their assumed differential contribution to racial tension (*race* was frequently used to refer only to coloreds, not to whites) clearly reproduced a class hierarchy whereby race was given concrete institutional expression.

In this transnational discursive formation of race, Chinese from Hong Kong were coloreds, yet they were clearly differentiated from Afro-Caribbean immigrants because of their significant role in overseas capitalism and their perceived docility under British rule in Hong Kong. In the 1960s, the restriction on immigration from the Commonwealth countries limited Hong Kong arrivals mainly to restaurant operators and employees.[39] In addition, thousands of students were sent by their parents for higher education in Britain. By the 1980s, fear of Hong Kong's imminent reversion to Chinese rule and the potential threat to the Hong Kong economy generated steady emigration, mainly to western countries. Soon the monthly outflow of Hong Kongers reached one thousand; this jeopardized confidence in the Hong Kong financial market, which British interests were heavily invested in. The colonial government saw the problem as one of "brain drain" and fought to stem the outflow by appealing to orientalist reason. An official commented that "the [Chinese] have an overwhelming pragmatic concern for family and personal development – the same pragmatic self-interest that has made the Hong Kong economy so successful."[40]

In England, immigration policy was modified in 1990 to grant British citizenship to some Hong Kong subjects, mainly as a gesture to stem the outflow from Hong Kong and stabilize faith in the Hong Kong economy. Again, biopolitical criteria that served market interests determined who was awarded citizenship. A nationality bill granted full citizenship or "the right of abode" to only fifty thousand elite Hong Kongers and their families (about a quarter-million out of a total Hong Kong population of almost six million). The members of this special subcategory of Chinese were carefully chosen from among householders (presumably predominantly male) who had connections in British government, business, or some other organization. A point system for different occupations, such as accountancy and law, discriminated among the applicants, who had to have a high educational standing and had presumably to speak fluent English. They were mainly in the age bracket of thirty to forty. Thus, these individuals were selected for their capacity to be normalized as British citizens and their ability to participate in the generation of transnational capital.

British immigration law thus produced a new discourse on overseas Chinese, who were eligible for citizenship only as *homo economicus*. Although the British Labour Party criticized the bill's "elitist" emphasis on the immigrants' educational and professional backgrounds, it did not address the larger subject of how interest in transnational capital colors the perception of race. Although still not fully implemented, the new nationality law constructs a different legal subjectivity of citizenship – as less than *homo economicus* – for Chinese already in the country.

Homi Bhabha has noted that English weather invokes the "most changeable and immanent signs of national character" and is implicitly contrasted to its "daemonic double": the hot, tropical landscapes of the former colonies. English weather represents an imagined national community under threat of "the return of the diasporic, the postcolonial."[41] Prime Minister Margaret Thatcher, anxious to quiet a restive public over the admission of more coloreds into the "bless'd isle," defended her bill in Parliament by wondering why the Chinese would trade sunny Hong Kong for Great Britain, "a cold and cloudy island." She reminded the British that the nationality bill was intended as an "insurance policy" to keep would-be Chinese citizens in Hong Kong up to and beyond 1997. In other words, full British citizenship for even those Chinese meeting the biopolitical criteria was citizenship indefinitely deferred; the nationality law operated as insurance against their ever becoming full British citizens. It was clear that a cold welcome awaited them.

China Recalls Prodigal Sons

Even before the "tidal wave" of emigration following the Tiananmen crack-down in 1989, China tried to stem the exodus of capital and professionals from Hong Kong. Through its mouthpiece, the Xinhua News Agency, the People's Republic repeatedly appealed to all Hong Kongers who had gone abroad to reconsider their decision, to "come back, to work for the prosperity of the land of [their] birth."[42] An official blamed the flight of Hong Kong Chinese on the instrumental ethos bred under western influence. He charged that Chinese residents had been led astray by capitalist countries offering investment opportunities to attract Hong Kong skilled labor and capital.[43] China viewed the British nationality law as a insult to Chinese sovereignty and a shameless attempt by Britain to cream off Hong Kong's talent. It threatened expulsion of those who possessed British citizenship after 1997.[44]

Generally, China took a paternalistic tone with errant Chinese capitalists, who it promised would be "forgiven" for seeking foreign citizenship; "prodigal sons" who returned were favorably contrasted with the "traitors" who had abandoned capitalism in China altogether. While China appealed to filial piety and held out promises of capitalist opportunities, thereby hoping to retain Hong Kong subjects, Britain held out promises of citizenship and democratic rights, thereby hoping to ensure a place for British interests in the Pacific Rim economies.

Many Hong Kongers opted to work in China while seeking citizenship elsewhere. Caught between British disciplinary racism and China's opportunistic claims of racial loyalty, between declining economic power in Britain and surging capitalism in Asia, they sought a flexible position among the myriad possibilities (and problems) found in the global economy. Flexible capital accumulation is dialectically linked to the search for flexible citizenship as a way to escape the regime of state control, either over capital or over citizens. In Hong Kong, a small industry arose to disseminate information about the legal requirements and economic incentives for acquiring citizenship abroad. Just as Hong Kong-registered companies sought tax havens in places such as Bermuda, well-off families accumulated passports not only from Canada, Australia, Singapore, and the United States but also from revenue-poor Fiji, the Philippines, Panama, and Tonga (which required in return for a passport a down payment of US $200,000 and an equal amount in installments).[45] The Hong Kong authorities uncovered a business scam that offered, for a sum of US $5,000, citizenship in a fictitious Pacific island country called Corterra. Wealthier travelers sought out actual remote islands, safe havens that issued passports with little commitment in return. Kenny Bao of the hotel family chain confided in me that his brother was a friend of the king of Tonga, who gave him citizenship in return for a major investment. A political refuge secured, his brother continued to operate the family's multinational hotel business out of their Hong Kong headquarters, managing properties in Britain and China but having citizenship in neither. Thus, Hong Kong Chinese, for whom the meanings of motherland, country, and family had long been discontinuous and even contradictory, sought legal citizenship not necessarily in the sites where they conducted their business but in places where their families could pursue their dreams. Among the elite and the not-so-elite, this meant a politically stable and secure environment where a world-class education could be found for the children and real estate was available for homesick housewives to speculate in.

Plotting Family Itineraries

Big-business families provide the clearest examples of a careful blending of discipline in familial practice and flexibility in business and citizenship. Li Kashing and the late Sir Y. K. Pao, both of whom rose from refugee poverty to immense wealth, are considered perhaps the most brilliant examples of entrepreneurial border running in the Chinese diaspora. Many tycoon families emerged in the 1960s, when businessmen amassed fortunes in real estate just as Hong Kong's manufacturing industries helped make the colony a household word for inexpensive consumer products.[46] In interviews with the sons of some of these wealthy families, I found the familial regime of control to be very firm, even as the family businesses were taking off overseas. Fame and business-power relations are inseparable, and the company founding father is a patriarch who regulates the activities of sons who must be trained and groomed to eventually take over the family business. Filial piety is instilled through the force of family wealth. From the top floor of his San Francisco high-rise, Alex Leong, a mild-mannered middle-aged investor, told me, "I remember, even when I was in junior high [in Hong Kong], my objective was to follow my father's footsteps and be in business . . . to take over the family business rather than to try to work for someone else or to do my own thing. Because I think it is very important for sons to carry on the family business, something that has been built up by your father. To me, that's the number one obligation. . . . If your family has a business, why would you go work for somebody else and leave a hired man to look after your family business? To me, that doesn't make any sense."[47]

Alex comes from a prominent family that traces its lineage back to a grand uncle who was once the governor of Guangdong Province. Alex's father went to school in Germany, but after the communist victory in 1949, he took his family to Australia. His father then explored business opportunities in Brazil, where the family lived for a few years. They finally returned to Hong Kong, where his father went into the real estate business and set up a firm called Universal Enterprises. Filial piety dictated that Alex and his brothers take on the roles mapped out by their father. Alex explained that it is a common practice for big-business families to distribute their sons across different geographic sites: "The fathers make a very clear subdivision whereby one brother doesn't infringe on the others, fearing that there would be too much fighting among them. For instance, my oldest brother works in Hong Kong. I take care of everything in North America. We always talk, but we know whose responsibility it is here and over there."[48]

In another wealthy family, the eldest son (who obtained a Tonga passport) remains in Hong Kong to run the family hotel chain in the Pacific region, while the second brother, based in San Francisco, takes care of the North American and European hotels. The youngest brother, who came on board later, is managing the family business in southern California. Daughters, no matter how qualified, are never put into management positions in the family business, which is considered their brothers' patrimony.[49] Three Hong Kong-born women are running investment businesses in the San Francisco Bay area, but they have established their own firms using seed money from their fathers. Their business are not part of the family enterprises founded by their fathers. Leong refers to one of these women as "one of the men" because she has been highly successful in what is still considered a male vocation.

Although Leong cannot imagine doing anything else, he confesses that he sometimes feels "stifled" by the fact that the reins of control are in his father's hands: "When you have a father as a boss, to me that's a double boss, right? You can't just say, 'I don't agree, I quit,' and resign. . . . You can't just walk away from your father. And then a father who has been in business for so long, he'll never recognize you as an equal, so you are always in a subordinate position." The familial regime is so powerful that even sons who try to slip its net are sometimes pulled right back into conformity. Leong's youngest brother graduated from college a few years ago, but having observed his older brothers' predicament, he has resisted working in the family business. The young man expressed his rebellion by working in a bank, but under the paternalistic eye of one of his father's wealthy friends. Leong expects that "eventually, when my youngest brother joins in, it is our objective to continue to expand here in the U.S. and to wind down in Hong Kong."[50] Scholars of rural China maintain that a man who has inherited family property rather than acquired his own fortune enjoys more power over his sons,[51] but here in the tumult of the global economy, it is the self-made tycoon who appears to exert strong control over his family throughout his lifetime. He directs and regulates the behavior of his sons, who are sent out across the world to carve out new niches for the family business empire. Leong's father has been retired for some years now, but the sons continued to consult him on major selling and buying decisions. A political analogue to this system of boss rule is the continuing power of the former prime minister of Singapore, Lee Kuan Yew, who still appears to exert tremendous *towkay* (boss) power over his state enterprise.[52]

Thus, the masculine subjectivity of this elite diasporan community is defined primarily in terms of the individual's role as a father or a son, that is, his role in maintaining the paternal/filial structure that both nurtures and expands family wealth. Unlike daughters, who inherit a small share of the family fortune (about a third of the sons' inheritance in Leong's family) and then have nothing to do with the male estates, sons must remain active, integral parts of the family business throughout their lives. To be passive – for example, to draw an income without being involved in the daily operation of the business – is to play a feminine role, like sisters (who marry out) or wives (who may manage the finances but rarely take on management roles). However, as uncertainties increase in Hong Kong and more sons break away and emigrate on their own, a few young women have taken over running their family businesses.[53] But the familial system has traditionally relied on men, and in families without sons, even "foreign devil" sons-in-law who have proved their loyalty to the family business can take the place of sons. For instance, the business empire of Sir Y. K. Pao, the late shipping and hotel magnate, is now run by his two Caucasian sons-in-law. One can say that filial piety has been bent and channeled to serve the governmentality not only of the family but of global capitalism as well.

Families in America, Fathers in Midair

The modernist norms and practices of diasporan Chinese anticipate their relocation, along with capital infusions, into the western hemisphere. Earlier Chinese immigrants to the United States were largely laborers, with a sprinkling of merchants. Today, Chinese investors and professionals arrive as cosmopolitans already wise in the ways of western business and economic liberalism.[54] With new modes of travel and communication, familial regimes have become more flexible in both dispersing and localizing members in different parts of the world. Hong Kong papers talk about the business traveler as an "astronaut" who is continually in the air while his wife and children are located in Australia, Canada, or the United States, earning rights of residence.

The turn toward the United States began in the 1960s, when teenagers from middle- and upper-middle-class families applied to American schools and colleges. Alex Leong's father often told him, "Your future is really going to be outside Hong Kong. So you should be educated outside, as long as you maintain some Chinese customs and speak Chinese."[55] The well-off used their children's overseas education as an entrée into a western democracy, buying homes for the children and setting up bank accounts and exploring local real estate. Upon graduation, sons were expected to help expand the family business in their country of residence. After graduating from the University of California, Berkeley, and the University of Wisconsin business school, Leong set up a local branch of his father's company in San Francisco. Because he is not yet a citizen, his parents plan to retire in Vancouver, Canada, where residential rights can be had for an investment of Can $300,000. They expect to join him eventually in the Bay Area, while the sons take greater control over running the family empire. This mix of family and business strategies allows them to weave in and out of political borders as they accumulate wealth and security.

Many entrepreneurs, however, continue to shuttle between both coasts of the Pacific (because it is still more profitable to do business in Hong Kong) while their wives and children are localized in North America. The astronaut as a trope of Chinese postmodern displacement also expresses the costs of the flexible accumulation logic and the toil it takes on an overly flexible family system. The astronaut wife in the United States is euphemistically referred to as "inner beauty" (*neizaimei*), a term that suggests two other phrases: "inner person," that is, wife (*neiren*) and "my wife in the Beautiful Country (America)" (*neiren zai Meiguo*). Wives thus localized to manage suburban homes and take care of the children – arranging lessons in ballet, classical music, Chinese language – sarcastically refer to themselves as "widows" (and computer widows), which expresses their feeling that family life is now thoroughly mediated and fragmented by the technology of travel and business.

In a Canadian suburb, some widows have formed a group called Ten Brothers to share domestic problems and chores in the absence of their husbands. "We have to start doing men's work like cutting grass in the summer and shoveling snow in the winter. So we call ourselves 'brothers' instead of sisters."[56] This sense of role reversal induced by flexible citizenship has also upset other prior arrangements. In the Bay Area, wives bored by being "imprisoned" in America parlay their well-honed sense of real estate into a business sideline. Down the peninsula, the majority of real-estate agents are immigrant Chinese women selling expensive homes to other newly arrived widows. Here, too, flexibility reigns as wives keep trading up their own homes in the hot residential real-estate market. A Hong Kong industrialist told me that he has moved five times over the past sixteen years as a result.

In some cases, the flexible logic deprives children of both parents. These are teenagers who are dropped off in southern Californian suburbs by their Hong Kong and Taiwan parents and who are referred to as "parachute kids." One such child who was left to fend for herself and her brother refers to her father as "the ATM machine" because he issues money but little else. Familial regimes of dispersal and localization, then, discipline family members to make do with very little emotional support; disrupted parental responsibility, strained marital relations, and abandoned children are such common circumstances that they have special terms. When the flexible imperative in family life and citizenship requires a form of isolation and disciplining of women and children that is both critiqued and resisted, claims that the "Confucian affective model" is at the heart of Chinese economic success are challenged.[57] The logic of flexibility expresses the governmentality of transnational capitalism within which many elite families are caught up, and their complex maneuvers around state regulations reveal the limits and pathos of such strategies.

American Liberalism and Pacific Rim Capital

I have argued elsewhere that in the United States, neoliberalism plays a role in shaping our notion of the deserving citizen. The history of racial conflict also tends to produce a perception that different kinds of ethnic and racial groups embody different forms of economic and political risks.[58] Following Foucault, I consider liberalism to be not merely an ethos but a regime of normalizing whereby *homo economicus* is the standard against which all other citizens are measured and ranked.

At the beginning of the twentieth century, the Chinese had the dubious distinction of being the first "racial" group to be excluded as undesirable and unsuitable immigrants to the United States. Earlier, Chinese immigrants had been welcomed by capitalists and missionaries as cheap, diligent, and docile laborers, but they were eventually attacked as unfair competitors by white workers in the railroad and mining industries. During the cold war, the public image of Chinese oscillated between that of the good Chinese, who were represented by America's Guomindang allies, and that of the bad Chinese, who were associated with "Red China."[59] In the 1960s, the emergence of a middle-class Chinese population provided contrast with the growth of a non-white "underclass," a term used mainly for inner-city blacks.[60] The media popularized the term *model minority* to refer to Asian Americans, who were perceived as having raised themselves up by their bootstraps, thus fitting the criteria for good, or at least deserving, citizens.[61] Images of Oriental docility, diligence, self-sufficiency, and productivity underpin contemporary notions that the Asian minority embodies the human capital that makes good citizens, in contrast to those who make claims on the welfare program.[62]

Through the next decade, the influx of immigrants from Hong Kong and Taiwan, many of them students bound for college, swelled the ranks of middle-class Asian Americans.[63] The rise of a Chinese-immigrant elite – many of them suburban professionals – coincided with the restructuring of the American economy and its increasing reliance on skilled immigrant labor and overseas capital. In the public mind, the Asian newcomers seemed to embody the desired disciplinary traits of an increasingly passé model of American character. For instance, in the aftermath of the Tiananmen crack-down, a letter to the *San Francisco Chronicle* defended the admission of Chinese (student) refugees: "The opportunity to welcome the best and the brightest of China and Hong Kong into our area is fantastic. These are motivated, energetic, courageous people, with strong cultural traditions of taking care of their families, working hard, and succeeding in business. We need more of these values in our midst, not less."[64] It appears to me that "traditional" American values are to be found in these newcomers, who are coming with different kinds of capital but perhaps not so strong "cultural traditions." Earlier images of the Chinese railroad worker, laundryman, houseboy, and garment worker have been replaced by the masculine executive, a *homo economicus* model inspired in part by the so-called neo-Confucian challenge from across the Pacific.[65]

Increasingly, the reception of skilled and capital-bearing Chinese newcomers represents the triumph of corporate discourses and practices that invoke the Pacific Rim and its Oriental productivity and new wealth. For instance, under pressure from corporate and Asian lobbies, US immigration laws were modified in 1990 to attract some of the Pacific Rim capital that was flowing toward Australia and Canada, where the laws are less stringent. A new "investor category" allows would-be immigrants to obtain a green card in return for a million-dollar investment that results in the creation of at least ten jobs. On Wall Street, seminars directed at Asian Americans offer suggestions on how to "get US citizenship through real estate investment and acquisition." A consultant urges, "Think of your relatives in Asia. If they invest in you, they get a green card and you get a new business."[66] As in other western countries with finance-based immigration, citizenship has become an instrument of flexible accumulation for the nation-state; it is a way for the nation-state to subvert its own regulatory mechanisms in order to compete more effectively in the global economy.

Narrating Cosmopolitan Citizenship

In what ways has the arrival of the diasporan Chinese reworked the cultural meaning of "Asian American" and produced a new discourse of Pacific Rim romanticism and even symbolic violence? Whereas Said has described orientalism as a one-sided and self-reifying process, I have tried throughout this chapter to represent the discursive objects themselves as co-creators in orientalism. This has been, after all, part of their flexibility in negotiating the multicultural worlds of European imperialism. For centuries, Asians and other peoples have been shaped by a perception and an experience of themselves as the other of the western world.[67] The new prominence of Asians in world markets has enabled Chinese subjects to play a bigger role in identifying what counts as "Chinese" in the West.[68] Diasporan-Chinese academics now use orientalist codes to (re)frame overseas Chinese as enlightened cosmopolitans who possess both economic capital and humanistic values. Wang Gungwu, the former chancellor of Hong Kong University, describes overseas Chinese living "among non-Chinese" as "a modern kind of cosmopolitan literati" who have embraced the Enlightenment ideals of rationality, individual freedom, and democracy.[69] Perhaps. Scholars based in the United States claim that "Confucian humanism" will create "an Oriental alternative" to the destructive instrumental rationality and individualism of the West[70] – in other words, a kinder and gentler capitalism for the twenty-first century. One wonders whether these scholars have bothered to visit factories run by Chinese entrepreneurs and observed whether their practices are really that "humanistic" and uninformed by the logic of capital accumulation.

These grand claims circle around and occlude the complex, wide-ranging realities of East Asian capitalism – or at least its Chinese variant. For instance, Hong Kongers hail from a colonial territory where there has been little nurturing of Confucian humanism and democratic values. Until Tiananmen, many had developed a radically apolitical stance toward the state. Just as Hong Kong is viewed as a place to maximize wealth, so the western democracies to which many Hong Kongers are bound are considered "gold mountains" of opportunity. The subcontracting system of production used in Hong Kong and Taiwan and now in China is among the most exploitative of women and children in the world.[71] In Hong Kong, "democracy," for many entrepreneurs, often means freedom from political constraints on making money; the state and wider society are of concern only when they can be made relevant to family interests.[72] In the view of the business elite, the modern social order is built upon the domination of those who possess intellectual and economic power, and wealthy people are models for envy and emulation rather than enemies of the poor.[73] Like investors all over the world, Chinese businessmen who engage in philanthropy are seeking to escape property taxes and to gain social status as prominent members of society; it is a stretch to construct these acts as acts of Confucian benevolence. As billionaire Li Kashing says, "There is no other criterion of excellence [except money]."[74] But such prideful discourses on diasporan-Chinese elites as humanistic citizens persist, and they are intervening in narratives about the role of Asian Americans in the United States.

From across the Pacific, corporate America answers the call to reconsider Chinese immigrants as exceptional citizens of the New World Order imaginary. Of course, the reception is not unambivalent, for global trade is viewed as war.[75] This contra-dictory attitude was expressed by David Murdock, chairman and CEO of Dole Foods, at a conference on Asian Americans in Los Angeles. Murdock personifies corporate America: his company has operations in more than fifty countries and employs thousands of employees in the Asia Pacific region. He warned that in a world of many big economic powers, the technological edge has shifted to the East. There are, however, more than seven million Asian Americans. He continued: "We need to be more competitive. We need people who understand the languages, cultures, the markets, the politics of this spectacular region. Many Asian Americans have language ability, cultural understanding, direct family ties, and knowledge of economic conditions and government practices throughout Asia. This knowledge and ability can help Americans achieve political and business success in the region. . . . Their insight and ability can [help] in opening doors for the US [and in] building a new structure for peace in the Pacific."[76] By defining a role for Asian Americans as good citizens and trade ambassadors, Murdock's speech situates them in the wider narrative of the Oriental as trade enemy.

At the same conference, Los Angeles City Councilman Michael Woo, who was then seeking to be the first Asian mayor of Los Angeles, picked up the narrative by reframing the question: "What then is this new person, this Asian American, in the new era of the Pacific?" The question, which is reminiscent of European queries about Anglos earlier in the century, subverts the view that whites are the undisputed key players on the West Coast. Woo, whose family has close ties with Asian capital, went on to propose "a new hybrid role" whereby new Asian immigrants (rather than long-resident Asian Americans, he seemed to suggest) can act as "translators, go-betweens [between] one culture and another, using skills that have brought us to such prominence and success in the business world and in the professions and entering into the public arena" to become mediators in community rela-tions.[77]

Asians are "bridge builders," Woo claimed.[78] In his view, the Asian American "middleman minority" is not the besieged ethnic group of academic theorizing.[79] Woo was using the term in the larger global sense, coming dangerously close to the meaning that evokes compradors, those members of the Chinese elite who acted as middlemen between colonial governments and the masses in Asia. Calling colonial go-betweens *muchachos*, Fred Chiu notes their role as "the ideal-typical mediating and (inter) mediating category/force in the reproduction of a world of – out-going as well as in-coming – nationalism and colonialism."[80] And of course the term "bridge" has gained new resonance for overseas Chinese in their new prominence as transnational capitalists. In Chinese, the word for bridge (*qiao*) puns with the term for overseas Chinese (the *qiao* in *huaqiao*), and as I have argued elsewhere,[81] diaspora Chinese have been quick to play on the metaphor of bridging political boundaries in their role as agents of flexible accumulation and flexible citizenship. The bridge-building metaphor appeals to the members of an Asian elite who set great store in being engineers, doctors, managers, and bankers and who see themselves as self-made men who are now building the infrastructures of modern affluence on both sides of the Pacific. Woo saw a continuity between Asian economic and cultural middleman roles. He noted that trading skills developed in the diaspora "in the midst of cultures very different from their own" included not just those of use in "the handling of money, but also skills in sizing up people, negotiating a deal, and long-term planning." He suggested that these "survival skills" could be "transferred" to non-Asians.[82] Woo thus echoed the *homo economicus* construction of Chinese immigrants and elevated their role in the American social order.

Such narrativization is never simply complicit with hegemonic constructions but seeks to reposition Asian immigrants and Asian Americans as new authority figures while suggesting declining human capital and leadership qualities among Anglos. By calling Asian Americans the new westerners, Woo implies that the Anglos have been surpassed in diligence, discipline, moral capital, and even knowledge of the changing multicultural world that is critical to America's success. His narrative carves out a space of Asian Americans as mediators in American race and class relations. The bridge-building citizen evokes the tradition of American communities and the ideal of a civil society in which neighbors look out for each other.[83] Asian American leaders, Woo seemed to suggest, could build bridges between racial minorities and the government. By identifying Pacific Rim bodies with Pacific Rim capital, the concept of bridge builders gentrifies Asian American identity in both its local and its global aspects – in moral contrast to less-privileged minorities, with their dependence on the welfare state.[84] When Woo's talk ended, the largely Asian audience rose up and clapped enthusiastically; they voted to replace the model-minority label with the label bridge-building minority, a term that apparently enables Asian Americans to share the transnational role of diasporan Chinese in building the Pacific Century.[85]

Conclusion

The emigration of Chinese corporate elites out of Asia has entailed the cultural work of image management as they seek wider acceptance in western democracies and in different zones of late capitalism. By revising the academic images of overseas Chinese as money handlers, trading minorities, and middlemen, corporate spokesmen paint a picture that mixes humanistic values with ultrarationalism and portrays the ideal *homo economicus* of the next century.[86] Such self-representations are not so much devised to collaborate in the biopolitical agenda of any nation-state as to convert political constraints in one field into economic opportunities in another, to turn displacement into advantageous placement in different sites, and to elude state disciplining in order to reproduce the family in tandem with the propulsion of capitalism.

Of course, whereas for bankers, boundaries are always flexible, for migrant workers, boat people, persecuted intellectuals, artists, and other kinds of less well heeled refugees, this apparent mix of humanistic concerns and capitalist rationality is a harder act to follow. For instance, Don Nonini has identified the tensions and pathos experienced by middle-class Malaysian Chinese whose familial strategies of emigration are intended to help them escape second-class citizenship as much as to accumulate wealth overseas.[87] Although Chinese small-business owners consider themselves locals in their Malaysian hometowns (e.g., as "natives of Bukit Merta-jam"), many are vulnerable to anti-Chinese policies and feel that they have no choice but to send their children overseas, where they may feel less discrimination. These businessmen postpone joining their children in places such as New Zealand that do not feel like "home." Their loyalty to home places in Malaysia is ironically disregarded by state policies that discriminate against them as lower-class ethnics in a way that does not affect wealthy Chinese, who are viewed as more "cosmopolitan" and open-minded about Malay rule. As Jim Clifford has reminded us, there are "discrepant cosmopolitanisms,"[88] and the cosmopolitanism of lower-class Chinese from Malaysia is fraught with tensions between sentiments of home and pressures to emigrate. This is not to say that members of the Hong Kong Chinese elite do not have patriotic feelings for the Chinese motherland but rather that the investor emigrants are well positioned to engage in a self-interested search for citizenship and profits abroad – a strategy that will enhance their economic mobility and yet sidestep the disciplining of particular nation-states.[89]

Among this elite group (though not limited to them), such a mix of ultra instrumentalism and familial moralism reveals a postnationalist ethos. They readily submit to the governmentality of capital, plotting all the while to escape state discipline. In the most extreme expressions, their loyalty appears to be limited to loyalty toward the family business; it does not extend to any particular country. A Chinese banker in San Francisco, explains that he can live in Asia, Canada, or Europe: "I can live anywhere in the world, but it must be near an airport." Such bravado constructs the bearable lightness of being that capital buoyancy can bring. Yet the politics of imagining a transnational identity that is dependent on global market mobility should not disabuse us of the fact that there are structural limits, and personal costs, to such flexible citizenship.

This essay should not be interpreted as an argument for a simple opposition between cosmopolitanism and patriotism (taken to an extreme, either is an undesirable or dangerous phenomenon). I have argued that a Confucian cultural triumphalism has arisen alongside modern Chinese transnationalism in Southeast Asia. Some scholars have been tempted to compare the role of the modern Chinese economic elite to that of medieval Jewish bankers, whose activities protected free trade, along with liberalism and other Enlightenment values, in the Dark Ages. We should resist such a comparison. Although contemporary Chinese merchants, bankers, and managers have burst through closed borders and freed up spaces for economic activities, they have also revived premodern forms of child, gender, and class oppression, as well as strengthened authoritarian regimes in Asia.[90] A different kind of cosmopolitical right is at play. The point is not that all Chinese are painted by the same broad brush of elite narratives but that the image of the border-running Chinese executive with no state loyalty has become an important figure in the era of Pacific Rim capital. What is it about flexible accumulation – the endless capacity to dodge state regulations, spin human relations across space, and find ever new niches to exploit – that allows a mix of humanistic relations and ultrainstrumentality to flourish? Indeed, there may not be anything uniquely "Chinese" about flexible personal discipline, disposition, and orientation; rather, they are the expressions of a habitus that is finely tuned to the turbulence of late capitalism.[91]

NOTES

1 Francis X. Clines, "In Burst of Fiendish Delight, Ukraine Topples a Monolith," *New York Times*, 31 August 1991, A1.

2 "The Silicon Valley Way of Divorce" (in Chinese), *Overseas Scholars' Monthly* (Taipei), January 1991.

3 See the two special issues of the journal *Daedalus* titled *The Living Tree: The Changing Meaning of Being Chinese Today* (120(2) spring 1991) and *China in Transformation* (122(2) spring 1993).

4 See Ong, *Flexible Citizenship*, ch. 2.

5 Said, *Orientalism*.

6 Harvey, *Condition of Postmodernity*, identifies our era as one of "flexible accumulation," but he underestimates the ways culture shapes material forces and the effects of political economy on culture.

7 This has been suggested by many scholars. See Miyoshi, "Borderless World?"; and Anderson, "Exodus."

8 By "governmentality," Michel Foucault means the deployment of modern forms of (nonrepressive) disciplining power by the state – especially in the bureaucratic realm – and other kinds of institutions that produce rules based on knowledge/power about populations. See Foucault, "Governmentality."

9 See Foucault, *Discipline and Punish*; and Foucault, *History of Sexuality*.

10 Nonini, "Shifting Identities," pp. 203–7.

11 See Yang, "The Modernity of Power," p. 416; and Barlow, "Theorizing Woman".

12 Barlow, "*Zhishifenzi*," pp. 214–15.

13 See Rabinow, *French Modern*, pp. 9–10.

14 For studies on Chinese merchant families in early modern China, when European powers dominated the coastal cities, see Elvin and Skinner, *Chinese City*.

15 Fei, "Peasant and Gentry," pp. 646–7. While Fei attacks the merchant class for its lack of responsibility toward society, other scholars maintain that the "hybrid" and "modernized" offspring of the compradors were people who might have brought about a capitalist revolution in China. See Murphey, "The Treaty Ports."

16 See Purcell, *Chinese in Southeast Asia*; and Trocki, *Opium and Empires*.

17 See Nonini and Ong, "Introduction."

18 In Southeast Asia, *huaqiao* became a generic term to refer in a diffused way to diasporan Chinese in general, regardless of their nationality. In this chapter, I use the terms *huaqiao*, *overseas Chinese*, and *diasporan Chinese* interchangeably.

19 Anderson, *Imagined Communities*, underplays the centrality of race in colonially inspired notions of nationalism in Southeast Asia and seeks instead to focus on the "good" kind of anti-imperialist, civic nationalism.

20 See Bourdieu, *Outline*, pp. 90–5.

21 See Chun, "Pariah Capitalism."

22 Bourdieu, *Outline*, pp. 190–7.

23 See, for example, Berger and Hsin-huang, *In Search of an East Asian Development Model*, and Tai, *Confucianism and Economic Development*.

24 American writers who contribute to this discourse include Kotkin, *Tribes*; and Fallows, *Looking at the Sun*. See Ong, *Flexible Citizenship*, ch. 2.

25 Hsiung, *Living Rooms as Factories*.

26 Edward A. Gargan, "A Giant Spreads Its Roots," *New York Times*, 14 November 1995, C3.

27 See Ong, *Flexible Citizenship*, ch. 1.

28 Foucault, *History of Sexuality*; and Foucault, "Governmentality."

29 See Deyo, *Political Economy of New Asian Industrialism*.

30 Lau, *Society and Politics in Hong Kong*.

31 Salaff, *Working Daughters of Hong Kong*.

32 See Ho, *Ladder of Success in Imperial China*.

33 See Lau, *Society and Politics*, pp. 95–6.

34 Chen, "The Economic Setting," pp. 3–4.

35 Brain Wong [pseud.], interview by author, San Francisco, June 1992.

36 See Gordon, "Governmental Rationality," pp. 1–51.

37 Miles, *Race*, pp. 84–5.

38 Ibid., pp. 85–6.

39 Watson, *Emigration*, 50–78.

40 Chan Chi-Keung, "Exodus Threat to H.K. Credibility," *South China Morning Post*, 28 January 1988. The most the official could hope for was that the Chinese emigrants would return to Hong Kong with their shiny new Canadian and Australian passports.

41 Bhabha, "DissemiNation," p. 327.

42 "Time Running Out to Stop the Brain Drain," *South China Morning Post*, 29 December 1987.

43 Ibid.

44 Sam Seibert et al., "Hong Kong Blues," *Newsweek*, 16 April 1990, p. 45.

45 For more details on finance-based immigration programs see *South China Morning Post*, 20 November 1988.

46 See Wong, *Emigrant Entrepreneurs*.

47 Alex Leong [pseud.], interview by author, San Francisco, March 1997.

48 Ibid.

49 For comparable practices in Chinese business families based in Singapore see Chan and Chiang, *Stepping Out*.

50 Leong, interview.

51 See, for example, Sung, "Property and Family Division."

52 *Towkay* is a transliteration of the Hokkien word for the head of a family business; it is commonly used in Southeast Asia to refer to Chinese entrepreneurs or any successful self-employed Chinese man. In Mandarin, the word is *toujia*.

53 See *New York Times*, 14 January 1996.

54 For a discussion of Chinese cosmopolitans in Vancouver see Mitchell, "Transnational Subjects."

55 Leong, interview, June 1994.

56 The name Ten Brothers is borrowed from the band of Robin Hood-type robbers in the Chinese classic *The Water Margin*. See *South China Morning Post*, 5 February 1994.

57 For an example of such claims see Tai, *Confucianism and Economic Development*, pp. 18–19.

58 See Ong, "Citizenship as Subject Making."

59 See Daniels, *Asian American*, pp. 129–54, 301.

60 Myrdal, *American Dilemma*, pp. 184–5.

61 Scholars often miss the ways neoliberal ideas about human worth have affected processes of racial formation in the United States. See, for example, Omi and Winant, *Racial Formation in the United States*.

62 Actually, the ideological divide was not so clearly cut, for Chinatown movements also came to be shaped by the Great Society programs, and many Chinese American students were radicalized by the African American struggle for civil rights in the 1960s. This new ethnic consciousness, which arose out of struggle, found expression in storefront programs to provide for the health care, housing, and other needs of new immigrants. Many of its advocates saw Chinese immigrants, most of whom were poor, as victims of racist capitalism, a view that was shaped by the Marxist framework of ethnic-studies programs that were being introduced on campuses.

63 The influx of poor immigrants also continued, helped by a 1962 law that allowed for the reunification of families; it provided a new infusion of people that revitalized many Chinatowns. See Nee and Nee, *Longtime Californ'*.

64 Letter to the Editor, *San Francisco Chronicle*, 16 June 1989.

65 Asian American writers such as Frank Chin and Maxine Hong Kingston have challenged the model-minority image by exploring Chinese American identity as formed from the tension between politics and aesthetics. See Chan et al. *The Big AIIEEEEE!* However, such literary works, together with more recent Asian American performative arts, have had less impact on the national consciousness than the media-borne and corporate renditions of Asians at home and abroad.

66 Through this opening, the US government hoped to attract $4 billion a year and to create as many as forty thousand jobs annually (see "Green-Card Law Means Business to Immigrants," *Wall Street Journal*, 21 February 1992, B1). The actual gains so far have fallen short of both goals. The Hong Kong investors I spoke to said that the investment figure is too steep, given that they can obtain a Canadian passport for Can $300,000. Furthermore, since the law was passed, great investment opportunities in China have sucked most of the overseas Chinese capital back to Asia. See Ong, *Flexible Citizenship*, ch.2.

67 Hall, "Cultural Identity and Diaspora," pp. 225–6.

68 The Japanese, of course, were the first economically significant Asians in the world economy, but other than by being featured in a few business tracts about superior Asian quality control, they have not participated as vigorously in western discourses about Orientals as one might have expected. But some have recently become more vocal, following the example of the newly assertive Southeast Asian leaders. See Mahathir and Ishihara, *The Voice of Asia*.

69 See Wang, "Among Non-Chinese," *Daedalus* 120, no. 2 (1991): 148–52. It is interesting that the term "non-Chinese" has emerged as a category in such self-orientalizing discourses as displayed in this special issue of *Daedalus*, which is titled *The Living Tree*. The term seems to herald the elevation of Chineseness to the global status enjoyed by westerners *vis-à-vis* less-developed parts of the world, which are commonly referred to as the conceptual and geographic South. By taking the East out of the underdeveloped category, this discursive move reinforces the model of global binarism.

70 See Tai, *Confucianism and Economic Development*; Tu, "The Rise of Industrial East Asia," "Cultural China."
71 See Salaff, *Working Daughters*; Greenhalgh, "De-orientalizing the Chinese Family Firm"; Lee, "Factory Regimes of Chinese Capitalism"; and Hsiung, *Living Rooms as Factories*.
72 Lau, *Society and Politics*, p. 118.
73 Ibid., p. 119.
74 Pan, *Sons of the Yellow Emperor*, pp. 366–7.
75 This view is promoted in the bestseller *Rising Sun*, by Michael Crichton and is suggested by James Fallows in Fallows, *Looking at the Sun*.
76 David Murdock, keynote speech delivered at the Asia Society conference "The Asian American Experience: Looking Ahead," Los Angeles, October 1991.
77 Michael Woo, keynote speech delivered at the Asia Society conference "The Asian American Experience: Looking Ahead," Los Angeles, October 1991.
78 Ibid.
79 See Bonacich, "Theory of Middleman Minorities."
80 Chiu, "Non-mediating Forces versus Mediating Forces."
81 See Ong, *Flexible Citizenship*, ch. 1.
82 Woo, keynote speech.
83 As a politician with a tiny Asian support base, Woo depended primarily on votes from multiethnic constituencies, especially Anglos and African Americans. There was something about his bridge-building metaphor that was reminiscent of the Confucian norm of relations between older and younger brothers, which he seemed to suggest as a model for city politics. This representation apparently found some acceptance among Los Angeles citizens because despite the failure of interethnic coalitions during the 1992 class and racial rioting, Michael Woo remained for a time the most popular candidate in the mayoral race.
84 See Hall and Held, "Citizens and Citizenship."
85 Citizenship rights are public entitlements, but does a citizen have the material and cultural resources to choose between different courses of action in public life? For Woo, Asian American citizenship seems irrevocably tied to Pacific Rim capital.
86 The academic terms were coined in Freedman, "Handling of Money"; and Wertheim, "Trading Minorities."
87 Nonini, "Shifting Identities."
88 Clifford, "Traveling Cultures," p. 108.
89 Roger Rouse ("Thinking Through Transnationalism") maintains that American class formation and cultural politics must be analyzed in relation to global capitalism, and yet he neglects to consider the role of foreign capitalists in reworking American race and class relations. Also, while he claims flexible subjectivities are fostered among the working classes by "the bourgeoisie" (p. 391), he does not discuss the flexible strategies of the latter in dealing with both global capitalism and the regulatory power of the nation-state.
90 Ong and Nonini, *Ungrounded Empires*.
91 See, for example, Lind, "To Have and Have Not."

REFERENCES

Anderson, Benedict. *Imagined Communities: Reflections on the Origin and Spread of Nationalism*, 2nd edn. London: Verso, 1991.
——. "Exodus." *Critical Inquiry* 20 (winter 1994): 314–27.

Barlow, Tani. "*Zhishifenzi* [Chinese Intellectuals] and Power." *Dialectical Anthropology* 16 (1991): 209–32.

——. "Theorizing Woman: *Funu, Guojia, Jiating*." *Genders* 10 (spring 1991): 132–60.

Berger, Peter, and Hsin-huang Michael Hsiao, eds. *In Search of an East Asian Development Model*. New Brunswick, NJ: Transaction Books, 1988.

Bhabha, Homi K. "DissemiNation: Time, Narrative, and the Margins of the Modern Nation." In *Nation and Narration*, ed. Homi K. Bhabha, pp. 291–322. New York: Routledge, 1990.

Bonacich, Edna. "A Theory of Middleman Minorities." *American Sociological Review* 38 (1973): 583–94.

Bourdieu, Pierre. *Outline of a Theory of Practice*. Cambridge: Cambridge University Press, 1977.

Chan, Jeffery Paul, Frank Chin, Lawson Fusao Inada, and Shawn Wong, eds. *The Big AIIEEEEE! An Anthology of Chinese American and Japanese American Literature*. New York: Meridian, 1991.

Chan Kwok Bun and Claire Chiang. *Stepping Out: The Making of Chinese Entrepreneurs*. Singapore: Simon and Schuster, 1994.

Chen, Edward K. Y. "The Economic Setting." In *The Business Environment in Hong Kong*. 2nd. edn., ed. D. G. Lethbridge, pp. 1–51. Hong Kong: Oxford University Press, 1984.

Chiu, Fred Y. L. "Non-mediating Forces versus Mediating Forces – New 'Subjecthood' in Local/Regional Resistances against Nation/Global Systemic Drives." Paper presented at the workshop "Nation-states, Transnational Publics, and Civil Society in the Asia-Pacific." University of California, Berkeley, 28–30 June 1996.

Chun, Allen. "Pariah Capitalism and the Overseas Chinese of Southeast Asia: Problems in the Definition of the Problem." *Ethnic and Racial Studies* 12(2) (1989): 233–56.

Clifford, James. "Travelling Cultures." In *Cultural Studies*, ed. Lawrence Grossberg, Cary Nelson, and Paula A. Treichler, pp. 96–116. New York: Routledge, 1992.

Crichton, Michael. *Rising Sun*. New York: Ballantine, 1992.

Daniels, Roger. *Asian American: Chinese and Japanese in the United States since 1850*. Seattle: University of Washington Press, 1988.

Deyo, Frederic C., ed. *The Political Economy of New Asian Industrialism*. Ithaca, NY: Cornell University Press, 1987.

Elvin, Mark, and G. William Skinner, eds. *The Chinese City between Two Worlds*. Stanford, CA: Stanford University Press, 1972.

Fallows, James. *Looking at the Sun: The Rise of the New East Asian Economic and Political System*. New York: Pantheon, 1994.

Fei Hsiao-tung. "Peasant and Gentry: An Interpretation of Chinese Social Structure and its Changes." In *Class, Status, and Power*, ed. Reinhard Bendix and Seymour M. Lipset, pp. 646–47. New York: Free Press, 1953.

Foucault, Michel. *Discipline and Punish: The Birth of the Prison*, trans. A. Sheridan. New York: Vintage, 1979.

——. *History of Sexuality, Volume 1*, trans. M. Hurley. New York: Pantheon, 1978.

——. "Governmentality." In *The Foucault Effect: Studies in Governmentality*, ed. Graham Burchell, Colin Gordon, and Peter Miller, pp. 87–104. Chicago: University of Chicago Press, 1991.

Freedman, Maurice. "The Handling of Money: A Note on the Background to the Economic Sophistication of the Overseas Chinese." *Man*, o.s. 19 (1959): 64–5.

Gordon, Colin. "Governmental Rationality: An Introduction." In *The Foucault Effect: Studies in Governmentality*, ed. Graham Burchell, Colin Gordon, and Peter Miller, pp. 1–51. Chicago: University of Chicago Press, 1991.

Greenhalgh, Susan. "De-orientalizing the Chinese Family Firm." *American Ethnologist* 21(4) (1994): 746–76.

Hall, Stuart. "Cultural Identity and Diaspora." In *Identity: Community, Culture, Difference,* ed. J. Rutherford, pp. 222–37. London: Lawrence and Wishart, 1990.

Hall, Stuart, and David Held. "Citizens and Citizenship." In *New Times: The Changing Face of Politics in the 1990s,* ed. Stuart Hall and M. Jacques, pp. 173–88. New York: Verso, 1989.

Harvey, David. *The Condition of Postmodernity.* Oxford: Blackwell Publishers, 1989.

Ho Ping-ti. *The Ladder of Success in Imperial China.* New York: Columbia University Press, 1962.

Hsiung, Ping-chun. *Living Rooms as Factories: Class, Gender, and the Satellite Factory System in Taiwan.* Philadelphia: Temple University Press, 1995.

Kotkin, Joel. *Tribes: How Race, Religion, and Identity Determine Success in the New Global Economy.* New York: Random House, 1992.

Lau, Emily Siu-kai. *Society and Politics in Hong Kong.* New York: St. Martin's Press, 1983.

Lee, Ching Kwan. "Factory Regimes of Chinese Capitalism: Different Cultural Logics in Labor Control." In *Ungrounded Empires,* ed. Aihwa Ong and Donald M. Nonini, pp. 115–42. New York: Routledge, 1997.

Lind, Michael. "To Have and Have Not: Notes on the Progress of American Class War." *Harper's* (June 1995): 35–47.

Mahathir, Mohamad, and Shintaro Ishihara. *The Voice of Asia: Two Asian Leaders Discuss the Coming Century,* trans. Frank Baldwin. Tokyo: Kodansha International, 1995.

Miyoshi, Masao. "A Borderless World? From Colonialism to Transnationalism and the Decline of the Nation-State." *Critical Inquiry* 19(4) (summer 1993): 726–51.

Miles, Robert. *Race.* London: Routledge, 1989.

Mitchell, Katharyne. "Transnational Subjects: Constituting the Cultural Citizen in an Era of Pacific Rim Capital." In *Ungrounded Empires,* ed. Aihwa Ong and Donald M. Nonini, pp. 228–58. New York: Routledge, 1997.

Murphey, Rhoades. "The Treaty Ports and China's Modernization." In *The Chinese City between Two Worlds,* ed. Mark Elvin and G. William Skinner, pp. 17–72. Stanford, CA.: Stanford University Press, 1974.

Myrdal, Gunnar. *The American Dilemma: The Negro Problem and Modern Democracy.* New York: Vintage, 1968.

Nee, Victor G., and Brett de Bary Nee. *Longtime Californ': A Documentary Study of an American Chinatown.* Stanford, CA: Stanford University Press, 1972.

Nonini, Donald M. "Shifting Identities, Positioned Imaginaries: Transnational Traversals and Reversals by Malaysian Chinese." In *Ungrounded Empires,* ed. Aihwa Ong and Donald M. Nonini, pp. 203–27. New York: Routledge, 1997.

Nonini, Donald M., and Aihwa Ong. "Introduction: Chinese Transnationalism as an Alternative Modernity." In *Ungrounded Empires,* ed. Aihwa Ong and Donald M. Nonini, pp. 1–33. New York: Routledge, 1997.

Omi, Michael, and Howard Winant. *Racial Formation in the United States.* New York: Routledge and Kegan Paul, 1986.

Ong, Aihwa. "Citizenship as Subject Making: New Immigrants Negotiate Racial and Ethnic Boundaries." *Current Anthropology* 37 (5) (December 1996): 737–62.

———. *Flexible Citizenship: The Cultural Logics of Transnationality.* Durham, NC: Duke University Press, 1999.

Ong, Aihwa, and Donald M. Nonini, eds. *Ungrounded Empires: The Cultural Politics of Modern Chinese Transnationalism.* New York: Routledge, 1997.

Pan, Lynn. *Sons of the Yellow Emperor: A History of the Chinese Diaspora.* Boston: Little, Brown, 1990.

Purcell, Victor. *The Chinese in Southeast Asia*, 2nd edn. Kuala Lumpur: Oxford University Press, 1965.

Rabinow, Paul. *French Modern: Norms and Forms of the Social Environment*. Cambridge, MA: MIT Press, 1989.

Rouse, Roger. "Thinking through Transnationalism: Notes on the Cultural Politics of Class Relations in the Contemporary United States." *Public Culture* 7(2) (1995): 353–402.

Said, Edward. *Orientalism*. New York: Pantheon, 1978.

Salaff, Janet W. *Working Daughters of Hong Kong: Filial Piety or Power in the Family?* Cambridge: Cambridge University Press, 1981.

Sung Lung-sheng. "Property and Family Division." In *The Anthropology of Taiwanese Society*, ed. Emily Martin and Hill Gates. Stanford, CA: Stanford University Press, 1981.

Tai, Hung-chao, ed. *Confucianism and Economic Development: An Oriental Alternative?* Washington, DC: Washington Institute Press, 1989.

Trocki, Carl. *Opium and Empires: Chinese Society in Colonial Singapore, 1800–1910*. Ithaca, NY: Cornell University Press, 1990.

Tu Wei-ming. "The Rise of Industrial East Asia: The Role of Confucian Values." *Copenhagen Papers in East and Southeast Asian Studies* (April 1988): 81–97.

——. "Cultural China: The Periphery as the Center." *Daedalus* 120(2) (1991): 1–32.

Wang Gungwu. "Among Non-Chinese." *Daedalus* 120(2) (1991): 148–52.

Watson, James L. *Emigration and the Chinese Lineage: The Mans in Hong Kong and London*. Berkeley and Los Angeles: University of California Press, 1975.

Wertheim, W. F. "The Trading Minorities of Southeast Asia." In *East-West Parallels*, pp. 39–82. The Hague: W. Van Hoeve, 1964.

Wong, Siu-lun. *Emigrant Entrepreneurs: Shanghai Industrialists in Hong Kong*. Hong Kong: Oxford University Press, 1988.

Yang, Mayfair Mei-hui. "The Modernity of Power in the Chinese Socialist Order." *Cultural Anthropology* 3(4) (1988): 408–27.

9

Arab Noise and Ramadan Nights: *Rai*, Rap, and Franco-Maghrebi Identities

Joan Gross, David McMurray, and Ted Swedenburg

Can't Take No Moor

For two thousand years, essentially the same people have posed the same dangers to us. Aren't the Iranian *mujahidin* the descendants of the Persians who were defeated at Marathon; isn't the Islamic World, now striking at Europe's frontiers and slowly penetrating her, composed of the sons of the Ottoman Turks who reached Vienna, and the Arabs whom Charles Martel routed at Poitiers? (Jean-Marie Le Pen)[1]

In the aftermath of the Berlin Wall's collapse, western Europe has been forced to rethink its identity. If in the recent past its conception of itself as a haven of democracy and civilization depended – in part – on a contrast to the evils of the Communist Empire, today an idea is being revived of Europe as Christendom, in contradistinction to Islam. Only this time around, the Islam in question is not being held back at Europe's Spanish or Balkan frontiers but has penetrated its very core, in the shape of new "minority" populations of Muslim background. Questions about the nature of Europe's identity and the place of Muslim immigrants within it are now among the most contentious on the Continent (Morley and Robins 1990). So acute is the anxiety about the ten to twelve million "immigrants" that many white western Europeans feel they are living under cultural and economic siege (Miller 1991: 33).

The Spanish novelist Juan Goytisolo brilliantly lampoons this European hysteria about "foreigners" in his hilariously provocative *Landscapes After the Battle*. It

From *Displacement, Diaspora and Geographies of Identity*, ed. Smadar Lavie and Ted Swedenburg, pp. 119–55. Durham, NC: Duke University Press. Copyright © 1996, Duke University Press.

opens with the inexplicable appearance of unintelligible scrawls on the walls of the Parisian neighborhood of Le Sentier. At first the natives assume the marks are the secret language of a gang of kids, but then someone spots a man with "kinky black hair" inscribing the mysterious messages. The natives conclude that the scrawls are written in a real alphabet – but backward – and are the handiwork of "those foreigners who, in ever-increasing numbers, were stealthily invading the decrepit buildings abandoned by their former tenants and offering their labor to the well-heeled merchants of Le Sentier" (1987a: 3). Then one morning, a working-class native of Le Sentier drops in at his local bar for a pick-me-up of calvados, to discover that the sign identifying his tavern has been replaced by one written in that incomprehensible script. Wandering through the neighborhood, he is horrified to find that every marker – the Rex Cinema's marquee, McDonald's, street signs, the placard on the district mayor's office – has been transformed. Even the sign outside the office of the newspaper of "the glorious Party of the working class," *L'Humanité*, now reads الإنسانيّة. A catastrophic, cacophonous traffic jam has broken out, for drivers cannot decipher the street signs, and the traffic police are no help. "Trying to hide his laughter, a swarthy-skinned youngster with kinky hair purveyed his services as guide to whichever helpless soul bid the highest" (1987a: 7). "Colonized by those barbarians!" the unnerved Le Sentier native thinks to himself (1987a: 5).

Goytisolo's send-up of the French nightmare about *immigrés* seems remarkably prescient today, more than a decade after its publication. For French antipathy is especially virulent toward those "foreigners" who have been coming from North Africa for decades and who utilize that "backward" script, Arabic. French society has never come to terms with the legacy of colonization or its bloody war against the Algerian national liberation movement, which cost one million Arab and ten thousand French lives.[2] Instead, one might imagine, from the frenzied reactions of so many white French men and women to all things "Arab" and "Islamic," that colonialism had been a magnanimous and bloodless project, and that Arabs in France live in the lap of luxury and have nothing to complain about.[3]

So severe are apprehensions about the *immigré* "problem" that during the "*hijab* affair" of 1989, when nine female Franco-Maghrebi students in state-run lycées demanded the right to wear Islamic headscarves, the media fused the signifiers "immigrant," "Muslim fundamentalist," and "invasion" together into a specter of an eventual Islamic France – a vision that horrified a good portion of the French population, on both the Left and the Right (Koulberg 1991).[4] Even President François Mitterrand, who postured as an anti-racist, was prompted to assert that the country had gone beyond "the threshold of tolerance" (Riding 1990: 1–16). Jacques Chirac, former prime minister, mayor of Paris, and leader of the right-wing Rally for the Republic (RPR), complained about the "overdose of immigrants" – a code word for "Arabs" – while former president Valéry Giscard d'Estaing warned of a foreign "invasion" (Gorce 1991: 30; Singer 1991: 814). These elite opinions lent legitimacy to widespread popular sentiments. Two 1991 surveys indicated that 71 percent of the populace thought there were too many Arabs in France and that over 30 percent of the electorate supported the platform of Jean-Marie Le Pen's far-right National Front, which calls for the expulsion of *immigrés* (*Le Monde*, March 22, 1991; Riding 1991).[5] And Chirac, in a now-infamous statement, expressed his sympathy for the decent French working people who are being driven "understandably crazy" by the "noise and smell" of foreigners (Drozdiak 1991; Hall 1991: 18).[6] (Chirac's RPR is the leading force in the center-Right French government that was brought to power in the March 1993 elections.)

"Noise and smell" – music and cuisine – are crucial cultural forms of expression, essential vehicles through which North Africans assert, sustain, and reconfigure their identities in France. And probably the best-known "Arab noise" blasting out of the boomboxes in Maghrebi neighborhoods of Paris and Marseilles is *rai*, a musical genre that arrived in the United States as part of the "World Music" wave in the late 1980s.

This essay tracks the complex trajectory of *rai*, from its origins and evolution in Algeria, to the transformations in its uses and meanings as migrant workers brought it to France, and as it has moved back and forth across the Mediterranean and into the World Music scene. We assess *rai*'s role in the construction of Franco-Maghrebi identities, particularly with regard to gender, tradition, and religion, seeing it as an exemplar of the various hybrid cultural practices that typify Maghrebi integration into French life. We compare the "defensive" cultural identities associated with *rai* against the assertive and multiethnic sensibilities affiliated with rap, the music now favored by young Franco-Maghrebis. Finally, we argue that, despite their marginality, Franco-Maghrebis and their expressive culture are integral to an understanding of contemporary French identity. France is being "Third-Worldized," for assimilation of Maghrebis into French life results not in their "acculturation" but in "cultural syncretism" (Gilroy 1987: 155). Against its will the country is shedding its Europeanness and becoming "mestizo, bastard, [and] fecundated" by formerly victimized civilizations (Goytisolo 1987b: 37–8; see Koptiuch 1991). Franco-Maghrebi expressive culture, in its most utopian moments, serves as a model of decentralized plurality and multiple affiliations, a means of recasting contemporary French identity and undermining French national exclusivism.

Algerian *Rai*: From Country to Pop, Bordello to Patrimoine National

Modern *rai* emerged during the 1920s, when rural migrants brought their native musical styles into the growing urban centers of northwestern Algeria, particularly the port town of Oran (Wahran in Arabic), Algeria's second largest city. In the new urban settings, *rai* developed as a hybrid blend of rural and cabaret musical genres, played by and for distillery workers, peasants dispossessed by European settlers, shepherds, prostitutes, and other members of the poor classes (Virolle-Souibès 1989: 51–2). Oran's permissive atmosphere proved congenial for *rai* artists, who found spaces to perform in its extensive network of nightclubs, taverns, and brothels, as well as in more "respectable" settings like wedding celebrations and festivals. Women singers were prominent from the genre's beginnings, and the performance of *rai*, unique among Algerian musical genres, was associated with dancing, often in mixed-gender settings (Benkheira 1986: 174).

Oran's proximity to Morocco and Spain and its port economy meant that its culture was permeated by multifarious influences. *Rai* musicians therefore absorbed an array of musical styles: flamenco from Spain, *gnawa* (a musical genre performed by Sufis of West African origin) from nearby Morocco, French cabaret, the sounds of Berber Kabylia, the rapid rhythms of Arab nomads. *Rai* artists sang in Orani, an Arabic dialect rich with French and Spanish borrowings and liberally seasoned with Berber.

As early as the 1930s, *rai* musicians reportedly were harassed by the colonial police for singing about social issues of concern to Algeria's indigenous inhabitants, such as typhus, imprisonment, poverty, and colonial oppression. Likewise, during the independence struggle, *rai* artists composed songs that expressed nationalist sentiments (Virolle-Souibès 1988b: 184–6). But throughout this period, *rai*'s main themes were wine, love, and the problems and pleasures of life on the margins. One of *rai*'s most renowned, and bawdy, singers was Cheikha Rimitti,[7] one of whose songs went:

> Oh my love, to gaze upon you is a sin,
> It's you who makes me break my fast.
> Oh lover, to gaze upon you is a sin,
> It's you who makes me "eat" during Ramadan.[8]
> (Virolle-Souibès 1988a: 208)

Another of Rimitti's songs went: "When he embraces me, he pricks me like a snake," and "People adore God, I adore beer" (Virolle-Souibès 1988a: 211, 214).

After Algeria won national independence in 1962, a state-sponsored Islamic reformist chill descended over all manifestations of popular culture until the late 1970s. In the wake of official puritanism, drastic restrictions were imposed on public performances by women singers (Virolle-Souibès 1989: 54). But the genre flourished on the fringes, at sex-segregated events like wedding parties and in the demimonde. Meanwhile, adolescent boys with high-pitched voices replaced female *rai* vocalists in the public arena. At the same time, musicians were supplementing and sometimes replacing the *gasba* (reed flute), the *rbaba* (single-stringed instrument played with a bow), the *gellal* and *derbouka* (Maghrebi drums) – the instruments that had typified the genre for decades – with the more "modern"-sounding *'ud* (Oriental lute), violin, and accordion.

In 1979, *rai* reemerged from the shadows, following President Chadhli Benjedid's loosening of social and economic restraints. By now, *rai* artists had incorporated additional musical influences – including the pop musics of Egypt, India, the Americas, Europe, and sub-Saharan Africa – and were performing and recording with trumpets and electric guitars, synthesizers and drum machines. A new sound known as "pop *rai*" was inaugurated, its stars a generation of young singers known as *chebs* (young men) and *chabas* (young women). In its "pop" incarnation, *rai* shed its regional status, and massive cassette sales quickly made it the national music for Algerian youth. Its popularity derived from its lively, contemporary sound and its raciness. Pop *rai* lyrics, just like "traditional" *rai*, dealt frankly and openly with subjects like sex and alcohol while at the same time challenging both official puritanism and patriarchal authority within the family. The "modernity" of its musical texture and the insubordinate spirit of its messages earned pop *rai* a substantial audience among a generation of disaffected and frequently unemployed youth, chafing at traditional social constraints and the lack of economic opportunities.

As cassette sales soared, producers tried to boost profits by insisting on more risqué lyrics (Virolle-Souibès 1989: 59). The pop *rai* star Chaba Zahouania, whose ruggedly sensual voice earned her the sobriquet "the Billie Holiday of Oran" (Virolle-Souibès 1988b: 197), sang: "I'm going with him, Mamma, I'm climbing in next to him," and "Call Malik so he'll bring the beer" (Virolle-Souibès 1988a: 211, 213). Chaba Fadela, another major pop *rai* star, similarly spiced up her lyrics: "I want to sleep with him, I want him to open up his shirts" (Virolle-Souibès 1988a: 210).

These racy lyrics not only spurred sales; they incurred government wrath in the early 1980s. The association of *rai* with dancing, particularly in mixed-gender company, also provoked the hostility of state officials who adhered to orthodox Islamic views that dancing is obscene (Benkheira 1986: 174–6). But more important, the government felt compelled to suppress an increasingly influential cultural practice that seemed to articulate the sentiments of insubordinate youth claiming new sexual and cultural freedoms – the "*rai* generation." Police rounded up single women patronizing night clubs featuring *rai*, while the government denounced *rai* as "illiterate" and lacking in "artistic merit," banned it from the state-run airwaves, and prohibited the import of blank cassettes in an attempt to halt distribution (Bizot 1988: 89; McMurray and Swedenburg 1991).

But in mid-1985 the government abruptly reversed its position. One reason for the volte-face was the lobbying of a former liberation army officer-turned-pop music impresario, Colonel Snoussi, who hoped to profit if *rai* could be mainstreamed. Another factor in officialdom's shift was the music's growing popularity in France, where the diasporic Maghrebi community provided an expanding market for the music, as well as facilities for production and a distribution network (via the massive to-and-fro movement of immigrants who smuggled cassettes). Pressure was also brought to bear by French Minister of Culture Jack Lang, who urged Algerian officials to grant exit visas to *rai* stars wishing to perform in France. Some sectors of the Algerian *nomenklatura*, moreover, argued that *rai* should be promoted as a counterweight to the growing militant Islamist trend among youth (Benkheira 1986: 177).

So the government relaxed its opposition, *rai* festivals were duly organized in Oran and Algiers, and the music began to receive radio and television exposure. But at the same time that officialdom brought *rai* in from the periphery and claimed it as part of the national patrimony, it attempted to tame, contain, and mainstream the music. A line originally sung by several *chebs* as "we made love in a broken-down shack" was broadcast on Algerian radio as "we did our military service in a broken-down shack" (Bizot and Dimerdji 1988: 133). The police tried to prevent audience members from dancing at the first Oran festival in 1985 (Benkheira 1986: 176). Such pressures prompted the music industry to practice self-censorship. The same producers who had so recently promoted bawdiness started vigorously cleaning up *rai* lyrics in order to get their product played on radio and television and to make it palatable to a wider audience. Rachid Baba, the producer of *Rai Rebels*[9] and other acclaimed *rai* releases for the US market, explained without a hint of irony: "In the beginning, I let a *cheb* sing the words as he wanted. Now I pay attention. When he sings a vulgarity, I say 'Stop.' If he doesn't obey, I cut it during the mixing" (quoted by Virolle-Souibès 1989: 60). The mainstreaming did succeed in increasing *rai*'s audience, for many who were previously put off by *rai*'s "dirty" reputation now found it pleasantly acceptable.

Rai and the Discourse of World Music

US World Music publicity – the CD or cassette jackets, the record reviews, and the critical articles – never tells such stories about *rai*'s self-censorship or its complex relation to the state. Instead, World Beat discourse on *rai* since its US arrival in 1988 has generally promoted it as a vehicle of resistance and compared its role within Algerian society to that of US or British rock music at oppositional moments – Elvis in the mid-1950s, the Beatles and Stones of the late 1960s, the Sex Pistols of the late 1970s. It is advertised as "the music of... Algerian rebel youth,"[10] and commentators claim that Cheb Khaled "is to *rai* what Elvis was to rock" (Bizot and Dimerdji 1988: 93) and that *rai* is a kind of "North African punk" (Eyre 1992: 19). Although there is some truth to such claims, they are essentially based on a projection of a white, Eurocentric model of the culture wars onto Algeria. Such a move allows us – World Music fans – to identify with the Algerian *rai* audience by assimilating their struggles to our models. We can thus sympathize with *rai* audiences who seem to be fighting battles we have already fought – as teenagers demanding more sexual freedom – or are still fighting – as rock fans opposed to religious fundamentalism or official puritanism.

This is not to deride some positive effects of *rai*'s late-1980s arrival on the US World Music scene, which until then had largely ignored or excluded Arabo-Islamic musics. The reputation that Arab musicians like Palestinian American '*ud* and violin virtuoso Simon Shaheen, Sudanese singer Abdel Aziz El Mubarak, and Moroccan *gnawa* artist Hassan Hakmoun have since gained in the West was greatly enabled by *rai*'s breakthrough. But that opening depended in part on a crucial discursive absence. World Music publicity has treated *rai* as a strictly Algerian phenomenon, as a musical genre that has merely absorbed western influences. A more subversive reading would see *rai* as part of the wider endeavor to bring about "the gradual dissolution of 'white' culture by all the peoples who, having been forcibly subjected to it, have assimilated the tricks, the techniques necessary to contaminate it" (Goytisolo 1987b: 38). It is symptomatic, therefore, that World Music publicity ignores the role of *rai* in France, where it has served as a central mode of cultural expression in minority struggles. Perhaps this silence can be attributed to the fact that it is much easier for benevolent white World Music fans to align with (imagined) young rockers or punks fighting the same battles as "us" than it is to express solidarity with racialized Others combating European racism.

The Varieties of Franco-Maghrebi Identity

The diaspora experience is defined, not by essence or purity, but by the recognition of a necessary heterogeneity and diversity: by a conception of "identity" which lives with and through, not despite, difference; by *hybridity*. (Stuart Hall 1989: 80)

As pop *rai* won over Algerian youth, it simultaneously gained adherents among Maghrebi immigrants in France and their offspring – the *Beurs*, as the second generation had come to be known. *Rai* emerged as a crucial cultural vehicle for a minority striving to carve out a space for itself in an inhospitable, racist environment. It became a veritable token of Maghrebi ethnic identity, and presence, in France.

In the summer of 1981, a series of dramatic events involving young Franco-Maghrebis was rapidly transformed by the media into staged spectacles that variously stunned, scared, and titillated an uncomprehending French public. Known as *rodeos*, they took place in the impoverished *banlieues* (suburbs) that encircle French cities and are where the bulk of the Franco-Maghrebi population is concentrated. Young *banlieusards* stole big-engined cars and proceeded to race and perform stunts at dusk for enthusiastic spectators. Before the police could catch them, they would stop, douse the vehicles with gasoline, and torch them. During July and August some 250 vehicles were immolated in these dramatic moments of defiance that were aimed at the hated police and that represented an angry affirmation of the minority's ghettoized existence (Jazouli 1992: 17–22).

This startling display of the drastic problems and incendiary mood of young *banlieue* Franco-Maghrebis was followed by a flurry of organizing and networking by Arab militants. Grassroots groups proliferated as the massive demonstrations organized in 1983 and 1984 thrust the socioeconomic problems and the racist treatment of *franco-maghrébins* upon the national stage. The French public could no longer pretend that the Arabs living in its midst were simply immigrant workers whose presence would be temporary. Here was a militant, visible generation of Maghrebis who spoke French fluently, who were permanent residents, not "visitors," and who were laying claim to full citizenship rights and equal participation in French cultural life.

But who, precisely, are these Franco-Maghrebis, whom French racist discourse usually lumps together into catchall categories like immigrants, Muslims, Maghrebis, Arabs, or foreigners? In fact they are a very heterogeneous group that encompasses Algerians, Moroccans, and Tunisians; Arabs and Berbers; citizens, "legal" noncitizen residents, and "illegals"; immigrants born in the Maghreb and their offspring born in France; *harkis* who fought for France during the Algerian War and their descendants, and Algerians who backed the FLN. An estimated 1.5 million North African "foreigners" (noncitizens) live in France, and tens of thousands more (no one is sure of the total) reside there without legal permission.[11] About one million French citizens are of Maghrebi origin, including from 400,000 to 600,000 *harkis* and their offspring (Etienne 1989: 107; Lanier 1991: 16–17). If we include Jews of North African ancestry, many of whom still identify with the Maghreb, this adds another 300,000 persons (Morin 1991: 535). We are speaking, then, of between 2.5 and 3.5 million persons, out of a total population of 60 million.

Economic conditions

The bulk of the Franco-Maghrebi population, both immigrant and citizen, is concentrated in the multiethnic *banlieues*. These isolated modernist architectural nightmares – bleak zones of high-rises, minimal public facilities, substandard schooling, and exceptional rates of unemployment (70 percent of the children of immigrants in Lyons aged sixteen to twenty-five have no jobs (Begag 1990:6)) – are the true loci of the "immigrant" problem.

Conditions in the *banlieues* are closely tied to the recent restructuring and "rationalization" of the French economy. The economy is moving in a "post-Fordist" direction: gradual state disengagement from economic affairs and the privatization of former state enterprises; decline of trade-union influence as well as of local administrative effectiveness; swelling of the service sector; diminution or flight of large-scale industries employing unskilled labor; the rise of industries using little unskilled labor.[12] The impact of these changes on the immigrant workforce is revealing: between 1973 and 1985 the proportion of working "immigrants" employed in industry fell from 45 percent to 36 percent, and in construction from 35 percent to 26 percent, while "immigrant" participation in the lower-paying service sector rose from 20 percent to 37.5 percent (Lanier 1991: 20).

The spatial marginalization of the Maghrebi population in France also reflects a socioeconomic shift toward the "ethnicization" of the labor force and an increased dependence on undocumented and "reserve" labor in the new era of "flexible specialization" (Naïr 1992: 39–46).[13] One facet of this shift is that the total number of working North African males has decreased by about 5 percent since 1975, whereas the number of Maghrebi women workers has shot up dramatically (by over 150 percent) during the same period. The fall in male employment and the coincident rise in the female workforce is integral to the process of economic restructuring, in which employers tap a "reserve army" of women and youth to maintain profits and ensure flexibility of labor allocation. This transformation in the makeup of the labor force is due in part to the government's halting of immigration in 1974 (until then predominantly a Maghrebi male activity) and its shift to a policy of family reunification (mainly involving Maghrebi women and youth). So sharp was the demographic turnabout that by 1982 more than 44 percent of the Maghrebi population in France was under seventeen years of age, compared with 22 percent for the population as a whole (Talha 1991: 497–9).

Authenticity and hybridity

We employ the term Franco-Maghrebi here as a convenient descriptive device. Although one occasionally encounters the designation *franco-maghrébin*, ethnic groups in France typically do not define themselves in terms of hyphenated identities. Whether one's background is Italian, Spanish, Jewish, or Polish, one is expected to be assimilated, to be simply "French." This requirement has proved difficult for residents and citizens of Third World origins to live up to. It is particularly problematic for North Africans, because memories of recent colonial violence in Algeria remain so vivid and because so many French people believe that the Maghrebis' Islamic heritage makes them unassimilable. Citizens or not, French Arabs tend to be regarded as foreigners.

Many first-generation immigrants would agree, at least in part, with this designation. They have never felt "at home" in France, and dream of returning to their villages of birth as they slowly lay aside savings to build homes there for comfortable retirement. Such *immigrés* often retain an image of an Algeria or a Morocco that continues to uphold the revered traditions and Islamic values. Then there are those Franco-Maghrebis, both immigrants and citizens, who have reacted to French

exclusivism by practicing their own form of isolationism. These are the ethnona-
tionalists, most prominent among them the militant Islamists.

But advocates of a separatist "authenticity" are probably a small minority. Most
Franco-Maghrebis, particularly the younger generation and especially those with
citizenship, dream neither of returning to the motherland nor of establishing an
isolated Maghrebi or Islamic enclave in France. Although all have felt the sting of
racism, few have contemplated departing France for a "home" in an unfamiliar
North Africa. Instead, their project is to create livable zones for themselves within
French society. Most therefore favor some form of integration that does not entail
total assimilation and the abandonment of their "Arabness." They seek to negotiate
integration on their own terms, maintaining their right to be different.

In the wake of the upsurge of Arab militancy in the early 1980s, Franco-Maghrebis born in France began to be known as *Beurs*, a *verlan*[14] term made by reversing
the sounds of *arabe*. Today many educated French Arabs consider this tag pejorative
and lacking in geographic specificity. They prefer the rather cumbersome appellation
"youths originating from North African immigration" (*jeunes issues de l'immigration maghrébine*).[15] Others simply refer to themselves as Algerians or as French. But
none of these terms seem to capture the complex positionality of those who feel
located somewhere "in-between." As one educated young Franco-Maghrebi told us:

We don't consider ourselves completely Algerian or completely French. Our parents are Arabs.
We were born in France (and visited Algeria only a few times). So what are we? French? Arab?
In the eyes of the French we are Arabs. But when we visit Algeria, some people call us emigrants
and say we've rejected our culture. We've even had stones thrown at us [in Algeria].

Such ambiguity is demonstrated in the various avenues of integration Franco-
Maghrebis have chosen to travel, all of which could be considered, in their different
ways, paths of hybridity.[16]

At one end of the hybridity spectrum are the quasi-assimilationists, who tend to
see France as the height of civilization, who frequently change their names from
Karima to Karine or Boubker to Bob, and who practice a kind of hyperconformism
to French societal norms. Members of this group tend to be successful, upwardly
mobile, and well educated, and frequently are of *harki* or *kabyle* (Algerian Berber)
background. They also have organized politically, most notably within the framework of France-Plus, an electoral pressure group that pushes for Franco-Maghrebi
electoral representation on all party tickets except those of Le Pen's National Front
and the Communists. Even Franco-Maghrebis who disapprove of France-Plus's
middle-of-the-road orientation admit it has markedly increased Arab visibility and
influence in the political arena. France-Plus managed to get 390 *Beurs* elected, about
equally divided between parties of the Right and the Left, in the municipal elections
of 1989, a major gain over 1983, when only 12 *Beurs* were voted in (Begag 1990: 9).
Two "*Beurettes*," Nora Zaïdi of the Socialist Party and Djida Tazdaït of the Greens,
were elected to the European Parliament in 1989. France-Plus, however, lacks a
social base in the *banlieues*, and is viewed as representing the interests of the
"*beurgeoisie*" (Aïchoune 1992: 15).

SOS-Racisme, France-Plus's chief competitor in the political sphere, occupies an
intermediate position. Founded in 1985 by activists with close ties to the ruling

Socialist Party, SOS-Racisme built on the wave of *Beur* militancy of the early 1980s, at the same time channeling and neutralizing its energies. The emergence of this multiethnic organization, according to many militants, represented a blunting of the Maghrebi-Arab specificity and orientation of earlier anti-racist struggles (Aïchoune 1991; Jazouli 1992). SOS-Racisme managed to deploy its connections with official-dom, superior organizing skills, media savvy, and ability to attract the financial support of government agencies, so as to position itself as *the* hegemonic group within the anti-racist movement. It gradually shifted the concerns of the anti-racist movement away from a platform stressing immigrants' rights to one that emphasizes individual ethics and diffuse "multiculturalism" (Jazouli 1992). SOS-Racisme evolved into the mediagenic organization of the anti-racist "establishment," the favorite of the ruling (until March 1993) Socialist Party. Although a vocal critic of racism, SOS-Racisme has often argued for quasi-assimilationist positions. Like France-Plus, it enjoys little grassroots support in the *banlieues*.

Arabs who have felt defeated or overwhelmed by an impossible social and economic environment have followed yet another route. These are the "delinquents," chiefly from the impoverished *banlieues*, whose response to the lack of decent educational or employment opportunities has been a resort to petty criminality, random acts of violence, rage, and drug use. Many of these Franco-Maghrebis regard the battle to establish a meaningful identity and comfortable space of existence as utterly hopeless. Yet the position of this group is unstable and contradictory, its members capable of actions, like the *rodeos*, at once nihilist and oppositional.

The opposite end of the spectrum from the *beurgeoisie* is populated by a diffuse array of community-based political and cultural groups that operate fairly autonomously, outside the framework of any overarching umbrella organization. It is these groups that carry on much of the organized activity with a specifically Franco-Maghrebi character. Franco-Maghrebis who hold this perspective aggressively assert their right to a place in France, regard racism as French society's problem, and reject out of hand the notion that they, the Arabs, are the "problem," as racist discourse would have it (see Gilroy 1987: 11). They consider themselves French citizens, just like anyone else, and they lay claim to the French heritage of democracy and freedom of speech. Their attitude might be summed up by the slogan "We're here, we're Beur, get used to it!"[17] They advocate a kind of affirmative identity politics that, at the same time, promotes syncretizing rather than essentializing practices.

Hybridity in Practice: Ramadan Nights in the Diaspora

Rai played a significant part in the story of Franco-Arab mobilization and identity formation. It was aired widely on the local radio stations, such as the celebrated Radio Beur in Paris, that sprang up to serve and instill pride into French North African communities. The music gained greater public visibility as a consequence of the upsurge of Franco-Arab anti-racist struggles of the 1980s, particularly when SOS-Racisme sponsored multicultural concerts featuring *rai*. Prominent Algerian *rai* performers started touring France, and young Franco-Maghrebis began forming their own *rai* bands.

Salah Eddine Bariki's study of Franco-Maghrebi radio stations, carried out in Marseilles – the site of France's largest concentration of Arabs – in 1984, highlights *rai*'s role in the complicated, syncretic processes of Franco-Maghrebi identity formation (Bariki 1986). The most popular radio programming, he discovered, was during Ramadan Nights, the evenings of feasting and celebration following daytime fasting during the holy month, when listeners stayed up late and called radio stations to request songs, tell jokes, engage in political or religious debates, or discuss the meaning of Ramadan for North Africans in France. Almost all callers to Arab stations spoke in "Musulman," as they termed the Arabic spoken in France (meaning they were probably immigrants rather than French-born). Bariki's survey of the everyday practices and beliefs of Marseilles's Arab radio audience showed that most drank alcohol, few condemned mixed marriages (with non-Muslims), about a third had eaten pork, and less than half fasted during Ramadan. But most of them still observed Ramadan, if rather idiosyncratically by orthodox standards. Many made special efforts to buy meat that was *halâl* (slaughtered according to strict Islamic precepts) during the holidays, and a large number claimed they did not drink alcohol for forty days prior to the holy month. Both practices were immigrant innovations.

Participants in the survey described Ramadan Nights radio programming as a nostalgia-laden return to an ambience resembling what they remembered or had heard about Ramadan celebrations in the home country – a time of plentiful food and pleasant relations between parents and children. The evenings of North African entertainment reduced the "burden of exile" by establishing a mood of community closeness. Many radio listeners reaffirmed their ethnic presence by phoning the station to dedicate a song to a relative or friend. Bariki's study shows that the near unanimous favorite of Ramadan radio audiences was Algeria's "King of Rai," Cheb Khaled.

That Arabs of Marseilles selected Cheb Khaled as their favorite vocalist during Ramadan merely underscores the complicated and contradictory nature of North African identity construction in France. For ever since launching his career at the age of fourteen in the mid-1970s, Cheb Khaled has cultivated the image of a swaggering, dissolute, worldly cabaret singer. "When I sing *rai*," Khaled proclaims, "I talk about things directly; I drink alcohol; I love a woman; I am suffering. I speak to the point... I like Julio Iglesias. But he just sings about women, whereas [I sing] about alcohol, bad luck and women" (Bizot 1988: 88; Eyre 1991: 44).

Although not sentiments one normally associates with Ramadan observance in the Arab-Islamic countries, they are consistent with *rai*'s demimonde, anti-puritanical heritage in Algeria. (Recall Cheikha Rimitti's song about "eating" during Ramadan.) According to Hocine Benkheira, during the mid-1980s Cheb Khaled typically opened his concerts in Algeria with a number about Muhammad, then followed it with songs about drink, women, and so on. Whether Khaled's subject was whiskey or the Prophet, the audience danced – and no one present considered this blasphemous (Benkheira 1986: 176). Such attitudes corresponded with cultural life in a tolerant country where, despite official puritanism and a growing Islamist movement, mosque attendance remained comparatively low and alcohol was consumed in open view of the street at the numerous taverns in central Algiers and Oran (Kapil 1990: 36).

In the spring of 1992, we made friends with twenty-three-year old Sonia, "modern" in outlook, a student of English at the University of Avignon, and recently married to Jeannot, the son of a *harki*. Her father left Algeria at age fourteen to work in France. Sonia is in charge of the family grocery store, and supplements her income by flipping Big Macs at Avignon's Golden Arches. She sells liquor in her shop – located in a rundown Maghrebi district where the usual clientele includes addicts and prostitutes – reasoning that although the Qur'an forbids handling alcohol, it is permissible to dispense wine sealed in glass or plastic bottles. But she does not peddle pork, which she would have to touch, an act that would be *harâm* (morally prohibited). Sonia fasts during Ramadan, but finds Islam's five daily prayers too cumbersome to integrate into everyday activities. "You've got to adapt to the society where you live," Sonia asserts, "but if I didn't observe Muslim holidays, there would be nothing to set me apart from any other French person."

Another young Franco-Maghrebi woman we met, *rai* singer Chaba Aïcha, feels strongly about being a Muslim although she does not cover her hair or pray five times daily. She fasts at Ramadan and observes dietary laws for forty days before Ramadan. In her opinion, Islam forbids alcohol not because of its substance but because of its effects. Therefore, she reasons, if one can maintain proper behavior, it is permissible to imbibe.

Such syncretizing attitudes and practices reflect a general secularizing trend within Franco-Maghrebi communities, in the course of which Islam – like Arab cuisine, language, and music – has become for many more a question of ethnic identification than of belief (Jazouli 1992: 133–4). Despite unceasing alarms raised by the mainstream press, the extent of militant Islamist mobilization in France is quite limited, and by some estimates, only 5 percent of the "potential" Islamic population are actually practicing, orthodox Muslims (Etienne 1989: 259–60; Singer 1988: 861).[18] Islamic observances like Ramadan, however, are widely commemorated – but in novel "ethnicized" forms (Safran 1986: 104). The focus of Ramadan has shifted away from daily fasting and praying to the celebratory nighttime meal. In this regard, the Franco-Maghrebi community resembles French society at large, which observes all former religious holidays chiefly as secular feasts. The head of the Paris mosque, for instance, has suggested that on 'Id al-Kabir (the commemoration of Abraham's sacrifice of a ram instead of his son), Muslim families slaughter chickens in the privacy of their homes rather than violate health laws and offend popular prejudice by slaughtering rams according to orthodox precepts (Brisebarre 1989). Lacoste-Dujardin (1992) reports that it is increasingly common for Franco-Maghrebis to imbibe champagne on festive occasions, including religious feasts like 'Id al-Kabir.

The secular, modern, and socially progressive lyrics and ambience associated with *rai* therefore appeal to young Franco-Arabs like Sonia, who desire to belong to a collectivity within France that endorses a tolerant sense of Arabo-Islamic identity. The sentiments of singers like Cheb Khaled resonate with the younger generation's dislike of the strictures imposed by their elders and Islamist orthodoxy:

I am against Islamic fundamentalists. Young people want to progress. Even now, I can't smoke in front of my father, not even a cigarette. Young people who want to speak with a girl or live with her can't talk about it with their parents. In rai music, people can express themselves. We break taboos. That's why fundamentalists don't like what we're doing. (quoted in Eyre 1991: 45)

But Khaled is not anti-Islam per se. "I'm a Muslim man, I love God, but I don't practice and I don't pray," he explains (Goldman 1993). Meanwhile, other *rai* artists incorporate religious themes into their songs. Cheb Anouar's "Bi'r Zem Zem" (from the video *La ballade d'Anouar*), for instance, refers to the famous well in Mecca that figures prominently in the hajj ritual. Anouar sings to his mother about leading the proper life and one day making the hajj. Vendors of *rai* cassettes and videos at Avignon's weekly Arab *sûq* (open-air market) claimed that "Bi'r Zem Zem" was merely Anouar's attempt to cash in on the heretofore ignored "Islamic" market niche. Many stalls in Avignon's *sûq* carry Islamist cassettes featuring Qur'anic recitations, sermons, and how-to guides for proper Islamic conduct, hard by *rai* recordings of Cheb Mami or Chaba Fadela that extol the virtues of libertine lifestyles.

Hybridity in Practice: Women and *Rai*

The analysis of *rai*'s uses within the North African diaspora reveals a great deal, not only about the changing valence of religion and tradition in Franco-Maghrebi identity construction, but also about gender relations, as the following examples illustrate.

Most of the women were sitting on low cushions along the wall at one end of the rented room in the Avignon *banlieue*. Those who felt uncomfortable squatting close to the floor were supported by chairs on the other side of the room. Older women were decked out in long, empire-waisted, shiny polyester Algerian dresses and gold marriage belts. Some younger ones were similarly clad in "traditional" outfits, while others sported slacks or miniskirts plus accessories like geometric earrings or necklaces hung with miniature pastel-colored pacifiers (a 1992 teenage fashion craze throughout Europe). Some women had flown in from Algeria specially for the wedding, while others had traveled north from Marseilles or south from St. Etienne. Only five of the sixty women present were not of North African origin.

Rai provided the sound track for the wedding festivities, but no one was paying much attention to the singers or the lyrics. "If you want to know the name of the singer or the song," they said, "go look at the cassettes." I picked up a bag full of home-dubbed tapes.[19] Most contained minimal or no information, but several Cheb Khaled tapes were clearly marked. When Khaled's 1992 hit "Didi" came on, many younger women jumped up to dance. The room was hopping when a power outage stopped us short.

Someone threw open the windows looking onto the courtyard where the men were gathered. A *rai* singer named Cheb Kader[20] started his set, accompanied by a single instrumentalist on a keyboard synthesizer equipped with drum machine. The dancing inside took up in earnest: a throng of shimmering sequins and beads, provençal skirts, satin and linen, bare shoulders and legs. Dance styles resembled what I had seen in northeastern Morocco in 1986, but occasionally younger women broke into disco steps and some girls seemed to be imitating cabaret belly dancers.

After midnight, over bowls of *chorba* and *tajine*, I asked some chicly accoutered lycée girls whether they liked the music. Not very much. What did they listen to?

Funk – African American. But they supposed that when their turns came, their weddings would be like this one. I tried to imagine James Brown's "Funky Drummer" blaring out amid the crowd of matrons who had flown in from Algeria for this gender-segregated event.

Rai was passé for, but tolerated by, the under-twenty set. But to the twenty-three-year-old bride and her generation, it signified a strong attachment to Algerian roots. The older women regarded *rai* as merely familiar Arabic music – perhaps not their first choice, but good for dancing. *Rai* was the musical form of expression uniting the generations in this community celebration.

Weddings like this remain major sites for *rai* performance and consumption. *Beur* radio stations in the major cities also serve up *rai* on a regular basis, often as part of astonishing sets that also feature African American funk, tunes from Berber Kabylia, Caribbean reggae, rap, and Zairean *soukous*. *Rai* is also disseminated via video technologies. Several videotapes sold in Arab stores and market stands feature live concert footage of *chebs* (male *rai* singers) at festivals in Oran or on European tour. Others show *chabas* or older *cheikhas* in staged settings, like Cheikha Rimitti's television-studio "wedding" performance.

Another video genre that focuses on gender relations is the narrative music video dealing with romantic love. Cheb Anouar's above-mentioned video, *La ballade d'Anouar*, not only pays homage to Mecca but also features numbers depicting teenage dating and the pain of separation from one's lover. Videos from the famous married couple of *rai*, Chaba Fadela and Cheb Sahraoui, often narrativize romantic relationships between boyfriend and girlfriend, in stereotypically western settings.

Such videos advocate a rejection of the "traditional" and patriarchal family power relations that continue to define the lives of so many young Franco-Maghrebi women. In fact, differences of opinion on how to integrate into French culture often focus on gender issues. The controversy about the appropriate behavior for women seems exacerbated both by the preference of French employers for female, as opposed to male, Franco-Maghrebi labor and the tendency of French society and media to treat young Franco-Maghrebi women as "model" citizens while subjecting Arab men to overt discrimination and denigration (Jazouli 1992: 179). Many ostensibly "integrated" Franco-Maghrebi males, who haunt the nightclubs and have white girlfriends, invoke traditional values when dealing with their own sisters and zealously police their movements in and outside the home. Parents, too, often attempt to uphold ethnic identity, at least within the domestic sphere, by insisting on controlling their daughters' extradomestic activities, by trying to choose their marriage partners, and by requiring that they wait on their brothers and fathers hand and foot when at home. Even young, unmarried Franco-Maghrebi women who appear completely at ease in French society assert that they would face tremendous problems if their families found out that they had been sitting with a man at a café. And for such young women, marriage to a non-Muslim would automatically cause a radical break with their families.[21]

Hence romantic love, involving dating before marriage and the option of choosing one's marriage partner without the interference of kin, is regarded as liberatory by many Franco-Maghrebi youth (as well as young people in North Africa).[22] But paradoxically, whereas many *rai* songs and videos promote romance as well as more freedom for women, the jackets of *rai* cassettes seem governed by normative codes that confine Maghrebi women to the private realm. The *cheb's* photograph almost invariably adorns his cassette, but tapes by *chabas* typically feature picturesque Algerian countryside vistas or photographs of women – sometimes lissome surfer girls with lush blonde hair and deep tans – who are more "conventionally" beautiful – by western standards – than the *chabas* who sing the music contained within.

Before we traveled to France, we heard several explanations for this absence in the World Music publicity on *rai*. An Algerian student claimed that the celebrated Chaba Zahouania, with the distinctive, vigorously husky voice and ribald lyrics, was unmarried, and forbidden by her family in Algeria to perform in public or to be photographed for album jackets. What resemblance, we wondered, did Zahouania bear to the exquisitely beautiful and exotic chiffon-draped belly dancer on the cover of her suggestively titled US release, *Nights Without Sleeping*?[23] We then came across another explanation: Zahouania did not sing in public because she was a divorcée with four children who did not want her ex-husband's family to be able to argue in court that she was an unfit mother and thereby win custody of the children (Rosen 1990: 23).[24] Wandering Paris' Arab district of Goutte d'Or in the summer of 1992, we found dozens of Chaba Zahouania cassettes for sale, none with a photograph of the elusive singer. But we did discover a video featuring Chaba Zahouania performing live before a television studio set. Zahouania looked about forty and wore a modest, western-style dress. Thick glasses magnified her conventional plainness. Later, acquaintances from the Netherlands told us that in an interview with a Dutch paper, Chaba Zahouania explained that her picture was not displayed on cassettes because she considered herself ugly! Perhaps *rai*'s advocacy of greater freedom for women is held back as much by the internalization of western standards of beauty as by "patriarchal" constraints.

We met *rai* artist Chaba Aïcha after seeing her perform, complete with disco globe and fog machine, at a modest hall near Avignon in August 1992. She claimed that *rai* is the music of women who have a great deal of experience in life, and that mothers with no husbands have traditionally sung *rai* to support their children. Aïcha's repertoire includes tunes about problematic love affairs, unemployment, parental restrictions, and undocumented immigrants. Her close-cropped hairdo and butch outfits projected an image unlike that of any other *chaba* we have come across, and reminded us of k.d. lang. Even the androgynous, progressive Chaba Aïcha did not want her photo to appear on the cover of her first release – but the Marseilles-based recording company insisted.[25] The photos of another female of *rai*, the chubby – by western standards – Chaba Fadela, also show up on cassettes. She usually wears unassuming dress (although sometimes a black leather jacket) and is always accompanied by her husband, *rai* singer Cheb Sahraoui.

In marked contrast to the *chabas*' public propriety, Franco-Maghrebi *rappeuse* Saliha strikes a pose that is at once defiant and seductive. On the cover of her 1991 recording, *Unique*, Saliha is fitted out in a sleek black mini, hands encased in black leather half-gloves. Romantic love as liberation does not feature prominently in the hip-hop emanating from the *banlieues*, nor does a wholesome image "sell" in the rap market. Yet French rappers appear unable to escape conventional expectations regarding female looks.

From *Rai* Thing to Rap Thang

By the mid-1980s, *rai* was breaking out of the strictly "ethnic" boundaries that characterized its uses in the Marseilles of Bariki's study. It gained greater public visibility during the upsurge of Franco-Arab struggles and through SOS-Racisme's concerts, which gained it an audience among anti-racist whites. In the late 1980s and early 1990s, *rai*'s star rose in French World Music circuits and then, via Paris, it was propelled into the international World Beat market.[26] By 1990, when Islamist campaigns against *rai*, as well as the lure of higher earnings and global exposure, prompted several of its leading figures (Cheb Khaled, Cheb Mami, Chaba Fadela, and Cheb Sahraoui) to relocate from Algeria to France, Paris became a major *rai* center.

More recently, *rai*'s fortunes in France have varied according to the trends within the Franco-Maghrebi community. For their part, the "*beurgeoisie*" and their benevolent white liberal and Socialist allies continue to sponsor concerts and festivals featuring Arab music, including *rai*. Such events, which celebrate the "authentic" culture or folklore of "the people," represent efforts to disguise the liberals' lack of a social base in the *banlieues*. State monies for such concerts were abundant under Socialist rule.

At the grassroots level, *rai*'s core audience has been somewhat diminished. It is now the music of choice principally for recent immigrants and "les jeunes issues de l'immigration maghrébine" over the age of twenty-five. *Rai* performers continue to tour the French-Arab communities, performing at modest local dance halls and at weddings. But none of the major figures – Cheb Mami, Cheb Kader, Chaba Fadela and Cheb Sahraoui, or Chaba Zahouania – managed to capitalize on their momentary successes on the World Music scene between 1988 and 1990, when a number of *rai* recordings were released on various US or international labels. Crossover success remains limited.

The exception is Cheb Khaled, who after years of performing for adoring Franco-Maghrebi audiences has finally, and spectacularly, "crossed over" into the French and international pop scene. His 1992 LP release, *Khaled*,[27] is a remarkable recording that manages to incorporate an impressive mélange of styles – traditional "folk" and "pop" *rai*, funk and reggae, flamenco and cabaret. But it is the hit single "Didi" that propelled Khaled into the international pop arena. Opening to *derbouka* rhythms, "Didi" switches to a deep-bass hip-hop underpinning, and is constructed around an instantly recognizable instrumental hook and a hummable chorus. In the spring of 1992 it was a dance-hall favorite throughout France.[28] The "Didi" video, aired frequently on French television and a key ingredient in the song's success, is a rapid-fire, MTV-style, cut-and-mix of images of a Moorish *mashrabiya* (wooden latticework screen), evocations of a Sufi music circle, and hip-hop steps performed by a multiethnic team of miniskirted dancers.[29]

In July 1992, some Franco-Maghrebi women we met in Avignon told us that mainstream French nightclubs and discos had finally, in the past two or three months, begun playing Arab music – but only Khaled. The Franco-Maghrebi men sitting with us had to take their word for it, for Arab men are still regularly turned away at the doors of French clubs. The first Arab voice to penetrate French discos failed to open the gates either for his Arab brothers who wish to dance there or for the discs of other *chebs* and *chabas*. It should be stressed that a key ingredient in the success of "Didi" – besides its intrinsic qualities – was Barclay's heavy promotion. A subsidiary of Virgin Records, Barclay is one of the big six recording companies (along with BMG, EMI, PolyGram, Sony, and Warner) that control 83 percent of the French market (Laing 1992: 129). Without such backing, commercial triumph is likely to continue to elude other *rai* artists.

As Khaled (who has now dropped the title Cheb, with its *rai* associations) captivated non-Arab music fans in France and elsewhere in Europe, he was abandoned by some of his original devotees. Some asserted that this occurred after Khaled was interviewed on television, where he expressed the same views about wine and women that he voices in his songs. Although Franco-Maghrebi fans did not object to Khaled singing about such subjects, some were offended when he discussed them on the air. Others claim that Khaled demonstrated disrespect for community values when he canceled a number of concerts scheduled for Arab audiences due to drunkenness and when he released a music video featuring "scantily dressed" dancers. Still others said that Khaled had "sold out" to western commercialism.

Although such complaints were voiced frequently in the summer of 1992, *Khaled* appeared to be selling briskly in the music stores we visited in Arab quarters in Paris and Marseilles. Meanwhile, "Didi" went high in the charts throughout Europe, sold well in the *sûqs* of northern Morocco, and ruled the airwaves in Israel, Jordan, and Lebanon. In October and November 1992, "Didi" occupied the number 1 spot on Egypt's official Top 40, and by May 1993, *Khaled* was said to have sold 2.5 million tapes there (de Neys 1993). By the spring of 1993, "Didi" was a certified global phenomenon (although one that seems to have bypassed the United States), and with the aid of video broadcasts on European and Asian MTV had sold 4.5 million copies (Dickey and de Koster 1993).

It is not yet clear what this unprecedented international popularity for a Franco-Maghrebi singer will ultimately mean. Will Khaled's move out of "ethnic" space contribute to a corrosion of dominant/white French culture, or will hegemonic western forces deploy Khaled as a convenient spokesman against "backward" Algerian traditions and Islamic "fundamentalism"?

Ironically, even as Khaled's reputation soared, French Arab youth had already largely abandoned *rai* for rap. This conversation with a group of twenty-something Franco-Maghrebis in Avignon suggests some of the continuities and differences between Khaled's *rai* and the new *rap français*:

Mehmed: Everyone listens to *rai*. It creates a festive atmosphere. Rap is for adolescents, fifteen to twenty years old, who have hard lives and feel lost. Rap is for their generation. *Rai* only talks about love, but rap speaks about society and how to change it.

Malika: I object. Rappers talk about their society because they are not doing well. Rappers are guys who don't have work, who don't have much, and they project messages about changing society. But in certain songs of Cheb Khaled, when you see that he speaks of love, of alcohol, of everything that is taboo in our culture, well, it's clear that he also wants a change. They're not only love songs. If they were, why would some of them be banned in Algeria? Umm Kalthum sings love songs and they're not banned.[30] *Rai* songs evoke emancipated, libertine women. They, too, contain messages.

Salah: Rap tries to change daily life, but *rai* tries to change a culture. Both rap and *rai* reclaim something which has been kept from us.

In a number titled "Do the Raï Thing," Malek Sultan of the rap group I AM likewise equates the social significance of *rai* and rap when he dubs Cheb Khaled "le Public Enemy arabe."[31] But this resemblance was all but lost on the second- and third-generation Franco-Maghrebi boys, between six and ten, at a birthday party Joan Gross attended in an Avignon *banlieue*. "No Arab music!" the boys yelled, whenever their mothers put "Didi" on the tape recorder. The moms appeased them with hip-hop, but periodically snuck the funky "Didi" back on the player. Eventually the boys were break dancing to the arabesque grooves of "le Public Enemy arabe."

Rapattitude

The late 1980s found the French media again training their lenses on the menacing youth of the *banlieues*. The focus of renewed concern was not *rodeos* but the apparent danger of suburban ghettos going the way of South Central Los Angeles and the South Bronx. What had become visible to the media, particularly after a wave of riots in *banlieues chaudes* like Vaulx-en-Velin and Sartrouville during 1990 and 1991, and the *banlieusard*-organized lycée strikes, demonstrations, and attendant "anarchic" violence of the fall of 1990, were the gangs (*bandes*) and their associated practices: "tagging," drug use, petty crime, and rap music.[32] The right-wing press sounded the alert, luridly suggesting links between *banlieue* youth and crack, AIDS, gang warfare, and welfare scrounging, all of which, the press suggested, inhered in immigrant culture. There were even intimations in the extreme-Right *Minute-La France* that the big (immigrant) drug dealers of Marseilles were using profits from heroin sales to finance "certain Arab movements in France" (Folch 1992: 19). In this latest version of the French nightmare, it was the illegible "tags" (*le graff*) of the *banlieue* posses that threatened to deface all the walls and monuments of *la civilisation française*.

For their part, most members of the French gangs or "posses," who give themselves names like Black Tiger Force or Black Dragons and turn out in continental hip-hop garb – Air Jordans, baseball caps, and baggy pants – regard themselves as part of an oppositional youth movement whose sonic expression is rap music. This new multiracial orientation reflects the ethnically diverse character of the predominantly "immigrant" *banlieues*. The *bandes*, whose argot is a distinctive blend of French *verlan* and US hip-hop vernacular,[33] often include Arabs (*rebeus* or *beurs* in *verlan*), Jews (*feujs*, from *juifs*), Blacks (*renois*, from *noires*), Portuguese (*tos*), and white French. The posses are vigorously anti-racist, and many try to project a positive image that marks them off from the *cailleras* (from *racailles*), "riffraff," gangs involved in criminal activities like drug dealing and theft (Aïchoune 1991: 79, 89). Franco-Maghrebis belonging to the *bandes* of the 1990s therefore appear markedly different from the "delinquent" Maghrebi youth of the early 1980s, whom Adil Jazouli (1982) described as being incapable of fashioning coherent identities, as trapped between two distinct cultural poles (French and Arab), neither of which could accommodate them.

French rappers achieved a remarkable proficiency (by US standards) and media visibility by the early 1990s.[34] Coming from *banlieue* backgrounds, *rappeurs* and *rappeuses* attempt to express, as well as to shape and mobilize, the sentiments of ghetto youth.[35] Their most salient messages are anti-racist, including the assertion of the need for interracial solidarity, for the unity of "Black, Blanc, *Beur.*" French rap groups, like the *bandes* of the *banlieues* but unlike rap groups or youth gangs in the United States, tend to be multiracial; the Marseilles rap group I AM, for instance, includes whites, Blacks, and Arabs. Their messages and historical sensibilities, however, tend to be pro-Black African; the backing tracks, as in US rap, are composed primarily of sampled African American riffs and beats. Yet while it articulates pro-Blackness, French rap is largely devoid of the Black nationalism so hegemonic within African American hip-hop. Saint Denis rappers Supreme NTM have even criticized Louis Farrakhan (head of the Nation of Islam, promoted by US rappers Public Enemy and Ice Cube), asserting that he is an agent of hatred just like Le Pen ("Blanc et Noir"). Such a contentious claim would be virtually unthinkable in the US hip-hop nation.[36]

But although they are anti-Le Pen, French rappers refuse to define themselves in terms of a hegemonic political discourse of Right, Center, or Left. They thereby manifest the disdain for traditional "politics" that is typical of the "new social movements" (Mercer 1990: 44). Rappers propose multiracial alliance and anti-racism as the alternative to the "old" politics, and often present music and dancing as the chief means to achieve these utopian ideals. According to *Beurette* rapper Saliha, "Seul le beat aujourd'hui nous lie et nous unit" ("Today only the beat links and unites us").[37] Rappers express total disdain for the state – "ce putain d'état," as I AM dubs it[38] – and the police. They dream of more money being allocated to the *banlieues* and of a cutoff in funds to the army while advocating equal rights for immigrants.[39] French homeboys and homegirls refuse all media discourses that brand them as criminals and barbarians. They promote a renewed spirit of militancy, anger, and menace, and self-consciously distinguish themselves from the pacifistic and mediagenic image projected by the state-friendly anti-racists of SOS-Racisme.[40]

The largest single constituent of the multiethnic *banlieue* posses and rap audiences is probably Franco-Maghrebi youth. Arab rappers (like Saliha, Malek Sultan of I AM, members of MCM 90, and Prophètes de Vacarme) occupy a significant position in the movement, although Black rappers appear to be preeminent. Rap numbers, whether by Black, white, or Maghrebi artists, are typically peppered with samples from Arabic music, positive references to Palestine and Islam, and the occasional Arabic expression ("Allahu akbar," "Salaam"). The name of one of the foremost rap groups, Supreme NTM, is short for *Nique ta mère* (Fuck your mother). This designation is symptomatic of the degree to which street slang has adopted Arabic terms (*nique*, sometimes spelled *nik*, is Arabic for "fuck").

But despite Maghrebis' significant involvement in the French rap scene, rap lyrics make few references to the history of French colonialism in the Maghreb. Instead, like US hip-hop, French rap expresses a hegemonic Afrocentric historical sensibility concerned mainly with sub-Saharan – not North or Arab – Africa. North Africa is mentioned only in the context of Afrocentric claims about the Black origins of civilization in ancient Egypt. (Most of I AM's members carry Pharaonic "tags": Kheops, Akhenaton, Imhotep, and Divin Kephren.) Rappers compose rhymes about the history of slavery, humanity's origins in Africa, Europe's destruction of African civilizations, and the struggle against apartheid – but almost none concerning Arabo-Islamic civilization,[41] colonial violence in North Africa, or the FLN-led independence struggle in Algeria.[42] Perhaps this absence stems in part from rap's roots in a diasporic, Afrocentric form of cultural expression that does not usually deal with specifically "Arab" subjects.[43] This hesitancy of otherwise militant rappers seems to echo the incapacity of society at large to confront the bloody colonial history that still poisons race relations in the metropole. The fact that a significant portion of rap's audience is composed of descendants of *harkis* (who fought along-side the *colons* in the Algerian War) also doubtless contributes to *rappeurs'* reticence concerning colonialism in Algeria.

While the Right fulminated about crack, rap, and immigrant hordes, the Socialist establishment's tactic was to try to co-opt the youth subculture. "Le rap, le graff; I believe in this generation," intoned Jack Lang, hip-hop's loudest elite cheerleader, during his tenure as culture minister. Lang's attempts to appropriate rap included arranging museum space for graffiti artists, subsidizing tours by hard-core rappers NTM, and inviting rap artists to perform at a prime minister's garden party before nonplussed National Assembly members (James 1991; Riding 1992). His justifica-tion was typically elitist: "A man of the theater such as myself would tell you that rap bears a relationship to *la commedia dell'arte* as it was practiced in the sixteenth and seventeenth century" (Labi et al. 1990).[44] But if such sponsorship earned hip-hoppers greater publicity, there are few signs that *banlieusard* youth are about to be tamed. "What gratitude should I have for France," raps NTM's Joey Starr, "I, whom they consider a barbarian?"[45]

Moor Better Blues

Beyond the realms of *rai* and rap, Franco-Maghrebis have actively invaded, created, or influenced an impressive range of expressive forms, from the humble local super-market – where canned couscous or tabbouleh may be purchased – to the pinnacle of high culture, the Paris Opera – where we find the star dancer Kader Bélarbi (Videau 1991: 39). The fiction of Tahar Ben Jelloun (1987 winner of France's most presti-gious literary award, the Prix Goncourt), Driss Chraïbi, and Abdelkebir Khatibi crowds the "Franco-phone" shelves in the bookstores (Hargreaves 1989). Arab comedians are making inroads as well. Tunisian-born Lilia is a prominent figure on the Paris stage, and the television and video sketches of the well-known comedy trio Les Inconnus frequently revolve around the misadventures of its *Beur* member.[46] The 1990–1 television season was enlivened by "La Famille Ramdan," a Cosby-ish sitcom (the oldest son was a doctor) about a *Beur* family (Hargreaves 1991). The most successful French Arab comedian, Smaïn, is often described as the successor to the late, and now canonical, figure Coluche.[47]

But it is to popular music, and not just in genres like *rai* and rap, that the Franco-Maghrebi contribution has been especially rich, complex, and contradictory. Among the expressive cultural forms, popular music seems particularly amenable to syncre-tization and cross-fertilization, because it is relatively unconstrained by the generic rules that fetter traditional or elite genres (see Barber 1987; Malkmus and Armes

1991: 23). Take the startlingly innovative heavy-metal band Dazibao, whose Mo-
roccan-born vocalist, Jamil, sings screeching Arabic vocals that cascade over grunge-
metal. Dazibao performed in June 1992 at a free outdoor music festival organized to
keep Marseilles's heavily "Maghrebized" 13th and 14th arrondissements "cooled
off."[48] Although the band inspired white head-bangers to thrash about wildly, they
seem to have left inner-city North Africans unmoved, despite Jamil's between-song
exhortations (in French) to be proud of one's Arabic heritage.

During the same month Radio Beur in Aix-en-Provence held a fund-raiser on its
first anniversary, attended by a casually attired but well-heeled, college-town Maghrebi crowd able to pay the 100 francs (approximately twenty dollars) admission. The
show's emotional peak was Parisian-Algerian blues-jazz-funk crooner Jimmy Oihid's
performance (in French) of "Ballade pour les enfants," his famous tribute to the
Palestinians.[49] The spots dimmed as hundreds of Bic lighters flickered on. Many
sang along with the chorus as the dance floor swayed solemnly to the lament's
measured beat. Although hybridized Franco-Maghrebis may care little for Arab
nationalism or Maghrebi "traditions," even the *beurgeoisie* identifies strongly with
Palestinian militancy.

There are other styles and cultural tendencies as well. Sapho, a French New Wave
jazz/rock singer raised in a Jewish household in Marrakesh, actively celebrates her
"Oriental heritage" as the source of her musical inspiration and performs with
North African string musicians and sub-Saharan percussionists (Billard 1987).
Mano Negra, whose members are of Spanish, Corsican, and Moroccan back-
grounds, belt out polyglot (Arabic, French, Spanish, and English) tunes to a frenetic
bouillabaisse of punk, rockabilly, reggae, flamenco, and *rai* styles – something like
The Clash gone pan-Mediterranean. Until recently the Franco-Maghrebi rock group
Carte de Séjour (meaning "residence card") vocalized in both French and Arabic,
and churned out guitar riffs tinged with subtle arabesques; their former leader,
Rachid Taha, continues to record in this vein as a solo artist. Finally, there is the
Franco-Tunisian Amina, France's representative at the mainstream 1991 Eurovision
contest, who sings cabaret ballads and disco-funk in French, Spanish, and Arabic,
and is backed by a band composed of Euro-French, West African, and North African
musicians.[50] Amina proclaims, "I will continue preaching for the mixture of cultures. . . . The more hybridization we have, the less we'll hear about claims to [a pure]
culture" (Attaf 1991: 52).

El Harba Wayn? (To Escape, but Where?)

Franco-Maghrebis deploy such syncretizing mechanisms to carve out a space for
themselves where they can identify simultaneously with French and Arab cultures
while rejecting French ethnocentrism and Algerian conservatism. Yet at times the
pressures from both French racists and Algerian traditionalists seem overwhelming,
and the Franco-Maghrebi border "zone" shrinks to a "line." Potent memories of
racist brutality, colonial and postcolonial, are relived with each new threat and
attack. Older Maghrebis still recall the horrific police massacre of three hundred
to four hundred Algerian immigrants in Paris in October 1961, after a demonstra-
tion organized in favor of the FLN – probably this century's bloodiest racial atrocity

against immigrants to occur in the West. The younger generation still remembers Habib Grimzi, an Algerian killed when French soldiers tossed him from a speeding train in November 1983, and carried his picture at the head of the 100,000-strong anti-racist march on Paris in December 1983. Similar incidents are a constant feature of Franco-Maghrebi existence, with over 250 Arabs killed in racist attacks since 1985 (Alcalay 1993: 12).[51]

Franco-Maghrebis felt especially vulnerable and beleaguered during the 1991 Gulf War, when French newspaper headlines howled about "the Arab Threat in France" and "Arab Terrorism in France," and Michel Poniatowski, who was interior minister during Giscard d'Estaing's presidency, suggested the mass expulsion of immigrants (Attaf 1991: 55). A poll in *Le Figaro*, taken during the war, showed that 70 percent of all French "Muslims" (i.e., Arabs)[52] feared they would become targets of terrorist attacks, and more than half felt that the war could lead France to deport Muslim immigrants (LaFranchi 1991; see also Ben Jelloun 1991). Rumors raged through southeastern France about Arab immigrants arming themselves and attacking whites, and caused a run on guns and ammunition by panicky French natives (Cambio 1991; Leblond 1991). During this period of heightened tensions, France-Plus urged Franco-Maghrebis to remain calm and not to organize demonstrations, and Arab stations like Radio-Gazelle in Marseilles and Radio-Soleil in Paris decided not to air recordings like "Vas-y Saddam!," the song by Algerian Mohammed Mazouni that was so wildly popular across the Mediterranean (Bernard 1991). To its credit, SOS-Racisme came out against the war, but it lost many liberal supporters as well as significant financial backing (Lhomea 1991).

Meanwhile, back in Algeria, hybrid cultural forms were also under assault from conservative forces who branded popular music – especially *rai* – not merely as "noise" but also as "illicit" and "immoral." *Rai* artists and consumers came under intense pressure in the wake of the sweeping municipal electoral victories of the Islamist party, Le Front Islamique du Salut (the Islamic Salvation Front, known as FIS), in 1990. The FIS-dominated city council of Oran canceled funding for the annual *rai* festival scheduled for August 1990, and its mayor banned a Cheb Mami concert on the grounds that his lyrics were offensive. Cheb Mami, Cheb Sahraoui, and other *rai* artists who returned from France to perform that summer were harassed and sometimes physically threatened by Islamists. As the Islamist movement emerged as a significant forum of expression for alienated Algerian youth in the late 1980s and early 1990s, it reportedly cut into *rai*'s audience, reducing it, according to some accounts, by over 50 percent.[53]

During Ramadan 1991 (which fell during March) FIS mounted a vigorous campaign against the public performance of music (*rai* and other genres). Fourteen persons were injured in Algiers on March 21 when young Islamists, attempting to torch a performance hall and halt a concert, clashed with police. On March 24, crowds led by FIS activists threw bottles and stones at another concert audience, injuring several fans.[54] An anti-*rai* plank was central to FIS's successful platform in the December 1991 elections (Ireland 1992). Franco-Maghrebi writer Mohamed Kacimi, attending a Friday prayer service in late 1990 at an Algiers mosque, reports hearing FIS second-in-command Ali Benhadj make the following remark: "As for the secularists, pseudo-democrats, atheists, feminists and francophones, and other evil-doers [*suppôts de Satan*], the day we gain power we'll put boats at their disposal which will take them to their motherland – France."[55] The crowd, according Kacimi, was entranced (Attaf 1991: 55). Writing at the time of the Gulf War, Kacimi wondered where – given virulent French anti-Arab sentiment and the rise of religious-based intolerance in Algeria – *franco-maghrébins* should go.

Kacimi's question recalls Cheb Khaled's celebrated song of alienated fury, "El harba wayn?" (To escape, but where?), released when *rai* was at its peak of popularity in Algeria. It was reportedly taken up as an anthem by rioting Algerian youths during the violent October 1988 urban insurgencies that resulted in over five hundred civilian deaths (Rosen 1990: 23). (Many rioters were since won over by FIS.) It goes:

> Where has youth gone?
> Where are the brave ones?
> The rich gorge themselves,
> The poor work themselves to death,
> The Islamic charlatans show their true face.
> So what's the solution? We'll check it out.
> You can always cry or complain
> Or escape. But where?[56]

Rai and rap are both possible "lines of flight" (Deleuze and Guattari 1983) for Franco-Maghrebis, cultural borderzones of syncretism and creative interminglings of French and Arab. At once "ethnic" and French, they are fronts in the wider cultural-political struggle to recast French national identity and force a kind of genetic mutation in French culture. Both *rai* and rap are practices of "inter-culturation" (Mercer 1987) or "transculturation," which George Yúdice describes as "a dynamic whereby different cultural matrices impact reciprocally – though not from equal positions – on each other, not to produce a single syncretic culture but rather a heterogeneous ensemble" (1992: 209).[57]

We should distinguish, within this heterogeneous ensemble, the relatively "defensive" and "ethnic" deployment of *rai* music by immigrants and twenty-plus Franco-Maghrebis, and the more assertive and multiethnic uses of rap by the younger generation of French Arabs. *Rai* represents a more cautious and separatist sensibility insofar as it reproduces cultural linkages with a remembered Algeria. With its cultural roots in Algeria, *rai* offers a kind of protective shield for immigrants who are experiencing the disruptions, dislocations, and insecurities of migration, who feel vulnerable to racist discrimination and economic marginality, and who wish to maintain an originary, imaginary communal identification. *Rai* is one tool that immigrants use in their attempts to "widen the margins," to expand their sphere of existence and identity beyond the claustrophobic confines imposed by the status of manual laborers (Balibar 1992). *Rai* performance and consumption re-create a relatively free and protected cultural zone, not unlike that of contemporary Oran or Algiers, in which Algerians in France can relax and feel "at home." *Rai* performances are also ritual occasions for the expression of pride and protest, where, as in music performances among African Americans and Black British, a "moral, even a political community" is defined (Gilroy 1990: 275, 277).

It is *rai*'s association with a progressive vision of Algeria – the contemporary, relaxed, sophisticated, tolerant, and urban image of the homeland that *rai* audiences selectively privilege – that attracts over-twenty, non-immigrant, French-born Magh-rebis. Equally important are *rai*'s modern, syncretic-pop sound and its danceability. The synthesizers, drum machines, and advanced production techniques combine to produce a musical texture that audiences regard as proof that Euro-Arab music is not quaintly "folkloric," but is as modern and advanced as any popular European music. As Khaled remarked about his "American sound" on the album *Khaled*:

I said to myself, if rock musicians in Europe can take our instruments and rhythms for their music, then why can't I do the same? I wanted to show people in France, where there's a lot of racism – they don't like us there, and that's a fact – that we can do anything they can, and better. (Goldman 1993)[58]

On the other hand, because *rai* is (virtually) always sung in Arabic and every recording is recognizably "Arab" in instrumentation and melody, it always carries an unmistakable air of "otherness" to the western ear. Today's *rai* is an expression of cosmopolitan "modernity" that self-consciously distances and distinguishes itself from Euro-pop (see Urla 1993). Franco-Maghrebis' attachments to *rai* also stem from its function as a marker of ethnic difference and its ability to evoke solidarity. *Rai* therefore manages to be at once "ethnic" and "intercultural."

Rap music, by contrast, is deployed in more volatile and intrusive ways, and expresses and mobilizes new forms of identity. It serves as the badge of a multiethnic minority youth subcultural movement that participates in the struggle against the new racism's attempts to impose rigid boundaries around French national culture. Rap is a key weapon in minority youths' attempts to invade from the margins and "dehomogenize" the French cultural core. (Khaled has invaded, too, but in a less threatening or incendiary manner.) Unlike the sometimes nostalgic and community-based appeal of *rai*, rap is aggressively deterritorializing and anti-nostalgic, even as it reterritorializes a multiethnic space. Rappers combine elements of the African-Caribbean musical diaspora with the specific concerns of the multiethnic French minorities, linking the diasporic Mediterranean to the diasporic Black Atlantic (see Gilroy 1992, 1993). It remains to be seen, however, whether rap will fully open up to assertions of Maghrebi identity, or will remain an ensemble that is heavily weighted toward the diasporic African cultural matrix.

The cultural milieus associated with both rap and *rai* provide alternative hetero-geneous discourses, clearing larger spaces in which formerly colonized subjects can live the multiplicity inherent in diasporic existences. In some of those intercultural zones, they contribute to the corrosion and mutation of dominant French identity. Maybe one day the "decent" people in France will listen avidly to the sounds of Chaba Zahouania or I AM, and consider the speeches of Le Pen and Chirac to be obnoxious "noise." Maybe one day French natives will decipher the graffiti, and learn that *l'humanité* and الإنسانيّة are synonyms, not mutually exclusive.

Postscript

In January 1992, the Algerian regime canceled the second round of national elec-tions after first-round results indicated that FIS would be the resounding winner. A military government with a civilian veneer was established, and quickly became embroiled in a "dirty war" against the Islamist militants.[59] Faced with daily attacks by Islamist guerrillas, who by the fall of 1992 were killing about one policeman per day,[60] the shaky regime attempted to enlist *rai* in an effort to win popular support. After disbanding FIS and dismissing Islamist mayors and city councils, the government permitted the annual *rai* festival to be held, once again, in Oran in the summer of 1992. On Thursday nights state-run television broadcast *rai* music videos on the program *Bled musique* (Country Music). Devout Muslims frequently called in to complain that the program promoted corrupt western values and was not "educational." They were particularly scandalized by the seductive dancing and miniskirts of Khaled's "Didi" video.

In 1994, after three years of struggle and a death toll of between ten thousand and fifteen thousand (Reuters, November 1, 1994), militant Islamists declared a sentence of death for "vulgar" singers. In September, Berber singer Lounes Matoub was kidnapped (but eventually released unharmed), and the popular *rai* singer Cheb Hasni was assassinated in front of his home in Oran. Although the twenty-six-year-old artist had remained in Algeria, he was a favorite among Franco-Maghrebis and had toured France, Scandinavia, Canada, and the United States (*Sud Ouest* [*Gers*], September 30, 1994). Several thousand fans and musicians reportedly joined in Cheb Hasni's funeral procession, carrying his portrait and chanting "Algeria free and democratic" – a cry that indicted all factions in the dirty war.

Meanwhile Khaled, riding on the sensational success of "Didi," toured the Arab world in the spring of 1993. But he was still unwelcome in Algeria, where he reportedly remains wanted for avoiding military service. A *Newsweek* report on the tour, "Rai Rocks the Mosques: Arab Pop Music Has Fundamentalists All Shook Up," resembled World Music discourse for its focus on Islamist antipathy to Khaled and its avoidance of Khaled's base in the Arab community in France (Dickey and Koster 1993). The article suggests how the western media may attempt to promote Khaled as a counterweight to Islamic "fundamentalism."

But we can be sure that the media will not boost Khaled as an opponent of French racism, recently invigorated by the Right's landslide electoral victory in March 1993. If Le Pen's popularity is on the wane, it is because the "respectable" Right has essentially embraced the National Front's program. The first few days of the Edouard Balladur premiership saw three young men killed by police in a space of four days (April 4–8), including a Maghrebi and a Zairean, and violent protest demonstrations. Since then, French police have been carrying out sweeps to round up undocumented immigrants and "delinquents." French Interior Minister Charles Pasqua introduced legislation to tighten immigration laws considerably, and his popularity rose accordingly, as many French citizens blamed rising crime rates and high unemployment (10.9 percent) on immigrants (read Arabs). Most recently, Jacques Chirac, the intrepid enemy of immigrant noise and smell, was elected French president.

NOTES

Thanks to Ruth Frankenberg, Smadar Lavie, Lata Mani, Fred Pfeil, and Miriam Rosen for their acute comments on various permutations of this piece. We are also grateful to Sonia Saouchi and her family, and to Aref al-Farra for loaning us a copy of the "Didi" video. Research for this article was funded in part by Oregon State University's College of Liberal Arts. The first version was presented in November 1991 at the American Anthropological Association meetings in Chicago and the Middle East Studies Association meetings in Washington, DC; shorter versions appeared in *Middle East Report* 22(5) (1992) and in *Diaspora* 3(1) (1994).

1 *Le Monde* (April 4, 1987), quoted in Stora 1992: 217 (our translation).
2 The figure of one million Arabs killed is commonly cited; our figure for French casualties comes from Dupuy and Dupuy (1986).
3 Etienne Balibar contends that the two European ideological schemata of colonialism and anti-Semitism converge in the racism against minority populations of Arab-Islamic origin, "so that imagery of racial superiority and imagery of cultural and religious rivalry reinforce each other" (1991: 12).
4 Koulberg (1991: 34) shows that, amid the media onslaught, it was ignored that 48 percent of French Muslims actually opposed wearing the *hijab*. A new furor over headscarves erupted in September–October 1994, after Education Minister François Bayrou issued a new ban on Islamic scarves and other "ostentatious religious symbols." In early October, Franco-Maghrebi students and their supporters clashed with teachers, parents, and police in Maintes-la-Jolie and in Lille (west and north of the capital). More than a dozen students were expelled for not complying with the new dress code.
5 One of the polls also found that 24 percent believe there are too many Jews in France. A March 1992 report by the National Consultative Commission on the Rights of Man found that nearly half of those polled expressed open antipathy toward North Africans, and 40 percent claimed to dislike North Africans born in France (*Minute-La France* (April 8–14, 1992): 15).
6 For more background on French racism, see Balibar (1992), Ben Jelloun (1984), Lloyd and Waters (1991), Taguieff (1991–2), and Wieviorka (1992).
7 On Cheikha Rimitti, see Virolle-Souibès (1993).
8 Muslims are required to abstain from sex as well as food from sunup to sundown during the month of Ramadan.
9 Virgin, 1988. Rachid Baba also produced *Pop Rai Rachid Style: Rai Rebels* (vol. 2) (Virgin, 1990), Chaba Fadela's *You Are Mine* (Mango, 1988), and Chaba Fadela and Cheb Sahraoui's *Hana Hana* (Island, 1989). The liner notes and song translations that accompany *Pop Rai Rachid Style* make a point of emphasizing that alcohol consumption and risqué female behavior are associated with *rai*.
10 This is how the 1990 World of Music and Dance Festival program advertised Chaba Fadela and Cheb Sahraoui (WOMAD 1990). Thanks to Rosemary Coombe for providing this source.
11 Estimates of "illegals" (Arab and others) in France range from 300,000 to 1 million (*al-Hayât* (April 30, 1993): 9). When the new Socialist government proclaimed amnesty for undocumented residents in 1981, 131,000 came forward to claim citizenship (Lanier 1991: 14).
12 This sketch is based on Balibar (1992), Naïr (1992), and Wieviorka (1992).
13 For an introduction to "flexible specialization" or post-Fordism, see Harvey (1991) and Hall (1991).

14 A type of slang that originated in criminal circles and is now used extensively by *banlieu-sard* youth, especially around Paris (see Sherzer 1976).

15 Some so-called *Beurs* are French citizens, some are foreign residents, and others are binationals. When we were in France in 1992, Algerians born in France after January 1, 1963, automatically received French citizenship, whereas those born before this date remained Algerian citizens. Children of Tunisian and Moroccan immigrants had to decide whether to opt for French citizenship at age twenty-one (Begag 1990: 4). Since the Right came to power in the 1993 elections, these regulations have become more restrictive.

16 Sociologist Adil Jazouli's typology (1982) of Franco-Maghrebi cultural orientations was very helpful in constructing this spectrum of hybridity.

17 Adapted from Queer Nation's slogan: "We're here, we're queer, get used to it!" Our discussions with members of La Rose des Sables, a Franco-Maghrebi theater group from Valence, helped us understand this orientation.

18 We are told, however, that adherence to Islamist groups has been on the rise since we left France.

19 The "I" in this section is Gross; McMurray and Swedenburg didn't attend this event.

20 A local musician, not the Cheb Kader heard on US *rai* releases (*From Oran to Paris*, Shanachie, 1990).

21 We realize that this does not tally with the Marseilles radio listeners' opinions on mixed marriages, discussed earlier. This leads us to believe that Bariki (1986) mainly questioned young men about their views on their own marriages, and not parents about their children's marriages.

22 Moroccan feminist Fatima Mernissi, for instance, regards the independent, companionate heterosexual marriage unit based on romantic love, in which partners are equal and share love for each other, as a real threat to the "Muslim system" (1987: 8).

23 Island, 1990.

24 McMurray and Swedenburg reproduced these stories uncritically in their 1991 article (1991: 40).

25 *Maman cherie* (Contact Music, 1991).

26 See Bizot 1987 for an early account of the Parisian World Music scene.

27 Barclay, 1992.

28 See Dominique Guillerm's review of "Didi" in *Max* (May 1992: 21). The album was recorded in Los Angeles with producers Don Was and Michael Brooks of 4AD Records. Don Was, a member of Was (Not Was), is well known in the US music industry for his production work with Bonnie Raitt, the B-52's, and Mick Jagger.

29 Since this writing, Khaled has released a new album (Mango, 1994) called *N'ssi N'ssi*. For an appreciative assessment, see Christgau (1994).

30 The late Umm Kalthum, most popular of all Egyptian singers, was probably the most canonical of those with a classical orientation. Among her lyrics: "Come and we will finish our love in one night." Muhammad 'Abd al-Wahhab, one of the few Egyptian singers who ranks with Umm Kalthum in terms of popularity and classicist orientation, sang "Life is a cigarette and a cup [of wine and liquor]." Neither singer, however, has a reputation for being "vulgar" (Armbrust 1992: 534).

31 From...*De la Planète Mars* (Labelle Noir/Virgin, 1991).

32 So-called delinquent youth seem to provide the media with ready suspects whenever violence erupts in the *banlieues*. See, for instance, Tourancheau (1991) on the March 1991 Sartrouville riots and Moreira (1990) on the November 1990 Vaulx-en-Velin riots, as well as the sensationalist media treatment of the "*Bandes de Zoulous*" (Vivier 1991c).

33 See Aïchoune (1991) for a flavor of the everyday speech of *banlieusard* posses.

34 Useful discussions of French rap are Lapassade (1991), Leibowitz (1992), Mézouane (1990), and Vivier (1991a, 1991b, 1991c, 1991d).

35 Our analysis is based primarily on the releases of Supreme NTM (*Authentik*, Epic, 1991) and I AM (... *De la Planète Mars*, Labelle Noir, 1991) – two of France's best-known rap groups – as well as two important anthologies (*Rapattitude*, Labelle Noir, 1990 and *Rapattitude 2*, Labelle Noir, 1992) and a recording by Franco-Maghrebi *rappeuse* Saliha (*Unique*, Virgin, 1991). We do not discuss the more celebrated and musically innovative rapper MC Solaar, whose lyrics are less confrontational.

36 As evidenced, for instance, by the angry reactions when presidential candidate Bill Clinton equated black nationalist rapper Sister Souljah with neo-Nazi David Duke.

37 From her song "Danse le beat."

38 On "Non Soumis à l'Etat."

39 On I AM's "Le Nouveau Président" and "Red, Black and Green."

40 For instance, NTM's "Freestyle."

41 One interesting exception is Siria Khan's "La Main de Fatma," on *Rapattitude 2*.

42 With the exception of Prophètes du Vacarme's politically ambivalent "Kameleon" on *Rapattitude 2*.

43 Although many prominent US rappers are avowed Muslims (Brand Nubian, Ice Cube, Poor Righteous Teachers, Rakim of Eric B and Rakim, Professor Griff, Big Daddy Kane, Wu Tang Clan, Nas), their rhymes almost never deal with specifically Arab subjects, except for an occasional mention of Palestine.

44 Other liberal "intellos" also feel compelled to establish rap's pedigree by comparing it with other canonical examples of verbal artistic performances. Mézouane (1990: 5) compares rappers with the West African griots, the *meddahs* (itinerant Berber poets), the *berrahs* (traditional *rai* announcers), and the reciters of *la chanson de geste* of the European Middle Ages. Georges Lapassade, the ethnographer of hip-hop who teaches at Paris VIII, likens rap performance to a Moroccan call-and-response ritual (*aît* and *daqa*) and the rapper to an Arab *majdoub* (a tranced-out religious ecstatic) (Loupias 1990). Another commentator claims that "the importance of rap today for the Black community perhaps approaches that of the story tellers of the nineteenth century in our [*sic*] society" (Bouillier 1990: 2).

45 On "Quelle Gratitude?"

46 One of their jokes: "What is the difference between 'migration' and 'immigration'?" Answer: "La migration c'est les oiseaux qui volent; l'immigration c'est les arabes qui volent" (Migration is birds that fly; immigration is Arabs who steal).

47 One of Smaïn's stand-up routines opens: "Okay, all French people in the audience, put your hands in the air. Now, all North Africans in the audience, take your hands out of their pockets."

48 Sayad et al. (1991) gives a breakdown on immigration to Marseilles by arrondissement.

49 On *Salam Alikoum* (Musidisc, 1992).

50 Amina played the prostitute in Bertolucci's *The Sheltering Sky*, a film she subsequently condemned as orientalist. She was the only Arab artist to participate in the remake of "Give Peace a Chance," an all-star recording organized by Julian Lennon to mobilize opinion against the 1991 Gulf War that went virtually unremarked in the United States. Her single US release is *Yalil* (Mango, 1989).

51 On the 1961 massacre, see Aïchoune (1991), Ben Jelloun (1984), Cockburn (1991), Einaudi (1991), and Hargreaves (1989); on racist violence in the 1980s, see Aïchoune (1991), Guidice (1992), and Jazouli (1992).

52 Although the Muslim population in France includes a growing number of Turks, as well as some Pakistanis and Black Africans, in this context "Muslim" means Arab.

53 Our thanks to the late Philip Shehadeh for this information.

54 *Foreign Broadcast Information Service*, Near East and South Asia Daily Reports, March 27, 1991, p. 5; *Libération*, March 28, 1991, p. 33. We heard quite different interpret-

ations of this event from Algerians living in Seattle. An engineer who loves *rai* and despises FIS returned from a visit to Algiers in March 1991 and claimed that several people were killed in one FIS attack on a music audience, and that one performance hall was burned down. We have been unable to confirm this story. A graduate student who is a sharp critic of the FLN claimed that the state was the aggressor in this battle, that it actively encouraged music performances during Ramadan in order to harass and provoke the Islamists. For instance, he claimed, the state would issue permits for concerts to be held during Ramadan prayer times, and it specifically promoted events at venues located next to mosques.

55 FIS's program would allow only widowed or divorced women, particularly those with children to support, to hold paid employment. In late December 1991, FIS leader Muhammad Said told a huge crowd that it was time for Algerian women in big cities to start wearing scarves to cover their hair and to stop looking like "cheap merchandise that is bought and sold" (Ibrahim 1991).

56 Adapted from Steve Arra's translation on the liner notes to Cheb Khaled's release *Fuir mais où?*

57 Yúdice draws this definition from the work of Cuban theorist Fernando Ortiz and Uruguayan theorist Angel Rama.

58 Goldman's article (1993) is unique in the music industry's coverage of Cheb Khaled for its mention of anti-Arab racism in France.

59 Useful accounts of the civil conflict in Algeria are Howe (1992), Bekkar (1992), Roberts (1994), and Human Rights Watch (1994).

60 According to a BBC news report, October 11, 1992. This should be understood in light of governmental repression of the Islamists. By March 1992, some twelve thousand Algerians had been banished to internment camps in the southern desert, and between one thousand and three thousand were still being held there in October 1993. Approximately twenty thousand Algerians had been jailed by late 1993, thirteen Islamists had been executed, and torture was rampant.

REFERENCES

Aïchoune, Farid. 1991. *Nés en banlieue*. Paris: Editions Ramsay.
——. 1992. "Une mouvance en question." *Qantara* 3 (April–June): 14–15.
Alcalay, Ammiel. 1993. *After Jews and Arabs: Remaking Levantine Culture*. Minneapolis: University of Minnesota Press.
Armbrust, Walter. 1992. "The National Vernacular: Folklore and Egyptian Popular Culture." *Michigan Quarterly Review* 31(4): 525–42.
Attaf, Rabha. 1991. "Ecoutez: Comment ferons-nous la paix?" *Actuel* (February): 49–57.
Balibar, Etienne. 1991. "Es gibt keinen Staat in Europa: Racism and Politics in Europe Today." *New Left Review* 186: 5–19.
——. 1992. *Les Frontières de la démocratie*. Paris: La Découverte.
Barber, Karin. 1987. "Popular Arts in Africa." *African Studies Review* 30(3): 1–78.
Bariki, Salah Eddine. 1986. "Identité religieuse, identité culturelle en situation immigrée." In Jean-Robert Henry et al., eds., *Nouveaux Enjeux culturels au Maghreb*, pp. 427–45. Paris: Editions du CNRS.
Begag, Azouz. 1990. " 'The Beurs,' Children of North-African Immigrants in France: The Issue of Integration." *Journal of Ethnic Studies* 18(1): 1–14.
Bekkar, Rabia. 1992. "Taking up Space in Tlemcen: The Islamist Occupation of Urban Algeria." *Middle East Report* 22(6): 11–15 (Interview by Hannah Davis).

Ben Jelloun, Tahar. 1984. *Hospitalité française. Racisme et immigration maghrébine*. Paris: Editions de Seuil.

——. 1991. "I Am an Arab, I Am Suspect." *Nation* (April 15): 482–4.

Benkheira, Mohamed Hocine. 1986. "De la musique avant toute chose: Remarques sur la raï." *Peuples méditerranéens/Mediterranean Peoples* 35–6: 173–7.

Bernard, Philippe. 1991. "Les Beurs, entre la fierté et la crainte." *Le Monde* (January 17): 5.

Billard, François. 1987. "Rock, Sapho." *Jazz Magazine* 359 (March): 24–5.

Bizot, Jean-François. 1987. "Ces Musiciens grandissent la France." *Actuel* (June): 145–55.

——. 1988. "Sex and Soul in the Maghreb." *The Face* 98: 86–93.

Bizot, Jean-François, and Fadia Dimerdji. 1988. "Le Blues de l'espoir." *Actuel* (March): 92–9, 132–3.

Bouillier, Grégoire. 1990. "Urban Rap." *Dire* 12 (Fall): 2–10.

Brisebarre, Anne-Marie. 1989. "La célébration de l'Ayd El'Kebir en France: Les enjeux du sacrifice." *Archives des sciences sociales des religions* 68(1) (July–September): 9–25.

Cambio, Sam. 1991. "Marseille: Verification d'une rumeur." *Actuel* (February): 33–8.

Christgau, Robert. 1994. "Goat-God Rising." *Village Voice* (April 26): 67.

Cockburn, Alexander. 1991. "Beat the Devil." *Nation* (December 23): 802–3.

De Neys, Anne. 1993. "Rai Rocks Egyptian Pop." *Al-Ahram Weekly* (May 13–19): 9.

Deleuze, Gilles, and Félix Guattari. 1983. "Rhizome." Trans. John Johnston. In *On the Line*, 1–65. New York: Semiotext(e).

Dickey, Christopher, and Beatrix de Koster. 1993. "Rai Rocks the Mosques: Arab Pop Has Fundamentalists All Shook Up." *Newsweek* (April 26): 53.

Drozdiak, William. 1991. "French at Odds over Immigrants." *Washington Post* (July 12): A24.

Dupuy, R. Ernest, and Trevor N. Dupuy. 1986. *The Encyclopedia of Military History*. New York: Harper & Row.

Einaudi, Jean-Luc. 1991. *La Bataille de Paris, 17 octobre 1961*. Paris: Editions du Seuil.

Etienne, Bruno. 1989. *La France et l'Islam*. Paris: Hachette.

Eyre, Banning. 1991. "A King in Exile: The Royal Rai of Cheb Khaled." *Option* 39: 42–5.

——. 1992. "Rai: North African Punk." *Option* 42: 19–20.

Folch, Arnaud. 1992. "Petit glossaire de la chasse aux vilains racistes." *Minute-La France* 1565 (April 8): 17–21.

Gilroy, Paul. 1987. *"There Ain't No Black in the Union Jack": The Cultural Politics of "Race" and Nation*. London: Hutchinson.

——. 1990. "One Nation under a Groove. The Cultural Politics of 'Race' and Racism in Britain." In David Theo Goldberg, ed., *Anatomy of Racism*, pp. 263–82. Minneapolis: University of Minnesota Press.

——. 1992. "Cultural Studies and Ethnic Absolutism." In Lawrence Grossberg et al., eds., *Cultural Studies*, pp. 187–98. New York: Routledge.

——. 1993. *The Black Atlantic: Modernity and Double Consciousness*. London: Verso.

Giudice, Fausto. 1992. *Arabicide: Une chronique française 1970–1991*. Paris: La Découverte.

Goldman, Antony. 1993. "The Man from Oran." *Focus on Africa* (April): 81.

Gorce, Paul-Marie de la. 1991. "Chirac joue du tam-tam." *Jeune Afrique* (July 3–9): 30–1.

Goytisolo, Juan. 1987a. *Landscapes After the Battle*. Trans. Helen Lane. New York: Seaver Books.

——. 1987b. *Space in Motion*. Trans. Helen Lane. New York: Lumen Books.

Hall, Stuart. 1989. "Cultural Identity and Cinematic Representation." *Framework* 36: 68–81.

——. 1991. "Europe's Other Self." *Marxism Today* 35(8): 18–19.

Hargreaves, Alec G. 1989. "Resistance and Identity in Beur Narratives." *Modern Fiction Studies* 35(1): 87–102.

——. 1991. "La Famille Ramdan: Un Sit-com 'pur beur'?" *Hommes et Migrations* 1147 (October): 60–6.

Harvey, David. 1991. "Flexibility: Threat or Opportunity?" *Socialist Review* 21(1): 65–77.

Howe, John. 1992. "The Crisis of Algerian Nationalism and the Rise of Islamic Integralism." *New Left Review* 196: 85–100

Human Rights Watch/Middle East. 1994. *Human Rights Abuses in Algeria: No One Is Spared*. New York: Human Rights Watch.

Ibrahim, Youssef M. 1991. "In Algeria, Clear Plans to Lay Down Islamic Law." *New York Times* (December 31): A4.

Ireland, Doug. 1992. "Press Clips." *Village Voice* (January 14): 8.

James, Barry. 1991. "French Rap and the Art of Vandalism." *International Herald Tribune* (July 4): 6.

Jazouli, Adil. 1982. *La Nouvelle Génération de l'immigration maghrébine: Essai d'analyse sociologique*. Paris: Centre d'Information et d'Etudes sur les Migrations.

——. 1992. *Les Années banlieues*. Paris: Editions du Seuil.

Kapil, Arun. 1990. "Algeria's Elections Show Islamist Strength." *Middle East Report* 20(5): 31–6.

Koptiuch, Kristin. 1991. "Third-Worlding at Home." *Social Text* 28: 87–99.

Koulberg, André. 1991. *L'Affaire du voile islamique: Comment perdre une bataille symbolique*. Marseilles: Fenêtre sur Cour.

Labi, Philippe, Marc Daum, and Crazy J.-M. 1990. "Jack Lang: Je crois à la culture rap." *VSD* (October 31): 40–1.

Lacoste-Dujardin, Camille. 1992. *Yasmina et les autres de Nanterre et d'ailleurs: Filles de parents maghrébins en France*. Paris: Editions La Découverte.

LaFranchi, Howard. 1991. "Immigrants Cool Toward Saddam – and the Coalition." *Christian Science Monitor* (January 3): 4.

Laing, Dave. 1992. "'Sadeness', Scorpions and Single Markets: National and Transnational Trends in European Popular Music." *Popular Music* 11(2): 127–40.

Lanier, Pierre. 1991. *Les Nouveaux Visages de l'immigration*. Lyons: Chronique Sociale.

Lapassade, Georges. 1991. "Qu'est-ce que le hip-hop?" *Hommes et Migrations* 1147 (October): 31–4.

Leblond, Renaud. 1991. "Les Folles rumeurs de grasse." *L'Express* (January 24): 61.

Leibowitz, Nicole. 1992. "Attali: 'Le Rap remplace le bal'." *Le Nouvel Observateur* (June 18): 20.

Lhomea, Jean-Yves. 1991. "Un Entretien avec le président de SOS-Racisme." *Le Monde* (June 8): 3.

Lloyd, Cathie, and Hazel Waters. 1991. "France: One Culture, One People?" *Race and Class* 32(3): 49–65.

Loupias, Bernard. 1990. "Le Rap français trouve ses mots." *Libération* (October 20–1): 44.

Malkmus, Lizbeth, and Roy Armes. 1991. *Arab and African Film Making*. London: Zed Books.

McMurray, David, and Ted Swedenburg. 1991. "Rai Tide Rising." *Middle East Report* 21(2): 39–42.

Mercer, Kobena. 1987. "Black Hair/Style Politics." *New Formations* 3: 33–54.

——. 1990. "Welcome to the Jungle." In Jonathan Rutherford, ed., *Identity: Community, Culture, Difference*, pp. 43–71. London: Lawrence and Wishart.

Mernissi, Fatima. 1987. *Beyond the Veil: Male–Female Dynamics in Modern Muslim Society*, rev. edn. Bloomington: Indiana University Press.

Mézouane, Rabah. 1990. "Le Rap, complainte des maudits." *Le Monde Diplomatique* 429 (December): 4–5.

Miller, Judith. 1991. "Strangers at the Gate." *New York Times Magazine* (September 15): 33–7, 49, 80–1.

Moreira, Paul. 1990. "La Mal-vie des jeunes." *Le Monde diplomatique* 429 (December): 4–5.

Morin, Georges. 1991. "Le Mosaïque des français du Maghreb et des maghrébins de France." In Camille Lacoste and Yves Lacoste, eds., *L'Etat du Maghreb*, pp. 533–7. Paris: Editions La Découverte.

Morley, David, and Kevin Robins. 1990. "No Place like *Heimat*: Images of Home(land) in European Culture." *New Formations* 12: 1–21.

Naïr, Sami. 1992. *Le Regard des vainqueurs: Les Enjeux français de l'immigration.* Paris: Bernard Grasset.

Riding, Alan. 1990. "A Surge of Racism in France Brings a Search for Answers." *New York Times* (May 27): I–1, I–16.

——. 1991. "Europe's Growing Debate over Whom to Let Inside." *New York Times* (December 1): E2.

——. 1992. "Parisians on Graffiti: Is it Vandalism or Art?" *New York Times* (February 6): A6.

Roberts, Hugh. 1994. "Algeria Between Eradicators and Conciliators." *Middle East Report* 24(4): 24–7.

Rosen, Miriam. 1990. "On Rai." *Artforum* (September): 22–3.

Safran, William. 1986. "Islamization in Western Europe: Political Consequences and Historical Parallels." *Annals of the American Academy of Political and Social Science* 485: 98–112.

Sayad, Abdelmalek, et al. 1991. *Migrance, histoire de migrations à Marseille.* Aix-en-Provence: Edisud.

Sherzer, Joel. 1976. "Play Languages: Implications for (Socio) Linguistics." In Barbara Kirshenblatt-Gimblett, ed., *Speech Play*, pp. 19–36. Philadelphia: University of Pennsylvania Press.

Singer, Daniel. 1988. "In the Heart of Le Pen Country." *Nation* (June 18): 845, 861–4.

——. 1991. "Le Pen's Pals – Blood and Soil." *Nation* (December 23): 814–16.

Stora, Benjamin. 1992. "L'Intégrisme islamique en France: Entre fantasmes et réalité." In Pierre-André Taguieff, ed., *Face au racisme*, vol. 2, pp. 216–22. Paris: Editions La Découverte.

Taguieff, Pierre-André, ed. 1991–2. *Face au racisme.* 2 vols. Paris: Editions La Découverte.

Talha, Larbi. 1991. "La Main-d'oeuvre émigrée en mutation." In Camille Lacoste and Yves Lacoste, eds., *L'Etat du Maghreb*, pp. 497–500. Paris: Editions La Découverte.

Tourancheau, Patricia. 1991. "'Assistance sécurité': Epinglée par police." *Libération* (March 30–1): 19.

Urla, Jacqueline. 1993. "Contesting Modernities: Language Standardization and the Production of an Ancient/Modern Basque Culture." *Critique of Anthropology* 13(2): 101–18.

Videau, André. 1991. "À la recherche de la culture immigrée." *Hommes et Migrations* 1144 (June): 35–9.

Virolle-Souibès, Marie. 1988a. "Le ray, côté femmes: Entre alchimie de la douleur et spleen sans idéal, quelques fragments de discours hédonique." *Peuples Méditerranéens* 44–5: 193–220.

——. 1988b. "Ce que chanter erray veut dire: Prelude à d'autres couplets." *Cahiers de Littérature Orale* 23: 177–208.

——. 1989. "Le raï entre résistances et récupération." *Revue d'Études du Monde Musulman et Méditerranéen* 51: 47–62.

——. 1993. "Le Raï de Cheikha Rimitti." *Mediterraneans* 4: 103–15.

Vivier, Jean-Pierre. 1991a. "Culture hip-hop et politique de la ville." *Hommes et Migrations* 1147 (October): 35–44.

——. 1991b. *Culture hip-hop et politique de la ville.* Paris: Centre d'Etudes et d'Actions Sociales de Paris.

——. 1991c. *"Bandes de zoulous" et culture hip-hop: Revue de presse (mai 1990–mars 1991).* Paris: Centre d'Etudes et d'Actions Sociales de Paris.

——. 1991d. *"Malaises" des jeunes et politique de la ville: Revue de presse (octobre 1990–août 1991).* Paris: Centre d'Etudes et d'Actions Sociales de Paris.

Wieviorka, Michel. 1992. *La France raciste.* Paris: Editions du Seuil.

WOMAD (World of Music and Dance). 1990. Festival program. Toronto, August.

Yúdice, George. 1992. "We Are Not the World." *Social Text* 31/2: 202–16.

Part IV

Roving Commodities

This section of the reader tracks the global flow of commodities, concentrating on the way the consumption of goods often mediates the "encounter" between peoples and cultures from around the world. Part of the aim of these essays is to suggest that the consumption of foreign goods does not necessarily lead to the eradication of local cultural traditions. They highlight how Third World consumers faced with a western cultural commodity will not simply or necessarily assimilate its values, ideologies, and lifestyle positions. Instead, these subjects will often bring their own cultural dispositions to bear on such cultural goods – interpreting, translating, and/ or rejecting them according to local conditions of reception. For example, Friedman's article shows how for Congolese subjects the process of consumption has become part of their broader cultural strategies of self-definition and self-maintenance, while Meyer's piece demonstrates how Ghanian pentecostalists often reject western commodities because, for them, consumption entails the danger of losing rather than gaining one's identity (specifically, one's Christian identity). More generally, the aim of these articles is just to call attention to the increasing commodification of the world, to how more and more spheres of human life have become subject to the logics of the market. Thus Nancy Scheper-Hughes's essay maps the late twentieth-century global trade in bodies and body parts, focusing on some of the principle countries – India, China, South Africa, and Brazil – that furnish these commodities.

SUGGESTIONS FOR FURTHER READING

Appadurai, Arjun, ed.
  1986   *The Social Life of Things: Commodities in Cultural Perspective.* Cambridge: Cambridge University Press.

Borooah, Romy
  2000 Transformations in Trade and the Constitution of Gender and Rank in Northeast
    India. *American Ethnologist* 27(2): 371–99.
Breckenridge, Carol A., ed.
  1995 *Consuming Modernity: Public Culture in a South Asian World*. Minneapolis: University of Minnesota Press.
Foster, Robert J.
  1996/7 Commercial Mass Media in Papua New Guinea: Notes on Agency, Bodies, and
    Commodity Consumption. *Visual Anthropology Review* 12(2): 1–17.
Friedman, Jonathan, ed.
  1994 *Consumption and Identity*. Chur, Switzerland: Harwood Academic Publishers.
Gewertz, Deborah, and Frederick Errington
  1996 On PepsiCo and Piety in a Papua New Guinea "Modernity." *American Ethnologist*
    23(3): 476–93.
Grewal, Inderpal
  1999 Travelling Barbie: Indian Transnationality and New Consumer Subjects. *Positions*
    7(3): 799–826.
Haugerud, Angelique, M. Priscilla Stone, and Peter D. Little, eds.
  2000 *Commodities and Globalization: Anthropological Perspectives*. Lanham, MD:
    Rowman & Littlefield.
Howes, David, ed.
  1996 *Cross-Cultural Consumption: Global Markets, Local Realities*. London: Routledge.
Miller, Daniel
  1994 *Modernity, an Ethnographic Approach: Dualism and Mass Consumption in Trinidad*. Oxford: Berg.
Miller, Daniel, ed.
  1998 *Material Cultures: Why Some Things Matter*. Chicago: University of Chicago Press.
Steiner, Christopher B.
  1994 *African Art in Transit*. Cambridge: Cambridge University Press.
Taylor, Timothy D.
  1997 *Global Pop: World Music, World Markets*. New York: Routledge.
Tobin, Joseph J., ed.
  1992 *Re-made in Japan: Everyday Life and Consumer Taste in a Changing Society*. New
    Haven: Yale University Press.
Watson, James E., ed.
  1997 *Golden Arches East: McDonald's in East Asia*. Stanford: Stanford University Press.

10

Globalization and Localization

Jonathan Friedman

Salman Rushdie has gone underground! From 1970 to 1980 the population of North American Indians increased from 700,000 to 1.4 million including the creation of several new tribes. The world network of stock markets is overcapitalized and lodged on the fluctuating brink of the threatening crash of 1990. The governments are there to stem disaster, by means of massive credit, whatever problem that may solve. In the Eastern bloc, large-scale ethnic mobilization threatens the monolithic face of empire while presenting new and even less manageable problems. The same T-shirt designs from Acapulco, Mallorca or Hawaii; the same watch and computer clones with different names, even Gucci clones; the nostalgic turn in the tourist trade, catering to a search for roots, even if largely simulacra, and the western search for the experience of otherness. Ethnic and cultural fragmentation and modernist homogenization are not two arguments, two opposing views of what is happening in the world today, but two constitutive trends of global reality. The dualist centralized world of the double East–West hegemony is fragmenting, politically and culturally, but the homogeneity of capitalism remains as intact and as systematic as ever. The cultural and by implication intellectual fragmentation of the world has undermined any attempt at a single interpretation of the current situation. We have been served everything from postindustrialism, late capitalism and postmodernism (as a purely cultural phenomenon expressive of an evolution of western capitalist society), to more sinister traditionalist representations of the decline of western civilization, of creeping narcissism, moral decay, etc. For years there has been a rampaging battle among intellectuals concerning the pros and cons of postmodernity, while imperialism theorists have become addicted admirers of all sorts of social movements, and the development elites have shifted interests, from questions of development to those of human rights and democracy. And if the Fernand Braudel Center continues to analyze long waves, there has been a growing interest in older civilizations, their rise

From *Cultural Identity and Global Process*, pp. 102–16. London: Sage Publications, 1994.

and fall, and in culture and identity. The intensive practice of identity is the hallmark of the present period. Rushdie's confrontation with fundamentalism highlights the volatile nature of this desperate negotiation of selfhood; the very consumption of modernist literature is suddenly a dangerous act. Global decentralization is tantamount to cultural renaissance. Liberation and self-determination, hysterical fanaticism and increasing border conflicts, all go hand in hand with an ever-increasing multinationalization of world market products. The interplay between the world market and cultural identity, between local and global processes, between consumption and cultural strategies, is part of one attempt to discover the logics involved in this apparent chaos.

Negotiating Selfhood and Consuming Desires

The aim of this discussion is to explore consumption as an aspect of broader cultural strategies of self-definition and self-maintenance. My use of the word 'cultural' is equivalent to 'specificity' as in a specific structure of desire expressed in a specific strategy of consumption that defines the contours of a specific identity space – such and such $\sum(a, \ldots n)$, a sum of products configured into an arrangement that expresses what I am. It is to be kept in mind that the currently conventional use of the concept culture to refer to maps, paradigms or semiotic codes would yield results that are diametrically opposed to the aims that I have set out, since they imply the existence of a text-like reality that provides a recipe for the organization of social life and thought. On the contrary, from this perspective, maps, paradigms and semiotic codes are all abstractions from social products whether dress fashions or forms of discourse. As such they merely reflect the products from which they are abstracted, but cannot generate those products. Strategies of consumption can only be truly grasped when we understand the specific way in which desire is constituted. And we shall assume for the time being that the latter is a dynamic aspect of the formation of personhood or selfhood.

   This argument parallels Bourdieu's modeling of the relation between *habitus* and practice, between the 'durably installed generative principle of regulated improvisation' (1977: 78) and specific strategies of consumption. But while Bourdieu seems to maintain a rationalist perspective on practice whereby it is ultimately reducible to the accumulation of cultural capital, that is, of power, we have suggested that this is tantamount to economism and fails to take into account the non-rational constitution of desire. Thus the (not so) explicitly Veblenesque model of *La Distinction* may tell us a great deal about the role of cultural differentiation in the definition of social position, a process whereby a particular 'class'-determined *habitus* distinguishes itself in the cultural marketplace by identifying itself with a clearly defined set of products and activities, a lifestyle:

Every condition is defined inseparably by its relational properties which are functions of its position within a system of conditions which is also a *system of differences*, of differential positions, designated, that is, in terms of everything that distinguishes it from that which it is not and more particularly from that to which it is opposed: social identity is defined and affirmed in difference. (Bourdieu 1979: 191)

But this kind of model cannot account for the more spectacular aspects of capitalist consumption in general, based on the desire for new identities and accompanying strategies that render any particular set of consumer-based distinctions obsolete after relatively short periods of stability.[1] Campbell's insightful analysis of the relation between modern individualism, romanticism and consumerism supplies a larger frame necessary to any understanding of strategies of consumption that display an instability that cannot be grasped in the terms set out by Bourdieu: 'The dialectic of conventionalization and romanticization is the personally concrete expression of the dialectic of class and capitalist reproduction in general, a dynamic contradiction between distinction and revolution, between other directed and self-directed images, between dandy and bohemian' (Friedman 1989: 129).

The common ground in these approaches to consumption is the explicit connection between self-identification and consumption. The former may be a conscious act, a statement about the relation between self and world, or it may be a taken-for-granted aspect of everyday life, that is, of a predefined identity. From this point of departure it is possible to envisage consumption as an aspect of a more general strategy or set of strategies for the establishment and/or maintenance of selfhood. Other practices of cultural self-constitution – ethnic, class, gender, and religious – paint and clothe bodies – consume specific objects and construct life spaces. These are higher-order modes of channeling consumption to specific ends. The latter is a means of identification.

The Struggle for Authenticity

Every social and cultural movement is a consumer or at least must define itself in relation to the world of goods as a non-consumer. Consumption within the bounds of the world system is always a consumption of identity, canalized by a negotiation between self-definition and the array of possibilities offered by the capitalist market. The old saying, 'you are what you eat,' once a characterization of a vulgar ecological view of humanity, is strikingly accurate when it is understood as a thoroughly social act. For eating is an act of self-identification, as is all consumption. Proteins and calories aside, consumption, the libidinous half of social reproduction, is a significant part of the differential definition of social groups and individuals. The act of identification, the engagement of the person in a higher project, is in one sense an act of pure existential authenticity, but, to the degree that it implies a consumption of self-defining symbols that are not self-produced but obtained in the marketplace, the authenticity is undermined by objectification and potential decontextualization.[2] Thus, while engagement authenticates, its consumption de-authenticates. The only authentic act inside of such a system is an act that encompasses both the authentic and its commodification, that is, an engaged cynicism, a distancing that is simultaneously at one with the world.

La Sape

The *sapeurs* of the People's Republic of the Congo and other similar groups recruit their members primarily from the lower ranks of the partially employed if not lumpenproletariat inhabiting Brazzaville and the second largest city, Pointe Noire. The dominant ethnic group is Bakongo, significant insofar as this former ruling group of southerners that identifies itself as the most civilized, that is, western, group in the Congo has been politically displaced by the Mbochi of the north. The latter represent a region that was very much outside of direct French administration and did not undergo the commercialization and concentrated missionary activity of the south. As such, Bakongo consider them to be backward if not barbarian, at least at a certain level of discourse, since in reality relations between north and south are more complex. *Les sapeurs* progress through a system of age grades that begins in Brazzaville with the acquisition of European ready-to-wear imports, and which then takes them to Paris where they accumulate, by any means available, famous designer clothes from France and highest-ranked Italy at tremendous expense. An occasional return to Brazzaville – Paris in the Congo, center in the periphery, the only *endroit* not to have had its name Africanized by the revolutionary national government – to perform the *danse des griffes*, with the great name labels that are sewn into the lapels of a jacket and displayed accordingly as part of the ritual of status.

It should be kept in mind here that such activities are an extreme form of a more general cultural strategy. In Brazzaville there are two kinds of Coke, one produced locally under license and consumed in bottles, and another more expensive variety imported in cans from Holland. The consumption of Coke in Brazzaville is locally significant! To be someone or to express one's position is to display the imported can in the windshield of one's car. Distinction is not simply show but is genuine 'cargo,' which always comes from the outside, a source of well-being and fertility and a sign of power. So in terms of western categories it might appear as the ideal type of the kind of Veblenesque ranking outlined in Bourdieu's *La Distinction*, but it is, in reality, much more than that. A Congolese can identify everyone's social rank in a crowd by their outward appearance. It is only by gaining some insight into the relation between local structures of desire and identity and the political and economic context that one can understand why a European professor of physics complained that she gained her prestige not from her academic position but from the fact that she invested all her savings in the acquisition of a fleet of taxis.

At one level *la sape* seems to be a commentary on modern consumerism. The French word is derived from the verb *se saper*, which means the art of dressing elegantly, connoting the *flâneur* of our own society, the other-directed dandy (Campbell 1987; Friedman 1989). La SAPE in its Congolese version is an institution. Société des Ambianceurs et Personnes Elégantes. But this is no cynical statement on hyperconsumerism, no punk parody of middle-class ideals. While the dandy may have been other-directed, his or her practice of self-identification was very much a question of the manipulation of appearances. And while the borderline narcissism involved in this may have been such that the dandy was relatively bound to the 'gaze of the other' for his or her own well-being, this entire world of activity occurred and occurs again today in a larger universe in which appearance and being are quite distinct from one another, that is, where there is, in principle at least, a 'real person' beneath the surface. Such is not the case for the Congolese, where tendentially, appearance and being are identical; you are what you wear! Not because 'clothes make the man' but because clothes are the immediate expression of the degree of life-force possessed by a person, and life-force is everywhere and always external. Consumption of clothing is encompassed by a global strategy of linkage to the force that provides not only wealth but also health and political power. Congolese medicine is very much focused on methods of maintaining or increasing flows of cosmic force to the body in order to maintain good health and defend the person against witchcraft. Western medicines, like any powerful substances, are not symbols for but aspects of God. Similarly clothing is not a symbol of social position but a concrete manifestation of such position.

The strategy of self-definition in *la sape* is in no sense cynical, nor is there a distancing, on the part of the participants, from the commodity as such, since the commodity is not 'as such' in this kind of strategy. Consumption is a life-and-death struggle for psychic and social survival and it consumes the entire person. If there is a fundamental desperation at the bottom of this activity it is perhaps related to the state of narcissistic non-being generated by a social crisis of self-constitution:

> How can I get to France?
> How can I get there?
> France, land of happiness.
> How can I get there?
> Perhaps I can get there, if God so wills.
> Perhaps I can get there?
> I shall go quietly,
> How can I get there?
> (from J. Missamou, 'Kua Kula,'
> translated in Gandoulou 1984: 195)

There is a certain family resemblance between this kind of intensified identification with European-defined success, which as we have argued can best be seen as a striving after well-being in a more general sense, and so-called cargo cults or any millenarism whose goal it is to overcome a lack in the present via the importation of life-force from the outside. *L'aventure*, as it is called, the great move to Paris, initiating the *sapeur* into the higher category, *parisien*, might be understood as the expression of a millenarian wish, as indicated in the above verses. But this dream is immediately destroyed by the realities of Paris for the Congolese. Living in squalor and eking out a bare subsistence, all and any cash is channeled into the installment purchase of the great names in menswear, from shirts and socks to trousers, suits and shoes. If consumption for us consists in the construction of life spaces for ourselves, for *la sape* it consists in the constitution of prestige, precisely without the lifestyle that such garments are meant to manifest. Thus it must be that the satisfaction gained does not lie in the lifestyle experience but in the constitution of self for others, the appearance of *les grands*, the powerful elites. And this strategy of acquisition is not simply a rational manipulation of appearances: 'It is as if we became drugged and were unable to give it all up' (Gandoulou 1984: 61).

The organization of *la sape* is such that immigrants, *parisiens*, attempt to accumulate *la gamme*, the set of famous-name *haute couture* that is necessary to make the *descente* to Brazzaville, where the *danse des griffes* must be performed to demonstrate the famous labels acquired. The latter is accomplished by sewing the labels on to the jacket lapel, where they can be exhibited for others. It is noteworthy that the word *gamme* means scale, indicating the ranked nature of prestige consumption. This enormously cosmopolitan strategy has its immediate effects in the production of a clear status demarcation: 'When the adventurer refers to the "peasant," the *ngaya*, he is referring to an inhabitant of Brazzaville who does not adhere to the value system of the *sapeurs*' (Gandoulou 1984: 152).

La sape is not a Congolese invention at odds with the very fabric of that society. On the contrary, it is a mere exaggeration of a strategy of prestige accumulation, but one that fundamentally negates its internal logic. It is thus a formula for success and a potential threat to the real power structure. While, as we have argued, the actual strategies of consumption are generated by a form of identity very different than that to be found in the modern West, the political implications have a clear historical parallel in European history: 'the different ranks of people are too much confounded: the lower orders press so hard on the heels of the higher, if some remedy is not used the Lord will be in danger of becoming the valet of his Gentleman' (Hanway 1756: 282–3).

But if the outcome of this confrontation ran in favor of the new consumers and a democratization of consumption, in the Congo the same kind of activity poses a more structural threat, since no such democratization is in the offing. On the contrary, lumpenproletarian dandyism is not a cheap imitation of the real thing, but a consumption of the highest orders of status that as such strikes at the heart of elite status itself from the bottom of society:

Scandal explodes as soon as unemployed youth, adventurers, in the extravagance of their aestheticism and dandyism challenge the truly powerful and place themselves *hors categorie*. They imitate the successful, and might expect that having done so they ought to be accepted and integrated into their rightful positions in Congolese society. (Gandoulou 1984: 188)

The European consumer revolution created a major threat to a system of class status that was previously impervious to imitation, but it resulted in a vast system of ranking in which the 'originals,' *la haute couture*, are the unassailable center in the clothing of social position. *La sape*, on the other hand, is thus a very expensive assault on the rank order of society and not merely on its symbolism. European dandyism was an individualistic affair, a practical manipulation of status symbols and rules of etiquette. The dandy's strategy was to subtly pass into the higher ranks. *La sape* is, in its systematic age-rank grading and explicit discourse of prestige, a subversion of the cultural classification of a political order. And it is logical that it is the product not of a western revolt against fashion, but of a Third World hypermodernity in which fashion is not merely representative but constitutive of social identity. The special kind of consumption that we have described here cannot be separated out as a sphere of activity distinct from the more general strategies that characterize modern Congolese society as an international phenomenon. The *sapeur* is not a *flâneur* because he is, in structural terms, authentic; that is, his identity is univocal. The outward appearance that he appropriates is not a mere project to fool the public, to appear as something other than himself. It is his very essence. It is this quality that renders it exotic to the westerner, for whom this apparent narcissism ought to be openly cynical, even in its desperation. But the point is that the narcissist whose identity partakes of a larger cosmology of life-forces is an authentic clothing freak and not a trickster.

Seeking a master

> At the post office I met a young man who attended the Lycée Technique in Brazzaville. He was from the Teke region to the north and lived in town with his maternal uncle. He demonstrated an unusually enthusiastic interest in developing a stable relation to me and expressed the hope of being able to come to Sweden after only a few minutes of conversation. He conveyed in no uncertain terms his interest in becoming my client or subordinate, a dependent for whom I would be responsible. The strategy is not reducible to subordination. It implies, for a student with a possible career, a connection that might enable him to establish his own clientele. Tapping into a source of social life-force is crucial: it explains why both Swedish and even American cars are ranked well above the more accessible French products, and why Sweden, origin of the major Protestant mission, is associated with 'heaven'.

If *la sape* is a specific expression of a more general praxis of consumption, the latter is in its turn an expression of a praxis of self-identification and self-maintenance that defines the nature of power, well-being and sickness. Over and above the seven official churches, there are ninety-five sects in Brazzaville, whose principal functions are therapeutic. Even the churches are very much engaged in what is called 'traditional medicine.' And there is clearly no undersupply of patients. Nor is it unusual for practitioners to don the white attire of western doctors and to flaunt western equipment and even medicines where possible. This is not mere status seeking, not a recognition of a supposed superiority (in a scientific sense) of western technique, but a real identification with higher and thus more powerful forms and substances. It would appear that cults increased dramatically in the 1970s after having declined during the 1960s wave of modernism. There is certainly evidence that a large percentage of the population is not 'well' and needs the source of life-force and protection from witchcraft that can be provided by the cult groups.

Even business enterprises make use of such 'magical' sources (Devauges 1977):

They use fetishism against me to take my clients away, especially X. I do the same thing against them – it's perfectly normal. (Shipper quoted ibid.: 150)

In order to succeed here, you need some means to attract clients (fetishes). Knowing one's work is not enough. (Tailor quoted ibid.)

I only use fetishes to protect myself and to protect my business. I have never used fetishes against my uncle (even though his family accuses me of sorcery). (Bar owner quoted ibid.)

There is a common core in these different domains of practice. There is an appropriation of modernity by means of a set of transformed traditional practices, transformed by the integration of the Congo into the French Franc Zone of the world economy. In all of this there is the invariant core whereby the maintenance and accumulation of self are dependent upon access to external life-force coming from the gods, from ancestors (also gods) and from Europe, the 'heavenly' source of such force. If the flow of force is distributed, fragmentation ensues, witchcraft and conflict abound, and 'fetishism' and cultism reach epidemic proportions, a massive and desperate attempt to survive.

The Ainu and the Hawaiians

The Ainu are a well-known ethnic minority of Japan, traditionally described by anthropologists in the general category of hunters and gatherers, primarily inhabiting the northern island of Hokkaido.[3] When discussing the present situation it is usually claimed that Ainu culture has largely disappeared and that they exist as a poorly acculturated and economically and politically marginal minority. Recent historical work would, however, indicate that the Ainu were at one time a hierarchical society with a mixed economy and that their present status, including the image of the hunter/gatherer, is a product of the long and painful integration of Hokkaido into the Meiji state. For the Japanese the Ainu do not have ethnic status, simply because no such status exists. All the inhabitants of the territory of Japan, Nihonjin, are variations of the Wajin people, some more developed than others. Ainu, like other deprived groups, are simply outcasts, a social category and not a definition. Their position can only be changed in Japanese official ideology via fuller integration into the larger economy and society. They must, in other words, enter modernity as the Japanese define it. There are many Ainu who attempt to do this, who deny their Ainu identity and attempt to become Japanese, which, of course, would imply consuming Japanese. This strategy has not been generally successful, owing primarily to discrimination against Ainu; for if, officially, Ainu are as Wajin as any other Japanese, they are still outcasts; that is, their social position, their aboriginal Japanese status, functions as effectively as any ethnic stigmatization. Sixty per cent of the Ainu depend on welfare to a greater or a lesser degree. As their lands were lost to the Japanese, they most often work for others, in agriculture and related industries, and in tourism and service sectors. Their unemployment rate is 15.2 per cent.

During the 1970s an Ainu cultural movement developed, whose aim has been to gain recognition as a separate ethnic group. There is no interest in political autonomy, but rather acceptance on equal terms with the majority population. While this might appear simple for the western observer, it is a very serious problem for a state whose very legitimacy is threatened by the existence of multi-ethnicity. The Ainu strategy is decidedly ethnic. They have established schools for the teaching of language and traditions to those who have lost them and, not least, for their children. But they do much more than that. In several areas they have established traditional village structures for the expressed purpose of producing traditional handcrafted goods and having tourists come and witness their traditional lifestyle. Although Ainu live in Japanese houses today, they have built traditional Ainu houses, *chise*, where important village activities, such as teaching of history and language, traditional dance, weaving and woodcarving, occur on a weekly basis. Many ritual activities are also held here, and it is usual to advertise their occurrence in order to get tourist attendance and newspaper coverage. Tourists are invited not only to buy Ainu products, but to see how they are made, even to learn how they are made and to experiment in making them themselves. They can also hear about Ainu mythology, ritual and history, taste Ainu food and live in Ainu homes, especially when the few boarding houses are full.

Tourist production and display have become a central process in the conscious reconstruction of Ainu identity. They emphasize the distinctive content of Ainu ethnicity for Japanese tourists in a context where such specificity is officially interpreted as a mere variation on Japanese culture and not a separate identity. The presentation of Ainu selfhood is a political instrument in the constitution of that selfhood:

My personal opinion is that the Ainu people have come to realize that in order to become a complete human being, an 'Ainu', one cannot repress one's origins. Instead one has to let it come into the open and that is exactly what is happening among the Ainu people today. They are eager to know about olden times, values, things, everything. They have been starving, mentally, for so many years now. There is nothing to stop their enthusiasm now. (Ainu leader quoted in Sjöberg 1993: 175)

One might suspect that placing that identity on the market would have a de-authenticating effect, but here again, as in the obverse case of the Congolese, commodification is encompassed by the larger authenticating project: 'Every Ainu man is a "Kibori man". We make carvings because we cannot stop. It is in our blood. If we can make a profit, well, we do not think there is anything wrong with this' (interview in Sjöberg 1993: 168).

The entire tourist project of an Ainu can be seen from this perspective, as a manifestation via a commodity form of a larger constitutive process of cultural identity, one that must, of course, be manifested for others if it is to have any real existence. It is in defining themselves for the Japanese, their significant other, that they establish their specificity:

They are arranging Ainu food festivals, where people can taste our food. *We have our own specialities you know.* The food is cooked in a traditional way and the people use traditional cooking utensils when they prepare the food. Now to be able to eat Ainu food we cannot use our land to cultivate imported crops only. We have to have areas where we can cultivate our own cereal. . . . Our food festivals are very popular and people come from all over Nihon to visit and eat. They say our food is very tasty and they will recommend their friends to come here and eat. *As a matter of fact we already have restaurants in Sapporo, Asahikawa and Hakodate.* (Ainu leader quoted in Sjöberg 1993: 175)

While food festivals, publicized rituals, courses in handicrafts and the sale of Ainu products in self-consciously organized villages-for-tourists create a public image for the Ainu, they are also instrumental in recreating or perhaps creating a traditional culture. The demand for land to grow Ainu crops, the revival of a great many rituals and other activities, the renaissance of Ainu history and language – these cannot be dissociated from the tourist-based strategy: 'the tourist villages forthwith shall function as research centers for the investigation of cultural and traditional varieties of the Ainu way of life. The vision is that the villages shall serve as information centers, with possibilities to provide lectures in various traditionally based activities' (interview in Sjöberg 1993: 175).

The Ainu would appear to be as extreme as the *sapeurs* in their strategy, even if their contents are diametrically opposed to one another. Just as we might suspect the apparent hyperconsumerism of the latter, the former's orientation to the tourist market would seem to be nothing short of cultural suicide. And this is not simply a western intellectual position.

The Hawaiian cultural movement, for example, is adamantly anti-tourist. The Hawaiian struggle for the revival of a traditional way of life is part of a struggle for sovereignty that might enable Hawaiian culture to be realized on the ground. It is a movement that began in the 1970s as an attempt to re-establish cultural identity and rights to land that would enable Hawaiians to practice that culture after more than a century of social disintegration and cultural genocide resulting from the forcible integration of the islands into an expanding United States hegemony. Following the decline of the Hawaiian monarchy's autonomy, a *coup d'état* made over the islands to the American missionary-planter class in 1892. The massive import of foreign plantation workers from Asia made the already dwindling Hawaiian population a minority in their own land. Their culture and language were forbidden and stigmatized. As most Hawaiians by the mid-twentieth century were 'part-Hawaiians' they often chose to identify as part-Chinese, part-Filipino, part-white. As Hawaii became thoroughly Americanized, Hawaiian cultural identity largely disappeared until the end of the 1960s when, as we have argued elsewhere, the decline of US and western hegemony in the world system led to a decline of modernist identity in general. The fragmentation of the world system is expressed at one level in the resurgence of local cultural identities, ethnicities and sub-nationalisms. The Hawaiian movement is very much part of this process. And since the tourist industry has been the absolutely dominant force in Hawaii following the demise of the plantation economy, an industry that does not express Hawaiian strategies, but which has done more to displace them than any previous colonial economy, the movement defines itself in strong opposition to that industry.

Contemporary Hawaiians do not feel a need to advertise their local culture. It has already been thoroughly advertised and continues to be depicted in the media, controlled by an enormous industry specialized in imaging and commodifying all aspects of Hawaiian tradition. Hawaiians are acutely aware of the potential de-authenticating power of commodification. The constitution of Hawaiian identity excludes tourism and especially the objectification of Hawaiianness implied by tourist commercialization. Western intellectual sympathies are congruent with Hawaiian attitudes. Hawaiians do not wish to be consumed as domesticated exotica, and the West has produced a massive amount of critical literature on so-called consumer culture. Both we and the Hawaiians would appear to share a similar cynicism with respect to the commercial product. But then both the Hawaiians and ourselves confront such products as externalities. The Ainu control the production of their culture-for-others. Their aim is not simply to sell commodities but to present their identity as they conceive it, in order to have it recognized by the larger world. They experience their products as extensions of themselves.

Transformations of Being-in-the-world and Global Process

Congolese consume modernity to strengthen themselves. The Ainu produce traditional goods in order to create themselves. The former appropriate otherness, while the latter produce selfhood for others. Hawaiians produce selfhood for themselves. In more concrete terms, the *sapeurs*, at the bottom of a hierarchy of ranked well-being defined as imported life-force, desperately struggle to appropriate the latter via the accumulation of what appear to us as the signs of status, but which for them are the substance of life. The verb *se jaunir* is often used of the *sapeurs*, referring to the use of bleach to lighten the skin but also to the more general whitening effect of status mobility. For the Congolese, identity is very much outside of the body, outside of the society. To realize oneself is to become *un grand*, and the latter is manifested in its highest form in the best of the West, the most modern and latest design and the least accessible. To obtain a Volvo or Saab in this Franc Zone monopoly would truly be a status coup. The practice of identity here is truly the accumulation of otherness.

The Ainu, unlike the Congolese, have no sovereignty, but are an oppressed minority whose ethnicity is officially denied. They are described as abject descendants of a proto-Wajin people that has since evolved into a great modern nation. If certain Bakongo are bent on being *parisiens*, their Ainu counterparts are striving to become Ainu. If *la sape* is about becoming 'modern' for one's own people, the Ainu movement is about becoming Ainu for modern Japanese. The contrast is one of symmetrical inversion: consumption of modernity vs. production of tradition; other-centered vs. self-centered; pilgrimage to Paris vs. struggle for land rights. The contrast in strategies of identity, I would suggest, is a question not simply of cultural difference but of global position. Bourdieu might perhaps be invoked here in referring to the way in which different conditions of existence generate different structures of *habitus*. The specific properties of these different strategies are, of course, clothed in cultural specificity, but I think it might well be argued that the strategies themselves can be accounted for by the particular local/global articulations within which they emerge. This does not imply that local cultural strategies are not crucial, but that to understand the strategies themselves it is necessary to account for their historical emergence. Congolese society was totally integrated as an already hierarchical system based on monopoly over imported prestige goods into a colonial system that was completely compatible with the former while becoming the major source of local wealth and welfare. It is important to note here that, while Congolese society was radically transformed throughout contact and colonization, the resultant product contains essential aspects of clanship and personhood that represent continuity with the past, and generate strategies expressive of a 'non-modern' organization of existence. The Ainu were defeated and their land was expropriated as the result of the unification of the formerly fragmented political systems of that island group. Their political autonomy disappeared in their integration as a stigmatized lower caste in the new 'nation' state. Hawaiians were also defeated – culturally, socially and demographically – by British and especially American colonial expansion. While the process here cannot be compared to that of the Ainu, the results were such that Hawaiians became a stigmatized minority in their own land, access to which they all but lost, along with their traditions and language. For both the Ainu and Hawaiians, as opposed to the Congolese, 'traditional' culture is experienced as external, as a past that has been lost and must be regained. They are both integrated into a larger modern society that is not their own. This fundamental rupture has not occurred in the Congo.

I would argue, then, that the differences among the above strategies cannot be accounted for by simply referring to different stable cultural paradigms, as Sahlins has been wont to argue. On the contrary, a consideration of the historical material would seem to imply that radical changes have indeed occurred. The early literature on contact with Hawaii indicates that the consumption of western goods by the chiefly class was an all-consuming pastime. Before 1820 American merchants engaged in the China trade

descended upon the islands in a swarm, bringing with them everything from pins, scissors, clothing, and kitchen utensils to carriages, billiard tables, house frames, and sailing ships, and doing their utmost to keep the speculating spirit at a fever heat among the Hawaiian chiefs. And the chiefs were not slow about buying; if they had not sandalwood at hand to pay for the goods, they gave promissory notes. (Kuykendall 1968: 89)

Lists of items imported include fine broadcloth, Chinese silks, cashmere and ladies' dresses, and there is an escalation of types of 'qualities': 'Everyone that comes brings better and better goods, and such as they have not seen will sell when common ones will not' (Bullard 1821–3: 4 July). While such goods are very much monopolized by the chiefs in what appears as a kind of status competition, a number of western and Chinese goods find their way into the lower ranks (Morgan 1948: 68). The image of the enthusiastic accumulation of western and Chinese goods is reminiscent of Central Africa. Even the adoption of European names, the identification with what is conceived as the source of power or *mana*, is common to both. Thus the description from the period 1817–19 of the Hawaiian king's men might ring true for many other parts of the globe: 'The soldiers around the King's house had swords and muskets with bayonets. Some of them wore white shirts, some waistcoats, and some were naked' (p. 68).

Early-contact Hawaii provides a model of the accumulation of western identity via acts of consumption of both goods and names. Chiefs attempt to identify as closely as possible with the *mana* that is embodied in such imports and which as such is simultaneously an accumulation of status (in our terms). But the disintegration of the Hawaiian polity and the marginalization of the Hawaiians in the colonial setting produce the kind of rupture, referred to above, whereby a separate identity emerges in conditions of stigmatized poverty:

The household is living at a poverty level.... Compared with this standard budget, the Hawaiian is high on food, particularly with the addition of payments on back food debts, low on household operation, and fortunately situated with no rent to pay. The tent shelter, in the midst of a sea of rubbish, is a shack that is neither beautiful nor probably very healthful. Clothes from the dump heaps may not be a good quality, but at least they are free and enable their wearers to be conventionally dressed for the most part. (Beaglehole 1939: 31)

Informant has bought no clothes for himself for many years. When he has need to dress up he wears suits made for him 20 years ago, the material of which is so good that it simply will not wear out. Prestige is acquired in this neighborhood by having a laundry van call each Monday morning. (ibid.: 32–3)

All the hats and clothes of the women are home-made. (ibid.)

Hawaiians in the early part of this century, a minority in a multi-ethnic society, develop a sense of their own culture of generosity, reciprocal feasting, egalitarianism and the extended family, as they are increasingly integrated into the larger society. Food as the stuff of social relations among Hawaiians acquires a special value, while things imported and the trappings of modernity lose very much of their function:

With their decreasing use, Hawaiian foods have increasingly become enveloped with that luscious haze which overhangs the golden age of Hawaiian glory. Thus, in one poor Hawaiian family, in which there is little food for many mouths, whenever there is not enough food to go around, the old Hawaiian mother requests her children to pretend they are eating the delicacies which the old Hawaiians love. The family thus fills its stomach on the golden age if not on the golden foods. Again, another older Hawaiian is fond of attributing the degeneration of the modern Hawaiian to his love of strange and exotic foods. ... This informant attributes his own vigor to the fact that he prepares his own foods himself. (Beaglehole 1939: 38)

Here we find the core of a developing ethnicity, a strategy of self-production and consumption which appears to be the foundation of modern Hawaiian identity and a strategy for cultural rebirth. This self-directedness is not something intrinsically Hawaiian but the specific product of the global transformation of the local society.

Conclusion

For several years now there has been an ongoing reconceptualization of processes of production and especially of consumption as more than simply material aspects of subsistence. Following a line of argument that began with the recognition that goods are building blocks of life worlds, I have suggested, as have others, that they can be further understood as constituents of selfhood, of social identity. From this point of view, the practice of identity encompasses a practice of consumption and even production. If we further assume a global historical frame of reference it is possible to detect and even to account for the differences among broad classes of strategies of identity and therefore of consumption and production as well as their transformations in time. This is the case, at least, to the extent that the different strategies of identity, which are always local, just like their subsumed forms of consumption and production, have emerged in interaction with one another in the global arena.

NOTES

1 One might even seriously question the validity of Bourdieu's differential model as applied to his own empirical data, where diametrically opposed categories are often represented by statistical differences of a more indeterminate nature – 49 per cent vs. 42 per cent – and where most of the defined categories of style correlated to 'class' linger in the 50 per cent range at best. Could it be that cultural identification is not so clearly linked to social position and that whatever linkages there are result from other kinds of systemic processes?

2 The most common examples are the tourist industry's capacity to commodify ethnicity, making once powerful symbols of cultural identity available to an international market.
3 The material about the Ainu is based on the work of K. Sjöberg (1993) which deals with Ainu cultural identity today and provides a brilliant analysis of the historical relationships between Ainu and Japanese.

REFERENCES

Beaglehole, E. (1939) *Some Modern Hawaiians*. Honolulu: University of Hawaii Research Publications, no. 19.
Bourdieu, P. (1977) *Outline of a Theory of Practice*. Cambridge: Cambridge University Press.
Bourdieu, P. (1979) *La Distinction*. Paris: Minuit.
Bullard, C. P. (1821–3) "Letterbook of Charles B. Bullard, Supercargo for Bryant and Sturgis at Hawaiian Islands and Canton, 20 March 1821–11 July 1823," typescript, Hawaiian Mission Children's Society Library, Honolulu.
Campbell, C. (1987) *The Romantic Ethic and the Spirit of Modern Consumerism*. Oxford: Blackwell Publishers.
Devauges, R. (1977) *L'Oncle, le Ndoki et l'entrepreneur: la petite entreprise congolaise à Brazzaville*. Paris: ORSTOM.
Friedman, J. (1989) "The Consumption of Modernity," *Culture and History* 4: 117–29.
Gandoulou, J. D. (1984) *Entre Paris et Bacongo*. Paris: Centre Georges Pompidou, Collection "Alors."
Hanway, J. (1756) "Essay on Tea," in *A Journal of Eight Days' Journey*. London.
Kuykendall, R. S. (1968) *The Hawaiian Kingdom*. Honolulu: University of Hawaii Press.
Morgan, T. (1948) *Hawaii: A Century of Economic Change 1778–1876*. Cambridge, MA: Harvard University Press.
Sjöberg, K. (1993) *The Return of the Ainu: Cultural Mobilization and the Practice of Ethnicity in Japan*. London: Harwood Academic Publishers.

11

Commodities and the Power of Prayer: Pentecostalist Attitudes towards Consumption in Contemporary Ghana

Birgit Meyer

In the course of my fieldwork among the Peki, who are part of the Ewe in South-eastern Ghana, I learned several remarkable things. One was that markets and shops are dangerous: they contain goods which one might long for, but alas, once bought, the things may turn against their owner and cause destruction. I was especially warned about the dangers imbued in commodities by a fervent pentecostalist preacher in his early thirties, who told me the following experience. One day he had bought a pair of underpants at the local market; since the day he started wearing them, he had been harassed by sexual dreams in which he had intercourse with beautiful ladies, although in daily life he was alone. Only after some time did he realize that the dreams were caused by the underpants; having thrown them away, he slept undisturbed by seductive women. Obviously I was not the only person to whom he related this experience: many members of the church in which he used to preach – the Evangelical Presbyterian Church 'of Ghana' – told me his story. Yet he did not stop at warning people about the possible danger inherent in goods, he also offered a remedy to neutralize it: prayer. All church members were called on to say a brief, silent prayer over every purchased commodity in their minds before entering their homes. They were to ask God to 'sanctify' the thing bought, thereby neutralizing any diabolic spirit imbued in it. Only in this way would it be possible to prevent the destructive powers incorporated in the objects from damaging their owners' lives.

From *Development and Change* 29(4) (1998), Blackwell Publishers. Copyright © Institute of Social Studies.

As I learned later, this intriguing attitude is not peculiar to pentecostalists in Peki, but is widely shared in Ghanaian pentecostalist circles, in both urban and rural areas. It is especially prevalent among members of classical pentecostal churches such as the Church of Pentecost and the Assemblies of God, as well as among members of prayer groups within mission churches and new pentecostalist churches such as the Evangelical Presbyterian Church 'of Ghana'.[1] Pentecostalism, a pre-eminently global religion (Poewe 1994), which has been increasing in popularity all over Africa since the late 1980s, offers a peculiar attitude towards the local market, that is, the place from which globally circulated products pass into private homes. It represents commodities offered in the market as animated and, at the same time, provides the means to transform them into mere objects to be used. This article is dedicated to an in-depth examination of this attitude. It focuses on the relationship between religion and consumption in the context of globalization, in other words, on people's (awareness of their) incorporation in global economic, political, social, cultural and religious processes.

While processes of conversion to world religions (for Africa, see for example, Horton 1971, 1975) and commodification (for example, Appadurai 1986; Parry and Bloch 1989; Thomas 1991) caught the attention of social scientists studying non-western people's experiences with colonialism and modernization a long time ago (even before globalization became a topic of investigation), the relationship between conversion to Christianity and consumption has been rather neglected. Yet the urge of Ghanaian pentecostalists to purify – or rather, de-fetishize – commodities through prayer suggests that a full understanding of both conversion and consumption requires an investigation of the relationship between the two.

This article provides a sketch of the relationship between Christianity and consumption at the grassroots level. On the basis of a detailed investigation of pente-costalist views and attitudes, it is shown that pentecostalists engage in a dialectic of enchantment and disenchantment. They represent the modern global economy as enchanted and themselves as agents of disenchantment: only through prayer can commodities cease to be fetishes and become mere commodities in the sense commonly accepted by social scientists and economists. I argue that taking for granted the meaning of terms such as 'commodities' and 'consumption' blocks the way for a better understanding of how the global economy is apprehended at the local level, by organizations such as pentecostalist churches. In order to grasp the developments which social scientists circumscribe as globalization, there is a definite need to approach economics as culture (Appadurai 1986; Gudeman 1986). The fruitfulness of this approach, which leads us beyond a reification of the economic, is revealed especially through recent anthropological studies of consumption as a cultural practice (see, for instance, Carrier 1995; Miller 1987, 1994). Yet in their eagerness to make us 'acknowledge' consumption (Miller 1995b), proponents of this approach tend to accept the rather instrumental view that in a globalizing world, consumption would serve the construction of modern identities. My research shows that con-sumption may not necessarily serve this positive goal; as commodities are considered able to impose their will on their owners, their consumption may also threaten to dissolve identity. Rather than assuming a knowledge of what consumption is and does, our investigations make us wonder how the people we study themselves view and deal with consumption. Only an anthropology which is prepared to keep on wondering about the meaning of its own vocabulary may claim to grasp what is going on in a globalizing world.[2]

Christianity and Consumption

Before looking at current pentecostalist attitudes towards prosperity, the global market and the consumption of foreign commodities, it is necessary to place pentecostalism in its proper historical perspective, by examining how nineteenth-century Ewe converts to Christianity appropriated the missionary stance towards goods that was communicated to them through both the sermons and material culture of the German Pietist missionaries of the Norddeutsche Missionsgesellschaft (NMG). This section briefly traces the history of the introduction of western consumer goods as part and parcel of missionization and examines Ewe Christians' attitudes towards western commodities.

In the course of the seventeenth century, the Ewe settled in the area lying between the rivers Volta and Mono and stretching from the coast some 200 km inland.[3] Through slave trade and the concomitant presence of European traders on the coast, the Ewe were part of a global system of trade; this entailed among other things that western goods found their way far into the hinterland. Yet the more frequent consumption of western goods on a day-to-day basis only occurred in the last decades of the nineteenth century in the course of the incorporation of the Ewe area into British Gold Coast and German Togo, when an increasing number of Ewe engaged in wage labour or the production of cash crops.

In this process mission societies played a crucial role. For the NMG, a German Pietist mission society which was active among the Ewe from 1847 onwards, the spread of the Gospel and world trade clearly belonged together. Unlike other Protestant mission societies such as the Basler Mission, which was active among the neighbouring Asante, the NMG did not run stores of its own. However, both at home and in the mission field it co-operated closely with the trading company Vietor which was owned by a Pietist trader (see Ustorf 1986). The NMG and Vietor company often settled at the same places and, at least for the local population, their association was evident, despite the usual disclaimers of NMG-missionaries who desperately tried to keep Christianity at a distance from worldly matters such as stores. While the Vietor company bought crops such as cotton and, from the turn of the century onwards, cocoa from the Ewe and, at the same time, offered European goods for sale, the NMG promoted paid labour through its educational system, including teachers, clerks, cash crop farmers and artisans.[4] Interestingly, the NMG did not favour converts' adoption of trade as a profession. Trade was to remain a European monopoly and the role of Africans was merely to sell raw materials to, and buy commodities from, western trading companies.[5]

This promotion of work for money, and the subsequent incorporation of people into world trade, either as producers of raw materials or as consumers of western commodities, was part and parcel of the propagation of a new Christian lifestyle. For the most visible characteristic feature of Christians was their material culture: the traditional compound housing the extended family was to be exchanged for a house for the nuclear family, which contained western furniture, china-ware, all

sorts of iron kitchen utensils, books and European cookies; Christians were expected
to wear clothes which were either imported from Europe (black coat and tie for the
men) or made from European materials (dresses in western or African styles for
women). To both the missionaries and the Ewe converts, the possession of western
goods was a self-evident feature of Christian life and their lack was regarded as a sign
of 'savagery'. Yet it seems that their ideas about consumption differed considerably.

The NMG held a complicated stance towards consumption. Although the mission
considered trade a civilizing strategy by which Africans could be lifted up from their
'heathen' life conditions, and thus favoured the *use* of western goods in Africa, it
associated the *pleasures* of consumption with an indulgence in worldly matters
which would prevent eternal salvation. In line with the popular lithograph depicting
the well-known image of 'The broad and the narrow path',[6] the missionaries
associated pleasures such as entertainment, beautiful clothes and good food and
drinks with the 'broad path', which would eventually end in hellfire, and abstinence
from these pleasures and indulgence in charity with the 'narrow path', which would
lead to salvation in the heavenly Jerusalem. As I have shown elsewhere (Meyer,
1995a: 24ff.), the Pietist NMG-missionaries were true exponents of Weber's innerworldly ascesis (1984/1920); that is, they promoted an ethic which favoured the
virtue of production above the pleasure of consumption. This, at least, was their
stance in their home base, Württemberg in southern Germany. The missionaries
from this area were highly suspicious of industrialization, urbanization and the new
possibilities offered by mass consumption, and the dream of the good, old, rural way
of life encouraged many of them to go to Africa (Jenkins 1978). Yet ironically, once
there, they contributed to sparking off the very same processes from which they
wanted to escape at home.

The attitudes of Ewe Christians towards consumption have to be deduced from
missionary sources. From the missionaries' frequent complaints it becomes clear that
for the Ewe, the mission was a road towards 'civilization', that is, a state of opened
eyes (*nku vu*) which implied the (striving for) possession of western goods.[7] The
missionaries were especially critical about Ewe staying on the coast near the commercial and administrative centres, who actively traded with Europeans and who
were wealthy enough to furnish themselves and their homes with all sorts of new
things (Ustorf 1989: 241ff.). Yet things that were ordinary, taken-for granted objects
of use for the missionaries, were new (and often luxury) goods to the Ewe. These
goods not only symbolized 'civilization', but also contributed to turning upside
down existing societal and familial structures. Western goods either replaced other
home-made things (in the case of clothes, for instance) or contributed to transforming customs and habits, as in the case of nuclear family houses which had an impact
on traditional patterns of production and distribution; western-styled furniture
contributed to the transformation of eating habits, and European clothes undermined existing patterns of co-operation between husbands and wives.[8]

The mission's emphasis on individual salvation and a certain material standard of
living were interrelated and contributed to the emergence of a group of people for
whom consumption became a practice to emphasize individuality at the expense of
forms of identity based on lineages or clans and the patterns of production, distribution and consumption related to them. Clearly, to Ewe converts western goods were
building blocks of a new type of lifestyle, by which they could distinguish themselves

from other people in society, for instance the traditional elites. This is not to say that Ewe converts' consumption of western goods is to be explained merely in terms of conspicuous consumption à la Veblen. Rather, western goods offered new 'means of objectification' (Miller 1987) by which Ewe converts could construct a new, modern identity – modern not only in the sense that they possessed hitherto unknown things, but, above all, in the sense of a change of notions of selfhood. They identified themselves as modern consumers, that is, persons with a 'consciousness that one is living through objects and images not of one's own creation' (Miller 1995a: 1). This meant that they wanted to go beyond mere subsistence, to enjoy things which they had not produced by themselves or in their surroundings, and to confine consumption to the nuclear family.

The mission represented those indulging in the pleasures of consumption as 'Halbgebildete' (semi-educated), that is, people who were merely imitating western ways, which was attributed to superficiality and a lack of profound character.[9] Although the mission did indeed regard western goods as a necessary ingredient of a Christian lifestyle, it expected converts to view material matters as subordinate to the 'true content' of the Christian message, and consumption as subordinate to production. Christians were expected to work hard and walk humbly on the 'narrow path', abstaining from 'worldly' pleasures. The mission's allegedly anti-materialistic stance also came to the fore in its feverish fight against the Ewe's materialist outlook in traditional religious matters and the denunciation of their worship as 'fetishistic'. The missionaries preached continuously that by worshipping rivers, stones and other objects, the Ewe were truly worshipping Satan (Meyer 1992, 1994, 1995a). Associating these 'fetishes' with the Devil, the missionaries asked the Ewe to burn all objects related to their old religion and adopt a much more spiritualistic and self-conscious attitude towards the divine. Converts were no longer to allow 'fetishes' to possess them, thereby drawing a strict boundary between people and things. A good Christian was to subject the object world to his or her own will and strive after higher, immaterial values.

Of course, by representing missionary Pietism as a non-materialistic form of worship and, at the same time, expecting converts to adopt a western lifestyle, the mission mystified its own actions. Ewe converts' attitudes towards consumption were so disturbing to the mission because they laid bare a characteristic feature of the Pietist mission: the fact that conversion to Christianity required western commodities. Rather than merely enabling people to buy commodities, Christianity itself was produced through consumption.

Until the 1940s, the lives of Ewe converts proved the association of Christianity and the ability to buy and consume western goods to be valid. In Peki, for instance, people became increasingly involved in the cultivation of cocoa. The popular nickname people gave to this crop, black gold, testifies to the relative ease by which cocoa farming yielded money. While the men planted the seeds and looked after the plants, women were responsible for the transport of the fruits to the cocoa merchants, from whom they then bought all sorts of western goods in return. In this way, women had money at their disposal which they could invest in trade; they thus became to some extent independent from subsistence production and contributed to the further spread of more and more western goods until even in the remotest village global commodities became accessible.

Although cocoa cultivation and trade were practised by Christians and non-Christians alike, for all those earning money in this way (or through other activities) it was relatively profitable to identify themselves as Christians. While traditionally, farming was organized by the patrilineal lineages and members were expected to share their wealth with their extended family, the mission emphasized the nuclear family as the unit of production and distribution and consumption. To the dismay of the missionaries, many people took up this emphasis for other reasons than intended by the mission, and converted because they thought 'that being Christians all their properties will be saved' (the Ewe teacher E. Buama, quoted in Meyer 1995a: 79). The implications of this remark become evident if one considers that among the Ewe there existed a fear that wealthy people might fall victim to witchcraft (*adze*) attacks inflicted upon them by poorer, envious relatives. This fear of witchcraft was part and parcel of an ethic which condemned a crude accumulation of wealth by individuals and which called for sharing one's gain with members of the extended family (Meyer 1995a: 135–6). Of course, rich people existed none the less, but they needed to protect themselves against destructive attacks, for instance by *dzo* (medicine, or 'magic'). By offering a way out of established patterns of production, distribution and consumption, missionary Pietism clearly undermined the previous moral order.

Even during the cocoa boom people occasionally experienced their dependence upon the world market in negative terms (for instance, when cocoa prices fell), but it was only during World War II that the disastrous aspects of this dependency become fully apparent. As a result of the war, European demand for cocoa slumped; Ghanaian producers were stuck with their products and were thus unable to continue buying western goods. After 1945, the situation improved in the colony as a whole, but not in Peki. As a result of an outbreak of the devastating cocoa disease 'swollen shoot', in the course of the 1950s cocoa cultivation ceased in the Peki area. Since there was no alternative cash crop to be cultivated for the world market, people had to either migrate to other parts of the colony or return to subsistence production, which, of course, severely limited their ability to buy western goods. Not surprisingly, this went along with a revaluation of the extended family and related ethics, at least by those at the poor end of the scale. Thus, after the decline of cocoa cultivation, migration became virtually the only way to make money. Those who stayed at home permanently – above all married women, children, and the elderly – were comparatively poor; they had enough to eat, but were more or less dependent on their richer relatives for cash. No longer linked to the world market as producers, villagers were severely limited in their possibilities for consumption.

Western goods continued to be available in Ghana, albeit only to a small elite. Especially as a result of the Structural Adjustment Programme of the late 1980s and early 1990s, goods from the global market became increasingly common in shops and markets. Yet to the majority of people, these goods remained unaffordable, only stimulating dreams of a better life. By the time of my fieldwork in Peki in 1991/2, the consumption of foreign goods had become highly problematic. Those who were old enough remembered the first half of the twentieth century as Peki's Golden Age, that is, as a time when they could enjoy western drinks, cigarettes and sweets, buy beautiful western furniture and wear modern clothes made from imported materials. Now poverty and the concomitant inability to consume in accordance with their desires were the rule. Women's trade really was 'petty' and revolved mainly around

American wheat flour for home baking; items such as sweets, mostly imported from Holland; cheap jewellery, mirrors, and batteries from Asian countries; powders, perfumes and soap from Europe, USA or neighbouring African countries; as well as sugar, cigarettes, candles and milk powder, and small items of clothing such as the underpants which brought such problems to the pentecostalist preacher.

Since for most people a whole kilo of sugar, a whole packet of cigarettes, or a whole tin of milk powder was too expensive, traders usually divided imported food items into affordable amounts. Through this peculiar division, petty trade thus played a crucial role in making available foreign goods to people who were unable to purchase a product as a whole, but who still longed to consume other things than those produced locally. Evidently, the purchase of a small sachet of sugar, a Dutch 'toffee' or a cheap pair of pants or bra were symbols of a longed-for lifestyle which asserted people's consumptive desires even more strongly. In a situation of scarcity, the presence of such articles in stores, as well as on films shown in video-cinemas or broadcast on TV (TVs being found in virtually every pub since the early 1990s), fed desire without ever granting satisfaction. To most people, the markers of 'civilization', which had played such a crucial role in the definition and production of Christian identity, were no longer part of real life but only the stuff of dreams.

Pentecostalism

In Ghana economic decline was paralleled by the rise of new churches. These so-called Spiritual churches, which promised their members not only salvation but also material well-being in this world, became increasingly appealing to mission church members after Independence in 1958. From the 1980s onwards (a disastrous period in Ghanaian socio-economic history which was marked by severe starvation), pentecostalist churches became increasingly popular.[10] This development also took place in Peki. The pentecostalist churches which I encountered there[11] are mostly attended by young educated people (a group which is worrying about the future and at the same time experiencing a great gap between dreams and actual possibilities), and middle-aged women, who are often thrown back upon themselves and have to take care of their children without receiving much assistance from their (absent) husbands. Socially speaking, the churches are most attractive to people who are relatively powerless in the male-oriented gerontocratic power structure which still prevails in Ewe society, and who attempt to move upward economically, mainly by business and trade. While in most cases the immediate reason for a person to join a pentecostalist church is an experience of affliction, the experience of healing as such cannot account for continued church membership. Rather, in these churches people find a perspective from which to look at the changing world and to address both modernity's malcontents and its attraction (Meyer 1995a).

Pentecostalism is not organized in one single association, but rather consists of a plethora of different, sometimes rival, churches, founded by different prophets who have seen the light.[12] All the same, I believe it is appropriate to speak of a pentecostalist complex because these churches have so much in common. Interestingly, the pentecostalist churches place much more emphasis on Christianity being a 'world religion' than the former mission churches whose theologians currently attempt to

Africanize Christianity.[13] The pentecostalist churches have little interest in typically African forms of expressing faith and rather organize services and prayer sessions according to established pentecostalist forms which are similar in, for instance, Sweden (Coleman 1996), Belgium (Roelofs 1994), America (Lindermaier 1995) and Ghana. There are frequent contacts with European and American pentecostalist associations, who assist in the setting up of so-called Bible Schools, where pentecostalist preachers are trained. Preachers such as the German Reinhard Bonnke or the American Morris Cerullo are well known in Ghana, and in many houses in Peki I saw posters advertising past 'crusades'.

The pentecostalist churches present themselves as representatives of global Christianity – some even have 'international', 'world' or 'global' in their name – and claim to be able to provide correct knowledge about the state of the world. People attending these churches are taken beyond the scope of local culture, which is denounced as limited, and provided with revelations about what is going on beneath the surface of the global political economy. The idea circulates – stimulated by the book of Revelation – that the end of the world has come near and that Satan is trying to prevent people from following God and being saved. There is, as it were, a worldwide conspiracy in which everybody on earth has become entangled, if only unconsciously. Since Satan can operate on a worldwide scale only by making use of local agents, local pentecostalist churches are to engage in the struggle against Satan's particular representatives. The global war against the Devil is to be fought everywhere.

The way the Ghanaian pentecostalist churches present themselves is in marked contrast to the established mission churches, which are criticized for failing to help their members to retain health and wealth, and to the Spiritual churches, which are accused of doing so by making clandestine use of traditional spirits, that is, Satan's demons. The pentecostalist churches claim to rely solely on the Word, which is thought to be able to both invoke and represent the Holy Spirit, and vehemently oppose reliance on objects such as amulets, candles and incense in healing practices. Representing the world in terms of an opposition between God and the Devil, they offer their members an elaborate discourse about evil spirits, which includes a whole range of local spiritual entities such as old deities, ancestor spirits, witchcraft, native medicines (*dzo*, a term translated as both 'magic' and 'juju' in popular discourse), as well as 'modern' magical powers derived from India or from the bottom of the ocean. All these entities are said to be servants of Satan whose worship will make a person's spirit and body accessible to his evil machinations, which will eventually result in destruction and death.

The obsession with demonology is one of the most salient features of the new pentecostalist churches (Gifford 1994; Meyer 1992, 1994). Although the belief in the existence of the Devil is central to many Ewe Christians irrespective of the church they attend, it is the pentecostalist churches which continuously dwell on the boundary between Christianity and 'heathendom'. In contrast to the mission churches they find it important to keep on fighting Satan, who is held to operate in the guise of evil spirits, and therefore offer their members rituals of exorcism which are to do away with poverty and sickness.

Pentecostalists distinguish between the realm of 'the physical' (in Ewe: *lenutilame*), that is, the visible world, and 'the spiritual' (in Ewe: *le gbogbome*), that is, the invisible world, and contend that the latter determines the former.

Consequently, sickness and mishaps are understood to be a result of evil spirits intruding into a person's spirit and body. In their view, there is a spiritual war going on between God and the Devil, and this is taking place both in the world as a whole and within a person's individual spirit. Pentecostalist preachers claim to be able to penetrate the invisible and to bring about physical healing and improvement of material conditions by fighting a spiritual battle against demons.

During prayer meetings members are protected against possible intrusions of evil spirits, so that they cannot be harmed by, for instance, *adze* or *dzo* which envious family members and neighbours may wish to inflict upon them. People experiencing bodily and spiritual weaknesses are called forward separately and if they are found to be possessed, attempts are made to deliver them from the powers of darkness which are disturbing them and to fill them with the Holy Spirit.[14] Deliverance is to ensure that a person is severed from all previous ties with spiritual entities, as well as from the social relations they imply. In the end, prayers create individuals whose spirits are fully possessed by the Holy Spirit and separated from the complex for which the Devil stands.[15] Significantly, demonic possession is not confined to the individuals experiencing it, but rather is a matter of public interest. The exorcism of demons takes place in front of the congregation, and pentecostalist churches offer their members the possibility to listen to testimonies from people who were involved with evil spirits in the past.

Pentecostalist Attitudes towards the Market and Consumption

Prosperity

One of the great concerns of the members of pentecostalist churches is to be successful in life. In the face of inflation and economic decline, pentecostalists seek divine protection to carry on and, if possible, progress. It will not come as a surprise, therefore, that money and goods are important themes in pentecostalist discourse.[16] Several authors have pointed out that all over the world pentecostalists embrace a so-called prosperity gospel (for example, Coleman 1996; Gifford 1994) which teaches that God will bless true 'born again' Christians with prosperity. During my fieldwork I saw how successful preachers proudly attributed their wealth to God, a claim which certainly attracted people into their churches.[17]

Most of the persons attending a 'National Deliverance Meeting' organized by The Lord's Pentecostal Church in April 1992 in its 'healing station' at Tokokoe,[18] were traders seeking success in business. In a fasting service organized by the same church in Peki Blengo I heard the pastor ask all members to rise, close their eyes and fill in a cheque in their minds which was then sent up to heaven; the people were assured that God would sign this cheque and that they would, in the future, receive the money requested – if only they believed. Afterwards a woman stood up and gave testimony that she had sent such an invisible cheque to the Almighty some time ago and that shortly afterwards a relative in Europe had sent her the very same amount for which she had asked, thereby implying that God had used the relative as his tool. One could hear similar testimonies in other pentecostalist churches whose congregations would all offer special prayers for success in business.

The contribution of pentecostalist churches to their members' financial efforts is above all symbolic. Unlike the NMG in the early days, pentecostalist churches do not actively support members in matters of production and do not run trading companies. It is emphasized that people should try to earn their money through hard work, and there are prayers in order to make these efforts successful; by just sitting down and praying one will not progress (though prayers may play an important part). In the sphere of accumulation and distribution the pentecostalist churches also play an important, although again symbolic, role. By offering protection for a person's individual business and by cutting symbolically the blood ties connecting a person with his or her family, pentecostalist churches promote economic individualism. In this way they lead people beyond the confines of their family, or accommodate those who already find themselves thrown back upon themselves, thereby translating the burden of being let down into the virtue of individual responsibility. In symbolic terms pentecostalist churches thus promote an ethics supporting the 'spirit of capitalism'. This, however, is of little consequence for the life conditions of the majority of the members. Pentecostalist churches cannot offer efficient remedies against economic misery on a large scale and most members definitely are not rich. Rather, pentecostalism provides an imaginary space in which people may address their longing for a modern, individual and prosperous way of life.

Yet, this positive attitude towards prosperity is only one aspect of pentecostalists' stance towards trade and consumption. Recalling the account of the sexy underpants with which we started, we may assume that goods also have a dark side; this side, which has been neglected in the literature on African pentecostalism at least, will occupy us in the remainder of this section.

The dangers of the market

As already noted, many women in pentecostalist churches engage in trade. They share the widespread fear of strange things going on in the market which would not meet the eye but which might have very severe consequences 'in the physical'. This links to the idea that, next to the visible, there is also an invisible witch market going on, in which meat is sold. This meat is taken 'spiritually' from human beings who are eventually 'eaten up' by witches until they fall sick and die. Of course, one has to take great care that one does not fall victim to these witches who are, above all, motivated by envy and seek to do away with successful traders or to prevent business women from ever prospering. Pentecostalists regard the Holy Spirit as the sole entity able to protect them against being eaten by witches and to provide at least some of them with the much-desired 'spirit of discernment', that is, the ability to peep into the otherwise invisible realm.

Another dangerous aspect of the market is the presence of successful trading women who are suspected of having made a deal with occult powers. There is, for instance, a rumour according to which certain traders carry a snake in their vagina which will make them rich in exchange for abstaining from having children (see Meyer 1995b: 245). Another rumour has it that certain women have a snake lying at the bottom of their pot from which they sell food, in order to make it taste so good that customers will become addicted and always return. Some of these cheats are said to have been exposed by brave pentecostalist preachers whose prayers have made the snake (a representative of the Devil, of course) appear at the surface of the pot; all customers ran away. Many women also complain that traders use other types of *juju* in order to attract customers; why otherwise would certain women prosper whereas others, who sell the very same items, do not?

Inquiring why pentecostalists are against this type of trade *dzo*, which after all works so well, I learned that the danger with the purchase of trade *dzo* is that the trader will be required to observe certain taboos and to humble himself or herself before the *dzo*'s spirit. The problem is that, once the traders are rich, they will forget these requirements, for this is how prosperous people are. As a result, the *dzo* that made them rich will turn against them and make them poor or mad. Against this background it is not surprising that pentecostalism is attractive to traders: by offering prayers for the progress of business it provides assistance which is in many respects complementary to popular trade magic while, at the same time, it does not involve a pact with a destructive power.

These types of rumours, which focus on the traders themselves, have circulated since cocoa cultivation was taken up on a massive scale and cocoa farmers became increasingly indebted to traders who offered them goods in advance for the forthcoming season's crop. Debrunner (1961: 71) reported that traders were regarded as people who made money through magical means and were therefore able to wield power over less rich and less influential people. In contrast to the mission churches, which discard such ideas as superstitions and propagate a secular view of the market, pentecostalist churches take the widespread fear of the market as a magical place as a point of departure, thereby engaging actively in the enchantment of the economy. By representing the market as a domain of possible activities of Satan's agents, and themselves as capable of providing adequate protection against these powers, they confirm people's fear that trade is a dangerous and insecure affair – a fear which is, of course, very much to the point since global trade works according to laws which are not transparent from a local perspective, but which nevertheless have very real (and often negative) consequences for one's own business. Next to the rumours about the dangers of the market there are nowadays an increasing number of narratives focusing on the dangers imbued in the commodities themselves. In this way, not only trade, but also consumption itself is represented as a dangerous matter.

The dangers of consumption

In pentecostalist circles many stories dealing with the dangers imbued in goods are spread through popular magazines, movies and songs, public sermons and confessions, and by way of gossip. In this context the realm of the sea is a matter of great importance. According to popular imagination, the bottom of the ocean is the dwelling place of *Mami Water*, that is, mermaids and mermen who may appear on earth in the shape of beautiful people and entice human beings to become their spouses. Once married to a *Mami Water* spirit, a person is no longer allowed to marry a human being and cannot have children, but in exchange for sacrificing the capability of sexual reproduction one will receive riches derived from the bottom of the ocean. This narrative, which circulates along the entire African coast (Drewal 1988; Fabian 1978; Wendl 1991; Wicker 2000), has recently been taken up by pentecostalists who have incorporated it in their imagination of the satanic and claim that *Mami Water* spirits are agents of the Devil.[19]

The confession laid down by the Nigerian Emmanuel Eni in his booklet *Delivered from the Powers of Darkness* (1988) is extremely popular in Ghanaian pentecostalist circles and even in the West African diaspora in Europe, because it is considered a first-hand account of the realm of darkness – Eni only became a 'born again' Christian after having a serious involvement with Satan.[20] In this confession, which I have examined in some detail elsewhere (Meyer 1995b; see also Marshall 1993: 227; Wicker 2000: 19), Eni makes some revealing remarks about the relationship between the Devil and consumption. Recounting his arrival in the realm of the *Mami Water* spirits at the bottom of the sea, which, as everybody knows, abounds with goods, he tells his readers that he even went into the scientific laboratory where scientists and psychiatrists joined forces to design 'flashy cars', the 'latest weapons', 'cloth, perfumes and assorted types of cosmetics', 'electronics, computers and alarms' (Eni 1988: 18). Eni does not tire of warning people that the Devil has told him 'that since man likes flashy and fanciful things he would continue to manufacture these things and make sure man has no time for his God . . .' (p. 22). Since one of the areas where the Devil would win souls was in the secondary schools, he would make sure to send satanic agents there who would tempt schoolgirls with 'cosmetics, dresses, underwear, books, provisions and money' (p. 32) to forget about God. Eni also warns his readers about the dangers of the market: 'The market is one of the major areas of operations . . . Certain fanciful products sold in the market e.g. necklaces, lipsticks, perfumes and food items such as sardines "queen of the coast" etc. have strange origin' (p. 54).

Eni is not very clear about how these objects 'of strange origin' work upon their owners: do they simply distract people's minds from God or do they connect people to Satan in a more active way? Put differently, do the fanciful things have a power of their own by which they can make their owner behave in a way in which he or she would not behave without them? Answers to these questions can be gained by a closer investigation of pentecostalist praxis. For, all over the country, pentecostalists not only read Eni's account, but also supplement it with similar experiences.

That there is a constant need to be suspicious about (fanciful) goods was one of the most important messages of the prayer sessions I encountered in Peki. During one prayer session I witnessed a preacher calling forward a seventeen-year-old girl who was wearing a western dress with a flowered design, a belt with a lock in the form of a butterfly, a necklace with a coloured heart and earrings in the shape of strawberries. According to the preacher she was related, through these adornments, to *Mami Water* spirits who would make her indulge in 'flirting' and spend money on fanciful things. Therefore he asked her to do away with these things; a request which she, however, refused to meet. The preacher warned the people present that by adorning themselves young women would risk devoting themselves to *Mami Water* spirits and thus forego marriage and childbirth in their future adult life. Clearly, for pentecostalist preachers the possession of fashionable jewellery amounts to more than mere distraction from God. It rather implies a state of being possessed by satanic powers.

In the same vein, during my stay in Ghana in 1996, pentecostalist preachers kept on warning female members to be very careful about Rasta-hair, through which they would be linked to *Mami Water* spirits. Hairdressers told me that while many customers would at least pray over the artificial hair before it was woven into their own hair, others would refrain from wearing it altogether. During deliverance services, too, preachers used to command women whom they suspected of being possessed by marine spirits to take off their Rasta look.

Pentecostalist discourse on consumption not only describes fashionable adornments as dangerous, but also targets other goods that are regarded as solid prestige items which many people aspire to possess. In Peki Avetile I heard a young man confess in public about his engagement with the powers of darkness prior to his conversion (for an elaborate presentation and discussion of this case see Meyer 1995c: 55ff.). Among other things he said that a demon had taught him to make appear before his mind's eye any place he wanted to see. He often gazed at shops in America and Europe which were filled with commodities such as bicycles, watches and TV sets – goods he longed for but did not possess in real life. The demon told him how 'to convert these goods into the demonic world', that is, to bring them under satanic control, by sprinkling lavender water on the ground in every shop he saw, thereby making sure that anybody buying any of these items would be tied to the Devil. Therefore the items would exert a destructive influence on their owners and could only be used to 'glorify' Satan. This implied that nothing productive could be done with these commodities, they would spoil easily, and eventually their owner would end up poor. He said that virtually nobody could ever be aware of what he had done to these objects because he operated in the 'spiritual realm' into which only those few people who 'were in the Holy Spirit' could penetrate.

Since the young man made his confession in public, many people were able to share his experiences and relate them to their own lives. Many were shocked to learn that western commodities with a commonly accepted use value such as watches, bicycles or TV sets – objects which pentecostalists also desired and which meant much more than certain types of cosmetics and jewellery 'from under the sea' – were also possible tools of Satan. In addition, the young preacher's account of what happened to him through his underpants made clear that consumption of objects 'converted to the Devil' or 'of strange origin' could also be dangerous for Christians. Thus, even 'born again' Christians were not safe and ran the risk of being subjected to Satan through consumption, even without being aware of it. I noticed a certain eagerness regarding revelations of the realm of darkness which were considered to be of great help for one's conduct in the world. In this way the world became increasingly insecure day by day, but at the same time pentecostalism offered appropriate remedies to ward off Satan's intrusive attempts. Hence the advice to abstain from the purchase of certain fashionable things and to purify all other commodities ranging from food items to electronic articles through prayer, that is, by predicating God's spirit upon the object.

De-fetishizing commodities

At first sight, the pentecostalist discourse on consumption may appear to be a misrepresentation of global economic facts and be dismissed as a product of fantasy which blurs the boundary between people and things. This is not a fruitful perspective, however: a closer look at the pentecostalist poetics of consumption can offer insight into people's experience and view of globalization.

Perhaps the most salient feature of the pentecostalist discourse on consumption is the emphasis laid on the possibly 'strange origin' of western commodities. It is due to this origin that a commodity may be dangerous. By pointing out that, since there is a gap between a commodity's creation and its appearance on the local market, each commodity encapsulates its origin and 'biography' (Kopytoff 1986), pentecostalist discourse problematizes the alienation which consumers experience *vis-à-vis* foreign commodities. The point here is not so much that under the condition of global capitalism people only have a very limited, partial view on the process in the course of which commodities are produced, marketed and consumed (Appadurai 1986: 54), but rather that they are unable to control this process. In short, the problem is not the inability to understand the market, but rather the inability to fully control it. This holds especially true in a country such as Ghana, where the value of imported foreign goods far outweighs that of exported raw materials, and where virtually all commodities (except locally produced foodstuff) are encountered only in a phase in which they are offered (and desired) as consumer goods, not in the phase of production.

By stressing that commodities may be dangerous because of their past, pentecostalism suggests that the appropriation of western goods through consumption is problematic and involves consumers in the danger zone of inverted possession: rather than possessing the commodity, the owner risks being possessed by the commodity. The commodity can thus not be properly possessed because it has itself become a thing which is directed by powers outside a person's own will and which exercises control over his or her body at certain moments, thereby defying the modern ideal of the autonomous self – a fetish (cf. Pietz 1985: 10ff.). This modern fetish is, ironically, similar to the religious objects burned by the missionaries earlier on. Fetishism, having shifted from the shrine to the market, strikes back. In both cases the fetish clearly is a material fixation of historical cross-cultural encounters which occupies a new space between the known and the unknown (Pietz 1985). Both are expressions of a tension between the striving for proprietorship of one's self and the notion that a person is to a large extent 'operated' through spiritual powers. Whereas the representation of local gods as fetishes criticizes the local religion for failing to let people own themselves (the main project of western missionary societies and their local converts), the representation of commodities as fetishes is a critique on capitalist consumption. In this way, the very means by which local converts were to achieve Christian identity (and thus proprietorship of the self) are suspected of making people lose this identity.

In order to grasp the pentecostalist notion of the animated commodity it is useful to turn briefly to the Marxist notion of commodity fetishism. I do not intend to discuss this in any detail (but see Carver 1987; Pietz 1993; Taussig 1980), but will merely summarize those aspects which are of immediate relevance to our comparison. Marxist theory regards commodity fetishism as the appearance of the products of human labour as autonomous entities and explains this 'false consciousness' as being based on an objective illusion which conceals a commodity's origin in exploitative social relations. Marx used the concept of fetishism primarily in order to reveal the true nature of commodities as a product of labour from which its producers have become alienated and which they are unable to appropriate. Here, making visible the exploitation from which a commodity originates destroys – or at least lays bare – its fetishistic appearance.

By contrast, pentecostalists actively fetishize commodities by referring to their unknown and hidden origin. Here awareness of the commodity's origin does not drive away the fetish, but rather makes it. By exposing the past, hitherto hidden life of the commodity, pentecostalist preachers claim to inform people about its true nature. In this view, commodities as they are found in the market truly are fetishes; the problem is that most people are not aware of this, and regard them as harmless goods. Fetishism here is not an illusory product of false consciousness, but an awareness which is able to explain, and eventually overcome, alienation. Only a commodity stripped of its past and embedded firmly in the present through prayer is a commodity in the sense of current economic discourse.

Of course, the origin referred to by pentecostalists is not the one which Marx had in mind, but a more spiritual one which is beyond the visible (albeit distanced) processes of production and marketing. For pentecostalists commodities become fetishes because the Devil appropriated them before they appeared in the market (or at the time when they are exposed in shops). Through the supposedly innocent act of buying, the consumer is linked with Satan. Entering into a relationship with the diabolic, owners lose their own will and identity, their spirits and bodies are reduced to signs which refer to, and even 'glorify', the power of the Devil. Consumption thus threatens to turn people into powerless signs – metonyms of the satanic – and in order to prevent this, one has to be aware of the fetish-aspect of commodities and prevent them from conquering one's spirit.

What is interesting here is the close association of Satan with the global market as the source and target of desire. It is through this circularity that people are drawn into its reach and come to adopt what Campbell (1987: 89) called the 'spirit of modern consumerism', that is, modern people's continuously frustrated hedonistic expectation that the purchase of the latest fashion would yield enduring pleasure. Pentecostalist preachers clearly leave no doubt that the Devil makes use of, above all, fanciful, designed goods which follow fashion and which are usually employed to attract the attention of the opposite sex. By allowing themselves to be charmed by such objects, people spend all their time feeding their desire for the new things which continually appear on the market. The true fetish, then, is the lust for pleasure and luxury which subverts a person's own individual will and locks him or her in the circularity of the market as the source and target of desire. Pentecostalists warn young people especially that their own (sexual) desire may eventually turn against them and make them forget and forego what really matters in life: instead of preparing themselves for marriage and childbirth they live in a dreamworld in which they are subordinated to spirits, bereft of a personality of their own.

With this warning, the pentecostalist stance towards consumption resembles that of the nineteenth-century Pietist missionaries. Contemporary pentecostalists' 'broad path', from which they struggle to stay away, is the splendid realm under the sea. As in the case of the missionaries, this puritan critique of fashion (and of sex as a means to acquire these prestigious commodities)[21] does not, of course, mean a general abstinence from consumption of western goods in practice. Rather, it signals that consumption is a dangerous matter which requires highly self-conscious consumers who should not keep running after everything new and who should rather control their desire.

Significantly, the pentecostalist discourse on consumption does not stop at exposing the dangers of commodities. It also claims to have the power to provide a safe alley towards consumption. By turning church members into vessels of the Holy Spirit, who are capable of fighting Satan and his demons through prayer, pentecostalism empowers believers to transform commodities into mere objects. It provides them with a ritual able 'to plumb the magicalities of modernity' (Comaroff and Comaroff 1993: xxx). By invoking God's power over every commodity bought, they perform 'exit rites' for the commodity, through which it is purified from its polluting past in the global market – in short, it is de-fetishized. Stripped of its history, it is safe to carry into its owner's house. Through this process, the object is subordinated to its owner; now it can no longer act as a fetish nor turn its owner into a satanic sign. Only through the act of prayer – the predication of the Word upon a thing – an owner thus truly becomes an owner, that is, a person able to overcome the alienating gap between a commodity's origin and its appearance on the local market, and to appropriate it through consumption.

Of course, this is not a linear project which results in the creation of self-determined persons who have for ever escaped the danger of inverted possession. It would be a regrettable omission to reduce the pentecostalist discourse on consumption to the successful construction of modern notions of selfhood and identity, firmly rooted beyond the powers of darkness which defy these notions. As I stated earlier, revelations about the realm of darkness, which bring about the, albeit imaginary, transgression into the forbidden zone of excessive sexual indulgence and waste of money and things, are extremely popular among pentecostalists. What is appealing here is 'the unspeakable mystique of the excessive, the abrogation of the useful, and the sensuous no less than logical intimacy binding overabundance to transgression in a forwards and backwards movement that is difficult to put in words' (Taussig 1995: 395). The pentecostalist discourse on consumption clearly not only addresses the dangers and possibilities of consumption, but also offers a virtual space – a dreamland located at the bottom of the ocean – to dream about its forbidden pleasures which defy any rational, utilitarian stance. It takes seriously people's wildest dreams in which they lose themselves in their desires, and offers them the possibility to claim ownership over things: a dialectic of being possessed and possessing.[22]

Conclusion

For obvious reasons, the study of consumption has recently been placed high on the anthropological agenda. Since it seems that people confront the global to a large extent through foreign commodities, consumption has become a privileged field in the study of the interaction between the local and the global. Advocating the 'acknowledgement' of consumption as a cultural practice which is located in time and space (Miller 1995b), these studies oppose the still common notion that mass consumption of global products would destroy cultural authenticity and result in homogenization.[23] Yet it is undeniable that in the context of globalization people increasingly consume resources which were not created in their own society – which are thus not 'authentic' – and, as Miller (1994) argues, have to be appropriated through mass consumption. In other words, consumption – and not, as Marx thought, production – entails the possibility of overcoming alienation and creating local identity.[24]

I agree that consumption may have the capacity to create identity at certain times and places (as, for instance, in the initial phase of missionization among the Ewe), but there is more to consumption than this constructive aspect. Our examination of the Ghanaian pentecostalist discourse on consumption reveals that the appropriation of commodities may be highly problematic. Yet until now, this aspect of consumption has hardly been an object of ethnography. Somehow the assumption prevails that globalization and the desire for western commodities go hand-in-hand,[25] and it looks as if the main problem which people face in the field of consumption is the unequal distribution of money to buy western commodities. While the witchcraft accusations and suspicions that may result from asymmetrical power relations and unequal consumptive possibilities have recently become an object of increased anthropological investigation,[26] consumption as a practice has not yet received the attention it probably deserves.

While not denying that people may strongly desire foreign goods, this article has concentrated on the problematic aspects of their consumption. It has shown that in order to retain control over western goods, a person has to strip them of their fetishistic properties, thereby making use of religion in order to produce them as commodities in the sense of western economists' prose. Here consumption does not merely entail a practice of appropriating objects, but also a highly complex reflection on the culturally specific nature of commodities in which anti-materialist and hedonistic inclinations are in conflict with each other – an interplay of anxiety and desire (cf. Taussig 1995). Rather than simply providing building blocks for the construction of identity and selfhood (Friedman 1994),[27] consumption entails the risk (or, perhaps, the temptation) of losing, rather than gaining, one's self (and hence one's Christian identity).[28]

Another important aspect of consumption which has not yet gained sufficient attention is its imaginary dimension in a situation of scarcity (but see Veenis 1994), as well as the capacity of religious organizations to take up the dreams arising in such a situation and control the consumptive practices of their adherents. As we saw, Christian missions successfully converted the Ewe into consumers of western goods which not only became symbols of 'civilization' but played an active part in the subversion of traditional patterns of production, distribution and consumption. While the desire for western goods, which was generated from the beginnings of missionization, remained, actual life conditions changed in such a way that Christians have become to a large extent unable to realize in practice the 'civilized' way of life which Christianity is supposed to entail. In a situation of material scarcity and bereft of their consumptive possibilities, Christians are forced into an extreme form of 'innerworldly ascesis' which does not even allow them to reproduce themselves as Christians in real life any longer. Hence many are virtually taken away into a dream world under the sea, where the things one's heart desires abound.

Pentecostalism helps people, albeit temporarily, out of this dream; not because it regards the *Mami Water* imagery as just fancy, but exactly because it confirms the spiritual reality of this imagery and maintains that *Mami Water* spirits may have effects on anybody, not only those who involve themselves in a spiritual marriage with these beings. By pointing out that the Devil may not only appropriate the abodes of local deities but also commodities as fetishes, the taken-for-granted association of western goods with Christian civilization is opened up (and this, of course, follows the actual state of things). Now it is possible to not only demonize local African religion, but also the global capitalist economy to which many people in Ghana – at least those who do not (or no longer) engage in cocoa cultivation – are basically linked as consumers.[29]

By representing commodities from the global market as enchanted by Satan's demons, and consumption as the major battlefield where the war between him and God takes place, pentecostalism in Ghana elaborates upon, and confirms, people's suspicions about the global market. Yet significantly, there is no advice to believers to abstain from the consumption of all imported goods (only from a very few things – a sort of symbolic abstinence). In pentecostalist discourse, no value judgement is predicated upon globalization. This is not a question of good or bad, but a matter of danger and control.[30] Pentecostalist discourse emphasizes the dangers imbued in commodities and, at the same time, presents itself as the sole instance which is truly able to help people *handle* globalization. It claims to connect people with a global community of 'born again' Christians whose form of worship follows more or less the same pattern (Johannesen 1994) and to offer true revelations about the state of the world. Local circumstances are understood in the light of this knowledge. Pentecostalist churches thus clearly offer people a scope of identification far beyond local culture. At the same time, the incorporation of the local into the global is problematized. The message is that people need pentecostalism in order to disenchant commodities and that neither the state nor the former mission churches would be able to achieve this; only through pentecostalism can people be connected with the 'world' without running the risk of being overrun. I contend that this version of Christianity is so successful in Ghana because it takes as a point of departure both the desire to have access to the world *and* existing fears about the nature of the global market and one's connection with it. Affirming that the market is an abode of invisible satanic forces, adherents can claim that a pentecostal religion is needed in order to profit from, rather than fall victim to, globalization.

NOTES

I would like to thank Gerd Baumann, Gosewijn van Beek, Remco Ensel, Peter Geschiere, Peter Pels, Peter van Rooden, Bonno Thoden van Velzen, Marja Spierenburg, Milena Veenis and Jojada Verrips for their comments on earlier versions of this article. It is based on fieldwork carried out in Peki and Accra in 1990, 1991 and 1996. This research would not have been possible without the financial assistance of the Amsterdam School for Social Science Research (ASSR) and the Netherlands Foundation for the Advancement of Tropical Research (WOTRO).

1 The so-called 'charismatic' churches, which represent a new pentecostalist branch which has become popular since the 1980s among the Ghanaian (aspiring) urban elite, appear to

be less concerned with dangers imbued in commodities (albeit on the level of the leaders) and more with gifts (cf. Van Dijk 1997).

2 I fully agree with Appiah's argument that understanding what happens in the world as a whole presupposes actual intercultural discussion. His statement concerning the understanding of modernity also applies to the understanding of 'globalization': 'the question what it is to *be* modern is one that Africans and westerners may ask together. And, as I shall suggest, neither of us will understand what modernity is until we understand each other' (Appiah 1992: 107, emphasis in original).

3 On Ewe history, see for example Amenumey 1964, 1986; Asare 1973; Spieth 1906; Wilks 1975; also my own brief overview (Meyer 1995a: 49ff.).

4 The NMG stimulated men much more than women to take up paid labour. Young women could only work as 'housegirls' at the mission posts or as childcare attendants in the kindergarten, and after marriage they were expected to devote themselves fully to their families. Against the wishes of the mission, however, many married women engaged in trade.

5 Ewe mission workers were not allowed to supplement their small incomes through trading activities. The only thing they were expected to do besides their job was to grow their own food.

6 For a detailed analysis of this lithograph, see Meyer 1995a: 25ff.

7 Elsewhere, I have dealt with the Ewe's striving for civilization through the consumption of western commodities in more detail; see Meyer 1997b.

8 In pre-colonial times there had existed a peculiar division of labour in the production of clothes between husband and wife. While spinning was the exclusive task of women, weaving was done only by men. In this way husband and wife had to co-operate in order to make clothes (Spieth 1906: 356).

9 On the NMG's use of the pejorative term 'Halbgebildete' see Meyer 1997a.

10 Between 1987 and 1992 the number of pentecostal churches grew by as much as 43 percent, the African Independent Churches by only 16 per cent. Growth rates of other types of churches also remained far below the growth rate of the pentecostal churches (Survey of the 'Ghana Evangelism Committee', 1993).

11 I conducted research in the Lord's Pentecostal Church (*Agbelengor*) and the Evangelical Presbyterian Church 'of Ghana'. These two churches split away from the Evangelical Presbyterian Church, the church resulting from the NMG, in 1961 and 1991 respectively. For the history of these secessions see Meyer 1995a: 184ff.

12 Only a restricted number of pentecostalist churches has been accepted into the Ghanaian Pentecostal Council. By pentecostalist churches, I mean all those churches within and outside this council which share the features outlined below.

13 The attempts of the Moderator N. K. Dzobo to Africanize the form and content of the Christian message in the Evangelical Presbyterian Church met so much resistance by a pentecostalist prayer group in the church that it split away from the mother church and became independent as the Evangelical Presbyterian Church of Ghana. On this conflict, see Meyer 1992.

14 Each exorcist attends to one person upon whom he lays his hand. In doing so the exorcists attempt to continue Jesus's work on earth, who also liberated people from evil spirits. As long as the afflicted person remains calm under the exorcist's hand, he or she is considered as being filled with God's Spirit. But if a person starts moving, this is attributed to the presence of evil spirits who feel disturbed by the power of the Holy Spirit touching the person through the mediation of the preacher. Once this occurs, the exorcist calls upon his colleagues to drive out the demon who is considered to harm the afflicted person (for a detailed account of this see Meyer 1995a: chs. 9 and 10).

15 Significantly, this contrasts sharply with traditional healing practices which aim at the restoration of social ties (on traditional Ewe religion see, for example, Rivière 1981; Spieth 1906, 1911; Surgy 1988). Pentecostalism's remedy against mishaps and sickness clearly is individualization. Elsewhere I have demonstrated this in more detail (1995a: 247–9). On deliverance, see also Meyer 1998.

16 Although not necessarily in a solely positive sense: on pentecostalist ideas about satanic riches (money achieved in exchange for sacrificing a beloved close relative) see Meyer 1995b.

17 In turn, an increase of members will make those running a church richer.

18 Like many other pentecostalist churches, this church runs a 'healing station' or 'prayer camp' because its leaders believe that in severe cases of possession persons can only be exorcised if they are taken out of their family's reach of influence. In this station, exorcism prayers are offered once a week. These prayers attract not only residents but also people from the surrounding area. Occasionally, the church organizes prayer sessions on a national scale.

19 The confessions of two pentecostalist girls about their involvement with *Mami Water* spirits inspired the Ghanaian script writer and film producer Socrate Safo to make 'Women in Love I and II' (released by Movie Africa Productions in 1997).

20 The fact that I once saw a person reading this pamphlet in a bus in Amsterdam testifies to the global spread of this account.

21 According to this Puritan view, sex should be used for reproductive, not consumptive ends.

22 Thus, pentecostalist discourse clearly goes further than the local rumours about devil-contracts described by Taussig. It not only permits transgression into a virtual realm of abundance and excess, but also enables people to consume without losing themselves.

23 For a critique of anthropologists' search for 'authentic culture' see especially Thomas 1991.

24 Although Miller emphasizes consumption's constructive aspects, he is aware that consumption may be problematic. He defines commodities which a person is unable to appropriate through consumption as fetishes (Miller 1990).

25 This may, of course, be so in particular cases. See for instance Gandalou 1989 on 'la Sape'; i.e. the struggle of young inhabitants of Brazzaville to accumulate famous designer clothes from France and Italy (cf. also Friedman 1994: 105ff.).

26 See, for instance, the work of Geschiere (for example, 1995) and Thoden van Velzen and Van Wetering (for example, 1988).

27 Friedman (1994: 104) views consumption as 'an aspect of a more general strategy or set of strategies for the establishment and/or maintenance of selfhood'. I disagree with this view not only because it leaves behind all too easily the problematic aspects of consumption to which I have tried to draw attention in this paper, but also because Friedman neglects the materiality of things by subsuming consumption under identity construction.

28 I strongly agree with the plea of Rouse (1995), not to regard identity construction as a universal concern of all cultures but rather to understand the globally occurring quest for identity as part and parcel of western bourgeois hegemonic projects. The pentecostalist concern with the fetish (both in the form of the local god and the western commodity) clearly testifies to a struggle for modern personhood without ever attaining it once and for all.

29 Given that people in this area are linked to the global market above all as consumers, not as producers, it is not surprising that consumption, not production, is represented as a field of satanic activity. Here lies the main difference between the present paper and studies such as the one by Taussig (1980) which focused on Columbian plantation workers' and Bolivian mineworkers' fantasies of devil contracts.

30 Comaroff and Comaroff (1993: xxx) have aptly caught the irony of 'modernity' (as 'a Eurocentric vision of universal teleology') in their statement that 'the more rationalistic

and disenchanted the terms in which it [modernity] is presented to "others", the more magical, impenetrable, inscrutable, uncontrollable, darkly dangerous seem its signs, commodities, and practices'. Yet I do not agree with their view that it is necessarily 'malcontent' which gathers 'in this fissure between assertive rationalities and perceived magicalities' (ibid). As this paper shows, people may also be striving to appropriate modernity because they find certain aspects very attractive.

REFERENCES

Amenumey, D. E. K. (1964) 'The Ewe People and the Coming of European Rule, 1850–1914'. MA thesis, University of London.

Amenumey, D. E. K. (1986) *The Ewe in Pre-Colonial Times: A Political History with Special Emphasis on the Anlo, Ge and Krepi*. Ho: E. P. Church Press.

Appadurai, Arjun (1986) 'Introduction: Commodities and the Politics of Value', in A. Appadurai (ed.) *The Social Life of Things: Commodities in Cultural Perspective*, pp. 3–63. Cambridge: Cambridge University Press.

Appiah, Kwame Anthony (1992) *In My Father's House: Africa in the Philosophy of Culture*. New York and Oxford: Oxford University Press.

Asare, E. B. (1973) 'Akwamu-Peki Relations in the Eighteenth and Nineteenth Centuries'. MA thesis, University of Ghana.

Campbell, Colin (1987) *The Romantic Ethic and the Spirit of Modern Consumerism*. Oxford: Blackwell Publishers.

Carrier, James C. (1995) *Gifts and Commodities: Exchange and Western Capitalism since 1700*. London and New York: Routledge.

Carver, Terrell (1987) *A Marx Dictionary*. Cambridge: Polity Press.

Comaroff, Jean, and John Comaroff (eds.) (1993) *Modernity and its Malcontents: Ritual and Power in Postcolonial Africa*. Chicago: University of Chicago Press.

Coleman, Simon (1996) 'All-Consuming Faith: Language, Material Culture and World-Transformation Among Protestant Evangelicals', *Etnofoor* IX(1): 26–47.

Debrunner, Hans W. (1961) *Witchcraft in Ghana: A Study of the Belief in Destructive Witches and its Effect on the Akan Tribe*. Kumasi: Presbyterian Book Depot.

Drewal, Henry John (1988) 'Performing the Other. *Mami Wata* Worship in Africa', *The Drama Review* 32(2): 160–85.

Eni, Emmanuel (1988) *Delivered from the Powers of Darkness*, 2nd edn. Ibadan: Scripture Union.

Fabian, Johannes (1978) 'Popular Culture in Africa: Findings and Conjectures', *Africa* 48(4): 315–34.

Friedman, Jonathan (1994) *Cultural Identity and Global Process*. London: Sage Publications.

Gandoulou, J. D. (1989) *Au Coeur de la sape: moeurs et aventures des Congolais à Paris*. Paris: L'Harmattan.

Geschiere, Peter (1995) *Sorcellerie et politique en Afrique: La viande des autres*. Paris: Karthala.

Ghana Evangelism Committee (1993) *National Church Survey, 1993 Update: Facing the Unfinished Task of the Church in Ghana*. Accra: Assemblies of God Literature Centre.

Gifford, Paul (1994) 'Ghana's Charismatic Churches', *Journal of Religion in Africa* 64(3): 241–65.

Gudeman, Stephen (1986) *Economics as Culture: Models and Metaphors of Livelihood*. London: Routledge & Kegan Paul.

Horton, R. (1971) 'African Conversion', *Africa* 41(2): 86–108.

——. (1975) 'On the Rationality of Conversion, Part I & II', *Africa* 45(3): 219–35, 373–99.

Jenkins, Paul (1978) 'Towards a Definition of the Pietism of Württemberg as a Missionary Movement'. Paper prepared for African Studies Association of the United Kingdom Conference 'Whites in Africa – Whites as Missionaries', Oxford.

Johannesen, Stanley (1994) 'Third Generation Pentecostal Language: Continuity and Change in Collective Perceptions', in K. Poewe (ed.) *Charismatic Christianity as a Global Culture*, pp. 176–99. Columbia, SC: University of South Carolina Press.

Kopytoff, Igor (1986) 'The Cultural Biography of Things: Commoditization as Process', in A. Appadurai (ed.) *The Social Life of Things: Commodities in Cultural Perspective*, pp. 64–91. Cambridge: Cambridge University Press.

Lindermaier, Orestis (1995) '"The Beast of the Revelation": American Fundamentalist Christianity and the European Union', *Etnofoor* 7(1): 27–46.

Marshall, Ruth (1993) '"Power in the Name of Jesus": Social Transformation and Pentecostalism in Western Nigeria "Revisited"', in T. Ranger and O. Vaughan (eds.) *Legitimacy and the State in Twentieth Century Africa*, pp. 213–46. Basingstoke: Macmillan.

Meyer, Birgit (1992) '"If You Are a Devil You Are a Witch and, If You Are a Witch You Are a Devil": The Integration of "Pagan" Ideas into the Conceptual Universe of Ewe Christians in Southeastern Ghana', *The Journal of Religion in Africa* 22(2): 98–132.

——. (1994) 'Beyond Syncretism: Translation and Diabolization in the Appropriation of Protestantism in Africa', in Ch. Stewart and R. Shaw (eds.) *Syncretism/Anti-syncretism: The Politics of Religious Synthesis*, pp. 45–67. London: Routledge.

——. (1995a) 'Translating the Devil: An African Appropriation of Pietist Protestantism. The Case of the Peki Ewe, 1847–1992'. Ph.D. thesis, University of Amsterdam.

——. (1995b) '"Delivered from the Powers of Darkness": Confessions about Satanic Riches in Christian Ghana', *Africa* 65(2): 236–55.

——. (1995c) 'Magic, Mermaids and Modernity: The Attraction of Pentecostalism in Africa', *Etnofoor* 8(2): 47–67.

——. (1997a) 'Christianity and the Ewe Nation: On the Encounter between German Pietist Missionaries and Ewe Mission Workers'. Paper presented at the Conference 'Identity in Africa', University of Leiden (22–3 May).

——. (1997b) 'Christian Mind and Worldly Matters: Religion and Materiality in Nineteenth-century Gold Coast', *Journal of Material Culture* 2(3): 311–37.

——. (1998) '"Make a complete break with the past": Memory and Post-colonial Modernity in Ghanaian Pentecostalist Discourse', *Journal of Religion in Africa* 28(3): 316–49.

Miller, Daniel (1987) *Material Culture and Mass Consumption*. New York: Blackwell Publishers.

——. (1990) 'Persons and Blue Jeans: Beyond Fetishism', *Etnofoor* 3(1): 97–111.

——. (1994) *Modernity: An Ethnographic Approach. Dualism and Mass Consumption in Trinidad*. Oxford: Berg.

——. (1995a) 'Introduction: Anthropology, Modernity and Consumption', in D. Miller (ed.) *Worlds Apart: Modernity through the Prism of the Local*, pp. 1–22. London and New York: Routledge.

——. (1995b) 'Consumption as the Vanguard of History', in D. Miller (ed.) *Acknowledging Consumption*, pp. 1–57. London and New York: Routledge.

Parry, J. and M. Bloch (eds.) (1989) *Money and the Morality of Exchange*. Cambridge: Cambridge University Press.

Pietz, William (1985) 'The Problem of the Fetish, I', *Res* 9: 5–17.

——. (1993) 'Fetishism and Materialism: The Limits of Theory in Marx', in E. Apter and W. Pietz (eds.) *Fetishism as Cultural Discourse*, pp. 119–51. Ithaca and London: Cornell University Press.

Poewe, Karla (ed.) (1994) *Charismatic Christianity as a Global Culture*. Columbia, SC: University of South Carolina Press.

Rivière, Claude (1981) *Anthropologie réligieuse des Evé du Togo*. Lomé: Les Nouvelles Éditions Africaines.

Roelofs, Gerard (1994) 'Charismatic Christian Thought. Experience, Metonomy, and Routinization', in K. Poewe (ed.) *Charismatic Christianity as a Global Culture*, pp. 217–33. Columbia, SC: University of South Carolina Press.

Rouse, Roger (1995) 'Questions of Identity: Personhood and Collectivity in Transnational Migration to the United States', *Critique of Anthropology* 15(4): 351–80.

Spieth, Jacob (1906) *Die Ewe-Stämme. Material zur Kunde des Ewe-Volkes in Deutsch-Togo*. Berlin: Dietrich Reimer.

——. (1911) *Die Religion der Eweer in Süd-Togo*. Leipzig: Dietersche Verlagsbuchhand lung.

de Surgy, Albert (1988) *Le système religieux des Évhé*. Paris: Éditions L'Harmattan.

Taussig, Michael T. (1980) *The Devil and Commodity Fetishism in South America*. Chapel Hill, NC: University of North Carolina Press.

——. (1995) 'The Sun Gives Without Receiving: An Old Story', *Comparative Studies in Society and History* 37(2): 368–98.

Thoden van Velzen, H. U. E., and W. Van Wetering (1988) *The Great Father and the Danger: Religious Cults, Material Forces, and Collective Fantasies in the World of the Surinamese Maroons*. Dordrecht: Foris Publications.

Thomas, Nicolas (1991) *Entangled Objects: Exchange, Material Culture, and Colonialism in the Pacific*. Cambridge, MA: Harvard University Press.

Ustorf, Werner (1989) *Die Missionsmethode Franz Michael Zahns und der Aufbau kirchlicher Strukturen in Westafrika (1862–1900). Eine missionsgeschichtliche Untersuchung*. Erlangen: Verlag der Ev.-Luth. Mission.

Van Dijk, Rijk (1997) 'The Pentecostal Gift: Ghanaian Charismatic Churches and the Moral Innocence of the Global Economy'. Paper Presented at the 13th Satterthwaite Colloquium on African Religion and Ritual (19–22 April).

Veenis, Milena (1994) ' "Only because of the Bananas . . . " Western Consumer Goods in East Germany', *Focaal* 24: 55–69.

Weber, Max (1984/1920) *Die protestantische Ethik I. Eine Aufsatzsammlung*. Herausgegeben von Johannes Winckelmann. Gütersloh: Gütersloher Verlagshaus.

Wendl, Tobias (1991) *Mami Wata oder ein Kult zwischen den Kulturen*. Münster: Lit Verlag.

Wicker, Kathleen O'Brien (2000) 'Mami Water in African Religion and Spirituality', in J. K. Olupona and Ch. H. Long (eds.) *African Spirituality*, New York: Crossroad Press.

Wilks, Ivor (1975) *Asante in the Nineteenth Century: The Structure and Evolution of a Political Order*. London: Cambridge University Press.

12

The Global Traffic in Human Organs

Nancy Scheper-Hughes

The urgent need for new international ethical standards for human transplant surgery in light of reports of abuses against the bodies of some of the most socially disadvantaged members of society brought together in Bellagio, Italy, in September 1995 a small international group of transplant surgeons, organ procurement specialists, social scientists, and human rights activists, organized by the social historian David Rothman. This group, the Bellagio Task Force on Organ Transplantation, Bodily Integrity, and the International Traffic in Organs, of which I am a member, is examining the ethical, social, and medical effects of the commercialization of human organs and accusations of human rights abuses regarding the procurement and distribution of organs to supply a growing global market.

At the top of our agenda are allegations of the use of organs from executed prisoners in China and elsewhere in Asia and South America for commercial transactions in transplant surgery; the continuing traffic in organs in India despite new laws which make the practice illegal in most regions; and the truth, if any, behind the global rumors of body stealing, child kidnapping, and body mutilations to procure organs for transplant surgery. My earlier research on the social and metaphorical truths underlying child-and-organ-stealing rumors in Brazil (see Scheper-Hughes 1991, 1992: ch. 6) and elsewhere (Scheper-Hughes 1996a) had led to my being invited to serve on the task force as its anthropologist-ethnographer. At its second meeting, in 1996, I was delegated to initiate ethnographic research on the social context of transplant surgery in three sites – Brazil, South Africa, and (through collaborations with my UC Berkeley colleague Lawrence Cohen) India – chosen because transplant surgery is currently a contentious issue there.

India continues to be a primary site for a lively domestic and international trade in kidneys purchased from living donors. Despite medical and philosophical debates about kidney sales (see Daar 1989, 1990 1992a, 1992b; Evans 1989; Reddy 1990;

From *Current Anthropology* 41(2) (2000): 191–224.

Richards et al. 1998) and medical outcome studies showing high mortality rates among foreign recipients of purchased Indian kidneys (see Saalahudeen et al. 1990), there have been no follow-up studies documenting the long-term medical and social effects of kidney sales on the sellers, their families, or their communities. In Brazil, allegations of child kidnapping, kidney theft, and commerce in organs and other tissues and body parts continue despite the passage in 1997 of a universal-donation law intended to stamp out rumors and prevent the growth of an illegal market in human organs. In South Africa, the radical reorganization of public medicine under the new democracy and the channeling of state funds toward primary care have shifted dialysis and transplant surgery into the private sector, with predictable negative consequences in terms of social equity. Meanwhile, allegations of gross medical abuses – especially the illegal harvesting of organs at police morgues during and following the apartheid years – have come to the attention of South Africa's official Truth and Reconciliation Commission. Finally, Sheila Rothman (1998) and a small team of medical students in New York City have initiated parallel research in New York City. Their preliminary findings indicate obstacles to the successful pre-screening of African-American, Latino, and all women as candidates for organ transplantation.

The first report of the Bellagio Task Force (Rothman et al. 1997) recommended the creation of an international human-donor surveillance committee that would investigate allegations of abuses country by country and serve as a clearinghouse for information on organ donation practices. As a first step toward that goal, Lawrence Cohen, David Rothman, and I have launched a new three-year project entitled Medicine, Markets, and Bodies/Organs Watch, supported by the Open Society Institute and housed at the University of California, Berkeley, and at the Medical School of Columbia University, New York, that will investigate, document, publicize, and monitor (with the help of international human rights activists and local ethnographers and medical students) human rights violations in the procurement and distribution of human organs. In 1999–2000 we expect to add new sites in Eastern Europe, the Middle East, Southeast Asia, and Latin America to our ongoing and collective research.

Anthropologists on Mars

This essay reports on our initial forays into alien and at times hostile and dangerous[1] territory to explore the practice of tissue and organ harvesting and organ harvesting and organ transplantation in the morgues, laboratories, prisons, hospitals, and discreet operating theaters where bodies, body parts, and technologies are exchanged across local, regional, and national boundaries. Virtually every site of transplant surgery is in some sense part of a global network. At the same time, the social world of transplant surgery is small and personalistic; in its upper echelons it could almost be described as a face-to-face community. Therefore, maintaining the anonymity of informants, except for those whose opinions and comments are already part of the public record, is essential.

The research by Cohen and myself took place between 1996 and 1998 during a total of five field trips, each roughly six to eight weeks in duration, in Brazil (Recife,

Salvador, Rio de Janeiro, and São Paulo), South Africa (Cape Town and Johannes-burg), and India. At each site, aided by a small number of local research assistants and anthropologist-colleagues, we conducted observations and interviews at public and private transplant clinics and dialysis centers, medical research laboratories, eye banks, morgues, police stations, newspaper offices, legal chambers and courts, state and municipal offices, parliaments, and other sites where organ harvesting and transplant surgery were conducted, discussed, or debated. In addition to open-ended interviews with transplant surgeons, transplant coordinators, nurses, hospital administrators, research scientists, bioethicists, transplant activists, transplant patients, and living donors in each of these sites, Cohen and I spent time in rural areas and in urban slums, townships, and shantytowns in the vicinity of large public hospitals and medical centers in order to discover what poor and socially margin-alized people imagined and thought about organ transplantation and about the symbolic and cultural meanings of body parts, blood, death, and the proper treat-ment of the dead body.

Of the many field sites in which I have found myself, none compares with the world of transplant surgery for its mythical properties, its secrecy, its impunity, and its exoticism. The organs trade is extensive, lucrative, explicitly illegal in most countries, and unethical according to every governing body of medical professional life. It is therefore covert. In some sites the organs trade links the upper strata of biomedical practice to the lowest reaches of the criminal world. The transactions can involve police, mortuary workers, pathologists, civil servants, ambulance drivers, emergency room workers, eye bank and blood bank managers, and transplant coordinators. As a description of our approach to this trade, Oliver Sacks's (1995) felicitous phrase "an anthropologist on Mars" comes immediately to mind. Playing the role of the anthropological court jester, we began by raising foolish but necessary first questions: *What is going on here?* What truths are being served up? Whose needs are being overlooked? Whose voices are being silenced? What unrecognized sacrifices are being made? What lies behind the transplant rhetoric of gifts, altruism, scarcities, and needs?

I will argue that transplant surgery as it is practiced today in many global contexts is a blend of altruism and commerce, of science and magic, of gifting, barter, and theft, of choice and coercion. Transplant surgery has reconceptualized social rela-tions between self and other, between individual and society, and among the "three bodies" – the existential lived body-self, the social, representational body, and the body political (see Scheper-Hughes and Lock 1987). Finally, it has redefined real/unreal, seen/unseen, life/death, body/corpse/cadaver, person/nonperson, and rumor/fiction/fact. Throughout these radical transformations, the voice of anthro-pology has been relatively muted, and the high-stakes debates have been waged among surgeons, bioethicists, international lawyers, and economists. From time to time anthropologists have intervened to translate or correct the prevailing medical and bioethical discourses on transplant practice as these conflict with alternative understandings of the body and of death. Margaret Lock's (1995, 1996) animated discussions, debates, and difficult collaborations with the moral philosopher Janet Radcliffe Richards (see Richards et al. 1998) and Veena Das's (2000) responses to the latter and to Abdullah Daar (Das 1996) are exemplary in this regard.

But perhaps what is needed from anthropology is something more akin to Donna Haraway's (1985) radical manifesto for the cyborg bodies and cyborg selves that we have already become. The emergence of strange markets, excess capital, "surplus bodies," and spare body parts has generated a global body trade which promises select individuals of reasonable economic means living almost anywhere in the world – from the Amazon Basin[2] to the deserts of Oman – a miraculous extension of what Giorgio Agamben (1998) refers to as *bios* – brute or naked life, the elementary form of species life.[3] In the face of this late-modern dilemma – this particular "end of the body" – the task of anthropology is relatively straightforward: to activate our discipline's radical epistemological promise and our commitment to the primacy of the ethical (Scheper-Hughes 1994). What follows is an ethnographic and reflexive essay on the transformations of the body and the state under conditions of neoliberal economic globalism.

The Global Economy and the Commodification of the Body

George Soros (1998a, 1998b) has recently analyzed some of the deficiencies of the global capitalist economy, particularly the erosion of social values and social cohesion in the face of the increasing dominance of antisocial market values. The problem is that markets are by nature indiscriminate and inclined to reduce everything – including human beings, their labor, and their reproductive capacity – to the status of commodities. As Arjun Appadurai (1986) has noted, there is nothing fixed, stable, or sacrosanct about the "commodity candidacy" of things. Nowhere is this more dramatically illustrated than in the current markets for human organs and tissues to supply a medical business driven by supply and demand. The rapid transfer of organ transplant technologies to countries in the East (China, Taiwan, and India) and the South (especially Argentina, Chile, and Brazil) has created a global scarcity of viable organs that has initiated a movement of sick bodies in one direction and of healthy organs – transported by commercial airlines in ordinary Styrofoam picnic coolers conveniently stored in overhead luggage compartments – often in the reverse direction, creating a kind of "kula ring" of bodies and body parts.

What were once experimental procedures performed in a few advanced medical centers (most of them connected to academic institutions) have become commonplace surgeries throughout the world. Today, kidney transplantation is virtually universal. Survival rates have increased markedly over the past decade, although they still vary by country, region, quality and type of organ (living or cadaveric), and access to the antirejection drug cyclosporine. In parts of the Third World where morbidity rates from infection and hepatitis are higher, there is a preference for a living donor whose health status can be documented before the transplant operation.

In general, the flow of organs follows the modern routes of capital: from South to North, from Third to First World, from poor to rich, from black and brown to white, and from female to male. Religious prohibitions in one country or region can stimulate an organs market in more secular or pluralistic neighboring areas. Residents of the Gulf States travel to India and Eastern Europe to obtain kidneys made scarce locally by fundamentalist Islamic teachings that will in some areas allow organ transplantation (to save a life) but draw the line at organ donation. Japanese patients travel to North America for transplant surgery with organs retrieved from brain-dead donors, a definition of death only recently and very reluctantly accepted in Japan. To this day heart transplantation is rarely performed in Japan, and most kidney transplants rely on living, related donors (see Lock 1996, 1997, n.d.; Ohnuki-Tierney 1994). For many years Japanese nationals have resorted to various intermediaries, sometimes with criminal connections, to locate donor hearts in other countries, including China (Tsuyoshi Awaya, testimony before the International Relations Committee, US House of Representatives, June 4, 1998) and the United States.

Until the practice was condemned by the World Medical Association in 1994, patients from several Asian countries traveled to Taiwan to purchase organs harvested from executed prisoners. The ban on the use of organs from executed prisoners in capitalist Taiwan merely opened up a similar practice in socialist China; the demand of governments for hard currency has no fixed ideological or political boundaries. Meanwhile, patients from Israel, which has its own well-developed but underused transplantation centers (see Fishman 1998, Kalifon 1995), travel elsewhere – to Eastern Europe, where living kidney donors can be found, and to South Africa, where the amenities in private transplantation clinics can resemble those of four-star hotels. Meanwhile, Turkey is emerging as a new and active site of illegal traffic in transplant organs, with both living donors and recipients arriving from other countries for operations. In all these transactions, organs brokers are the essential actors. Because of these unsavory events, the sociologist-ethnographers Renée Fox and Judith Swazey (1992) have abandoned the field of organ transplantation after some forty years, expressing their dismay at the "profanation" of organ transplantation over the past decade and pointing to the "excessive ardor" to prolong life indefinitely and the move toward financial incentives and purchased organs. More recently, Fox (1996: 253) has expressed the hope that her decision will serve as moral testimony against the perversion of a technology in which she had been a strong believer.

Cultural notions about the dignity of the body and of sovereign states pose some barriers to the global market in body parts, but these ideas have proven fragile. In the West, theological and philosophical reservations gave way rather readily to the demands of advanced medicine and biotechnology. Donald Joralemon (1995: 335) has noted wryly that organ transplantation seems to be protected by a massive dose of cultural denial, an ideological equivalent of the cyclosporine which prevents the individual body's rejection of a strange organ. This dose of denial is needed to overcome the social body's resistance to the alien idea of transplantation and the new kinds of bodies and publics that it requires. No modern pope (beginning with Pius XII) has raised any moral objection to the requirements of transplant surgery. The Catholic Church decided over thirty years ago that the definition of death – unlike the definition of life – should be left up to the doctors, paving the way for the acceptance of brain-stem death.

While transplant surgery has become more or less routine in the industrialized West, one can recapture some of the technology's basic strangeness by observing the effects of its expansion into new social, cultural, and economic settings. Wherever transplant surgery moves it challenges customary laws and traditional local practices bearing on the body, death, and social relations. Commonsense notions of embodiment, relations of body parts to the whole, and the treatment and disposal of the dying are consequently being reinvented throughout the world. Not only stock markets have crashed on the periphery in recent years – so have long-standing religious and cultural prohibitions.

Lawrence Cohen, who has worked in rural towns in various regions of India over the past decade, notes that in a very brief period the idea of trading a kidney for a dowry has caught on and become one strategy for poor parents desperate to arrange a comfortable marriage for an "extra" daughter. A decade ago, when townspeople first heard through newspaper reports of kidney sales occurring in the cities of Bombay and Madras, they responded with understandable alarm. Today, Cohen says, some of these same people now speak matter-of-factly about *when* it might be necessary to sell a "spare" organ. Cohen argues that it is not that every townsperson actually knows someone who has been tempted to sell a vital part of the self but that the idea of the "commodified" kidney has permeated the social imaginary: "The kidney [stands] . . . as the marker of one's economic horizon, one's ultimate collateral" (1999). Some parents say that they can no longer complain about the fate of a dowry-less daughter; in 1998 Cohen encountered friends in Benares who were considering selling a kidney to raise money for a younger sister's dowry. In this instance, he notes, "women flow in one direction and kidneys in the other." And the appearance of a new biomedical technology has reinforced a traditional practice, the dowry, that had been waning. With the emergence of new sources of capital, the dowry system is expanding, along with kidney sales, into areas where it had not traditionally been practiced.

In the interior of Northeast Brazil, in response to a kidney market that emerged in the late 1970s, ordinary people began to view their matched organs as redundancies. Brazilian newspapers carried ads like this one published in the *Diario de Pernambuco* in 1981: "I am willing to sell any organ of my body that is not vital to my survival and that could help save another person's life in exchange for an amount of money that will allow me to feed my family." Ivo Patarra, a São Paulo journalist with whom I have been collaborating on this project, traced the man who placed this ad to a peripheral suburb of Recife. Miguel Correia de Oliveira, age 30, married and the father of two small children, was unemployed and worried about his family's miserable condition. His rent was unpaid, food bills were accumulating, and he did not even have the money to purchase the newspaper every day to see if there had been a response to his ad. He told Patarra (1982: 136)

I would do exactly as I said, and I have not regretted my offer. I know that I would have to undergo an operation that is difficult and risky. But I would sell any organ that would not immediately cause my death. It could be a kidney or an eye because I have two of them. . . . I am living through all sorts of crises and I cannot make ends meet. If I could sell a kidney or an eye for that much money I would never have to work again. But I am not stupid. I would make the doctor examine me first and then pay me the money up front *before* the operation. And after my bills were paid, I would invest what remains in the stock market.

In 1996 I interviewed a schoolteacher in the interior of Pernambuco who had been persuaded to donate a kidney to a distant male relation in exchange for a small compensation. Despite the payment Rosalva insisted that she had donated "from the heart" and out of pity for her cousin. "Besides," she added, "wouldn't you feel obligated to give an organ of which you had two and the other had none?" But it had not been so long before this that I had accompanied a small procession to the municipal graveyard in this same community for the ceremonial burial of an amputated foot. Religious and cultural sentiments about the sacredness and integrity of the body were still strong. Rosalva's view, less than two decades later, of her body as a reservoir of duplicate parts was troubling.

India: Organs Bazaar

A great many people – not all of them wealthy – have shown their willingness to travel great distances to secure transplants through legal or illegal channels, even though survival rates in some of the more commercialized contexts are quite low. For example, between 1983 and 1988, 131 patients from just three renal units in the United Arab Emirates and Oman traveled to India to purchase, through local brokers, kidneys from living donors. The donors, mostly from urban shantytowns, were paid between $2,000 and $3,000. News of incipient "organs bazaars" in the slums of Bombay, Calcutta, and Madras appeared in Indian weeklies (Chengappa 1990) and in special reports on US and British television. It was not clear at the time how much of this reporting was to be trusted, but in the early 1990s scientific articles began to appear in *The Lancet* and *Transplantation Proceedings* reporting poor medical outcomes with kidneys purchased from individuals infected with hepatitis and HIV (see Saalahudeen et al. 1990).

The first inklings of a commercial market in organs appeared in 1983, when a US physician, H. Barry Jacobs, established the International Kidney Exchange in an attempt to broker kidneys from living donors in the Third World, especially India. By the early 1990s some 2,000 kidney transplants with living donors were being performed each year in India, leading Prakash Chandra (1991) to refer to India as the "organs bazaar of the world." But the proponents of paid living donors, such as K. C. Reddy (1990), a urologist with a thriving practice of kidney transplantation in Madras, argued that legalizing the business would eliminate the middlemen who profit by exploiting such donors. Reddy described the kidney market as a marriage bureau of sorts, bringing together desperately ill buyers and desperately poor sellers in a temporary alliance against the wolves at their doors.

The overt market in kidneys that catered largely to wealthy patients from the Middle East was forced underground following passage of a law in 1994 that criminalized organ sales. But recent reports by human rights activists, journalists, and medical anthropologists, including Cohen and Das, indicate that the new law has produced an even larger *domestic* black market in kidneys, controlled by organized crime expanding out from the heroin trade (in some cases with the backing of local political leaders). In other areas of India the kidney business is controlled by the owners of for-profit hospitals that cater to foreign and domestic patients who can pay to occupy luxuriously equipped medical suites while awaiting the appearance of a living donor. Investigative reporters (see *Frontline*, December 26, 1997) found that a doctor–broker nexus in Bangalore and Madras continues to profit from kidney sales because a loophole in the new law permits unrelated kidney "donation" following approval by local medical authorization committees. Cohen and others report that these committees have been readily corrupted in areas where kidney sales have become an important source of local income, with the result that sales are now conducted with official seals of approval by local authorization committees.

Today, says Cohen (1999), only the very rich can acquire an unrelated kidney, for in addition to paying the donor, the middlemen, and the hospital they must bribe the authorization committee members. As for the kidney sellers, recruited by brokers who often get half the proceeds, almost all are trapped in crippling cycles of debt. The kidney trade is another link, Cohen suggests, in a system of debt peonage reinforced by neoliberal structural adjustment. Kidney sales display some of the bizarre effects of a global capitalism that seeks to turn everything into a commodity. And though fathers and brothers talk about selling kidneys to rescue dowry-less daughters or sisters, in fact most kidney sellers are women trying to rescue a husband, whether a bad one who has prejudiced the family by his drinking and unemployment or a good one who has gotten trapped in the debt cycle. Underlying it is the logic of gender reciprocity: the husband "gives" his body in often servile and/or back-breaking labor, and the wife "gives" her body in a mutually life-saving medical procedure.

But the climate of rampant commercialism has produced rumors and allegations of organ theft in hospitals similar to those frequently encountered in Brazil. During an international conference I organized in April 1996 at the University of California, Berkeley, on the commerce in human organs, Veena Das told a National Public Radio reporter for the program *Marketplace* the story of a young woman in Delhi whose stomach pains were diagnosed as a bladder stone requiring surgery. Later, the woman charged that the attending surgeon had used the "bladder stone" as a pretext to operate and remove one of her kidneys for sale to a third party. True or false – and allegations like these are slippery because hospitals refuse to open their records to journalists or anthropologists – such stories are believed by many poor people worldwide, who therefore avoid public hospitals even for the most necessary and routine operations.

China: The State's Body

China stands accused today of taking organs from executed prisoners for sale in transplant surgeries involving mostly foreign patients. Human Rights Watch/Asia (1995) and the independent Laogai Research Foundation have documented through available statistics and the reports of Chinese informants, some of them doctors or prison guards, that the Chinese state systematically takes kidneys, corneas, liver tissue, and heart valves from its executed prisoners. While some of these organs are used to reward politically well-connected Chinese, others are sold to transplant patients from Hong Kong, Taiwan, Singapore, and other mostly Asian nations, who will pay as much as $30,000 for an organ. Officials have denied the allegations, but they refuse to allow independent observers to be present at executions or to review transplant medical records. As early as October 1984, the government published a directive stating that "the use of corpses or organs of executed criminals *must be kept strictly secret*... to avoid negative repercussions" (cited in Human Rights Watch/Asia 1995: 7).

Robin Monroe, the author of the Human Rights Watch/Asia report (1995), told the Bellagio Task Force that organs were taken from some 2,000 executed prisoners each year and, worse, that number was growing, as the list of capital crimes in China had been expanded to accommodate the growing demand for organs. These allegations are supported by an Amnesty International report claiming that a new "strike hard" anticrime campaign in China has sharply increased the number of people executed, among them thieves and tax cheaters. In 1996 at least 6,100 death sentences were handed down and at least 4,367 confirmed executions took place. Following these reports, David Rothman (1997) visited several major hospitals in Beijing and Shanghai, where he interviewed transplant surgeons and other medical officers about the technical and the social dimensions of transplant surgery as practiced in their units. While they readily answered technical questions, they refused to respond to questions regarding the sources of transplant organs, the costs for organs and surgery, or the numbers of foreign patients who received transplants. Rothman returned from China convinced that what lies behind its anticrime campaign is a "thriving medical business that relies on prisoners' organs for raw materials."

Tsuyoshi Awaya, another Bellagio Task Force member, has made five research trips to China since 1995 to investigate organs harvesting in Chinese prisons. On his most recent trip, in 1997, he was accompanied by a Japanese organs broker and several of his patients, all of whom returned to Japan with new kidneys that they knew had come from executed prisoners. Awaya told the US House International Relations Committee in 1998 that a great many Japanese patients go overseas for organ transplants. Those who cannot afford to go to the West go to one of several developing countries in Asia, including China, where purchased organs from executed prisoners are part of the package of hospital services for a transplant operation. Since prisoners are not paid for their "donation," organs sales per se do not exist in China. However, taking prisoners' organs without consent could be seen as a form of body theft.

Finally, Dr. Chun Jean Lee, chief transplant surgeon at the National Taiwan University Medical Center and also a member of the Bellagio Task Force, is convinced that the allegations about China are true because the practice of using organs from executed prisoners is fairly widespread in Asia. He says that until international human rights organizations put pressure on his institution, it too had used prisons to supply the organs it needed. China has held out, Lee suggests, because of the desperate need for foreign dollars and because there is less concern in Asia for issues of informed consent. In some Asian nations the use of prisoners' organs is seen as a social good, a form of public service, and an opportunity for them to redeem their families' honor.

Of course, not all Chinese citizens embrace this collectivist ethos, and human rights activists such as Harry Wu, the director of the Laogai Foundation in California, see the practice as a gross violation of human rights. At the 1996 Berkeley conference on traffic in human organs, Wu said,

In 1992 I interviewed a doctor who routinely participated in removing kidneys from condemned prisoners. In one case, she said, breaking down in the telling, that she had even participated in a surgery in which two kidneys were removed from a living, anesthetized prisoner late at night. The following morning the prisoner was executed by a bullet to the head.

In this chilling scenario brain death followed rather than preceded the harvesting of the prisoner's vital organs. Later, Wu introduced Mr. Lin, a recent Chinese immigrant to California, who told the National Public Radio reporters for *Marketplace* that shortly before leaving China he had visited a friend at a medical center in Shanghai. In the bed next to his friend was a politically well-situated professional who told Lin that he was waiting for a kidney transplant later that day. The kidney, he explained, would arrive as soon as a prisoner was executed that morning. The prisoner would be intubated and prepared for the subsequent surgery by doctors present for the execution. Minutes later the man would be shot in the head and the doctors would extract his kidneys and rush them to the hospital, where two transplant surgery teams would be assembled and waiting.

Wu's allegations were bolstered by the result of a sting operation in New York City that led to the arrest of two Chinese citizens offering to sell corneas, kidneys, livers, and other human organs to US doctors for transplant surgery (*Mail and Guardian*, February 27, 1998: *San Jose Mercury News*, March 19, 1998; *New York Times*, February 24, 1998). Posing as a prospective customer, Wu produced a videotape of the two men in a Manhattan hotel room offering to sell "quality organs" from a dependable source: some 200 prisoners executed on Hainan Island each year. A pair of corneas would cost $5,000. One of the men guaranteed this commitment by producing documents indicating that he had been deputy chief of criminal prosecutions in that prison. Following their arrest by FBI agents, the men were charged with conspiring to sell human organs, but the trial has been delayed because of concerns over the extent to which the defendants were entrapped in the case (*New York Times*, March 2, 1999). As a result of this story, Fresenius Medical Care, based outside Frankfurt, announced that it was ending its half-interest in a kidney dialysis unit (next to a transplant clinic) in Guangzhou, noting its suspicion that foreign patients there were receiving "kidneys harvested from executed Chinese criminals" (*New York Times*, March 7, 1998).

Bioethical Dilemmas

While members of the Bellagio Task Force agreed on the human rights violations implicit in the use of executed prisoners' organs, they found the issue of organ sales more complex. Those opposing the idea of sales expressed concerns about social justice and equity. Would those forced by circumstance to sell a kidney be in a roughly equivalent position to obtain dialysis or transplant surgery should their remaining kidney fail at a later date? Others noted the negative effects of organ sales on family and marital relations, gender relations, and community life. Others worried about the coarsening of medical sensibilities in the casual disregard by doctors of the primary ethical mandate to do no harm to the bodies in their care, including their donor patients.

Those favoring regulated sales argued against social science paternalism and on behalf of individual rights, bodily autonomy, and the right to sell one's organs, tissues, blood, or other body products, an argument that has gained currency in some scholarly circles (see Daar 1989, 1992a, 1992b, n.d.; Kervorkian 1992; Marshall et al. 1996; Richards et al. 1998). Daar argues from a pragmatic position that *regulation* rather than *prohibition* or moral condemnation is the more appropriate response to a practice that is already widely established in many parts of the world. What is needed, he argues, is rigorous oversight and the adoption of a "donor's bill of rights" to inform and protect potential organ sellers.

Some transplant surgeons on the task force asked why kidneys were treated differently from other body parts that are sold commercially, including skin, corneas, bones, bone marrow, cardiac valves, blood vessels, and blood. The exception was based (they suggest) on the layman's natural aversion to the idea of tampering with *internal* organs. Influenced by Daar's "rational-choice" position, the Bellagio Task Force report (Rothman et al. 1997: 2741) concluded that the "sale of body parts is already so widespread that it is not self-evident why solid organs should be excluded [from commercialization]. In many countries, blood, sperm and ova are sold. . . . On what grounds may blood or bone be traded on the open market, but not cadaveric kidneys?"

But the social scientists and human rights activists serving on the task force remain profoundly critical of bioethical arguments based on Euro-American notions of contract and individual choice. They are mindful of the social and economic contexts that make the choice to sell a kidney in an urban slum of Calcutta or in a Brazilian *favela* anything but a free and autonomous one. Consent is problematic with the executioner – whether on death row or metaphorically at the door – looking over one's shoulder. A market price on body parts – even a fair one – exploits the desperation of the poor, turning their suffering into an opportunity, as Veena Das (2000) so aptly puts it. And the argument for regulation is out of touch with social and medical realities in many parts of the world, especially in Second and Third World nations. The medical institutions created to monitor organ harvesting and distribution are often dysfunctional, corrupt, or compromised by the power of organs markets and the impunity of the organs brokers.

Responding to Daar during the Berkeley conference on the question of regulating organ sales, Das countered the neoliberal defense of individual rights to sell by noting that in *all* contracts there are certain exclusions. In family, labor, and antitrust law, for example, anything that would damage social or community relations is generally excluded. Asking the law to negotiate a fair price for a live human kidney, Das argued, goes against everything that contract theory represents. When concepts such as individual agency and autonomy are invoked in defending the right to sell a spare organ, anthropologists might suggest that certain living things are not legitimate candidates for commodification. The removal of nonrenewable organs leads to irreparable personal injury, and it is an act in which, given their ethical standards, medical practitioners should not be asked to participate.

While to many surgeons an organ is a thing, an expensive "object" of health, a critical anthropologist like Das must ask, "Just what is an organ?" Is the transplant surgeon's kidney seen as a redundancy, a "spare part," equivalent to the Indian textile worker's kidney, seen as an "organ of last resort"? These two "objects" are not comparable, and neither is equivalent to the kidney seen as that precious "gift of life" anxiously sought by the desperate transplant patient. And, while bioethicists begin their inquiries with the unexamined premise of the body (and its organs) as the unique property of the individual, anthropologists must intrude with our cautionary cultural relativism. Are those living under conditions of social insecurity and economic abandonment on the periphery of the new world order really the "owners" of their bodies? This seemingly self-evident first premise of western bioethics would not be shared by peasants and shantytown dwellers in many parts of the Third World. The chronically hungry sugar plantation workers in Northeast Brazil, for example, frequently state with conviction, "We are not even the owners of our own bodies" (see Scheper-Hughes 1992: ch. 6).

Nonetheless, arguments for the commercialization of organs are gaining ground in the United States and elsewhere (Anders 1995; Schwindt and Vining 1986). Lloyd R. Cohen (1989, 1993) has proposed a "futures market" in cadaveric organs that would operate through advance contracts offered to the general public. For organs successfully transplanted at death such contracts would provide a substantial sum – $5,000 per organ used has been suggested – to the deceased person's designee. While gifting can always be expected among family members, financial inducements might be necessary, Cohen argues, to provide organs for strangers. The American Medical Association is considering various proposals that would enable people to bequeath organs to their own heirs or to charity for a price. In a telephone interview in 1996, Dr. Charles Plows, chair of the AMA's Committee on Ethical and Judicial Affairs, said that he agreed in principle with Cohen's proposal. Everyone, he said, except the organ donor benefits from the transplant transaction. So, at present the AMA is exploring several options. One is to set a fixed price per organ. Another is to allow market forces – supply and demand – to establish the price. The current amalgam of positions points to the construction of new desires and needs, new social ties and social contracts, and new conceptions of justice and ethics around the medical and mercantile uses of the body.

Artificial Needs and Invented Scarcities

The demand for human organs – and for wealthy transplant patients to purchase them – is driven by the medical discourse on scarcity. Similar to the parties in the international market in child adoption (see Raymond 1989; Scheper-Hughes 1991), those looking for transplant organs – both surgeons and their patients – are often willing to set aside questions about how the "purchased commodity" was obtained. In both instances the language of "gifts," "donations," "heroic rescues," and "saving lives" masks the extent to which ethically questionable and even illegal means are used to obtain the desired object. The specter of long transplant waiting lists – often only virtual lists with little material basis in reality – has motivated physicians, hospital administrators, government officials, and various intermediaries to employ questionable tactics for procuring organs. The results are blatant commercialism alongside "compensated gifting," doctors acting as brokers, and fierce competition between public and private hospitals for patients of means. At its worst, the scramble for organs and tissues has led to gross human rights violations in intensive care units and morgues. But the idea of organ scarcity is what Ivan Illich would call an artificially created need, invented by transplant technicians for an ever-expanding sick, aging, and dying population.

Several key words in organ transplantation require radical deconstruction, among them "scarcity," "need," "donation," "gift," "bond," "life," "death," "supply," and "demand." Organ scarcity, for example, is invoked like a mantra in reference to the long waiting lists of candidates for various transplant surgeries (see Randall 1991). In the United States alone, despite a well-organized national distribution system and a law that requires hospitals to request donated organs from next of kin, there are close to 50,000 people currently on various active organ waiting lists (see Hogle 1995). But this scarcity, created by the technicians of transplant surgery, represents an artificial need, one that can never be satisfied, for underlying it is the unprecedented possibility of extending life indefinitely with the organs of others. I refer, with no disrespect intended to those now patiently waiting for organ transplants, to the age-old denial and refusal of death that contributes to what Ivan Illich (1976) identified as the hubris of medicine and medical technology in the face of mortality.

Meanwhile, the so-called gift of life that is extended to terminal heart, lung, and liver patients is sometimes something other than the commonsense notion of a life. The survival rates of a great many transplant patients often conceal the real living-in-death – the weeks and months of extended suffering – that precedes actual death.[4] Transplant patients today are increasingly warned that they are not exchanging a death sentence for a new life but rather exchanging one mortal, chronic disease for another. "I tell all my heart transplant patients," said a South African transplant coordinator, "that after transplant they will have a condition similar to AIDS and that in all probability they will die of an opportunistic infection resulting from the artificial suppression of their immune system." While this statement is an exaggeration, most transplant surgeons I interviewed accepted its basic premise. Dr. N of South Africa told of major depressions among his large sample of post-operative heart transplant patients, some leading to suicides following otherwise successful transplants. For this and other reasons he had decided to give up heart transplant surgery for less radical surgical interventions.

The medical discourse on scarcity has produced what Lock (1996, 1997) has called "rapacious demands." Awaya (1994) goes even farther, referring to transplant surgery as a form of "neo-cannibalism." "We are now eyeing each other's bodies greedily," he says, "as a source of detachable spare parts with which to extend our lives." While unwilling to condemn this "human revolution," which he sees as continuous with, indeed the final flowering of, our evolutionary history, he wants organ donors and recipients to recognize the kind of social exchange in which they are engaged. Through modern transplant technology the "biosociality" (see Rabinow 1996) of a few is made possible through the literal incorporation of the body parts of those who often have no social destiny other than premature death (Biehl 1998, 1999; Castel 1991; Scheper-Hughes 1992).

The discourse on scarcity conceals the overproduction of excess and wasted organs that daily end up in hospital dumpsters in parts of the world where the necessary transplant infrastructure is limited. The ill will and competitiveness of hospital workers and medical professionals also contributes to waste of organs. Transplant specialists whom Cohen and I interviewed in South Africa, India, and

Brazil often scoffed at the notion of organ scarcity, given the appallingly high rates of youth mortality, accidental death, homicide, and transport death that produce a superabundance of young, healthy cadavers. These precious commodities are routinely wasted, however, in the absence of trained organ-capture teams in hospital emergency rooms and intensive care units, rapid transportation, and basic equipment to preserve "heart-beating" cadavers and their organs. And organ scarcity is reproduced in the increasing competition between public and private hospitals and their transplant surgeons, who, in the words of one South African transplant coordinator, "order their assistants to dispose of perfectly good organs rather than allow the competition to get their hands on them." The real scarcity is not of organs but of transplant patients of sufficient means to pay for them. In India, Brazil, and even South Africa there is a superabundance of poor people willing to sell kidneys for a pittance.

And, while "high-quality" organs and tissues are scarce, there are plenty of what Dr. S, the director of an eye bank in São Paulo, referred to as usable "leftovers." Brazil, he said, has long been a favored dumping ground for surplus inventories from the First World, including old, poor-quality, or damaged tissues and organs. In extensive interviews in 1997 and 1998, he complained of a US-based program which routinely sent surplus corneas to his center. "Obviously," he said, "these are not the best corneas. The Americans will only send us what they have already rejected for themselves."

In Cape Town, Mrs. R, the director of her country's largest eye bank (an independent foundation), normally keeps a dozen or more "post-dated" cadaver eyes in her organization's refrigerator. These poor-quality "corneas" would not be used, she said, for transplantation anywhere in South Africa, but they might be sent to less fortunate neighboring countries that requested them. Nearby, in his office at an academic hospital center, Dr. B, a young heart transplant surgeon, told me about a human organs broker in southern California who promises his clients delivery of "fresh organs" anywhere in the world within 30 days of placing an electronic mail order.

Because commercial exchanges have also contributed to the transfer of transplantation capabilities to previously underserved areas of the world, transplant specialists I interviewed in Brazil and South Africa are deeply ambivalent about them. Surgeons in São Paulo told me about a controversial proposal some years ago by Dr. Thomas Starzl of the University of Pittsburgh Medical School to exchange his institution's transplant expertise for a regular supply of "surplus" Brazilian livers. The public outcry in Brazil against this exchange, fueled in large part by the Brazilian media (see *Isto É Senhor*, December 11, 1991; *Folha de São Paulo*, December 1, 1991), interrupted the agreement.

Although no Brazilian livers were delivered to Pittsburgh, many other Third World organs and tissues have found their way to the United States in recent decades. In the files of an elected official in São Paulo I found results of a police investigation of the local morgue indicating that several thousand pituitary glands had been taken (without consent) from poor people's cadavers and sold to private medical firms in the United States, where they were to be used in the production of growth hormones. Similarly, during the late military dictatorship years, an anatomy professor at the Federal University of Pernambuco in Recife was prosecuted for having sold thousands of inner-ear parts taken from pauper cadavers to the US

National Aeronautics and Space Administration for its space training and research programs.

Even today such practices continue. Abbokinase, a widely used clot-dissolving drug, uses materials derived from kidneys taken from deceased newborns in a hospital in Cali, Colombia, without any evidence of parental consent, informed or otherwise (Wolfe 1999). In South Africa, the director of an experimental research unit in a large public medical school showed me official documents approving the transfer of human heart valves taken (without consent) from the bodies of the poor in the morgue and shipped "for handling costs" to medical centers in Germany and Austria. These permissible fees, I was told, helped defray the costs of the unit's research program in the face of the downsizing of advanced medical research facilities in the new South Africa.

But a great many ordinary citizens in India, South Africa, and Brazil protest such commercial exchanges as a form of global (South-to-North) "bio-piracy" (see Shiva 1997). Increasingly, one hears demands for "nationalizing" dead bodies, tissues, and body parts to protect them from global exploitation. The mere idea of Brazilian livers going to US transplant patients gives Dr. O, a Brazilian surgeon, "an attack of spleen." A white South African transplant coordinator attached to a large private hospital criticized the policy that allowed many wealthy foreigners – especially "ex-colonials" from Botswana and Nambia – to come to South Africa for organs and transplant surgery. "I can't *stop* them from coming to this hospital," she said, "but I tell them that South African organs *belong* to South African citizens and that before I see a white person from Namibia getting their hands on a heart or a kidney that belongs to a little black South African child, I myself will see to it that the organ gets tossed into a bucket." The coordinator defended her harsh remarks as following the directives of Dr. N. C. Dlamini Zuma, then minister of health, to give preferential treatment, as it were, to South Africa's long-excluded black majority. Such nationalist medical sentiments are not shared by hospital administrators, for whom other considerations – especially the ability of foreign patients to pay twice or more what the state or private insurance companies will allow for the surgery – are often uppermost. In one academic and public hospital in Cape Town a steady stream of paying foreigners from Mauritius was largely responsible for keeping its beleaguered transplant unit solvent following the budget cuts and the redirection of state funds toward primary care.

The Death that Precedes Death

Death is, of course, another key word in transplantation. The possibility of extending life through transplantation was facilitated by medical definitions of irreversible coma (at the end of the 1950s) and brain-stem death[5] (at the end of the 1960s), when death became an epiphenomenon of transplantation. Here one sees the awesome power of the life sciences and medical technology over modern states. In the age of transplant surgery, life and death are replaced with surrogates, proxies, and facsimiles, and ordinary people have relinquished the power to determine the moment of death, which now requires technical and legal expertise beyond their ability (see Agamben 1998: 165).[6]

Additionally, the new biotechnologies have thrown conventional western thinking about ownership of the dead body in relation to the state into doubt. Is the Enlightenment notion of the body as the unique property of the individual still viable in light of the many competing claims on human tissues and genetic material by the state and by commercial pharmaceutical and biotechnology research companies (see Curran 1991; Neves 1993; Rabinow 1996)? Can it exist in the presence of the claims of modern states, including Spain, Belgium, and, now, Brazil to complete authority over the disposal of bodies, organs, and tissues at death? What kind of state assumes rights to the bodies of both those presumed to be dead and those presumed to have given consent to organ harvesting (see Berlinger and Garrafa 1996; Shiva 1997)? Since the passage of the new compulsory donation law in Brazil, one hears angry references to the dead person as "the state's body." Certainly, both the family and the church have lost control over it.

While most doctors have worked through their own doubts about the new criteria for brain death, a great many ordinary people still resist it. Brain-stem death is not an intuitive or commonsense perception; it is far from obvious to family members, nursing staff, and even some medical specialists. The language of brain death is replete with indeterminacy and contradiction. Does brain death *anticipate* somatic death? Should we call it, as Agamben does, "the death that precedes death"? (1998: 163)? What is the relation between the time of technically declared brain death and the deadline for harvesting usable organs? In a 1996 interview, a forensic pathologist attached to the Groote Schuur Hospital in Cape Town, where Christiaan Barnard experimented with the first heart transplants, vehemently rejected the medical concept of brain death:

There are only two organic states: living and dead. "Dead" is when the heart stops beating and organs decompose. "Brain-dead" is not dead. It is still alive. Doctors know better, and they should speak the truth to family members and to themselves. They could, for example, approach family members saying, "Your loved one is beyond any hope of recovery. Would you allow us to turn off the machines that are keeping him or her in a liminal state somewhere between life and death so that we can harvest the organs to save another person's life?" Then it would be ethical. Then it would be an honest transaction.

Dr. Cicero Galli Coimbra of the Department of Neurology and Neurosurgery at the Federal University of São Paulo, where he also directs the Laboratorio de Neurologia Experimental, has written several scientific papers questioning the validity of the criteria established in 1968 by the Ad Hoc Committee of the Harvard Medical School to Examine the Definition of Brain Death. During interviews with me in 1998, Coimbra reiterated his claims, backed by his own research and his clinical work, that brain-stem death, as currently defined, is applied to a number of patients whose lives could be saved. Moreover, he claims that "apnea testing" as widely used to determine brain-stem death actually *induces* irreversible brain damage. All the so-called confirmatory tests, he said, "reflect nothing more than the detrimental effects of doctor-induced intercranial circulatory arrest." Coimbra, who refused anonymity, is a major critic of Brazil's new compulsory donation law, which he sees as an assault on his clinical population of brain-traumatized patients.

The body may be defined as brain-dead for one purpose – organ retrieval – while still perceived as alive for other purposes including family ties, affections, religious beliefs, or notions of individual dignity.[7] Even when somatic death is obvious to family members and loved ones, the perceptual shift from the dead body – the "recently departed," the "beloved deceased," "our dearly departed brother" – to the anonymous and depersonalized cadaver (as usable object and reservoir of spare parts) may take more than the pressured "technical time" allowed to harvest organs usable for transplantation. But as the retrieval time is extended with new conservation methods, the confusion and doubt of family members may increase.

The "gift of life" demands a parallel gift – the "gift of death," the giving over of life before its normally recognized time. In the language of anthropology, brain-stem death is social, not biological, death, and every "gift" demands a return (Mauss 1966). To Coimbra and some of his colleagues, brain-stem death has created a population of living dead people. It has yet to be embraced as common sense even in a great many industrialized societies, including Japan, Brazil, and the United States (see Kolata 1995), let alone in countries where transplant surgery is still rare. And yet the public unrest in Brazil following passage of the country's new "presumed-consent" law in 1997 is an exception to the general rule of public apathy toward the state's assumption of control over the dead body. Transplant surgeons often explain popular resistance in terms of a cultural time lag that prevents ordinary people from accepting the changes brought about by new medical technologies.

While the postmodern state has certainly expanded its control over death (see Agamben 1998: 119–25) through recent advances in biotechnology, genetics, and biomedicine, there are many antecedents to consider. The Comaroffs (1992), for example, showed the extent to which British colonial regimes in Africa relied on medical practices to discipline and civilize newly colonized peoples. The African colonies became laboratories for experiments with medical sciences and public health practices. And the medical experiments under National Socialism produced, through applied eugenics and death sentencing, a concentration-camp population of walking cadavers, living dead people (Agamben 1998: 136) whose lives could be taken without explanation or justification. Agambem dares to compare these slave bodies to the "living dead" candidates for organ donation held hostage to the machine in today's intensive care units.

The idea of organ scarcity also has historical antecedents in the long-standing "shortage" of human bodies and human body parts for autopsy, medical training, and medical experimentation (see Foucault 1975; Richardson 1989, 1996). Who and what gets defined as "waste" in any given society often has bearing on the lives of the poorest in countries with a ready surplus of unidentified, unclaimed pauper bodies, as in Brazil (see Scheper-Hughes 1992, 1996a, 1992b; Biehl 1998), South Africa (Lerer and Matzopoulos 1996), and India. In Europe during the sixteenth, seventeenth, and eighteenth centuries, the corpses of gallows prisoners were offered to barbers and surgeons to dispose of as they wished. "Criminal" bodies were required then, just as they are now, for "scientific" and medical reasons. In Brazil as in France (Laqueur 1983) during the early phases of modernity, paupers had no autonomy at death, and their bodies could be confiscated from poorhouses and workhouses and sold to medical students and to hospitals. Because the body was considered part of the estate of the dead man and could be used to cover outstanding debts, the bodies of paupers were often left unclaimed by relatives to be used for medical research and education. Indeed, medical claims to "surplus" bodies have a long history. To this day many rural people in Northeast Brazil fear medicine and the state, imagining that almost anything can be done to them either before or at the hour of their deaths. Those fears – once specific to the rural and shantytown poor – have spread today to working-class Brazilians, who are united in their opposition to Brazil's universal donation law, fearing that it will be used against them to serve the needs of more affluent citizens. Such fears, we have learned, are not entirely ground-less.

The Organ-stealing Rumor

The poor and disadvantaged populations of the world have not remained silent in the face of threats and assaults to their bodily integrity, security, and dignity. For those living in urban shantytowns and hillside *favelas*, possessing little or no sym-bolic capital, the circulation of body-stealing and organ-theft rumors allowed people to express their fears. These rumors warned of the existence and dangerous proxi-mity of markets in bodies and body parts (Pinero 1992). As Das (1998: 185) has noted, there is a substantial literature in radical social science on the role of rumor in mobilizing crowds. Some scholars in this tradition have seen in rumors a special form of communication among the socially dispossessed. Guha (1983: 256, 201, cited by Das 1998: 186) identified various features of rumor, including "its capacity to build solidarity, and the overwhelming urge it prompts in listeners to pass it on to others...the performative power of [rumor] circulation results in its continuous spreading, an almost uncontrollable impulse to pass it on to another person."

The latest version of the organ-stealing rumor seems to have begun in Brazil or Guatemala in the 1980s and spread from there like wildfire to other, similar political contexts (see Scheper-Hughes 1996a). The South African variants are so different, however, that they should be considered independent creations. I first heard the rumor when it was circulating in the shantytowns of Northeast Brazil in the 1980s. It warned of child kidnapping and body stealing by "medical agents" from the United States and Japan, who were said to be seeking a fresh supply of human organs for transplant surgeries in the First World. Shantytown residents reported multiple sightings of large blue-and-yellow combi-vans scouring poor neighbor-hoods in search of stray youngsters. The children would be nabbed and shoved into the trunk of the van, and their discarded and eviscerated bodies – minus heart, lungs, liver, kidneys, and eyes – would turn up later by the roadside, between rows of sugarcane, or in hospital dumpsters.

At first I interpreted this rumor as expressing the chronic state of emergency (see Taussig 1992, citing Walter Benjamin) experienced by desperately poor people living on the margins of the newly emerging global economy. I noted that it coincided with a covert war against mostly black and semi-abandoned street children in urban Brazil (see Scheper-Hughes and Hoffman 1998) and with a booming market in international adoptions (see Scheper-Hughes 1991). The rumor confused the market in "spare babies" for international adoption with the market in "spare parts" for transplant surgery. Poor and semi-literate parents, tricked or intimidated into surrendering their babies for domestic and/or international adoption, imagined that their babies were wanted as fodder for transplant surgery. The rumor condensed the black markets for organs and babies into a single frightening story.

It is the task of anthropologists working in these murky realms to disentangle rumors from the realities of everyday life, which are often horrific enough. In the following analysis I am not suggesting that all rumors and urban legends about body stealing and organ theft can be reduced to specific historical facts. These rumors are part of a universal class of popular culture dating back to at least medieval Europe (see Dundes 1991), and they serve multiple ends. But the current spate of organ-stealing rumors seem to constitute what James Scott (1985) has called a classic "weapon of the weak." The rumors have shown their ability to challenge and interrupt the designs of medicine and the state. They have, for example, contributed to a climate of civil resistance toward compulsory organ donation in Brazil and caused voluntary organ donations to drop precipitously in Argentina (Cantarovitch 1990). The organ-theft rumors, combined with media reports of rampant commercialism in the procurement of organs, have contributed to a growing backlash against transplant ethics and to demoralization among some transplant surgeons themselves.

Dr. B, a heart transplant surgeon in Cape Town, said during an interview in February 1998 that he was disheartened about his profession's decline in prestige and popular confidence:

Organ transplantation has moved from an era back in 1967 when the public attitude was very different.... People then spoke about organ donation as that fantastic gift. Our first organ donor, Denise Ann Darvall, and her family were very much hallowed here; they were honored for what they did. Today, organ donation has lost its luster. The rumors of organ stealing are just a part of it. The families of potential donors throughout the world have been put under a lot more pressure. And there have been some unfortunate incidents. So we've begun to experience a sea of backlash. In Europe there is a new resistance toward the state's demand to donate. Suddenly, new objections are being raised. The Lutheran Church in Germany has started to question the idea of brain death, long after it was generally accepted there. And so we are seeing a drop of about 20 percent in organ donations in Europe, most acutely in Germany. And what happens in Europe has repercussions for South Africa.

Bio-Piracy: The State and its Subcitizens

It is important to note the timing and the geopolitical mapping of these organ-theft rumors. While blood-stealing (see Dundes 1991) and body-snatching rumors have appeared in various historical periods, the current generation of rumors arose and spread in the 1980s within specific political contexts. They followed the recent history of military regimes, police states, civil wars, and "dirty wars" in which abductions, disappearances, mutilations, and deaths in detention and under strange circumstances were commonplace. During the military regimes of the 1970s and 1980s in Brazil, Argentina, and Chile, the state launched a series of violent attacks on certain classes of "subcitizens" – subversives, Jewish intellectuals, journalists, university students, labor leaders, and writers and other social critics – whose bodies, in addition to being subjected to the usual tortures, were mined for their reproductive capacities and sometimes even for their organs to serve the needs of "supercitizens," especially elite military families.

During the Argentine "dirty war" (1976 to 1982) infants and small children of imprisoned dissidents were kidnapped and given as rewards to loyal childless military families (see Suarez-Orozco 1987). Older children were abducted by security officers, brutalized in detention, and then returned, politically "transformed," to their relatives. Other children of suspected subversives were tortured in front of their parents, and some died in prison. These forms of state-level "body snatching" were justified in terms of saving Argentina's innocent children from communism. Later, revelations of an illegal market in blood, corneas, and organs taken from executed political prisoners and mental patients in Argentina appeared in the *British Medical Journal* (Chaudhary 1992, 1994). Between 1976 and 1991 some 1,321 patients died under mysterious circumstances, and another 1,400 patients disappeared at the state mental asylum of Montes de Oca, where many "insane" political dissidents were sent. Years later, when some of the bodies were exhumed, it was found that their eyes and other body parts had been removed.

Despite these grotesque political realities, Felix Cantarovitch (1990: 147), reporting from the Ministry of Health in Buenos Aires, complained in a special issue of *Transplantation Proceedings*:

In Argentina between 1984 and 1987 a persistent rumor circulated about child kidnapping. The rumor was extremely troublesome because of its persistence sustained by the exaggerated press that has always been a powerful tool to attract attention of people about the matter. In November 1987 the Secretary of Health gathered the most important authorities of justice, police, medical associations and also members of Parliament with the purpose of determining the truth. As a result it was stated that all the rumors and comments made by the press were completely spurious.

Similarly, in Brazil during the military years, adults and children were kidnapped, and now it appears that their organs were sometimes appropriated as well. Organ transplant surgeries and organ sales reached a peak in São Paulo in the late 1970s during the presidency of General Figueiredo. According to my well-placed sources, during the late military dictatorship period a covert traffic in bodies, organs, and tissues taken from the despised social and political classes was supported by the military state. A senior physician attached to a large academic hospital in Brazil said that the commerce in organs there in the late 1970s was rampant and "quasi-legal." Surgeons like himself, he charged, were ordered to produce quotas of "quality" organs and were protected from any legal actions by police cover-ups: "The transplant teams in [X and Y] hospitals were real bandits after money. They were totally organ-crazy. The transplant team of hospital [Y] would transport freshly procured organs by ambulance from one region to the next via Super Highway Dutra. The ambulance was accompanied by a full military police escort so that the organs would arrive quickly and safely."

Sometimes, Dr. F continued, organs were acquired by criminal means. He told of surreal medical scenarios in which doctors and transplant teams met their quotas by "inducing" symptoms of brain death in seriously ill patients. The donors, he said, were the usual ones – people from the lowest classes and from families unable to defend them. The doctors would apply injections of strong barbiturates and then call on two other unsuspecting doctors to testify, according to the established protocols, that the criteria for brain death had been met and the organs could be harvested. Because of this history of abuses, Dr. Fadamantly opposes Brazil's law of presumed consent, calling it a law against the poor. "It is not the organs of the supercitizen that will disappear but those of people without any resources."

Similar allegations of body tampering and organ theft against doctors working in hospitals and morgues in South Africa during the late apartheid years surfaced during the hearings of the South African Truth and Reconciliation Commission. In these accounts we can begin to see some material basis for the epidemics of organ-stealing rumors. They surfaced at a time when the military in each country believed that it could do as it pleased with the bodies, organs, and progeny of its subcitizens, people perceived as social and political "waste."

In Argentina, Brazil, and Guatemala the organ-stealing rumors surfaced during or soon after the democratization process was initiated and in the wake of human rights reports such as *Nunca Más* in Argentina and *Brazil Nunca Más*. They appeared during a time when ordinary people became aware of the magnitude of the atrocities practiced by the state and its military and medical officials. Given that the poor of urban shantytowns are rarely called upon to speak before truth commissions, the body-theft rumors may be seen as a surrogate form of political witnessing. The rumors participated in the spirit of human rights activism, testifying to human suffering on the margins of "the official story."

The body- and organ-stealing rumors of the 1980s and 1990s were at the very least metaphorically true, operating by means of symbolic substitutions. They spoke to the ontological insecurity of poor people to whom almost anything could be done, reflecting everyday threats to bodily security, urban violence, police terror, social anarchy, theft, loss and fragmentation. Recently, new variants of the organ-stealing rumor, originating in the impoverished periphery of the global economic order, have migrated to the industrialized North, where they circulate among affluent people through e-mail chain letters despite the efforts of an organized US government disinformation campaign to kill them (see USIA 1994). Indeed, a great many people in the world today are uneasy about the nature of the beast that medical technology has released in the name of transplant surgery (see White 1996). But in our "rational," secular world, rumors are one thing, while scientific reports in medical journals are quite another. In the late 1980s the two narratives began to converge as dozens of articles published in *The Lancet, Transplantation Proceedings*, and the *Journal of Health, Politics, Policy and Law* cited evidence of an illegal commerce and black market in human organs. Indeed, urban legends and rumors, like metaphors, do sometimes harden into ethnographic facts.

Finally, in 1996, I decided to track down the strange rumors to their most obvious but least studied source: routine practices of organ procurement for transplant surgery. But as soon as I abandoned more symbolic analyses for practical and material explanations, my research was discredited by social scientists and medical professionals, who suggested that I had fallen into the assumptive world of my uneducated informants. Indeed, a great deal is invested in maintaining a social and clinical reality denying any factual basis for poor people's fear of medical technologies. The transplant community's narrative concerning the absurdity of the organ-stealing rumors offers a remarkably resilient defense against having to respond seriously to allegations of medical abuses in organ harvesting.

For example, a transplantation website (TransWeb) posts the "Top Ten Myths About Donation and Transplantation" with authoritative refutations of each. The "myth" that "rich and famous people get moved to the top of the waiting list while regular people have to wait a long time for a transplant" is refuted with the following blanket statement: "The organ allocation system is blind to wealth or social status." But our preliminary research indicates that this, like some other transplant myths, has some basis in contemporary transplant practices. The director of his region's transplant center in southern Brazil explained exactly how wealthy clients (including foreigners) and those with political and social connections managed to bypass established waiting lists and how patients without resources were often dropped, without their knowledge, from "active status" on such lists.

Even the most preposterous of the organ-stealing rumors, which the TransWeb authors say has never been documented anywhere – "I heard about this guy who woke up the next morning in a bathtub full of ice. His kidneys were stolen for sale on the black market" – finds some basis in lawsuits and criminal proceedings, some still unresolved or pending. In Brazil, for example, the case of the theft of the eyes of Olivio Oliveira, a 56-year-old mentally ill man living in a small town near Porto Alegre, has never been solved. The story first surfaced in local newspapers in November 1995 and soon became an international cause célèbre. The case was investigated by doctors, surgeons, hospital administrators, police, and journalists. While some experts claimed that the man's eyes were pecked out by *urubus* (vultures) or gnawed away by rats, others noted that they seemed to have been carefully, even surgically removed. More recently, Laudiceia Cristina da Silva, a young receptionist in São Paulo, filed a complaint with the city government requesting a police investigation of the public hospital where in June 1997 one of her kidneys was removed without her knowledge or consent during a minor surgery to remove an ovarian cyst. Her loss of the kidney was discovered soon after the operation by her family doctor during a routine follow-up examination. When confronted with the information, the hospital surgeon explained that the missing kidney had been embedded in the large ovarian cyst, a highly improbably medical narrative. The hospital refused to produce its medical records and said that the ovary and kidney had been "discarded." Representatives of the São Paulo Medical Council, which investigates allegations of malpractice, refused to grant us an interview; the director told us in a telephone call that there was no reason to distrust the hospital's version of the story. Laudiceia insists that she will pursue her case legally until the hospital is forced to account for what happened, whether it was a gross medical error or a case of kidney theft.

South Africa: Bodies of Apartheid

A stone's throw from the Groote Schuur Hospital, residents of black townships express fearful, suspicious, and negative attitudes toward organ transplantation. Among older people and recent arrivals from the rural homelands the very idea of organ harvesting bears an uncanny resemblance to traditional witchcraft practices, especially *muti* (magical) murders, in which body parts – especially skulls, hearts, eyes, and genitals – are removed and used or sold by deviant traditional practitioners to increase the wealth, influence, health, or fertility of a paying client. An older Xhosa woman and recent rural migrant to the outskirts of Cape Town commented in disbelief when my assistant and I confronted her with the facts of transplant surgery: "If what you are saying is true, that the white doctors can take the beating heart from one person who is dead, but not truly dead, and put it inside another person to give him strength and life, then these doctors are witches just like our own."

Under apartheid and in South Africa's new, democratic, and neoliberal context, organ transplant practices reveal the marked social and economic cleavages that separate donors and recipients into two opposed and antagonistic populations. Paradoxically, both witchcraft and witchhunting (see Ashforth 1996; Niehaus 1993, 1997) have been experiencing a renaissance in parts of South Africa since the democratic transition. These seeming "gargoyles" of the past testify, instead, to the "modernity of witchcraft" (Geschiere 1997; Taussig 1997) and to the hypermodern longings and magical expectations of poor South Africans for improved life chances since the fall of apartheid and the election of Nelson Mandela. Long-frustrated desires for land, employment, housing, and a fair share in the material wealth have fostered a resurgence of magic.

In 1995 an angry crowd of residents of Nyanga township in Cape Town tore down the shack of a suspected *muti*-murderer after police, tipped off by a local informer, discovered the dismembered body of a missing five-year-old boy smoldering in the fireplace and stored in medicine jars and boxes in the suspect's shack. On June 8, 1995, Moses Mokgethi was sentenced in the Rand Supreme Court, Gauteng, to life imprisonment for the murder of six children between the ages of four and nine whose bodies were mutilated for hearts, livers, and penises, which Mokgethi claims he sold to a local township businessman for between 2,000 and 3,000 rands to strengthen his business (see Ashforth 1996: 1228). Such widely publicized incidents are often followed by anxious rumors of luxury cars prowling squatter camps in search of children to steal for their heads and soft skulls or rumors of body parts stolen or purchased by "witch doctors" from corrupt doctors and police officials for use in rituals of magical increase. These rumors are conflated with fears of autopsy and organ harvesting for transplantation.

Younger and more sophisticated township residents are critical of organ transplantation as a living legacy of apartheid medicine. "Why is it," I was asked, "that in our township we have never met or even heard of such a person who received a new heart, or eyes, or a kidney? And yet we know a great many people who say that the bodies of their dead have been tampered with in the police morgues?" Township residents are quick to note the inequality of the exchanges in which organs and tissues have been taken from young, productive black bodies – the victims of excess mortality caused by apartheid's policies of substandard housing, poor street lighting, bad sanitation, hazardous transportation, and the overt political violence of the apartheid state and the black struggle for freedom – and transplanted into older, debilitated, affluent white bodies. In their view, organ transplantation reproduces the notorious body of apartheid. Even in the new South Africa, transplant surgery and other high-tech medical procedures are still largely the prerogative of whites.

During the apartheid years, transplant surgeons were not obligated to solicit family consent before harvesting organs (and tissues) from cadaver donors. "Up until 1984 the conditions for transplantation were easier," said Dr. B, a heart transplant surgeon at Groote Schuur Hospital. "We didn't worry too much in those days. We just took the hearts we needed. But it was never a racial issue. Christiaan Barnard was very firm about this. he was one of those people who just ignored the government. Even when our hospital wards were still segregated by law, there was no race apartheid in transplant surgery." But what he meant was that there was no hesitation in transplanting black and colored (mixed-race) "donors" hearts – taken without consent or knowledge of family members – into the ailing bodies of their mostly white male patients.

Up through the early 1990s about 85 percent of all heart transplant recipients at Groote Schuur Hospital were white males. Transplant doctors refused to reveal the "race" of the donors of hearts to concerned and sometimes racist organ recipients, saying that "hearts have no race." "We always used *whatever* hearts we could get," the doctor concluded, whether or not the patient feared he might be getting an "inferior organ." When asked why there were so few black and mixed-race heart transplant patients, Dr. B cited vague scientific findings indicating that "black South Africans coming from rural areas did not suffer the modern urban and stress-related scourges of ischemic heart disease, which primarily affects more affluent white males in urban settings." But this medical myth was difficult to reconcile with the reality of the forced migrations of South African blacks to mines and other industries in the periurban area and the history of forced removals to urban squatter camps, worker hostels, and other highly stressful urban institutions. And by 1994, the year of the first democratic elections, for the very first time a significant percentage (36 percent) of heart transplants at Groote Schuur Hospital were assigned to mixed-race, Indian, or black patients. With the passage of the Human Tissue Act of 1983, requiring individual of family members' consent at the time of death, organ harvesting became more complicated. South African blacks are reluctant organ, blood, and tissue donors (see Palmer 1984; Pike et al. 1993), and few voluntary donations come from the large Cape Malay Muslim community because of perceived religious prohibitions.

In 1996 and again in 1998 I began to investigate allegations of body-part theft at the state-run police mortuary in Cape Town. During the anti-apartheid struggle years many physicians, district surgeons, and state pathologists working with police at the mortuaries collaborated in covering up police actions that had resulted in deaths and body mutilations of hundreds of "suspected terrorists" and political prisoners. Meanwhile, rumors of criminal body tampering were fueled by several cases that came to the attention of journalists. On July 23, 1995, the Afrikaans-language newspaper *Rapport* (July 23, 1995) ran a story about a private detective who testified in the Johannesburg Regional Court that a policeman had shown him the mutilated body of Chris Hani in a Johannesburg mortuary the day after the black activist and political hero was murdered in 1993. A human heart alleged to be Hani's was sold for 2,000 rand by a mortuary worker to disguised investigative reporters. The heart was subsequently handed over to police, and Sergeant Andre Schutte was charged with defiling and corrupting the body of the slain leader. Because of stories such as these, the morgue remains a place of horror for township residents.

In the course of my investigations I learned that corneas, heart valves, and other human tissues were harvested by state pathologists and other mortuary staff and distributed to surgical and medical units, usually without soliciting family members' consent. The "donor" bodies, most of them township blacks and coloreds and victims of violence and other traumas, were handled by state pathologists attached to morgues still controlled by the police (see also NIM 1996). Some pathologists held that these practices were legal, if contested, but others considered them unethical.

A state pathologist attached to a prestigious academic teaching hospital spoke of his uneasiness over the informal practice of "presumed consent." A loophole in the 1983 Organ and Tissue Act allows the "appropriate" officials to remove needed organs and tissues without consent when "reasonable attempts" to locate the potential donor's next of kin have failed. Since eyes and heart valves need to be removed within hours of death and given the difficulty of locating families living in distant townships and informal communities (squatter settlements) without adequate transportation and communication systems, some doctors and coroners use their authority to harvest the prized organs without giving too much thought to the feelings of the relations. They justify their actions as motivated by the altruistic desire to save lives. In return these organ providers gain, minimally, the gratitude, professional friendship, and respect of the prestigious transplant teams, who owe them certain professional favors in return. Since harvested corneas and heart valves are sometimes sold to other hospitals and clinics – domestically and, in the case of heart valves, internationally – that request them, the possibility of secret gratuities and honoraria paid on the side to cooperating mortuary staff cannot be discounted. Small gratuities were paid, for example, by a local independent eye bank to transplant coordinators for the favor of carrying donor eyes designated for air transport to the local airport.

Currently, the South African Truth and Reconciliation Commission (TRC) is considering allegations of gross human rights violations at the Salt River Mortuary by the parents and survivors of 17-year-old Andrew Sitshetshe of Guguletu township, who failed to get a response to their complaint from the ethics committee and administrators at Groote Schuur Hospital. The case was taken up by the TRC in its health-sector hearings in June 1997 (see Health and Human Rights Project: Professional Accountability in South Africa, Submission to the TRC for Consideration at the Hearings on the Health Sector, June 17 and 18, 1997, Cape Town). Andrew Sitshetshe had been caught in the fire of township gang warfare in August 1992. Badly wounded, he had been taken to the Guguletu police station, where his mother, Rosemary, found him lying on the floor with a bleeding chest wound. By the time the ambulance attendants arrived he was dead, and the police had him taken to the Salt River Mortuary. They advised Mrs. Sitsheshe to go home until the morning, when she could claim her son's body for burial. When Andrew's parents arrived at the mortuary the following morning, the officials turned them away, saying that the body was not yet ready for viewing. When later in the day they were finally allowed to view the body, they were shocked.

As Mrs. Sitsheshe testified, "The blanket covering the body was full of blood, and he had two deep holes on the sides of his forehead so you could easily see the bone. His face was in bad condition. And I could see that something was wrong with his eyes. . . . I started to question the people in charge and they said that nothing had happened." In fact, Andrew's eyes had been removed at the morgue, and when members of the Sitsheshe family returned to confront the staff they were treated abusively. A few days later, Mrs. Sitsheshe, unable to rest, went to the eye bank to confront the director and request what was left of her son's eyes. The director informed her that her son's corneas had been "shaved" and given to two recipients and his eyes were being kept in the refrigerator. She refused to surrender them to Andrew's mother for burial. Consequently, Andrew Sitsheshe was buried without his eyes. Mrs. Sitshetshe asked, "Although my son is buried, is it good that his flesh is here, there, and everywhere, that part and parcel of his body are still floating around? . . . Must we be stripped of every comfort as well as our dignity? . . . How could the medical doctor decide or know what was a priority for us?" Leslie London, a professor of health at the University of Cape Town, testified on behalf of the Sitsheshes: "These were not events involving a few bad apples. . . . These abuses arose in a context in which the entire fabric of the health sector was permeated by apartheid, and in which basic human rights were profoundly disvalued."

In response to this case, the TRC raised two questions of central concern: How, under the new Bill of Rights, might the new government ensure equal access to organ transplantation for all of South Africa's people in need, especially those not covered by medical aid schemes? And how might the state institute equitable harvesting and transplantation? The relevant section in the Bill of Rights dealing with bodily integrity specifies "the right of all citizens to make decisions about reproduction and their bodies free from coercion, discrimination and violence." The inclusion of the words "and their bodies" was intended to refer directly to organ harvesting.

Popular sentiments against organ harvesting and transplantation practices in the African community may have contributed to the health minister's transfer of public support away from tertiary medicine to primary care – a move not without its own contradictions. At present, organ transplantation is moving rapidly from state hospitals and the academic research centers where organ transplantation was first developed in South Africa to new, relatively autonomous private, for-profit hospitals. Soon only the wealthy and those with excellent private medical insurance will have access to any transplantation.

In November 1997 the Constitutional Court of South Africa decided against a universal right to dialysis and kidney transplant (see *Soobramoney v. Minister of Health, Kwa Zulu-Natal*), a decision that Judge Albie Sachs described to me as necessary given the country's limited economic resources but "wrenchingly painful." The court was responding to the case of a 41-year-old unemployed man from Durban who was a diabetic with kidney failure. The man had used up his medical insurance and was denied dialysis at public expense at his provincial hospital following a stroke. The high court upheld the South African Ministry of Health's policy that restricts public support of dialysis to that small population approved for kidney transplant and awaiting the surgery. Candidates must be free of all other significant physical or mental disease, including vascular disease, chronic liver disease, or lung disease, alcoholism, malignancies, or HIV-positivity. Therefore Soobramoney was sent home to die.

As organ transplantation has moved into the private sector, commercialism has taken hold. In the absence of a national policy regulating transplant surgery and of any regional, let alone national, official waiting lists, the distribution of transplantable organs is informal and subject to corruption. Although all hospitals and medical centers have ethics boards to review decisions concerning the distribution of organs for transplant, in fact transplant teams are allowed a great deal of autonomy. Public and private hospitals hire their own transplant coordinators, who say that they are sometimes under pressure from their surgeons to dispose of usable hearts or kidneys rather than give them to a competing institution following the rather informal rules set up between and among hospitals and transplant centers.

The temptation "to accommodate" patients who are able to pay is beginning to affect both public and private hospitals. At one large public hospital's kidney transplant unit, there is a steady trickle of kidney patients and their live donors arriving from Mauritius and Namibia. Although claiming to be "relatives," many are, according to the nurses, paid donors, and since they arrive from "across the border" the doctors tend to look the other way. While I was in Cape Town in 1998, a very ill older businessman from Cameroon arrived at the kidney transplant unit of a public hospital accompanied by a paid donor he had located in Johannesburg. The donor was a young college student who had agreed to part with one of his kidneys for less than $2,000. When the two failed to cross-match in blood tests and were turned away, they returned to the hospital the next day, begging to be transplanted in any case; the patient was willing to face almost certain organ rejection. They were turned away, but would private hospitals be as conscientious in refusing such hopeless cases among those willing to pay regardless of the outcome?

Meanwhile, those acutely ill patients who live at a distance, for example, in the sprawling townships of Soweto outside Johannesburg or Khayalitsha outside Cape Town, have little chance of receiving a transplant. The rule of thumb among heart and kidney transplant surgeons in Johannesburg is "No fixed home, no phone, no organ." The ironies are striking. At the famous Chris Hani Bara Hospital on the outskirts of Soweto, I met a sprightly and playful middle-aged man, flirting with nurses during his dialysis treatment, who had been on the hospital's waiting list for a kidney for more than twenty years. Not a single patient at the huge Bara Hospital's kidney unit had received a transplant in the past year. But the week before I had met with Wynand Breytanbach, once deputy minister of defense under President P. W. Botha, who was recuperating at home outside Cape Town from the heart transplant he had received on his government pension and health plan after less than a month's wait. Meanwhile, at Groote Schuur Hospital a virtual if unofficial moratorium had brought "public" heart transplantation to a standstill in February 1998.

Brazil: From Theft and Sale to Compensated Gifting and Universal Donation

There are several distinct narratives concerning abusive and deviant practices of organ procurement for transplant surgery in Brazil. The first narrative, already discussed, concerns the gross human rights violations of the bodies of poor subcitizens, living and dead, during the later years of the Brazilian military dictatorship. With the transition to democracy in the mid-1980s these violations were replaced by softer forms of organ sales and compensated gifting between family members and strangers.

Democratization and valiant attempts to centralize organ harvesting and distribution regionally in the cities of Rio de Janeiro, São Paulo, and Recife, among others, have eroded but not eliminated the many opportunities available to the wealthy to obtain organs months and years ahead of ordinary citizens who depend on the national health service or on inadequate medical insurance programs. From the industrialized south to the rural interior of Northeast Brazil, transplant surgeons, patients, organ recipients, and transplant activists told us how laws and hospital regulations were bent, "negotiated," "facilitated," or circumvented by means of personal contacts and *jeitos* (a popular expression for ways of getting through obstacles by means of wit, cunning, trickery, bribery, or influence). A young informant reported to my assistant, Mariana Ferreira, in São Paulo in December 1997 that after being told he would need a cornea transplant he was reassured by the doctor: "I can refer you to some friends of mine at X Hospital. You will still need to register with the cornea waiting list, but if you have $3,000 cash you can cut through the list and be placed up front." A kidney transplant activist in São Paulo showed us her files on the hundreds of ordinary citizens and candidates for kidney transplant who, despite medical exams and multiple referrals, have never been called to the top of any transplant list, herself included. She was cynical about the wealthy people who arrive in São Paulo from elsewhere in the country and return home with the organ sought, often within weeks. "The waiting list makes donkeys out of us," she said. "Sometimes I think we are just there to 'decorate' the list." Her criticisms were supported by transplant surgeons in public and private medical centers, who complained that affluent patients were hard to come by, since most traveled to Europe or the United States to get "quality organs" at up-scale medical centers. And, of course, they said, money "paved the way" for them, whether in Houston, New York, or São Paulo. Transplant surgeons at the large public hospitals in Recife, Rio de Janeiro, and São Paulo that I visited in 1997 and 1998 seemed to be engaged in a slowdown as they waited for the real scarce commodity – paying patients – to arrive. In the meantime, few transplants were done under the system of national health insurance.

The complicated workings of Brazil's two-tiered health care system – a free national health care system, universally available and universally disdained, and a booming private medical sector, available to the minority and coveted by all – generates ideal conditions for a commerce in organs and for bribes and facilitations to speed up access to transplant procedures. In the absence of a unified organ-sharing network comparable to UNOS in the United States and Eurotransplant in western Europe, private transplantation clinics compete with public-sector hospitals for available organs. Since financial incentives are so much greater in the private sector (where surgeons can be paid many times the standard fee for transplant surgery allowed by the health service), private hospitals are more aggressive in locating and obtaining organs (see Pereira Coelho 1996). The national system pays the hospital $7,000 for a kidney transplant, of which the medical team receives $2,000, while in a private hospital the same surgery can reap between $25,000 and $50,000. In the case of liver transplants, the system pays the hospital $24,000, while in a private clinic this surgery ranges from $50,000 to $300,000, depending on the complications. The chief nurse responsible for the transplant unit of a private hospital in São Paulo said that the above-quoted average costs per transplant surgery pertained only to the hospital expenses. "Medical honoraria," she said, "are negotiated between the patient and the surgeons. We do not interfere in those details."

So, though the Brazilian constitution guarantees dialysis and organ transplants to Brazilian citizens who need them, waiting lists are filled with people who have been "on hold" for decades, since the fee payment schedule hardly makes the surgery worth doing. Dr. J, a young transplant surgeon in Rio de Janeiro, took me for a tour of the empty transplant unit of a huge public hospital. "It is a shame," he said, "but there is simply no motivation to operate under the state system [of payment]. Most [surgeons] just bide their time here during their weekly shifts. Their real work is with paying patients in private clinics."

But even at smaller, private hospitals, most kidney transplant patients were local and of modest means. "Why would a wealthy person come here?" asked the irritated director of the kidney transplant unit at one such hospital in Recife in answer to my questions about commercialization in his unit. Although trained abroad at the best academic hospitals, Dr. P claimed that his kidney transplant unit was slighted by the "bourgeoisie," who went south to São Paulo or north to the United States for their operations. His unit survived largely through living kidney donations, mostly kin-related but also from compensated friends and strangers.

While the global business in organs has received extensive media attention, most organs trade is domestic, following the usual social and economic cleavages and obeying local rules of class, race, gender, and geography. According to an elderly Brazilian surgeon interviewed by my assistant in São Paulo in 1997, a "shadow" commerce in organs has long been a reality among Brazilians. "Those who suffer most," he said, "are the usual ones, mostly poor and uneducated, who are tricked or pressured into donation through private transactions that rarely come to the attention of the doctors." During the 1970s and 1980s there was evidence of the kind of rampant commercialism found in India today. I interviewed Dr. L, a nephrologist in private practice in Rio, who denounced the medical climate in his city in those days: "The [organs] traffic was practically legalized here. It was a safe thing, taking place in both large and small hospitals, with no concern over its illegality." The commerce reached a "scary peak," he said, in the 1980s, when newspapers were publishing an alarming number of ads of organs for sale: "There were just too many people offering to sell kidneys and corneas at competitive prices, not to mention the 'bad' [i.e., HIV-contaminated] blood that was also being sold to private blood banks." Beginning in the 1990s, in an improved economic climate, such blatant ads disappeared, but, according to Dr. L, "The commerce has not stopped. It is simply less visible today." According to Dr. M of São Paulo, organ donors still show up, unannounced, at transplant centers. The wording of the exchanges is more discreet: from "selling" and "buying" organs to "offers" of help. "The price of kidneys varies. If it is an economist in need of money, naturally the price is higher. If it is a simple person, it will be cheaper." For example, he said, from time to time a patient arrives dressed in the latest fashion with expensive jewelry and brings with her a "donor" wearing rubber sandals. "She describes him as her cousin from the interior of the state. We refuse to operate, and when they insist I send them to a judge to decide and leave it to him to authorize the transaction or not."

In addition to these wholly private transactions between live donors and recipients, which most doctors tolerate as "having nothing to do with them," there are organized crime rings that deal in human body parts from hospitals and morgues. Brazil's leading newspaper, the *Folha de São Paulo*, carried several stories in 1997 of police investigations of a "body Mafia" with connections to hospital and emergency room staff, ambulance drivers, and local and state morgues that traded in blood, organs, and human tissues from cadavers. In one case, falsified death certificates were provided to conceal the identities of multilated corpses in the Rio de Janeiro morgue. Investigations resulted in criminal proceedings against a ring of criminal mortuary workers.

Even where there is no explicit commerce in organs, the social inequity inherent in the public medical care system interferes with the harvesting of organs and produces an unjust distribution. Transplant specialists such as Dr. F from São Paulo note a common occurrence:

Sometimes a young patient dies in the periphery and is identified as a potential donor. A mobile intensive care unit arrives and takes him to the hospital so he can be placed in better [clinical] conditions to become a donor body. The family is confused and does not understand what is going on. Before this, there was no room for him in the public hospital. Suddenly, he is put into a super-modern intensive care unit in a private hospital or an academic research hospital. This is why the poor so often say – and with some reason – that they are worth more dead than alive.

Although the earlier law regulating living organ donors (Law No. 8489, issued in 1992) required special judicial authorization for nonrelated living donation, loopholes were common, especially in small, private hospitals where living kidney donors remain the rule. In July 1997 and August 1998 I spent time in a private hospital in Recife where 70 percent of all kidney transplants relied on living donors. Hospital statistics for the past decade listed 37 "unrelated" living donors in addition to a larger number of highly suspect "cousins," "godchildren," "in laws," "nieces," and "nephews." Hospital administrators, social workers, and the psychologist were not defensive about their practice, which was legal as long as a local judge was willing to authorize an exception. Brazil has 117 medically certified centers for kidney transplant, 22 for heart transplant, 19 for liver transplant, and a large number of cornea transplant centers, of which only 17 are certified (*Censo* 1997). Keeping these clinics operating cost-effectively has meant greater tolerance for various informal incentives to encourage organ donation by relatives and friends. The lines between "bought" and "gifted" organs are fuzzy. Rewarded gifting is accepted by some transplant surgeons as an ethically "neutral" practice. Although most transplant surgeons avoid patients they suspect of having arranged for a paid donor, others turn a blind eye to such exchanges. A transplant surgeon in Rio de Janeiro said, "I am a doctor, not a policeman."

The compensation offered to living donors varies from small lump sums of $1,000 to privileges over inheritance. A São Paulo surgeon explained: "Yes, of course, sometimes people get things. A brother who donates his kidney will receive a private financial bonus. Later we learn that he got a car. Or a son who donates a kidney to the father – a situation we don't usually encourage – gets extra privileges within the family." A nephrologist in Rio de Janeiro told of a young woman who agreed to donate a kidney to her uncle in exchange for a house. The surgeons resisted because the patient was a poor candidate for transplant and noncompliant, but he eventually found a private clinic that would accept him. The outcome? "The man suffered various crises of kidney rejection, wound up back in dialysis, and was dead within the year. And there was the niece, minus a kidney but enjoying her new home."

In addition to rewarded gifting within families, there may be considerable pressure, especially on lower-status, poor, or female relatives, to volunteer as kidney donors (see De Vasconcelos 1995). Dr. N, a transplant surgeon in Salvador, Bahia, interviewed in June 1998, told of the case of a young woman whose brother had threatened to kill her if she refused to give him a kidney. He said, "The whole issue of organ capture occurring within the family involves an intensely private dynamic that often escapes the control of the most careful medical professionals."

The pressure exerted on lower-status, poor, or female relatives to volunteer as donors is especially problematic in that these vulnerable social groups have a much smaller chance of being organ recipients themselves.[8] A transplant surgeon in São Paulo explained that "the tendency, often unconscious, is to choose the least productive member of the family as a kidney donor. One might choose, for example, the single aunt." And by and large living related kidney donors tend to be female. A surgeon in São Paulo with a large pediatric kidney transplant practice defended his clinic's statistics: "Of course, it is only natural that the mother is the primary donor. But I usually try to enlist the father first. I tell him that the mother has already given life to the child, and now it is his turn. But the men tend to feel that organ donation is a womanly thing to do."

Zulaide, a working-class physical education teacher from a small town in Pernambuco, was approached by her older brother to be a kidney donor in the mid-1990s. He had been in dialysis for years awaiting a cadaveric organ. Because of his distance from the medical center and the national health system's low fees and refusal to pay for blood-matching tests, Roberto's chances of receiving an "official" organ were slim. Along with the other 15,000 Brazilians waiting for cadaveric kidneys, Roberto would have to remain wedded to an antiquated dialysis machine. Ever since the much publicized medical disaster of 1995, in which 38 dialysis patients from the interior town of Caruaru, Pernambuco, died of a bacterial infection transmitted through just such poorly maintained public machines, kidney patients have been willing to do almost anything to avoid dialysis and obtain a transplant.

Balking at the suggestion that he find a paid donor, Roberto agreed to allow his sister, a healthy young married woman with three children, to help him out. Although Zulaide freely donated her kidney – "I gave it from the heart," she said, "and not for gain" – the operation was not a success, and Roberto died within the year. Complications arose in her own recovery, and she had to give up her physically demanding job. But when she went to the private transplant clinic in Recife looking for follow-up medical attention she was rebuffed by the doctors. She was selected as a donor, the surgeons insisted, because she was healthy. Her complaints, they said, were probably psychological, a syndrome one doctor called "donor regret" – a kind of "compensatory neurosis." Zulaide scoffed at this interpretation: "I miss my brother, not my kidney," she maintains.

On the other side of town, when Wellington Barbosa, an affluent pharmacist in his late sixties, was told that he needed a heart transplant, his private doctor was able to facilitate his move to the top of the waiting list at a prestigious medical center in São Paulo. Consequently, Wellington's new heart was beating inside his chest within a matter of weeks.

Meanwhile, in the crowded hillside shantytown which practically looks down into Wellington's property, Carminha dos Santos was engaged in a fruitless pursuit of transplant surgery for her son Tomas, who had lost his sight at the age of seven following the medical maltreatment of an eye infection. Carminha was certain that her son's condition could be reversed by a cornea transplant. The obstacle, as she saw it, was that the "eye banks, like everything else in the world, were reserved for those with money." She first took the boy to Recife, and when that failed she traveled with him by bus to Rio de Janeiro, where the two of them went from hospital to hospital and doctor to doctor. Throughout she persisted in the belief that somewhere she would find "a sainted doctor," a doctor of conscience who would be willing to help. "Don't they give new eyes to the rich?" And wasn't her own son "equal in the eyes of God"? In the end she returned home angry and defeated. Her only hope was to get a trained seeing-eye dog for her son through a Catholic charity.

According to legislators interviewed, Brazil's new law[9] of presumed consent, issued on February 4, 1997, was designed to produce a surplus of organs for transplant surgery, guarantee an equilibrium between supply and demand, establish equity in the distribution of organs, and end any commerce in organs. But almost immediately, the law was contested from above and below, by surgeons and by the popular classes (see also Gabel 1996). Most transplant specialists attributed the real problems of organ transplantation to the lack of medical and technological infra-structure for organ capture, distribution, and transplant surgery. The head nurse of the largest private transplant center in São Paulo explained:

The government wanted the population to believe that the real problem was the family's refusal to donate. The truth is that the national health care system does not have the technical capacity to maintain the donor's body, and so we lose most donors. When we think we have found a perfect donor, a 25-year-old man who suffered a car accident, who is brain-dead but otherwise perfect, it is a weekend and there is no public surgeon available, and the perfect heart goes into the garbage.

The new organ law, similar to compulsory donation laws in Belgium and Spain, makes all Brazilian adults into universal organ donors at death unless they officially declare themselves "nondonors of organs and tissues." The state has assumed the function of monitoring the harvesting and distribution of cadaveric organs. But still there is nothing to prevent a continuing commerce in organs, because the new law eliminated the key requirement of court authorization for nonkin-related trans-plants. The pertinent section of the law reads: "Any able person according to the terms of civil law can dispose of tissues, organs and body parts to be removed in life for transplant and therapeutic ends" (Federal Law No. 9, 434, Chapter 3, Section 2, Article 15). As Dr. B explained, "If you want to sell a kidney to somebody, it is no longer my duty as a doctor to investigate. According to the new law, all responsi-bility resides in the state alone."

And, despite the new law, those who are better off economically will continue to refuse cadaveric organs. A strong preference for a known, living donor will keep the market for kidneys alive. According to a nephrologist in private practice in Rio de Janeiro, only poorer clients will "accept" a cadaveric kidney for transplant: "In my experience the rich always want a kidney from a living person about whom something is known.... Deep down, there is a visceral disbelief in our national health system. The fear of contracting AIDS or hepatitis from public corpses is extreme." And, in fact, he concluded, these fears are not entirely groundless.

The director of Rio de Janeiro's notorious state morgue welcomed the new law of presumed consent as a thoroughly modern institution which offered an opportunity to educate the "ignorant masses" in the new democracy. But to the proverbial man and woman on the street in São Paulo, Rio, Recife, and Salvador, the new law is just another bureaucratic assault on their bodies. The only way to exempt oneself was to request new identity cards or driver's licenses officially stamped "I am not a donor of organs or tissues." People formed long lines in civil registry offices all over the country to "opt out" of the pool of compulsory organ donors. At registry offices in Rio de Janeiro, São Paulo, Salvador, and San Carlos, they expressed anger and resentment over an imperious act of the state against "little people" like themselves. Here and there individuals expressed some support for the "good intention" of the law, but they doubted the moral and organizational capacity of the state to implement it fairly.

"Doctors have never treated us with respect before this law," said Magdelena, a domestic worker, referring to the scandal of sterilizations performed on poor women without their consent. "Why would they suddenly protect our rights and our bodies after this law?" Carlos Almeida, a 52-year-old construction worker, saw the law as driven by profit: "Who can guarantee that doctors will not speed up death, give a little *jeitinho* for some guy to die quicker in order to profit from it? I don't put any faith in this business of brain death. As long as the heart is beating, there is still life for me." Almeida advised his adult sons not to become donors: "I told them that there are people around like vultures after the organs of young and healthy persons." A retired accountant, Inácio Fagundes, asked, "Does this law mean that when I die they can take my body, cut it up, take what they wish, even if my family does not agree?" On being told that this was more or less the case, he told the civil registrar: "Stamp it very large on my identity card: "Fagundes will *not* donate anything!"

Conclusion

Under what social conditions can organ harvesting and distribution for transplant surgery be fair, equitable, just, and ethical? Organ transplantation depends on a social contract and social trust, the grounds for which must be explicit. Minimally, this requires national laws and international guidelines outlining and protecting the rights of organ donors, living and dead, as well as organ recipients. Additionally, organ transplantation requires a reasonably fair and equitable health care system.

It also requires a reasonably democratic state in which basic human rights are guaranteed. Organ transplantation, even in elite medical centers by the most conscientious of physicians, that occurs in the context of an authoritarian or police state can lead to gross abuses. Similarly, where vestiges of debt peonage persist and where class, race, and caste ideologies cause certain kinds of bodies – whether women, common criminals, paupers, or street children – to be treated as "waste," these sentiments will corrupt medical practices concerning brain death, organ harvesting, and distribution.

Under conditions such as these the most vulnerable citizens will fight back with the only resources they have – gossip, rumors, urban legends, and resistance to modern laws. In this way, they act and react to the state of emergency that exists for them in this time of economic and democratic readjustments. They express their consciousness of social exclusions and articulate their own ethical and political categories in the face of the "consuming" demands which value their bodies most when they can be claimed by the state as repositories of spare parts. While for transplant specialists an organ is just a "thing," a commodity better used than wasted, to a great many people an organ is something else – a lively, animate, and spiritualized part of the self which most would still like to take with them when they die.

NOTES

This essay is offered as a "transplanted" surrogate for the Sidney Mintz lecture, "Small Wars: The Cultural Politics of Childhood," which I was honored to present at Johns Hopkins University, October 28, 1996. A revised and expanded version of that lecture was published as the introduction to *Small Wars: The Cultural Politics of Childhood*, edited by Nancy Scheper-Hughes and Carolyn Sargent (Berkeley and Los Angeles: University of California Press, 1998). I hope that traces of Mintz's historical and ethnographic sensibility can be recognized in my analysis of the commodification of human organs, yet another variant of the global trade in bodies, desires, and needs (see Mintz 1985). This article has emerged from a larger comparative and collaborative project entitled "Selling Life," codirected by Nancy Scheper-Hughes and Lawrence Cohen at the University of California, Berkeley, and funded by an individual fellowship from the Open Society Foundation in New York City.

1　Although I have been harassed in the field with respect to other research projects, this was the first time that I was warned of being followed by a hit man representing a deeply implicated and corrupt judge.

2　At the Hospital das Clínicas, Mariana Ferreira and I were able to follow the relatively uncomplicated transplant surgery of Domba, a Suya religious leader with end-stage renal disease who had been flown to São Paulo from his small reserve in Amazonas. Domba was, in fact, considerably less anxious about the operation than the local businessman who shared his semiprivate hospital room. He was certain that his spirit familiars would accompany him into and through the operation.

3　I am indebted to João Biehl for the reference to Agamben's recent work and for pointing out its relevance to this project.

4　The suffering of transplant patients caused by the blend of clinical and "experimental" liver transplant procedures has led one noted bioethicist (M. Rorty, personal communication) to stipulate an exception in her own living will: All "usable" organs – *minus her liver* – are to be donated to medical science. Likewise, Das (2000) refers to "the tension between the therapeutic and the experimental" in liver transplant surgeries performed in parts of India.

5 Brain-stem death implies that there are no homeostatic functions remaining; the patient cannot breathe spontaneously, and support of cardiovascular function is usually necessary. However, the criteria used in defining brain death vary across states, regions, and nations. In Japan only 25 percent of the population accepts the idea of brain death, while in Cuba the fact of irreversible damage to the brain stem is sufficient to declare the person dead. Some doctors accept brain-stem death alone, while for others the upper brain, responsible for thought, memory, emotions, and voluntary muscle movements, must also have ceased to function.

6 I recall how recently it was in rural Ireland that it was customary to call the priest, not the doctor, when a parishioner began to approach death – a situation that every villager recognized. Dr. Healy would berate a villager for calling him to attend to a dying person. "Call the priest," he would say. "There's nothing that I can do here." Thus the passage to death was mediated by spiritual, not medical, rituals.

7 A young farmer from the Dingle Peninsula shared with me in the 1970s the wisdom that informed the country people's practice of long wakes: "It just wouldn't be right or seemly to put 'em into the hole when they are still fresh-like. You see, you never know, exactly, when the soul leaves the body." One thing was certain: the soul, the spirit force and persona of the individual, could hover in and near the body for hours or even days after the somatic signs of death were visible. One can scarcely imagine what he would have to say today about brain-stem death after his 60-odd years of sitting up with the dying and keeping company with the dead and their resistant, hanger-on spirits.

8 A survey of the distribution of renal transplants in Europe and North America (Kjellstrand 1990) shows that women and nonwhite patients had only two-thirds the chance of men and white patients of receiving a transplant. A study by the Southeastern Organ Procurement Foundation in 1978 (cited in Callender et al. 1995) noted a disparity in the United States between the large numbers of African-American patients on dialysis and the small numbers of African-American transplant patients. The preliminary research of Sheila Rothman (1998) reveals a pattern of unintended discrimination in the screening of African-American and Latino transplant candidates in New York City.

9 The problem of presumed consent for organ retrieval from cadavers is not limited to countries in the South, where vast segments of the population are illiterate or semi-literate. In the United States today there is considerable resistance to cadaveric organ donation (Kolata 1995), and James Childress (1996: 11) notes that the laws regarding organ harvesting from cadavers are "marked by inconsistencies regarding rights holders, whether these are the individual while alive or the family after the individual's death." In practice, the state assumes rights over any cadavers presumed to have been "abandoned" by kin. In addition, in many states there is "presumed consent" for the removal of corneas, skin, pituitary glands, and other tissues and parts even under ordinary circumstances and without informing the next of kin, but this presumption of consent is called into question whenever people become aware of routine organ and tissue harvesting practices.

REFERENCES

Agamben, Giorgio. 1998. *Homo Sacer: Sovereign Power and Bare Life*. Stanford: Stanford University Press.

Anders, George. 1995. On sale now at your HMO: Organ transplants. *Wall Street, Journal*, January 17.

Appadurai, Arjun, ed. 1986. *The Social Life of Things*. New York: Cambridge University Press.

Ashforth, Adam. 1996. Of secrecy and the commonplace: Witchcraft and power in Soweto. *Social Research* 63 (Winter).

Awaya, Tsuyoshi. 1994. The theory of neo-cannibalism (in Japanese). *Japanese Journal of Philosophy* 3: 29–47.

Berlinger, Giovanni, and Volnei Garrafa. 1996. *O mercado humano: Estudo bioetico da compra e venda de partes do corpo*. Brasília: Editora Universidade de Brasília.

Biehl, João. 1998. A morte da sonhadora: Iluminismo, A. Guerra Mucker e o campo do inconsciente no sul do brasil, século XIX. In *Psicanálise e colonização*. Edited by Edson Souza. Porto Alegre: Artes e Oficios.

——. 1999. Other life: AIDS, biopolitics, and subjectivity in Brazil's zones of social abandonment. Ph.D. diss., University of California, Berkeley, CA.

Callender, C. A., A. S. Bey, P. V. Miles, and C. L. Yeager. 1995. A national minority organ/tissues transplant education program. *Transplantation Proceedings* 27: 1441–3.

Cantarovich, F. 1990. Organ commerce in South America. *Transplantation Proceedings* 24: 146–8.

Castel, Robert. 1991. From dangerousness to risk. In *The Foucault Effect: Studies in Governmentality*. Edited by G. Burchell, C. Gordon, and P. Miller. Chicago: University of Chicago Press.

Censo nacional de transplantes de orgáos. 1997. Brasília: Ministry of Health.

Chandra, Prakash. 1991. Kidneys for sale. *World Press Review*, February, p. 53.

Chaudhary, V. 1992. Argentina uncovers patients killed for organs. *British Medical Journal* 34: 1073–4.

——.1994. Organ trade investigators seize hospital records in Buenos Aires. *Guardian*, June 22.

Chengappa, Raj. 1990. The organs bazaar. *India Today*, July, pp. 30–7.

Childress, James. 1996. The gift of life: Ethical considerations in organ transplantation. *Bulletin of the American College of Surgeons* 81: 10–220.

Cohen, Lawrence. 1999. Where it hurts: Indian material for an ethics of organ transplantation. *Daedalus* 128: 135–65.

Cohen, Lloyd R. 1989. Increasing the supply of transplant organs: The virtues of a futures market. *George Washington Law Review*.

——. 1993. A futures market in cadaveric organs: Would it work? *Transplantation Proceedings* 25: 60–1.

Comaroff, John, and Jean Comaroff. 1992. "Medicine, colonialism, and the black body," in *Ethnography and the Historical Imagination*. Boulder: Westview Press.

Curran, W. J. 1991. Scientific and commercial development of the human cell lines: Issues of property, ethics, and conflicts of interest. *New England Journal of Medicine* 324: 998–1000.

Daar, A. S. 1989. Ethical issues: A Middle East perspective. *Transplantation Proceedings* 21: 1402–4.

——. 1990. Rewarded gifting or rampant commercialism: Is there a difference? In *Organ Replacement Therapy: Ethics, Justice, Commerce*. Edited by W. Land and J. B. Dossetpor. Berlin: Springer-Verlag.

——. 1992a. Nonrelated donors and commercialism: A historical perspective. *Transplantation Proceedings* 25: 2087–90.

——. 1992b. Rewarded gifting. *Transplantation Proceedings* 24: 2207–11.

——. n.d. Living-organ donation: Time for a donor charter. MS, Department of Surgery, Sultan Qaboos University, Sultanate of Oman.

Das, Veena. 1996. Organ transplants: Gift, sale, or theft? Paper read at the international conference "Selling Life: Commerce in Human Organs," Berkeley, CA, April 20–8.

——. 1998. Wittgenstein and anthropology. *Annual Review of Anthropology* 27: 171–95.

——. 2000. The practice of organ transplants: Networks, documents, translations. In *Living and Working with the New Medical Technologies: Intersections of Inquiry.* Edited by Margaret Lock et al., pp. 263–87. Cambridge: Cambridge University Press.

De Vasconcelos, Maria Odete. 1995. Contribução ao estudo antropológico do doador renal. MA thesis, Postgraduate Program on Anthropology, UFPE, Recife, Brazil.

Dundes, Alan, ed. 1991. *The Blood Libel Legend.* Madison: University of Wisconsin Press.

Evans, M. 1989. Organ donations should not be restricted to relatives. *Journal of Medical Ethics* 15: 17–20.

Fishman, Rachelle H. B. 1998. Israeli kidney swap unites Jews and Muslims. *Lancet* 351 (9116): 1641.

Foucault, Michel. 1975. *The Birth of the Clinic.* New York: Vintage Books.

Fox, R. C. 1996. Afterthoughts: Continuing reflections on organ transplantation. In *Organ Transplantation: Meanings and Realities.* Edited by Stuart Younger, Renée Fox, and Laurence O'Connell, pp. 251–74. Madison: University of Wisconsin Press.

Fox, R. C., and J. Swazey. 1992. *Spare Parts: Organ Replacement in American Society.* New York: Oxford University Press.

Gabel, H. 1996. How presumed is presumed consent? *Transplantation Proceedings* 28: 27–30.

Geschiere, Peter. 1997. *The Modernity of Witchcraft: Politics and the Occult in Postcolonial Africa.* Charlottesville: University Press of Virginia.

Guha, Ranajit. 1983. *Elementary Aspects of Peasant Insurgency in Colonial India.* Delhi: Oxford University Press.

Haraway, Donna. 1985. A manifesto for cyborgs. *Socialist Review* 80: 65–108.

Hogle, Linda. 1995. Standardization across non-standard domains: The case of organ procurement. *Science, Technology, and Human Values* 20: 482–500.

Human Rights Watch/Asia. 1995. An executioner's testimony. Supplementary submission by HRW/A to the US Senate Committee on Foreign Relations May 4, 1995, hearing on China's use of executed prisoners' organs.

Illich, Ivan. 1976. *Medical Nemesis.* New York: Pantheon.

Joralemon, Donald. 1995. Organ wars: The battle for body parts. *Medical Anthropology Quarterly* 9: 335–56.

Kalifon, S. Zev. 1995. The shortage of donor organs in Israel: Cultural symbols and consensus. Paper presented at the annual meetings of the American Anthropological Association, Washington, DC, November 15–19.

Kevorkian, Jack. 1992. A controlled auction market is a practical solution to the shortage of transplantable organs. *Med Law* 11: 47–55.

Kjellstrand, C. 1990. The distribution of renal transplants: Are physicians just? *Transplantation Proceedings* 22: 964–5.

Kolata, Gina. 1995. Why organs aren't donated. *San Francisco Chronicle*, July 7.

Laqueur, Thomas. 1983. Bodies, death, and pauper funerals. *Representations* 191: 109–31.

Lerer, Leonard, and Richard Matzopoulos. 1996. *A Profile of Violence and Injury: Mortality in the Cape Town Metropole.* Tygerberg: South African Medical Research Council.

Lock, Margaret. 1995. Transcending mortality: Organ transplants and the practice of contradictions. *Medical Anthropology Quarterly* 9: 390–9.

——. 1996. Deadly disputes: Understanding death in Europe, Japan, and North America. *Doreen B. Townsend Center Occasional Papers* 4: 7–25.

——. 1997. Culture, technology, and the new death: Deadly disputes in Japan and North America. *Culture* 17(1–2): 27–42.

——. n.d. *Twice Dead: Circulation of Body Parts and Remembrance of Persons*. Berkeley and Los Angeles: University of California Press. In press.

Marshall, P. A., D. C. Thomas, and A. S. Daar. 1996. Marketing human organs: The autonomy paradox. *Theoretical Medicine* 17(1): 1–18.

Mauss, Marcel. 1966. *The Gift*. London: Cohen and West.

Mintz, Sidney. 1985. *Sweetness and Power*. New York: Penguin.

Neves, L. Moreira. 1993. Patentes para a vida? *O Estado de São Paulo*, April 21.

Niehaus, Isak. 1993. Coins for blood and blood for coins: Toward a genealogy of sacrifice in the Transvaal Lowveld. Paper presented at the meeting of the Society for South African Anthropology, Johannesburg.

——. 1997. Witchcraft, power, and politics: An ethnographic study of the South African Lowveld. Ph.D. dissertation, University of the Witwatersrand, Johannesburg, South Africa.

NIM (Network of Independent Monitors). 1996. *Breaking with the Past: Reports of Alleged Human Rights Violations by South African Police*. Cape Town.

Ohnuki-Tierney, Emiko. 1994. Organ transplantation: Cultural bases of medical technology. *Current Anthropology* 35: 233–54.

Palmer, Robin. 1984. *Blood Donation in the Border Region: Black Donors, Exdonors, and Nondonors*. Grahamstown: Rhodes University Institute of Social and Economic Research.

Patarra, Ivo. 1982. *Fome no nordeste do Brasil*. São Paulo: Editora Marco Zero.

Pereira Coelho, Vera S. 1996. Interesses e instituições na política de saúde: O transplante e a diálise no Brasil. Ph.D. dissertation, Universidade Estadual de Campinas, Brazil.

Pike, R. E., J. A. Odell, and D. Kahan. 1993. Public attitudes to organ donation in South Africa. *South African Medical Journal* 83 (February): 91–4.

Pinero, Maite. 1992. Enlèvements d'enfants et trafic d'organes. *Le Monde Diplomatique*, August, pp. 16–17.

Rabinow, Paul. 1996. *Essays on the Anthropology of Reason*. Princeton: Princeton University Press.

Randall, T. 1991. Too few human organs for transplantation, too many in need, and the gap widens. *Journal of the American Medical Association* 265: 1223–7.

Raymond, Janice. 1989. Children for organ export? *Reproductive and Genetic Engineering* 2: 237–45.

Reddy, K. C. 1990. Organ donation for consideration: An Indian viewpoint. *Organ Replacement Therapy: Ethics, Justice, and Commerce (Proceedings of the First Joint Meeting of ESOT and EDTA/ERA, December)*. Berlin: Springer-Verlag.

Richards, Janet Radcliffe, et al. 1998. The case for allowing kidney sales. *Lancet* 51: 1950–2.

Richardson, Ruth. 1989. *Death, Dissection, and the Destitute*. London: Penguin Books.

——. 1996. Fearful symmetry: Corpses for anatomy, organs for transplantation. In *Organ Transplantation: Meanings and Realities*. Edited by Stuart Younger, Renée Fox, and Laurence O'Connell, pp. 66–100. Madison: University of Wisconsin Press.

Rothman, David. 1997. Body shop. *The Sciences*, November/December, pp. 17–21.

Rothman, David, et al. 1997. The Bellagio Task Force report on transplantation, bodily integrity, and the international traffic in organs. *Transplantation Proceedings* 29: 2739–45.

Rothman, Sheila. 1998. Monitoring kidney donations from living donors: A pilot study in the New York metropolitan region. Paper presented at the World Bioethics Meetings, Tokyo, Japan.

Saalahudeen, A. K., et al. 1990. High mortality among recipients of bought living-unrelated kidneys. *Lancet* 336 (8717): 725–8.

Sacks, Oliver. 1995. *An Anthropologist on Mars*. New York: Knopf.

Scheper-Hughes, Nancy. 1991. Theft of life. *Transaction: Society* 27(6): 57–62.

———. 1992. *Death without Weeping: The Violence of Everyday Life in Brazil*. Berkeley: University of California Press.

———. 1994. Embodied knowledge: Thinking with the body in medical anthropology. In *Assessing Cultural Anthropology*. Edited by Rob Borofsky, pp. 229–42. New York: McGraw-Hill.

———. 1996a. Theft of life: Globalization of organ-stealing rumors. *Anthropology Today* 12(3): 3–11.

———. 1996b. Small wars and invisible genocides. *Social Science and Medicine* 43: 889–900.

Scheper-Hughes, Nancy, and Daniel Hoffman. 1998. "Brazilian apartheid: Street kids and the struggle for urban space," in *Small Wars: The Cultural Politics of Childhood*. Edited by Nancy Scheper-Hughes and Carolyn Sargent. Berkeley and Los Angeles: University of California Press.

Scheper-Hughes, Nancy, and Margaret Lock. 1987. The mindful body: A prolegomenon to future work in medical anthropology. *Medical Anthropology Quarterly* 1: 1–60.

Schwindt, Richard, and Aidan Vining. 1986. Proposal for a future delivery market for transplant organs. *Journal of Health, Politics, Policy, and Law* 11: 483–500.

Scott, James. 1985. *Weapons of the Weak*. New Haven: Yale University Press.

Shiva, Vandana. 1997. *Biopiracy: The Plunder of Nature and Knowledge*. Boston: South End Press.

Soros, George. 1998a. Toward a global open society. *Atlantic Monthly*, pp. 20–32.

———. 1998b. *The Crisis of Global Capitalism: Open Society Endangered*. New York: Public Affairs.

Suarez-Orozco, Marcelo. 1987. The treatment of children in the dirty war: Ideology, state terrorism, and the abuse of children in Argentina. In *Child Survival*. Edited by Nancy Scheper-Hughes, pp. 227–46. Dordrecht: D. Reidel.

Taussig, Michael. 1992. *The Nervous System*. New York: Routledge.

———. 1997. *The Magic of the State*. New York: Routledge.

USIA. 1994. The child organ trafficking rumor: A modern urban legend. Report submitted to the UN Special Rapporteur on the Sale of Children.

White, Luise. 1996. Traffic in heads. Paper presented at the international conference "Selling Life: Commerce in Human Organs," Berkeley, CA, April 26–8.

Wolfe, Sidney. 1999. Letter to Dr. Jane Henney, Commissioner, US Food and Drug Administration, February 10. www.citizen.org/public_citizen/hrg/WHAT'SNEW/1473.

Part V

Traveling Media

This section of the book deals with the meanderings of the mass media, highlighting the increasingly important role they play in the quotidian realities of people all over the world. Just as the chapters in Part IV were on commodity flows, this section illustrates that people in the periphery are not passive in their encounters with foreign cultural products. For example, the essay by Michaels shows how Warlpiri Aborigines in the western Central Desert region of Australia actively participate in constructing the meaning of any given American/western film and television program they watch and do not simply absorb its values.

In addition, Part V shows that, when it comes to global cultural influence, the West is not the only player in town. There are also quite a number of Third World countries – India, Mexico, and Taiwan, to name only a few – that exert a powerful cultural influence around the world, particularly on other countries of the periphery. Thus Yang's essay shows that for the Chinese state the specter of Americanization or westernization is less disconcerting than, say, the prospects of Taiwanization. And the piece by Larkin highlights how Indian films provide Nigerian men and women with meaningful cultural alternatives to the mass media productions of the West – alternatives that permit them to fashion modern forms of existing in the world without being weighed down by the ideological baggage of western cultural imperialism.

SUGGESTIONS FOR FURTHER READING

Abu-Lughod, Lila
  1995 Movie Stars and Islamic Moralism in Egypt. *Social Text* 42: 53–67.
  1997 The Interpretation of Culture(s) after Television. *Representations* 59: 109–34.

Abu-Lughod, Lila, ed.
  1993   Screening Politics in a World of Nations. Special section. *Public Culture* 5(3): 463–604.
Armbrust, Walter, ed.
  2000   *Mass Mediations: New Approaches to Popular Culture in the Middle East and Beyond*. Berkeley: University of California Press.
Ginsburg, Faye
  1991   Indigenous Media: Faustian Contract or Global Village? *Cultural Anthropology* 6(1): 92–112.
  1997   "From Little Things, Big Things Grow": Indigenous Media and Cultural Activism. In *Between Resistance and Revolution: Cultural Politics and Social Protest*. Richard G. Fox and Orin Starn, eds. Pp. 118–44. New Brunswick, NJ: Rutgers University Press.
Kolar-Panov, Dona
  1997   *Video, War, and the Diasporic Imagination*. London: Routledge.
Mankekar, Purnima
  1999   *Screening Culture, Viewing Politics: An Ethnography of Television, Womanhood, and Nation in Postcolonial India*. Durham, NC: Duke University Press.
Michaels, Eric
  1994   *Bad Aboriginal Art: Tradition, Media, and Technological Horizons*. Minneapolis: University of Minnesota Press.
Miller, Daniel
  1992   The Young and the Restless in Trinidad: A Case of the Local and the Global in Mass Consumption. In *Consuming Technologies*. Roger Silverstone and Eric Hirsch, eds. Pp. 163–82. London: Routledge.
Morley, David, and Kevin Robins
  1995   *Spaces of Identity: Global Media, Electronic Landscapes, and Cultural Boundaries*. London: Routledge.
Naficy, Hamid
  1993   *The Making of Exile Cultures: Iranian Television in Los Angeles*. Minneapolis: University of Minnesota Press.
Rofel, Lisa
  1994   Yearnings: Televisual Love and Melodramatic Politics in Contemporary China. *American Ethnologist* 21(4): 700–22.
Thompson, John B.
  1995   *The Media and Modernity: A Social Theory of the Media*. Stanford: Stanford University Press.
Wilk, Richard R.
  1993   "It's Destroying a Whole Generation": Television and Moral Discourse in Belize. *Visual Anthropology* 5(3–4): 229–44.

13

Hollywood Iconography: A Warlpiri Reading

Eric Michaels

Isolated Aboriginal Australians in the Central Desert region, where traditional language and culture have survived a traumatic hundred-year contact period, began to view Hollywood videotapes in the early 1980s and are now beginning to receive television from the new national satellite, AUSSAT. This situation raises many issues for humanistic research, including questions about the ability of the traditional culture to survive this new electronic invasion. I spent three years living with Warlpiri Aborigines of the Yuendumu community undergoing this imposed transition, partly engaged in applied research and development leading to the birth of an indigenous community television station that challenged government policy and licensing. In the process, I noted what many other field-workers in nonliterate, Third World, and indigenous enclaves are recognizing: that electronic media have proved remarkably attractive and accessible to such people where often print and literacy have not.

We are used to selling literacy as a prosocial, prodevelopment medium. We are used to denigrating video and television as antisocial and repressive. In this essay I want to examine these biases and their sources in an effort to see if our thinking on these matters can't be brought more in line with indigenous peoples' own capabilities and preferences, to lead to a perspective that might prove more helpful and less protectionist.

This is of theoretical interest as well, because we have come to regard the western world's media development sequence as somehow natural: from orality to literacy, print, film, and now electronics. But Aborigines and other "developing" peoples do not conform to this sequence, and produce some very different media histories. For

From *Bad Aboriginal Art: Tradition, Media, and Technological Horizons*, pp. 81–96. Minneapolis: University of Minnesota Press, 1994.

philosophers and historians such as Ong, Innis, or even Lévi-Strauss, who posit special equivalencies between oral and electronic society, these ethnographic cases ought to prove especially revealing.

The Fallacy of Unilineal Evolution of Culture

Despite our best efforts, anthropologists have been unable to undo the racist damage of the unilineal theory of cultural evolution developed by our discipline's founding fathers. The Victorian passion to classify encouraged Edward Burnett Tylor and Lewis Henry Morgan, for example, to borrow from Darwinian biology a vulgar theory of evolution and apply it to the very different problem of cultural variation. This produced the idea that people too unlike the Victorian English represented less evolved stages in a single great chain of culture.

This thinking was then used to justify both a dismissal of the value of non-western cultures and the evangelical urge to civilize heathens and savages. The *reductio ad absurdum* of the fallacy was realized by the 1940s in Nazi cosmology. By then, anthropology had well and truly repudiated the theory of unilinealism and had produced evidence of the authenticity and distinctness of cultural types. The theory of cultural relativism that replaced unilinealism now seems naive, but its basic tenet – that cultures do not arise in a single historical sequence – remains established in the canon of anthropological thought. This revision has not been conveyed to the popular mind, however, or even much to other disciplines. (The problem is a bit like Lamarckism in biology. Despite the evidence, and the theoretical incompatibility with accepted theory, the possibility of inheritance of acquired traits persists, even in biology textbooks that sometimes talk as if the giraffe got its long neck from stretching for leaves; certainly, almost everybody else talks this way.)

Evidence of the persistence of unilinealism is everywhere, from popular thinking about "primitives" (aided and abetted by the etymology of the very word), to Third World development agendas, to a remarkable variety of humanist scholarship. It matters not whether the value-loading is Rousseauesque romanticism, or native advancement, or simple garden variety racism. The point is that very few people believe what anthropology teaches: that indigenous, small-scale traditional societies are not earlier (or degenerate) versions of our own. They are rather differing solutions to historical circumstances and environmental particulars that testify to the breadth of human intellectual creativity and its capacity for symbolization.

In the case of Aboriginal Australians, it may be said that comparative isolation from the network of world cultures for perhaps 40,000 years encouraged a continuous cultural sequence such as is to be found nowhere else. By contrast, modern European culture is assumed to have recent points of disjuncture (the industrial revolution, the world wars, the electronic revolution), so that certain of our own cultural forms may prove only a few generations old. If Aborigines have had 40,000 years (or more) to elaborate a continuous cultural tradition, certainly there must be respects in which this degree of elaboration produces results of extraordinary value. We can hardly justify a claim that Europeans proved more sophisticated than the Aborigines, unless we take the technology and the will to subjugate as privileged measures of human values.

Unilinealism surely persists in our theories of media history. The idea that media are either signals or engines of cultural sequence is familiar at least since Innis and McLuhan. Both, in accounting for European media, simplify histories of development to a unilineal historical causality for the West. And both are guilty of generalizing from here to some universal evolutionary sequence, using "primitive" societies in curious and usually uninformed ways to illustrate their points. But the fault cannot be attributed to these scholars alone. The very commonest terms we use to distinguish our civilization from others – "historical" from "prehistorical" – are semantically loaded with precisely the same ammunition, and refer to writing as the pivotal event in this presumed sequence. It seems telling that when we searched for a new, nonpejorative term to describe the distinction that would contain contemporary nonwriting cultures as well as ancient ones in a class contrastive to our own, "literate" and "preliterate" gained the widest currency. Attempts to unbias the matter by substituting "nonliterate" never really caught on. And the descriptor "oral," itself mostly unexamined, became confused with "tribal," a word whose technical meaning is inappropriate for many of the groups so classified.

All these terms underscore western society's perhaps Judeo-derived cultural emphasis on our own writing skills and reveal our opinion that people who can't write are backward. This very deeply rooted conceptualization is now being challenged as we move from writing to electronic coding as the central symbolizing system of our age. Marshall McLuhan (1962) looked for precedents and claimed that this new age would make us more akin to "preliterate," "tribal" societies. And whether the public read McLuhan or not, it began to panic, aware that something was happening to our reliance on reading. Illiteracy rates appeared to be rising among our own young. The very fabric of culture and society was being sundered, and we risked degenerating into some new form of savagery.

One problem with this literate myopia has been that we haven't paid much attention to what other people do instead of writing, and how information is processed, stored, transmitted, shared, or received in its absence. This paper offers a reconsideration of the sequence of media history in a society that doesn't write, or at least has been believed not to.

Aboriginal Australian Media

Contemporary Aboriginal Australians have generally resisted several generations of concerted literacy teaching, first from Bible-toting missionaries and then from an "enlightened" school system. Wherever their traditional law, language, and culture are viable in Australia, literacy rates remain well below 25 percent, even when bilingual and special education services have been available. I believe this implies that there is something essential to cultural maintenance associated with *not* writing, which is yet to be understood. But in this same population, video recorders have appeared in the last few years, and during my three years of fieldwork I was able to observe the rapid adoption of electronic media by people who rejected print. This provides us with the intriguing but perhaps no longer so unusual situation of a people's moving rapidly from "oral" to electronic society, but bypassing print literacy. Attention to the particulars of both the traditional system and the accommodation to the imposed one offers insights into the limitations of our unexamined theories of unilineal media evolution.

Traditional Aboriginal society did not employ, and presumably did not discover, alphabetic writing. It is probably accurate to classify this culture as "oral," and elsewhere I have discussed at some length some of the nature and consequences of this central feature of the society (Michaels 1985). Yet Aborigines were not without resources for codifying experience and inscribing it in various media.

The Warlpiri people of the Yuendumu community with whom I worked are noted particularly for a rich graphic design tradition described to us at length by Nancy Munn (1970, 1973). This design system extends throughout the central region of Australia and across most of the western Desert, although symbols and techniques vary in particulars from community to community. It appears that the northern coastal communities employed an appreciably different design system, which may correspond partly with the classification of many groups in this area as comprising a language family distinct from most of the rest of the continent. Graphic systems in the southeast quadrant are apparently defunct, along with most of the languages, so that rock art and artifacts contain suggestive clues but probably are insufficient for reconstructing the system as a whole, compared with the opportunity to observe the system in full use, as among the Warlpiri. It will be difficult to generalize accurately from the Warlpiri example, but I suspect that the basic graphic system described for them will prove to apply fairly widely in general outline to many Aboriginal societies.

Warlpiri Graphics: A Traditional Medium

Warlpiri design is a form of inscription that operates quite differently from more familiar writings. It provides neither phonological symbols that combine to record speech (alphabets), nor pictorial glyphs that denote specified objects or ideas (picto/ideographs). If anything, it poses a sort of mediation between the two. It does provide pictographic symbols that are recombined to express ideas and things, but unlike Oriental ideographic writing, and more like alphabets, it abstracts elements so combined and reduces them to comparatively few. Attempts to provide lexicons that associate the symbols with discrete words or even with broad semantic domains prove unsuccessful and ultimately misleading, as Munn seems to have discovered.

The system relies on a fairly discrete but polysemous inventory of graphic symbols: circles, dots, lines, semicircles (additional representational depictions of a specific tree leaf or animal body can be included – attempts by reviewers such as Dubinskas and Traweek (1984) to treat Munn's corpus as an exhaustive generative system are incorrect). These are combined in ground paintings (made of soils, ochres, feathers, flowers), body decoration (ochres, pipeclay, animal fats), utilitarian objects and weapons, and special ceremonial objects (boards, stones, sticks), as well as being painted and carved on caves and rock faces. In recent years, traditional designs have been translated to acrylics and applied to canvas, objects, and murals, and women have developed a batik technique. Most of my experience of Warlpiri graphics comes from assisting in the formative stages of this transition to modern media for sale to contemporary art markets.

The distinctive features of Warlpiri graphics are many: I want to focus on some of the features that contrast this system to contemporary writing systems. This is not the approach taken by Munn, or more recently by her critics. The grammatical structures and social-psychological functions of the design system for the Warlpiri that are discussed by these authors are accepted here as evidence of the richness of that system, which can support various interpretations. Instead, I want to ask, as Havelock (1982) might: What kind of writing system is this? And I will conclude that it is as close to what we call writing (logo/ideographic or alphabetic) as you can get without compromising the authority of human speakers and interpreters – that is, it is a writing in the service of orality. Havelock would call Warlpiri graphics *solipsistic*: they record ideas rather than speech, are evocative rather than denotative, and do not assure a given reading. Unfortunately, such systems do not attract his attention except to remark that others have been most careless in their classification and attentions to such systems, a point well taken.

Some differences between Warlpiri graphics and other writing systems are immediately and visibly apparent. For example, both western alphabets and pictographic writing systems arrange symbols in linear sequence and are biased toward surfaces, such as scrolls and book pages, which frame and support the cumulative string so produced. For Warlpiri, the relationship between the symbol and the surface is more creative. The painter-writer arranges the designs in a manner that relates them to the shape of the object, body, or ground contour on which they are applied. Perhaps this is why Warlpiri graphics get reviewed as art, not writing. But this attention to the inscription surface is appropriate because the contents typically inscribed are Dreaming stories, which are the myths accounting for the land, its objects, and its people. This is like bricolage in Lévi-Strauss's (1966) sense, where components enlisted in the service of an abstract recombinative system still retain their associations with their origins. Warlpiri graphics might be called a "meta-bricolage" because the inscribing media, the messages, and the surfaces to be inscribed are all meaningful bricolage elements of a dynamic intertextuality.

Another way to describe these graphic constructions is as maps. As stories of the landscape they are also images of that landscape. To this extent, spatial relationships of the symbols are constrained by a compositional and topographical system that the artist must respect. For a painting to be deemed a "proper law one," its elements must be in a correct proxemic arrangement. Scale and relationship are conventional, but obviously in terms quite distinct from western linear writing.

The adage "the map is not the territory" may not prove accurate for the Warlpiri. Where the land, a rock face, or even a body is embellished, the result sometimes may be an articulation of actual or perceived features of the thing itself. This is one area in which the transition to portable painted surfaces like canvas took some working out. Early acrylic paintings by traditional artists, for example, do not reduce large designs in scale to smaller surfaces. To achieve complexity in a painting, very large canvases had to be provided. Small canvases tended to depict what proved to be only small sections of large design complexes, like a single window in a computer spreadsheet. Only after some time and experience is an artist likely to scale down large designs to smaller, marketable surfaces.

Because the "icon," the inscription medium, and the surface are all meaningful semiotic elements to be considered in the reading of Warlpiri graphics, it begins to appear that the system contains too many functioning semiotic levels to achieve either the denotation of pictographs or the abstract creativity of alphabets. But there are more levels than this. Eight are listed by Dubinskas and Traweek. (The additional ones are sociolinguistic matters of the performance event in which the design is produced and used.) We have now a problem like the one Bateson (1972) considers exemplified by the croquet game in *Alice in Wonderland*: If the balls, the wickets, and the mallets are all independently motivated moving elements, the game is too unpredictable to play. It is therefore an organic system, not a mechanical one, he concludes. Writing, if it is to accomplish the functions it achieves in the western world, must be a mechanical system, rule-bound and predictable. Reading must become automatic, transparent, or, as Havelock says, "the purely passive instrument of the spoken word." The system must detach itself from its human author and operate more or less equivalently for all literate users. This is precisely what Warlpiri graphics do not attempt. Warlpiri designs remain attached to their authors, as their property, and to paint another's design may be regarded as theft of a particularly troublesome kind.

To call the owners of these designs their authors is not precisely correct, however. Warlpiri cosmology is staunchly conservative. It insists that truth preexists human apprehension. The creation and recreation of the world is an established eternal process; the stories, songs, dances, and designs that contain and explain these truths are likewise unchanging. What one paints or sings or dances is what your fathers and mothers and their fathers and mothers painted, danced, and sang before you (although one may acquire additional information about these truths through revelation or exchange). Your rights to do the same are determined by your position in an elaborately structured system of kin, itself handed down along with these expressive arts from the ancestors themselves.

In terms of what we know of cybernetic systems, this is impossible, a prescription for total cultural entropy. To explain how novelty enters the system, so that it can respond to environmental circumstances and remain viable, we have to step outside the explanations the system offers us.

Ethnology takes this vantage point when it notes ways in which the system does respond to change. Hale (1984) has described how pedagogic events may permit creativity. Wild (1975) has discovered ethnomusicological equivalents. Morphy (1983) has described the public display of secret designs. Rose (1984) has documented a historical account of Captain Cook becoming a legend, and I have analyzed elsewhere elements of a history transforming to Dreaming construction in which videotape has become involved (Michaels and Kelly 1984). What we have not so readily pursued is how our own activity in inscribing these in literate print may prove subversive of these traditions.

It is precisely the point that Warlpiri graphics are a writing system that does not subvert the authority of living people, and does not permit the identification of historical change as western literacy does. Warlpiri graphics oppose publication and public access. They do this partly by limiting denotation, operating instead as an evocative mnemonic, recalling stories without asserting any authorized text or privileged reading. They also do this by restricting access to both the production and viewing of designs. In the "sand stories" described by Munn, which are women's casual accounting of dreams, daily life, and folk tales, the public designs in this ephemeral, shifting medium are mostly illustrative and serve as entertainment and to introduce children to the system. In ritual, sacred and often secret designs are applied to bodies, objects, and the ground, and the rules governing the construction and viewing of these designs are highly constrained, and permit less creativity. Most of these designs are obliterated after the ritual performance. Kolig (1982) observes that the secret designs painted on bodies may remain dimly visible in camp for days afterwards, undecipherable to the uninitiated, but testimony to the existence of secret lore nonetheless. It would seem that the most secret designs, those inscribed on sacred boards (*tjuringa*) and rock faces are also the most permanent. They are tended, and rock paintings and boards are ritually renewed cyclically. These are the only permanent texts, and their locations are rigorously guarded. For uninitiated or otherwise inappropriate people to view these, even accidentally, is punishable by death. Other than these, Warlpiri graphics are mentally stored and sociologically guarded, and emerge only in ceremonial and storytelling performances.

These constraints on ownership and meaning become clear when, in the Yuendumu artists' association studio, we try to identify paintings in preparation for sales. Usually, people refuse to provide the stories for any paintings but their own, or sometimes for designs owned by their kin group. However, understanding our relative naïveté and the economic incentive, sometimes when the painter is out of the community another senior man or woman may try to provide a story for the painting. Remarkably, they sometimes fail, and more often come up with a reading that proves to be at variance with the "correct" version provided later by the painter.

For a full, "correct" version, a male painter will assemble other senior men of his patrimoiety associated with the same or adjacent land as himself, and negotiate the interpretation along with a set of men from the opposite patrimoiety who maintain rights as "witnesses" or caretakers (*kurdungurlu* – see Nash 1982), but not performers or owners of the story.

Glenn (1963), in an insightful but overlooked note, provides an explanation. Comparing Munn's early reports of Warlpiri iconography to "State Department graphics," he suggests that Warlpiri symbols seem much like the unique shorthand that translators and state department staff take of speeches during top-level meetings. These provide a means of recall of speech texts to be transcribed shortly after the event and prove quite accurate. But despite great similarities in the symbols used, rarely could a reporter reconstruct a speech from another's notes. Even the author might have difficulty as time elapsed. The difference between these idiolectic glyphs and Warlpiri symbols is partly in the collectivity of the Warlpiri system, where shared meanings are emergent in the interpretive negotiations that occur in graphic display events very much more than in the text itself.

Munn described these iconographs as devices for mediating symbolically between essential dualities expressed in Warlpiri cosmology, including subject/object, individual/collectivity, and especially Dreaming Time/present time. In the last instance, my analysis suggests there is more than a structuralist abstraction operating here: this writing system functionally reconciles a conservative ideology, where things are always the same, with the contradictory lived evidence of a changing world. If this proves true, then the changes imposed on Aborigines since European invasion must present the most fundamental challenge to this system, and we begin to suspect that the dismal literacy rates represent more than just a failure of effort or will on the part

of teachers or students. The failure of literacy might be seen as a resistance as well –
not to change, but to a threat to the culture's capacity to manage change.

Certainly, many senior people feel this way. They complain about the school and
about writing. They say it makes the kids "cheeky," so they don't listen to their
elders. Especially interesting is the attitude of the middle-aged people who succeeded
at the school in the 1950s and 1960s, before the bilingual program was established.
They say that the bilingual program is holding up the kids, wasting their time with
Warlpiri when they should be learning English, presumably as they did, usually by
rote. (This contradicts all of the evaluation and testing evidence collected at Yuendumu, which demonstrates that English is being learned better and more quickly in
the bilingual program.) Because this generation now operates in a uniquely powerful
role in the community as spokespeople and leaders of the Council and other
European-inspired institutions (and thereby commands and channels substantial
resources), they have been capable of engineering a considerable political challenge
to bilingual education. The fact is, they themselves usually cannot read Warlpiri.
These community leaders often are themselves in an anomalous cultural situation,
and probably take the brunt of "civilization" – ennui, alcoholism, corruption –
harder than anyone else. But from a distance, what we observe is a classical
Aboriginal situation: generations in competition with each other. What is new is
that the resource that the society afforded the most senior people to control –
intellectual property in the form of Dreaming Law – is now subverted by the intellectual property accessible to younger people, through the medium of literacy.

TV and Video

In the last few years, another medium of inscribing and accessing information has
entered Warlpiri life: video and television. Within a year of the first VCR coming to
Yuendumu (and sufficient tape-rental services opening in Alice Springs to support
these), videotape penetration was effectively total in the community. Only nine
VCRs were reported in Aboriginal camps in 1983, for a population of 1,000, but
these meant that essentially every extended family had access to at least one machine
and could view in appropriate groupings, respecting avoidance restrictions and other
traditional constraints on congregating. (When similar contents were screened as
films at the school or church twenty-five years earlier, mass viewing required violations of traditional avoidance and association rules, which produced considerable
stress and often ended in chaos or fighting. This hardly encouraged the acquisition of
cinema literacy.)

My Aboriginal associate and I (Michaels and Japanangka 1984) surveyed the
situation and discovered, among other things, that it was costing at least $5,000
annually to maintain a VCR here, which exceeded annual per capita income. The
difficulties of equipment purchase, maintenance, and program supply in desert
camps 300 km. along a mostly dirt road from the nearest repair or tape-rental
shop proved enormous. Indeed, we found communities without electricity where
ingenious generator installations were rigged up for the first time, not for lights or
heat but to play video. By the summer of 1985, the glow of the cathode ray tube had
replaced the glow of the campfire in many remote Aboriginal settlements. There

could be no question of motivation. Of all the introduced western technologies, only rifles and four-wheel-drive Toyotas had achieved such acceptance.

The situation was reported with predictable alarm by the press, but also by Aborigines themselves (noting no contradiction in the fact that many of the most articulate objectors were themselves video-watchers/owners). People were predicting "culturecide" and claimed that Aborigines appeared helpless to resist this new invasion. The analogy to alcohol was quickly made, and the received wisdom was that the electronic damage was already done, the pristine culture ruined, and so forth. These "facts" were used with great ingenuity to support a wide and contradictory array of agendas, schemes, and proposals, none, as far as I could tell, having much to do with the actual situation.

During this time I was watching Aborigines view video and watching them make video. It became quite clear that here was a situation where the bankruptcy of the "effects" fallacy was amply demonstrated. From my observations, a very different "uses and gratifications" picture emerged than the passive victimization of Aboriginal audiences suggested by the alarmists.

One kind of insight was available by asking my associates what any given videotape was "about," in the most usual, conversational way. This produced what were to me quite extraordinary readings of Hollywood programs I thought I was already familiar with. Additional evidence came from school children and creative writing exercises. Another kind of evidence came from assisting in the production of indigenous Warlpiri video programs along the lines of Worth and Adair's (1973) studies of Navajo filmmaking, and analyzing both production style and product (see Michaels and Kelly 1984). The evidence from these two sources proved complementary and permitted the beginnings of a theory of Aboriginal interpretation of imported television. Here, I will summarize some of the elements of this theory, which I have treated more fully elsewhere (Michaels 1987).

The most suggestive finding was that Aboriginal people were unfamiliar with the conventions, genres, and epistemology of western narrative fiction. They were unable to evaluate the truth value of Hollywood cinema, to distinguish, for example, documentary from romance. This may be because all Warlpiri stories are true, and the inscription and interpretation processes that assure their preservation also ensure their truthfulness (or at least engineer a consensus on what is true at each re-creation, which amounts to the same thing). Thus I was observing the impact of fiction on Aborigines much more than the impact of television *per se*.

Comparisons between Warlpiri story form and imported video fictions demonstrated that, in many instances, content (what is supplied in the narrative) and context (what must be assumed) are so different from one system to the other that they might be said to be reversed. For example, Warlpiri narrative will provide detailed kinship relationships between all characters as well as establishing a kinship domain for each. When Hollywood videos fail to say where Rocky's grandmother is, or who's taking care of his sister-in-law, Warlpiri viewers discuss the matter and need to fill in what for them is missing content. By contrast, personal motivation is unusual in Aboriginal story; characters do things because the class (kin, animal, plant) of which they are members is known to behave this way. This produces interesting indigenous theories, for example, of national character to explain behavior in *Midnight Express* or *The A-Team*. But it is equally interesting that it tends to ignore narrative exposition and character development, focusing instead on dramatic action (as do Aboriginal stories themselves).

Violence, for instance, described by some as TV's cheap industrial ingredient overlaid on narratives mainly to bring viewers' attention to the screen for ultimately commercial purposes, is for Aboriginal viewers the core of the story. The motivation and character exposition that the European viewer is expected to know, to explain why someone was mugged or robbed or blown up, is missing. It is more likely in Aboriginal accounts to be supplied by what we would consider supernatural reasons, consistent with the reasons misfortunes befall people in Aboriginal cosmology.

These brief examples should make it clear that it will be very difficult to predict the effects of particular television contents on traditional Aboriginal audiences without a well-developed theory of interpretation. To advance a theory of interpretation, it may be helpful to consider now what kind of writing system television is that makes it so accessible and attractive to these people whose traditional preference was for writing systems of the sort explained above. An analysis of the videotapes the Warlpiri made themselves provides some insight.

Warlpiri videotape is at first disappointing to the European observer. It seems unbearably slow, involving long landscape pans and still takes that seem semantically empty. Much of what appears on screen, for better or worse, might easily be attributed to naive filmmaking. Finally, the entire corpus of 300 hours of tape shot at Yuendumu is all documentary-type "direct cinema." The only exceptions, when events were constructed and people performed expressly for the camera, were the result of my intervention for experimental purposes.

Yet Warlpiri audiences view these tapes with great attention and emotion, often repeatedly, beyond what could be expected from a fascination with "home movies." If this is attributable to novelty, it has yet to wear off in the three years I've been involved. In fact, the limits to some tapes' lifespan are the limits of the lifespan of the characters. A mortuary rule prohibiting the mention of the names of dead people now applies as well to their recorded images, which means that when a tape contains pictures of someone deceased, that tape is no longer shown.

Producers and viewers will describe the tape, its purposes and meanings, in ways not immediately apparent from the recorded images themselves. For example, proper videotape production for a particular story may require the presence of several families including many people. But not only do most of these people not appear on the tape, but a proportion of them (related to the on-screen "owner" of the story through the mother's patrilineage) must not appear on screen. They may, however, operate the camera. This is consistent with equivalent rules in ceremonial performance. But what attracts our attention is that everybody seems to know how that tape was made and whether these rules were observed, and therefore if the tape is a "proper" and "true" story, without any apparent evidence on the tape itself. Similarly, what are to the European observer semantically empty landscape pans are explained by Aboriginal producers and viewers as full of meaning. The camera in fact traces "tracks" or locations where ancestors, spirits, or historical characters traveled. The apparently empty shot is quite full of life and history to the Aboriginal eye. The electronic inscription process may be said to be operating for the Warlpiri in a way not unlike their graphic system, providing mnemonic, evocative symbols amenable to interpretation and historical accuracy when viewed in the proper social and cultural context.

Video-viewing is a very active interpretive social event, particularly in groups, made possible by private ownership of VCRs. In fact, ownership of VCRs is not quite private in the European sense, and our early survey determined that these machines were corporate purchases and circulated along traditional exchange/obligation routes, usually within families. This means that viewing groups, as described above, are appropriate assemblages of kin, and provide a suitable setting for events of social interpretation, not unlike what was described for Warlpiri artists explaining their paintings. One interesting difference between groups viewing Warlpiri productions and those viewing European ones is the placement of the elders. With the former, elders sit toward the front, turned half around to interpret to the younger people. With Hollywood videos, the children sit in front, often interpreting and explaining to their elders.

Conclusions

Warlpiri Aborigines have perhaps discovered some comfortable analogies between their experience of video production and viewing and their own traditional graphic system. For Warlpiri viewers, Hollywood videos do not prove to be complete, authoritative texts. Rather, they are very partial accounts requiring a good deal of interpretive activity on the part of viewers to supply contents as well as contexts with which to make these stories meaningful. When home video made it possible for Warlpiri to control the place and membership of viewing groups, it became possible to assemble the small, interpretive communities that are associated with other performances in which stories are told and their associated graphics displayed. At this point, video-viewing became a most popular and persuasive camp activity.

By contrast, reading and literature did not. While this article has not expanded a theory of literacy except by contrast to Warlpiri graphics, a historical point is worth making. Current literary criticism now questions the notion that there are correct or even privileged readings of literary texts; reader-centered criticism claims that readers will make diverse interpretations. But the Warlpiri were introduced to literature through that most privileged of texts, the Christian Bible, by missionaries who took the Calvinist position that every word therein had one and only one "commonsense" meaning. Thus literature may well be associated by Aborigines with a dogmatism, a certitude, a sense of revealed and inscribed truth that would prove subversive of their own Dreaming history and law. That history and law required a different mode of writing to maintain the continuity of its authority.

The evidence from Warlpiri graphics and Warlpiri video proves useful to the reexamination of the "oral/electronic" analogy proposed by my media historians. It would be important in this reexamination to note first that some "oral" societies, for example the Warlpiri, do have writing of a particular sort: a writing subservient to, and in the service of, oral performance and living authorities. The writings that became the source of western literacy are distinguished functionally from "oral writing" in that they subverted and replaced orality as the interpreting mode of symbolization for society.

We may now question whether written texts are in fact so authoritative as we have been used to considering them. But we raise this question at a time when another inscription system competes for centrality in our information processing and imaginative symbolizing: electronics. It seems particularly interesting that this new inscription process is proving more accessible, and perhaps less culturally subversive, to people in those remaining enclaves of oral tradition. The most useful first question to ask may be: "What about their writing systems is like electronic writing?", rather than "How is their society like ours?"

At least one result of this kind of inquiry is to suggest some useful considerations for dealing with commercial video narratives and emergent television genres. Although historically the sources for plot and character are found in earlier novel and literary forms, Warlpiri viewers, and perhaps now many others, put video fictions to quite different uses and make quite different sense of them. What Warlpiri viewers require is a good deal of visual and visceral action, a rich familial and kinship context, and a means of combining these into a classificatory universe whose truth is partly in the structures they can produce with these elements and partly in the opportunities the texts provide for negotiation and social discourse. As western television develops its own conventions, themes, and genres, reaching out for the vastest pancultural (or acultural) mass audiences, it is clearly offering more of these kinds of materials to its viewers. To the horror of literacy-biased critics, it is stripping away cultural denotation, culture-specific motivations and psychologies, and their place in character development. Its commitment to "inscribed truth" is gone. Indeed, we might seem to be realizing Lévi-Strauss's prophecy:

This universe made up of meanings no longer appears to us as a retrospective witness of a time when: "...*le ciel sur la terre marchait et respirait dans un peuple de dieux*," and which the poet evokes only for the purpose [of asking] whether it is to be regretted. This time is now restored to us, thanks to the discovery of a universe of information where the laws of savage thought reign once more: "heaven" too, "walking on earth" among a population of transmitters and receivers whose messages, while in transmission, constitute objects of the physical world and can be grasped from without and within.[1]

That video now proves acceptable and accessible in a way that alphabetic literature did not could prove to be partly a transitional feature of Aborigines' recent encounter with the medium. Warlpiri-produced video may preserve these features, if its unique properties are recognized and encouraged (a difficult proposition when overzealous "professional" trainers intercede, and media institutions force competition between indigenous and imported programs). It is likely that Warlpiri people will develop greater sophistication in European genres and the interpretation of imported narrative fiction that will bring them closer to European readings. In so doing, it may be that the "gaps" I have identified will fill up, and the medium will become more denotative and less evocative and, finally, less Warlpiri.

It could prove promising that the most popular genres appear to be action/adventure, soaps, musicals, and slapstick. Whatever our educated palates may think of these forms, they have advantages in the context of this analysis. As the least character-motivated, most formulaic fictions, they may encourage active interpretation and cross-culturally varied readings. The trend in popular TV and international video marketing continues to be in favor of those entertainments in which universal familial relationships are highlighted, action is dominant, and culture-specific references are either minimal or unnecessary for the viewer's enjoyment. From this perspective, it would seem difficult to see in the introduction of imported video and television programs the destruction of Aboriginal culture. Such a claim can only be made in ignorance of the strong traditions and preferences in graphics, the selectivity of media and contents, and the strength of interpretation of the Warlpiri. Such ignorance arises best in unilineal evolutionism.

NOTE

This paper was presented at the Second International Television Studies Conference, British Film Institute, London, 1986. My appreciation to the Australian Institute for Aboriginal Studies for funding to undertake this study.

1 Lévi-Strauss, *The Savage Mind*, p. 267, quoting Alfred de Musset [from "Rolla," in *Poesies nouvelles, 1836–1852*, Paris: Charpentier, 1908].

REFERENCES

Bateson, G. 1972. "Why Do Things Have Outlines?" *Steps to an Ecology of Mind*. New York: Ballantine.

Dubinskas, F., and S. Traweek. 1984. "Closer to the Ground: A Reinterpretation of Warlpiri Iconography." *Man* 19(1).

Glenn, E. 1963. "Walbiri and State Department Graphics." *American Anthropologist* 65: 1113–35.

Hale, K. 1984. "Remarks on Creativity in Aboriginal Verse." In *Problems and Solutions*, ed. J. Kassler and J. Stubington. Sydney: Hale & Iremonger.

Havelock, E. 1982. *The Literate Revolution in Greece and its Cultural Consequences*. Princeton, NJ: Princeton University Press.

Kolig, E. 1982. *The Silent Revolution*. Philadelphia: Institute for the Study of Human Issues.

Lévi-Strauss, C. 1966. *The Savage Mind*. Chicago: University of Chicago Press.

McLuhan, M. 1962. *The Gutenberg Galaxy*. Toronto: University of Toronto Press.

Michaels, E. 1985. "Constraints on Knowledge in an Economy of Oral Information." *Current Anthropology* 26(4): 505–10.

——. 1987. "The Indigenous Languages of Video and Television." In *Visual Explorations of the World: Selected Proceedings of the International Visual Communication Conference*, ed. Martin Taureg and Jay Ruby. Aachen: Rader Verlag.

Michaels, E., and L. Japanangka Granites. 1984. "The Cost of Video at Yuendumu." *Media Information Australia* 32: 17–25.

Michaels, E., and F. Kelly. 1984. "The Social Organisation of an Aboriginal Video Workplace." *Australian Aboriginal Studies* 1: 26–34.

Morphy, H. 1983. "'Now you understand': An Analysis of the Way Yolngu Have Used Sacred Knowledge to Retain their Autonomy." In *Aborigines, Land and Land Rights*, ed. N. Peterson and M. Langton. Canberra: Australian Institute of Aboriginal Studies.

Munn, N. D. 1970. "The Transformation of Subjects into Objects in Warlpiri and Pitjantjat-jara Myth." In *Australian Aboriginal Anthropology*, ed. R. Berndt. Nedlands, WA: University of Western Australia Press, pp. 141–63.

——. 1973. *Walbiri Iconography*. Ithaca, NY: Cornell University Press.

Nash, D. 1982. "An Etymological Note on Warlpiri Kurdungurlu." In *Languages of Kinship in Aboriginal Australia*, ed. J. Heath et al. Sydney: University of Sydney Press.

Rose, D. B. 1984. "The Saga of Captain Cook." *Australian Aboriginal Studies* 2.

Wild, S. 1975. "Warlpiri Music and Dance in their Social and Cultural Nexus." Unpublished Ph.D. thesis, University of Indiana, Bloomington.

Worth, S., and J. Adair. 1973. *Through Navajo Eyes: An Exploration in Film Communication and Anthropology*. Bloomington: Indiana University Press.

14

Mass Media and Transnational Subjectivity in Shanghai: Notes on (Re)Cosmopolitanism in a Chinese Metropolis

Mayfair Mei-hui Yang

In thinking about the history of the Roman empire, Marshall McLuhan noted that writing and paved roads brought about "the alteration of social groupings, and the formation of new communities" (McLuhan 1994: 90). They enabled the formation of an empire that broke down the old Greek city-states and feudal realms in favor of centralized control at a distance. A similar process can be seen in the history of the Chinese empire, where writing enabled the bureaucracy to hold together diverse ethnic and linguistic groupings. However, it is with modernity and its new mass media that local and kinship identities come to be radically dissolved by a more powerful national space of identity. Anthony Giddens has noted that an important feature of modernity is the "disembedding of social systems," or the "'lifting out' of social relations from local contexts of interaction and their restructuring across infinite spans of time-space" (Giddens 1990: 21). In twentieth-century China, the mass media's disembedding operations have constituted first a new national community and then a powerful state subjectivity. This essay is an initial inquiry into a *third* disembedding process: the reemergence of a transnational Chinese global media public and its effects on the modernist project of the nation-state.

Benedict Anderson's (1991) thesis that a nation, a unit of identification larger than a village, local community, or region, could be conceptualized only through the medium of mass print such as newspapers and novels is borne out by China's early-

From *Ungrounded Empires: The Cultural Politics of Modern Chinese Transnationalism*, ed. Aihwa Ong and Donald M. Nonini, pp. 287–319. New York: Routledge, 1997.

twentieth-century experience, in which print culture was intricately tied in with May fourth, republican, and Communist nationalism.[1] However, the point I would like to make is that the mass media are vehicles for imagining not only the nation but also the larger space beyond the national borders – that is, the wider world. This transnational aspect of media must not be neglected, because it harbors potentials for liberation from hegemonic nationalism and statism. Although both nationalism and internationalism composed the narratives of modernity, nationalism exerted a much more powerful influence, as it became implicated in nation-state territorial imperatives. However, with postmodernity, increasing transnational electronic linkages "all presage a delocalized, potentially nomadic future" (Friedland 1994: 15) which can offer postmodern challenges to state modernity. In post-Mao China, what can be discerned is a process in which the modern mass media, which had been (and continues to be) a central constitutive force for state projects of modernity and nation-state, has now also begun to construct a Chinese transnational imaginary world order.

Since media provide ways for audiences to traverse great distances without physically moving from local sites, they are crucial components of transnationalism. In China in the 1980s and 1990s, the media increasingly enable national subjects to inhabit trans-spatial and trans-temporal imaginaries that dissolve the fixity and boundedness of historical nationhood and state territorial imperatives. What is occuring via the mass media in China today is no longer the simple picture of a third-world culture "locked in a life-and-death struggle with first-world cultural imperialism" (Jameson 1987: 68) but a more complex variegated process of eager accommodation, appropriation, and resistance to foreign cultures. What can be detected is a culture now more confidently and creatively constructing a "third space" (Bhabha 1994) of transational Chinese identity through interaction with Hong Kong and Taiwanese mass culture. From a nationalist anticolonial culture, what is now starting to get created is a Chinese "traveling culture" (Clifford 1992) reaching out around the globe.

In recent scholarly literature, writings on diaspora comprise a body of work that deals with the traversing of vast distances of space (Chow 1993; Clifford 1994; Rouse 1991, 1995b). They chart an important phenomenon of modernity: the global movements of populations, especially from postcolonial places to the West. However, most of this writing is about how postcolonials become minorities in the West and the multicultural changes and challenges they introduce to western hegemony, national identity, and academic curricula. While challenging the West, there is still a focus on the West as the central place of concern, the primary actor, and the key place of action. There is another important spatial transformation taking place among those who have stayed within their homelands, because a similar displacement is taking place there – people in imaginary travel increasingly look outward and participate via mass media in what is going on with their fellow nationals in other parts of the world. This essay will document another reaction to colonialism besides nationalism: the increasing cosmopolitanism of the homeland.

The experiences of modernity and mass-media-induced consciousness in China challenge at least three common conflations dominant in western critical theory. These conflations are those of *nation and state, state and capitalism, capitalism and the West*. In China we find that in each pair, the two processes have not always been the same, nor are they necessarily parallel; rather they have often been in conflict with each other. Understanding twentieth-century China requires the deconstruction of these ahistorical conflations, whose origins stem from the western experience, for an approach emphasizing the historical fluidity of different forces that wax and wane, combine, diverge, counteract, and overpower each other (Deleuze 1980).

Shanghai's History as Media Capital[2]

As a treaty port opened up for trade and shipping with the West in 1842, Shanghai's history was inextricably tied up with the history of western (and Japanese) colonialism as well as the development of native and western capitalism in China.[3] Its western influence meant that Shanghai always maintained a certain distance from the political centers of an agrarian bureaucratic state order, first the Qing imperial government and then the republican Kuomintang (Ding 1994). In the 1920s and 1930s, before the devasting dual processes of Japanese imperialist invasion in 1937 and the Chinese civil war, the city was the most urban, industrial, and cosmopolitan city in all of Asia.

In this bustling metropolis, there emerged what one historian has called "a new tradition, that of Chinese modernism" (Bergere 1981: 2). Shanghai saw the birth of a new modern, urban, commercial, and popular culture that, despite its foreign influences, was nevertheless Chinese. Shanghai was home to China's main publishing companies and printing presses, and to the greatest number of newspapers and magazines in the country. The city was also the cradle of a dynamic Chinese film industry in the 1920s and 1930s and had China's largest movie-going audiences (Leyda 1972).[4] Virtually all of the major film companies in the country were established in this city, and Shanghai films were distributed not only to all other regions of the country but also in Southeast Asia.

After the Communist victory, even an open port such as Shanghai became like the rest of China: closed to most foreign and overseas contact. While Shanghai continued to be the major industrial center creating wealth for the whole nation, urban cosmopolitan cultural life saw a radical curtailment when, in the new ethos of revolutionary asceticism, it came to be labeled a decadent "bourgeois culture." With tight fiscal and political control by the center, the city focused on heavy industry rather than cultural production.

The Spatialization of National and State Subjects

Too often in western academic discourse, *nation* and *state* are used interchangeably. Two exceptions are Arjun Appadurai (1990, 1993), who argues that diaspora populations around the world comprise emerging "post-nations" that deterritorialize states, and Katherine Verdery (1994), who has shown how, after the collapse of a super-state such as the Soviet Union, (re)emergent ethnic nationalist imaginaries (whose subjects are spread out across different East European states) seek to define and bolster themselves territorially with new and separate state apparatuses. My own concern to distinguish between nation and state stems from a different historical situation as well as from as a different set of political and theoretical concerns.

Rather than a nation in search of a state, I think that the Chinese situation in the twentieth century requires that we examine how a powerful state apparatus came to overcode itself onto the nation, and how a reemergent nation or alternative community has now begun to decode or elude the state.

In China's transition from a traditional dynastic order to a modern nation-state, there was a "flattening" of a centripetal and hierarchical social realm, whose borders were hazy and indistinct, into a novel social space defined by horizontal linkages of comradeship inside and by distinct outer borders (Anderson 1991: 15; Chun 1994b; Foster 1991: 253). In the first three decades of the twentieth century, through the print medium, the urban reading public was exposed to the literature and culture of the West and Japan (Chow 1960) and came to share a growing alarm at the desperate poverty, "ignorance," and "backwardness" of China as compared to these foreign lands. At the same time, print also fanned the growing nationalist outrage at the imperialism of these same countries. The task of "saving the nation" (*jiuguo*) in the Darwinian struggle for existence between nations became a rallying cry that interpellated (Althusser 1971) patriotic subjects into the project of making the Chinese nation "prosperous and strong" (*fuqiang*).[5]

There is a historical significance to the fact that China's opening to the world was forced and its entrance into the world of nations was not on equal terms. China's encounter with global forces was disastrous for cultural self-esteem, and out of this was born nationalism. The violations of the empire's territorial space, first by western powers in the Opium Wars and Treaty Port systems of the mid-nineteenth century, and then in the Japanese seizure of Shandong in 1914, annexation of Manchuria, and invasion of East China in 1937, propelled this traumatized new nation-state to close its doors for the first three decades after the Communist revolution of 1949. There followed the tight sealing of state borders. Outside contact was limited to government exchanges with the Soviet bloc and the non-aligned third world. Foreign visitors and returning overseas Chinese were relatively rare, as were emigrants leaving China. Few foreign films were shown; reading foreign literature was also frowned upon as submitting oneself to bourgeois culture; even letter-writing to people in foreign countries was severely curtailed. During the Cultural Revolution, it was politically dangerous to have "overseas connections" (*haiwai guanxi*) in one's family or personal past, and those who tried to flee across the borders in south China were often executed as "traitors" (*pantu*).

The first half of the twentieth century in China saw the emergence of nationalist consciousness and a concern for cultural survival in a colonial context. At the same time, the new nation sought to disengage itself from an older imperial state order and dynastic system. With the strengthening of the Kuomintang, a new state organization captured and harnessed nationalism to the project of the state. With the Communist revolution in the second half of the century, nation and state became fully coterminous, and the state took charge of all aspects of life. Beginning with Mao's historic talks at the Yan'an Forum on Literature and Art in 1942, all cultural and artistic production was harnessed to the task of state indoctrination and the upholding of party policies. Henceforth, nationalism as a critical discourse became a state discourse (A 1994). The Maoist period can be seen as the full appropriation of nationalism by the state, in which nation and state came to be fully integrated into a single entity.

By the mid-1950s, all private publishing firms, newspaper companies, radio stations, and film companies had come under centralized state administration, so that all the paths and networks of print and electronic media led to Beijing. The Central People's Broadcasting Station was established in Beijing in December 1949. All provincial, municipal, and local radio stations were required to transmit its news, commentary, and political programs (Chang 1989: 55) in Mandarin, the national language. Film in the Maoist era can be described in Walter Benjamin's (1969: 242) terms as both the politicization of art and the aestheticization of politics, but the former was more dominant than the latter, since aesthetic standards were often deemphasized (Clark 1984). The audience was constructed as an undifferentiated monolithic whole of "the masses" or "the people," so that gone were the variety and diversity of styles and tastes in the arts. During the Cultural Revolution, audiences across the country were restricted to a repertoire of nine "revolutionary model operas" (yangbanxi). In Maoist China, the mass media helped create a homogeneity of culture that played down regional identities, promoted the voice of the central government in Beijing in Mandarin, and reiterated the same state messages in all media, whether radio, newspapers, or film.

In almost all films of the Maoist era, family ties and personal sentiments were played down in favor of national and class commitments. The elevation of class also erased gender and gender discourse, as shown by Meng Yue's (1993) analysis of how *White Haired Woman* transformed the rape of a peasant woman Xi-er from a gender issue into a class issue. Film scholar Dai Jinhua (1995) has also noted the strange paradox whereby the Chinese film industry boasts many women film directors, but virtually none of their films have a female perspective. Although the state championed women's liberation, it did so by substituting for women's discourse a state discourse that was no longer as patriarchal but was part of a new masculinist national project (Yang 1995).

Running through many media messages was an "us vs. them" construction in which the sacred national space is constantly being threatened (as in the United States in the 1950s) and encroached upon by foreign interests and internal enemies who serve them. A binary classificatory system was set up of pure/impure and inside/outside forces of peasant and landlord, native and foreigner, in which the class opposition was made parallel with the native/foreign opposition as both struggle over the space of the state.[6] Thus, along with the centralization of all media in the Maoist era, the national identity that was first constructed by print capitalism in the early twentieth century came to coincide with the contours and logic of the state.

Mass Media Development in Post-Mao Shanghai

It can be said without exaggeration that in the post-Mao era there has been an explosion in the development of mass media. If the Maoist period can be described as a period in which the mass media sought to level, uniformitize, and homogenize the Chinese public, the post-Mao period can be said to have brought about the pluralization, differentiation, and stratification of media publics according to class, educational level, region, locality, gender, occupation, and leisure interests, fragmenting the state's mass public.

In Shanghai, radio culture was transformed with the establishment of the new Eastern Broadcast Station (*Dongfang Guangbotai* or DFBS) in January 1993, which quickly drew listeners away from the more "official" (*guanfang*) Shanghai Broadcast Station. When I first listened to this station in June 1993, I could not believe that I was in China. The Chinese media culture I was familiar with elsewhere in the country still featured broadcasters with solemn voices speaking in the standard Mandarin dialect about portentous affairs of the state. On DFBS, the serious voice and style had changed into a soft, fast-paced chatty style resembling that of Taiwan media culture. Programming content had switched to more market news, international news, and Shanghai local news (as opposed to Beijing news); there were interviews with Taiwanese, Hong Kong, and domestic stars of the film and popular music scene, and several times a day the stock market quotes would be read. What was different about DFBS was that all of its programming was live and it constantly solicited call-in comments and opinions from its listeners, so that all day long the voices of ordinary people talking about their everyday problems and dreams, in Shanghainese accents, filled the air (Bao 1993). I would walk into someone's home or get into a taxi, and eight times out of ten, this station would be playing in the background. A further novelty was that several late-night programs brought issues of the private sphere, such as marriage, romance, and the hitherto unmentionable topic of sexual life, to the public arena of radio.

At Shanghai Film Studio, the career of Xie Jin, its most well-known and successful director, spans the entire period from 1949 to the present. His films have always followed the changing Party policies and political vicissitudes of the country; however, in *The Last Aristocracy* (*Zuihou de guizu*), a 1987 film, Xie for the first time departs from politics and takes on the new theme of personal identity and cultural displacement in a foreign land. *The Last Aristocracy* embodies the very transformation of media addressed in this essay: a movement away from affairs of state toward personal issues and transnational wanderings of the imagination. The film expresses both the territorial restlessness and the longing for home experienced by a cosmopolitan Chinese woman whose identity is unmoored from her homeland. She flees war-torn Shanghai to study abroad. Prevented from returning home because of the Communist victory, she is cast adrift in a foreign land (the United States) to lead a lonely and alienated life. The nostalgia for old Shanghai is evident not only in the 1940s setting but also in the fact that the story is based on a novel of the same title by the Taiwanese ex-mainlander Kenneth Pai (Bai Xianyong), who now resides in Santa Barbara. The fact that the film was also shot on location in the United States and Venice, Italy, also exemplifies the growing transnational forays of Chinese media production. This combination of reconnecting with Old Shanghai, with Taiwan, and with the overseas world encapsulates the transformation of the imaginary taking place in Shanghai today.

New Technological Media and Publics

At least four important new media technologies have now become widely available: the cassette recorder, the telephone, the television, and the VCR. Two significant changes have accompanied the widespread adoption of these new media forms.

First, in their contexts of use or reception, they have greatly expanded the private, personal and familial spheres. Take the telephone. In the Maoist era, telephones were very few and found mainly in work units, to be used in a public context for public business. Nowadays, of the 39 million telephones found in China in 1995 (up from 6.26 million in 1985), 70 percent are residential phones (*China News Daily*, May 17, 1995). For those who lived in China in the early 1980s, it is astounding to find that in some prosperous coastal cities today, 25 percent of the population now owns a phone. Urban neighborhood phone stands and booths have also multiplied, making it increasingly easy to transact personal business and weave countless *guanxi* or personal networks independent of state administrative organizations.

Whereas in the Maoist era information usually came from a centralized source, such as official newspapers and editorials, state documents (*wenjian*), or the radio, new media such as the telephone, cassette recorder, and VCR tend to decentralize information sources, making information flow more along the lines created by personal relationships (cassettes and videotapes are often circulated via personal and *guanxi* networks). In the Maoist era, state directives and didactic art were usually received in collective contexts: state directives were transmitted and newspaper editorials were often read in political study group sessions at the work unit; filmgoing was often organized as a work unit collective outing; revolutionary operas were viewed by the whole community in local theaters. Television viewing now, however, takes place in the private sphere among family, neighbors, and friends. Whereas in the public state-monitored context, one had to show one's acceptance of what was received from the state, in a private context of reception, one could also debate, mock, or reject the messages with one's family and friends, thus reducing the capacity for state media to sustain state subjects.

Another significance of these new media is that they have brought about increasing transnational connections for ordinary people. In the late 1970s and early 1980s, when cassette recorders and tapes first became widespread, they were primarily used to listen to music and to practice a foreign language such as English. Anyone wishing to listen to the sweet crooning voice and love songs of Taiwan's popular female singer Deng Lijun (Gold 1993: 909) had to have access to a cassette recorder because her songs were not played on the official radio stations. At that time most tapes were smuggled in from offshore, very similarly to how it is done today with videotapes. Now that telephone service has been established with Hong Kong, Taiwan, and virtually all countries of the world, those with relatives abroad can be constantly connected with life overseas. Via telephone, cassette, and videotape, they can be transported across the borders to be with their kin.

The television documentary *Their Home is Shanghai* (*Jia zai Shanghai*) illustrates well the role of the media in keeping people connected to their kin or fellow Chinese nationals in foreign lands. Its gripping portrayal of the lives and thoughts of Shanghainese studying and laboring in Tokyo emptied the streets in Shanghai as viewers crammed in front of televisions when it first aired in early 1994 (Guo 1994: 48). Shot on location in Tokyo by a Shanghai Television Station crew led by woman filmmaker Wang Xiaoping, with most of the interviews conducted in Shanghainese dialect, it made documentary more vivid and fascinating than fiction. In part 3 there is a poignant interview of a Shanghainese man who lives by himself in a cramped apartment and works three jobs a day to send money to his family back in Shanghai.

He sits on the floor watching his daughter, whom he has not seen for four years, on a videotape the camera crew has brought from Shanghai, and tells the interviewer that he calls home once a week. Meanwhile, the Shanghai audience watching him being interviewed on their own screens collectively and vicariously experience not only his separation from and longing for home but also the foregrounding of his Shanghai-nese identity over his national identity in a foreign land, since he speaks in Shanghaiese. Furthermore, in a more subtle way, they also experience his displacement from the confines and strictures of the Chinese state and the habitus of state subjects.

The Post-Mao Transnational Disembedding of Culture

The post-Mao era can be seen as a period in which a decoupling of nation from state takes place, so that Chinese identity becomes more culturally defined instead of defined only in terms of the state. While capitalism has brought back many disturbing tendencies to a state socialist society, such as increasing income disparities, the return of prostitution and child labor, and government corruption, it has also started the transnationalization of Chinese identity out of the confines of the state. What is developing in urban China, and especially in cities along the eastern seaboard such as Shanghai, is a fascination with and a hunger to learn about the world outside of the state borders. The new mass media both cater to and create this interest and longing for the outside world, through linking up with the market economy and its global forays. The new Oriental Television Station (*Dongfang dianshitai*), which started broadcasting in Shanghai, is an example of this change in that its revenues come mainly from advertising, and it caters more to popular taste than the more official station. No longer relying on state subsidies, the media become increasingly independent of the state and dependent on the market.

Critiques of capitalism often assume that the logic and interests of *state* and *capital* are the same, or that they are coextensive. For advanced capitalist systems such as those in the United States and Japan, I would agree with Roger Rouse that "by and large, corporations and the state, as differently mediated forms of bourgeois practice, have worked together" (Rouse 1995a: 368) to serve as crucial media for a ruling bloc. The current situation in China of a transition from a state redistributive power to a new social form is different from this in that the moments of antagonism between state and capital are more evident and structurally deeper than they are in the United States and Japan. There is a major difference between theorizing a welfare state such as the United States and theorizing the state in state socialist systems. The Maoist state was not a welfare state in a capitalist mode of production, where the state regulates competition, assuages class tensions, and cleans up the environment. It was a system in which the state itself was the form that mode of production took, controlling not only production and distribution but also the determination of needs.[7] Therefore in the current period, when market forces are being introduced, the encounter between capital and state in state socialism will be marked by more conflict than that between capital and the welfare state.

What we find in post-Mao China is a new, complex political economy in which state and capital both converge and diverge at different moments. On the one hand, it is the state that initiates and sustains the new market-oriented policies and which eagerly lays out the welcome mat to overseas capital. On the other hand, the state also finds that the new forces it has unleashed often have a logic quite threatening to its own desire of fixing culture within territorial borders. The state redistributive economy of the Maoist period was a process whereby the state made the economy operate according to the logic of the state – just the reverse of what is going on in the United States on Capitol Hill, where the Republicans are engineering a deeper capitalist penetration of the state. It seems to me that since state logic classifies the population to enable it to measure, account for, and control it, therefore it would favor stability and a certain rigidity. This would be at odds with the nature of capitalism, which is restless and fluid in its class conflicts, constant overturning of productive forces, search for profit and new markets, and breaking up of established social relations. Marx himself pointed out the corrosive power of capitalism toward all traditional societies and values. What makes capitalism a deterritorializing culture is "the encounter between flows of convertible wealth owned by capitalists and a flow of workers possessing nothing more than their labor capacity" (Deleuze and Guattari 1983: 140) and the flows of desire which consumer capitalism unleashes. Just as "capitalism has haunted all forms of society [and] haunts them as their terrifying nightmare, [because of] the dread they feel of a flow that would elude their codes" (p. 140), so capitalism is often threatening to state-centered systems and the logic of state order and regulation over a delimited space.

There are countless examples of this tension between state and capital in the cultural realm (M. Yang 1993). Until 1995, the state limited the number of foreign (including Hong Kong and Taiwanese) films imported into the country to sixty films per year, chosen by the state film distribution bureaucracy. In the early 1990s there developed a widespread craving for American Oscar-winning films, which were seldom shown in Chinese theaters. Video technology solved the problem through the illegal private circulation of videotapes, most of which were smuggled in from Hong Kong or by Chinese returning from overseas. Although it was illegal to bring in videotaped programs from abroad, airport customs inspections were often lax. Often these videos were barely viewable, being second- and third-generation copies already viewed countless times before. College students were perhaps the biggest audience for such videos, and student entrepreneurs acquired videos and laser discs through various means and showed them in campus theaters on large video screens for four yuan a person. Sometimes there were no subtitles, but only a translator at the front of the cinema. At times it seemed that the films had been recorded on video directly in a Hong Kong cinema, because the sound quality was bad, and once in a while one could even see the heads of the Hong Kong audience on the screen or hear their laughter. *Lady Chatterley's Lover* was shown on one campus, but since it was considered a pornographic or "yellow film" (*huangse pian*), the police raided the crowded theater and stopped the showing halfway through the film. As a result of allowing Hollywood films to be shown in theaters, China's cinema attendance in 1995, especially in Shanghai, increased for the first time since its steady decline from the mid-1980s, almost doubling 1994 attendance (*China News Daily*, January 23, 1996).[8]

With television came the greatest exposure to the outside world and to the "culture industries" of Asia, the West, and other places. The Chinese urban television audience was only formed in the first half of the 1980s, and the rural audience in the second half (Zhang 1992). However, the growth of the television industry is quite astounding in this short period, contributing to the decline in the film audience. Already in 1986, 95 percent of all urban families owned at least one television set (Lull 1991: 23). Imported television programs from Taiwan, Hong Kong, the United States, and Japan (in that order), broadcasts of transnational sports and competitions, and TV guided tours of foreign cities all respond to a keen appetite on the part of the Chinese audience.[9] Many people have told me that when a domestically produced show (*guochan pian*) comes on screen, they or their children immediately change channels or turn off the television without bothering to check what it is about. Zhou Yigong, a division head at one of the two Shanghai TV stations, informed me that they often receive directives from the Municipal Party Propaganda Department to decrease their advertising for Hong Kong and Taiwan songs and TV shows, and to avoid showing them during prime time (*huangjin shijian*).

The Chinese audience's interest in the world outside China finds an economic expression and ally in the growing advertising industry and the business interests, both domestic and foreign, that it represents. Besides, pressures from the government, Zhou's station must also respond to those who buy commercial time on their shows. Businesses refuse to buy ad time if there is a domestically produced show: "They don't even bother to check out the show to see if it's any good; they just don't want to have anything to do with it," he said. The reason domestic films are not welcome by most viewers is perhaps because people no longer wish to plug themselves into the state imaginary; rather, they wish to cast their imagination outward.[10] Another reason is the poor quality of the technical production, the plot and narrative structure, and the stilted acting.

The pursuit of advertising patrons is why the station ignored a long-standing state regulation requiring stations to limit their imported TV series to two per year. Instead, they actually show about twenty per year, Zhou said. The authorities usually chose not to make an issue of this. Therefore, advertising has exerted a powerful influence on television programming, decreasing officially sanctioned, domestically produced didactic and political drama in favor of foreign and overseas Chinese products, as well as a new generation of innovative domestic dramas and soap operas.

Another point of contention between the public and the state is the issue of personal satellite television dishes, which receive programs from Hong Kong, Taiwan and Japan and (on more powerful receivers) from the United States, Russia, and Europe. In the early 1990s, many private Shanghai homes were equipped with satellite dishes, most of them made in China by rural factories hoping to profit from this highly valued product. State regulations forbid the setting up of personal satellite dishes, permitting only those work units dealing with international business to set up dishes (Anonymous 1993). The Public Security Bureau mounted periodic raids in Shanghai to confiscate private dishes, but the dishes always went back up after a while and the police chose to ignore it.

Thus the usual theory that conflates state and capital must be modified to one that can account for the changing moments or historical phases of convergence and divergence between state and capital and for the structural and discursive tensions that erupt in different situations. The case of China is especially illustrative of this tension, as it has experienced a shift from a state economy with territorially sealed activity and identity to a mobile capitalist transnational consumer economy without abandoning many features of state centralized control.

"The advent of modernity," writes Anthony Giddens, "increasingly tears space away from place by fostering relations between 'absent' others, locationally distant from any given situation of face-to-face interaction" (Giddens 1990: 18). Through the mass media of a growing consumer culture, the space of the state is becoming disembedded by transnational spaces of orientation. In the Maoist era, the "absent others" were the voice of the state and its symbolic leaders in Beijing. In the current commercialized period, Party leaders are being replaced in popular culture by new icons: pop singers and film stars located outside the national borders in Taiwan, Hong Kong, and beyond.

At least two mechanisms of spatial mobility of subjectivity can be discerned operating in the mass media and constructing a transnational Chinese imaginary. First, there is the mainland identification with roles played by Taiwanese and Hong Kong stars in films, TV shows, and popular songs. Second, there is the transnational Chinese imaginary at play, in the identification of the audience with a mainland character who goes to foreign lands.

Identifying with overseas Chinese others

Although American film and television have made some headway in China, they cannot compare with the influence of Hong Kong and Taiwan popular culture. One most vivid indication of this cultural invasion can be found in the pop songs that young people listen to and the popularity of karaoke singing. There is something mesmerizing about the repetition of endless stories of love and disappointment. Hong Kong and Taiwan popular culture has gained a firm foothold in the mainland (Gold 1993; Zhen 1992), with visiting singers giving concerts to packed halls filled with adoring fans paying high prices for tickets. Sixteen- and seventeen-year-old girls want to embrace and kneel in the footsteps of such male idols as Tong Ange and Tang Yongling. The longing to be a star oneself can be temporarily satisfied using the imported karaoke audiovisual systems now found in karaoke bars and in many work units, schools, and restaurants. Music stores have sprung up to sell this music on cassettes. Hong Kong songs are sung in Cantonese by young Shanghainese whose point of comparison these days is not Beijing but Hong Kong.[11]

A radio program host in his thirties who introduces Anglo-American rock music explained to me the appeal of Hong Kong and Taiwanese pop music in Shanghai: "It represents the modern for young people, and that is why it has replaced folk music [*minge*]," which used to dominate the airwaves during most of the 1980s. Chinese folk music is also about love between men and women, and the lyrics also depict scenes of nature, but "there is something old-fashioned about it; it's for middle-aged and old people, it feels rural and quaint now. In contrast, Hong Kong and Taiwanese pop feels new, advanced, and urban." It represents what young people aspire to, a faster-paced, prosperous life outside of the borders of the mainland. This life is thought to possess the cachet of sophistication.

In watching Hong Kong and Taiwanese shows, and in listening and singing its songs, the mainland mass media audience can be said to be undergoing four processes simultaneously: (1) identification with Hong Kong and Taiwanese people; (2) internalization of another kind of Chinese culture not so tied in with a statist imaginary; (3) differentiation of gender in identification and performance; and (4) insertion into a discourse of love and sexuality. In these four processes, karaoke singing has a deeper impact, because it involves the active performance and enactment of a different way to be Chinese, where state identity diminishes in importance and female and male genders become salient categories.[12]

Here J. L. Austin's speech act theory and Judith Butler's performance theory on the staging of gender and sexuality are relevant in thinking about the construction of the subject in karaoke.

> If the "I" is the effect of a certain repetition, one which produces the semblance of a continuity or coherence, then there is no "I" that precedes the gender [or national identity] that it is said to perform; the repetition, and the failure to repeat, produce a string of performances that constitute and contest the coherence of that "I." (Butler 1991:18)

It is through repeated performances that gender and national identity are constructed and reconstructed and that subjects sometimes come to realize that no essence lies beneath or outside of performance. To be sure, karaoke singing in China is putting into place a new regime of normalized heterosexual male and female objects of imitation, but it is also instituting different ways of being Chinese. The subjectivities produced by karaoke singing and those produced by the Maoist loyalty dance are vastly different. Whereas Maoist subjectivity sought to merge the self with the body of the state and its embodiment, Mao's body (Yang 1994c), karaoke places the subject in a narcissistic dynamic between self and the love object through which it learns to desire, and whose desire it needs, to fulfill and strengthen the fragile self. This Other through which the self yearns to be completed is no longer the larger and powerful collective "I" of the nation, but a Chinese cultural Other of Taiwan or Hong Kong who has a gender.

The longing to be reunited with or merged with the Chinese Other outside the borders of the Chinese state is given full expression in a popular song of the nineties, "My 1997 Hong Kong," written and sung by Ai Jing, a young mainland female singer who is also popular in Taiwan and Hong Kong. I translate some excerpts:

> The year I was seventeen, I left my hometown, Shenyang,
> Because I felt that the place didn't fulfill my dreams ...
> I sang from Beijing to Shanghai,
> And from Shanghai I sang to the South that I had dreamed of.
> My stay in Guangzhou was rather long,
> Because my Other, he is in Hong Kong.
> When will we have Hong Kong?
> When will we know what Hong Kong people are like?
> My boyfriend can come to visit Shenyang,
> But I can't go to Hong Kong.
> Hong Kong, oh, that Hong Kong!
> I should have gone out into the world to broaden myself when I was young ...

Let me go to that dazzling world,
Give me that big red official seal of approval to go abroad.
1997! May that year arrive quickly!...
Then I can go with him to the night markets.
1997! May that year arrive quickly!...
Then I can go to Hong Kong!

(Ai 1993)

This song sends shivers of anxiety through the hearts of Hong Kong Chinese because it reminds them of 1997, when China will become Hong Kong's new master. However, mainland Chinese are impatient for the day when Hong Kong's dazzle, wealth, and cosmopolitanism will become accessible to them. In contrast to mainland official discourse about 1997, which stresses Hong Kong's "return to the embrace of the motherland" (*huidao zuguo de huaibao*), the song expresses a yearning to break out of the motherland and to cross the state borders that forbid another way of being Chinese, although this alternative involves becoming a consuming Chinese. Along with the strengthening of the desiring "I," what comes into being is not only a culture of individualism but also a culture of desiring, consuming individuals yearning to be fulfilled.

The incursions of Hong Kong and Taiwanese popular culture, called *gangtai wenhua* (Gold 1993), into mainland state culture also show that it is no longer adequate for critical theory to identify *capitalism* only as a *western* force. What post-Mao China is encountering is the regional or transnational ethnic capitalism of overseas Chinese in Hong Kong, Taiwan, and Southeast Asia. In the past two decades, overseas Chinese economic investment has dramatically increased on the mainland (Ash and Kueh 1993; Harding 1993; Ong 1997). In 1990 Hong Kong surpassed Japan and the United States as the number-one investor in China, and Taiwan became the second-largest investor (Hsiao and So 1994: 2). As a Chinese scholar friend said to me, "For Chinese people today, cultural imperialism no longer means western imperialism, because it's now also coming from Taiwan and Hong Kong."

Increasingly the West is no longer the only, or even the primary, outside influence in local cultures, as Leo Ching's (1994) work on the importance of Japanese mass culture in Taiwan shows. Rather than a center-periphery framework of the West versus the rest, or capitalism versus the third world, it now looks as if the West is just another node in a system of other nodes (Appadurai 1990). The outside capital moving in is not western but of the same ethnicity as the labor force it is appropriating. Furthermore, while Hong Kong and Taiwan are the capitalists exploiting mainland labor, they must also answer to a powerful mainland state that has military superiority over them, as evidenced in the mainland's readiness for military action against Taiwan. Thus previous simple models of western cultural imperialism overrunning the third world through capitalist expansion cannot capture the complex situation in China today, where critique must be directed at a Chinese state as well as Chinese capital.

Recent critiques of multinational capitalism (Jameson 1987; Miyoshi 1993; Wallerstein 1974, 1984) often suffer from the very same problem they are against. That is, in seeing the world engulfed by multinational capitalism, they do so from a very western-centric perspective. They fail to take an on-the-ground perspective of the particular cultural formations that undergo this complex process. Their models fail to take into account how at the same time transnational capitalism introduces a new regime of power into China, it also serves to dislodge an entrenched and deeply rooted state power.[13] The binary constructions of center versus periphery and West versus the rest prove inadequate, as the outside "center" that is having the most impact on China today is not the West but the modernized and commercialized Chinese societies of Taiwan, Hong Kong, and overseas Chinese. In this second spurt of capitalist culture, China is not being ground underfoot by western cultural or economic imperialism, but is being drawn into a regional or ethnic Chinese capitalist mode of power in which China is both the victim as well as a host that benefits, manipulates, and calls the shots.

Following mobile Chinese subjects in other lands

The second mechanism for constructing a new transnational identity is the imagining of a mobile Chinese identity moving through foreign lands. This is a process in which the media audience identify with main characters who are mainland Chinese experiencing life in an alien culture. In recent years bookstores in Chinese cities have been selling a new genre of semi-autobiographical and semi-fictional writing: accounts or stories by people who have lived in the United States or Japan of their experiences and fortunes. Theater, film, and television productions have also taken up these themes.[14]

The "leave-the-country fever" (*chuguore*) reached a peak after the Tiananmen tragedy of 1989. The phenomenon of urban Chinese going abroad to live, whether as students and scholars, émigrés, laborers, or entrepreneurs, has been satirically called "joining a brigade overseas" (*yang chadui*). This expression conjures up the image of city people in the Cultural Revolution going down to the harsh life of physical labor in the countryside. Like their predecessors in the Cultural Revolution, today's Chinese are going to alien lands where they must struggle to survive through their own labor and wits.

The most famous book in this genre is *A Beijing Native in New York*, written by Cao Guilin, which was made into the first television drama series shot entirely on location in New York City.[15] This popular show aired in China in October 1993 and was made by Beijing Television Production Center. The story is about Wang Qiming, a cello player in the Beijing Symphony, who goes with his wife, Guo Yan, to New York City. There they do not receive the help of their relatives and have to start life at the bottom of American society, he as dishwasher in a Chinese restaurant, she as a seamstress in a sweatshop owned by an ambitious American named McCarthy. In his uphill climb to become a wealthy sweatshop owner himself, Wang Qiming employs some ruthless tactics, loses his wife to McCarthy, and joins up with his employer, A Chun, an astute, independent single businesswoman from Taiwan.

By listening to the discussion of this series by twenty members of a workers' film criticism group in Shanghai, we can get an idea of how this show has engendered multiple effects, such as: transnationalizing the audience, tapping into feelings of unease and suspicion about capitalism, giving vent to yearnings for a better life in the United States, disseminating a new model of independent womanhood that is sensual and hard-edged at the same time, and providing a forum in which to critique state policies.

Everyone agreed this was a popular series, and people were very interested in seeing what American streets and building interiors looked like. They were very curious about the life of Chinese abroad, especially since many of them had relatives or friends abroad. Five themes emerged in the discussion. First, a middle-aged man said that a feature of this film is international exchange. America is a place that is not xenophobic (*paiwai*) and in which everyone is treated equally; different races and cultures in the United States are engaged in competition. The lives of Chinese in America are not ones of luxury, for they must work hard in order to get anywhere. Just as he was learning about America, he thought Americans could also learn about life in China from watching a hypothetical show called *An American in Beijing* or *An American in Shanghai*. What can be detected in this statement is a subjectivity traversing great distances as well as a change of perspective that follows upon this. Through the medium of television, this man could imagine himself in another land, observing people there, and could even reverse the process and imagine himself as an American coming to China. The latter move of stepping out of his taken-for-granted subjectivity and assuming another would enable him to defamiliarize his native surroundings, to look at them with a fresh and different perspective. Indeed, in a popular-magazine discussion of the program, one reviewer quoted the old Chinese adage "Not knowing the real nature of Mt. Lushan is due to one's fate of living only in its midst" (*bushi Lushan zheng mianmu, zhi yuan shen zai cishan zhong*) to say that the show enabled Chinese to metaphorically leave China to come to a new understanding of their own country from a new vantage point (R. Yang 1993: 12).

A second theme was that of losing one's status, privileges, and support network, things that give one an identity and social role at home, and being propelled into a different status in America, where everyone starts out equal and only some rise up to the top through their own efforts. Several people commented on how once Wang Qiming entered the United States he could no longer enjoy the "aristocratic" (*guizu*) status that being a musician brought him in China; instead he had to use those refined musician's hands to wash dishes, because in the United States one is judged not by one's status (*shenfen*) but by one's efforts and talents. One man said that it doesn't matter whether one is a professor or worker in China, for in the United States none of this is recognized. It was also an eye-opener for them to see how Wang's relatives treated the couple in such a distant impersonal fashion. In the show the relatives were late to pick up Wang and Guo Yan at the airport and did not take the new arrivals to their homes but unceremoniously dumped them in a wretched basement apartment for which they expected the rent to be repaid. One man said that the show smashed not only the Chinese fantasy that one could pick up gold on the streets in America but also the fantasy that one could rely on one's relatives abroad. What seems to be operating in this line of thinking is that viewers of the show see the stripping away of familiar ways of being Chinese, such as relying on prescribed social status and on relatives. Through imagining these different ways of being Chinese abroad, the possibility is opened up for a reconstructing of both subject and society at home. So, for example, one man said that Chinese should learn to be more self-sufficient, and he called for a different way to raise children so that they will not rely on their parents.

A third theme was the ferociousness of capitalism and its ruthless cutthroat competition of "big fish eat little fish." A middle-aged man repeated a refrain of the theme song: "America is neither heaven nor hell, it is a battleground." Several people commented on the intense competitiveness of American society. They said that a newspaper had started a lively discussion soliciting letters debating the question of whether Wang Qiming is a good or bad man and whether he deserves sympathy or not. Sun, a factory office worker in his thirties, identified two issues in the show: the conflict between a planned economy and a market economy, and the conflict between Chinese and western culture. Sun thought that Wang Qiming had to compete in order to survive, and he resorted to some ruthless methods, such as using his wife to destroy a competitor. Sun could sympathize with Wang: Wang won the economic battle but lost his personal integrity. He became dehumanized in the struggle; his "human nature became twisted [*niuqu*]." This showed how deeply western culture has penetrated Chinese culture, he thought. Why did Wang, a person from a culture over two thousand years old, lose himself to a culture only three hundred years old? Because he was shocked at finding out about the West's economic might. Sun consoled himself that the Chinese market economy will not be as twisted and dehumanizing as that in the United States.[16] What was perhaps being worked out through this show and through the discussions it generated was the anxiety and ambivalence of plunging into capitalism and into the global society it represents. There was the fear of being corrupted by alien outside forces, of losing one's self and identity. At the same time there was the feeling that this was the only way to go, that it was necessary to overcome one's scruples and hesitations and make the leap.

There was also a fourth discussion of the female characters in the show. A Chun, the Taiwanese lover, and Guo Yan, the mainland wife, were compared. A Chun won the admiration of both men and women for her economic astuteness and her knowledge of the market and western culture. As a soft-spoken traditional woman who could endure hardships, Guo Yan won the approbation of the male film discussants, who thought she represented "Eastern beauty and virtue" (*dongfang meide*). A Chun was considered very Americanized, and there was the belief that she too had once been like Guo Yan when she first went to the United States. The men thought women like A Chun, who are astute business women, are good to have in a market economy, but they would not like to have her for a wife. Sun said that in China it is not common to find a woman like A Chun, who is so successful in the market. He confessed that his "world view" had still not completely turned around to fully accept her, although he admired her. "It's as though we have to tear off a layer of skin before we can completely turn around," he said. It would seem that the disturbing thing about capitalism is not only the cutthroat competition but also the new kind of independent women, like A Chun.

In separate discussions with women, I found that women generally liked the A Chun character. They admired her independence, her no-nonsense toughness, and the way she managed to separate the economic relationship from her romantic relationship with Wang. However, one of the women said that she did not want to challenge the men openly about their preference for Guo Yan at a public forum, and that even though men and women are now equal, it was still not easy for women to speak out in public. Perhaps it was easier for Chinese audiences to accept A Chun's novel combination of toughness, feminine sexual allure, and caringness when it was presented in the character of a Taiwan Chinese.[17]

Finally, this television series also provided an opportunity for these film discussants to question the wisdom of past state policies, such as political campaigns, that have caused so many people to want so desperately to leave China in the hope of finding a better future. Referring to a well-known phenomenon, one man declared, "There is something deeply wrong when some Shanghai women want to flee abroad so much that they are even willing to become prostitutes in someone else's country in order to survive." Since this was a public discussion, criticizing the government for past mistakes, which have made material and spiritual life so harsh in China, was a delicate and still potentially risky undertaking. This theme was expressed in so roundabout a fashion that I almost missed it until I sought clarification in separate private discussions.

This discussion of *A Beijing Native in New York* may seem to many in the West who have seen the show to be discrepant with the pervasive allegory of big-state rivalry and capitalist competition between China and the United States, personified by the characters Wang Qiming and David McCarthy. However, as Stuart Hall has shown, the process of audience *decoding* of media messages often "does not constitute an 'immediate identity'" with the process of authorial *encoding* of the messages, for there is a "relative autonomy" in decoding due to "the structural differences of relation and position between broadcasters and audiences" (Hall 1980: 131). As the recent flood of audience reception studies show (Ang 1990; de Certeau 1984; Radway 1988; Yang 1994a), a sole reliance on textual criticism by academics of media products cannot get at the full range of their social effects, because audiences selectively misread or read past the intentions of the producers. What I discerned in doing fieldwork on this film discussion group in 1993 was not a tendency to identify with the Chinese state against the United States, but rather an interest in exploring the possibilities of transnational mobility and displacement.

A deterritorialized Chinese subjectivity

In these two examples of a pop song and a television series can be detected a deterritorialized Chinese subjectivity that cannot be contained by the state apparatuses of either mainland China or Taiwan. What Homi Bhabha (1994) calls a "third space" of cultural hybridity has begun to spill out over the constrictive molds of a fixed, state-spatialized Chinese identity and homogeneous national culture. This "third space" is the "intervention of the 'beyond'. . . . [which] captures something of the estranging sense of the relocation of the home and the world – the unhomeliness – that is the condition of extra-territorial and cross-cultural initiations" (Bhabha 1994: 9). Whereas only a tiny proportion of people in Shanghai have been able to physically cross state boundaries and venture into the outside world, it is through the proliferating media that the mass of the people now also occupy a "third space" of transnational encounters.[18] In this space, the lines between home and world, one's own nation-state and another country, Chinese and foreign, socialism and capitalism get blurred through traveling identities.

The song "My 1997 Hong Kong" is heard on the airwaves of cities in mainland China, Taiwan, and Hong Kong, so that we may begin to speak of the emergence of a set of Chinese audiences who are viewing an increasingly common set of programs, although they are separated by state boundaries. This sharing of a common set of media products is developing across a broad space of the globe and creating a linked Chinese community of media audience stretching from China to overseas Chinese in Southeast Asia and the United States. So although it is still not fully or directly connected by satellite, transnational subjectivity in Shanghai has already entered into a shared space of a common nexus of Chinese popular culture programming around the globe. Don Nonini describes two new Chinese-Malaysian public spheres that look outward from Malaysia for news and entertainment: cosmopolitans who have traveled and worked abroad (including in China) and whose children attend universities in the West, and the Sino-internationalists who are involved in Chinese-language new media of videotapes, cassettes, films, and karaoke (Nonini 1995: 16). Here in the United States there are now three Chinese-language satellite television stations: North American TV, a station airing Taiwanese but also some mainland programs; Jade Channel/TVB, a Hong Kong channel; and the new Eastern Satellite TV, founded by mainland Chinese in Chicago and airing mainland shows (Hamilton 1995; Qiu 1993; Sheng 1995). Thus in Shanghai, Taiwan, Hong Kong, Malaysia, and the United States, there are increasing overlaps and commonalities in the programming that Chinese in these various places are viewing, making for the emergence of a transnational (read trans-state) Chinese-language imagined community in the next century (Lee 1993).

Since the media is caught up with the commercial promotion and celebration of material consumption, its detaching of subjects from the state is often at the price of what Benjamin (1969: 240) called the "distraction" of these liberated subjects from serious social reflection and critique. However, in the present historical moment, despite the commercialism, there is something implicitly oppositional about the new media. Most intellectuals I spoke with had a pained expression when asked about the influx of overseas popular culture. They were disturbed by this sudden shift to the vulgar, the shallow, and the commercial. Lan Tian, a college professor, had his own explanation: "Mainland Chinese are like children who have been shut up at home for years. When finally you let them out, everything outside is good in their eyes." However, he also saw the potential in this imported culture for a challenge to state culture. This wave of another type of Chinese culture is a relief from the "linguistic violence" or "rape" (*yuyan qiangbao*) that people were subjected to before, he thought. Popular culture threatens both "official discusive power" (*guanfang huayu quanli*) and "central core culture" (*zhongxin wenhua*). "Money knows no center," he said, with some sarcasm.

Zhang Daoming, a writer in his late thirties, was even more affirming of Hong Kong and Taiwanese popular culture. He wanted higher dosages of it: "Let's have more of this cultural garbage [*wenhua laji*], so that it becomes a flood and disaster, then people will get sick of it. It will make people feel isolated and displaced so that they can throw off this great monolithic unity [of the nation] (*da yi tong*)." Zhang is much more willing for people to be trodden down by economics rather than by politics. "At least in karaoke pop songs, people are singing their individual hearts, not that of the state."

Conclusion

The historical specificities of modern China have led me to challenge several assumptions in critical theory on the question of the spread of capitalism, modern mass media, and globalism. I have pointed out that three common conflations must be challenged when we look at the particular situation of China today. What I have outlined is a case of a newly created nation, or nationalist imaginary of print, first throwing off an old state (the imperial dynastic order), then adopting, or being adopted by, a new socialist state, which sealed the national borders and homogenized the interior with print, radio and film. More recently, new forms of mass media and popular culture have generated sentiments toward eluding and transcending this new state once again with the creation of a transnational cultural subjectivity in the exposure to an ethnic overseas Chinese capitalism. The recosmopolitanizing of Shanghai is part of this counter movement of a transnational Chinese cultural identity that shuts off state messages to wander imaginatively across the globe.

The focus here has been to show how transnational media have enabled the detaching of Chinese subjectivity from the state and its mobilization across imaginary space to link up with alternative Chinese subjectivities far away. Through the new mass media, those who have stayed in the country have started to undergo a change in subjectivity that is perhaps just as dramatic as that of those who have traveled abroad, so that returning Chinese often find themselves strangers upon their return. While the nation and state continue to be imagined, now they must contend with the splintering of subjectivities into pluralized media audiences of gender, class, and rural–urban differences, as well as the emergence of a regional overseas Chinese imaginary. However, even while liberated transnational Chinese subjects have begun to displace state subjects, they immediately face the danger of getting trapped in new and different tentacles of power.

It seems to me that today China is poised between two dangers, neither of which is western, although both are shaped by forces of modernity that the West first launched. First, there is the state centralized power of the Maoist era, which was largely indifferent to the high toll in human lives and psychic misery produced by its various political campaigns to strengthen the state and ensure that state subjectivity was the only form of consciousness. This danger has not fully retreated, although there have been recent cultural departures from its grip. Second, the new danger is that this same state will adopt the model of Asian state capitalism in the rest of Asia, which Aihwa Ong has suggested is an emerging counter-West Asia-Pacific hegemony of the twenty-first century (see Ong 1997). In this second mode of power, there is a smoother alliance of state and capital, a novel appropriation of cultural tradition such as state Confucianism (Chun 1994a; Heng and Devan 1992; Ong 1996) as legitimizing device, a state management of labor through the deployment of consumerism, and the dominance of a male business culture that tolerates women as business partners but more often casts them in roles servicing men in a commercialized culture of male sexuality. In this period of transition, the second mode challenges and offers relief from the first; however, this should not prevent us from seeing what Foucault (1980) realized with the early-twentieth-century discourse of sexual liberation: that liberation is always a prelude to a new insertion into another mode of power.

NOTES

I wish to thank Aihwa Ong and Roger Rouse for providing me with insightful and helpful suggestions on my paper. Thanks also to Don Nonini for his incisive comments and for the idea of the title, and to Lydia Liui and Zhang Yuehong for their careful reading of the manuscript. This paper was also presented at the Chicago Humanities Institute, University of Chicago, in January 1996, and I would like to thank the many scholars there who provided stimulating comments.

1 Anderson's work has also had an impact on studies of electronic media and national identity, such as recent works by feminist anthropologists who show how television is an important means of constituting national identity through gender, albeit through a contestatory process (Abu-Lughod 1993; Brownell 1995; Mankekar 1993; Rofel 1994). These works point to an important effect of print and television: the knitting together of a readership and audience scattered across vast regions into a national identity, sharing the same language, emotions, narrative structures, and political messages.

2 Fieldwork and interviews on recent developments in mass media and media publics in the post-Mao market economy era were conducted over five months in the city of Shanghai between 1991 and 1993 among mass media professionals and intellectuals and among working-class film and television criticism groups (see Yang 1994a).

3 In the 1920s, Shanghai's international settlement zones housed 23,307 foreign residents (out of a Chinese population of 2.5 million) (Bergere 1981: 6), the largest collection in any Chinese city. Shanghai was also the city with the largest Chinese migrant population from other parts of China (Ding 1994), and perhaps the city with the largest number of Chinese to go abroad and return from abroad. Shanghai factories in 1934 accounted for half of China's modern industrial production, and in 1935 the city received 46.4 percent of all foreign investments in China (Bergere 1981: 21–2).

4 It was in the Shanghai film industry that the figure of the "modern woman" emerged as a new site of culture production. Zhang Yingjin has shown how it provided critiques of tradition and expressions of sexuality for male desire as well as new objects for modern male disciplinary knowledge (Zhang 1994: 605). See also Pickowicz 1991 for a discussion of themes of urban and foreign decadence vs. native rural purity in 1930s Shanghai films.

5 In its iconoclastic attacks against the traditional Chinese family, kinship, and religion and in its promotion of the individual and the nation, May fourth discourse laid the foundation for what later became "the masses," atomised individual state subjects (Wu 1992) who were more equal, and at the same distance from the political center (Yang 1994c; 1996).

6 The category of "third world brothers" softens this dichotomy but retains the sense of state border separations.

7 See Feher et al. 1983 for a Marxist critique of Soviet-type state-centralized economic systems.

8 Shanghai film ticket sales in 1995 were 230 million yuan, up from 140 million in 1994 (*China News Daily*, January 23, 1996). One Chinese intellectual I spoke with said that many people are concerned about the damage done to the domestic film industry by foreign films, but others argue that what Hollywood films will do is to draw the Chinese audience back into the theaters, so that Chinese films will in the future find a more conducive climate among domestic, as opposed to foreign, financers for their films.

9 Here is a sampling of some international programs on the four television channels in Shanghai in the week of November 1–7, 1993: World Heavyweight Boxing Championship live from Las Vegas; tours of Hong Kong, Japan, and Hollywood with various Shanghai TV hosts; a history of the world trade agreement; Japanese and English language

classes; the American program *Matlock* (*Bianhu lushi*), dubbed into Mandarin; a Taiwan television serial *The Capital City and Four Youths* (*Jingchen sishao*); an American documentary about the KGB and CIA; a Japanese children's cartoon, *Hero of the Universe: Jack Automan*, dubbed into Mandarin; and *The News in English* every night at 1 a.m.

10 One exception to advertisers' reluctance to buy commercial time on domestic programs are those shows made by Wang Shuo and crew at the Beijing Television Production Center, which produced the very popular *Yearning* (*Ke wang*, 1990) (Rofel 1994; Zha 1995), *Stories from the Editing Department* (*Bianjibu de gushi*, 1992), and *A Beijing Native in New York* (*Beijingren zai niuyue*, 1993).

11 Of course, the cultural impact is not just one-way; mainland media and popular culture have also influenced Taiwan and Hong Kong (see Shih 1995 on the impact of the mainland on Taiwanese TV and popular music).

12 See two other discussions of karaoke by Vincanne Adams (1994) and Aihwa Ong (1996).

13 The assumption that the center (which is always figured as the West) always dominates the periphery means that "we get the history of the impact of the center on the periphery, rather than the history of the periphery itself" (Hannerz 1989: 207). The actual interactive process of cross-cultural negotiation, interpretation, and specific strategies of appropriation are not examined at all.

14 The books of this genre come with titles such as *Chinese Educated Youth Abroad; Manhattan's China Lady; The Moon Back Home is Brighter; A Beijing Woman in Tokyo; The Bright Moon of Another Land*; and *A Shanghainese in Tokyo*. There are also two successful plays, one called "The Wife Who Came Back from America" (*Meiguo lai de qizi*), by Zhang Xian, and "The Woman Left Behind" (*Liu shou nüshi*), by Yue Meiqin, both of which I saw in a small theater in Shanghai. The latter was made into a film of the same title by Shanghai Film Studio in 1992. Another play titled "Tokyo's Moon" (*Dongjing de yueliang*) was written by Sha Yexin, and a TV documentary shot by Wang Xiaoping on location in Tokyo called "Their Home is Shanghai" (*Jia zai shanghai*), depicting the everyday life of Shanghainese working in Japan, was aired to great acclaim on STV.

15 For a critique of how this show promotes the consumerism of transnational corporate products and becomes implicated in the movements of transnational (western) capital, see Liu 1995.

16 In an analysis highly critical of the show and of his compatriots who accept it, a Chinese expatriate living in the United States wrote that the picture the show paints of an immoral dog-eat-dog society in America merely serves as an excuse for Chinese to practice a ruthless kind of capitalism, which they conveniently imagine exists in the United States (Ye 1994). I think the fact that Wang Qiming's moral character is the subject of debate shows that many people cannot accept him.

17 In the imaginary of travel and transnational crossings taking hold in the coastal Chinese cities, there is a gender differential whereby women are imagined to be more mobile and successful in adapting to foreign cultures and places, whereas men are seen as more rooted to the culture and national space. Space limits require a separate treatment of this theme in another publication (Yang 1995).

18 Mike Featherstone also has a similar notion of "third cultures," or transnational cultures that are oriented beyond national boundaries; however, his application of this concept is narrower than what I am trying to conceive. By "third culture" he means the world of transnational professionals in architecture, advertising, film, global financial markets, international law, and other international agencies (Featherstone 1990: 6–8; 1992: 146). I would like to include the transnational mass cultures created by mass media.

REFERENCES

A Cheng. 1994. *Xianhua xianshuo: Zhongguo shisu yu Zhongguo xiaoshuo* (Leisurely Chats: Chinese Customs and the Chinese Novel). Taipei: Shibao wenhua chubanshe.

Abu-Lughod, Lila. 1993. "Finding a Place for Islam: Egyptian Television Serials and the National Interest." *Public Culture* 5(3).

Adams, Vincanne. 1994. "Karaoke as Modern Lhasa, Tibet: A Western View." Paper presented at the American Anthropological Association meetings in Atlanta, Georgia.

Ai, Jing 1993. *Wode yijiujiuqi xianggang* (My 1997 Hong Kong). Cassette tape distributed by Beijing Film Academy Sound Production and Distribution.

Althusser, Louis. 1971. "Ideology and Ideological State Apparatuses." In *Lenin and Philosophy: Notes Towards an Investigation*, trans. Ben Brewster. London: New Left Books.

Anderson, Benedict. 1991. *Imagined Communities: Reflections on the Origin and Spread of Nationalism*, rev. edn. New York: Verso.

Ang, Ien. 1990. "Culture and Communication: Towards an Ethnographic Critique of Media Consumption in the Transnational Media System." *European Journal of Communication* 5(2–3).

Anonymous. 1993. "Guanyu weixin dianshi dimian jieshou wenti" (On the question of on-the-ground satellite reception). *Mei zhou guangbo dianshi*, November 1–7.

Appadurai, Arjun. 1990. "Disjuncture and Difference in the Global Cultural Economy." *Public Culture* 2(2): 1–24.

——. 1993. "Patriotism and Its Futures". *Public Culture* 5(3).

Ash, Robert, and Y. Y. Kueh. 1993. "Economic Integration within Greater China: Trade and Investment Flows between China, Hong Kong and Taiwan." *China Quarterly* 136.

Bao, Ming. 1993. "Shanghai shiting dazhan" (The great wars of television and radio in Shanghai). *Zhongguo shibao* 66.

Benjamin, Walter. 1969. "The Work of Art in the Age of Mechanical Reproduction." In *Illuminations*, ed. Hannah Arendt. New York: Schocken.

Bergere, Marie-Claire. 1981. "The Other China: Shanghai from 1919 to 1949." In Christopher Howe, ed., *Shanghai: Revolution and Development in an Asian Metropolis*. Cambridge: Cambridge University Press.

Bhabha, Homi K. 1994. *The Location of Culture*. London: Routledge.

Brownell, Susan. 1995. "Women Who Represent the Nation: Sportswomen and Sports Media in Chinese Public Culture." Paper presented at the conference on Mass Media, Gender, and a Chinese Public: Mainland, Taiwan, and Hong Kong, University of California at Santa Barbara, April 1–3.

Butler, Judith. 1991. "Imitation and Gender Insubordination." In Diana Fuss, ed., *Inside/Out: Lesbian Theories, Gay Theories*. New York: Routledge.

Chang, Won Ho. 1989. *Mass Media in China: The History and the Future*. Ames: Iowa State University Press.

Ching, Leo. 1994. "Imaginings in the Empires of the Sun: Japanese Mass Culture in Asia." *Boundary 2* 21(1).

Chow, Rey. 1993. *Writing Diaspora: Tactics of Intervention in Contemporary Cultural Studies*. Bloomington: Indiana University Press.

Chow, Tse-ts'ung. 1960. *The May Fourth Movement: Intellectual Revolution in Modern China*. Cambridge, MA: Harvard University Press.

Chun, Allen. 1994a. "From Nationalism to Nationalizing: Cultural Imagination and State Formation in Postwar Taiwan." *Australian Journal of Chinese Affairs* 31.

———. 1994b. "Discourses of Identity in the Politics of the Modern Nation-State: Spaces of Public Culture in Taiwan, Hong Kong, and Singapore." *Culture and Policy 5.*

Clark, Paul. 1984. "The Film Industry in the 1970s." In Bonnie McDougall, ed. *Popular Chinese Literature and Performing Arts in the People's Republic of China, 1949–79.* Berkeley: University of California Press.

Clifford, James. 1992. "Traveling Cultures." In Lawrence Grossberg et al., eds., *Cultural Studies.* New York: Routledge.

———. 1994. "Diasporas." *Cultural Anthropology* 9(3).

Dai, Jinhua. 1995. "Invisible Women: Women's Films in Contemporary Chinese Cinema," trans. Mayfair Yang, *Positions* 3(1).

de Certeau, Michel. 1984. *The Practice of Everyday Life*, trans. Steven F. Rendall. Berkeley: University of California Press.

Deleuze, Gilles. 1980. *Nietszche and Philosophy.* New York: Columbia University Press.

Deleuze, Gilles, and Felix Guattari. 1983. *Anti-Oedipus: Capitalism and Schizophrenia.* Minneapolis: University of Minnesota Press.

Ding, Yi. 1994 "Shanghai shiluo 50 nian?" (Has Shanghai fallen behind by 50 years?) *Zhongshi zhoukan*, November 13–19.

Featherstone, Mike. 1990. "Global Culture: An Introduction." In Mike Featherstone, ed., *Global Culture: Nationalism, Globalization, and Modernity.* London: Sage Publications.

———. 1992. *Consumer Culture and Postmodernism.* London: Sage Publications.

Feher, Ferenc, Agnes Heller, and Gyorgy Markus. 1983. *Dictatorship over Needs: An Analysis of Soviet Societies.* Oxford: Blackwell Publishers.

Foster, Robert J. 1991. "Making National Cultures in the Global Ecumene." *Annual Review of Anthropology* 20.

Foucault, Michel. 1980. *The History of Sexuality, Volume 1: An Introduction*, trans. Robert Hurley. New York: Random House.

Friedland, Roger. 1994. "NowHere: An Introduction to Space, Time and Modernity." In Roger Friedland and Deirdre Boden, eds., *NowHere: Space, Time and Modernity.* Berkeley: University of California Press.

Giddens, Anthony. 1990. *The Consequences of Modernity.* Stanford: Stanford University Press.

Gold, Thomas. 1993. "Go with Your Feelings: Hong Kong and Taiwan Popular Culture in Greater China." *China Quarterly* 136: 907–25.

Guo, Ke. 1994. "'Jilupian bianjishi' zhendong Shanghaitan ([The show] 'Documentary Editing Room' shakes Shanghai). *Zhongshi zhoukan*, August 14–20: 48–9.

Hall, Stuart. 1980. "Encoding/Decoding." In Stuart Hall et al., eds., *Culture, Media, Language.* London: Hutchinson

Hamilton, Denise. 1995. "Providing a Space Link to Homeland: Chinese-Language Satellite TV Gets a Good Reception Among Immigrants in U.S." *Los Angeles Times*, August 2.

Hannerz, Ulf. 1989. "Culture Between Center and Periphery: Toward a Macroanthropology." *Ethnos* 54: 200–16.

Harding, Harry. 1993. "The Concept of 'Greater China': Themes, Variations and Reservations." *China Quarterly* 136.

Heng, Geraldine, and Janadas Devan. 1992. "State Fatherhood: The Politics of Nationalism, Sexuality, and Race in Singapore." In Andrew Parker, Mary Russo, et al., eds., *Nationalisms and Sexualities.* New York: Routledge.

Hsiao, Hsin-Huang Michael, and Alvin Y. So. 1994. "Taiwan-Mainland Economic Nexus: Socio-Political Origins, State-Society Impacts, and Future Prospects." Hong Kong: Institute of Asia-Pacific Studies, Chinese University of Hong Kong.

Jameson, Fredric. 1987. "Third-World Literature in the Era of Multinational Capitalism." *Social Text* 15: 65–88.

Lee, Benjamin. 1993. "Going Public." *Public Culture* 5(2).

Leyda, Jay. 1972. *Dianying: An Account of Films and the Film Audience in China.* Cambridge, MA: MIT Press.

Liu, Lydia. 1995. "Disjuncture of Theory: Transnationals, (Im)migrants, and/or Diaspora?" Paper presented at the Conference on Mass Media, Gender, and a Chinese Public, University of California at Santa Barbara, April 1–3.

Lull, James. 1991. *China Turned On: Television, Reform, and Resistance.* New York: Routledge.

Mankekar, Purnima. 1993. "Television Tales and a Woman's Rage: A Nationalist Recasting of Draupadi's 'Disrobing.'" *Public Culture* 5(3).

McLuhan, Marshall. 1994. *Understanding Media: The Extensions of Man.* Cambridge, MA: MIT Press.

Meng, Yue. 1993. "Female Images and National Myth." In Tani E. Barlow, ed., *Gender Politics in Modern China: Writing and Feminism.* Durham: Duke University Press.

Miyoshi, Masao. 1993. "A Borderless World? From Colonialism to Transnationalism and the Decline of the Nation-State." *Critical Inquiry* 19.

Nonini, Donald. 1995. "The Chinese Public Sphere and the Cultural Boundaries of the Malaysian Nation-State." Paper presented at the American Ethnological Society Meetings, Austin, Texas.

Ong, Aihwa. 1996. "Anthropology, China, and Modernities: The Geopolitics of Cultural Knowledge." In Henrietta Moore, ed., *The Future of Anthropological Knowledge.* London: Routledge.

——. 1997. "Chinese Modernities: Narratives of Nation and Capitalism." In Aihwa Ong and Donald M. Nonini, eds., *Ungrounded Empires: The Cultural Politics of Modern Chinese Transnationalism.* New York: Routledge.

Pickowicz, Paul. 1991. "The Theme of Spiritual Pollution in Chinese Films of the 1930s." *Modern China* 17(1): 38–75.

Qiu, Xiuwen. 1993. "Heima chuangjing beimei huayu dianshi shichang [A black horse charges into the North American Chinese-language television market]. *Zhongguo shibao*, September 12–18.

Radway, Janice. 1988. "Reception Study: Ethnography and the Problems of Dispersed Audiences and Nomadic Subjects." *Cultural Studies* 2(3).

Rayns, Tony. 1991. "Breakthroughs and Setbacks: The Origins of the New Chinese Cinema." In Chris Berry, ed., *Perspectives on Chinese Cinema.* London: British Film Institute.

Rofel, Lisa. 1994. "Yearnings: Televisual Love and Melodramatic Politics in Contemporary China." *American Ethnologist* 21(4).

Rouse, Roger. 1991. "Mexican Migration and the Social Space of Postmodernism." *Diaspora* 1(1).

——. 1995a. "Thinking Through Transnationalism: Notes on the Cultural Politics of Class Relations in the Contemporary United States." *Public Culture* 7(2).

——. 1995b. "Questions of Identity: Personhood and Collectivity in Transnational Migration to the United States." *Critique of Anthropology* 15(4).

Sheng, Feng. 1995. "Beimei shangkong de Zhongwen dianshi dazhan" [Chinese-language television wars in North American outer space]. *Huaxia wenzhai* (Chinese electronic news service), April 15.

Shih, Shu-mei. 1995. "The Trope of 'Mainland China' in Taiwan's Media." *Positions* 3(1).

Verdery, Katherine. 1994. "Beyond the Nation in Eastern Europe." *Social Text* 38.

Wallerstein, Immanuel. 1974. *The Modern World System.* New York: Academic Press.

——. 1984. *The Politics of the World Economy.* Cambridge: Cambridge University Press.

Wu, Xiaoming. 1992. "Ershi shiji Zhongguo wenhua zai xifang mianqian de ziwo yishi" [Cultural self-identity in the face of the West in twentieth-century China]. *Ershiyi shiji* 14: 102–12.

Yang, Mayfair Mei-hui. 1993. "Of Gender, State Censorship and Overseas Capital: An Interview with Chinese Director Zhang Yimou." *Public Culture* 5(2): 1–17.

——. 1994a. "State Discourse or a Plebeian Public Sphere? Film Discussion Groups in China." *Visual Anthropology* 10(1).

——. 1994b. *Gifts, Favors, and Banquets: The Art of Social Relationships in China.* Ithaca, NY: Cornell University Press.

——. 1994c. "A Sweep of Red: State Subjects and the Cult of Mao." In *Gifts, Favors, and Banquets: The Art of Social Relationships in China.* Ithaca, NY: Cornell University Press.

——. 1995. "From Gender Erasure to Gender Difference: State Feminism, Mass Media, and Public Culture in China." Paper presented at the conference "Mass Media, Gender, and a Chinese Public: Mainland, Taiwan, Hong Kong," University of Santa Barbara, April 1–3.

——. 1996. "Tradition, Traveling Anthropology, and the Discourse of Modernity in China." In Henrietta Moore, ed., *The Future of Anthropological Knowledge.* London: Routledge.

Yang, Rujie. 1993. "Jingcai yu wunai – cong 'Beijingren zai Neuyue' tan dongxifang wenhua chongji" [Gripping and frustrating: on East-West collisions in 'A Beijing Native in New York']. *Dianying wenxue* 12.

Ye Ren. 1994. "Xi 'Beijingren zai niuyue' de shehui xiaoguo" [An analysis of the social effects of 'A Beijing Native in New York']. *Zhongguo zhi chun* 14.

Zha, Jianying. 1995. *China Pop: How Soap Operas, Tabloids, and Best-sellers are Transforming a Culture.* New York: New Press.

Zhang, Hong. 1992. "TV, TV, fangcun shijie de jingcai yu wunai [TV, TV, the brilliance and frustration of that square world]. *Shehui* 92.

Zhang, Yingjin. 1994. "Engendering Chinese Filmic Discourse of the 1930s: Configurations of Modern Women in Shanghai in Three Silent Films." *Positions* 2(3): 603–28.

Zhen, Hanliang. 1992. "Wo liaojie sandi de Zhongguoren: zhuanfang Luo Dayou" [What I understand of the Chinese in the three Chinas: an interview with Luo Dayou]. *Zhongguo shibao*, August 23.

15

Indian Films and Nigerian Lovers: Media and the Creation of Parallel Modernities

Brian Larkin

God make him rich so he can go to India.
  Mallam Sidi, husband of Hotiho.
Sidi's ambition is for God to make him rich so he can go to India.
  Mallam Sidi, husband of Hotiho.
His ambition is to see Hotiho . . .
  Mallam Sidi, husband of Hotiho.
He swears if he sees Hotiho then no problems can move him.
  Mallam Sidi, husband of Hotiho.

Mamman Shata, '*Mallam Sidi, mijin Hotiho*'
'Mallam Sidi is the husband of Hotiho'[1]

The sight of a 15 foot image of Sridevi, dancing erotically on the screens of the open-air cinemas of northern Nigeria, or the tall, angular figure of Amitabh Bachchan radiating charisma through the snowy, crackly reception of domestic television, have become powerful, resonant images in Hausa popular culture. To this day, stickers of Indian films and stars decorate the taxis and buses of the north, posters of Indian films adorn the walls of tailors' shops and mechanics' garages, and love songs from Indian film songs are borrowed by religious singers who change the words to sing praises to the Prophet Mohammed. For over thirty years Indian films, their stars and fashions, music and stories have been a dominant part of everyday popular culture in northern Nigeria. If, as Bakhtin (1981) writes, communication is fundamental to human life, if self and society emerge in dialogue with others surrounding them,

From *Africa* 67(3) (1997): 406–39.

then Indian films have entered into the dialogic construction of Hausa popular culture by offering Hausa men and women an alternative world, similar to their own, from which they may imagine other forms of fashion, beauty, love and romance, coloniality and postcoloniality.

Before I began my research I read all I could find by Nigerian and western scholars on media and film in Nigeria. For the most part, this scholarship dealt with the complex and continuing problem of cultural imperialism – the dominance of western media and most especially Hollywood films. When I first visited Kano, the major city in northern Nigeria, it came as a surprise, then, that Indian films are shown five nights a week at the cinemas (compared with one night for Hollywood films and one night for Chinese films); that the most popular programme on television was the Sunday morning Indian film on City Television Kano (CTV); and that most video shops reserved the bulk of their space for Indian films (followed by western and Chinese films, Nigerian dramas and religious videos). The question of why Indian films are so popular among Hausa viewers has occupied much of my research since that time.[2] What pleasures do Hausa viewers take from films portraying a culture and religion that seem so dissimilar and are watched usually in a language they cannot understand? Why has such a prominent part of the popular culture of many African societies received so little attention from academics?[3] This article attempts to answer these questions by taking seriously the significance of Indian films in Hausa culture. It explores the influence of Indian cinema on Hausa social life through the medium of Hausa *littatafan soyayya* (love stories). This pamphlet-type market literature, which began as recently as 1989, has created a popular reading public for wilful, passionate heroes and heroines who mimic a style of love and sexual interaction found in Indian films. *Soyayya* books, and videos based on their plots, produce a world where the imagined alternative of Indian romance is incorporated within local Hausa reality.

The popularity of Indian film in Nigeria highlights the circulation of media within and between non-western countries, an aspect of transnational cultural flows that has been largely ignored in recent theories of globalisation. Indian films offer Hausa viewers a way of imaginatively engaging with forms of tradition different from their own at the same time as conceiving of a modernity that comes without the political and ideological significance of that of the West. After discussing reasons for the popularity of Indian films in a Hausa context, I account for this imaginative investment of viewers by looking at narrative as a mode of social enquiry. Hausa youth explore the limits of accepted Hausa attitudes to love and sexuality through the narratives of Indian film and Hausa love stories. This exploration has occasioned intense public debate, as *soyayya* authors are accused of corrupting Hausa youth by borrowing from Indian films foreign modes of love and sexual relations. I argue that this controversy indexes wider concerns about the shape and direction of contemporary Nigerian culture. Analysing *soyayya* books and Indian films gives insight into the local reworking and indigenising of transnational media flows that take place within and between Third World countries, disrupting the dichotomies between West and non-West, coloniser and colonised, modernity and tradition, foregrounding instead the ability of media to create parallel modernities.

Parallel Modernities

I use the term 'parallel modernities' to refer to the coexistence in space and time of multiple economic, religious and cultural flows that are often subsumed within the term 'modernity'. This formulation resonates with the term 'alternative modernities' used by Appadurai (1991),[4] but with a key difference. Appadurai links the emergence of alternative modernities with the increased deterritorialisation of the globe and the movement of people, capital and political movements across cultural and national boundaries. While deterritorialisation is important, the experience of parallel modernities is not necessarily linked with the needs of relocated populations for contact with their homelands (Appadurai 1991: 192). My concern, by contrast, is with an Indian film-watching Hausa populace who are not involved in nostalgic imaginings of a partly invented native land but who participate in the imagined realities of other cultures as part of their daily lives.

By stressing the importance of modernities that run parallel to the classical paradigm of the West I want to criticise recent work in African studies and media studies that has been dominated by the focus on local 'resistance' to various forms of 'dominant culture'. Abu-Lughod has warned that the 'romance of resistance' tends to focus on the creativity of resistors and fails to explore fully the effectiveness of systems of power (1990). My concern is different, arguing that concepts of resistance in African studies and elsewhere often depend on a reductive binary distinction between oppression and resistance. The effect of this is that phenomena that cannot be neatly organised within that binary distinction then fall out of view. In a recent review essay on African historiography Frederick Cooper addresses some of these concerns:

The difficulty [in contemporary Africanist historiography] is to confront the power behind European expansion without assuming it was all-determining and to probe the clash of different forms of social organisation without treating them as self-contained and autonomous. The binaries of coloniser/colonised, Western/non-Western and domination/resistance begin as useful devices for opening up questions of power but end up constraining the search for precise ways in which power is deployed and the ways in which power is engaged, contested, deflected, and appropriated. (Cooper 1994: 1517)

Cooper wishes to move away from what he sees as monolithic constructions of civilised coloniser and primitive colonised (and the related labels of modernity and tradition) by asserting the heterogeneity of both colonial rule and African resistances. While complicating the picture, he nevertheless remains wedded to a structural binarism that looks at the organisation of African experience in terms of its response to western rule and its consequences.

Recent theories of postcolonialism have also unintentionally tended to reify this distinction in that the term 'postcolonial', despite a variety of different definitions, connotes a historical periodisation based on the core period of colonialism.[5] Northern Nigeria, for example, was colonised by the British in 1903, and achieved independence in 1960. A history of over a thousand years is divided into the period pre-colonial, colonial and postcolonial which centres less than sixty years of British rule at the heart of Hausa experience. Even while criticising the role of the West in postcolonial Nigerian life, theorists of cultural imperialism and postcolonialism often view Nigerian reality largely in terms of its relation to the West, with the resulting irony of reaffirming cultural imperialism at the same moment as critiquing it. It is as if the periphery could not have an experience independent of its relation to metropolitan centres. Shohat and Stam criticise this contemporary insistence on resistance for producing an 'inverted European narcissism' positing a monolithic West as the source of all evil in the world, and which 'reduces non-western life to a pathological response to western domination' (Shohat and Stam 1994: 3). The widespread popularity of Indian films in Nigeria necessitates a revision of conceptions of global cultural flows that privilege the centrality of the West and refuse to recognise the common historical process of centres and peripheries engaged in contemporary cultural production.

The narrow conception of cultural imperialism has left little place for the study of phenomena such as Hong Kong or Indian film which cannot be as easily tied to a wider economic hegemony as is the case with Hollywood film.[6] This myopia has also been the result of the disciplinary boundaries of contemporary scholarship, which has little ethnographic understanding of cross-cultural media environments. Recent groundbreaking works in African cinema, such as Diawara (1992) and Ukadike (1994; see also Ekwuazi 1987; Ekwuazi and Nasidi 1992), deal largely with production by African film makers and are less concerned with what African film audiences are actually watching. Until recently anthropologists, with their disciplinary focus on indigenous cultural production, have been suspicious of foreign mass-mediated cultural forms, no matter how popular they may be (cf. Abu-Lughod 1993b; Ginsburg 1991; Hannerz 1992). Karin Barber, for instance, in her seminal definition of African popular arts argues that 'imported commercial entertainments ... symbolize western culture (though they include Chinese Kung Fu movies and Indian romantic melodramas)' (1987: 25; her parenthesis). As well as reducing foreign media to a subset of Hollywood, Barber is reluctant to admit any real engagement by African audiences with these texts. Because they do not originate from an African reality she suggests they have little meaning in African life. '[E]ntertainment films that are least mediated by African culture ... [she concludes] are also the most easily replaced' (ibid.). Barber's observations are probably influenced by her experience among Yoruba, where indigenous videos have provided a popular alternative to imported cinema in recent years. She fails, however, to appreciate the complicated identifications that allow audiences to engage with media forms no matter how superficially 'foreign'. The popularity of Indian films in Africa has fallen into the interstices of academic analysis, as the *Indian* texts do not fit with studies of African cinema; the *African* audience is ignored in the growing work on Indian film; the films are too non-western for Euro-American-dominated media studies, and anthropologists are only beginning to theorise the social importance of media.

My intent is not to downplay the importance of the cultural struggle of Nigerians against foreign media, or to minimise the hegemony of western culture, but to stress that this is only part of the cultural reality of many African nations. It is necessary to move toward a more ethnographic understanding of the range of the media environments that offer Hausa youth the choice between watching Hausa or Yoruba videos, Indian, Hong Kong or American films, or videos of Qur'anic *tafsir* (exegesis) by local preachers. In this my work has been influenced heavily by participation in the Program in Culture and Media and its affiliates within the department of anthropology at New York University. Borrowing from media and cultural studies as well as from traditional anthropological theory the Program is developing a variety of critical anthropological perspectives that examine the social relations within which media are embedded and enacted (Abu-Lughod 1993b, 1995; Ginsburg 1991, 1993, 1994; McLagan 1996; Sullivan 1993). Examining the significance of Indian films in an African context, and the processes of identification by which the ideas, values and aesthetics of another culture are incorporated within an African quotidian, is a step further in this developing field. With other approaches to transnational cultural studies such as that emerging from the journal *Public Culture*, this work is building a sophisticated and supple theoretical frame to deal with what Appadurai terms a 'new cosmopolitanism' that unites the cultural, financial and political flows within and between western and non-western countries into a single conceptual whole. 'Modernity,' Appadurai and Breckenridge assert, 'is now everywhere, it is simultaneously everywhere, it is interactively everywhere' (1995: 2).

Appadurai argues that the new cosmopolitanism brought about by movements of people and capital in the contemporary era has created a deterritorialised world that has new significance for the understanding of media and of imagination (1990, 1991). Media figure prominently in creating interconnections between different peoples who can now consider alternative lives based not on experiences in their own locality but on a range of experiences brought to them through international mass media. As more people throughout the world see their reality 'through the prisms of possible lives offered by the mass media', Appadurai argues that contemporary ethnography must now expand to find ways of understanding the social reality of imagination: 'fantasy is now a social practice; it enters, in a host of ways, into the fabrication of social lives' (1991: 198).

The concept of imagination as outlined by Appadurai is helpful in gaining insight into the pleasures that Indian films offer Hausa viewers. (I shall discuss this further below.) It also provides a theoretical way to understand the complicated identifications of audiences and cultural forms that cross expected racial, cultural and national lines. For Hausa viewers, Indian films offer images of a parallel modernity to the West, one intimately concerned with the changing basis of social life, but rooted in conservative cultural values. Characters in Indian films struggle over whether they should speak Hindi or borrow from English, whether they should marry the person they love or wed the person their parents choose. In these and many other decisions like them the narrative tensions of Indian films raise, consider and resolve minor and major anxieties within contemporary Indian society, anxieties that are relevant to Hausa viewers. Moreover, when Hausa youth rework Indian films within their own culture by adopting Indian fashions (such as the headscarves or jewellery of Indian actresses), by copying the music styles for religious purposes, or by using the filmic world of Indian sexual relations to probe the limitations within their own cultural world they can do so without engaging with the heavy ideological load of 'becoming western'. The popularity of Indian films rests on this delicate balance of being situated between Nigerian 'tradition' and western 'modernity', offering a mediating space for postcolonial Hausa viewers from which they may reflect on and consider the nature of contemporary social change.

Indian Films and Hausa Viewers

One result of the myopia regarding the presence of Indian films in West Africa is that hard data regarding their distribution and exhibition are extremely difficult to come by. Ekwuazi, for instance, borrows from UN statistics to write that in 1978–9, 86 per cent of all films imported into Nigeria were of American origin (1987: 121). Yet earlier in the same book he acknowledges that many films come in through a grey market that escapes official notice, and unofficially 'the all-time favourite is the Indian, not the American film' (1987: 44).[7] Whereas all American films were imported through the American Motion Picture Exporters and Cinema Association (AMPECA), later the Nigerian Film Distribution Company (NFDC), Indian films were imported by a host of entrepreneurs in different countries, including the Middle East, England and India. British censorship records reveal that Indian films were first introduced by Lebanese exhibitors in the 1950s who were eager to see whether the diet of American and English films could be supplemented by the odd Arab or Indian one.[8] These exhibitors speculated that Arabic films would be popular in the north because of the many religious links between northern Nigeria and the Islamic world. As the language of religious practice and debate Arabic carried immense authority, but despite these links the films never became popular on northern Nigerian screens while Indian films came to dominate them.[9]

The lack of information on the political economy of Indian film obscures the relation between the economic and symbolic reasons for its popularity (but see Pendakur and Subramanyam 1996). It seems likely that the disappearing presence of American films is related to the increasing cost of American film prints, which makes the cheaper Indian films more attractive. However, Hausa, Lebanese and Indian film and video entrepreneurs I interviewed all accounted for the dominance of Indian film in symbolic and cultural, rather than economic, terms. In an interview with Michel Issa, manager of the Cinema Distribution Circuit, which owns cinemas throughout northern Nigeria, Issa argued that Indian films were popular because 'their culture is the same' as Hausa culture.[10] One Indian video entrepreneur posited that it was the (allegedly) common linguistic roots of Hindi and Hausa that accounted for the sense of cultural familiarity (an argument supported by Muhammad 1992).[11] Uninterested in my questions about why Indian films were more popular, Issa finally said he had no idea why Arab films had not been accepted. All he knew was that from the beginning Indian films gained a massive popular following in the north. Even before American films stopped being distributed in Nigeria, he pointed out, they had been largely replaced by Indian films on northern screens.

Indian film fans and theorists refer to contemporary Hindi films as *masala* films. Referring to the blend of spices used in Indian cooking, popular Indian cinema often mixes the genres of romance, melodrama, action, musical and comedy within the same film. For a considerable time this eclectic mix was seen by both western and Indian academics as evidence of the inability of Indian film makers to make 'proper' American-style films. More recently, Indian film scholars have come to view Bombay films not as poor imitations of American films but as based on a distinct narrative style and structure (see Chakravarty 1993; the special issue of *India*

International Centre Quarterly 1980; Mishray 1985; Thomas 1985, 1995). Rosie Thomas argues that:

A form has developed in which narrative is comparatively loose and fragmented, realism irrelevant, psychological characterization disregarded, elaborate dialogues prized, music essential and both the emotional involvement of the audience and the pleasures of sheer spectacle privileged throughout the three hour long duration of the entertainment. (Thomas 1995: 162; see also Thomas 1985)

Indian films, or at least the Hindi ones that are imported into Nigeria, are made for a pan-Indian audience, and the makers of the films are aware of the necessity of constructing a filmic style that crosses both linguistic and cultural boundaries. Even so, these films are embedded in a cultural specificity that presupposes familiarity with Indian cultural values, Hindu religion, and a strong sense of Indian national-ism. They are also playfully intertextual, making constant reference to classical Indian mythology, folk drama and literature and Hindu religious practice. Chakra-varty (1993) argues that Indian films have created a 'communal' mode of address, a 'we-ness' of common cultural and national concerns that accounts for their appeal but which is largely a fiction in a country as large and diverse as India. Indian films are subtitled in English at Hausa cinemas, but the majority of those on television (which has the largest audience) are broadcast in Hindi only. This means that most Hausa viewers are watching Indian films in a language of which they have little understanding. After thirty years of watching Indian films Hausa audiences are, of course, sophisticated at understanding the narrative style of the films, and many families have several members who claim they can 'speak' Hindi, but inevitably there is a considerable cultural gap between the intertextual references to local cultural and religious values by Indian films and a Hausa viewing audience.

Despite the cultural gap between the Hindu Indian audience to which the filmic text is being addressed and the Muslim Hausa one watching in northern Nigeria, what is remarkable is how well the main messages of the films are communicated. This problem is made easier by the narrative structure of Indian films, which is borrowed from the Indian religious epics the *Mahabarata* and *Ramayana* (Mishray 1985). The dependence upon the epics means that there is usually a fixed range of plots with clear moral contrasts that make the outlines of Indian films familiar to their viewers. The regularity of character types whose actions fall within a limited range of behaviour such as the hero, the mother, the comedic friend or the evil boss, with many of the lesser roles (such as boss or the mother) played by the same people in film after film, further aids the fixed parameters of plot structure within which the spectacle unfolds. This dependence on religious epics for narrative structure pro-vides an easily comprehended moral guide for characters' actions and creates a limited set of narrative possibilities facilitating the easy 'translation' of Indian films across cultural, linguistic and national boundaries.[12]

Talking to many friends about their love of Indian films, I was struck by the common refrain that Indian culture was 'just like' Hausa culture. I found it surpris-ing that staunchly Muslim Hausa should identify so strongly with Hindu Indian culture, but over time different cultural similarities became clearer. Most obvious are the many visual affinities between Indian and Hausa culture. Men in Indian films, for instance, often dress in long kaftans, similar to the Hausa *dogon riga*, over which they wear long waistcoats, much like the Hausa *palmaran*. Women are also dressed in long saris and scarves which veil their heads and accord with Hausa ideas of feminine decorum. The iconography of Indian "tradition", such as marriage celebrations, food, village life and so on, even when different from Hausa culture, provides a similar cultural background that is frequently in opposition to the spread of "westernisation". Indian films place family and kinship at the centre of narrative tension as a key stimulus for characters' motivations to a degree that rarely occurs in western films. They are based on a strict division between the sexes, and love songs and sexual relations, while sensuous, are kept within firm boundaries. Kissing is rare and nudity absent. These generic conventions provide a marked difference from Hollywood films, and many Hausa viewers argue that Indian films 'have culture' in a way that American films seem to lack.

More complexly, Indian films are based upon negotiating the tension of preserving traditional moral values in a time of profound change. Ashis Nandy argues, in terms as relevant for Nigerians as they are for Indians, that Indian films are successful with Indian masses because despite their spectacle and rich settings they are based in a moral universe of action that is grounded in a traditional world view.

The basic principles of commercial cinema derive from the needs of Indians caught in the hinges of social change who are trying to understand their predicament in terms familiar to them. (Nandy 1995: 205)

Nandy argues that commercial cinema tends to

reaffirm the values that are being increasingly marginalized in public life by the language of the modernizing middle classes, values such as community ties, primacy of maternity over conjugality, priority of the mythic over the historical. (ibid.: 202)

Characters in Indian films have to negotiate the tension between traditional life and modernity in ways that Hausa, in a similar postcolonial situation, can sympathise with. The choice of wearing Indian or western-style clothes; the use of English by arrogant upper-class characters or by imperious bureaucrats; even the endemic corruption of the postcolonial state, are all familiar situations with which Hausa viewers can engage.

The familiarity that Hausa viewers experience when watching Indian films is reinforced by changes over time in the style and themes of Indian film. Contemporary films are more sexually explicit and violent, and borrow heavily from the styles of western film genres. Nigerian viewers comment on this when they compare older Indian films of the 1950s and 1960s that 'had culture' with newer ones which are more westernised. Older films were more often set among the rural poor than contemporary films. Characters, for instance, were more likely to wear traditional clothes, to keep animals or to travel by oxen. Not only did visual iconography change but musical styles, once based mainly on Indian classical forms, began to incorporate disco beats and western instrumentation. This perceived shift toward a growing materialism in Indian film echoed a similar shift in Nigerian society brought about by the radical dislocations of the oil boom of the mid-1970s. For Nigerian audiences the evolution of Indian film style thus corresponded with developments within their own society that brought home the similarities between the two. This has been a contentious process, and as difficult for Hausa viewers to accept in Indian films as to accept in their own culture. One young friend, who was a fan of Indian film, complained to me about this shift:

> When I was young and watching films, the Indian films we used to see were based on their tradition. You wouldn't see something like disco, going out to clubs, making gangs. Before, they didn't do it like that. But now Indian films are just like American films. They go to discos, make gangs, go out for picnics.[13] They'll do anything in a hotel and they play rough in romantic scenes where before you could never see things like that.

The perceived rise in violence, in sexual immorality and in materialism are all represented in my friend's complaint. Clubs, hotels and discos are symbols in Indian film and in Hausa popular culture of corrupt immoral spaces frequented by the rich. They are emblems of western life and stand in moral contrast to the Indian or Hausa social spaces such as the temple, mosque or village. Indian films depict an ambivalent attitude to such spaces, exploiting their use as spectacle while at the same time ensuring that the heroes and heroines are at some moral distance from them. Nandy argues that Indian films stand against the vicissitudes of the postcolonial state by grounding the shifts in materialism, urbanisation and apparent westernisation within a moral universe that is structured around familiar religious values. This is why, despite apparent westernisation, Indian films depict moral dilemmas strikingly different from Hollywood or other western films.

The reasons why Hausa viewers recognise commonalities between their culture and Indian culture are many and varied. In an Islamic African society the films are popular because they engage with the disjunctures of social change elaborated in terms that are familiar to Hausa society yet also distinct from it. This coexistence between likeness and dissimilarity is important because it is in the gap that the narratives of Indian film allow the exploration of social relations. I now discuss in greater detail this aspect of narrative and offer suggestions why it has become so controversial in *soyayya* books.

Imagination, Narrative and Social Change

The narratives of Indian films allow the exploration of attitudes and social possibilities that are still controversial in everyday Hausa social life. The psychoanalyst Sudhir Kakar has discussed this phenomenon in India, arguing that Hindi films are successful because they engage everyday fantasy. 'The power of fantasy…,' he argues, 'comes to our rescue by extending or withdrawing the desires beyond what is possible or reasonable' in the social order (1989: 27). He defines fantasy as 'that world of imagination which is fuelled by desire and which provides us with an alternative world where we can continue with our longstanding quarrel with reality' (ibid.). My concern in this article is with the narrative tension between love marriages and arranged marriages which is a dominant theme of both Hindi cinema and Hausa *soyayya* books. There is much more to Hindi films than this – the spectacle of beauty and wealth, the difficulty of reconciling responsibility to kin in a rapidly urbanising bureaucratic world or the problem of operating with honesty and honour in a corrupt postcolonial world – but this one genre of Indian film gives insight into broader conflict between desire and responsibility to a wider social order.

The romantic insistence on the potentially subversive power of imagination has been explored in two recent works on African oral literature and social structure. Beidelman (1993) argues that imagination has both an individual and a group importance. On the one hand, 'it relates to the ways that people construct images of the world in which they live . . . a cosmology that . . . presents a picture in which they measure, assess and reflect upon the reality of their experiences' (1993: 1). On the other hand, imagination offers a space from which to reflect upon the social order: 'In this sense imaginative exercise constitutes means for criticism, for distortion, even subversion of the moral social order' (ibid.). Michael Jackson, in his study of Kuranko oral literature, puts forward a similar picture of the power of narrative to explore ambiguities in social life. 'Kuranko narratives,' he argues, 'initiate a dialectic of doubt and uncertainty . . . [that] promote ambivalence and exploit ambiguity as a way of stimulating listeners to resolve problems of choice' (Jackson 1982: 2). Jackson stipulates that narratives are a secure way to bring up ambiguous situations, allowing readers the imaginative space to explore multiple resolutions of narrative tensions, before resolving them (in the case of oral literature) safely within the limits of accepted norms.

What Jackson and Beidelman see as a function of oral literature Kakar views as part of the collective fantasy provided by the mass culture of Indian films. I argue that the engagement with themes of romantic love revealed in *soyayya* books and Indian films exemplifies precisely this desire to explore the limits of social norms during a period of rapid change. The tension between arranged marriages and love marriages is not new to Hausa society, nor is the idea that romantic love may be subversive of the moral order, as many Hausa folk tales exemplify. What is new, however, is the speed of contemporary social change that has placed the issues of love, marriage and sexuality squarely at the forefront of social concern. The increase in conflicts over the style and nature of courtship, the appropriate age and conditions of marriage and over what is seen as the increased materialism of marriage partners condenses fears about the pace of social change. As Indian films and *soyayya* books are the main mass cultural forms that provide a sustained engagement with these issues over a long period of time, it is unsurprising that they have become a topic of public controversy. To account for the intensity of this controversy it is first necessary to outline the boundaries of social transformation in contemporary Hausa society.

Youth and Marriage in Contemporary Kano

The oil boom of the 1970s thrust Nigeria into the fast capitalism of an oil economy, transforming not only the economic basis of the country but the pace of urbanisation, consumption habits and the political system. Watts and Pred (1992) have borrowed from Benjamin to label this revolutionary change the 'shock of modernity'. As well as making the country dependent upon imports of basic foodstuffs, the boom internationalised the consumption habits of the middle classes, creating the easy assumption that fast capitalism meant fast westernisation. The economic crash which followed the oil boom exacerbated these transformations and contributed to a growing self-consciousness about the changing nature of Nigerian society, marked by Islamic revitalisation and criticism of secular westernisation. The transformative impact of the boom and bust of the oil economy continues to affect all classes of Nigerian society, but the position of youth has become an issue of considerable concern (Barkindo 1993; 'Dan Asabe, n.d.; Said and Last 1991).

The 'problems' of contemporary youth are evidenced in different realms, from the perceived rise in violence to theft, drug-taking, disrespect for elders and materialism. Even the rise in Islamic participation of youth has been a key moral discourse by which youths have challenged the authority of government and elders.[14] Important religious scholars such as Sheikh Isa Waziri in Kano preached regularly against the changing attitudes and behaviour of Hausa youth, and it is these social tensions that are indexed by the debate about *soyayya* books. At the forefront of this concern is the problem of changing marriage patterns in northern Nigeria, and more especially the concern over regulating female sexuality.

The collapse in the Nigerian economy has made the cost of the *lefe*, the gifts each man must give his wife before marriage, economically difficult for many young men. The *lefe* forms only part of the rising cost of marriage, and this inflation has been vehemently attacked as one of the most visible markers of the growing materialism of Hausa society. Religious leaders have complained regularly against the practice and there have even been attempts by state governments to regulate the costs involved, but to little avail. The result is that young men are delaying marriage until a later age when they have the income to afford the expense. Meanwhile the marrying age of women has also been moving upward. The introduction of compulsory primary-school education in 1976 affected the traditional practice of arranging marriages for girls before the onset of puberty, at around 13 years of age (Callaway 1987). Nowadays it is more common for parents to wait until a child has finished school, around the age of 16 or 17, before choosing a marriage partner. Callaway, in her study of Hausa women in Kano, sees the rise in both western and Islamic education as the source of potential change in the status of women (ibid.). As women are more enlightened as to their rights as women under Islamic law, she asserts there may be more room to resist Hausa cultural practices from the point of view of Islamic orthodoxy. One consequence is that increased education and the rise in marriage age mean that women may be more prepared to assert some measure of control over the choice of their marriage partners.

For parents and religious leaders the increase in the number of sexually mature young people outside the bounds of marriage is not only contrary to a proper Islamic social order but has become an issue demanding public regulation. In 1987 the Kano state government set up state committees to find solutions to contemporary social problems. Along with the rise in crime, hooliganism and begging, the "problem" of unmarried women was the subject of state examination. Two years later, in his Ramadan sermon, Sheikh Isa Waziri, one of the prominent Islamic leaders in Kano, addressed the same issue when he sent out a call for rich men to marry more wives in order to solve what he termed the 'calamity' of unmarried women (Barkindo 1993: 96). A perceived rise in sexual activity before marriage, as well as in the growing number of prostitutes (seen as a moral rather than an economic problem), has neatly conflated the issues of westernisation, materialism, the need to regulate sexuality, and the immorality of the secular Nigerian state, for northern political and religious leaders.

In her discussion of Hausa female marriage and sexuality Callaway points out that there is no acceptable space within Islamic society to be of childbearing age and unmarried. As more women occupy this 'unacceptable' space, relations between the sexes are evolving. Callaway, for instance, describes traditional Hausa interaction between the sexes as extremely limited. Compared with the West, she argues, Hausa men live separate physical and emotional lives. She concludes,

Thus, men and women live in two separate worlds, normally do not share their thoughts or their lives, and function fairly independently of each other in their different spheres. Even husbands and wives do not normally socialize together or with each other; in order to show respect in the home, they do not eat together, seldom interact and avoid addressing each other by name. (Callaway 1987: 44)

As a result of this sexual segregation, Callaway argues, 'The experience of romantic love is not normally part of an Islamic marriage'; "Love" and "Romance" are western concepts and have little real meaning in this [Hausa] culture' (1987: 36, 40). Callaway's comments caricature and devalue the complex emotions of Muslim marriages,[15] but she does represent problems that many Hausa experience. Many soyayya authors discussed the issue with me as they talked of the massive changes in the way young men and women interact with each other in contemporary Hausa society. Ideally, both women and men in Hausa society are expected to exhibit kunya, a sense of modesty and shame. Adamu Mohammed,[16] author of the novel Garnak'ak'i ('Uncompromising') explained what this meant in terms of sexual interaction. Traditionally, he said, all meetings between boys and girls would be chaperoned by older relatives. Frequently the couple involved might be too embarrassed even to speak to each other, and women, especially, would communicate reluctantly, if at all. Another author, 'Dan Azumi 'Yan Gurasa,[17] confirmed this. 'When I was young,' he said, 'and came across the girl I loved I couldn't face her and tell her. Instead I would send someone who could talk to her about it.' Nowadays, both authors agreed, this sense of shyness has been transformed, and both men and women act in a manner that would have been unacceptable twenty years previously.

In their plots, soyayya authors examine some of the issues made contentious by the shift in gender interaction. The common narrative conflict between youth wishing to marry for love and parents who wish to organise marriage partners reveals how romance narratives allow a form of moral enquiry for Hausa youth. The fantasy encoded in fictional narratives succeeds, as Beidelman points out, 'by presenting a version of experience and things that is both less and more than what we ordinarily encounter', allowing, in part, 'a luxuriation of qualities and possibilities not encountered in reality' (1993: 5). For over thirty years Indian films provided a dominant forum for the creation of an imaginary space where real social tensions over love and responsibility, individual desire and social control, appeared and various resolutions of these tensions were considered. Indian films could do this successfully only by engaging with issues that were meaningful to Hausa viewers yet at the same time providing enough of a difference for alternative resolutions to be possible. This engagement with the conflict of love and courtship in contemporary society is what has defined the plots of *soyayya* books for both their admirers and their critics. Examining these stories reveals the intertextual presence of Indian films and its appropriation within Hausa popular culture.

Market Literature in the Vernacular: The Rise of *Soyayya* Books

In the last six years there has been a near-revolution in the publishing of Hausa literature. A whole new genre of *littatafan soyayya*, love stories, has emerged, published by authors themselves and sold through markets and small shops all over the northern region. During the time of the Structural Adjustment Programme (SAP), when the cost of imported goods (such as paper) has been soaring and the purchasing power of incomes has been collapsing, *soyayya* authors have published over 200 books, and created a system of publishing and distribution that keeps book prices within the range of ordinary people. Earlier books have achieved the status of 'best-seller', giving their authors a great deal of fame. Many of them are read out on the radio, on the extremely popular programme *Shafa Labari Shuni* (meaning 'a person exaggerates what he hears'), and adaptations of successful books form a significant proportion of the vibrant new market in Hausa videos. While the debate rages over whether *soyayya* books are a beneficial addition to Hausa culture, their great achievement has been to create a popular Hausa reading public for fiction.

In his major survey of Hausa literature Furniss (1996: 54–5) argues that *soyayya* writers 'appear to owe more to the English language publishing of Mills and Boon, and James Hadley Chase...than to any Hausa precedent'. Furniss is correct in assessing the innovativeness of this new style of literature but mistaken in seeing it as based solely on western precedents. *Soyayya* authors and their critics cite many sources for their books, including English romances and Hollywood 'best-sellers', but they also admit the important influence of Arabian tales, Nigerian romance magazines and Indian films. I concentrate on the influence of Indian films, not to ignore these other media, but as part of my larger point in analysing the flow of media within and between non-western countries. The great appeal of Indian films across class, education and gender, along with the recognised similarities in culture, make them a significant precedent for contemporary writers and readers.

Soyayya books are pamphlets little more than fifty pages in length. Many run to two or three parts in order to keep costs down. They are badly typeset, badly printed and, from the point of view of critics, badly edited and written. Furniss argues that authors adopted the practice of publishing their own work, using offset litho printers, following the example of religious *ajami*[18] poets. Print runs are typically small, running from 2,000 to 5,000, but successful books will go into multiple printings. Originally, *soyayya* books were sold from shops and vendors selling school books. As they have become more established it is not uncommon to see market stalls devoted solely to *soyayya* books, or to see hawkers wandering round markets and business districts balancing books on their heads. The authors, unlike earlier generations of Hausa writers, come from neither an elite nor even a well educated background. Some have never received western education and most of those who have, left after primary level, remaining only in Islamic schools, and consequently their knowledge of English, and with it their integration into existing literary culture, is often poor. Women make up a significant proportion of *soyayya* authors and some, like Hajiya Balaraba Ramat Yakubu (*Alhaki Kwikwiyo*, meaning 'Retribution is like a puppy, it follows its owner', 1990a, and *Budurwar Zuciya*, 'The heart's desire', 1990b), are among the most famous *soyayya* authors. Second-ary-school leavers make up a significant proportion of the readers (though perhaps not as great a proportion as people claim) and there is a strong association in the public mind between *soyayya* books and women readers. Despite this, many young men I knew were avid readers of the literature, and the high percentage of men who write fan letters to the authors suggests that there is a significant male relationship.

Soyayya books first emerged from Kano, the metropolitan centre of northern Nigeria. Originally authors came together to organise writers' clubs modelled on the famous drama clubs organised by heroes of independence in the north, Mallam Aminu Kano, Sa'adu Zungur and Maitama Sule. The first and most famous clubs were Raina Kama ('Deceptive Appearances')[19] and Kukan Kurciya ('The Cry of a Dove'), created in order to exchange mutual aid and advice among neophyte authors. Since that time new writers' clubs have appeared in many major cities and contemporary *soyayya* authors come from all northern urban centres. Many authors began by basing their first novel on an experience that had happened to them or their friends, often an affair of love. *In da so da K'auna* I, II (meaning 'Where there's love and desire') by Ado Ahmad (1989) or *Garnak'ak'i* I, II by Adamu Mohammed (1991) are both examples of this. Many authors go on to write about other issues, whether it be politics in Bala Anas Babinlata's *Tsuntsu Mai Wayo* I, II ("The Clever Bird", 1993) or *'yan daba* [thugs] and crime in 'Dan Azumi Baba's *Rikicin Duniya* I, II, III ('This Deceptive World', 1990). The dominant theme with which most books are identified remains the conflict over love.

Soyayya books dramatise the problems of contemporary sexual relations, criticis-ing forced marriages and the increasing material demands of both lovers and parents. Many authors claim a didactic purpose for their writing, arguing that they are educating young people and their parents against the problems that beset contemporary youth. The fact that many authors begin writing as a direct result of a personal experience underscores the close relation between the stories and perceived social problems. Adamu Mohammed explained to me that he began writing books when the parents of the girl he loved married her off, against the wishes of both the lovers, to a wealthier man. As a poor man, Mohammed argued, he had no means of fighting the decision except by writing his book *Garnak'ak'i* – 'Uncompromising'. The sense of outrage and vindication is common to many of the early *soyayya* writers. A similar event sparked off the career of Ado Ahmad. As Maigari Ahmed Bichi (1992) reports, the arrangements for Ahmad's first marriage were broken off despite the fact that he and his fiancée were in love and her parents were happy about the marriage: 'a misunderstanding between their two families... was caused by the grandmother of the girl, who... had arranged for the girl to be given to one Alhaji[20] for marriage' (1992: 7). Bichi continues that as a result Ahmad intended his first novel to 'show how love is played in Hausa society and the role of parents in marriage affairs' (ibid.). One fledgling author from Kaduna, Adamu Ciroma, who also began writing after a personal experience, argues that many if not most *soyayya* authors begin writing this way:

Our writers today we share experiences which makes us start writing. . . . An experience happens to me and so I decide to write about it in order to enlighten people on what has happened. . . . Nine out of ten writers begin writing *soyayya* because they have experienced it. (personal communication)

For *soyayya* authors there is a didactic and moral purpose to their discourse on love that gives their novels a sense of social responsibility. They argue that incompatibility in the choice of marriage partner leads daughters to run away from their parents to become 'independent women' (and hence prostitutes), or to attempt suicide, or to go through an unhappy marriage and an early divorce – even if the partner chosen is wealthy. But as the author 'Dan Azumi Baba argues, 'now everything has changed [and] because of reading such books [*soyayya* books] no girl agrees with forced marriage and parents understand that if they force their daughter to marry somebody she will eventually go and become a prostitute' (interview, 28 June 1995). He continued, 'the main problem of marriage is lack of love', adding that most women now are wise to the fact that 'if there is love, they will not mind about any problems.' The concerns aired by 'Dan Azumi and others over the increasing commodification of contemporary love and the iniquities of forced marriage are not just the province of *soyayya* books but have formed staple themes of Indian films. For over thirty years Indian films have provided an extended narration of the problems of arranged marriages and of the place of materialism in a 'traditional' society that mimics real events in everyday Hausa lives. Before discussing *soyayya* books themselves it is worth returning briefly to the concept of fantasy and imagination to give an example of the investment of viewers in Indian narratives.

The possibility of imaginative investment was brought home to me one day when I was talking to an older Hausa friend in his forties. Knowing he liked Indian films, I was surprised to hear him say that they had a negative influence on Hausa culture. He cited the example of his own marriage. He said that when he was young, in the 1970s, he went to see lots of Indian films. He, like many other men, liked the commitment of Indian films to the family, the importance of marriage and children, and many other cultural values in the films. The problem, he said, was that in Indian films women are very supportive of their husbands. He explained that what he meant was that when an Indian man sees his love they talk about their problems. He declares his love for her, she declares hers for him, and they embrace. In the 1970s men who went to the cinema were expecting or wanting similar behaviour from their wives. It was what he had wanted when he got married. But when he returned home and tried to talk to his wife she would turn away, answer as briefly as possible and try to leave the room. He told me women in Hausa society were taught that their husband is everything and they should be in awe of him. His wife was acting with the modesty that a good Hausa wife should have, whereas he wanted the sort of relationship he had seen in Indian films. As a result he had encountered many problems early in his marriage and that was why, he argued, the films could be harmful. Indian films, he said conveyed ideas about marriage and relationships that local culture could not support.

My friend's anecdote is a striking example of the complicated ways in which transnational media flows become incorporated into individual experience and affect larger social constructions such as gender. It is even more fascinating as it is so clearly dated. In the early 1970s the exhibition of Indian films was largely restricted to the cinema. The practice of female seclusion (*kulle*) meant that women were absent (for the most part) from the male arena of cinema and it was not until the growth of domestic technologies such as television and video that women gained access to the popular culture of Indian films. Since that time Indian films have become identified as 'women's films' because of their huge popularity. The stereotype now is that it is *women* who demand that their partners act more like lovers in Indian films and *men* who complain that Indian films create demands that cannot be met. This complaint has become all the more controversial as people accuse *soyayya* authors of dramatising the Bombay melodrama style of love within a Hausa context.

All You Need Is Love...

To give some sense of the tone and structure of the texts I am dealing with I briefly outline the plots of two *soyayya* books. The books I discuss are *In Da so da K'auna* I, II by Ado Ahmad (1989) and *Kishi Kumallon Mata* (meaning 'Jealousy is the nausea of women') by Maryam Sahabi Liman (1993). *In Da* is a two-part volume that was abridged and translated into English as *The Soul of my Heart* in 1993. Its author, Ado Ahmad, says it is the best-selling of all *soyayya* books, selling over 50,000 copies, and has since been adapted into a three-part Hausa video and remains one of the few *soyayya* books to have been translated into English. (I cite from this text.)[21] *In Da*, as one of the earliest and most popular books, has been the subject of great attention and discussion, and exemplifies many of the major themes associated with *soyayya* books. *Kishi* is a more recent novel, published after *soyayya* books had received a great deal of public criticism. Because of this, Liman is careful to avoid many of the themes that have led to *soyayya* books being dismissed as a form of *iskanci* (immorality, loose living) and provides a good counterpoint to *In Da*.

In Da tells the story of Sumayya, a rich girl who falls in love with a much poorer boy, Mohammed. Unfortunately Sumayya herself is the object of the affections of Abdulkadir, a wealthy young businessman. When Abdulkadir is rejected by Sumayya he visits her grandmother, taking gifts and money, and persuades her to intervene on his behalf with Sumayya's parents. Accordingly she threatens to withdraw her blessing from her son if Sumayya is not wed to Abdulkadir. Abdulkadir, meanwhile, arranges to have Mohammed beaten up by thugs to warn him off Sumayya. Sumayya and Mohammed are crushed by the news of the arranged marriage. As the wedding nears, Sumayya throws herself down a well in a desperate attempt at suicide. She survives and is taken to hospital, where her life is saved by a timely blood transfusion from Mohammed. Her parents, seeing this, feel that now the couple should be united and agree to the marriage. They are wed and Mohammed goes into business, becoming rich, while Abdulkadir, returning from a business deal in Abuja, is pursued by armed robbers who force his Mercedes off the road and rob him of all his money, leaving him a pauper.

Kishi describes the problems that derive from jealous co-wives. It tells the story of a rich man, Usman, who falls in love and marries Ruk'ayya. They live happily together until it is found out that Ruk'ayya cannot conceive. After consulting both western doctors and religious teachers, Ruk'ayya selflessly advises her husband that he should take a second wife. Ruk'ayya persuades her good friend Saratu to attract the attentions of her husband so that he will marry her, arguing that if she has to have a co-wife it should be someone she is friends with. Usman and Saratu marry and Saratu becomes pregnant. Immediately, though, she accuses Ruk'ayya of trying to poison her from jealousy. Usman comes to side with Saratu's accusations of poison and witchcraft against Ruk'ayya. He moves Saratu to a different house and later, when he travels to America on business, he leaves his affairs in the hands of Saratu's grasping father. After his departure, Ruk'ayya discovers she is two months pregnant. Months later, while Usman is still away, she gives birth and while she is in hospital Saratu is admitted because of a miscarriage. Usman returns home to discover that his and Saratu's baby has died, that Saratu orchestrated the accusations of poison and witchcraft against Ruk'ayya and that her father has been ruining his business. Usman divorces Saratu and returns to Ruk'ayya, who accepts him lovingly and without recrimination.

Soyayya books create a utopian world where the norms of sexual relations are inverted and transformed. *In Da* and *Kishi* recount the love stories of young people of equal age. Unlike usual Hausa sexual relations, men and women not only share social space with each other, but they spend recreational time together and lead a shared emotional life. The traditional sense of shyness that regulates social interaction is transformed. Men openly declare their love for women, and women, more shockingly, are equally vocal in expressing their love in return. In *In Da*, for instance, Sumayya is the first to look at Mohammed. She initiates contact with him through letters and when they finally meet:

'Mohammed,' she said shyly, 'I must confess that you are always on my mind. I love you very much.' (Ahmad 1993a: 10)

Similarly, in *Kishi*, Usman and Ruk'ayya address each other in phrases that are new to Hausa love-making: in one scene Ruk'ayya approaches a worried Usman and asks, 'O my lover, the milk that cools my heart, what is worrying you?' (Liman 1993: 20). Usman replies, 'There is nothing, light of my heart' (ibid.).

Soyayya books portray a field of sexual interaction very different from 'traditional' Hausa ideals. Open declarations of love, expressed in an elaborate and highly formalised way, are one of the most visible markers of the shift in styles of love among Hausa youth. In fact *In Da* represents a reversal of the norms of Hausa sexual hierarchy, with Sumayya, by virtue of her money and status, narratively more active and passionate than Mohammed. This subversive link between materialism and sexuality is another common theme of *soyayya* books, and reiterates the fears of many Hausa young about the difficulties of marriage. At the beginning of *In Da*, when his friends notice that Sumayya is eyeing Mohammed, it sets off an exchange among his friends, who dismiss Mohammed's concern that Sumayya is too rich for him. They make the familiar claim among male Hausa youth that there are too many unmarried women and lament the fact that they cannot afford to marry:

'Husbands are hard to come by now, anyway.'

'Exactly,' Garba agreed. 'The table has now turned. It is the girls that now court. Men are extremely scarce you know.' (Ahmad 1993a: 3)

Garba discusses the reason for this unnatural state of affairs:

'The fault lies squarely on the parents. They try to commercialise marriages. It goes to the highest bidder. . . . [A]ll of us here crave marriage but it is the demands that scare us away.' (ibid.: 4)

The commodification of religious affairs such as marriage that Garba refers to is represented by the figure of the grandmother. Her age should represent the accrual of wisdom and authority but she loses the respect she is due when she commodifies her authority by accepting bribes from Abdulkadir. Instead of representing what is best about tradition she comes to stand for what is worst about the corruption of contemporary times. It is this illegitimate act that allows Sumayya's rebellion against parental authority to remain within the bounds of an ideal moral universe.

The tension between tradition and modernity that materialism represents in the story is mimicked in the conflict over individual desire and social responsibility. Early in the book, Mohammed points out to Sumayya that her parents are likely to view the possibility of their marriage negatively, owing to their unequal social status. Sumayya reveals her commitment to modern social values as she dismisses his argument:

Please do understand that nothing is permanent, riches or otherwise. Are we the ones who determine our destinies? I assume that our creator has that singular quality. He gives to whomever he wishes and refuses whomever he wishes. Besides, talking about parental inter-ference, I think that has by now been one of the bygones. They now accept what the boy and girl want. The evils of forced marriages are too clear for all to see. (ibid.: 10–11)

Sumayya is overconfident in believing forced marriage a thing of the past, and that parents will readily cede autonomy to their children. She makes the religiously acceptable argument that it is Allah who determines destiny, but she does so as she sloughs off concern for parental authority and asserts the right to control her own destiny.

While overt rebellion against parental authority is missing, this sense of individual control also marks the storyline of *Kishi*. *Kishi* was intended overtly to avoid the criticism that surrounded early *soyayya* books such as *In Da*. The suicide attempt by Sumayya, for instance, was alleged to have inspired other young girls to follow her example, and critics accused Ahmad of teaching girls to rebel against their parents (Giginyu 1992). Liman is careful not to advocate rebellion and attempts to articulate the new subjectivity of youth, and the fascination of romantic love, within an accepted Hausa framework. *Kishi* is full of platitudinous statements about ideal behaviour which are immediately contradicted by the logic and tension of narrative development. Unlike *In Da*, all the youths in *Kishi* respect and obey their parents and never contemplate rebelling against their decisions. But Liman never puts them in a position where they have to. Usman and Ruk'ayya meet and court by them-selves. When they fall in love *they* decide to tell their parents, who are delighted and form no embarrassing obstacles. Significantly, though, control over the decision as to marriage partner is left to the young people themselves. This is the case even with Usman's second marriage, to the devious but beautiful Saratu.

Liman creates a utopian world of rich and beautiful youth who fly to Europe for medical treatment, who act selflessly and love passionately, but always in the context of proper Hausa behaviour. It may be that the characters drive fancy cars, go to western-style hotels for their honeymoon and live in large houses filled with the latest in electronic consumer goods, but Liman accompanies this spectacle of material wealth with moral homilies referencing key Hausa virtues. When Alhaji Lawal, Usman's grandfather, instructs him that now is the time to be thinking of marriage and to begin looking for a bride, he tells him, 'Even though I won't prevent you from looking for beauty, you should make sure it's religion that leads you to marriage and not your heart' (Liman 1993: 2). Usman agrees to this obvious insertion of 'ideal' Hausa values, but in the next paragraph he sees a girl, their eyes meet and he falls in love, asking himself if she will agree to marry him before he has ever said a word to her, let alone found out about her religious values. Similarly, Usman announces his wedding to his grandfather with:

'Grandfather, today something wonderful has happened to us.' Then he told him the story from the beginning to the end. Fortunately Alhaji Lawal knew Mallam Haruna [Ruk'ayya's father] and knew him for an upright character who doesn't care about worldly things. (Liman 1993: 9–10)

Liman protects Usman's desire for control over his own life and Alhaji's concern for proper Hausa values, as individual desire and parental will coincide in a perfect world.

The dominant melodramatic tension in *Kishi* revolves around the moral of sacrifice. This theme constitutes part of the basic genre of Indian film and depends for its significance on the tension between modernity and tradition in postcolonial societies. Sacrifice, as it is mobilised in *Kishi* and many Indian films, depends upon a moral choice between individual desire and social responsibility, taking on a cultural as well as an individual resonance. Ruk'ayya, in *Kishi*, is the supreme example of the self-sacrificing wife. Not only does she accept the unjust accusations of her co-wife uncomplainingly, the very fact that as a wife she insists on her husband marrying a second wife reveals how willing she is to sacrifice her individual happiness for the good of the family. In Hausa the name for co-wife, *kishiya*, derives from *kishi*, the Hausa word for jealousy, and is particularly identified with women (as the proverb and title of the book, 'Jealousy is the nausea of women', implies). Most Hausa readers I spoke to thought it highly unlikely that any husband and grandfather would not look for a second wife if the first were barren (again reiterating the utopian nature of the book), but this device is necessary to highlight the individual nature of Ruk'ayya's sacrifice.

Jackson argues that narratives function by raising 'ethical dissonance' (1982: 2), situations of doubt and uncertainty through which the audience can reflect upon the nature of the social order. He argues that this is especially true in folk tales about love. In many societies the choice of marriage partner is an important decision affecting the entire family and so is rarely left to the individuals directly concerned. Love affairs, Jackson points out, are based on individual choices. 'Love,' he states, "like all strong emotions, is difficult to control, and its course is unpredictable" (ibid.: 202). In consequence love can be wild and a potential threat to the social order. To make sure the passing fancies of men and women are regulated for the common good, love has to be reined in and controlled by authorities, usually elder kin. Abu-Lughod makes a similar point in her discussion of the poetry of love and emotions among Bedouin. 'Succumbing to sexual desire, or merely to romantic love,' she asserts, 'can lead individuals to disregard social convention and social obligations' and threaten social values of honour and the authority of elders (1986: 147–8). Stories of romantic love raise questions about the importance of individual action versus familial obligation, but precisely how these stories are resolved varies. When, in *Kishi*, Ruk'ayya decides to regulate her emotions and sacrifice her desires for the good of the family she makes a choice in favour of the social order. Conversely, when Sumayya decides to reject what she sees as the illegitimate decision of her parents, she refuses their authority in an attempted suicide.

By presenting two radically different solutions to comparable problems these books bear out Jackson's argument that narratives promote ambivalence and ambiguity as a way of allowing readers to imaginatively explore social tensions in their multiple connotations. Jackson argues that this process occurs in the development of a single narrative, but it is my point that the mass culture of *soyayya* books and Indian films develops the process of ambiguity by presenting various resolutions of similar predicaments in thousands of narratives extending over many years. By engaging both with individual stories and with the genre as a whole, narratives provide the ability for social inquiry. Sacrifice is significant to postcolonial societies negotiating the rapidity and direction of social change because it is for their readers and viewers that the conflict between parental authority and individual desire is most keenly felt. This is one reason why the theme of sacrifice is so prevalent in Indian films and *soyayya* books and relatively absent from western genres such as Hollywood films. Precisely because this theme has such relevance to Hausa society, the success of *soyayya* books has occasioned a powerful backlash against them, and even, by proxy, against Indian films, which previously were a relatively unremarked part of the Hausa cultural landscape. To finish my discussion of transnational media and social change I now outline the contours of the public debate that surrounds the success of *soyayya* books. This controversy reveals how conflict over the direction of social change is condensed around issues of changing sexual relations among youth, and the place of Indian films as a cultural third space situated between Hausa tradition and western modernity.[22]

Soyayya Books, Youth and Social Change: The Controversy

Right from your book cover the design is sinful. . . . Similarly when somebody reads your books he will see that inside consists of sin and forbidden things. And when it comes to letters in the books to believe in them will make somebody deviate from the teachings of his religion. Quotations like 'my better half' [*rabin raina*], 'the light of my heart' [*hasken zuciyata*] and other lies makes you wonder whether the writer should not be lashed. (*Zuwa ga marabutan Soyayya*, 'An open letter to *soyayya* authors', from the editor, *Gwagwarmaya* ('Struggle') 2: 19)

The strong moral lessons embedded in *soyayya* books have gained enormous popularity with a young Hausa audience. Yet it is often youth who are the bitterest opponents of this new form of fiction. The success of *soyayya* books has created a public discourse that includes a profusion of articles in Hausa-language magazines and newspapers, letters to the authors themselves, and the everyday conversation of fans and critics. The tone and passion of the public discourse indicate the volatility of response to the popular culture of romance. One letter to the editor of the Hausa-language newspaper *Nasiha* 'Advice') is typical of the debate:

Dear Sir,

I wish to take space in your widely read newspaper to appeal to the Federal Government and the State Government. In truth, it would be better if the Government took steps regarding the books that certain notorious elements are writing everywhere in Nigeria, especially in the north. (19 May 1995: 8)

The letter writer continues, 'These books only succeed in corrupting our youth, especially girls," and adds that it has become necessary for the government to take action.

When I was in Nigeria the idea that the state government was about to take radical action 'against' *soyayya* books was widely believed by young men who were opposed to their continued distribution. Such youths had two main complaints against the books. The first was that the material world of fine clothes, expensive cars and generous lovers that the books presented encouraged girls to demand presents from their boyfriends and lovers that they could not afford. In consequence boys who may court a girl for years, giving her small presents and supporting her education, lose out to a rich Alhaji who meets and marries the girl within just a few months. The second complaint is that girls demand a different style of behaviour from their lovers. In a reverse of the complaints made against Indian films cited earlier, girls both demonstrate and demand greater sophistication in the language and behaviour of love. One friend of mine who attacked *soyayya* books vehemently said that in the past if you tried to kiss a girl before you were married she would scream and call for her brothers. Now, he said, if you don't kiss her by the second time you meet she will think you are 'bush" (backward) and this is the result of reading *soyayya* books. As well as calls for the government to intervene, some secondary school headmasters are said to have embarked on a campaign to expel any girls found with *soyayya* books in their possession. The discourse around the books then, has touched on an issue of considerable public passion.

The press debate was sparked by the efforts of two journalists (both fiction writers themselves) working at the newspaper *Nasiha*: Ibrahim Sheme and Ibrahim Malumfashi. Sheme initiated a regular literary page in the newspaper which, soon after *soyayya* books began to appear in northern markets, published an interview with one author, Hauwa Ibrahim Shariff (6 September 1991). Thus began the public debate over the pros and cons of *soyayya* books, including a seminal exchange of articles between Ibrahim Malumfashi (then at Usman Dan Fodio University in Sokoto) and Ado Ahmad. Malumfashi opened the debate with an attack on *soyayya* writers, 'On the need to change the style of Hausa literature' (November 1991: 7). In this article he charged *soyayya* writers with dwelling on themes of escapism that had little or no relevance to the problems of poverty and deteriorating life style that dominated everyday existence. He argued that the books shamelessly borrowed from other cultures, creating situations that could never possibly exist in Hausa society. Later, Malumfashi extended his critique of cultural borrowing in an article entitled 'Between second-hand and original' (*Nasiha*, 7 August 1992: 4; 14 August 1992: 4) where he argued that *soyayya* books were 'second-hand' and that if Ado Ahmad 'watches Indian films he will realise that it is these films that are being translated into Hausa and claimed to have happened in Kano, Kaduna, Katsina or Sokoto. Most of these books are filled with rubbish' (14 August 1992: 4).

Ahmad responded to Malumfashi as chairman of the main *soyayya* writing group, Raina Kama. His article 'Let's go with modern times! (*Nasiha* 24, 31 July 1992) makes the powerful point that for the first time Hausa markets are filled with books written in Hausa that, far from copying foreign cultures, represent an efflorescence of Hausa culture. Times have changed, Ahmad argues, and *soyayya* books call for the betterment of society rather than corrupting it. Ahmad's argument stems from the fact that many *soyayya* writers who create stories from personal experience are writing about issues that are important to contemporary culture and should not be ignored for the sake of more 'relevant' issues. It is a point of view echoed by Yusuf Adamu Mohammed when he asks why contemporary authors write love stories:

The contemporary generation of readers are more interested in what concerns them: stories of ancient empires and jinns [spirits] are no longer appealing to them.[23] Second, many of these young authors are young and unmarried... [and they suffer] from the misdeeds of autocratic rich men in society... Since the young novelists are also among the downtrodden, in real life they are virtually helpless. Yet they can use their pens to fight for their rights and the rights of the oppressed. (*Association of Nigerian Authors Review*, October 1994: 9, 10)

The debate between Ahmad, Malumfashi and others sparked an outpouring in the pages of *Nasiha* and other Hausa-language magazines and newspapers. Sheme, who had initiated the debate, finally had to ask for no more submissions because the paper was inundated (*Nasiha*, 28 August 1992), though the debate still continues regularly. The debate in the press was supplemented by letters to the authors themselves. Many *soyayya* authors include a postal address on all books published, and popular authors such as Ahmad, 'Dan Azumi Baba and Adamu Mohhammed get an enormous response. Ahmad has received more than 2,000 letters covering a range of topics from requests for free copies, to expressions of love, to requests for advice on how to manage relationships, and compliments and criticism. One such letter from a recent (male) school graduate stated:

Among all the writers of Hausa *soyayya* books you [Ado Ahmad] are the best of them. This is because you are aware of what is going on nowadays. And you are more devoted Islamically and culturally than all of them.... [Your popularity is] because of your struggle to educate youth on marriage and not only children but parents too. The books stop parents making arranged marriages for their children and give freedom of choice to each and everybody irrespective of tribe or culture. This is of course the major aspect of your books that impresses and encourages people to read more *soyayya* books. (3 November 1993)

It is interesting and unsurprising that the writer registers Ahmad's devotion to religion and to culture, as these are the grounds on which *soyayya* authors are attacked most strongly. Many other letter writers have praised Ahmad for his stand against materialistic parents. One said that contemporary youth were sick of the greed of money mongers (*mai idon cin naira*) like Sumayya's grandmother and grateful for the 'educative' nature of *soyayya* books. Another said that the books showed him the wrongs of forced marriage (*auren dole*) and the importance of individual choice. The books, he continued, 'teach us how to live successfully in the world . . . how parents should take care of their children and be careful in letting their daughters choose the person they love and admire' (no date).

The insistence on individual choice curbing parental authority is cited by many critics as the prime reason for the pernicious effect of *soyayya* books. 'I swear, Mallam Ado,' wrote one youth in response to reading *In Da*, 'most of the crises that are occurring nowadays are caused by your writings. Our youths are spoiled by reading your books.' He continued:

[Ado Ahmad] you are among those who mobilise our youth, especially our girls, to start feeling freedom of choice by force, and that they should start doing everything according to their own interest and to forget about their parents' interest, and that they should only marry the person they love. For example, mostly in your books you write about a girl running away from her parents, because of someone she loves and chooses to be with. And, as you see, this is a great deviation from the teachings of Islam and culture, as you forget that girls are under the thumb of their parents religiously and culturally. (29 January 1994)

The response of letter writers to Ahmad and other authors indicates how closely people view the relation between *soyayya* books and everyday life. One writer to Ahmad said he became a fan of his books when his girlfriend insisted he read them because there were so many things he could learn from them. Similarly, Baba and Ahmad receive many letters asking for advice in matters of love. It is unsurprising, then, that these books generate such passion, as fans of *soyayya* writers and their critics are both responding to the mundane concern about contemporary social change. *Soyayya* books effectively dramatise this change within the realm of romance and sexuality. The profusion of articles both for and against *soyayya* books in the press has taken what was mainly a controversy among young people (reading *soyayya* books would be considered too demanding for older men) into a wider public arena.

Conclusion

One Friday night I went with a friend to see the classic Indian film *Mother India* (1957, directed by Mehboob Khan) at the Marhaba. A Lebanese distributor had explained to me how despite the fact that he had been screening the film for decades it could still sell out any cinema in the north, and he made me curious to see whether it was true. Sure enough, on Friday night at the Marhaba, the busiest night (usually reserved for new films) at the newest and largest cinema in Kano, all the seats were full. As the film started the friend I went with turned to me and said, 'Besides you, everyone in the cinema has seen this film at least fifteen times.' I relate this anecdote to give some sense not just of the pervasiveness of Indian film but of the fan culture that surrounds it. This comes across strongly when you watch a film where everyone knows the songs, when people laugh at the comedy routines almost before they are finished, and where the dialogue, the narrative and the emotions invoked carry the familiarity and comfort of a well-known and well-loved film.[24] When I returned home that night another friend in his late twenties asked me where I had been. I told him and asked if he knew when the film was made. He laughed, saying, 'I don't know, but as soon as I knew film I knew *Mother India*.' Just as I, growing up in London in a cinematic world dominated by American stars, incorporated American media as part of English popular culture, so it is for Hausa audiences. Indian films have been reworked and incorporated to form an integral part of contemporary Hausa social life.

The long struggle against cultural imperialism has not so much criticised the influence of Indian films as ignored it. While the politics of representation, and the effects of cultural imperialism, are highly politicised topics in Nigeria, Indian films, by virtue of their traditions and 'culture', have created a space which largely side-steps criticism. This is because for Hausa viewers Indian films have been situated in cultural space that stands outside the binary distinctions between tradition and modernity, Africa and the West, resistance and domination. The images of moder-nity they offer are mediated through a concern for maintaining traditional social relations and so they run parallel to, similar yet different from, the modernity offered by westernisation. Hausa viewers managed to engage with texts that showed a culture that was 'just like' Hausa culture as long as it was also irreducibly different. It is no surprise that, when the difference collapsed through the rise of *soyayya* books, Indian films became controversial in a way they never were before. As one writer to Ado Ahmad put it, 'In truth, Ado, you are among those who spread this modern love to our young people, not the films they watch, because in those films they don't usually understand what they are about. But now you are telling us in our own language' (letter to Ahmad, 29 January 1994).

The tendency of many Africanists to see resistance as the underlying cause of a vast range of social and cultural phenomena led, in its reductionism, to the elision of other cultural flows that did not fit neatly into the pattern. How else do we account for the absence of Indian films from analyses of African popular culture? The understandable tendency for anthropologists and others to concentrate on the vibrancy of popular arts produced by the people, though laudable, has elided some forms of mass-mediated culture from academic purview. Barber, for instance, asks, 'What exactly does an African audience get out of, say, a film in a foreign language, about culturally remote people who perform a series of actions almost invisible to the naked eye on a dim and flickering screen. Do these shows perhaps represent novelty itself in its most concentrated form?' (Barber 1987: 25). What audiences take from these films is considerable. Indian film has been a popular form of entertainment in urban West Africa [since at least the mid-1950s] and commands viewers because it engages with real desires and conflicts in African societies. Instead of indulging in a blanket dismissal of these forms it is necessary to take them seriously in their textual, cultural and historical specificities. The task that remains is to theorise adequately the complexity and heterogeneity of contemporary national and transnational cul-tural flows. Why are Indian films more popular in northern than in southern Nigeria? Are the reasons for their popularity the same elsewhere in West Africa? Why have influential film genres such as Egyptian films had so little impact in

Nigeria? These are questions that need to be answered, for, as Appadurai and Breckenridge (1988) observe, transnational cultural flows emerge from many centres and flow into many peripheries. In this article I have been concerned to articulate why one media form – Indian film – has resonance in the very different cultural environment of northern Nigeria. Indian films are popular because they provide a parallel modernity, a way of imaginatively engaging with the changing social basis of contemporary life that is an alternative to the pervasive influence of a secular West. Through spectacle and fantasy, romance and sexuality, Indian films provide arenas to consider what it means to be modern and what may be the place of Hausa society within that modernity. For northern Nigerians, who respond to a number of different centres, whether politically to the Nigerian state, religiously to the Middle East and North Africa, economically to the West, or culturally to the cinematic dominance of India, Indian films are just one part of the heterogeneity of everyday life.

NOTES

Acknowledgements: Funding for this research was provided by the Wenner-Gren Foundation and a Dean's Research Grant from New York University. I am grateful to Faye Ginsburg, T. O. Beidelman, Lila Abu-Lughod and Meg McLagan, who all commented on drafts of this article. I also thank Karin Barber and Murray Last for their editorial comments. The article relies heavily on the generous help given by the *soyayya* authors 'Dan Azumi Baba, Yusuf Lawan and Adamu Mohammed. I especially thank Ado Ahmad and Yusuf Mohammad Adamu, who initiated me into the world of *soyayya* literature. This article could not have been written without them. Ibrahim Sheme and Ibrahim Malumfashi added their critical view of *soyayya* books to the picture. Finally, I thank Usman Aliyu Abdulmalik and Abdullahi Kafin-Hausa for help with translation.

1 Mamman Shata is one of the most famous Hausa singers. This song was written as a satire on his friend, Mallam Sidi, who 'fell in love' with an Indian film actress.
2 I use the term 'Indian film' throughout as it is how Hausa viewers describe what is, in actuality, Bombay Hindi film. 'Indian film' should properly refer to the variety of Indian-language films.
3 To my knowledge, the only Nigerian film critics to discuss Indian films are Ekwuazi (1987), who criticises them, and Muhammad (1992), who praises them. For a journalist's view see Sheme (1995a, 1995b). Fugelsang (1994) discusses viewing of Indian videos by Lamu youth.
4 Abu-Lughod (1993a) also argues for increased attention to global flows that do not originate in Euro-American centres.
5 My use of the term 'postcolonial' in this article is historical rather than theoretical, referring to the aftermath of the experience of colonialism for ex-colonised nations.
6 The success of Brazilian *telenovelas* in China, the Soviet Union and elsewhere, and the regional dominance of Egyptian film and soap operas among Arabic-speaking countries, are other examples of the phenomenon. See McNeely and Soysal (1989) for a discussion of this trend. See Sreberny-Mohammadi (1991) for a critique.
7 Ekwuazi, while admitting the widespread popularity of Indian film, argues that 'its impact on the cultural landscape is relatively minimal' (1987: 44). In almost direct contrast to this

article, he argues that the reason is that Indian films are unable to offer a 'feasible model for (teenage) dreams' (ibid.). That Ekwuazi comes to what I see as a mistaken conclusion is a marker of the devalued position that popular Indian cinema has among scholars. (See Thomas 1985 for a discussion of this phenomenon.) Ekwuazi views Indian film as a cheap copy of American film and, rather than considering Indian narratives, stars or spectacles as governed by an alternative filmic style he judges them by their failure to live up to western standards: 'To anyone who has seen the real thing, the Indian imitation film is an aesthetic offense; it makes even the worst American film a sight for sore eyes' (ibid.).

8 History and Culture Bureau, Kano (HCB): Edu/14, Cinematograph and Censorship of Films, Exhibition of Films.

9 The reason why this is so is unclear. Arab films have long been successful internationally, and popular Egyptian films have a wide audience outside their own country. Perhaps it was precisely because Arabic is a religious language that its association with such a profane domain as cinema (as it is seen in northern Nigeria) made it impossible to attract an early viewing public. The recent introduction of satellite television in Nigeria has made channels from Saudi Arabia and Egypt available. As this comes at the same time as a revival in Arabic-language learning it may give Arab media a new popularity.

10 Interview, Michel G. Issa, Manager, Cinema Distribution Circuit, May 1995.

11 Many Arabic loan words are common to both Hindi and Hausa, which creates an oft-remarked sense of linguistic similarity.

12 It is no accident that the two other popular genres of film in Nigeria are Chinese Kung-fu and gangster films, and American action films. Action films depend more heavily on visual sequences than on complex narrative development, which makes them easier to understand across linguistic barriers.

13 Going out for picnics is a disreputable activity because it refers to increased mixing between unrelated men and women. This goes against the traditional norm of sexual segregation and is widely seen (and criticised) as an index of growing immorality.

14 The participation of youth in Islamic religious movements has been part of the history of northern Nigeria. Contemporary challenges, revealed in movements as diverse as the *'yan tatsine* (see Lubeck 1987; Watts and Pred 1992) and the Muslim Brothers illustrate how oppositional contemporary religious movements can be for the *status quo*.

15 Consider, for instance, that, during the time Callaway was researching and writing, Indian films were already established as a common part of everyday female popular culture. Often referred to as 'women's films', the concentration of romance and melodrama was and is seen as the prime reason for female identification. Only two years after Callaway's book was published, the efflorescence of a Hausa romance literature identified primarily with women readers (and with a significant number of women writers) makes her assertion that romance cannot exist in Islamic marriages untenable. Abu-Lughod (1986) provides a much more nuanced analysis of the romance, the poetry of love and emotional attachments among an equally sexually segregated Bedouin society.

16 Interview, December 1994.

17 Interview, June 1995.

18 Hausa can be written in either Arabic or Latin script. *Ajami* refers to Hausa written in Arabic script, *boko* to Hausa written in Latin script.

19 For the sake of consistency, wherever possible I follow (as here) the translation of *soyayya* clubs and books in Furniss 1996.

20 *Alhaji* strictly means a man who has made the pilgrimage (*hajj*) to Mecca. In common Hausa usage it refers to any person of wealth or status.

21 Ahmad abridged and translated his book into English in order to tap into a wider Nigerian English-speaking audience (interview, May 1995). Following its publication he did begin

to receive letters in English from fans from many other Nigerian ethnic groups, indicating its success. In 1995 he abridged and published *Masoyan Zamani* I, II ('Modern Lovers', 1993) as *Nemesis*. The only other English-language *soyayya* book is *The Sign of the Times* (1994) by Tijani Usman Adamu. Adamu's book was written in English and no Hausa version exists.

22 Indian films present an alternative to both Hausa tradition and western modernity in that, while they depict a culture 'just like' Hausa culture, their popularity resides in the fact that Indian culture is also precisely *unlike* Hausa culture. Indian films portray an alternative world where actions that would not be tolerated within Hausa social norms are raised without attracting widespread condemnation. A comparison with Hausa reception of Yoruba or Igbo films is helpful here. Onitsha market literature, Yoruba and Igbo videos, and popular romance magazines such as *Hints*, all suggest how popular the theme of love remains in southern Nigeria. Clearly many of the Yoruba and Igbo films are set in locations with cultural references that are familiar to and have similarities with Hausa audiences. Yoruba and Igbo films, however, are often sexually more explicit in their themes than either Hausa videos or Indian films. While many Hausa viewers watch and enjoy these videos, for others their themes are too explicit for comfort. The attitude of one Hausa video shop owner I talked to, who sold Igbo and Yoruba films but was reluctant to let members of his family watch them, is not exceptional.

23 Mohammed is here referring to the subject matter of stories which make up classic Hausa fiction such as Abubakar Imam's *Ruwan Bagaja* (1934) or *Gand'oki* by Bello Kagara (1934). For further discussion of these works see Furniss 1996; Rahim 1990; Sani 1990; Yahaya 1988.

24 This familiarity is one reason why *bandiri* singers have drawn on popular Indian film songs for religious music. These sufi adepts will take the songs from a popular film, such as *Mother India, or Kabhi, Kabhie* (1976, directed by Yash Chopra), and change the words to sing praises to the Prophet Mohammed.

REFERENCES

Abu-Lughod, Lila. 1986. *Veiled Sentiments: Honor and Poetry in a Bedouin Society.* Berkeley, CA: University of California Press.
——1990. 'The romance of resistance: tracing transformations through Bedouin women', *American Ethnologist* 17(1): 41–55.
——. 1993a. 'Editorial comment: screening politics in a world of nations', *Public Culture* 5(3): 465–7.
——. 1993b. 'Finding a place for Islam: Egyptian television serials and the national interest', *Public Culture* 5(3): 493–514.
——. 1995. 'The objects of soap opera: Egyptian television and the cultural politics of modernity', in Daniel Miller (ed.), *Worlds Apart: Modernity through the Prism of the Local*, pp. 190–210. London: Routledge.
Adamu, Tijani Usman. 1994. *The Sign of the Times.* Kano: Gidan Dabino.
Ahmad, Ado. 1989. *In da so da K'auna.* Kano.
——. 1993a. *The Soul of my Heart.* Kano.
——. 1993b. *Masoyan Zamani.* Kano.
——. 1995. *Nemesis.* Kano.
Appadurai, Arjun. 1990. 'Disjuncture and difference in the global cultural economy', *Public Culture* 2(2): 1–24.

——. 1991. 'Global ethnoscapes: notes and queries for a transnational anthropology', in Richard Fox (ed.), *Recapturing Anthropology: Working in the Present*, pp. 191–210. Santa Fe, CA: SAR Press.

Appadurai, Arjun, and Carol A. Breckenridge. 1988. 'Why public culture?' *Public Culture* 1(1): 5–9.

——. 1995. 'Public modernity in India', in Carol A. Breckenridge (ed.), *Consuming Modernity: Public Culture in a South Asian World*, pp. 1–20. Minneapolis: University of Minnesota Press.

Baba, 'Dan Azumi. 1990. *Rikicin Duniya*. Kano.

Babinlata, Bala Anas. 1993. *Tsuntsu Mai Wayo*. Kano.

Bakhtin, Mikhail. 1981. *The Dialogic Imagination*. Austin: University of Texas Press.

Barber, Karin. 1987. 'Popular arts in Africa', *African Studies Review* 30(3): 1–78.

Barkindo, Bawuro M. 1993. 'Growing Islamism in Kano City since 1970', in Louis Brenner (ed.), *Muslim Identity and Social Change in Sub-Saharan Africa*, pp. 91–105. Bloomington: Indiana University Press.

Beidelman, T. O. 1993. *Moral Imagination among Kaguru Modes of Thought*, Bloomington, Ind.: Indiana University Press. 1st edn. 1986. Washington, DC: Smithsonian Institution Press.

Bichi, Maigari Ahmed. 1992. 'The author's imagination' II, *The Triumph*, 17 March, p. 7.

Callaway, Barbara. 1987. *Muslim Hausa Women in Nigeria: Tradition and Change*. New York: Syracuse University Press.

Chakravarty, Sunita. 1993. *National Ideology in Indiana Popular Cinema, 1947–87*. Austin: University of Texas Press.

Cooper, Frederick. 1994. 'Conflict and connection: rethinking African colonial history', *American Historical Review* 99(5): 1516–45.

'Dan Asabe, Abdul Karim. n.d. 'The way youth organise themselves: a study of clubs in Kano metropolis, Nigeria'. Kano (unpublished).

Diawara, Manthia. 1992. *African Cinema: Politics and Culture*. Bloomington: Indiana University Press.

Ekwuazi Hyginus. 1987. *Film in Nigeria*. Jos: Nigerian Film Corporation.

Ekwuazi, Hyginus, and Nasidi Yakubu (eds.) 1992. *Operative Principles of the Film Industry: Towards a Film Policy for Nigeria*. Jos: Nigerian Film Corporation.

Fugelsang, Minou. 1994. *Veils and Videos: Female Youth Culture on the Kenyan Coast*. Studies in Social Anthropology, Stockholm: Gotab.

Furniss, Graham. 1996. *Poetry, Prose and Popular Culture in Hausa*. Edinburgh: Edinburgh University Press; Washington, DC: Smithsonian Institution Press, for the International African Institute.

Giginyu, Nasiru Mudi. 1992. 'A little knowledge is a dangerous thing: a reply to Ado Ahmad, Gidan Dabino', *Nasiha*, 28 August.

Ginsburg, Faye. 1991. 'Indigenous media: Faustian contract or global village?' *Cultural Anthropology* 6(1): 92–112.

——. 1993. 'Aboriginal media and the aboriginal imaginary', *Public Culture* 5(3): 557–78.

——. 1994. 'Embedded aesthetics: creating a discursive place for indigenous media', *Cultural Anthropology* 9(3): 365–82.

Hannerz, Ulf. 1992. *Cultural Complexity: Studies in the Social Organization of Meaning*. New York: Columbia University Press.

Imam, Abubakar. 1934. *Ruwan Bagaja*. Zaria: NNPC.

India Interanational Centre Quarterly. 1980. Special issue, 8(1).

Jackson, Michael. 1982. *Allegories of the Wilderness: Ethics and Ambiguity in Kuranko Narratives*. Bloomington: Indiana University Press.

Kagara, Bello. 1934. *Gand'oki*. Zaria: Literature Bureau.

Kakar, Sudhir. 1989. *Intimate Relations: Exploring Indian Sexuality*. Chicago: University of Chicago Press.

Lawan, Yusuf. 1993. *Komai Wahalar So*. Kano.
——. 1995. *Mai Hakuri...Kano*.
Liman, Maryam Sahabi. 1993. *Kishi Kumallon Mata*. Gusau: Bushara Publishing House.
Lubeck, Paul. 1987. 'Islamic protest under semi-industrial capitalism: Yan Tatsine explained',
    in J. D. Y. Peel and C. C. Stewart (eds.) *Popular Islam South of the Sahara*, pp. 369–89.
    Manchester: Manchester University Press, for the International African Institute.
McLagan, Meg. 1996. 'Computing for Tibet: virtual politics in the Cold War era', in
    G. Marcus (ed.) *Connected: Engagements with Media at Century's End*. Late Editions 3.
    Chicago: University of Chicago Press.
McNeely, Connie, and Yasemin Muhoglu Soysal. 1989. 'International flows of television
    programming: a revisionist research orientation', *Public Culture* 2(1): 136–45.
Mishray, Vijay. 1985. 'Toward a theoretical critique of Bombay cinema', *Screen* 26(3–4):
    133–46.
Mohammed, Adamu. 1991. *Garnak'ak'i*. Kano: Kamfanin Kwabon Masoyi.
Muhammad, Bala. 1992. 'The Hausa film: a study of slow growth, problems and prospects',
    in Hyginus Ekwuazi and Yakubu Nasidi (eds.) *Operative Principles of the Film Industry:
    Towards a Film Policy for Nigeria*, pp. 179–204. Jos: Nigerian Film Corporation.
Nandy, Ashis. 1995. *The Savage Freud and other Essays on Possible and Retrievable Selves*.
    Princeton, NJ: Princeton University Press.
Pendakur, Manjunath, and Radha Subramanyam. 1996. 'Indian cinema beyond national
    borders', in John Sinclair, Elizabeth Jacka and Stuart Cunningham (eds.) *New Patterns in
    Global Television: Peripheral Vision*, pp. 67–82. Oxford: Oxford University Press.
Rahim, Oba Abdul (ed.) 1990. *Essays on Northern Nigerian Literature* 1. Zaria: Hamdan
    Express Printers.
Said, H. I., and Murray Last. 1991. *Youth and Health in Kano Today*. Special issue of *Kano
    Studies*.
Sani, Abba Aliyu. 1990. 'The place of Rupert East in the culture and literature of northern
    Nigeria', in Oba Abdul Raheem (ed.) *Essays on Northern Nigerian Literature*, pp. 12–21.
    Zaria: Hamdan Express Printers.
Sheme, Ibrahim. 1995a. 'Indian films and our culture', *New Nigerian*, 13 May: 7.
——1995b. 'Zagon K'asar da fina finan Indiya ke yi wa al'adanmu' ('The danger of Indian
    films to our culture'), *Gaskiya ta fi kwabo*, 15 May: 5.
Shohat, Ella, and Robert Stam. 1994. *Unthinking Eurocentrism*. New York: Routledge.
Sreberny-Mohammadi, Annabelle. 1991. 'The global and the local in international commu-
    nications', in James Curran and Michael Gurevitch (eds.) *Mass Media and Society*. London:
    Edward Arnold.
Sullivan, Nancy. 1993. 'Film and television production in New Guinea: how the media
    become the message', *Public Culture* 5(3): 533–55.
Thomas, Rosie. 1985. 'Indian cinema: pleasures and popularity', *Screen* 26(3–4): 116–31.
——. 1995. 'Melodrama and the negotiation of morality in mainstram Indian film', in
    Consuming Modernity: Public Culture in a South Asian World, pp. 157–82. Minneapolis:
    University of Minnesota Press.
Ukadike, Nwachukwu Frank. 1994. *Black African Cinema*. Berkeley, CA: University of
    California Press.
Watts, Michael and Allan Pred. 1992. *The Shock of Modernity: Capitalisms and Symbolic
    Discontent*. New Brunswick, NJ: Rutgers University Press.
Yahaya, Ibrahim Yaro. 1988. *Hausa a Rubuce: tarihin rubuce rubuce cikin Hausa*. Zaria:
    NNPC.
Yakubu, Hajiya Balaraba Ramat. 1990a. *Alhaki Kwikwiyo*. Kano.
——. 1990b. *Budurwar Zuciya*. Kano.

Part VI

Nomadic Ideologies

This final part of our reader explores the circulation of western ideologies and discourses, focusing on how these narratives both constrict the lives of and create new subject positions for the peoples of the periphery. Adams's article looks at how Tibetans are forced to embrace universalistic and individualistic positions to ensure that their claims for human rights are heard – while ironically expressing ideas about suffering that challenge such universalistic positions. Donham's piece focuses on how globally circulating narratives, specifically those related to 'gayness,' have become particularly relevant in understanding the formation of sexual communities in black South Africa. These are narratives that have helped to create new 'gay' subject positions. And Abu-Lughod's essay shows how 'western' feminist ideologies have engendered a tension in Egypt between those who endeavor to locate women's emancipation, however articulated, at the heart of the constitution of the nation and those who would call into question such an undertaking as an alien cultural imposition.

SUGGESTIONS FOR FURTHER READING

Bielefeldt, Heiner
   2000 'Western' versus 'Islamic' Human Rights Conceptions? A Critique of Cultural Essentialism in the Discussion on Human Rights. *Political Theory* 28(1): 90–121.
Boellstorff, Tom
   1999 The Perfect Path: Gay Men, Marriage, Indonesia. *GLQ: A Journal of Lesbian and Gay Studies* 5(4): 475–509.
Comaroff, John L., and Jean Comaroff
   1997 Postcolonial Politics and Discourses of Democracy in Southern Africa: An Anthropological Reflection on African Political Modernities. *Journal of Anthropological Research* 53(2): 123–46.
Hammar, Lawrence
   1996 Brothels, Bamu, and Tu Kina Bus in South Coast New Guinea: Human Rights Issues and Global Responsibilities. *Anthropology and Humanism* 21(2): 140–58.
Holston, James
   2001 Urban Citizenship and Globalization. In *Global City-Regions*. Allen J. Scott, ed. Pp. 325–48. New York: Oxford University Press.

Liechty, Mark
  1996 Paying for Modernity: Women and the Discourse of Freedom in Kathmandu. *Studies in Nepali History and Society* 1(1): 201–30.
Malkki, Liisa
  1994 Citizens of Humanity: Internationalism and the Imagined Community of Nations. *Diaspora* 3(1): 41–68.
Richard, Nelly
  1993 The Latin-American Problematic of Theoretical-Cultural Transference: Postmodern Appropriations and Counterappropriations. *South Atlantic Quarterly* 92(3): 453–9.
Rofel, Lisa
  1999 Qualities of Desire: Imagining Gay Identities in China. *GLQ: A Journal of Lesbian and Gay Studies* 5(4): 451–74.
Weeratunge, Nireka
  2000 Nature, Harmony, and the Kaliyugaya: Global/Local Discourses on the Human–Environment Relationships. *Current Anthropology* 41(2): 249–68.
Wilson, Richard A., ed.
  1997 *Human Rights, Culture and Context: Anthropological Perspectives.* London: Pluto Press.

16

Suffering the Winds of Lhasa: Politicized Bodies, Human Rights, Cultural Difference, and Humanism in Tibet

Vincanne Adams

In its own eyes, Western humanism is the love of humanity, but to others it is merely the custom and institution of a group of men, their password, and sometimes their battle cry.
(Maurice Merleau-Ponty)

Liberal Humanism

Veena Das once observed that globalization does not necessarily mean universalization. One meaning of this comment is that even though a culture is globalized, it still might not partake of certain universalist privileges. For example, Tibetan culture is known around the world today (spawned at least in part by the 1959 diaspora of refugees over at least three continents), but Tibetans do not share equally with other cultural groups, or even uniformly within their culture, the privileges of universal human rights, particularly the right not to be imprisoned or tortured for their politics. This situation, in part, inspires Das to ask questions not about the means necessary to ensure universalization but rather about the utility of universalist rights discourse itself.[1] In a related fashion, I ask in this article questions about the universalist potential of a specific intersection of human rights discourse, anthropology, and a politics of engagement in the case of Tibetan suffering. I take *human rights discourse* as currently one of the most popular rubrics of liberal humanism, *anthropology* as among other things a persistent concern with identifying and valorizing cultural difference, and *a politics of engagement* as that which is required of humanism. My goal is to explore how a politics of engagement might move

From *Medical Anthropology Quarterly* 12(1): 74–102. Copyright © 1998, American Anthropological Association.

beyond the paralyzing polemic that situates universalism in opposition to cultural specificity when it comes to human rights, politicized bodies, and suffering in Tibet.

Adopting the position that universalism can and should be a basis upon which to promote a contemporary liberal agenda in an era when globalization seems to engage so many people so unequally in transnational projects, I ask here how such a project might also suggest rethinking the very category of "universal" in the case of human rights in Tibet. I do this not to revert to or adopt the conventionally recognized position that opposes universalism in human rights – namely that human rights are not universal but culturally specific – although that would seem inevitable given that the debate is already cast in these polarized terms. I do not want to reproduce the dualism. Rather, I ask how a humanist agenda might be combined with anthropological concerns for identifying cultural difference in ways that constructively disentangle and disempower both sides of this polarized debate. As such, my discussion focuses on three discourses of difference: universal versus culturally specific human rights, individualist versus collective subjectivities, and Tibetan versus Chinese, and Tibetan versus western identities.

My motivation stems partially from what I see as a complicated politics of identity in Tibet wherein various constructions of Tibetan identity issue from western and Tibetan refugee activists who desire a free Tibet. I see this not as a civilizing agenda but as a politicizing one that impacts on both Tibetans who are and those who are not already politically active about their identity. My motivation also stems partially from a desire to move away from what I see as a tendency to exclude from the western and foreign view the idea (or even the possibility) that at least some Tibetans are less interested in liberation by independence from China than they are in the delivery of modernization by the Chinese or anyone else.[2] At the same time, I also note that "ethnic" and class tensions and conflict between Chinese and Tibetans are extant and pervasive on the plateau,[3] and that official PRC policies toward Tibetans seem to be driven by a good deal of paranoia (Craig Janes, personal communication December, 1996), leading to a situation in which what gets construed by both sides as political conflict is always near the surface. I also note that the resulting suffering can be very great indeed. The polarization of political views when it comes to human rights in Tibet parallels the identity politics found there: the debate on human rights in Tibet is constructed by advocates as a polar contest of cultural specificity versus universalism, in the same way that "Chineseness" is characterized as the polar opposite of "Tibetanness." This is the background to the following exploration of human rights discourse and what it might be able to accomplish for Tibetans in Tibet, and for others.

My point of departure is a discussion of the polarization of human rights discourse concerning Tibet. The central argument of the article, however, is made in and through an exploration of Tibetan experiences of bodily suffering that result from political imprisonment and torture, and of expressions of ill health heard at the traditional Tibetan medical hospital of Lhasa (Mentsikhang). I draw upon Tibetan utterances from both locales in order to gain insights into a Tibetan subjectivity that intersects and potentially disrupts the human rights discourse as it is presently constructed. Specifically, expressions of Tibetan subjectivity found in utterances and theories of karma and the diagnostic category "winds" (see also Janes 1995) reveal a subject who is at least partially collective, and this fact might suggest a need for alternative ways of discussing the human rights agendas mobilized on behalf of Tibet and Tibetans. Data for this article are drawn from two field visits to Lhasa, Tibet in 1993 and 1995 and from published and unpublished sources on Tibetan medicine and human rights collected in Tibet and in the United States.[4] In its use of the medical domain to explicate conceptualizations of subjectivity in a contested political field, I suggest that cultural analysis in medical anthropology is important to larger international debates about human rights.

Human Rights Discourse

Since the 1960s, but prolifically since the 1980s, human rights discourse has supplied a language through which activists working for a free Tibet have enunciated and legitimized their politics. Accounts of human rights abuses in Tibet focus on cultural genocide, political imprisonment and torture, the illegitimacy of China's sovereignty in the region, and the Chinese (PRC) government's disregard for universalist definitions of human rights.[5] Tibetan refugees, Tibetans in Lhasa, and western activists offer these sorts of descriptions of human rights abuses to concerned observers:

The Chinese keep saying they gave us human rights, but in reality we don't even have freedom of speech. And when you end up in prison, they mercilessly torture you, using all kinds of materials. They simply regard you as an animal. They suspend you in the air and shackle your limbs, rub ice on your skin and touch you with an electric prod. (unnamed Tibetan man from Lhasa, from Schell 1992)

The Chinese are trying to swallow our country and eradicate [the Tibetan] people. So the only way for us to challenge the Chinese is with historical fact and international laws and by following the nonviolent path led by his holiness the Dalai Lama. (another unnamed Tibetan man from Lhasa, from Schell 1992)

Since China gained control over Tibet in 1950, the Chinese government has been responsible for murdering one-fifth of the Tibetan population – a staggering 1.2 million lives. (the Dalai Lama, quoted by Senator George Mitchell from the 137 Cong. Rec. S10517 daily ed. July 22, 1991, in Drinan and Kuo 1992: 28)

In most thorough accounts, human rights violations are presented as taking the form of cultural genocide: the complete eradication of a distinctive Tibetan way of life. During the Cultural Revolution, it is argued, the Chinese government practiced cultural genocide in Tibet and throughout China by attempting to eliminate all traces of the Tibetan religion and the folk culture associated with it. Accounts today confirm that Tibetans who demand the right to practice Buddhism as they wish, who have in their possession images of the Dalai Lama, or who advocate at any time a non-Chinese Tibet are often imprisoned. Cultural genocide is portrayed by advocates of an independent Tibet as taking place through massive sinicization programs. These include the unrestricted inflow of Chinese peasants to the Tibetan Autonomous Region, the suppression of use of Tibetan language,[6] and the systematic privileging of only those who speak Mandarin for educational, economic, and social rewards issued by the state.

That is the threat we face today: the complete assimilation and absorption of our people by a vast sea of Chinese settlers streaming across our borders. (H. H. the Dalai Lama 1985)

The most serious accounts draw attention to the ways that cultural genocide is enacted through the physical bodies of Tibetans. This occurs, critics say, through forced sterilization, forced intermarriage between Chinese and Tibetans, and the attempt to transform native Tibetans into a culturally and physically "broken" minority in their homeland. Reflecting on her experiences in Tibet, one Tibetan refugee said:

The Chinese want our land, but they don't want the Tibetan people. The women in our village were called to be sterilized, one by one. Those who refused must pay a fine. They have no money, so they have no choice. (Tsultrim Doma, Buddhist nun, from Bruno 1993)

Another account states it this way:

Tibetan women are subjected to mandatory sterilization and forced abortion as a means of reducing the Tibetan population. (US Tibet Committee 1994)

In general, the assumption made by human rights advocates, both Tibetan and western, is that the political situation in Tibet makes it different from the rest of China. The enforcement of Chinese policies in Tibet leads to cultural and physical genocide in contrast to the enforcement of its policies in the rest of China where they are seen in many accounts as enabling the *survival* of China's people. At the same time, human rights advocates also believe generally that if *universal* human rights standards were applied and enforced in all of China, and particularly in Tibet, Tibetans would suffer less, their culture could be saved, and they would come closer to political independence from the PRC. In some accounts, cultural survival is seen as contingent upon political independence. Refugee Tibetans in diaspora are understandably among the most vocal advocates of this position.

Implicit in westerners' adoption of this position is a valorization of Tibetan culture as both distinctive and different enough from their own that it merits saving, yet similar enough to their own that they can identify with Tibetan suffering and establish a universalist basis for political action. The adoption of a universalist human rights discourse to promote the Tibetan cause thus reflects these *shared* western and Tibetan assumptions: (1) that persons involved in a movement for a free Tibet, regardless of their culture, can, as human subjects, come to a mutual understanding and recognition of the moral and physical limits to cultural difference; and (2) that they are able to share a recognition of right, wrong, and the meanings of human suffering around which to mobilize a political agenda. Implied in this discourse is the understanding that many Chinese who oppress them do not share in this mutuality. Official Chinese accounts of government efforts to preserve Tibetan culture are believed by many westerners and Tibetans to be spurious (see Goldstein 1997).

The persistent violation of human rights in Tibet by the PRC government is generally attributed to the fact that China, since it took up the human rights rubric, insists on a *relativist* definition of human rights organized around the collective.

Chinese human rights are based, officials maintain, on the rights of the "citizen" and the distinctive Asian value of the preeminence of society over the individual. At least officially, the significance of this position has been associated with sentiments of nationalism that were articulated through utilitarian principles of Marxism and Confucianism during the last years of the Maoist era. The position maintained that individual rights were articulated in bourgeois western societies in order to protect the privileges of the bourgeoisie. Chinese scholars draw upon the 1776 American Declaration of Independence and the 1789 French Declaration of the Rights of Man to make their point: "both [documents] advocated freedom, the right of property and equality among others as natural rights," but individual human rights "advocated by the bourgeoisie," they felt, "can only be enjoyed by the latter, who own the means of production and thus enslave and exploit the proletarians" (Chiu 1989: 10–11).

In the early post-Maoist era (after 1977) many Chinese scholars rejected the view that human rights discourse was only an instrument of the bourgeoisie, and instead argued that it could be used as a weapon against the bourgeoisie, particularly in the prosecution of Cultural Revolution criminals (e.g., the Gang of Four). Human rights, they said, *could also be used against* feudal fascist regimes: in a society ruled by the proletariat, concerns of the collective reign supreme over those of the individual; thus human rights can be used to promote the needs of the collective-minded proletariat over those of the individualist-minded bourgeoisie. Marxist idealization of the collective privileges of a revolutionary society were also merged in human rights discourse in China with Confucianist principles of mutual duty to others in society, as opposed to equal rights shared by individuals and protected by law.[7] Rejecting internationalist United Nations positions on human rights, which they called "instruments of imperialism," and seeing such universalist rhetoric as potentially authorizing imperialist intervention into and against their socialist society (Thurston 1988), Chinese officials have persistently rejected the assumptions of individualism and universalism in human rights discourse.[8]

Westerners and refugee Tibetans feel PRC official discourse on human rights exemplifies the dangers of a relativist position. They maintain that a position that advocates *cultural specificity* and that consequently acknowledges only collectivist rights *for only its citizens* can easily justify violations. Those persons whose conduct is considered politically dangerous by the state because it violates the "social good" can be reidentified as enemies of the state – as counterrevolutionaries – and therefore as noncitizens and thus not entitled to the same securities afforded to citizens. Additionally, actions carried out for the benefit of society and state security, including forced fertility control, intermarriage, and bans of politically oppositional speech, are in this model considered vehicles for the protection of citizen rights, rather than violations of them. In metropole terms (that is, the international terms adopted by multilaterals like the UN),[9] China's position enables the state to justify its actions against its people and leads to the violation not just of international law but of universal humanity.

To reiterate, critics of China's position cleave to the idea that human rights are *universally* agreed upon and that they articulate around the *individual*. Officially, China persistently rejects this notion, and holds fast to a *collectivist* and *culturally* (*in fact, Asia-*) *specific* stance on human rights. The position adopted by China is consistent with the position of other Asian governments that signed the Bangkok Declaration of Human Rights in March 1993. That declaration holds that Asian governments

recognize that while human rights are universal in nature, they must be considered in the context of a dynamic and evolving process of international norm-setting, bearing in mind the significance of national and regional particularities and various historical, cultural and religious backgrounds. (Chan 1995: 25)

Most critics contend that the use of the word *universal* here is purely rhetorical, for its *only* operational valences are those that invoke particular historical, religious, or cultural conditions. Chan notes that the relativism is based on the fact that

Asian societies in general seem to embrace a set of attitudes toward issues of values and morals that is different from that of the West. Many Asians do not value personal autonomy as highly as Western liberals do. In Asian political moralities, we can see a stronger emphasis on the stability, harmony and prosperity of society and a greater reverence for traditions, elders and leaders. (Chan 1995: 35)

Underlying China's position is the supposition that people from different cultures can have completely different though not necessarily *mutually noncomprehensible* understandings of the subject, indeed of what it means to be human – that different constitutions of subjectivity demand different kinds of state interventions to either "protect" or "prohibit" certain human behaviors.

There is ample evidence that metropole discourse on human rights can encompass rights of individuals *and* rights of the group or collective (whether defined in terms of national self-determination, or rights of indigenous peoples). But in the case of China's Tibet, the discussions of a right to national identity and self-determination become articulated among anti-PRC activists in terms of individualist human rights. One reason for this is that China's official discourse claims the intellectual and rhetorical space of nationalist determination and collectivism for itself. For example, PRC policy notes that self-determination is only an issue under conditions of foreign slavery and colonial rule, and therefore is not applicable to Tibet. PRC policy makers also note that issues concerning nations within states are a matter of domestic jurisprudence. And PRC policy recognizes and publicly valorizes separate nationalities within its greater nation-state. In fact, the government devotes considerable attention to and investment in the problems of identifying, valorizing, promoting, and integrating its officially recognized regional and national minorities. Chinese official discourse also attests to guarantees of ethnic nationalist preservation by making sure local governments are comprised of local representatives of the national territories – a form of self-administration – and in the case of Tibet, this is evidenced most dramatically in the government's establishment of the Tibetan Autonomous Region.

Thus, regardless of potential overlap, the notion of individual rights becomes "owned" by the metropole and "free Tibet" activists while the notion of collectivism becomes "owned" by China (and other Asian official positions) as instruments in the political battle over rights in Tibet. Activists perceive that in order to take an oppositional stance, they must cleave to one rhetorical strategy, and more often than not, this has meant pointing out that China ignores individual rights and that the cultural survival of Tibetans is contingent above all else on the enforcement of individually based, universally accepted rights. Tibetans, by recruiting avid westerners and others (Tibetophiles, political and human rights activists, and Buddhists) to their cause, are persistently invited to promote the movement for a free Tibet through use of the metropole terms that insist on universalism and individualism, even when cultural survival is seen as the goal. This enables advocates to position themselves against China. In this act, suffering and political violence are displaced from the particular circumstances of Chinese prisons and cultural destruction on the Tibetan plateau onto the framework of international law and justice. In what follows, I turn the focus back upon the particulars of suffering. I inquire further into the idioms through which Tibetans' suffering is experienced – idioms that are both provoked and yet often displaced by or subordinated to the internationalist terms of the debate.

Body Politics

In human rights discourse in Lhasa, activists specifically identify not just bodies but *encultured* bodies as the sites for universalist suffering. This is most clear in cases of the imprisonment and torture of nuns and monks. Because they are bearers of religion, they, above all others, are *seen* by many as embodying traditional Tibetan culture and therefore as being the most likely to be suspected of political criminality in the new era. They are also identified by China's critics as among the most appropriate authorities on human rights violations in Tibet, whether occuring in daily life or behind prison walls. This is surely because so many of them have been imprisoned for political actions against the state. In their accounts, suffering is the natural result of living in a world wherein the very act of practicing their religion has been, at some times more than others, made into a legal matter. This is also because Tibetan culture has come to be defined by many activists and others *as religion.* Suffering is often depicted as a uniform experience among Tibetans in Tibet, because it is said that all Tibetans are, by cultural identity, religious and because religious culture has been largely suppressed. The problems of religious essentialism notwithstanding, the idea that Tibetan culture has been historically formulated within a culture of Buddhism is not the same as the idea that Tibetans are uniformly religious. The former may be more true than the latter. It is thus not surprising that suffering is often depicted by Tibetans in Buddhist terms, because Buddhism has formed a foundation for Tibetan culture despite wide variation in lay religious knowledge and practice (and despite wide variation in what constitutes Tibetan culture today). Among nuns, religious sensibilities are very audible. Consider these passages about suffering recorded in a film by Ellen Bruno, *Satya: A Prayer for the Enemy:*[10]

When I was a child, there was so much darkness in Tibet. When someone died, we couldn't say a word of prayer or light a butter lamp to show the soul which path to take. My father told me that after the Chinese invasion, everything turned to the opposite way. Monks and nuns were forced to marry. But many kept their vows separately. . . . Buddhism is deep within us.

The Chinese say religion gets in the way of progress. They think only of this life, they don't think about the next. They say when you die you become rock and soil and nothing else. But our path leads through many births and deaths. What we do in this lifetime will influence our lives to come. This is the law of *karma*.

Monks and nuns have become the real enemy of the Chinese. The strength of our devotion frightens them.

A nun who had been imprisoned said,

When we went to demonstrate we were ready for death. We are fighting for truth and for this we must be ready to die. The truth will find its way. We never doubt this. I felt no fear. I felt strength from all the people who were killed before me. I became less attached to my own life and courage and determination rose up in me. After all, from the moment we are born, we are headed toward death. Death is inescapable.

Other former nun prisoners say, remembering as if reliving the experience,

For a month and ten days, they do not let me see the sky. I do not know night from day. When the guards have passed. I listen for a whisper, faint like wind, any sign that I am not alone. They wanted to know who was behind us, but no one was behind us. It was our own idea, and I told them so. But they insisted someone put us up to it. Then they stripped me completely naked. They stood me up and kicked me in the groin. They made me stick out my tongue and pushed an electric cattle prod in my mouth. They hit me again and again.

It is as though I am every Tibetan. The full wrath of China upon me. They try to break us. It is our will against their might. Sometimes they give a drug which makes us dream and we can no longer hold in our thoughts.

They wrapped wires around my fingers. Then they turned on the electric current. The shock was unbearable. My whole body contracted, and sharp pains shot up from my feet. It was more painful than the cattle prod. If I was sitting like this when they turned on the current I was thrown across the room. I was shaking and screaming. I didn't know how it was done. . . . They tortured me every day, and then they set my sentence. They gave me two years.

The one who tortures me is made to believe that what he is doing is right. He must stay blind to my pain in order to carry on. At the end of the day, he returns to his family; with arms that beat me he embraces his women, wraps loving arms around his child, protecting her with his strength.

No one can escape the consequences of their actions. This darkness will not last. Like all things, it too will change. In the solitude of our cell we imagine ourselves in meditation caves, high on the roof of the world. Our enemy is our greatest teacher. . . teacher of patience and compassion. Our imprisonment our greatest test of faith. Through the force of my prayers, I ask that those who imprison us be freed from the darkness of ignorance, that the clouds which obscure the truth give way to clarity.

At first I was angry at all the birds, all the plants and all the animals. Then my anger spread to all living beings, to all the six realms of existence. I tried to imagine what would happen if we fought a war with the Chinese. Causing confusion, thinking something good might come of it. Such thoughts entered my mind. But in war it is not only the humans who die. . . . All the living beings, all the birds, and animals, and insects suffer along with humans. . . . This I remember.

The path of nonviolence may seem long and tiresome, but what is a single lifetime in this endless cycle of birth and death? The teachings of Buddha are deep like an ocean. As anger and hatred arise, I pray that the minds of the Chinese become gentle and calm, that through love and compassion those who are drunk with delusions, lost in the darkness of ignorance, acquire the wisdom eye to see what is right and what is wrong. May all living beings be free from suffering. (Printed, by permission, from Bruno 1993)

Heard by activists outside of Tibet, these accounts are interpreted as utterances of suffering, not simply of the sort that can bring spiritual salvation, but of the sort that can bring about a political revolution. Suffering in this latter sense is about creating a space of shared meaning between Buddhist and non-Buddhist, Tibetan and Tibetan refugee, Tibetan and foreign activist, Tibetan refugee and foreign activist.[11] Suffering has to be made into something that for non-Tibetans and Tibetans alike can transform the religious into the political by the fact that it results from a presumed universally shared understanding. Suffering is asked to speak in the language of the one who is perceived as being able to alleviate it. Thus the nuns respond to the western filmmaker, and in their voices we perceive both something that is produced by the western gaze and some things that may be contrary to it.

Universalist claims to human rights presuppose an ability to identify with and acquire a shared meaning of suffering that is sometimes cross-national and often cross-cultural. In the lexicon of uttered and heard suffering, people (who are frequently culturally different) reach agreement about the limits of acceptable behavior, the threshold of intolerable violence, and the right of individuals to maintain and practice their culture. In order to legitimize and render credible the moral and political universalist claims against the Chinese government, suffering in Lhasa must at some level mean the same thing as suffering anywhere else in the world. The universal body links these worlds: it is a body that is violated and made to suffer, and deprived of its culture, freedom, integrity, and comfort.

In the metropole terms used by most advocates, this body is individualized and derives at least part of its authority to express pain from the authenticity invested in its individuality. Firsthand accounts "count" for everything in human rights discourse and so suffering bodies are made to say, "it is not that someone else contends that there was suffering but that it was *me* who suffered, *I* who spoke and speak of my own pain." Or, "it is not that someone told me that violations occurred, but that *I saw* them occurring myself." Individual pain can be shared by others who hear of it, but pain's authenticity is invested in its being uttered by the one who knows it as his or her own or who sees it for him or herself. The individualized body in pain speaks, "It is the violation of the integrity of my own body that compels me to speak"; its flesh exposed, bruised, and torn opened as it should not be. The directory of Political and Religious Prisoners, published by Asia Watch, lists the names of each and every political prisoner in Tibet, each one a named individual (Asia Watch 1994). It is as though, for them and us, without such a list, without actual names, the strong case for Tibetan oppression could not be made; it is as though gains in human rights are accountable only in terms of individuals; each person counts, each person is accounted for.

In internationalist human rights terms, the individual is the indivisible unit of symbolic currency; it is the individual's rights that are always at stake, for it is at the level of the individual (not the level of society or culture) that shared humanism is found. Shared humanism requires a transcendance of cultural difference. Difference is perceptible when bodies are enculturated, when a *body* becomes an enculturated *person*. Individualized and to some extent objectified by the presence of *a body* tortured, bodies can be universalized and suffering can go to work for human rights politics. Were the body not universalized, we might not be able to agree upon a tolerable degree of inhumanities against it, and suffering could not then be used for legal claims, let alone transnational politics.

But the particular meanings in Tibetan human rights discourse suggest that if suffering is at least partly shared across cultures, it is also at least partially not entirely the same "here" as "there." Travel with me momentarily to another site of suffering on the plateau, to a place where suffering is treated, Tibetan-style, in order to see how else bodies can be heard, or even to see how we might be able to hear those utterances already spoken on a more subtle level. Along the way I ask whether Tibetan understandings might interrupt the human rights discourse of violations already occurring on the plateau. Can a desire for the persistence and valorization of cultural difference also be useful in arguing for the enforcement of rights, even without the lexicon of universalism versus cultural specificity, individualism versus collectivity, as we currently know it?

Embodied Suffering: Tibet

In order to understand Tibetan suffering and the politicization of it for human rights, we might first try to understand Tibetan conceptions of the body and subjectivity as gleaned from the medical setting. In particular, one idiom through which suffering is expressed among Tibetans in Lhasa's traditional Tibetan medical hospital is that of *rlung* (wind) (see also Janes 1995). Rlung can literally refer to the winds inside the body and outside, in which wind has a more general meaning that encompasses social, cultural, and political as well as physical and psychological forces (Adams 1992). Feelings of anger and frustration are *as important* as the cold foods one has eaten, the changing climate, and political oppression when it comes to explicating rlung disorders. Tibetan theories of medicine hold an expansive notion of the body in relation to the world around it, a body in which distinctions between mental and physical, and self and society are very unlike those found in western epistemology (and human rights discourse). Listen to the accounts of suffering as told to me by women patients in Lhasa's Traditional Tibetan Medical Hospital for utterances of a body that is constituted by the social and experienced at least sometimes as "collective."

In the halls of the Mentsikhang, Tibetan doctors called *men pa* (*sman-pa* (physician) or *amchi* (doctor)) tend to suffering Tibetans; they are promoted and almost entirely paid for by the Chinese government, at some financial cost to only some patients. Here the medical system is still based on the *rGyud bZhi*, the four tantras, borne from the words of Vairocana, a student of Padmasambhava, one of the seventh-century Indian pandits credited with introducing Buddhism to Tibet and who was said to have acquired his medical knowledge from the Indian Ayurvedic physician Candranandana (Dash 1976; Fenner 1996). One finds continuities with the Tibetan Buddhist past in these practices – continuities that are embedded in notions of the body, causes of suffering, and modes of efficacious healing (Adams n.d.; Clifford 1984; Dhonden 1986; Dhonden and Kelsang 1983; Rinpoche 1973). These continuities are audibly expressed by teachers, practitioners, and patients in their surprisingly public sentiments about self, body, and suffering.[12]

The first patient I met was a 30-year-old woman named Dolma who was diagnosed with both *gnyan kha* (hereafter written as pronounced: *nyenga*) and *snying rlung* (pronounced *nying loong*, hereafter written as *nying rlung*). Nyenga means inflammation, in this case in the pelvic region, and nying rlung translates to an imbalance of the "heart wind." The doctor explained to me that Dolma had had an intrauterine device (IUD) iserted at the Lhasa People's Hospital (biomedical) nearly two years ago and began to feel pain three months later. She got medicine from that hospital for her symptoms but it made her sick. The pain, meanwhile, subsided and only seemed to arise during her menstruation. Now it was two years later and when she began to feel unbearable pain twenty days ago she decided to come to the Mentsikhang, remembering that she had been successfully treated there for hepatitis about a year before.

This explained Dolma's nyenga, but she also had a nying rlung "heart wind" problem. In Tibetan medicine, rlung is the most important of the body's humors. Just as with winds outside the body, winds inside of the body are responsible for any and all movement. Its circulations result in linkages between the body's seven essential constituents (the nourishment in food and drink, blood, flesh, fat, bones, marrow, and semen) and also between what are known in Tibetan as five heaps or essences (*phung-bo lnga*) that make up the human being.[13] As such, winds take a variety of forms, some related to more subtle, physical conditions of being (discussed in *tantric* theory). Some are related to less subtle, physical conditions of being (discussed in medical theory). Winds are the responsible force that moves the body and its substances through and out of the body (Clifford 1984). The winds of the being are all related to one another in that the force of one will have effects on others. Trying to explain this to me in terms of organ systems that I would understand, one doctor explained, "In Tibetan medicine, there is no separate department for heart, bone, lungs, these separate things. In Tibetan medicine," she said, "all of these things are related to one another. For each patient, we look for all things." She then went on to reveal that winds are not simply an effect of the quality of the person's health in this life. "When Dolma was born, she had a problem with rlung and now when she gets unhappy, cold, eats poorly, she gets this rlung problem. Then, if she is not happy, very sad, she will not eat well and she will get nyenga." Dysfunctioning winds, it seems, affected the body systemically and, surprisingly, could be inherited from one's past lives.

Janes (1995), doing research in the same hospital in 1991 and 1993, found that rlung disorders were among the most commonly diagnosed in this hospital. The same was true in the ward devoted to women's health where I was working in 1993 and 1995. In addition to noting that symptoms of rlung derived from disorders of rlung in different parts of the body,[14] rlung is an indicator of the problem recognized in Tibetan Buddhism as "desire" (Adams 1992; Janes 1995). Rlung imbalances spring from unfulfilled desires, revealing a connection between one's sense body and one's physical being. In its most religious valences, desire is seen as inevitable once one is born to this world of material essence; the sense body is responsible for one's feelings of attraction to material forms, things, and so on. In less esoteric terms, the formation of the fetus is itself an outcome of the presence of desire in the transmigrating consciousness (a "most subtle mind"). Tibetan beliefs in rebirth hold that until reaching enlightenment, all beings will be endlessly reborn into the world. A sentient consciousness transmigrating from one life to the next is compelled by a force called *srog* (explained below), but the motivation for this force is desire. Desire is manifest as wind, thus as the wind humor in the developing being, just as ignorance gives rise to the body's *bad ken* (phlegm) humor, and aversion gives rise to its *mkhris* (bile) humor. From these humors emerge the body's seven constituents and finally a fully formed human being. Without the initial desire for rebirth on the part of a subtle mind transmigrating through the intermediate state from death to rebirth, the winds would not be aroused, nor would the physical being emerge therefrom. Without the presence of desire, anger and ignorance, there would be no physical form of the being. Thus, strong expressions of any of these characteristics-cum-emotions lead to and reflect imbalances of the formed body's humors of wind, bile, and phlegm, respectively.

Tibetan medical texts originally derived from religious perspectives that hold that desire can only be completely eliminated by taking refuge in the Buddha, the *dharma* (religion), the *sangha* (community of practitioners), and a life of steadfast practices enabling achievement of enlightenment. But again not all problems of desire are articulated in such esoteric terms. Indeed, few are for patients at the Mentsikhang (Janes 1995). Most are related to more immediate material concerns. One doctor told Janes, "People want to have good living conditions, enough food, obedient children, peace in the family, and so on. However, when they do not have these things that they desire, it leads to mental agitation, and these in turn cause rlung imbalance" (p. 30).

Turning back to Dolma, I asked, "What has made you sad?" She tells me that she works in an office, but the office is very busy. "I am always working, very hard work, and I have so much to do," she said. "In my office we translate Tibetan from Chinese, Chinese from Tibetan. It is a government office. The letters come in Chinese and I translate them into Tibetan. I have worked there for seven years. But we are too busy." The doctor interrupts to tell me that Dolma's nyenga is already better but her "wind" problem is still there. She was born with this problem, and because her work is hard, there is not much that she can do to prevent it from recurring. The doctor says that she has told Dolma to stay warm, wear warm clothes, and avoid overworking and hard physical labor. Dolma tells us that she often works overtime. If she does not finish the job during the day, she works into the night. The doctor says Dolma will probably stay another month or two in the hospital before going back to work.

One patient after another, I learn, has a problem related to rlung. One 36-year-old woman named Lhamo is in the hospital because dizziness caused her to fall down the stairs and hurt her hands and head. She had a great deal of fear since then. She had been in the hospital for two months already. She also had nyenga. Lhamo ate chilis and potatoes a few days earlier and these cold foods exacerbated her rlung. She was very unhappy. The doctor explained, "She fell down because she had the rlung problem and then after falling down, the rlung was made worse. It also made her get nyenga. She is sad because she is not married." I ask why she never married and she did not answer, but later I was told that people in government work units needed permission to marry and she had probably been refused.

Lhamo worked in one of the large hotels in Lhasa, a place with "too much noise and too many people," she said. She tells me they had political meetings there every Thursday night and these were hard for her. Nearly two thousand people come and go from them and she has so much work for them, day and night, day and night. It is difficult. Work units in Lhasa all held weekly political meetings at which attendance was mandatory. These were political "pep talks" and confessionals, a scheduled time for party cadres to remind Tibetans of their role as dutiful citizens and for citizens to confess politically suspicious or praiseworthy behaviors. Lhamo's concerns were not in her words about the political demands of the meetings so much as the physical demands of preparing for them and cleaning up after. "Can you change your work?" I ask. "It is difficult." She told me she would like to change work, and would apply, but it would be hard.

The amchi told me that this type of disease takes a long time to treat. "There is no set time, but it takes a long time. She can get better here, but when she goes back to her work, she will be around noise and all the people and the same situation again, and she will get sick again." Lhamo's rlung problem would always be there. Just then, the doctor pointed out to me that Lhamo was now not talking again and was thinking too much. She had stopped talking because "she thinks many things inside and gets sad." The doctor quickly takes my hand and wants me to place it on the body of Lhamo, letting me feel for myself where her rlung disease is. She places my hand at the back of her head, the base of her skull. There is the rlung imbalance. Also, she points out, there is a problem of rlung down the back and front in the center of her body; Lhamo's work situation was "worn" internally.

Another woman I met on my visit was a 50-year-old woman who earned her living as a street sweeper. She had been sick for the last five or six years and periodically came to the hospital for treatment. On her last visit, she stayed twenty days. This time, she was diagnosed with *kema* (*mkhal ma:* a kidney disease). Her face, hands, and legs were swollen. She also suffered from *srog rlung* (pronounced *sok loong*), the most dangerous sort of rlung – wind in the "life vein" – potentially leading to madness. "Too much work," the doctor said. "She has too much hard work." "She has rlung, srog rlung... any noise can make her mad. She gets sad feelings from rlung. If people get rlung [problems] then all other diseases come: *thiwa* [bile], nyenga, *pagin* [phlegm]."

One of the last patients suffering from nyenga and rlung with whom I spoke became sick after having an abortion. She had three children and did not want another. She had the abortion at two months. After the procedure, she got nyenga. The amchi explained that she probably got sick from unsanitary instruments. The doctor also told me that

She has many babies and that is why she has rlung [disorder]. Anyone who has so many babies has rlung. They cannot afford them. They cannot raise them nicely or provide food for all of them. They are farmers. They are poor. Their rlung will become worse from this. If they had one baby, they could raise it nicely, but with more, they cannot raise them nicely. So, they get [have] rlung disease.

The doctor's words at least partially blur the distinctions between Tibetan and Chinese perspectives on the causes of suffering and fertility. But it was not a complete match. The patient suffered because she was too poor to have so many children, and thus would have benefited from following China's strict birth control policy earlier in her life. But the testimony of Tibetan nuns addresses another problem faced by women who are forced or compelled to have abortions. Here, following the policy could be deleterious.

When you marry you will have as many children as is written in your fate. If you stop the spirit of a child from entering this world, you will not be reborn as a human being for many lifetimes. It is there in all the teachings. (Bruno 1993)

The visible and audible links between conditions of living and physiological suffering were found in each of the patients I met who had rlung disorders. The social disruptions of their everyday lives were drawn on their bodies, making their bodies physical maps of the social universes in which they existed. The rlung was there at the center of Lhamo's torso but that was where her difficult social conditions also existed. Conditions of physiological suffering were an expression of difficult social relations. Not surprisingly, these conditions were also expressed in terms of political oppression. A doctor who spoke to Janes was explicit: "Of course, rlung must be more common nowadays because Tibet is no longer free. The Chinese government is the government of rlung. The Chinese government makes people unhappy, and so rlung must be more common . . . Tibetans have rlung because they are not free" (1995: 31).

When I accompanied the senior physician on her rounds one day, she explained how difficult it is to explain rlung, especially to the Chinese. "The Chinese think that rlung means *angry* – we say 'No, this is not rlung. It refers to an internal not external state.' How can we explain it? In the Chinese language it is very hard."[15] Saying that rlung is "not an external state" was perhaps this doctor's way of avoiding scrutiny by a politically repressive regime that would be offended by a medical system that claimed to identify "social or political anger."[16] But there are other ways to interpret this doctor's reticence to describe rlung as an external state. Her statement is a comment on an at least partial incommensurability of Chinese and Tibetan views of the subject, stated for me, a westerner. She perceived that I too regarded the Chinese and Tibetan views as incommensurate. But she also understood that my culture's view of the subject might be as incommensurate with hers as was the Chinese view. For the amchi and her patient, rlung really was not about "external" anger, as if it could be seen as separate from an "internal" anger. Rather, it was about the way that anger permeates the world of the body at the same time that it is experienced as an external psychological and/or social assault. A bidirectionality of cause and effect suggests a form of simultaneity largely unfamiliar to me. For her, anger emerges as much from one's *internal* predisposition to being angered over even the most minor disruptions of the social world, because one is *born* with weak winds, as it does from the *internalizations* of what might be agreed upon as heinous conditions of *external* conflict. Here, an official Chinese position that aims to eliminate religion from medicine *and* my own biomedical Cartesianism would strip this relationship of its bidirectionality and simultaneity. Internal and external causes and effects are manifested in the same way because the external world is in some sense found at the site of the internal. But also a "flawed" internal world can create an oppressive and conflictual external one. That Tibetans think of their bodies as social milieus finally then directs our attention to the possibility of a collective subjectivity.

Tibetan Subjectivities, Karma, and Epistemology

In Tibetan theories of the body, a lexicon of winds makes it difficult to draw the stark distinctions between self and society, and mind and body, which are generally made by westerners and found in western biomedical epistemology. For example, when Tibetans talk about foods and job frustrations as similar disruptions to their winds, they are telling us that, in terms of bodily experience, these two things are in the same category. Likewise, becoming upset by one's poverty is experienced in the same visceral manner as falling and hitting one's head from dizziness. The body records these as at once internal *and* external events. The condition of falling down is produced by the same circumstance that produces the condition of becoming upset. Both are caused by winds. Just as social problems are worn internally as disruptions of winds, internal imbalances cause one to experience and relate to the world as conflictual and problematic, that is, as filled with disruptive winds. The skin is not a boundary between external and internal; it is a porous passageway connecting worlds made up of the same elements and forces.

One of the most vivid examples of the way that lay Tibetans conceptualize the porous boundary between internal and external is in the practice of raising prayer flags (*rlung rta*) as a means of strengthening one's own rlung. Interestingly, the term *rlung rta* is Chinese in origin, meaning "luck." It was transliterated into the Tibetan term *wind horse* but has come to stand for the good luck and protection one garners from meritorious religious action, such as raising prayer flags (i.e., practicing Buddhism). For lay Tibetans, the luck gained from external "winds," as conceptualized in the religious effects of placing written prayers in the winds, is simultaneously the luck gained by one's bodily winds. Since external winds are also internal bodily winds, raising flags in the winds is thought to confer direct benefit on one's health, making one less susceptible to disorders.[17]

One might argue that even among westerners social distress is experienced in physiological symptoms (e.g., in theories of somatization, or the biologization of psychology). But compelling evidence of at least one difference between Tibetan and western medical epistemologies, and similarity with traditional Chinese theory, is that Tibetans have a conceptual category that synthesizes the internal and external event/experience. Biomedicine refers to psychosomatic, or somatopsychic, as materially distinct phenomena, while the Tibetan category of winds (and other humors) treats them as indistinct. Winds outside the body are the winds inside the body; they are of the same substance and potentiality – effects outside are effects inside. Whether one experiences winds as climatic change, political or family trouble, or the fruition of *karma* from past lives, these experiences are understood not simply as internal responses to external conditions but also as internal imbalances *manifesting as* external distressors.

As has been shown in other Asian societies (Daniels 1984; Farquhar 1994; Kuriyama 1994; Obeyesekere 1976; Ots 1994; for Iran, see Good 1994), and particularly for Zhongyi, traditional Chinese medicine theories of the body often merge psychological and physical domains; this makes it problematic to assume the cross-cultural validity of an epistemological method that separates psychological from physiological domains.[18] Among Tibetans, too, the physical body is the site of mental emotions. That is, the heart (physically) is considered the seat of the mind, the source of mental insight. But if an epistemiology that posits a mind/body dualism is inappropriate here, then an epidemiology that presupposes a social/individual dualism is also problematic. The physical body for Tibetans is the site for social relationships among people who are believed to be connected to one another as a *physical* rather than a sociological fact. That is, if Tibetan medical epistemology conceptualizes the social at the location of the body, then the Tibetan body must be seen as physiologically constituted as a multitude of beings. This is better explained through the specificity of Tibetan notions of embryology and the karma that is believed responsible for producing life.

In Tibetan medicine, the basis for human life is not biology but ethics. Stated better, in the Tibetan view, the basis for *biology is ethics*. Tibetans believe that the human being comes into existence as a result of something called the *srog* (life force). The srog is the "spark of life" that enables the sentient mind, *sems*, to remain connected to the physical form – the life force that brings the living being into existence. The srog, riding on a wind (that is, desire), gives rise to the fetus (three humors and seven constituents) at the heart (*chakra*). The srog is literally the ignition, the enlivening of material substance. The quality of the srog is determined by karma – by the inevitability of consequences for all of our actions and all of our intentions. Karma, as action producing results, is understood by Tibetans very clearly: actions from one's past life bear fruit in one's present or future lives, and actions from one's present life will bear fruit in one's future lives. The srog, in other words, is *an ethical possibility from which emerges a biological form*. It both rides upon winds and *determines* their quality and strength. Hence karma determines one's susceptibility to wind disorders and one's predisposition to avoiding them. The discourse is strangely alternative to and contrasted with the discourse on genetics in biomedicine.[19]

Recognizing that physicality is a matter of ethics does not mean that biology is something that can be discarded or treated as transcendable by a purely mental state of being – by a purely ethical stance. On the contrary, in the Tibetan view biology is made all the *more* important because here in the phenomenal world the body is the site for the expression of the ethical, and therefore the social. "No one can escape the consequences of their actions," the nun reminds us. I would guess that many westerners think of karma as a metaphysical principle, an individualized moral accounting system that will make certain that there are consequences of one's actions in a spiritually and self-contained sense. Indeed, even most Tibetans would agree that karma reveals the continuity of *a person* from one life to the next and that this might be thought of as tied to an individual, or to a singular "mind stream," a consciousness. But most Tibetans also recognize that because karma works in a physical more so than a metaphysical manner, its field of operation is the *social* realm, and it is thus an extraordinary expression of collectivity. In the first instance, karma concerns morality in terms of how one behaves *in relation to* others. In the second instance, karma concerns morality as an expression of how one behaves *as others* – the actions of one person produce results in another. This second sense is more subtle. Karma explains how all phenomena, and especially living beings, are contingent on their causes; human bodies are themselves contingent on other beings; they could not exist without prior actions of other beings.

The effects of one's karma are both produced and expressed primarily in relation to other people with whom one is connected, in the Tibetan view, in a physical sense through rebirth. A person's current life represents an accumulation of his or her actions toward others in previous lives, but also as others in previous lives. These lives are typically viewed as being in some important sense both the same as and *other than the self* (they can even be nonhumans). The sems (sentient mind) is the physical expression of a collection of various persons who are present at once in the living being. These beings – who were not flesh, bone, blood, the same as "you" – are now present in you in the sense that it was their actions that produced your physical existence. Their lives make up your life. Collectively, they are the physical foundation of the self. The most subtle mind is thus inseparable from the body and it is a collectivity of *bodies*.[20] This most subtle mind must be seen as the expression of the accumulated *karma* that derives from these body forms in past lives.[21]

Karma enables the materialization of ethical behavior that concerns, at heart, one's social relations with others and *as* others. That is, for Tibetans, one's srog reflects the way one behaves not only *toward* others but also as an expression *of* these other people. At rebirth, social relations with other persons become embodied in the physical presence of the person, especially in the strength of one's wind humor. In more esoteric religious accounts this sensibility is tied to ideas about compassion; because one's rebirths are potentially infinite, one should recognize that at any point in time any living being could have been or will be one's own mother. Thus, our relationships to one another are all essentially like those between mother and child and should be filled with compassion and loving kindness. Tibetans say, whether we are able to accomplish this or not, we remain connected to the persons from our past lives upon inheriting the potential for the expression of their *karmic* effects in this life in our very physical bodies. Thus acting toward all others as if they were our mothers or children can only help to achieve a better rebirth in the next life. One might think of the ability to accomplish this as tantamount to the greatest achievement of collective subjectivity: ethical responsibility to others is both personalized and collectivized in a principle that is taken by Tibetans to be a universal law.

Tibetan medicine and traditional Tibetan notions of the subject held by most, but certainly not all, Tibetans were formed under the overarching cultural system of Buddhism.[22] Buddhism historically formed a substrate from which both scholarly and lay epistemology derived in general, and this is still true today despite various infringements at different historical times on Tibetans' ability to practice religion. This becomes audible in accounts patients give about their ailments that they attribute to karmic causes, especially in reference to innate humoral imbalances. It is also heard in other ways, and is thus worth exploring the lay expressions of collective subjectivity that have resonance with more esoteric Buddhist ideas.

Evidence of a collective subjectivity among Tibetans comes from patients who describe their health problems in terms of the actions of both karma and spirit beings. Many Tibetans believe that one's person is constituted by a collection of a variety of gods: from one's place of birth (*ziptak*), lineage (*gyurpa lha*), and past lives (*gyaptak*). For instance, a person who is born in a particular locale will *contain* the god of that locale who, if offended by things done by the person, may make the subject sick. These gods are shared by all those persons who are born in the same locale, or, in the case of lineage gods, who are members of the same lineage. This fact does not suggest the "partibility" of the person but rather that the person's subjectivity is constituted by the collective. It is the same god who resides in numerous people, making some aspect of the person the "same person" as others.

Tibetans also generally believe that each person is made up of numerous beings (who have become ghosts, for example, or other spirit entities) who become attached to the person at the moment of the person's death in a former life. These entities (*gyaptak* and *shrindi*) can have gyaptak of their own, who become attached to them at the moment of the former's death. A man who dies because he has offended a deity (a water goddess, *klu*, for example) can be reborn with that goddess inside of him. During his life, this gyaptak can cause him enormous sickness. Upon his death, he may himself become a spirit entity who, upon being violently disturbed, may cause the untimely death of another living being. Thus, during possession rituals performed by shamans among culturally Tibetan people (Adams 1996a), one finds that even when a shaman is possessed by one supernatural being, over the course of that single possession he may manifest as several different beings, each one a different gyaptak who is embodied in the same initial spirit visitor.

One can become ill as a result of the suffering of a god or supernatural being who is "housed" in, or rather who makes up, the self. Often, when Tibetans witness something that makes them sad, for example, they do not refer to themselves as being sad, but to having offended one of their "gods" (*lha*) or having made him sad. Making one's god sad is dangerous because, they note, one's ability to have a good future rebirth is tied to the amount of comfort experienced by one's gods in this life. Two gods who sit atop one's shoulders keeping track of one's merits and demerits are particularly important here.

The convergences between these "folk" conceptions of subjectivity in relation to health are not far from more doctrinal Buddhist practices found in tantric pedagogy. Tibetan Buddhist or Vajrayana practices of meditation take as foundational the possibility of manifesting oneself as multiple beings at one time. Whether invoking the presence of one's lineage teacher inside of oneself, or acknowledging the presence of religious teachings as a product of historical adepts who manifested in the form of their disciples, conceptualizations of beings as collectivized are essential to the practices. Again, practitioners' abilities to understand how this works is generally associated with theories of karma, of the dependent origination of phenomena, and of the idea that the self has no essential fixed nature – it is impermanent and dependent upon causes. The exercises provide a subtle reminder of both the "empty" nature of the self – the subject does not exist as a thing with self-nature – and the simultaneous and undeniable *presence* of a being who appears as a result of countless actions and karmic effects of others. The Buddha's achievement of enlightenment was his emanating consciously as an infinite number of beings in the world. These manifestations of collectivities within the singular being are in their most adept form not simply psychological states, as most westerners are inclined to surmise; rather, they are *physiological* embodiments.

The idea that collective subjectivity is the only way that Tibetans conceptualize subjectivity would be an exaggeration, for individualism exists as a Tibetan epistemological foundation for subjectivity as well.[23] Surely Tibetan Buddhist scriptures would not be so concerned with teaching practitioners how to overcome a grasping of the idea of the self (*bdag bdzin*) if the average practitioner had already transcended this tendency. But it would be even more of an exaggeration to suggest that a sensibility of collectivism is only an ideal for Tibetans, aspired to but seldom achieved, as Buddhist scriptural materials would suggest. Rather, a sensibility of collectivism operates in this culture and manifests itself every day, but particularly at liminal moments, such as when the body suffers (Comaroff 1981 and Turner 1968). It becomes visible at moments of bodily crisis when the body – this body that is a collection of social relationships – actualizes the presence of other beings who both cause and alleviate suffering.[24] It is present when concerns about morality and violations of it are aroused and experienced in imbalances of wind (rlung). Here, a theory of karma becomes a basis for understanding Tibetan subjectivity and might be seen as operating at the level of epistemology in Tibetan culture.

The nuns' prayers for clarity for their Chinese oppressors in the passages opening this article become even more compelling when one notes that karma expresses itself in an extraordinarily materialist and collectivist sense. They saw their jailers and torturers not as absolutely wrong, but as part of a universe that is intact, connected in ways that reveal their Chinese oppressors' actions as inevitably wrongheaded, unclear, and "backward" because of their lack of awareness of the karma that connects all beings together into physically dependent relationships. The suffering body in Tibetan culture is thus the extraordinary expression of the unity of what westerners generally divide into the physical, moral, social, political, and/or religious aspects of a person's life. The Tibetan body does not simply "house" a transcendent consciousness or "soul" that is self-contained by boundaries that ascribe differences between one individual and another. On the contrary, it is occasionally experienced as a repository for the universe as a whole, a source for its production and perpetuation, and held together by *karma* and therefore connected to other, many other, sentient beings. This might have important implications for an anthropological politics of engagement.

In Tibetan culture, the category of rlung encompasses the political as part of bodily suffering, and as expressions of the social and moral connections among people. Its expression in ailing Tibetans thus reveals that they experience their subjectivity as at least partially collective, based on notions of karma and an inseparability of body, mind, and society. In much of Tibetan culture the body is thus an extremely visible site for politics while politics itself persistently refers to, and is transposed onto, the physical body, religion, the social collective, and more importantly, the karma that binds it. The notion of "political" that emerges in this world is expressed in ways that make it relevant when it pertains to a collective body and that body's potential for moral responsibility to others. This is a moral field that reaches far beyond the immediate realm of both Chinese politics and metropole human rights agendas. Finally, a Tibetan view of morally based biology reveals suffering in terms that may resonate as easily with Chinese medical ideas of subjectivity and collectivist constructions of healing (Farquhar 1994) as it does with metropole individual rights. At the same time, this suffering resists an easy conflation with either Chinese or metropole conceptions.

Collective Subjectivity and Human Rights Politics

We are not paying enough attention to activists and intellectuals who often appear to be of an oppositional nature and are also formed by Western modernist discourse. They are the same and of the same fate as the repressive regimes of the postcolonial states which they are criticizing....
The most recent example to appear in Indonesia is the argumentation between New Order Bureaucrats and a few human rights leaders concerning the understanding of the issue as a universal one or not. Both sides have unconsciously and without intent, both so very harsh and uncompromising, mutually shaped and reproduced the discourse of Western modernism.

(Ariel Heryanto, *Indonesian Intellectual*, translated by John MacDougal)

The utterances about suffering issued by Tibetans are made in a lexicon that is both familiar and unfamiliar to most people who are in the centers of global economic, social, and political power where human rights discourse is articulated for international use. The Tibetan nuns are as concerned with the effects of karma on their oppressors, their actions on all living beings, their next lives, turning their enemy into their greatest teacher, and freeing all living beings from suffering, as they are with making sense of their experience in the terms of the United Nations or Geneva Convention. A nun says "I pray that the minds of the Chinese become gentle and calm, that through love and compassion those who are drunk with delusions, lost in the darkness of ignorance, acquire the wisdom eye to see what is right and what is wrong" (Bruno 1993). The discourse of women in the wards of the Tibetan medical hospital helps draw our attention to Tibetan notions of subjectivity that are expressed in "winds," karma, and a person's unalterable connectedness to others. Their utterances of suffering reveal Tibetan conceptions of what it means to be human and suggest that human rights violations produce suffering and are effective upon Tibetans in unique ways. Freedom from violations for Tibetans, then, may ironically be understood best in terms of ideas about the collective.

Since metropole human rights discourse ultimately references domains of experience that are shared cross-culturally, such as shared understandings of suffering, they are seldom phrased in terms of cultural differences. What, then, can be gained by an inquiry into cultural differences in the experience and expression of suffering? There is much at stake in questioning the concept of universalism articulated around individualism in human rights, for in Tibet a universalist discourse has made it possible to hear the voices of Tibetans. I also note that if you are being tortured, you do not care as much about your cultural survival as you do about your physical survival. So why should we be concerned with a human rights that can attend to this particular cultural specificity?

My focus is overdetermined in three ways. First, the violations of human rights in Tibet consistently direct us to the issue of *cultural* survival. Second, the victims themselves suggest that we should pay attention to these specificities; differences are another basis upon which political claims are made and differences explain how notions of physical survival might be envisioned. Finally, the practicality of embracing a politics *for* human rights, as opposed to a politics *of* human rights, on the Tibetan plateau might ironically require us to move away from a notion of universalism as we know it. If the western response to Tibetan suffering reinforces the polarization of options, it could lead to a situation in which adopting universalism may lead to furthering the Chinese government's violations of Tibetans. To the extent that even nonindependence-oriented Tibetans pay for this polarization in increased restrictions and violence against them, this is problematic.

This article asks whether realigning difference and similarity can be a means of entering into the debate about human rights in alternative and productive ways. The international human rights discourse emerging from the metropole remains contingent on notions of subjectivity that are primarily individualist, and on notions of truth that are principally universal. The particular prophecy it brought to life out of the Cold War[25] was that there would be a way in which to derive and then deploy an institutionalized belief in universalism. For some Tibetans, the presence of this discourse means that since China is the oppressor, the "western" metropole can only be a liberator and *its* terms of liberation have to be the ones used. But using medical anthropology as a means of investigating the cultural expressions of bodily suffering, I have brought to the fore Tibetan understandings of collective subjectivity in ways that suggest odd and ironic juxtapositions and potential erasures when it comes to the discourses of human rights in Tibet. International human rights discourse emerging from activists for an independent Tibet compels Tibetans to make their claims heard, and we interpret them as calls for the deployment of the metropole idioms: those of individualism and universalism. Here humanism operates at the level of the individual, not the culture. But are not Tibetan subjectivities *also* about being collective, not individual? Does not this bring Tibetan views closer to Chinese than metropole or western internationalist views? Does not this disrupt the neat and tidy polarization of the human rights politics so clear in so many advocates' minds?

On the one hand, one could argue that erasures of cultural specificity resulting from the human rights activism are far less than the erasures of Tibetan culture that results from the Chinese revolution and modernization, however officially designated as beneficial. And, to be sure, Chinese configurations of collectivism may share even less with Tibetan notions of collectivism than do western notions of individualism and universalism when compared with Tibetans'. The amchi told us, after all, that it was hard to explain Tibetan suffering in Chinese terms. It would be naive to assume that an account of the ways in which the distance between Tibetan and western conceptualizations of subjectivity is greater than between Tibetan and Chinese conceptualizations of subjectivity could make much of a difference in the realpolitik of Chinese concerns over secessionist activism in Tibet. So long as there is a desire for independence on the Tibetan plateau, the restrictions on some Tibetans' freedoms of expression will remain. On the other hand, metropole human rights discourse is partly about sustaining cultural differences by creating a political and moral space within which people are allowed to practice their cultures as they wish.

So what can come from a recognition of cultural differences when one is persistently concerned with steering them away from the "Chinese" and collectivist, cultural-specific terms of the debate? Tibetans offer a particularly *karmic* vision of the universe that acknowledges a partially collective identity. They call for the world to recognize the applicability of Tibetan culture universally. Thus, we must ask, can recognizing the difference between the metropole discourse about suffering and the experiences of suffering among Tibetans make a difference in how metropole advocates think about human rights politics? If Tibetans are answered, humanism might have to operate at the level of the culture, not the individual, and universalism might have to operate at the level of a recognizable, ethically collective subject. In some sense this conceptualization may be more in keeping with the sentiment expressed by the nuns as the "law of karma."

My aim in this article has been to bring Tibetan voices into the existing polarized debate on human rights in Tibet in a manner that shows the relevance of medical anthropology to this larger political debate. I have sought to accomplish this not by reinforcing the conflict between universalism and particularism, Tibetanness and Chineseness, but perhaps by displacing it with one that highlights the blurriness between these polarized categories when one focuses on bodies and subjectivities that suffer rather than on international agendas and transnational politics. If Tibetan concerns can disrupt the polemicization of discourses already in place, then my aim would be to illustrate Tibetans' recognition of the collective within the individual, and the universalist potential of their very specific culture.

NOTES

Acknowledgments. A version of this article was originally prepared for the conference entitled "Universalizing from Particulars: Islamic Views of the Human and the UN Declaration of Human Rights in Comparative Perspective," sponsored by the Center for Transregional Studies, Princeton University, May 1996. I would like to thank Abdellah Hammoudi for including me in the conference, Princeton University for providing me with funds for the preliminary research upon which this article is based, and three anonymous reviewers whose suggestions greatly improved the essay. Either by their dissent or approval, other readers have also shaped my views here. These include Veena Das, Robert Desjarlais, David Maybury-Lewis, Alan Klima, Peter Moran, Mahmood Mamdani, Abdellah Hammoudi, Kay Warren, Gay Becker, and Norman Fineman. I alone take responsibility for the final essay and do not imply agreement with its final form on the part of any of the persons listed here.

1 Veena Das, personal communication, May 1996, in commentary for panel presentation at the American Anthropological Association 94th Annual Meeting, Washington, DC. Das (1996) made the point that a discourse of rights might itself produce uneven effects for persons who are differentially privileged to begin with. For example, rights of the individual to self-determination may legitimize the right of individuals to sell their organs, when in fact some people are more likely to be forced into this out of economic desperation than others. She notes here and elsewhere (for example, rape trials *vis-à-vis* women) that the discourse of rights under patriarchy can itself exacerbate oppression of women.

2 This is not to say that these Tibetans might not *also* be interested in a politics of independence. See Adams 1996b in which I describe one aspect of identity politics in Lhasa, especially urban youth, who have adopted this position. I point out that western romantic assumptions about the uniformity of Tibetan identity can be misleading, for Tibetans have responded unevenly to the current presence of Chinese communist hegemony.

3 One might consider that the contours of the conflict could be better described as "racial." Some international human rights discourses, and even some refugee Tibetans, view it this way. But the term has little relevance from the Chinese perspective since they consider Tibetans to be a "nationality," or *minzu*, a term also used for the Han majority. Tibetans are considered a minority nationality, *shaoshu minzu*. I use the term *ethnic* but acknowledge that from some perspectives it cannot capture the full range of sentiments and concerns that

arise from the perception of ascribed differences between Tibetans and Chinese found among both Tibetans and Han Chinese.

4 I have been collecting materials on Tibet, the Tibetan diaspora, and Tibetan medicine since 1981. In this article, I draw from materials collected on two preliminary field visits to Tibet and from extensive fieldwork experience over more than two years among culturally Tibetan Sherpas in Nepal. During four months of research in Tibet, I worked principally in Lhasa with physicians and patients at the outpatient Mentsikhang (College of Medicine and Astrology) where I was allowed to interview women and their family members with a tape recorder. In addition to taped interviews with patients and physicians, I also interviewed women and health care employees outside of the hospital context regarding their knowledge of women's disorders and their health concerns. Additional information about contemporary Tibetan medicine is taken from an unpublished manuscript on women's health and the treatment of common disorders written by a physician from the Mentsikhang that was translated by Art Engle of Howell, New Jersey.

5 For a review of the situation in Tibet from a western and refugee perspective, and one that does not deploy the rhetoric of human rights, see various coverage of the Tibet issue in *Cultural Survival Quarterly:* Hampton 1985; Smith 1986; Thurman 1988; Wangyal 1986. For additional views on human rights violations and cultural survival see Ackerly 1988; Avedon 1984a, 1984b, 1988; Congressional Records 1992; International Campaign for Tibet 1992; Lowry 1988; The Office of Tibet 1983; Schwartz 1992; UN Commission on Human Rights 1985; Van Walt Van Praag 1988; and Wangyal 1986. Articles here also mention that despite the oppression in Tibet, Tibetans persistently hold onto their culture, inside and outside of their homeland. Also, the 1988 collection of articles contain lengthy reviews of the debate over the historical yet contested facts about Tibet's sovereignty. I should note here that the terms used for the debate are not mapped easily onto regions or nations of the world. *Metropole*, in my use, refers to agencies like the UN, which tend to be dominated by western interests; but the category of "advocates" for a free Tibet is larger than metropole or westerners. It should also be noted that although the terms of the discourse on human rights were initially articulated by the UN, these terms are used by advocate groups today, and the UN general assembly (at which Tibetan refugees have no representation) has not been consistent in recognizing and supporting discussion of resolutions concerning human rights violations in Tibet (see Goldstein 1989).

6 Many accounts attest to a cultural genocide by state design. Until 1989 educational opportunities and chances for social advancement in Tibet were only available to those who spoke fluent Mandarin. The Chinese attempted to eliminate the need for Tibetan language and sought to turn it into a secondary, token language of a premodern era spoken by the most economically and socially underdeveloped people. The accounts note that the majority of students graduating from Lhasa university were, and still are, Chinese, not Tibetans. Although this changed somewhat in 1989 when officials called for the use of Tibetan language textbooks in schools, especially higher education schools (Asia Watch 1990; also see Goldstein 1997), this effort was itself disrupted by the move toward liberalization that directed greater state funds to coastal regions rather than to rural minority regions in China more generally, leading to a gross underfunding of educational projects in general on the plateau.

7 Thanks are owed to Clara Han (Princeton class of 1997) who collected references on this topic.

8 The Chinese position articulates in some ways with debates between "northern" and "southern" nations over the prioritizing of civil and political rights (negative rights) versus economic, social, and cultural rights (positive rights), but only partially and for different motivations. Chinese official discourse considers political and civil rights to be "bourgeois" rights because they prioritize individual needs over the needs of society. It therefore

disregards them, as opposed to simply making them lower priority, as is the case in many "Southern" nations. Economic and social rights, on the other hand, because they are collectivist, are preserved and protected for citizens in China. In fact, few western critics fault China for failing to attend to the economic and social needs of its citizens, through the provision of health care, housing, employment, and social security. Many "southern" nations argue that these rights are more important than civil and political rights. This also serves as a critique of dependency spawned by postcolonial development era inequalities that are also seen as a form of human rights violations.

9 *Metropole* refers to the term used in world systems theory and underdevelopment literature (by Andre Gunther Frank and others) to identify the international agencies brought into existence by western industrialized nations as instruments of global development, capitalism, and political dialogue.

10 This film is available from Film Library, 22-D Hollywood Ave., Ho-Ho-Kus, NJ 07423, 1-800-383-5548.

11 Some of the most vocal activists among Tibetan refugees are Tibetans who know very little about life in Tibet other than what they hear from newly arrived refugees, news resources, short visits, and in some cases, their memories of their early childhood on the plateau. Nevertheless their claims are legitimate. The nuns' commentaries need to be understood as a product of what can be called a romantic western gaze – a desire for a particularly religious and oppressed Tibetan (Adams 1996b). But this does not entirely discredit their views, for Tibetan desires for difference are built into the discourse on human rights (Adams 1996a). Also I do not want to use the nuns' utterances in a voyeuristic manner that might add to the oppression of these women by valorizing their words as an instrument for my own theoretical or ethnographic gain. One way to work through the problem of voyeurism is to acknowledge the power of their statements to induce emotional responses that compel me to think about how we can do justice to them in the ethical framings they suggest. No doubt some will accuse me of offering a romanticism of my own.

12 Janes (1995) argues that the fact that one ward of the hospital is devoted specifically to women's health is a visible sign of the steady effort to incorporate organizational and structural components of biomedicine and its sinicized counterpart into this traditional cultural system. Indeed, the medical practices have been purged of many of their religious underpinnings, and there has been steadfast recuperation of some of them in scientized as well as sinicized form.

13 These are the physical being (*gzugs*), sense being (*tshor wa*), discerning being (*du shes*), intentional being (*du byed*), and consciousness (*rnam shes*).

14 He wrote that

the discrete symptom clusters of rlung imbalance are related to the spatial orientation of rlung in the body. Symptoms that derive from disorders of rlung in the brain, heart, and chest are most frequently experienced. In the brain, rlung may disrupt the "life vein," causing disordered thinking, depression, and insanity. In less severe forms, rlung causes dizziness, insomnia, dysphoria, fainting, ringing in the ears, and impaired sensory perception. In the heart, rlung contributes to palpations, heart swings, and a rapid fluttering heart beat. In the chest area, rlung causes shortness of breath and symptoms of pain in the sternum that often go through to the upper spine. (Janes 1995: 29–30)

15 One reviewer for this essay indicated that the Chinese interpretation of rlung as anger is too narrow. In fact, s/he notes that the Chinese have "initiated a few, small propaganda campaigns aimed at rlung, calling it 'altitude disease' or the result of 'air pollution from fires (usually from incense)'" (anonymous). Also, Tibetans do refer to people with hot temper as *rlung tsha bo*, or hot winded.

16 Janes (1995) suggests this.

17 Especially disorders caused by malevolent spirit entities and ghosts (Adams 1996a).

18 Thus, I would distinguish this idea from that of somatization developed by Kleinman (1980) for whom the model of cultural distress treated psychological diseases as separable from biological substrates. I would say a theory of somatization disregards traditional Chinese medical understandings of the body. Tibetan bodies experience *srog rlung* as a physical disease that is at the same time social and psychological. There is no way to treat the social and psychological as cultural or symbolic – as epiphenomenal to biology. Kleinman's early approach reproduced a Cartesian dualism (tied to the problem of subject-object dualism) not present in the Tibetan case.

19 The *srog* determines the quality of one's wind humor. This is not the only contributing factor to the quality of one's winds. Events occurring during pregnancy and childbirth can have an effect on one's winds, in the same way that events in one's lifetime can have an effect on them, producing health or disease.

20 There are theories of tantric practice that explain methods by which living beings can become skilled in techniques that separate mental faculties from coarse bodily forms, but the average practitioner or layperson, and even most skilled ones, would not be able to achieve this.

21 Although I suggest that many Tibetans understand the basic idea about rebirth as on some level an ultimate truth, it is important to note that few Tibetans, or others for that matter, could make use of this knowledge in any profound religious way. The theory holds that beings who have achieved great spiritual accomplishment can actually remember their past lives and appear in this life as emanations of their past lives. They are called *tulkus* *(sprul kus)*, who, because of the unpredictable but (in this case) favorable ripening of karma from past lives, are able to emanate into this life in a particular human form. The Dalai Lama(s), for example, is a very high level tulku. Tulkus are embodiments of the same and yet "different" beings. Few persons have the ability to become emanation beings insofar as this means "remembering" one's past life, but the fact that rebirth entails a continuity of mind, or *sems*, and that this sems is the expression of continuity for past bodies, is tacitly accepted by all Buddhist Tibetans. In any life the *sems* thus represents the collection of the different beings into a single consciousness, while the living entity represents a single life in a collective temporal continuity involving endless rebirth until enlightenment.

22 Some Buddhologists, who rely on texts to the exclusion of ethnographic data, as well as ethnographers, who are not familiar enough with religious texts to see religious foundations in many "cultural" practices, often fail to see the grounds for a claim to a Tibetan epistemology based on the Buddhist foundations of Tibetan culture (see French 1995 as exception). Tibetans who do identify as Buddhist do so by culture, not simply by observance of religious practices. This is true for most Tibetans in Tibet, I would say, despite thirty years of intensive reforms by the Chinese government including ten years of a Cultural Revolution (which targeted Tibet's "feudalistic" religion for eradication), despite the fact that among Tibetans one finds differential levels of practice and awareness of Buddhist teachings, not to mention divided and diverse loyalties to different schools of Tibetan Buddhism, and despite the presence of many (especially urban young) Tibetans who in the rush toward modernization have adopted different attitudes toward religion than their parents and many others of their generational cohort (Adams 1996b).

23 The question of collective subjectivity in Buddhist and some South Asian cultures has been discussed in numerous sources (Dumont 1970; McHugh 1989; Obeyesekere 1990; Ortner 1998; Tambiah 1984). Often, the idea of collective subjectivity is presented as a subject position that is in tension with other tendencies revealed in social behaviors and intentions, such as the tendency toward individualism and selfishness. Indeed, Tibetan

scriptural sources and practices devote a great deal of attention to the problem of over-coming the idea of a self – a person with self-existent nature from which derive selfish desires – thus suggesting that the inherent tendency of all living beings is toward mis-takenly thinking of themselves as having self-nature, as being individuals with essential nature. Indeed, realizing the implications of collective subjectivity from the perspective of *karma* is a great achievement and should be seen as an ideal of sorts (pace Ortner 1978). At the same time, it would be a misunderstanding to underestimate Tibetan epistemolo-gical foundations for subjectivity. The logic followed is the reverse of western assump-tions: whereas we begin with the assumption of individualism and work to overcome this with ethics, codes of morality, cultural codes, and so on. I believe Tibetans begin with the assumption of a universe contained within the subtle mind, which, with development, learns to develop sensibilities of individualism, attachment, and desire. Again, these tendencies can be overcome through practices of religion. In a Foucauldian manner, one might argue that Buddhism among Tibetans has to continually establish the presence of individualism as an object of concern and as a problem in order to teach people to avoid it, and to recover their original state of being (Adams 1992).

24 This is one reason that healers in Tibetan medicine are ideally meant to establish relation-ships of interdependency with their patients: in religious training they assume the position of the healing Buddha as a teacher of their student, the patient.

25 I am aware that "rights" discourse is older than the postcolonial geopolitical climate.

REFERENCES

Ackerly, John, and Blake Kerr
   1988   Reflections on a Riot. *Cultural Survival Quarterly* 12(1): 45–8.
Adams, Vincanne
   1992   The Social Production of the Self and the Body in Sherpa and Tibetan Society. In *Anthropological Approaches to the Study of Ethnomedicine*. Mark Nichter, ed. Pp. 149–90. New York: Gordon and Breach.
   1996a   *Tigers of the Snow and Other Virtual Sherpas: An Ethnography of Himalayan Encounters*. Princeton, NJ: Princeton University Press.
   1996b   Karaoke as Modern Lhasa, Tibet. *Cultural Anthropology* 11(4): 510–46.
   N.d. Epistemologies of the Modern: Treating Women's Disorders in Lhasa, Tibet. [Paper given at] Conference at the Department of Sociology and Anthropology, University of Newcastle, Australia.
Asia Watch
   1990   *A Report: Merciless Repression: Human Rights Abuses in Tibet*. New York: Human Rights Watch.
   1994   *Detained in China and Tibet: A Directory of Political and Religious Prisoners*. New York: Human Rights Watch.
Avedon, John F.
   1984a   Tibet's "Exile Generation." *New York Times Magazine*, February 26: 34–42.
   1984b   *In Exile from the Land of Snows*. New York: Alfred A. Knopf.
   1988   Tibet Today: Current Conditions and Prospects. *Cultural Survival Quarterly* 12(1): 52–60.
Bruno, Ellen
   1993   Satya: A Prayer for the Enemy. Ellen Bruno Productions. Video. Ho-Ho-Kus, NJ: Film Library.

Chan, Joseph
    1995   The Asian Challenge to Universal Human Rights: A Philosophical Appraisal. In *Human Rights and International Relations in the Asia-Pacific Region*. James T. H. Tang, ed. Pp. 25–38. London and New York: Pinter.

Chiu, Hungdah
    1989   Chinese Attitudes toward International Law of Human Rights in the Post-Mao Era. Occasional Papers/Reprint Series in Contemporary Asian Studies, no. 5. Baltimore: School of Law.

Clifford, Terry
    1984   *Tibetan Buddhist Medicine and Psychiatry: The Diamond Healing*. York Beach, ME: Samuel Weiser.

Comaroff, Jean
    1981   Medicine: Symbol and Ideology. In *The Problem of Medical Knowledge*. Peter Wright and Andrew Treacher, eds. Pp. 49–68. Edinburgh: Edinburgh University Press.

Congressional Records
    1992   *Refugee Reports of Conditions in Tibet*. Section IV. Washington, DC, August 12.

Dalai Lama
    1985   A Vast Sea of Chinese Threatens Tibet. *New York Times*, August 9.

Daniels, E. Valentine
    1984   *Fluid Signs: Being a Person the Tamil Way*. Berkeley: University of California Press.

Das, Veena
    1996   The "Human" in Human Rights: Universalization versus Globalization. Unpublished manuscript delivered at the Conference, "Universalizing from Particulars: Islamic Views of the Human and the UN Declaration of Human Rights in Comparative Perspective." Center for Transregional Studies, Princeton University, NJ, May 24–6.

Dash, Bagwan
    1976   *Tibetan Medicine*. Dharamsala, India: Library of Tibetan Works and Archives.

Dhonden, Yeshi
    1986   *Health through Balance: An Introduction to Tibetan Medicine*. Jeffrey Hopkins, trans. Ithaca, NY: Snow Lion Publications.

Dhonden, Yeshi, and Jampel Kelsang
    1983   The Ambrosia Heart Tantra. *Journal of Tibetan Medicine*. Dharamsala, India: Library of Tibetan Works and Archives, 6.

Drinan, Robert F., and S. J. Teresa T. Kuo
    1992   The 1991 Battle for Human Rights in China. *Human Rights Quarterly* 14(1): 21–42.

Dumont, Louis Homo
    1970   *Hierarchicus, An Essay on the Caste System*. Chicago: Chicago University Press.

Farquhar, Judith
    1994   Multiplicity, Point of View, and Responsibility in Traditional Chinese Healing. In *Body, Subject and Power in China*. A. Zito and T. Barlow, eds. Pp. 78–99. Chicago: Chicago University Press.

Fenner, Tom
    1996   The Origin of rGyud bshi: A Tibetan Medical Tantra. In *Tibetan Literature*. Ithaca, NY: Snow Lion Publications.

French, Rebecca Redwood
    1995   *The Golden Yoke: The Legal Cosmology of Buddhist Tibet*. Ithaca, NY: Cornell University Press.

Goldstein, Melvyn C.
    1989   *A History of Modern Tibet, 1913–1951: The Demise of the Lamaist State*. Berkeley: University of California Press.

1997   *The Snow Lion and the Dragon: China, Tibet, and the Dalai Lama*. Berkeley: University of California Press.

Good, Byron
   1994   *Medicine, Rationality, and Experience*. Cambridge: Cambridge University Press.

Hampton, Francesca
   1985   Tibetans in India – A New Generation in Exile. *Cultural Survival Quarterly* 9(2): 13–15.

Heryanto, Ariel
   1991   Postmodernisme: Which One? Concerning Criticism and Confusion within the Postmodernisme Debate in Indonesia. From *Postmodernism amongst/around Us, Kalam* 1: 91.

International Campaign for Tibet
   1992   *Tibetan Environment and Development News Issue* 6. Washington DC, November.

Janes, Craig
   1995   The Transformation of Tibetan Medicine. *Medical Anthropology Quarterly* 9: 6–39.

Kleinman, Arthur
   1980   *Patients and Healers in the Context of Culture*. Berkeley: University of California Press.

Kuriyama, Shigehisa
   1994   The Imagination of Winds and the Development of the Chinese Conception of the Body. In *Body, Subject and Power in China*. A. Zito and T. Barlow, eds. Pp. 23–41. Chicago: Chicago University Press.

Lowry, Haynie
   1988   A Chinese Press Conference on Tibet. *Cultural Survival Quarterly* 12(1): 49–51.

McHugh, Ernestine
   1989   Concepts of the Person among the Gurungs of Nepal. *American Ethnologist* 16: 75–86.

Obeyesekere, Gananath
   1976   The Impact of Ayurvedic Ideas on the Culture and the Individual in Sri Lanka. In *Asian Medical Systems: A Comparative Study*. Charles Leslie, ed. Pp. 201–26. Berkeley: University of California Press.
   1990   *The Work of Culture: Symbolic Transformation in Psychoanalysis and Anthropology*. Chicago: University of Chicago Press.

The Office of Tibet
   1983   *Summary of Recent Events in Tibet*, 3 October 1983.
   1984   *The Story of Ani Kalsang*. Palmo: Human Rights Violation.

Ortner, Sherry
   1978   *Sherpas through their Rituals*. Cambridge: Cambridge University Press.
   1998   The Case of the Disappearing Shamans, or No Individualism, No Relationalism. In *Selves in Time and Place: Identities, Experience, and History in Nepal*. Debra Skinner, Alfred Pach III, and Dorothy Holland, eds. Pp. 239–67. Lanham: Rowman and Littlefield.

Ots, Thomas
   1994   The Silenced Body – the Expressive Lieb: On the Dialectic of Mind and Life in Chinese Cathartic Healing. In *Embodiment and Experience*. T. Csordas, ed. Pp. 116–36. Cambridge: Cambridge University Press.

Rinpoche, Rechung
   1973   *Tibetan Medicine*. Berkeley: University of California Press.

Schell, Orville
   1992   Frontline: Red Flag Over Tibet. Public Broadcasting Service. Video.

Schwartz, Ronald David
  1992   Travelers under Fire: Tourists in the Tibetan Uprising. *Annals of Tourism Research*, excerpts from *Tibet Press Watch*, April.
Smith, Warren
  1986   The Survival of Tibetan Culture. *Cultural Survival Quarterly* 10(3): 43–4.
Tambiah, Stanley
  1984   *Buddhist Saints of the Forest and the Cult of the Amulets*. Cambridge: Cambridge University Press.
Thurman, Robert A. F.
  1988   Tibet: An Introduction and An Outline of Tibetan Culture. *Cultural Survival Quarterly* 12(1): 42–4, 65–6.
Thurston, Anne F.
  1988   The Chinese View of Tibet – Is Dialogue Possible? *Cultural Survival Quarterly* 12(1): 70–3.
Turner, Victor
  1968   *Drums of Affliction: A Study of Religious Processes among the Ndembu of Zambia*. New York: Oxford University Press.
UN Commission on Human Rights
  1985   *Tibet: The Facts*. A Report prepared by the Scientific Buddhist Association for the UN Commission on Human Rights. London.
US Tibet Committee
  1994   *Tibet: An Independent State under Illegal Occupation*. New York: US Tibet Committee.
Van Walt Van Praag, Michael
  1988   The Legal Status of Tibet. *Cultural Survival Quarterly* 12(1): 67–9.
Wangyal, Tsering
  1986   Tibetan Culture in Exile. *Cultural Survival Quarterly* 10(3): 45–6.

17

Freeing South Africa: The "Modernization" of Male–Male Sexuality in Soweto

Donald L. Donham

Identity is formed at the unstable point where the "unspeakable" stories of subjectivity meet the narratives of history, of a culture.

(Stuart Hall, *Minimal Selves*)

Of Dress and Drag

In February 1993, a black man in his mid-thirties named Linda (an ordinary male name in Zulu) died of AIDS in Soweto, South Africa. Something of an activist, Linda was a founding member of GLOW, the Gay and Lesbian Organization of the Witwatersrand. Composed of both blacks and whites, GLOW was and is the principal gay and lesbian organization in the Johannesburg area. Because Linda had many friends in the group, GLOW organized a memorial service at a member's home in Soweto a few days before the funeral.

Linda's father, who belonged to an independent Zionist church, attended and spoke. He recalled Linda's life and what a good person he had been, how hard he had worked in the household. But then he went on, in the way that elders sometimes do, to advise the young men present: "There was just one thing about my son's life that bothered me," he said. "So let me tell you, if you're a man, wear men's clothes. If you're colored, act colored. Above all, if you're black, don't wear Indian clothes. If you do this, how will our ancestors recognize [and protect] you?" Linda had been something of a drag queen, with a particular penchant for Indian saris.

To Linda's father and to his church, dress had ritual significance. One might even say that there was an indigenous theory of "drag" among many black Zionist South

From *Cultural Anthropology* 13(1): 3–21. Copyright © 1998, American Anthropological Association.

Africans, albeit one different from that in North America. To assume church dress not only indicated a certain state of personhood, it in some real sense effected that state.[1] Writing on Tswana Zionists, who like the Zulu have been drawn into townships around Johannesburg, Jean Comaroff (1985) asserted, "The power of uniforms in Tshidi perception was both expressive and pragmatic, for the uniform instantiated the ritual practice it represented" (1985: 220).[2]

If dress had one set of associations within Zionist symbolism, it had others for a small group of young black South African activists who saw themselves as "gay." To the members of GLOW present, most of whom were black, Linda's father's comments were insulting. Most particularly, they were seen as homophobic. As the week wore on, GLOW began to organize to make their point and to take over the funeral.

As Saturday neared – nearly all Soweto funerals are held on the weekend – tensions rose. There were rumors that there might be an open confrontation between the family and GLOW. Along with Paul, a member of GLOW from Soweto, I attended, and the following is a description of what transpired, taken from a letter that I wrote home a few days later to my American lover:

The funeral was held in a community center that looked something like a run-down school auditorium. There was a wide stage on which all of the men of the church, dressed in suits and ties, were seated behind the podium. In front of the podium was the coffin. And facing the stage, the women of the church were seated as an audience – dressed completely in white. (Independent churches have distinctive ways of dressing especially for women, but also sometimes for men.) To the right (from the point of view of the seated women) was a choir of young girls – again all in white: white dresses and white hats of various kinds (most were the kind of berets that you have seen South African women wear). I stood at the very back of the hall, behind the seated women, along with most of the members of GLOW and various other men and women, most dressed up. This last group was apparently made up of friends and relatives who were not members of the church.

I had arrived late, about 9:30 in the morning (the service had begun at about 9:00). I was surprised to see, behind the coffin, in front of the podium, a GLOW banner being held by two members. There were flowers on the coffin and around it. Throughout the service, including the sermon, the two GLOW members holding the banner changed periodically. From the back, two new people marched up through the ladies in white to take the place of the two at the banner. Then those who had been relieved came back through the congregation to the back of the church.

One GLOW member videotaped the funeral from the back. About six or seven of the members who had come were white. It was hard to tell exactly, but there were probably 10 or 15 black members. Quite a few, both white and black, wore GLOW T-shirts (the back of which said, "We can speak for ourselves"). Finally, two or three of the black members wore various stages of drag. One, Jabu, was especially notable in complete, full regalia – a West African-style woman's dress in a very colorful print with a matching and elaborately tied bonnet, one edge of which read, "Java print." Wearing a heavy gold necklace, she walked up and down the aisle to hold the banner at least twice – in the most haughty, queenly walk. It was almost as if she dared anybody to say anything. She made quite a contrast with the stolid, all-in-white ladies seated in the audience (one of whom was heard to comment to a neighbor, "She's very pretty, isn't she [referring to Jabu]? But look at those legs!").

When we arrived, Simon Nkoli, one of the first black gay activists in South Africa, was speaking. Simon was dressed in an immaculately white and flowing West African (male) outfit with gold embroidery. He spoke in English, and someone translated simultaneously (into Zulu). His speech was about gay activism in South Africa and the contributions that Linda, his dead friend, had made. At points in his speech, Simon sang out the beginning lines of hymns, at which point the congregation immediately joined in, in the [style] of black South African singing, without instruments and in part-harmony.

After Simon, there were other speeches by the ministers of the church. They emphasized that Linda was a child of the church, that his sins had been forgiven, and that he was in heaven. Diffusing any trace of tension between the church and GLOW, one of the ministers rose and apologized on behalf of Linda's father for offending the group earlier in the week.

Toward the end of the service, the gay people congregated on the front steps outside the community center and began singing in English a song that began with "We are gay and straight together…" When the people came pouring out and finally the coffin was carried out, the GLOW members in their T-shirts took the handles of the casket from the men of the church and placed it in the hearse. The several hundred people present boarded two very large transport buses hired for the occasion and probably 20 private automobiles to go to the cemetery.

Because there are so many funerals in Soweto on the weekend (probably 200 at Avalon cemetery alone) and because the cemetery had only one entrance (the better to control people), the roads were clogged and it took us an hour to go a few miles. The members of GLOW got out of the bus and *toi toied*, the distinctive, punctuated jogging-dancing that South African blacks have developed in anti-apartheid demonstrations. While waiting for the caravan to move, a giant *caspir*, one of those armored tank-like vehicles that the South African police use in the townships, passed us by, and then another police car with two white police-men inside. The temperature was not so hot, but the sun was blazing. At Johannesburg's elevation, it feels like the sun is closer (it is summer here).

Suddenly, we sped up (the cortege ahead had gone past) and we almost raced to the gravesite. There was a long row of freshly dug graves and several services were going simultaneously, side by side. Luckily for me, I was able to share someone's umbrella.

There was something about the routinized way that so many people had to bury their dead and leave (others were waiting) that brought home to me, in a way that I had not anticipated, what apartheid still means in many black people's lives…. The South African police stood in the background. Continually, another and another group arrived, and as each rushed to its gravesite, red dust began to cover us all. The sun got hotter.

In the middle of the brief graveside service for Linda (I was too far away to hear more than the few hymns that were sung), another group of buses arrived with chanting students. I was told that they were burying a young boy who had been killed by the police. Suddenly, shots rang out. Someone among the students shot into the grave and then into the air. As quickly as they had come, the kids were back on the buses, some of them dancing on the top with an ANC [African National Congress] flag. As the buses lumbered down the road, the ones on the top managed not to fall off. They were "comrades" – political activists. Things get more serious when a *tsotsi*, or gangster, is buried. It's not unusual for his friends to steal a car, fire an AK-47 into the air at the cemetery, cut figure-eights with the car after the burial, and on the way out of the cemetery, leave the stolen car burning.

After the graveside service, GLOW members gathered at one of the members' houses in Soweto and proceeded to get drunk. I had had enough. Driving back to Johannesburg (it's a little over 30 minutes), I almost had an accident. Tired and with my reflexes not working for left-hand-of-the-road driving, I turned into oncoming traffic. By the end of the day, I felt overwhelmed. Another gay man dead – yet another. And his burial had brought together, for me, a mind-numbing juxtaposition of peoples and projects, desires and fears – Zionist Christians and gay activists, the first, moreover, accommodating themselves to and even apologizing to the second. Could anything comparable have happened in the United States? A gay hijacking of a funeral in a church in, say, Atlanta?

Apartheid and Male Sexuality

Although engaged in another research project, in my free time with friends like Paul, I thus stumbled onto a series of questions that began to perplex me: Who was Linda? In the letter quoted above, I had unproblematically identified Linda as "gay." But in *his* context, was he? And if so, how did he come to see himself as so? And I quickly confronted questions of gender as well. Did Linda consider himself as male? And if so, had he always done so?

As issues like these began to pose themselves, I soon realized that for black men in townships around Johannesburg, identifying as gay was both recent and tied up, in unexpectedly complex ways, with a much larger historical transformation: the end of apartheid and the creation of a modern nation; in a phrase, the "freeing" of South Africa.

This story, more than any other, constitutes for most South Africans (certainly black South Africans) what Stuart Hall, in the epigraph at the beginning of this paper, referred to as a "narrative of history." It structures identity, legitimates the present, and organizes the past. There are indeed few places on earth in which modernist narratives of progress and freedom currently appear so compelling. This undoubtedly results, at least in part, because apartheid itself was an antimodernist project that explicitly set itself against most of the rest of the "developed" world.

As Foucault (1980) has argued, current western views on sexuality and modernity are inextricably intertwined.[3] After Foucault, it would be difficult to interpret the conjugated transitions in South Africa as merely the result of the end of a repressive regime – a denouement that opened up spaces in which black men could, at last, claim their gayness, as if being "gay" were naturally pregiven. But if such a conclusion looks implausible, Foucault's own explanation of the formation of modern notions of sexuality also does not capture the full dynamic of the black South African case.

According to Foucault, current western notions of homosexuality – that is, the concept of the homosexual as a distinct species of person – developed during the nineteenth century out of the sexual sciences and the dividing practices of modern states. Foucault's method, what he first called archaeology and later genealogy, was to work "across" time – within the same spatial unit. But what happens when one proceeds across space as well as time?[4] At a minimum, a series of new dynamics come into view – ones involving the transnational flow of persons, signs, commodities, and I shall argue, narratives that (help) create new subject positions. Of late, communications technologies have accelerated and intensified these flows to create what seem to be qualitatively new cultural phenomena.

So how did Linda become gay? I never met or interviewed Linda, but fortunately, for the purposes of this article, before he died Linda wrote an extraordinarily self-revealing article with Hugh McLean entitled "*Abangibhamayo Bathi Ngim-nandi* (Those Who Fuck Me Say I'm Tasty): Gay Sexuality in Reef Townships" (McLean and Ngcobo 1994). The collaboration between Hugh and Linda – both members of GLOW – was itself a part of the transformations I seek to understand: the creation of a black gay identity, Linda's "coming out," and the "freeing" of South Africa.

To begin with, Linda did not always consider himself – to adopt the gender category appropriate at the end of his life – to be "gay." If anything, it was female gender, not sexuality as such, that fitted most easily with local disciplinary regimes and that made the most sense to Linda during his teenage years. Indeed, in apart-heid-era urban black culture, gender apparently overrode biological sex to such a degree that it is difficult, and perhaps inappropriate, to maintain the distinction between these two analytical concepts below.[5]

Let me quote the comments of Neil Miller, a visiting North American gay journal-ist who interviewed Linda:

Township gay male culture, as Linda described it, revolved around cross-dressing and sexual role-playing and the general idea that if gay men weren't exactly women, they were some variation thereof, a third sex. No one, including gay men, seemed to be quite sure what gay meant – were gay men really women? men? or something in between? . . . When Linda was in high school word went out among his schoolmates that he had both male and female sex organs. Everyone wanted to have sex with him, he claimed, if only to see if the rumors were true. When he didn't turn out to be the anatomical freak they had been promised, his sexual partners were disappointed. Then, there was the male lover who wanted to marry Linda when they were teenagers. "Can you have children?" the boy's mother asked Linda. The mother went to several doctors to ask if a gay man could bear a child. The doctors said no, but the mother didn't believe them. She urged the two boys to have sex as frequently as possible so Linda could become pregnant. Linda went along with the idea. On the mother's orders, the boys would stay in bed most of the weekend. "We'd get up on a Saturday morning, she'd give us a glass of milk, and she'd send us back to bed," Linda told me. After three months of this experiment, the mother grew impatient. She went to yet another doctor who managed to convince her that it was quite impossible for a man, even a gay man, to bear a child. Linda's relationship with his friend continued for a time until finally the young man acceded to his mother's wishes and married a woman, who eventually bore the child Linda could never give him. (Miller 1993: 14–15)

The description above uses the word *gay* anachronistically. In black township slang, the actual designation for the effeminate partner in a male same-sex coupling was *stabane* – literally, a hermaphrodite. Instead of sexuality in the western sense, it was local notions of sexed bodies and gendered identities – what I shall call sex/gender in the black South African sense – that divided and categorized. But these two analytical dimensions, gender and sex, interrelated in complex ways. While she was growing up, Linda thought of herself as a girl, as did Jabu, the drag queen at Linda's funeral about whom I shall have more to say below. Even though they had male genitalia, both were raised by their parents as girls and both understood themselves in this way.[6]

If it was gender that made sense to Linda and Jabu themselves (as well as to some others close to them, such as parents and "mothers-in-law"), strangers in the township typically used sex as a classifactory grid. That is, both Linda and Jabu were taken by others as a biologically-mixed third sex. Significantly, as far as I can tell, neither ever saw themselves in such terms.

I explored these issues with the regal drag queen who had turned everyone's eyes at Linda's funeral. In English, Jabu explained,

When I grew up, I thought I was completely... I thought I was a woman. The girls I grew up with, when they were 13 or 14, they started to get breasts. Why didn't I? And they were different sexually. What is this? I don't have that. But they have that.

If an urban black South African boy during the 1960s and 1970s showed signs of effeminacy, then there was only one possibility: she was "really" a woman, or at least some mixed form of woman. Conversely, in any sexual relationship with such a person, the other partner remained, according to most participants, simply a man (and certainly not a "homosexual").[7]

This gendered system of categories was imposed on Linda as she grew up:

I used to wear girls' clothes at home. My mother dressed me up. In fact, I grew up wearing girls' clothes. And when I first went to school they didn't know how to register me. (quoted in McLean and Ngcobo 1994: 170)

Miller recorded the following impressions:

Linda didn't strike one as particularly effeminate. He was lanky and graceful, with the body of a dancer. The day we met he was wearing white pants and a white cotton sweater with big, clear-framed glasses and a string of red African beads around his neck. But even as an adult, he was treated like a girl at home by his parents. They expected him to do women's jobs – to be in the kitchen, do the washing and ironing and baking. "You can get me at home almost any morning," he told me. "I'll be cleaning the house." There were girls' shopping days when he, his mother, and his sister would go off to buy underclothes and nighties. Each day, he would plan his mother's and father's wardrobes. As a teenager, Linda began undergoing female-hormone treatments, on the recommendation of a doctor. When he finally decided to halt treatments, his father, a minister of the Twelfth Apostle Church, was disappointed. It seemed he would rather have a son who grew breasts and outwardly appeared to be a girl than a son who was gay. Even today, Linda sings in the choir at his father's church – in a girl's uniform.

"What part do you sing?" I asked him.

"Soprano, of course," he replied. "What did you think?" (1993: 15)

The fact that Linda wore a girl's uniform in church into the early 1990s offers some insight into his father's remarks that caused such a stir in GLOW. His father was not, it seems, particularly concerned with "cross-dressing." Phrasing the matter this way implies, after all, a naturally given bodily sex that one dresses "across." To Linda's family, he was apparently really a female. What the father was most upset about was dressing "across" race, and the implications that had for ancestral blessings.

In sum, black townships during the apartheid era found it easier to understand gender-deviant boys as girls or as a biologically mixed third sex. By the early 1970s, a network of boys who dressed as girls existed in Soweto, many of whom came to refer to themselves in their own slang as *skesana*.[8] Jabu was a few years younger than Linda. After the funeral, he recounted to me how he had first met Linda:

I didn't know Linda. He heard about me. Those years, I was...among blacks, people didn't know about gay people. I was young and people didn't know whether I was a boy or a girl, and those days people thought if someone is gay he is hermaphroditic, you know. I was actually so famous, I don't know. But everyone knew that there is this child called Jabu; there is this boy called Jabu and they thought that I had two sex organs and wherever I went people got excited just to see or whatever. One day, it was a Wednesday or a Thursday, I was home with my mother, and there came this Linda. "Oh my goodness, what is this?" You know you didn't really realize as well whether he was a boy or a girl. With me, I used to tell myself I am the only one. And I was very proud of being myself. Wherever I used to go, everyone used to stare at me, and I said to myself that there is this special thing that I have, you know. And then when Linda came, I said, "Oh no, I don't want to associate with him." Luckily my mom was there. She called him and they talked. After he left, my mom called me and said, "You see, you're not the only person who is like that. That guy is also like you." "What do you mean he's like me? He's a guy. I'm not a guy, I'm a girl."

Skesanas dressed as women and adopted only the receptive role in sexual inter-course. Here is Linda speaking:

In the township they used to think I was a hermaphrodite. They think I was cursed in life to have two organs. Sometimes you can get a nice *pantsula* [tough, macho guy] and you will find him looking for two organs. You don't give him the freedom to touch you. He might discover that your dick is bigger than his. Then he might be embarrassed, or even worse, he might be attracted to your dick. This is not what a *skesana* needs or wants. So we keep up the mystery. We won't let them touch and we won't disillusion them....I think it makes you more acceptable if you are a hermaphrodite, and they think your dick is very small. The problem is, the *skesanas* always have the biggest dicks. And I should know.... (quoted in McLean and Ngcobo 1994: 168–9)

It would be a mistake to view this system of sex/gender categories as *only* being imposed upon skesanas. In adopting their highly visible role, skesanas sometimes used the traditional subordinate role of the woman to play with and ultimately to mock male power. According to Linda,

On a weekend I went to a shebeen [informal drinking establishment] with a lady friend of mine. I was in drag. I often used to do this on the weekends – many *skesanas* do it. We were inside. It seemed as if four boys wanted to rape us, they were *pantsulas* and they were very rough. One of them proposed to my friend and she accepted. The others approached me one by one. The first two I didn't like so I said no! I was attracted by the third one, so I said yes to him. As we left the shebeen, my one said to me, "If you don't have it, I'm going to cut your throat." I could see that he was serious and I knew I must have it or I'm dead. So I asked my friend to say that she was hungry and we stopped at some shops. I went inside and bought a can of pilchards [inexpensive fish]. I knew that the only thing the *pantsula* was interested in was the hole and the smell. *Pantsulas* don't explore much, they just lift up your dress and go for it. We all went to bed in the one room. There were two beds. The one *pantsula* and my friend were in one and I was in the other bed with this *pantsula*.... Sardines is one of the tricks the *skesanas* use. We know that some *pantsulas* like dirty pussy, so for them you must use pilchards, but not Glenrick [a brand] because they smell too bad. Other *pantsulas* like clean pussy, so for them you can use sardines. For my *pantsula* I bought pilchards because I could see what kind he was. So before I went to bed I just smeared some pilchards around my anus and my thighs. When he smelled the smell and found the hole he was quite happy. We became lovers for some months after that. He never knew that I was a man, and he never needed the smell again because he was satisfied the first time. (quoted in McLean and Ngcobo 1994: 172–3)

Although the connection would have been anathema to the Puritan planners of apartheid, skesana identity was finally tied up with the structure of apartheid power – particularly with the all-male hostels that dotted Soweto. In these hostels, rural men without the right to reside permanently in Soweto and without their wives lived, supposedly temporarily, in order to provide labor to the white-dominated economy. From the nineteenth century onward, there is evidence that at least some black men in these all-male environments saw little wrong with taking other, younger workers as "wives." In these relationships, it was age and wealth, not sex, that organized and defined male–male sexual relationships; as boys matured and gained their own resources, they in turn would take "wives." This pattern has been described among gangs of thieves on the Rand in the early twentieth century (van Onselen 1982) and among gold mine workers into the 1980s (Moodie 1989).

Certainly, in Soweto in the 1960s, hostels populated by rural men had become notorious sites for same-sex sexual relations. Township parents warned young sons not to go anywhere nearby, that they would be swept inside and smeared with Vaseline and raped (see also Mathabane 1986: 68–74). To urban-raised skesanas like Linda, however, these stories apparently only aroused phantasy and desire. Linda described a "marriage ceremony" in which she took part in one of the hostels, as follows:

At these marriage ceremonies, called *mkehlo*, all the young *skesanas* . . . sit on one side and the older ones on the other. Then your mother would be chosen. My mother was MaButhelezi. These things would happen in the hostels those days. They were famous. The older gays [*sic*] would choose you a mother from one of them. Then your mother's affair [partner] would be your father. Then your father is the one who would teach you how to screw. All of them, they would teach you all the positions and how to ride him up and down and sideways. . . . (quoted in McLean and Ngcobo 1994: 163)

Modernity and Sexuality in the "New" South Africa

By the early 1990s, a great deal had changed in South Africa and in Linda's life. Nelson Mandela had been released from prison. It was clear to everyone in South Africa that a new society was in process of being born. This clarity had come, however, only after more than a decade and a half of protracted, agonizing, and often violent struggle – a contest for power that upended routines all the way from the structures of the state down to the dynamics of black families in Soweto. As a result, the cultural definitions and social institutions that supported the sex/gender system in which Linda had been raised had been shaken to its roots.

By the 1990s, Linda and his friends no longer felt safe going to the hostels; many rural men's compounds in the Johannesburg region had become sites of violent opposition to the surrounding black townships, the conflict often being phrased in terms of the split between the Inkatha Freedom Party and the ANC. Also, as the end of apartheid neared, rural women began to join their men in the hostels, and the old days of male–male marriages were left behind. Looking back from the 1990s, Linda commented,

This [male–male marriage] doesn't happen now. You don't have to be taught these things. Now is the free South Africa and the roles are not so strong, they are breaking down. (quoted in McLean and Ngcobo 1994: 164)

I will make explicit what Linda suggested: with the birth of a "free" South Africa, the notion of sexuality was created for some black men, or more precisely, an identity based on sexuality was created. The classificatory grid in the making was different from the old one. Now, *both* partners in a same-sex relationship were potentially classified as the same (male) gender – and as "gay."

Obviously, this new way of looking at the sexual world was not taken up consistently, evenly, or completely. The simultaneous presence of different models of same-sex sexuality in present-day South Africa will be evident by the end of this article. Whatever the overlapping ambiguities, it is interesting to note who took the lead in "modernizing" male–male sexuality in black South Africa: it was precisely formerly female-identified men like Linda and Jabu.[9] But if female-identified men seem to have initiated the shift, a turning point will be reached when their male partners also uniformly identify as gay. It is perhaps altogether too easy to overstate the degree to which such a transformation has occurred in the United States itself, particularly outside urban areas and outside the white middle and upper classes.

If one sexual paradigm did not fully replace another in black townships, there were nonetheless significant changes by the early 1990s. Three events, perhaps more than others, serve to summarize these changes. First was the founding of a genuinely multiracial gay rights organization in the Johannesburg area in the late 1980s – namely, GLOW. Linda was a founding member. Second, around the same time, the ANC, still in exile, added sexuality to its policy of nondiscrimination. As I shall explain below, the ANC's peculiar international context – its dependence on foreign support in the fight against apartheid – was probably one of the factors that inclined it to support gay rights. According to Gevisser (1994),

ANC members in exile were being exposed to what the PAC's [Pan-Africanist Congress] Alexander calls "the European Leftist position on the matter." Liberal European notions of gender rights and the political legitimacy of gay rights had immense impact on senior ANC lawyers like Albie Sachs and Kader Asmal, who have hence become gay issues' strongest lobbyists within the ANC. (1994: 75)

Finally, a third event that heralded change was the first gay pride march in Johannesburg in 1990, modeled on those held in places like New York and San Francisco that celebrated the Stonewall riots of 1969. Linda and his friends participated, along with approximately one thousand others. This annual ritual began to do much, through a set of such internationally recognized gay symbols as rainbow flags and pink triangles, to create a sense of transnational connections for gay South Africans.

How was Linda's life affected by these changes? Exactly how did sexuality replace local definitions of sex/gender in her forms of self-identification? According to Linda himself, the black youth uprising against apartheid was the beginning:

Gays are a lot more confident now in the townships. I think this happened from about 1976. Before that everything was very quiet. 1976 gave people a lot of confidence.... I remember when the time came to go and march and they wanted all the boys and girls to join in. The gays said: We're not accepted by you, so why should we march? But then they said they didn't mind and we should go to march in drag. Even the straight boys would wear drag. You could wear what you like. (quoted in McLean and Ngcobo 1994: 180)

As black youth took up the cause of national liberation and townships became virtual war zones, traditional black generational hierarchies were shaken to the core. Black youth came to occupy a new political space, one relatively more independent of the power of parents. But as such resistance movements have developed in other times and places, gender hierarchies have sometimes been strengthened (Landes 1988; Stacey 1983). In resisting one form of domination, another is reinforced. In the black power movement in the United States during the 1960s, for example, masculinist and heterosexist ideals were sometimes celebrated.[10]

Why did this reaction, with respect to gender, *not* take place in South Africa? One respect in which the South African case differs, certainly compared to the United States in the 1960s, is the extent to which the transnational was involved in the national struggle.[11] Until Mandela was released, the ANC was legally banned in South Africa. Leaders not in prison were based *outside* the country, and there can be no doubt that the ANC could not have accomplished the political transition that it did without international support. In this context, the international left-liberal consensus on human rights – one to which gay people also appealed – probably dampened any tendency to contest local racial domination by strengthening local gender and sexuality hierarchies. Any such move would certainly have alienated antiapartheid groups from Britain to Holland to Canada to the United States.

But the significance of the transnational in the South African struggle was not only material. The imaginations of black South Africans were finally affected – particularly, in the ways in which people located themselves in the world. And it was precisely in the context of transnational antiapartheid connections that some skesanas like Linda, particularly after they were in closer contact with white gay people in Johannesburg, became aware for the first time of a global gay community – an imagined community, to adapt Benedict Anderson's phrase, imaginatively united by "deep horizontal bonds of comradeship" (1991: 7).[12]

How did this occur? Perhaps the incident, more than any other, that catalyzed such associations, that served as a node for exchange, was the arrest of Simon Nkoli.[13] Nkoli, by the 1980s a gay-identified black man, was arrested for treason along with others and tried in one of the most publicized trials of the apartheid era – the so-called Delmas treason trials. After Nkoli's situation become known internationally, he became a symbol for gay people in the antiapartheid movement across the globe. For example, in December of 1986, while he was in prison, Nkoli was startled to receive more than 150 Christmas cards from gay people and organizations around the world (Nkoli 1994: 255).

According to Gevisser,

In Nkoli, gay anti-apartheid activists found a ready-made hero. In Canada, the Simon Nkoli Anti-Apartheid Committee became a critical player in both the gay and anti-apartheid movements. Through Nkoli's imprisonment, too, progressive members of the international anti-apartheid movement were able to begin introducing the issue of gay rights to the African National Congress. The highly respectable Anti-Apartheid Movements of both Britain and Holland, for example, took up Nkoli's cause, and this was to exert a major impact on the ANC's later decision to include gay rights on its agenda. (1994: 56)

These cultural connections and others eventually helped to produce changes in the most intimate details of skesanas' lives. To return to Linda, gay identity meant literally a new gender and a new way of relating to his body. In Linda's words,

Before, all skesanas wanted to have a small cock. Now we can relax, it does not matter too much and people don't discuss cocks as much....Before, I thought I was a woman. Now I think I'm a man, but it doesn't worry me anyway. Although it used to cause problems earlier. (quoted in McLean and Ngcobo 1994: 168–9)

In addition to how he viewed his body, Linda began to dress differently:

I wear girl's clothes now sometimes, but not so much. But I sleep in a nightie, and I wear slippers and a gown – no skirts. I like the way a nightie feels in bed. (quoted in McLean and Ngcobo 1994: 170)

Consider the underneath-of-the-iceberg for the intimacies that Linda described; it is difficult to reconstruct the hundreds of micro-encounters, the thousands of messages that must have come from as far away as Amsterdam and New York. Gevisser outlines some of the social underpinnings of this reordering:

The current township gay scene has its roots in a generalised youth rebellion that found expression first in 1976 and then in the mid-1980s. And, once a white gay organisation took root in the 1980s and a collapse of rigid racial boundaries allowed greater interaction between township and city gay people, ideas of gay community filtered into the already-existent township gay networks. A few gay men and lesbians, like Nkoli, moved into Hillbrow. As the neighborhood started deracialising, they began patronising the gay bars and thus hooking into the urban gay subculture – despite this subculture's patent racism. GLOW's kwaThema chapter was founded, for example, when a group of residents returned from the Skyline Bar with a copy of *Exit* [the local gay publication]: "When we saw the publicity about this new non-racial group," explains Manku Madux, a woman who, with Sgxabai, founded the chapter, "we decided to get in touch with them to join." (1994: 69)

The ways in which an imagined gay community became real to black South Africans were, of course, various. In Jabu's case, he had already come to see himself differently after he began work in a downtown hotel in Johannesburg in the late 1970s:

Well, I joined the hotel industry. I started at the Carlton Hotel.... There was no position actually that they could start me in. I won't say that being a porter was not a good job; it was. But they had to start me there. But I had some problems with guests. Most of them actually picked up that I'm gay. How, I don't know. Actually... how am I going to word this? People from foreign countries, they would demand my service in a different way... than being a porter.... We had Pan Am, British Airways, American Airways coming. Probably the whole world assumes that any male who works for an airline is gay. I used to make friends with them. But the management wasn't happy about that, and they transferred me to the switchboard.

The assumption of a gay identity for Jabu affected not only his view of the present but also of the past. Like virtually all forms of identification that essentialize and project themselves backward in history, South African black gay identity unites the past with the present (and future) in an unchanging unity. According to Jabu, being gay is "natural"; gay people have always been present in South African black cultures. But in his great-grandmother's time, African traditional cultures dealt with such things differently:

I asked my grandmother and great-grandmother (she died at the age of 102). Within the family, the moment they realized that you were gay, in order to keep outside people from knowing, they organized someone who was gay to go out with you, and they arranged with another family to whom they explained the whole situation: "Okay, fine, you've got a daughter, we have three sons, this one is gay, and then there are the other two. Your daughter is not married. What if, in public, your daughter marries our gay son, but they are not going to have sex. She will have sex with the younger brother or the elder brother, and by so doing, the family will expand, you know." And at the end of the day, even if the next person realizes that I am gay, they wouldn't say anything because I am married. That is the secret that used to be kept in the black community.[14]

Foucault in a Transnational World

> One of the distinctive features of modernity is an increasing interconnection between the two "extremes" of extensionality and intentionality: globalising influences on the one hand and personal dispositions on the other.
>
> (Anthony Giddens, *Modernity and Self-Identity*)

In the West so relentlessly analyzed by Foucault, sexual identity was produced by a long, internal process of disciplining and dividing. Visiting airline stewards were not part of the story. What is striking about black South Africa is the transparency with which the transnational is implicated in and imbricated with gay identity formation. When asked to date the beginning of the gay movement in Soweto, some young black men answered that it commenced when a gay character appeared on *Dynasty* on local South African television (McLean and Ngcobo 1994: 180).

It goes without saying that the category of gay people that this process has produced in South Africa is hardly homogeneous, nor is it the same as in western countries. Being black and gay and poor in South Africa is hardly the same as being black and gay and middle-class, which is again hardly the same as being white and gay and middle-class, whether in South Africa or in North America. Despite these differences, there is still in the background a wider imagined community of gay people with which all of these persons are familiar and, at least in certain contexts, with which they identify. How this imagined community becomes "available" for persons variously situated across the globe is a major analytical question.

In Paul Gilroy's (1993) analysis of the black diaspora, he writes suggestively of the role of sailors, of ships, and of recordings of black music in making a transnational black community imaginatively real. As black identity has been formed and reformed in the context of transnational connections, black families have typically played some role – complex to be sure – in reproducing black identity. Gay identity is different to the degree that it does not rely upon the family for its anchoring; indeed, if anything, it has continually to liberate itself from the effects of family socialization.[15]

This means, ipso facto, that identifying as gay is peculiarly dependent upon and bound up with modern media, with ways of communicatively linking people across space and time. In North America, how many "coming out" stories tell about trips to the public library, furtive searches through dictionaries, or secret readings of novels that explore lesbian and gay topics (Newton 1984)? A certain communicative density is probably a prerequisite for people to identify as gay at all, and it is not improbable that as media density increases, so will the number of gay people.[16]

In less-developed societies of the world today, then, transnational flows become particularly relevant in understanding the formation of sexual communities. Sustained analysis of these connections has hardly begun, but I would suggest that we start not with ships but with airplanes, not with sailors (although they undoubtedly played their role here as well, particularly in port cities) but, in the South African case, with tourists, exiled antiapartheid activists, and visiting anthropologists; and finally not with music, but with images, typically erotic images – first drawings, then photographs, and now videos, most especially of the male body.

Given the composition of the global gay community, most of these images are of the *white* male body. For black men, then, identifying as gay must carry with it a certain complexity absent for most white South Africans. Also, the fact that international gay images are overwhelmingly *male* probably also affects the way that lesbian identity is imagined and appropriated by South African women, black and white. In any case, it could be argued that these kinds of contradictory identifications are not exceptional under late capitalism; they are the stuff of most people's lives. And lately the flow of images has been greatly accelerated; South African gays with access to a modem and a computer – admittedly, a tiny minority so far – can now download material from San Francisco, New York, or Amsterdam.

Each niche in this flow has its own characteristics. For North Americans, the national struggle was separated by two centuries from the gay struggle.[17] In South Africa, these two occurred more-or-less simultaneously, at least for black people. The resulting unevenness of the global-in-the-local disrupts ordinary notions of political "progress." In relation to economic development, Trotsky emphasized long ago that previously "backward" areas can leapfrog ahead of "advanced" ones. At present, the constitution in South Africa prohibits discrimination on the basis of sexual orientation. Who could imagine anything similar happening in the United States?

The overlapping of the national and gay questions means that gay identity in South Africa reverberates – in a way that it cannot in the United States – with a proud, new national identity. Let me quote the reaction of one of the *white* gays present at Linda's funeral:

As I stood in Phiri Hall behind the black gay mourners behind the hymn-singing congregants, I felt a proud commonality with Linda's black friends around, despite our differences; *we were all gay, all South African.* (Gevisser 1994: 17, emphasis added)

In conclusion, let me suggest that a fuller understanding of sexual identity, in South Africa and elsewhere, requires a revitalized attention to ethnography. Foucault's work remains in many ways foundational in this enterprise, but it also presents serious limitations. Even for the "West," Foucault overstressed what Sedgwick (1990: 44–8) has called a unidirectional narrative of supersession. In fact, cultural change tends to be more various, more fractured, more incomplete. What I am calling the "modernization" of male–male sexuality involves, then, not so much the replacement of one cultural system by another, but the addition of a new cultural model to older ones – with a certain splintering, a certain weighting of new schemas in the lives of at least a few particularly visible actors.

The second limitation of Foucault's work on sexuality stems from his overreliance on the text of medical specialists to infer the categories and commitments of ordinary people. Both Chauncey (1985) and Duggan (1993) have shown that notions about homosexuality in the United States emerged in a more complex dialectic than Foucault supposed. Popular notions, sometimes spread and reinforced in press accounts of spectacular events like trials, often formed the substratum for medical notions – which, after being inflected in certain ways, eventually affected, but only partially so, particular layers of the population. How these factors play out in any context is to be determined by textured historical ethnography, not, as Foucault seems to have sometimes imagined, by abstract philosophy.

Finally, and most important for the case at hand, Foucault did not problematize the role of cultural exchange across space, of transnational connections that bring, at ever quickening speeds, "unspeakable" stories of subjectivity into relationship with narratives of history. Ethnography is required to meet this goal, an ethnography that traces the global in the local, that analyzes the interplay between globally circulating narratives that persuasively cast past sufferings and offer future liberations, on the one hand, and the local technologies of communication that help conjure up the imagined communities that will enact those liberations, on the other.

But let me give Linda the last say. Here he uses sexuality as a point of self-identification, but in a way that is not unrelated to her previous notions of gender and sexuality:

The thing that has done most for gays in the township are the marches we have had for gay and lesbian rights. These have been very important and I hope that we will be legalised with an ANC government. Then maybe we can even get married in Regina Mundi [one of Soweto's principal churches, one particularly associated with the struggle against apartheid] and they won't be throwing in the teargas. (quoted in McLean and Ngcobo 1994: 181)

NOTES

Acknowledgments: I would like to thank Mark Auslander, Jacqueline Nassey Brown, Carla Freeman, Bruce Knauft, Esther Newton, and Luise White for their comments and suggestions on earlier versions of this article, as well as the editor and reviewers for *Cultural Anthropology*. As I make clear below, this article could not have been written without Gevisser and Cameron 1994, and most particularly, without the article by McLean and Ngcobo therein. See also Krouse 1993.

1 This notion of what might be called the production of personhood – that who one is can be transformed and worked upon by dress – appears to mirror, in important ways, local concepts of sex/gender. That is, notions of sex and gender are not understood as being simply given by nature. Rather, sex/gender is created, in part, through dress, gesture, and demeanor.

2 The classic studies on Zulu Zionists are Sundkler 1961 and 1976.

3 Parts of Foucault's argument were prefigured in McIntosh 1968 and developed more-or-less independently in Weeks 1977.

4 Stoler (1995) has posed this question in a different way, one focused more precisely upon race and colonialism.

5 For an early statement of the position that the distinction between sex and gender may reflect western culture rather than a useful analytical device, see Collier and Yanagisako 1987: 14–50.

6 As Jabu points out below, he could not understand why he did not develop breasts at puberty. And Linda's boyfriend's mother could not understand why he could not bear children. What is striking from a western point of view is how little gender categories seem to have been constrained by sex.

7 That a special label existed (at least by the 1980s, although the timing of this development is not clear) for *injonga*, men who sexually penetrated other men, indicates that at another level, matters were more complex. According to McLean and Ngcobo (1994), "The man who calls himself an *injonga* is someone who consciously adopts the role of a man who has sex with men. He is different from the 'accidental' homosexual, the *pantsula* (macho township guy) who sleeps with what he believes to be a hermaphrodite or with someone who pretends, and who he pretends, is female" (1994: 166). Again, according McLean and Ngcobo, "Many *injongas* were *skesanas* once" (1994: 166). *Skesana*, as I shall explain below, is a slang term for men who are women, men who are penetrated by other men. Such age-related progression through sexual roles recalls the arrangements of rural black South African migrant workers described in Moodie's classic article (1989).

8 According to Linda, "A *skesana* is a boy who likes to be fucked" (quoted in McLean and Ngcobo 1994: 164).

9 For a moment when female-identified men took the lead in gay identity politics in the United States, consider the Stonewall rebellion in New York City during 1969. See Duberman 1993.

10 See Eldridge Cleaver's reaction to James Baldwin (1968: 97–111). At the same time, it is important to remember that there were other voices in the black resistance movement. Black Panther Huey P. Newton, before the 1970 Revolutionary People's Constitutional Convention in Philadelphia, called for an alliance with the gay liberation movement. See Stein 2000.

11 Perhaps the most interesting case to which to compare South Africa would be Israel. There also, politics is peculiarly transnationalized, with many local political actors anxious to be seen as "progressive." And there also, gays and lesbians enjoy relative legal protection, for example, the opportunity to serve openly in the Israeli military. I thank Esther Newton for calling my attention to the Israeli case.

12 The link between Anderson's work and sexual identity has been made by Parker et al. 1992.

13 Trials often seem to serve a notable role in making "public" what is ordinarily kept "private," in circulating images of same-sex sexuality. See in particular Duggan 1993.

14 Whether this characterization – what one might call families "passing" rather than individuals "passing" – accurately represents the past in southern Africa I do not know. It appears, at least, as not inconsistent with what anthropologists know of rural African social organization. However, the terms in which the argument is stated are clearly those of the present, designed to rebut claims that homosexuality is un-African.

15 Whether heterosexually-based families must necessarily inculcate homophobic norms is an interesting question. Clearly, individual families can create non-homophobic environments. But to date, I am unaware of any society that accomplishes such an ideal across the board.

16 Historians have emphasized the urban connections of gay culture for some time; see Boswell 1980 and D'Emilio 1992: 3–16.

17 This does not mean that the connections between the gay movement in the United States and previous political currents of the 1960s can be neglected. The link with the women's and black civil rights movements is obviously crucial.

REFERENCES

Anderson, Benedict
    1991   *Imagined Communities: Reflections on the Origin and Spread of Nationalism.* Revised edn. London: Verso.
Boswell, John
    1980   *Christianity, Social Tolerance, and Homosexuality.* Chicago: University of Chicago Press.
Chauncey, George Jr.
    1985   Christian Brotherhood or Sexual Perversion? Homosexual Identities and the Construction of Sexual Boundaries in the World War I Era. *Journal of Social History* 19: 189–212.
Cleaver, Eldridge
    1968   *Soul on Ice.* New York: McGraw-Hill.
Collier, Jane, and Sylvia Yanagisako, eds.
    1987   *Gender and Kinship: Essays Toward a Unified Analysis.* Stanford, CA: Stanford University Press.
Comaroff, Jean
    1985   *Body of Power, Spirit of Resistance.* Chicago: University of Chicago Press.
D'Emilio, John
    1992   Capitalism and Gay Identity. In *Making Trouble: Essays on Gay History, Politics, and the University.* New York: Routledge.
Duberman, Martin
    1993   *Stonewall.* New York: Plume.
Duggan, Lisa
    1993   The Trials of Alice Mitchell: Sensationalism, Sexology, and the Lesbian Subject in Turn-of-the-Century America. *Signs* 18: 791–814.
Foucault, Michel
    1980 [1976]   *The History of Sexuality Volume 1: An Introduction.* Robert Hurley, trans. New York: Vintage Books.

Gevisser, Mark
    1994   A Different Fight for Freedom: A History of South African Lesbian and Gay
        Organisation – the 1950s to the 1990s. In *Defiant Desire: Gay and Lesbian Lives in
        South Africa*. Mark Gevisser and Edwin Cameron, eds. Pp. 14–88. Johannesburg: Ravan
        Press.
Gevisser, Mark, and Edwin Cameron, eds.
    1994   *Defiant Desire: Gay and Lesbian Lives in South Africa*. Johannesburg: Ravan Press.
Gilroy, Paul
    1993   *The Black Atlantic: Modernity and Double Consciousness*. Cambridge, MA:
        Harvard University Press.
Krouse, Matthew, ed.
    1993   *The Invisible Ghetto: Lesbian and Gay Writing from South Africa*. Johannesburg:
        COSAW Publishing.
Landes, Joan B.
    1988   *Women and the Public Sphere in the Age of the French Revolution*. Ithaca, NY:
        Cornell University Press.
McIntosh, Mary
    1968   The Homosexual Role. *Social Problems* 16: 182–92.
McLean, Hugh, and Linda Ngcobo
    1994   Abangibhamayo Bathi Ngimnandi (Those Who Fuck Me Say I'm Tasty): Gay
        Sexuality in Reef Townships. In *Defiant Desire: Gay and Lesbian Lives in South Africa*.
        Mark Gevisser and Edwin Cameron, eds. Pp. 158–85. Johannesburg: Ravan Press.
Miller, Neil
    1993   *Out In The World: Gay and Lesbian Life from Buenos Aires to Bangkok*. New
        York: Vintage Books.
Mathabane, Mark
    1986   *Kaffir Boy: The True Story of a Black Youth's Coming of Age in Apartheid South
        Africa*. New York: Macmillan.
Moodie, T. Dunbar, with Vivien Ndatshe and British Sibuyi
    1989   Migrancy and Male Sexuality on the South African Gold Mines. In *Hidden From
        History: Reclaiming the Gay and Lesbian Past*. Martin Bauml Duberman, Martha
        Vicinus, and George Chauncey Jr., eds. Pp. 411–25. New York: New American Library.
Newton, Esther
    1984   The Mythic Mannish Lesbian: Radclyffe Hall and the New Woman. *Signs* 4: 557–75.
Nkoli, Simon
    1994   Wardrobes: Coming Out as a Black Gay Activist in South Africa. In *Defiant Desire:
        Gay and Lesbian Lives in South Africa*. Mark Gevisser and Edwin Cameron, eds. Pp.
        249–57. Johannesburg: Ravan Press.
Parker, Andrew, Mary Russo, Doris Sommer, and Patricia Yaeger, eds.
    1992   *Nationalisms and Sexualities*. New York: Routledge.
Sedgwick, Eve
    1990   *The Epistemology of the Closet*. Berkeley: University of California Press.
Stacey, Judith
    1983   *Patriarchy and Socialist Revolution in China*. Berkeley: University of California
        Press.
Stein, Marc
    2000   *City of Sisterly and Brotherly Loves: Lesbian and Gay Philadelphia, 1945–1972*.
        Chicago: University of Chicago Press.
Stoler, Ann
    1995   *Race and the Education of Desire: Foucault's* History of Sexuality *and the Colonial
        Order of Things*. Durham, NC: Duke University Press.

Sundkler, Bengt G. M.

    1961   *Bantu Prophets in South Africa*. London: Oxford University Press.

    1976   *Zulu Zion and Some Swazi Zionists*. Oxford: Oxford University Press.

van Onselen, Charles

    1982   *Studies in the Social and Economic History of the Witwatersrand, 1886–1914*, vol. 2, *The Regiment of the Hills – Umkosi Wezintaba: The Witwatersrand's Lumpenproletarian Army, 1890–1920*. London: Longman.

Weeks, Jeffrey

    1977   *Coming Out: Homosexual Politics in Britain*. New York: Quartet Books.

18

The Marriage of Feminism and Islamism in Egypt: Selective Repudiation as a Dynamic of Postcolonial Cultural Politics

Lila Abu-Lughod

In the context of her analysis of the East/West dialectic that has secured the veil as a loaded symbolic marker of cultural identity and women's status in the contemporary Muslim world, Leila Ahmed has argued that "[c]olonialism's use of feminism to promote the culture of the colonizers and undermine native culture has ever since imparted to feminism in non-western societies the taint of having served as an instrument of colonial domination, rendering it suspect in Arab eyes and vulnerable to the charge of being an ally of colonial interests."[1]

I want to explore here one facet of this vexed relationship between feminism and cultural nationalism, reexamining that familiar dynamic of postcolonial politics in which "the woman question" animates political and ideological contests couched in the language of cultural authenticity versus foreign influence.[2] In Egypt ever since the late nineteenth century when reformers and nationalist modernizers took up the question of women's status and role in society, there has been a struggle between those who seek to locate women's emancipation, variously defined, at the heart of the development of nation and of society and those who try to dislocate such a project as an alien western import. However, the contemporary form this debate takes reveals something that is often overlooked: those who claim to reject feminist ideals as western imports actually practice a form of selective repudiation that depends on significant occlusions.

From *Remaking Women: Feminism and Modernity in the Middle East*, ed. Lila Abu-Lughod, pp. 243–69. Princeton: Princeton University Press, 1998.

Islamists today are the best examples of those who condemn feminism as western, although Arab feminists complain that their progressive male colleagues can be just as dismissive.[3] I will argue, however, that what is characteristic of the Islamists is that they stigmatize sexual independence and public freedoms as western but much more gingerly challenge women's rights to work, barely question women's education, and unthinkingly embrace the ideals of bourgeois marriage. Yet the latter three are elements of the turn-of-the-century modernist projects that might well carry the label "feminist" and whose origins are just as entangled with the West as are the sexual mores singled out in horror. This leads one to ask how the component parts of the modern feminism that developed in Egypt have become disaggregated such that only certain aspects can today be made to stand for a western-tainted female emancipation – something groups like the Islamists gain such symbolic capital by denouncing.

One clue can be uncovered through a questioning of the Islamists' rhetorical claims to cultural authenticity and traditionalism. I will first describe some contemporary positions in Egypt on the question of women. Then I will present a critical reading of the work of Qasim Amin, the turn-of-the-century reformer known for his advocacy of women's emancipation. Through this I hope to show how dependent the Islamists, like their secular progressive counterparts, are on the ideas of such early modernizing reformers as these ideas have become transmuted, widely disseminated, and grounded in people's lives through the socioeconomic transformations of the last century.

Modernist Visions

Many Egyptian secularist liberals and progressives fear that women's rights are now under threat. They see signs of this in the growing popularity in the last two decades of the new forms of dress called Islamic or modest dress and the adoption in particular of the form of head covering called the *hijab*, institutionalized in the reversion to more conservative personal status laws, and publicized in calls made in Parliament, mosques, and the media for women's return to the home and their "traditional" roles.

Among the most influential sites for the articulation of their views are print media and television. Secularists have enjoyed access to these media since the 1950s and 1960s, although they have had to contend with government censors and periodic political repression. Thus one can look to state-controlled forms such as the enormously popular evening dramatic television serials for representations of their views on women – views that do not take the form of polemics and may not be completely conscious, and thus are especially revealing.[4]

As I have analyzed them elsewhere, television serials may not be as powerful and effective in influencing people as urban critics and those involved in producing them believe.[5] Yet they are both representative of the values of an influential segment of the middle class and enough subject to censorship to be in line with basic assumptions about social morality. Television writers are a diverse group, in their views and their politics, but the work of some recognized screenwriters who have been involved in television since the 1960s and regularly take up women's issues in their dramas is especially interesting to consider.

The two writers whose productions and views I will examine here are considered progressive and secular, sharing a disdain for the commercial values and productions of recent years, a deep concern about the increasingly conservative social climate in Egypt, and a fundamental belief in television drama as a tool of social education, a reflection of the fact that they came of age during the era of Nasser, Egypt's first president. They take up the key issues for women, issues that have been the subject of debate and transformation since the turn of the century: education, work, and marriage.

The mark of their progressive positions is that they treat the issue of women's work positively. Usama Anwar 'Ukasha, for example, widely regarded as the most brilliant writer of television serials, provides a glimpse of this in his most spectacular and complex serial, *Hilmiyya Nights (Layali al-Hilmiyya)*, aired in the late 1980s and early 1990s. In over a hundred episodes its rich group of characters, people originally from a traditional Cairo neighborhood called Hilmiyya, were taken through the events of modern Egyptian history.

His unqualified support for education is reflected in his positive depiction of the achievements of the daughters of two working-class protagonists, women who went to university and began careers, one teaching in the university and the other working as a medical doctor whose goal was to open a clinic in her own community.

An important theme of *Hilmiyya Nights*, like many of his serials, is how women are to balance work and love, careers and marriage. The intractability of this social problem is dramatized most fully in the story line of the semi-tragic relationship between the young protagonists 'Ali and Zohra. 'Ali and Zohra are in love; they share their dreams and aspirations. Zohra finds in 'Ali the love and support she has never experienced. Others try to thwart the relationship, but it is finally Zohra's apparent dedication to her career that spells its end. In their conversations, Zohra has confided in 'Ali about the importance of an independent career for someone whose life circumstances have forced her to rely on herself. When 'Ali is offered a fellowship to do graduate study abroad, he asks Zohra to marry him and accompany him. Her father resists, and after a while, somewhat mysteriously, she stops pressuring her father. 'Ali gives up his opportunity to go abroad but then gets arrested while attending a political meeting.

It then becomes clear that behind Zohra's growing coldness to 'Ali is the fact that her boss, through flattery about her talents as a journalist and promises to promote her career, is seducing her. She agrees to a secret marriage with him, but when she gets pregnant, her family forces a shotgun public wedding, and then she goes abroad. An innocent 'Ali gets out of prison, discovers that Zohra has betrayed him, and, disillusioned in love and politics, becomes an unscrupulous businessman. He is made to represent in *Hilmiyya Nights* the corrupt and materialistic entrepreneurs who made fortunes under the free-market policies initiated by President Sadat after the death of Nasser.

Despite the negative message about women's career ambitions that this plot line might suggest, consideration of a later stage in 'Ali's and Zohra's lives and other relationships in *Hilmiyya Nights* shows 'Ukasha to be more balanced. The most telling defense of women's rights to careers comes in the marital troubles that develop between 'Ali and Shireen. She is the beautiful, talented, and principled young journalist of modest background 'Ali finally marries. Increasingly he tries to control her activities and to restrict her career. He demands, while he has fled the country to escape prosecution for his business crimes, that she give up her work. As 'Ukasha portrays these events, 'Ali looks like an unreasonable patriarchal bully. He spoils his second chance for happiness in love by treating his wife like a possession in an age, the 1980s, when women's rights to professions have been firmly established.

'Ukasha knows how to touch emotions through the deployment of familiar popular images, like that of the *ibn al-balad*, the noble salt of the earth of urban Egypt, and the mobilization of shared assumptions; meanwhile he pushes ordinary people a little beyond their usual aspirations by holding up as models values that are more "enlightened" and modernist (and middle-class) than those of many of his viewers – and of the political conservatives who capitalize on these.[6] In *Hilmiyya Nights* one familiar chord he sounds is the shared aspiration for conjugal love and devotion to the nuclear family. We only finally begin to sympathize with an aristocratic protagonist's third wife when she shows her motherly concern by running away with her son because her husband is neglecting him. This is the cause, she accuses, of their son's brush with recreational drugs. 'Ukasha also knows how to inculcate values by shaping and giving emotional depth to viewers' fantasies. Our unfulfilled longing for a happy ending for 'Ali and Zohra works to intensify the sense of the desirability of a marriage based on true love and understanding.

Yet 'Ukasha pushes his viewers by showing that love and marital happiness should not be incompatible with women's work. He does not pretend that the resolution of the tension between the two is easy. He wants to make a distinction, however, the same defensive distinction that most Egyptian modernist reformers from the nineteenth century on have tried to make: between women's rights to work and to develop themselves and the dangerous forms of illicit sexuality that the mixing between the sexes might ignite. Unlike the Islamists to be discussed below, however, 'Ukasha paints his fallen characters like Zohra with sympathy. He shows the social genesis of the human weaknesses that led to their mistakes, rather than blaming the West, or the Devil, as might Islamists.

One of the few women writers of television serials of her generation, Fathiyya al-'Assal also uses her serials to present progressive views on social issues. A vivacious woman of sixty, mother of grown children, and committed political activist in Hizb al-Tagammu' (the leftist party), she is adamant that feminist issues cannot be divorced from general social and political issues. She criticizes fellow Egyptian feminist Nawal El-Saadawi, lionized in the West, for her exclusive focus on women's issues like marital abuse. This focus, she notes, corresponds (too) nicely to the depoliticized agenda of the American-based Ford Foundation, which sponsored El-Saadawi's short-lived feminist organization, the Arab Women's Solidarity Union. As Al-'Assal explains, "I'm against men beating their wives and women submitting to being beaten, of course. But that is not the only issue. For me the issue is how women can be liberated economically, politically, and intellectually; then they will be automatically liberated from men."[7]

Literacy and education for women are long-standing interests of Al-'Assal's. In fact, she traces her beginnings as a drama writer to her days as a literacy instructor who was frustrated that her students escaped the classroom to sit with the janitor whenever the radio serials were broadcast. She decided to try her hand at radio drama in 1957 and went on to television in 1967. She deplores the fact that people watch television more than they read, and tries to encourage reading in her television serials.

Al-'Assal is more uncompromising than 'Ukasha both on the importance of women's work – as a means of fulfillment *and* domestic bliss – and of companionate marriage. She looks to her controversial 1982 serial, *She and the Impossible* (*Hiya wa al-mustahil*) as the best example of her views. In it she combined her perennial push for education and economic independence for women with a strong vision of love as the only proper basis of marriage. The serial, as she described it, was about a man who divorced his illiterate wife once he got educated. After he left her, she persevered and got a job and then went to university while raising her son on her own.

After twelve years, the husband came back and wanted to remarry her because she was no longer uneducated ("ignorant"). As Al-'Assal explained,

She refused and told him that the Zaynab whom he had chosen in the past now rejected him.... The husband then suggested they should return to each other in order to raise their son. She argued that they should get back together only if they loved each other, in which case they could live under one roof and raise the boy together.... My point was to emphasize the value of a home as a home. That is to say, a man and a woman should enter only on the condition that they love one another; otherwise it would be sheer betrayal. These are new values, of course.

While most serials on Egyptian television take for granted that the ideal form of marriage is one based on shared values and mutual love and respect, and all depict the core social units as couples, it is the more politically progressive Al-'Assal who seems most explicit in her promotion of the companionate marriage. Asked about the lessons on love and marriage she tries to teach in her serials, she said:

Regarding love, marriage, or anything for that matter, I try to force people to be honest with themselves.... Marriage is not a question of a diploma or a house. It is a form of understanding between you and the person you are marrying, that you actually love each other. Any other form of marriage I consider sinful and a betrayal.... That is my opinion on love. Economic necessity often leads a woman to marry a man who can support her well, because she cannot do so herself. What I want is for her to be able to set up a household herself. Then she won't have to sell her body to a man, under the guise of marriage.[8]

Islamists: The Other End of the Spectrum?

Those supporting some sort of self-consciously Muslim identity and associated with a range of positions regarding the importance of structuring society and the polity in more Islamic terms now also produce popular forms of public culture. While progressive television writers and other intellectuals have worked through the official state-run instruments of mass media, the Islamists (except a few associated with the state) are forced to disseminate their messages through magazines, books, and booklets sold in bookstores and street stalls, pamphlets distributed in mosques, and sermons and lessons, often recorded on cassettes carrying notices like "Copyright in the name of all Muslims."

These two sets of politically motivated culture producers can be thought of as in dialogue with each other, although both conceive of themselves as oppositional voices in Egypt. What a comparison between their output on women suggests, however, is that there are surprising areas of overlap, even as they define their projects quite differently *vis-à-vis* modernity and the West.

The television writers just discussed define their projects as modernist. They respect aspects of the West and are quite familiar with its literature and culture, but see themselves as nationalists with Egypt's social good at heart. Englightenment, advancement, and progress are central to their vocabularies, and they share a sense that their most dangerous adversaries on social issues are the Islamists who do not use the lexicon of "modernity" and yet target the same "masses" they try to uplift. For example, Wafiyya Kheiry, a liberal screenwriter, expresses her worries about the direction Egypt is taking by bemoaning the way that the social climate has changed television programming since the progressive 1960s and 1970s. Referring to a serial she had written in 1975 about the difficulties of establishing collegiality between men and women in the workplace, she said, "If I were to write a serial along these lines today, men would simply respond by asserting that women should go back to the home; then all these problems would be avoided. Now the fundamentalists would claim that all these problems are due to the fact that women are going out to work in the first place."[9] To these imagined conservatives Kheiry retorted, "Just because someone gets run over by a car, should I forbid people to walk on the streets? Of course there are problems created [by female employment], but we must confront them."

She also expressed her anger about a recent confrontation with the television censors. She was working on a serial based on short stories by Egyptian women writers. The script of one story called "An Emancipated Woman" ("Imra'a muta-harrira") was turned down. As she described it, the story was about a liberal man who returns from abroad and falls in love with a conservative woman, always challenging her conservative views. She defends herself, saying that her conservativism is just the way she is. He then gets to know a more liberated woman and leaves the first. Once the first woman realizes that she has lost him, she changes herself radically and becomes quite cosmopolitan. When his relationship with the second woman fails to work out, he returns to the first, only to find her completely changed. He then leaves her too. The story was meant to show how men do not know what they want. But the censors rejected the episode, with the explanation that, as Kheiry put it, "it would create problems with the fundamentalists. . . . It would be problematic to depict a woman as moving from conservatism to liberalism. In fact, it was impossible for a woman to do so."

Al-'Assal, on the other hand, though she has had many run-ins with the censors, reserves her contempt for another group of veiled women involved in media: the so-called repentant artists who have captured the press and the imaginations of many in the past few years. These are a small group of famous actresses, singers, and belly dancers, stars of film and stage, who have given up their careers and taken on the new head covering called the *hijab*. In small booklets the decisions of these born-again stars are explored and marketed, one book sensationalizing the phenomenon by portraying these women as embattled. The blurb on the back cover reads, "After more than twenty actresses and radio personalities had adopted the veil (*hijab*)...war was declared on them....Those carrying the banner of this war are 'sex stars' and 'merchants of lust.'"[10]

These actresses have done what an increasing number of urban Egyptian women have done: adopted the new modest Islamic dress as part of what they conceive of as their religious awakening.[11] Because they are such well-known figures, their actions have been publicized and capitalized on by the Islamists to further legitimize the trend toward women's veiling and to support their call for women's return to the home. Secularists and progressives, those opposed to veiling as a sign of "back-wardness," suspiciously accuse these actresses of taking fat salaries from the Islamic groups for hosting study groups at which conservative religious authorities or unqualified women proselytize. Fathiyya al-'Assal sees them as gullible victims of the Islamic groups, who have preyed on their guilt about their genuinely dissolute lives with fiery talk about "Hell, God, and Judgment Day."

But such study groups have cropped up everywhere, and the decision to adopt the *hijab*, while initially, in the late 1970s, mostly a form of political action by intelligent university women, usually the first in their families to be educated, has now spread down to working women of the lower middle classes and up to a few rebellious upper-class adolescents and movie stars. In rural areas, educated girls declare their difference from their uneducated relatives without jeopardizing their respect-ability by means of this form of dress.[12] In short, adopting the *hijab* now has an extraordinary number of meanings and complications that need to be distin-guished.

Analysis of the discourse of these repentant stars suggests the complexity of the meanings and brings into relief a crucial dimension of the debates on women and cultural authenticity in contemporary Egypt. The women's narratives dramatically denounce performing as the work of the Devil and remorsefully regret their years in the milieu of the (night) world of "art," fame, and the limelight. The women express their joy at having become closer to God through renunciation of their professions.

I examine elsewhere ordinary Egyptians' responses to these stars, showing how media stars' wealth, independence from family, and links with western lifestyles are conflated with sexual immorality to make them objects of ambivalence.[13] Recently the Islamist attacks on stars as symbols of sexual immorality have gained strength, Egypt's most famous and westernized actress, Yusra, now having to fight a lawsuit that charges her with offending public morals. Her crime was appearing on the cover of a film magazine in skimpy clothes.[14]

Here I want to point out only one interesting aspect of the reformed actresses' self-presentations. A recurring theme in their narratives, bolstered by the interviews with their husbands that accompany their stories, is how their careers had caused them to neglect their husbands and children. In the book *Repentant Artists and the Sex Stars!*, Shams al-Barudi, a former film star introduced as someone "associated with seduction roles," is reported as saying, "I now live a happy life in the midst of my family, with my noble husband who stood by me and encouraged me and congra-tulated me on each step...and my three children."[15] Her husband, a former actor and movie director, explains, "I had long wished that Shams would retire from acting and live for her household." In talking about how she had changed, he said, "Shams has now become a wife who cares for her husband...and a mother who tends her children and lives her life like any other wife...she is a mother with a calling [to raise her children in a Muslim way]."[16] In a recent interview where he modifies his position on art and justifies his return to acting, he nevertheless ends with a similar statement: "My wife is the wealth God has bestowed on me. My beloved wife shares my life, for better or worse, and we adore our children, care for them, and show them every concern."[17]

This husband is echoing the conservative sentiments that have been widely expressed especially [since the early 1970s] in the press and other media, sentiments perhaps widely felt, that women's proper place is in the home with their families. Actresses and other show business personalities epitomize the challenge to that model, and they are targeted because they represent the moral nightmare of the sexual looseness of professional women.

The problem is often presented as one affecting the next generation. As Soha Abdel Kader notes, when in 1985 a draft law was presented to Parliament calling for women to quit their jobs, keeping half their salaries, "the rationale behind the draft law was that working women were neglecting the care and upbringing of their children, thereby contributing to an increase in the incidence of juvenile delinquency and drug addiction among the young."[18] A short article by Anis Mansour, an establishment journalist, in the official government newspaper *Al-Ahram* in 1989 lays out the links between careerist mothers and unhappy children who turn to drugs, brothels, and "deviation." He stresses film stars' special culpability as people who send their children away to boarding school to feel unwanted.[19]

This call for women's "return" to the roles of wife and mother, also harped on by popular religious authorities such as Shaykh al-Sha'rawi and the younger Dr. 'Umar 'Abd al-Kafi, who preaches his message on cassettes, is a cornerstone of a program constructed as "Islamic" or authentic. Such figures claim to be radically different from the progressive television writers who see women's work as essential to national development and social progress. Although there are important differences among Islamists that should not be ignored, I would still argue that the Islamists and other conservatives, and especially their women followers, are not as different from the liberals as they might think.[20] In particular, although they may claim to represent a "return" to the culturally authentic, rejecting the emancipation of women as a western corruption, their positions are no more "traditional" than those of the progressives. They are certainly less positive about women's work than are the progressive television writers whose productions I described above, but on the value of education and conjugal love they hardly disagree.

As is often the case, men, and especially the male religious authorities, seem to be more conservative than the women to whom they preach. Someone like Shaykh al-Sha'rawi is obsessive in his condemnation of western corruption and his insistence on the importance of women's veiling. He tries to persuade women that their place is in the home, using odd arguments – asserting, for example that Marilyn Monroe herself had wished she had been able to be a housewife.[21] Women's work is problematic for these figures because it involves them in a public world now distinctly separate, as it is in all modern capitalist societies, from the private world of home and family.

There has indeed been a backlash against working women, which many analysts relate to high levels of unemployment for men (exacerbated in Egypt by the dismantling of the public sector after Sadat's open-door policy and by fewer opportunities for migration to the Gulf). Many Islamists argue that women should not work outside the home, God having given them the noblest of occupations – raising His creatures. The reality is, however, that most of the women who have taken on the veil are in fact working or expect to work. Most families aspiring to achieve or maintain middle-class status cannot do without a second income.[22] And Egyptians have become used to women professionals in all areas. As Zuhur puts it, work for the Islamists is one of the "negotiable" issues.[23] Given these realities, at most what figures like Shaykh al-Sha'rawi can do is tell women that if they must work, they should comport themselves properly and have no physical contact with men in work situations.[24] This, of course, is not so different from what 'Ukasha suggests in *Hilmiyya Nights* in showing the sexual perils of working or what Wafiyya Kheiry suggests in showing the difficulties of establishing cross-sex collegiality (although both, it must be stressed, are more positive about professional women's work as an avenue for personal development).

The findings of one of the few serious surveys of veiled university women, reported on by both Leila Ahmed and Mervat Hatem and conducted in the early 1980s by Zaynab Radwan, show that the survey's subjects actually accept many components of what we might consider the modernist feminist project.[25] As Ahmed has noted, Radwan's study, while confirming that unveiled women were more feminist than their veiled counterparts on matters of women's education, work, political participation, and rights in marriage, showed that on most issues the majority of women shared what could be called feminist goals.[26] The margin of difference between the veiled and unveiled groups was often only slight. For example, 99 percent of unveiled women thought work outside the home was acceptable, but so did 88 percent of the veiled students. Badran has argued that in the late 1980s, there has even been a liberalization on gender issues within Islamist ranks. She points to Islamist women like Safinaz Kazim and Hiba Ra'uf who insist on women's rights to the public sphere.[27]

The support for women's education is more consistent. Radwan's 1982 study showed that 98 percent of unveiled women believed that women had the right to pursue the highest level of education possible; the figure for veiled women was 92 percent. And even the most conservative new charismatic religious figures, such as Dr. 'Umar 'Abd al-Kafi, whose daily appearance on a television show during Ramadan 1993 (hosted by Kariman Hamza, the only veiled public broadcaster) made him a media star, barely attack education for women.[28] He insisted only that women should not go far from home unaccompanied to attend university, and that wives should not work hundreds of miles away from their families.[29]

It is on matters of marriage, however, that one sees the most overlap between the liberal secular and Islamist positions. Although the television writers place more stress on women's equality and dignity in marriage and say little about motherhood, those advocating a "return" to Islam and tradition see conjugal love and the nuclear family as ideal.[30] Although much more research needs to be done before we can speak with confidence about expectations concerning love, marriage, and motherhood among those in the Islamic groups and the broad base of young people who find appealing an explicitly Islamic identity, the "born-again" stars and their supportive husbands quoted above suggest some of the ideals of domesticity that seem to be part of being pious in Egypt today. Hatem has also written about how central the husband–wife relationship was deemed by Zaynab al-Ghazali, influential leader of the Muslim Women's Association, to the "happy [Muslim] home," her advice going so far as to suggest that "the affairs of the couple and their marital agreements should not go beyond the couple."[31] And one could read Shayk Al-Sha'rawi's interpretation of the Islamic requirement of social equivalence (*takafu'*) of marriage partners as referring not to wealth but to "an equality in essential nature, such as the mind, health, character, and values," and thus framing an ideal of companionate marriage in Islamic terms.[32] Elsewhere, Hatem has accused him of a "startling embrace of heterosexual (emotional) intimacy" because he regards women's care of men as "more primary than their reproductive task."[33]

Evidence of Islamists' concern with marital love can be found in the articles and advice columns that appear on the women's page of the newspaper published by Al-Azhar, *Al-Luwa' al-Islami*. These articles, on themes like how to achieve marital happiness or a stable and calm marital life, urge husbands and wives to be patient, forgiving, and tolerant of each other.[34] Although those interviewed, like the Islamist thinker Yusuf Qaradawi, outline women's duties as including serving their husbands, raising children, and keeping house – with statements like "virtuous women care only about satisfying, pleasing, and serving their husbands, taking good care of their home and family"[35] – they also urge husbands to be good-natured and to remember their wives' rights to kind words and tender gestures;[36] describe the proper management of household affairs as involving mutual consultation and cooperation rather than the domination of one partner;[37] condemn forced marriage; and, like the progressive writer Al-'Assal, assert that financial considerations should not be paramount in spouse selection.[38]

There is certainly no single Islamist voice on these matters. For example, although Qaradawi and 'Aliyya al-'Asqalani, the woman writer and interviewer responsible for many of the articles on the women's page, characterize marriage as properly based on the emotions of amity (*mawadda*) (described as a higher emotional state than love) and mercy (*rahma*) and meant to produce peace of mind (*sakina*) and serenity (*tamanina*), others, like Muhammad Ibrahim Mabruk, are happy to use the word love (*hubb*). In his recent book, *Islam's Position on Love: A Revolt against the Materialism of Our Age, the Love of Man toward Woman and Woman toward Man*, he denounces forced marriages and declares that Muslims, unlike westerners, have always agreed about the value of love because they know it is not an illusion but a spiritual matter.[39] With images as trite as a Hallmark greeting card, he describes true love in the following terms: "A lover accepts the beloved's personality as a whole; he wishes the subject to stay just as it is, without trying to reform, guide, or advise";[40] "love is a constant attachment to and affection for the other... an ever renewing activity. It does not seek to possess the other...."[41]

What all these Islamists share is the fact that the framework is religious, marriage being characterized as a spiritual blending (*imtizaj ruhi*) or as a resemblance between lovers' souls (*mushakala bayn nufus al-'ushaq*), and all their positions are justified and supported by reference to Islamic texts, whether the Qur'an or traditions of the Prophet, or to the example of the Prophet. This is not insignificant, even when they readily use the authority of sexologists, psychologists, and medical scientists to confirm their points of view (as in Mabruk's arguments about the greater sexual fulfillment of those who have sex in the context of love).[42] Yet I would still maintain that their image of the ideal marriage shares its basic contours with the less explicitly religious norm.

From a somewhat bizarre television experience comes another kind of confirmation of the importance for Islamists of these "modern" values for marriage. One evening in 1990 there was a fleeting episode of a television serial that was not continued the following day. It began innocently enough, resembling any evening serial, with parents discussing with their grown children possible marriage partners, an outdoor scene at a club where a meeting had been arranged between a fashionably dressed young couple, and a slight twist on a predictable theme with the parents urging their handsome son to consider the daughter of their wealthy neighbors.

But suddenly all the usual terms of the evening serials were unsettled. The young man went to complain to his grandparents about his parents' materialistic motives. In language rich with pious phrases he revealed his dilemma. Quoting the well-known tradition of the Prophet Muhammad about what qualities to value in a woman, he asserted that he too valued piety above wealth and beauty. He confessed that he already knew who he wanted to marry. She was a pious woman, a veiled woman who was a classmate of his in medical school. This episode pitted arranged marriage against the love match, but it was the secular modern parents who wanted to arrange the match for their son and the Islamist son who wanted the love marriage with his colleague.

Although I was never able to discover the story behind this unusual drama, it was easy to see why it was yanked from the air, apparently after two episodes. Made by a private Islamic production company, it violated the segregation of religious from secular programming in its heavy incorporation of quotations from the Qur'an and the traditions of the Prophet. And it made positive mention of the modern urban religious men and women who, until 1992, were strictly ignored in television drama.[43] Yet what is so revealing about it is its suggestion that for the pious, educated, middle-class youths, the ideals of companionate marriage are just as vital as they are for the progressive secular nationalist feminists like Fathiyya al-'Assal.[44] In fact, sharing the values of a new generation and being, as the Islamist Zaynab al-Ghazali put it, comrades within a movement, should strengthen the bonds of marriage.[45]

Historical Roots

Many characterize the current call by conservatives for women to return to the home as a call for the "retraditionalization" of women's status and roles.[46] And indeed the assertion of the proper role of a woman as wife and mother, with the assumption of a happy nuclear family, husband and wife devoted to each other and to their children, is now – as the comment of the husband of the born-again film star Shams al-Barudi suggests, and the writings of Islamist thinkers indicate – couched in an Islamic religious idiom that gives it a pedigree. The duty of the mother is to raise good Muslim children, and the love between husband and wife is described in terms of emotions with Qur'anic resonances like mercy and amity.

But I would argue that this vision of family and women's proper relation to husband and children is profoundly modern and its sources are entwined with the

West as surely as are the negatively perceived public freedoms of women the Islamists denounce. Yet this bourgeois vision of women's domesticity, rooted in a much earlier phase of western and Egyptian feminist reform, has become so ensconced in upper-, middle-, and even lower-middle-class Egyptian society that none of those arguing for a rejection of western ways seek to dislocate it. Instead, they assimilate it to "tradition" and try to find Islamic bases for it while vilifying as foreign the other side of what being a western emancipated woman might mean. This is not to say that the Islamist inflection or translation of the ideals does not change the model in important ways; it is merely to note that the claims to a pure indigenous tradition are spurious.

To understand why I say this, one needs to understand the historical context of contemporary debates and the situation of women. A good place to begin is with a critical examination of the ideas of the most prominent instigator of Egyptian debates on women, the elite reformer Qasim Amin, whose controversial *The Liberation of Women*, published in 1899 while Egypt was under British occupation, has led many to consider him the father of Egyptian feminism. More recently, a reassessment of his contributions has begun, with Timothy Mitchell questioning the colonial roots of his feminism and showing its link to a large-scale modernizing project intended to open up the women's world to the same surveillance and individualized subjection to the state as was imposed on the rest of the population, and to organize the family into a house of discipline for producing a new Egyptian mentality.[47] Leila Ahmed has followed, although without criticizing the overall projects of modern power in which Amin and his class were engaged, by accusing him of being "the son of Cromer [the British consul general] and colonialism," who used a particular kind of feminism to undermine his own culture along lines desired by the colonial powers.[48]

I will take up another aspect of his project, arguing that although he spoke of women's rights, education, and work, what he ultimately was most interested in promoting was the modern bourgeois family with its ideal of conjugal love and scientific child rearing. This is a form of family that some western feminists, Marxists, and social theorists of the second half of the twentieth century have now come to criticize as a source of women's subjection because of the way it divides women from one another, gives them new tasks, places them under the control of husbands, and opens up the family to capitalist exploitation, state control, and new forms of discipline.

Like many reformers produced in the colonial encounter, Amin linked women's status to the progress of the nation, arguing that it was not an "exaggeration to claim that women are the foundation of the towering constructs of modern civilization."[49] He held up for admiration Europe and America where "women have contributed shoulder to shoulder with men to every branch of trade and industry, to every branch of knowledge and the arts, to every philanthropic activity, and to every political event."[50] Advocating especially an end to the veiling and seclusion of women, he detailed the potential gains for household heads and for the nation in the contributions women could make. "Our country," he wrote, "would benefit from the active participation of all its citizens, men and women alike."[51]

Despite the references to European women's public achievements, however, in the end he argued only for primary education for girls (albeit to be consolidated through later participation in public life) and never actually suggested that anyone except poor women and those without male support should have full educations and professions, the latter needing this opportunity so as not to turn to "improper occupations."[52] So how were women to help the nation develop?

For Amin, the principal benefits of Egyptian women's becoming educated and exposed to the world seemed to be two: they would become better mothers, capable of bringing up the kinds of good citizens required by the modern nation; and they would become better marriage companions for the educated modern man, capable of truly loving and understanding him. Both notions, informed child rearing and companionate marriage, can be considered novel imports, cultural forms transplanted from the West.

[Omnia Shakry has explored] the way that he linked motherhood and nationalism and the fascination his contemporaries had with new ideas about the importance of child rearing.[53] As Mitchell has pointed out, and Shakry has elaborated, his criticism of Egyptian women's methods of child rearing is shot through with the obsessions with hygiene, rationality, and discipline that characterized the "enlightened" West and were adopted by colonial modernizers, indigenous or foreign.

Here I will be more concerned with his views on marriage. Although defensive throughout his book about his intent to stay within an Islamic framework, giving women only the rights they had according to the true principles of Islam, the Paris-educated Amin is blatant in his admiration for European society. Scathing in his condemnation of contemporary Egyptian women who were, in his words, incapable of truly loving their husbands, and of Islamic scholars who had reduced marriage to a contract by which a man has the right to sleep with a woman, he devotes many pages to painting a romantic picture of the kind of spiritual, mutual love he envisions between husbands and wives. He uses a passage from the Qur'an again to justify this: "He created for you helpmeets from yourselves that ye might find rest in them, and He ordained between you love and mercy." But the sources of this saccharine vision are clearly western, and he uses the model of intense friendship to characterize it.[54] He dedicated his second book on the subject of women to his fellow nationalist Sa'd Zaghlul, whose friendship, he says, had led him "to consider the value of such a love when shared between a man and his wife" and which he then offers as "the secret of happiness that I declare to the citizens of my country, men or women."[55]

His call to end veiling and seclusion as well as to ban polygamy can be read as means to nurture the marital bond. Anticipating the anxieties about fidelity and chastity these reforms would incite, he again turns to the superiority of Europeans, arguing that they had realized, as their knowledge increased and "they began to evaluate and measure their way of life against rational criteria and accurate, unbiased information" that the chastity belt and other forms of control over women they had used in the past did not work or "guarantee their happiness. They concluded that their only route to happiness lay in having their wives share with them in their endeavors, assisting them in straightening out their muddled affairs, and complementing their inadequacies. To achieve this they began to prepare their women through education for their new role."[56]

Echoing the European Christian marriage vows, and quoting John Stuart Mill, he asks in *The New Woman*, "What better situation is there for a man than living with a companion who accompanies him day and night, at home and abroad, in sickness and in health, through good and bad, a companion who is intelligent, educated, and knowledgeable of life's challenges?...Can a man be happy if he does not have a woman next to him to donate his life to and who personifies perfection through her friendship? This type of life – which our men do not comprehend – is one of the greatest inspirations to great works."[57]

Amin in vivid terms portrayed the dismal state of marriage in his era. He argued that marital unhappiness was the rule, although he believed it was the upper- and middle-class urban men who suffered the most because the gap between themselves and their ignorant (uneducated) women was the greatest. They wanted order and systematically arranged homes; they wanted to share the ideas they cherished, their concerns about the society they served and the country they esteemed, their joys and pain. When they found their wives ignorant, wanting only money or attention from them, they came to despise them and turned away. This made their wives hate them. He concluded, "From then on life is like hell for both of them."[58]

One must wonder at the sources of his strange and negative depiction of marital life and the condition of women in Egypt. The resemblances between his descriptions and those of the missionaries and colonial officials, for example, are striking. Although the missionary women working in the Muslim world blamed the men as well as the system of seclusion, they too described the Muslim family as loveless and described upper-class women as idle. As evidence for the absence of love in marriage, besides numerous anecdotes about miserable marriages, they noted that "there is no word in the Arabic language for home." In a nice circulation of ideas, Annie Van Sommer's introduction to a 1907 collection of missionary women's accounts of their experiences in Muslim lands (*Our Moslem Sisters: A Cry of Need from Lands of Darkness*) cites the "Egyptian gentleman" Qasim Amin as an authority on the lovelessness of Muslim marriage.[59]

To highlight the novelty of Amin's vision of the proper role of wife and mother, a vision to which I suggest the current call to "retraditionalization" as well as the progressive vision of television writers are deeply indebted, I would like to pursue two strategies. One is to read against the grain Amin's complaints about women in his era, particularly the upper-class women with whom he is most concerned. This will suggest what one form of "traditional" (in the sense of pre-twentieth-century) gender relations might have been like. The second, and trickier, strategy is to sketch in what women's roles in one contemporary, nonurban community in Egypt are like. My intent is not to suggest that this community represents the past, whether pre-nineteenth-century or the Prophet's time, but rather to cautiously indicate the kinds of models of marriage and motherhood that developed in communities less affected by the modernizing reforms of the state. It should become clear that the current calls for "retraditionalization" do not have this kind of "tradition" in mind.

Amin's first complaint is that wives are too clingy, not respecting the work their husbands do, not granting them the freedom to read quietly. This may suggest that they expected more attention from husbands than the modern educated husband, with his ideological and social (read extrafamilial) concerns, now wished to provide.

He also thinks that women do not run their households efficiently and complains that they "have become accustomed to idleness...the source of all evil."[60] He proposes that the proper administration of large households is a serious occupation. Can one suggest that he would like to impose on women a new form of industriousness and new standards of household work that are more demanding of their time, keeping them bound to the home rather than permitting them time for visiting?

He accuses seclusion of being a source of moral corruption because it encourages upper-class women to mix with lower-class and less respectable women, to talk freely to peddlers ("women who are ignorant of their roots, their background, or their condition, and who have not adopted any points of good character"), and to be exposed to prostitutes (dancers) at wedding celebrations. He finds it problematic that "[t]he woman of the house sees no harm in visiting her servant's wife; in fact, she may be entertained by conversing with her and listening to her tales. She gives minimal consideration to the appropriateness or inappropriateness of the topics of conversation."[61] This anxiety over women's talk surfaces elsewhere in his complaint that idle women spend their time talking to their friends: "While with friends and neighbors, her deep sighs ascend with the cigarette smoke and coffee steam as she talks loudly about her private concerns: her relationship with her husband, her husband's relatives and friends, her sadness, her happiness, her anxiety, her joy. She pours out every secret to her friends, even those details associated with private behavior in the bedroom."[62]

Here I would like to suggest that Amin is signaling his desire to undermine the solidarities of a relatively separate women's world, distinguishing an emergent middle class, and dividing women by placing them into separate bourgeois nuclear families. He also seems to want to put an end to the sexually explicit language of that world that is often hostile to men. In her eloquent analysis of the parallel movement to modernize Iranian women, Najmabadi has argued that as women became educated and unveiled, they lost the rich and expressive language of their former homosocial world and imposed on themselves new forms of silence.[63]

Although he specifically distinguished the women of his class who were the main objects of his proposed reforms from rural women and desert Bedouin, women he saw as more the equals and partners of their men, I think that such women even today can offer further clues about what was novel about his notions of the proper charges of wives and mothers. This is not to deny that such groups themselves have undergone significant transformations in the last century. But since these communities have been positioned differently within colonial and postcolonial Egypt, they have followed paths separate from those of the urban middle and lower classes. Their assumptions about gender relations can offer hints about what might be included in the repertoire of "the traditional" or "indigenous."

I have shown in great detail elsewhere how one such community, the Awlad 'Ali Bedouin of Egypt's Western Desert, work with very different ideas about marriage and child rearing from those of contemporary urban middle-class Egyptians.[64] Marriages are arranged, in many cases between relatives, and love and respect can develop between marital partners if each fulfills his/her tasks well and respects the honor and dignity of the other. The basic loyalties, however, of men and women, are to kin. And the basic day-to-day socializing is oriented around same-sex groups, with women experiencing great freedom from the surveillance of men and expressing vibrant irreverence and resistance to the control of men in their separate sphere.

Women do most of the caring for children, but they do not see themselves as molding the characters of their children, making them industrious, or exposing them to proper stimulation and experience. They see their children's characters as in part due to heredity, in part influenced by the example set around them, but mostly God-given. Women take seriously their Qur'anic duty to suckle their children for two years, but after that their main charge is to make sure that their children's behavior by their adolescent years is socially appropriate with regard to showing respect to others. Child rearing is not considered an occupation but only one of the many things, such as cooking, weaving, getting water, and paying social calls, that women do. They get help with the children from other women in the household but mostly from older children. If anyone is responsible for children's religious training, it is their fathers. And these women are certainly not trying to raise the future citizens of a proud Egypt or even good members of the Muslim *umma*, although they might sympathize with the latter concept.

In short, women are wives and mothers, but these roles do not require them to be devoted to their husbands or dedicated to the proper training of their children; and these roles are balanced by women's significant involvement in the affairs of their kin and of the women's community. Other studies of Arab women have suggested that in kin-based societies "public" and "private" do not have the same meanings they bear in other sorts of societies, and that in the former women's involvement in family affairs is a form of significant public action.[65]

Only now, with a younger generation of women who are becoming educated in state schools and gaining the literacy that allows them to be influenced by national ideologies, as well as being exposed to mass media, can one detect the entrance of the modernist ideals of marriage. Young, educated Awlad 'Ali women talk about mutual understanding (*tafahum*) as what they want most in a marriage. The only young woman in the community I lived in to achieve secondary education was also the only one to aspire to living with her new husband in a nice clean apartment alone, having only two children. She cherished her postcard collection, which like the collections of similarly educated girls in rural Upper Egypt, included romantic scenes of brides and grooms looking deep into each others' eyes.[66]

Amin's program, one can now see clearly, was for a liberation of women that would make of them good bourgeois wives and mothers in a world where state and class ties would override those of kin, capitalist organization would divide the world into the distinct spheres of private and public, and women would be subjected to husbands and children, cut off from their kin and from other women. His was a project of domesticating women that relied heavily, as Shakry and Najmabadi show,[67] on western models of the time. Clearly it is this modernist and "feminist" tradition within which the Islamists work, even as they transform some of its elements. They do not gesture toward the sex-segregated world Amin denounced or toward the alternative model with different cultural and political roots that I have described for the contemporary Awlad 'Ali Bedouin in Egypt. As Homi Bhabha has argued for other postcolonial societies, access to any sort of real "tradition" has been made impossible by the historical cultural encounter with the West.[68]

Conclusion: Beyond the Rhetoric

It has been about a hundred years since Qasim Amin published his two controversial books. As feminist scholars have recently documented, he wrote in a context where women writers were already raising many of the concerns he raised. The struggles for women's rights and the transformation of women's lives were carried forward by a range of women writers and activists and an impressive series of feminist organizations in the early to mid-twentieth century, led by women like Huda Sha'rawi, Saiza Nabarawi, and later Doria Shafik, who were far more radical than Amin in their demands for education and women's rights to the public sphere.[69]

Mostly tied by class to Europe and Europeans, even as many were anti-imperialist, they adopted not just the "feminist" projects of education and public roles for women but also the ideals of uplifting the lower classes and the key components of a new domesticity – companionate marriage and scientific child rearing. They thus retained and elaborated many of the ideals Amin promoted. Their journals carried dire stories about the tragedies of forced marriage and polygyny, carried information on how to run a proper household, and provided advice about child rearing. In short, as part of their call for awakening women and transforming their lives and possibilities, they encouraged modern bourgeois "rational" modes of housewifery and child rearing, similar to the modes of domesticity being developed and marketed through magazines in Europe and the United States at the time.[70] Most telling, they promoted the ideal of the conjugal couple, arguing against arranged marriage, polygyny, men's rights to easy divorce, and women's lack of access to the same. Their motives were different from Amin's, since they did not put themselves in the place of the modern man looking for a companion or blame women for marital unhappiness. They were more concerned with abuses of women. But they idealized companionate marriage as much as he did.[71]

It was Nasser who in the 1950s and 1960s could be said to have nationalized many of these feminist projects, removing at least from the goals of women's education and employment the taint of foreign influence with his own impeccable nationalist credentials. It was during his presidency that what Hatem calls "state feminism" was introduced, and independent women's organizations were suppressed.[72] His policies of mass education and guaranteed employment for graduates, regardless of sex, were based on a conception of woman as worker and citizen whose participation was essential for national development.

As many of Nasser's policies are being dismantled in the wake of Sadat's rapprochement with the United States and *infitah* (the opening up of Egypt to western investment) and the restructuring that international agencies are requiring of Egypt under current president Mubarak, women are finding themselves at the center of debate again. But because of the history of reforms for women in Egypt and the socioeconomic transformations of the last century, the terms have changed.

Urban women today, of a variety of classes, veiled and unveiled, are generally more radical than Qasim Amin was on issues of education, work, and participation in some aspects of the public sphere, such as politics. If they were informed enough about Egyptian history to know about the early-twentieth-century Egyptian feminists whose activities and views have been so crucial, they would probably denounce them.[73] Yet they are the inheritors of the political gains made for women by these women who took up where Amin left off, as they are the beneficiaries of Nasser's policies of mass education and employment.[74]

Their views on motherhood and their romance with companionate marriage can be traced further back. These are arguments that Marilyn Booth and Omnia Shakry show very clearly to have been part of the nationalist rhetoric of an earlier part of the century.[75] The positive expectations about the marital couple carry the telltale signs of the bourgeois dreams of reformers like Amin and the women writers who advocated companionate marriage. For the conservatives of the middle classes these views are just the shared widespread assumptions about marriage of their class, assumptions that, as Baron has indicated, developed in the early twentieth century.[76] Although she asserts that these developed indigenously and were not influenced by the West, she provides no evidence of this alternative genealogy. I would suggest instead that it is very hard to deny their sources in the West, where they had developed historically as part of deep social and economic shifts. One would also have to explore the local socioeconomic conditions that favored this shift in ideology. Furthermore, as Dipesh Chakrabarty does for the Bengali adaptation of European ideals of companionate marriage, one should examine the important ways that the European ideals were reshaped when translated into the emerging Egyptian context, not to mention how they are inflected by being framed within an Islamic discourse.[77]

For the upwardly mobile lower middle classes, from whom the Islamists draw much of their support, I suspect it is changes in the nature of the economy and social organization that combine with the middle-class images offered as models by television and magazines that underpin this vision. After all, even the progressives' serials, which clearly reinforce the Nasserist legacy of support for women's work and education, take for granted, if they do not glorify, the ideals of the "modern" couple and the companionate marriage. It could well be argued that the religious leaders' stress on the couple arises from a need to accommodate to and appropriate widely shared popular attitudes and demographic realities, not just of the upper and middle classes but increasingly of the lower classes as well.[78]

Just as the *hijab* and the modest dress being adopted around the Middle East are modern forms of dress, representing, despite the rhetoric, not any sort of "return" to cultural traditions but rather a complex reaction to a wide set of modern conditions (including, to be sure, a confrontation with western consumerism), so the Islamist call for women to return to their roles as wives and mothers does not represent anything resembling what could be considered "traditional." These roles were fundamentally altered in the twentieth century. To "return" to the home after the world has become fundamentally divided between a domestic and public sphere, after wage labor for all has transformed social and economic relations, after kin-based forms of social and economic organization have been attenuated, and after being a wife and mother has come to be thought of by some as a career, is to go to a new place and take on a radically new role.

The enmeshment with the West of an earlier period of such notions about the organization of family and the roles of women, like the colonial roots of many of the socioeconomic transformations that went along with these, are conveniently forgotten by the Islamists. This occlusion enables them to gain the moral high ground by seeming to reject the West, in their fixation on the chimera of sexual or public freedom, while not fundamentally challenging widely held ideals – like conjugal love, the nuclear family, the companionate marriage, and women's education – and economic necessities, like women's work, of late-twentieth-century middle- and lower-middle-class life in Egypt.

Cultures cannot simply displace or undermine each other, as the quotations with which this chapter opened might suggest. The complex processes of borrowing, translating, and creating new mixtures – what some theorists prefer to call cultural hybrids – cannot be subsumed under this sort of dichotomous image.[79] Nor can the ways in which new ideas are given firm bases by social and economic transformations as well as ideological familiarization, especially now through powerful forms of mass media. What the case of feminism in Egypt shows, however, is that the elements of borrowed, imported, or imposed "culture" are susceptible to disaggregation for political purposes. Elements that apply to only a tiny minority can be singled out for self-serving vilification as foreign, while those widely accepted, especially by the large middle and lower middle classes, are less likely to find themselves carrying the tainted label, "Made in the West."

It seems to be a common dynamic of postcolonial cultural politics that cultural transplants are selectively and self-consciously made the object of political contest. As analysts, we need to stand outside these struggles, writing the history of feminism in Egypt with an awareness of its multifaceted nature, historical stages, and complex intertwinement with the West while regarding the claims of the Islamists to cultural authenticity or countermodernity with healthy suspicion.

NOTES

For support in 1989–90 and 1993 for the research in Egypt on which this paper is based, I am grateful to the American Research Center in Egypt, the Near and Middle East Committee of the Social Science Research Council, and New York University (Presidential Fellowship). I have accumulated many debts for help with research and conceptualizing the issues since I wrote it in 1994. In particular I want to thank Iman Farid Abdel Karim, Hala Abu-Khatwa, Janet Abu-Lughod, Soraya Altorki, Fathiyya Al-'Assal, Beth Baron, Elwi Captan, Mervat Hatem, Deniz Kandiyoti, Wafiyya Kheiry, Saba Mahmood, Hasna Mekdashi, Tim Mitchell, Afsaneh Najmabadi, and Omnia Shakry. It goes without saying that none of these people or institutions is responsible for the views presented here.

1   Leila Ahmed, *Women and Gender in Islam* (New Haven: Yale University Press, 1992), p. 167.
2   For an early discussion, see Kumari Jayawardena, *Feminism and Nationalism in the Third World* (London: Zed Books, 1986). Partha Chatterjee in *The Nation and Its Fragments* (Princeton: Princeton University Press, 1993), Amrita Chhaachhi in "Forced Identities: The State, Communalism, Fundamentalism and Women in India," in *Women, Islam and the State*, ed. Deniz Kandiyoti (Philadelphia: Temple University Press, 1991), pp. 144–75, Lata Mani in "Contentious Traditions: The Debate on Sati in Colonial India," in *Recasting Women: Essays in Indian Colonial History*, ed. Kumkum Sangari and Sudesh Vaid (New Brunswick, NJ: Rutgers University Press, 1990), pp. 88–126, and others have explored with acuity the way "the woman question" has figured centrally in anticolonial and now communal politics in India; Aihwa Ong in "State versus Islam: Malay Families, Women's Bodies, and the Body Politic in Malaysia," *American Ethnologist* 17(2) (1990): 558–82, has shown how in Malaysia today a public obsession with the sexual freedom of (westernized) young women factory workers is used to reinforce the trend toward Islamic veiling; and Deniz Kandiyoti in *Women, Islam and the State* has argued most forcefully about how

crucial women, as symbols and pawns, have been to nationalist politics across the Muslim world. For a recent collection on the Muslim world, see Valentine Moghadam, ed., *Gender and National Identity: Women and Politics in Muslim Societies* (London: Zed Books, 1994).

3 Margot Badran has written that even Egyptian professional women often resist the label "feminist" because of this taint. Margot Badran, "Gender Activism: Feminists and Islamists in Egypt," in *Identity Politics and Women: Cultural Reassertions and Feminisms in International Perspective*, ed. Valentine M. Moghadam (Boulder, CO: Westview Press, 1993), pp. 202–27.

4 Literacy rates still make newspaper (and book) reading the habit of a minority, while radios are in every home, popularized by Nasser (the first president of postindependence Egypt) in the 1950s and 1960s as a political instrument. Most people have access to television. Among the most widely watched television programs are the evening dramatic serials, which provide the occasion for a good deal of national discussion and debate of major social issues.

5 Lila Abu-Lughod, "The Objects of Soap Opera: Egyptian Television and the Cultural Politics of Modernity," in *Worlds Apart: Modernity through the Prism of the Local*, ed. Daniel Miller (London and New York: Routledge, 1995), pp. 190–210.

6 For more on *ibn al-balad*, see Sawsan El-Messiri, *Ibn al-Balad: A Concept of Egyptian Identity* (Leiden: Brill, 1978). For a discussion of this figure in another of 'Ukasha's television serials, see Walter Armbrust, *Mass Culture and Modernism in Egypt* (Cambridge: Cambridge University Press, 1996), ch. 2.

7 This and all other quotations are from two interviews with the author on June 27 and 28, 1993.

8 'Ukasha has also expressed his concern over the materialistic motives of those contracting marriages, in an interview with Sawsan Al-Duwayk, "Al-hubb fi al-musal-salat." *Al-Idha'a wa al-tilifizyun*, January 23, 1993, p. 15. This is a theme that echoes early-twentieth-century arguments against arranged marriage.

9 All quotations are from an interview with the author on June 22, 1993.

10 The book was coauthored by 'Imad Nasif and Amal Khodayr and entitled *Fannanat ta'ibat wa nijmat al-ithara!* It listed no publisher, but its publication date was 1991 and it was in its eighth printing in January 1993.

11 The phenomenon of "the new veiling" is extremely complex. Among those who have written insightfully on it, showing clearly how the religious motivation for it, stated by many as the reason, needs to be balanced by an understanding of how veiling contributes to greater freedom of movement in public, easier work relations in mixed-sex settings, respectability in the eyes of neighbors and husbands, greater economy, and social conformity, are Ahmed, *Women and Gender in Islam*; Fadwa El Guindi, "Veiling Infitah with Muslim Ethic," *Social Problems* 28 (1981): 465–85; Mervat Hatem, "Economic and Political Liberalization in Egypt and the Demise of State Feminism," *International Journal of Middle East Studies* 24 (1992): 231–51; Valerie Hoffman-Ladd, "Polemics on the Modesty and Segregation of Women in Contemporary Egypt," *International Journal of Middle East Studies* 19 (1987): 23–50; Arlene MacLeod, *Accommodating Protest: Working Women, the New Veiling, and Change in Cairo* (New York: Columbia University Press, 1991); and Sherifa Zuhur, *Revealing Reveiling: Islamist Gender Ideology in Contemporary Egypt* (Albany: State University of New York Press, 1992). Elizabeth Fernea's documentary film *A Veiled Revolution* is especially good at revealing many meanings of the new modest dress.

12 See Lila Abu-Lughod, "The Romance of Resistance: Tracing Transformations of Power through Bedouin Women," *American Ethnologist* 17 (1990): 41–55 and "Movie Stars and Islamic Moralism in Egypt," *Social Text* 42 (1995): 53–67.

13 Abu-Lughod, "Movie Stars and Islamic Moralism in Egypt."

14 John Lancaster, "Cloudy Days for Cairo Star: Film Celebrity Sued by Islamic Right, Stalked by Alleged Ex-Lover," *Washington Post*, January 31, 1996, p. 12.

15 Nasif and Khodayr, *Fannanat ta'ibat*, pp. 49, 61.

16 Ibid., pp. 60–1.

17 Interview of Hasan Yusuf with Amal Surur and 'Umar Tahir, *Nusf al-dunya*, May 4, 1997, p. 21.

18 Soha Abdel Kader, *Egyptian Women in a Changing Society, 1899–1987* (Boulder, CO: Lynne Reinner Publishing, 1987), pp. 137–8.

19 This article was warranted important enough to be translated and published in the English-language newspaper. Anis Mansour, "Victims," *Egyptian Gazette*, November 6, 1989, p. 3.

20 See Mervat Hatem, "Egyptian Discourses on Gender and Political Liberalization: Do Secularist and Islamist Views Really Differ?" *Middle East Journal* 48 (4) (1994): 661–76, for an important assessment of this convergence.

21 Barbara Stowasser, "Religious Ideology, Women and the Family: The Islamic Paradigm," in her *The Islamic Impulse* (Washington, DC: Center for Contemporary Arab Studies, Georgetown University, 1987), pp. 262–96.

22 See MacLeod, *Accommodating Protest*.

23 Zuhur, *Revealing Reveiling*.

24 Stowasser, "Religious Ideology, Women and the Family," p. 269.

25 Ahmed, *Women and Gender in Islam*, and Hatem, "Economic and Political Liberalization."

26 Ahmed, *Women and Gender in Islam*, pp. 226–7.

27 Badran, "Gender Activism," pp. 205, 211–14.

28 For more on this announcer, see Fedwa Malti-Douglas, "A Woman and Her Sûfîs" (Washington, DC: Center for Contemporary Arab Studies Occasional Papers, Georgetown University, 1995).

29 This conservative's views are critically described in two articles by Ibrahim 'Issa, "Mashayikh Kariman Hamza," *Roz al-Yusuf*, March 15, 1993, p. 23, and "D. 'Umar 'Abd al-Kafi shaykh al-nisa' . . . wa al-fitna al-ta'ifiyya," *Roz al-Yusuf*, March 29, 1993, pp. 23–5.

30 One should, perhaps, distinguish more carefully among ideals of marriage, noting the differences between a bourgeois notion of the couple and what could more accurately be called companionate marriage, carrying implications of equality between marital partners. But for the purposes of this argument, I am simply trying to locate the ideal of the couple.

31 Mervat Hatem, "Secularist and Islamist Discourses on Modernity in Egypt and the Evolution of the Post Colonial Nation-State," in *Islam, Gender and Social Change*, ed. Yvonne Haddad and John Esposito (New York and Oxford: Oxford University Press, 1998), pp. 85–99. Zuhur in *Revealing Reveiling*, p. 93, also argues that "the image of the veiled woman idealizes love within marriage."

32 Stowasser, "Religious Ideology, Women and Family," p. 277.

33 Hatem, "The Secularist and the Islamist Discourses on Modernity," p. 93.

34 Maha 'Umar, "Min ajl hayat zawjiyya mustaqirra wa hadi'a," *Al-Luwa' al-Islami*, August 8, 1996, p. 17. I am grateful to Mervat Hatem and Saba Mahmood for guiding me to this material.

35 "'Indama tarfud al-mar'a khidmat zawjiha wa al-qiyam bishu'un al-manzil," *Al-Luwa' al-Islami*, August 8, 1996, p. 16.

36 Yusuf al-Qaradawi, *Fatawa mu'asira li-lmar'a wa al-usra al-muslima* (Cairo: Dar al-Isra', n.d.), p. 65; 'Aliyya al-'Asqalani, "Li kul mushkila hal," *Al-Luwa' al-Islami*, December 21, 1995, p. 17.

37 'Aliyya al-'Asqalani, "Al-Tasallut yudammir al-'alaqa al-zawjiyya: sultat al-rajul fi al-bayt la tu'add istibdadan," *Al-Luwa' al-Islami*, July 6, 1995, p. 16.

38 Al-Qaradawi, *Fatawa mu'asira*, pp. 33–4.

39 Muhammad Ibrahim Mabruk, *Mawqif al-Islam min al-hubb* (Cairo: Al-Nur al-Islami, 1996), p. 19.

40 Ibid., p. 21.

41 Ibid., p. 26.

42 Ibid., p. 25.

43 For more on this exclusion, see my "Finding a Place for Islam: Egyptian Television Serials and the National Interest," *Public Culture* 5 (3) (1993): 493–513. See my "Dramatic Reversals," in *Political Islam*, ed. Joel Beinin and Joe Stork (Berkeley and Los Angeles: University of California Press, 1996), for a discussion of how this policy of exclusion shifted such that there is now a media campaign against "extremists."

44 Note also the similarities to the feminist discourse in the Egyptian press in 1930, which Badran summarizes as scorning "marriages made with an eye toward material advance or elevation in status." Margot Badran, *Feminists, Islam, and Nation: Gender and the Making of Modern Egypt* (Princeton: Princeton University Press, 1995), pp. 139–40.

45 See Zuhur, *Revealing Reveiling*, pp. 93–5. Deniz Kandiyoti (personal communication) also notes that marital choice within the circle of activists versus an older generation's attempts to control and arrange marriages on other bases is a classic theme in the political subculture of the Turkish Islamist youth.

46 See for example, Abdel Kader, *Egyptian Women in a Changing Society*, p. 137.

47 Timothy Mitchell, *Colonising Egypt* (Cambridge: Cambridge University Press, 1988), pp. 111–13.

48 Ahmed, *Women and Gender in Islam*, p. 153. Mervat Hatem's "Toward a Critique of Modernization: Narrative in Middle East Women Studies," *Arab Studies Quarterly* 15 (2) (1993): 117–22, also reassesses the meaning of education for women, criticizing the narrative of modernization shared by most feminist scholars of the Middle East that assumes that the introduction of education and other "modern" institutions has been absolutely positive for women.

49 All quotations are from Samiha Sidhom Peterson's translation of Qasim Amin, *The Liberation of Women* (Cairo: American University in Cairo Press, 1992). This one is from p. 58.

50 Ibid., p. 73.

51 Ibid., p. 10.

52 Ibid., pp. 47–8 and p. 13.

53 Omnia Shakry, "Schooled Mothers and Structured Play: Child Rearing in Turn-of-the-Century Egypt," in *Remaking Women: Feminism and Modernity in the Middle East*, ed. Lila Abu-Lughod (Princeton: Princeton University Press, 1998), pp. 126–70. See also Beth Baron, "Mothers, Morality, and Nationalism in Pre-1919 Egypt," in *The Origins of Arab Nationalism*, ed. Rashid Khalidi, Lisa Anderson, Muhammad Muslih, and Reeva Simon (New York: Columbia University Press, 1991), pp. 271–88.

54 Amin, *The Liberation of Women*, p. 20.

55 Qasim Amin, *The New Woman*, trans. Samiha Sidhom Peterson (Cairo: American University in Cairo Press, 1995), p. xi.

56 Amin, *The Liberation of Women*, p. 58.

57 Amin, *The New Woman*, p. 55.

58 Amin, *The Liberation of Women*, p. 17.

59 Annie Van Sommer and Samuel M. Zwemmer, *Our Moslem Sisters: A Cry of Need from Lands of Darkness* (New York: Fleming H. Revell Company, 1907), esp. pp. 7 and 28.

60 Amin, *The Liberation of Women*, p. 32.

61 Ibid., p. 55.

62 Ibid., p. 33.

63 Afsaneh Najmabadi, "Veiled Discourse – Unveiled Bodies," *Feminist Studies* 19(3) (1993): 487–518.

64 Lila Abu-Lughod, "A Community of Secrets," *Signs* 10(4) (1985): 637–57; *Veiled Sentiments* (Berkeley and Los Angeles: University of California Press, 1986); and *Writing Women's Worlds: Bedouin Stories* (Berkeley and Los Angeles: University of California Press, 1993).

65 For example, see Soraya Altorki, *Women in Saudi Arabia* (New York: Columbia University Press, 1986), and Cynthia Nelson, "Public and Private Politics," *American Ethnologist* 1(3) (1974): 551–63.

66 For more on this young Bedouin woman's views, see Abu-Lughod, *Writing Women's Worlds*, ch. 5; for similar examples from Upper Egypt, see Lila Abu-Lughod, "The Interpretation of Culture(s) after Television," *Representations* 59 (1997): 109–34.

67 Shakry, "Schooled Mothers and Structured Play," and Afsaneh Najmabadi, "Crafting an Educated Housewife in Iran," in *Remaking Women*, ed. Abu-Lughod, pp. 91–125.

68 Homi Bhabha, *The Location of Culture* (London and New York: Routledge, 1994), p. 2.

69 Badran, *Feminists, Islam, and Nation*; Beth Baron, *The Women's Awakening in Egypt* (New Haven: Yale University Press, 1994); Cynthia Nelson, "Biography and Women's History: On Interpreting Doria Shafik," in *Women in Middle Eastern History*, ed. Nikki Keddie and Beth Baron (New Haven: Yale University Press), pp. 310–33, and *Doria Shafik, Egyptian Feminist: A Woman Apart* (Gainesville: University Press of Florida, 1996).

70 Marilyn Booth in "'May Her Likes Be Multiplied': 'Famous Women' Biography and Gendered Prescription in Egypt, 1892–1935," *Signs* 22(4) (1997): 827–90, presents rich detail on the contents of these journals, and particularly the use of biographies of famous women to suggest models for young women of the future.

71 For more on women's campaigns and writing on marriage, see Badran, *Feminists, Islam and Nation*, esp. pp. 135–40, and Beth Baron, "The Making and Breaking of Marital Bonds in Modern Egypt" in Keddie and Baron, *Women in Middle Eastern History*, pp. 275–91, esp. pp. 277–8. Badran notes that the 1930s saw a shift in emphasis from concern with the maternal role to that of the wife.

72 Hatem, "Economic and Political Liberalization."

73 Mervat Hatem's "Egypt's Middle Class in Crisis: The Sexual Division of Labor," *Middle East Journal* 42(3) (1988): 407–22, p. 419, reports that most of the veiled college women surveyed denounced Qasim Amin but so did many of the unveiled women.

74 As a result, like just about everyone else in Egypt, they unthinkingly presume that education is good, despite the facts that the benefits of such a poor quality of education as is available in the overtaxed state system, leading to poorly paid employment at best, are dubious, and that the continuing debt to the West for the development of secular education is easy to see for those who want to. For example, none of those asserting the new Islamic identities complain that in the competitive university faculties where the veiled women are concentrated the influence of the West is most direct; it is there, in the scientific fields of medicine, engineering, and pharmacy that English is even the language of instruction.

75 Marilyn Booth, "The Egyptian Lives of Jeanne d'Arc," in *Remaking Women*, ed. Abu-Lughod, pp. 171–211; and Shakry, "Schooled Mothers and Structured Play."

76 Baron, "The Making and Breaking of Marital Bonds in Modern Egypt," pp. 275–91.

77 See Deniz Kandiyoti, "Gendering the Modern," in *Rethinking Modernity and National Identity in Turkey*, ed. Sibel Bozdoğan and Reşat Kasaba (Seattle: University of Washington Press, 1997), pp. 113–32, for an argument that the shift to new forms of marriage in

Turkey may have preceded westernization and calls for reform. Dipesh Chakrabarty, "The Difference-Deferral of a Colonial Modernity: Public Debates on Domesticity in British Bengal," *Subaltern Studies* VIII, ed. David Arnold and David Hardiman (Delhi: Oxford University Press, 1994), pp. 50–88.

78 See Marcia Inhorn, *Infertility and Patriarchy* (Philadelphia: University of Pennsylvania Press, 1996), esp. pp. 148–50. It would be worth exploring demographically the class breakdown of historical shifts from extended to nuclear households. For instance, Judith Tucker, in *Women in Nineteenth Century Egypt* (Cambridge: Cambridge University Press, 1985), p. 100, has argued in her study of the Egyptian peasantry and urban lower classes that even in the nineteenth century "[i]t was the small nuclear family, the husband and wife unit, that formed the basis of much business and property holding, not the large extended family of received wisdom and inheritance law logic."

79 Bhabha, *The Location of Culture*, has pursued this idea furthest.

Editorial note: This essay by Anna Tsing was not written specifically as a conclusion for this reader. However, since it does such a wonderful job reflecting on the anthropological discourse of globalization – on its strengths, limitations, and possibilities – we felt it was an appropriate piece with which to end the book.

Conclusion

The Global Situation

Anna Tsing

Click on worldmaking.interconnections. Your screen fills with global flows.

Imagine a creek cutting through a hillside. As the water rushes down, it carves rock and moves gravel; it deposits silt on slow turns; it switches courses and breaks earth dams after a sudden storm. As the creek flows, it makes and remakes its channels.

Imagine an internet system, linking up computer users. Or a rush of immigrants across national borders. Or capital investments shuttled to varied offshore locations. These world-making "flows," too, are not just interconnections but also the recarving of channels and the remapping of the possibilities of geography.

Imagine the landscape nourished by the creek. Yet even beyond the creek's "flows," there are no stable landscape elements: Trees sprout up, transforming meadows into forests; cattle browse on saplings, spreading meadows past forest edges. Nor are forests and meadows the only way to divide up the landscape. Consider the perspective of the earthworm, looking for rich soils, or the weed, able to flourish in both meadow and forest, though only when each meets certain conditions. To tell the story of this landscape requires an appreciation not only of changing landscape elements but also of the partial, tentative, and shifting ability of the storyteller to identify elements at all.

Imagine ethnic groups, corporations, refugees, nongovernmental organizations (NGOs), nation-states, consumers, social movements, media moguls, trade organizations, social scientists, international lawyers, and bankers, all swarming alongside creeks and earthworms to compose the landscape, to define its elements, carve its channels of flow, and establish its units of historical agency. We live in a time of self-consciousness about units and scales: Where shall we draw the boundaries of regions? How are local communities composed? And, most important for this essay, what is this thing we call the globe? If social scientists have had a lot to say

From *Cultural Anthropology* 15(3): 327–60. Copyright © 2000, American Anthropological Association.

about these questions of late, so have other people. Contestants form themselves in shifting alliances, mobilized for reasons of power, passion, discipline, or dis-ease and mounting campaigns for particular configurations of scale. Some of the most excited campaigning [since the mid-1970s] has concerned the globe, that planet-wide space for all humanity and its encompassing habitat. Moreover, in the last ten years, talk about the globe has heated up to the point that many commentators imagine a global *era*, a time in which no units or scales count for much except the globe. "Globalization," the process taking us into that era, has caught up enthusiasts ranging from corporate managers to social activists, from advertisers to cultural theorists.

For many years, the creek makes only gradual changes in the landscape. Then a storm sweeps the flux beyond its accustomed boundaries, shifting every bank and eddy. Trees are uprooted, and what was once on the right side is now on the left. So, too, the social world has shifted around us. Market enthusiasms have replaced communism; national governments prostrate themselves before international finance; social movements market "culture" on a global scale. How should social scientists analyze these changes? This question is muddied by the fact that social science changes too. "Global" practices challenge social scientists to internationalize their venues, as North American and European scholars are brought into discussion with scholars from the South. Social science theories no longer take western genealogies for granted but, rather, require fluency with a wider range of perspectives, from Latin American dependency theories to South Asian subaltern studies. The excitement of this internationalization of scholarship encourages many of us to throw ourselves into endorsements of globalization as a multilayered evolution, drawing us into the future. Sometimes our critical distance seems less useful than our participation. And yet, can we understand either our own involvement or the changing world without our critical skills? This essay argues that we cannot.

Is Globalization like Modernization?

Consider another moment in which social science was remade together with the world: the period after World War II, when social scientists were called on to participate in the international project of modernization and development. Modernization frameworks brought together scholars, policy makers, politicians, and social activists in a common program for social betterment. It offered the hope of moving beyond the colonial segregation of Europeans and natives to a world in which every nation could aspire to the highest standards of livelihood and culture. Even social scientists who feared its destructiveness or despised its imperiousness thus came to imagine modernization as the world-making process of the times. The charisma of the notion of an era of globalization is comparable in many ways to the charm of modernization in that postwar period. Like modernization theory, the global-future program has swept together scholars and public thinkers to imagine a new world in the making. Do globalization theories contain pitfalls for engaged social scientists similar to those of modernization theory?

Modernization, like globalization, was seductive. It was many years before social scientists moved beyond endorsements, refusals, and reforms of modernization to describe modernization as a set of *projects* with cultural and institutional specificities and limitations. Only when the shine of modernization began to fade did scholars ask how it managed to capture the hopes and dreams of so many experts, how its formulas were communicated to such a variety of social groups and within such a diversity of situations, and how its features were transformed in the process for multiple uses. Recent literature on modernization in its guise as "development" for the Third World is exemplary in this regard. A number of analysts, including Escobar (1995) and Ferguson (1990), have shown the discursive specificities of development, which often thrived more through the coherence of its internal logic than through any insight into the social situations in which it was expected to intervene. The commitment of experts to development drew material and institutional resources to its programs even when they were quite obviously destructive of the human well-being that formed its ostensible goal. Meanwhile, development was also reformulated through its constant negotiation and translation within particular settings, and it assumed multiple forms. Recent studies have shown how development policies diversified as they become entangled in regional political struggles (e.g., Peters 1994) and as they were reinterpreted in varied cultural settings (e.g., Pigg 1992). This rich literature has inspired new attention to the making of modernization. Its example can stimulate attention to the multiple projects of imagining and making globality.

Studies of modernization as a set of projects look in at least three directions. First, analysts attend to the cultural specificity of commitments to modernization. They may make these commitments seem exotic to remove them from the reader's common sense. (How odd, the analyst might say, that sitting in uncomfortable chairs is considered more modern than squatting.) Analysts explore the elements through which modernization projects make assumptions about the world. For example, modernization projects create notions of time through which groups and activities can be situated in relation to stories of progress. Second, analysts attend to the social practices, material infrastructure, cultural negotiations, institutions, and power relations through which modernization projects work – and are opposed, contested, and reformulated. Modernization projects do their work through educational practices, military coercion, administrative policies, resource entitlements, community reorganization, and much more; these arenas and practices both make and are transformed by modernization. To examine the effects of modernization commitments requires attention to the social worlds both of and beyond modernization visions. Third, analysts use the promise of questions and dilemmas brought up in modernization programs without becoming caught in their prescriptions for social change. For example, through its emphasis on critical reflection as a mode of "modern" thought, modernization draws attention to the awkward relationship between representation and its object and to the craft and creativity through which social life must be described. Analysts of modernization projects make use of this insight without assuming the framework of progress that helped generate it.

These directions of analysis seem equally useful to understanding projects of imagining and making globality. Certainly, commitments to globalism are strange enough to warrant cultural analysis. Furthermore, as globalization becomes institutionalized as a program not only in the academy but in corporate policy, politics, and popular culture, it is important to attend to these sites to understand what projects of globalization *do* in the world – and what else goes on with and around them. Finally, I think there is enormous analytic promise in tracing global interconnections without subsuming them to any one program of global-future commitments. A global framework allows one to consider the making and remaking of geographical and historical agents and the forms of their agency in relation to movement, interaction, and shifting, competing claims about community, culture, and scale. Places are made through their connections with each other, not their isolation: this kind of analysis seems too important to relegate only to studying the best-promoted "global" trends; indeed, among other uses, we can employ it to specify the uneven and contested global terrain of global promotion.

In this essay, I use these three directions of analysis to learn something about social science commitments to the newly emerging significance of a global scale. First, I examine the charisma of social science globalisms. By *globalism*, I refer to endorsements of the importance of the global. I want to know how the idea of the global has worked to excite and inspire social scientists. I pick out a number of elements that add to this charisma and argue for their obfuscating as well as enlivening features.

Second, to see how this charisma produces effects in the world, I examine reading and discussion practices in the field of anthropology, as these produce and reproduce commitments to globalization. As an observer, I try to track the excitement of my students and colleagues; yet, as a participant, I want to argue for a *better* use of the charisma of global frameworks.

Thus, third, I show how questions about global interconnections might be detached from the most problematic globalist commitments to offer a more nuanced and critical analysis of culture and history, including recent shifts that have turned attention to the global. I argue that we can investigate globalist projects and dreams without assuming that they remake the world just as they want. The task of understanding planet-wide interconnections requires locating and specifying globalist projects and dreams, with their contradictory as well as charismatic logics and their messy as well as effective encounters and translations.

Globalization draws our enthusiasm because it helps us imagine interconnection, travel, and sudden transformation. Yet it also draws us inside its rhetoric until we take its claims for true descriptions. In the imagery with which I began, flow is valorized but not the carving of the channel; national and regional units are mapped as the baseline of change without attention to their shifting and contested ability to define the landscape. We lose sight of the coalitions of claimants as well as their partial and shifting claims. We lose touch with the material and institutional components through which powerful and central sites are constructed, from which convincing claims about units and scales can be made. We describe the landscape imagined within these claims rather than the culture and politics of scale making. This essay suggests approaches to the study of the global that seem to me to hold onto the excitement of this endorsement of planetary interconnection without trading our critical stance for globalist wishes and fantasies.

Hurtling through Space

To invoke the global at the turn of the second millennium is to call attention to the speed and density of interconnections among people and places. In this imagery, the planet overwhelms us in its rush toward the future; we must either sit on top of it or be swamped and overcome.[1] It seems worth hesitating for a moment to consider the difference between this aggressive globe, hurtling through space, and an only slightly earlier fragile planet, floating gently in its cloud cover. This fertile yet vulnerable green planet was conjured by the global environmentalism that emerged in the United States and Europe at the end of the 1960s and blossomed in the 1970s, 1980s, and early 1990s. As Yaakov Garb (1990) has shown, the global environmentalists' globe gained its power from the visual image of the earth first seen in photographs from space in the 1960s; this awe-inspiring image was repeated in many forms and contexts to mobilize sentiment for the kind of nature that most needed our respect, love, and protection.[2] It became possible to imagine this nature as extending across the planet because global environmentalism brought together the universalist morality of 1960s social justice politics and the transboundary expertise of an emergent ecological science (Haas 1992; Taylor and Buttel 1992). Politics and science, working together, conjured an earth worth studying, managing, and fighting for at multiple but compatibly stratified scales and levels of advocacy and analysis.

Global environmentalism also participated in building another image of the global, in which globality represented the goal of a *process* of building transnational political and cultural ties. Beginning most intensely in the 1980s, social movements – including environmentalism, human rights, indigenous rights, and feminist causes – extended themselves through NGOs; they sought to work around the restrictions of nation-states by forging transnational lines of financial, scientific, and political support (Keck and Sikkink 1998). Activists put pressure on their respective governments with these resources; national policies were also pressed to respond to international agreements. The global here is a never-ending process of "networking" and building lines of support. Annelise Riles (1998b) has shown how the aesthetics of global network formation developed such charisma within NGOs that it became a major objective in itself. Global process here encourages participants to speak up, to learn from each other, and to extend themselves. But it does not yet push us over the edge of an evolutionary abyss.

It was only at the beginning of the 1990s that the process of "globalization," as the definitional characteristic of an *era*, became popular in the media and advertising. The triumph of the capitalist marketplace had been proclaimed with the dismantling of the Soviet Union, and enthusiasm ran high for national economic deregulation and privatization in the North and more thorough forms of structural adjustment in the South. In this atmosphere, *globalization* came to mean an endorsement of international free trade and the outlawing of protected or public domestic economies (Chomsky 1998). Yet the term came to encompass much more. Corporate reorganizations required not just markets but also the ability to transfer operations and finances transnationally to find the most profitable conditions; these kinds of corporate transfers, although reaching several decades back, became caught up in the talk of globalization. Furthermore, social commentators reminded the public that the new mobility of labor was tied to capital mobility and global market guarantees (e.g., Sassen 1998; Schiller et al. 1992). Cosmopolitan connoisseurs have delighted in the new availability of West African music, Brazilian martial arts, and Thai cuisine, as Southern arts blossomed in wealthy Northern cities (e.g., Appiah and Gates 1997). A variety of public debates and discussions came to be seen as "globally" interconnected: not only labor-and-capital-oriented fights about immigration, unionization, downsizing, subcontracting, and impoverishment but also debates about the worldwide spread of US media productions, the role of national governments, the dangers and promises of multiculturalism, and the growing influence and proper management of new computer-based communications technologies. Indeed, the popularity of "global" terms and approaches drew from their evocation of multiple causes, agendas, and historical layers of imagery.[3]

At the turn of the century, then, globalism is multireferential: part corporate hype and capitalist regulatory agenda, part cultural excitement, part social commentary and protest. Within this shifting agenda, several features attract and engage an expanding audience for imagining the globe: first, its futurism, that is, its ability not only to name an era but to predict its progress; second, its conflations of varied projects through which the populist and the corporate, the scientific and the cultural, the excluded margins and the newly thriving centers, all seem wrapped up in the same energetic movement; and, third, its rhetoric of linkage and circulation as the overcoming of boundaries and restrictions, through which all this excitement appears positive for everyone involved. These elements are worth examining separately.

Futurism

Globalization is a crystal ball that promises to tell us of an almost-but-not-quite-there globality. This is powerful stuff for experts, politicians, and policy makers. Social scientists are particularly caught by the force of this charisma. The rush of prescience returns social science to the period after World War II, when the field charted the development of the new nations of the South and, in the North, the welfare state. Since then, social scientists have been better known – like economists and sociologists – as technicians of the present or – like anthropologists and geographers – as collectors of ancient survivals. Now the opportunity has come to look forward with a new expertise. The crystal ball inspires us to rush anxiously into the future, afraid to be left behind.

The future orientation of this discussion of the global requires the assumption of newness. If global interconnections do not define the contemporary era, setting it off from the past, to examine these interconnections shows us complexity rather than direction. Analysts of globalization force attention to the break that differentiates the present from the past because in the context of that break they can see forward.[4] The assumption of newness has other benefits. It can help us see the distinctiveness of a historical moment. It can inspire a "bandwagon" effect whereby unexpected and creative alliances among different kinds of analysts may be forged.[5] In this spirit, it can break up too-comfortably established fields, inspiring new forms of discussion.[6]

However, the assumption of newness can also stifle other lines of inquiry and disallow questions about the construction of the field for which it forms the starting line. In history and anthropology, for example, the idea that global interconnections are *old* has only recently been revitalized, muffled as it was for much of the twentieth century by the draw of nationally contained legacies, in history, and functionally contained social worlds, in anthropology; it seems unfortunate to lose this insight so quickly.[7]

Perhaps the worst fault of the assumption of global newness is that it erects stereotypes of the past that get in the way of appreciating both the past and the present. This fault has been particularly glaring in the discussion of the nation inspired by talk of globalization.[8] In interpreting the defeat of various national attempts to control financial capital, analysts have imagined an unprecedented world-historical defeat of the nation, as if nations, until now, were unquestioned, consistent, and everywhere hegemonic. Yet national control of finance may itself have been a recent, ephemeral product. After World War II, economic regulations emerging from the Bretton Woods agreement made it possible for nation-states to control domestic financial capital, providing funding for welfare states. An earlier free-flowing internationalization of finance was cut off, as national capitalisms were set in place (Helleiner 1993).

Similarly, political commitment to national territorial boundaries and the importance of regulating population movements across national borders has a particular history. The new nation-states that emerged after World War II in Africa and Asia, for example, developed special concerns for territorial sovereignty to declare their autonomy from the colonial condition; their national histories and geographies stress self-development, not regional and transregional flow.[9] To turn nationalist visions from this period into a description of a homogeneous past seems likely to lead to distortions.

Given long-term commitments in the humanities to tracing intellectual lineages and civilizational commitments, it is perhaps surprising that literary critics have embraced the assumption of era-making global newness to put together anthologies on "the cultures of globalization" (Jameson and Miyoshi 1998).[10] The anthologies they have created are in many ways extremely exciting. Here are a variety of themes, a breadth of places discussed, and a diversity of scholars that form a striking intervention into the narrowly western, textual orientation of most humanities. This is not scholarship as usual; it has the political energy and passion of cultural studies. This development is so important that it is awkward to say anything else. But I am suspicious of cultural stage theories, with their determinations of who is at the peak of human evolution and who will be left behind. Without denying their contribution, it may be useful to question how the articles in these anthologies are connected to each other. To discuss globalization, the editors make the a priori assumption of a cultural political era.[11] The era must have a cultural logic, and the descriptions of culture gathered in the book must form part of that logic.[12] I think we can discuss global projects, links, and situations with a better frame: one that recognizes the making and unmaking of claims about the global, even as it examines the consequences of these powerful claims in the world we know, and one that recognizes new and surprising developments without declaring, by fiat, the beginning of an era.[13]

Yet global futurism is seductive. It can be conjured equally by a technical mathematics or by an enthusiastic and suggestive vagueness. Frederic Jameson (1998b: xi) is perhaps the most up-front about all this, claiming that questions about the definition of the global era to which he devotes his book are not only premature but decidedly uncool. Surely, we will find that the disparate cultural and political processes we investigate in these times will turn out to be the trunk, limbs, and tail of that elephant not recognized as a single beast by the blind men. He disarms critics: Anyone who has questions about the elephant must certainly be a curmudgeonly old elephant hater, who believes that there is nothing new under the sun; this exhausts, for him, the options for dissent (1998a: 54). And yet, might it not be a *newly* productive strategy to pay close and critical attention to these different limb-like global projects and agendas, to appreciate their articulations as well as their disengagements and mismatched encounters?

Conflations

Jameson (1998a) argues that globalization is best understood through the Hegelian dialectic: its ideological logic produces both a dark and a light side. This is a useful reminder that the global developments that we, as social commentators, find promising are often deeply connected to those we find dangerous. But why jump quite so quickly into the assumption that the vast array of transcommunal and transnational ideas and activities around us form a single ideological system? There are some important advantages. Overlaps among ideological projects produce an added intensity all around. When the machinery of corporate and state publicity has converged on a single image, it is doubly hard to avoid the sense of complicity, for better or worse. In analyzing recent developments, it would be silly to argue for autonomous institutional, regional, or political-cause domains. It is clear that the appreciation of synergy among varied globalist projects is at the heart of the new enthusiasm about the globe. My point is that this very search for overlaps, alliances, collaborations, and complicities is one of the most important phenomena we could study. We might look at how particular projects become formulated, how they are tied and transformed in the process, and how they sometimes interrupt each other despite themselves. The "globalization" that is formed from these hit-and-miss convergences would be considerably more unstable, and more interesting, than the one posited by any single claimant as a world-making system. One step in looking for this kind of globalization must be to recognize that there are varied agendas, practices, and processes that may or may not be deeply interconnected at a given historical moment.

Two recent studies of the cultural logic of global "network" formation are useful to compare in this regard. Roger Rouse (1997) analyzes a series of advertisements produced for the telephone company MCI that promote the company's ability to build an interactive multimedia communications network. This communication network is advertised as part of a world-changing, future-making revamping of space and time, in which instantaneous communications within a personalized web of ties will replace geographically grounded routes and central-place hierarchies. The "network" MCI promotes is simultaneously the material technology of telephones, computers, and the like and the individualized, flexible, transnational set of contacts and associates that citizens of the future will be able to maintain through these technologies.

A similar but contrasting global network-in-the-making is analyzed by Annelise Riles (1998b), who studied women's organizing in Fiji in preparation for the United Nations-sponsored international conference on women in Beijing in 1995. The women she studied had formed NGOs addressing gendered concerns; these organizations were connected to sister organizations, funders, and other kinds of political supporters all over the world. What they learned from this system of ties, Riles shows, is the importance of "networks," that is, webs of imagined interconnection through which groups in one area were to exchange information and support with other groups on what was seen as an egalitarian, voluntary basis. Riles argues that networks took on a formal aesthetic value and, through this formalism, the Fijian women organizers saw themselves as part of an emergent global process.[14]

These two globe-making projects have a lot in common. Both have educational goals to teach people to visualize a future globalism in which "networks" – rather than nations or bureaucracies – will be the organizing aesthetic. Both value personal contacts over long distances and individual initiative over the recognition of preset roles. Yet it is also clear that each project has come into being along a different historical trajectory, with different material and political resources and objectives, and their convergence is broken by those differences. As Rouse shows, MCI's presentation of its product as a "network" separates wealthy professionals (i.e., those in the network) from the underpaid workers and other poor people to whom they have some responsibility in the public space of the nation. Only through this separation can they build a constituency for the global mobility of corporate resources and the wealthy niche marketing of corporate products. The globalization this network promotes, then, is one that ties privileged consumers and their corporate sponsors in a self-conscious forgetting about the rest of the world. In contrast, the NGO networks discussed by Riles are intended to build a transnational women's solidarity that brings women's rights *into* particular national contexts rather than excluding network builders from participation in nations. Attention to national and regional "levels" of network building is supposed to strengthen the call of public responsibilities within these units rather than eviscerate them. Even as they bypass state bureaucracies, the women are called on to act as national representatives; in this capacity, Riles argues (1998a), the Fijian women bring national cultural sensibilities to the imagination of global network activities by focusing on a formal aesthetics grounded in other Fijian cultural work.

One further striking contrast between these two images of the network is their differential gender content. MCI's network, as Rouse explains it, rescues vulnerable young girls through the patriarchal security of a privatized globe. The Fijian women's NGO network creates new arenas of all-female sociality that draw on but extend local forms in transnational translations. The contrast provides rich grounds for thinking about emergent forms of subjectivity and agency in varied global projects. There is a lot going on, and it does not all match up. Were we to limit ourselves to one of these visions as a description of the new global landscape, we would miss the pleasures and dangers of this multiplicity. Furthermore, we might overvalorize connection and circulation rather than attending to the shifting, contested making of channels and landscape elements.

Circulation

Interconnection is everything in the new globalisms. And interconnection is created through circulation. Many things are said to circulate, ranging from people to money; cultures to information; and television programs, to international protocols, to the process called globalization itself. "Circulation" is in global rhetoric what the "penetration" of capitalism was in certain kinds of Marxist world-systems theory: the way powerful institutions and ideas spread geographically and come to have an influence in distant places. The difference is significant; where *penetration* always evokes a kind of rape, a forcing of some people's powerful interests onto other people, *circulation* calls forth images of the healthy flow of blood in the body and the stimulating, evenhanded exchange of the marketplace.

Both bodies and markets as models for understanding social process have been much criticized in social theory in the twentieth century. Images of society as organically interconnected like a body were important in establishing the social sciences, but they have been largely discredited as disallowing the study of power, meaning, conflict, disjuncture, and historical change. Images of society as a market have had a different kind of lasting power. Caught up in the endorsement of capitalism as an economic system and free trade as its ideal political context, they have been revived and given new authority in celebration of the end of communism and the Cold War. Marxist scholarship, however, continues a substantial record of criticism of these images. Market models assume a "level playing field" of exchange that erases the inequalities of property and the processes of labor exploitation. Market models appear to be inclusive, but they privilege social actors who, because of their economic resources, are able to participate in markets. Most importantly in the context of the post-Cold War enthusiasm for market models, Marxist scholars have shown how bourgeois governments and social institutions have promoted market thinking to naturalize class and other social distinctions. By training the attention of citizens on the equalities and opportunities of circulation and exchange, they justify policies of domination and discrimination. Recent endorsements of "global circulation" as the process for making the future partake in the obfuscations of inequality for which market models are known.

Global circulation is not just a rhetoric of corporate expansion, however. Leftist social commentators often find as much good use for circulation models as capitalist apologists. Circulation is used to discuss the breaking down of oppressive barriers among cultures, races, languages, and nations, including immigration restrictions and segregation policies. Diasporas circulate, bringing the wealth of their cultural heritage to new locations. Authoritarian regimes prevent the circulation of information, inspiring democratic movements to create underground channels of flow. The circulation of film inspires creative viewing practices. Circulation is thus tapped for the endorsement of multicultural enrichment, freedom, mobility, communication, and creative hybridity.

In part, the acceptability of circulation rhetoric among liberal and leftist social scientists derives from a self-conscious rejection of the Marxist emphasis on capitalist production and its consequent de-emphasis on market exchange and consumption (e.g., Appadurai 1986; Baudrillard 1975). Leftist critics of corporate globalization point to the importance of marketing and consumption in contemporary corporate strategies for reaching out to new fields of operation (e.g., Jameson 1998a); these are topics that need to be discussed. The growth of managerial and service professions (e.g., Ong 1999; Sassen 1998) also calls out to critics to abandon an exclusive analytic focus on factory production to attend to the variety of economic forms of contemporary capitalism.

The form and variety of capitalist economic activities are not, however, the only issues to raise about the use of the rhetoric of circulation as a ruling image for global interconnections. There are hidden relations of production here that may have nothing to do with labor in factories: the making of the objects and subjects who circulate, the channels of circulation, and the landscape elements that enclose and frame those channels. A focus on circulation shows us the movement of people, things, ideas, or institutions, but it does not show us how this movement depends on defining tracks and grounds or scales and units of agency. This blindness may not be inherent in the idea of circulation itself but, rather, may be caused by the kinds of circulations that have delineated the model. For historically layered political reasons, the model has been closed to attention to struggles over the terrain of circulation and the privileging of certain kinds of people as players. We focus on the money – the *ur* object of flow – instead of the social conditions that allow or encourage that flow. If we imagined creeks, perhaps the model would be different; we might notice the channel as well as the water moving.

In this spirit, Saskia Sassen (1998) has addressed channel making in relation to global circulations of corporate communications as well as labor. She argues that "global cities" have developed as centers for transnational corporate operations because of the density of corporate real estate, professional service workers, and telecommunication connection grids. Corporate rhetoric aspires to an infinite decentralization and deterritorialization of management operations, but this rhetoric ignores the material requirements for dispersed communication, for example, telephone and computer connections, as well as the specialized labor of advertising, finance, and other services, all of which is concentrated in particular cities. The much touted mobility of information, capital, products, and production facilities depends on these coordinating centers. Similarly, Sassen shows that immigration, often discussed as the mass product of individual mobility, requires the creation of institutional ties linking sending and receiving areas. Histories of direct foreign investment or military intervention, for example, have predictably produced flows of immigrants from the targeted regions to the United States. "Flow" is movement stimulated through political and economic channels.

Sassen's work shows that the alternatives to conventional models of circulation are not just to close off our attention to travel and trade. Analysts can also examine the material and institutional infrastructure of movement and pay special attention to the economic coercions and political guarantees that limit or promote circulation. In order to do this, however, we would need to redefine the common distinction between the "local" and the "global." Most commonly, globalist thinkers imagine the local as the stopping point of global circulations. It is the place where global flows are consumed, incorporated, and resisted (Pred and Watts 1992). It is the place where global flows fragment and are transformed into something place bound and particular (Wilson and Dissanayake 1996b). But if flow itself always involves making terrain, there can be no territorial distinctions between the "global" transcending of place and the "local" making of places. Instead, there is place making – and travel – all around, from New York to New Guinea.[15]

Place making is always a cultural as well as a political-economic activity. It involves assumptions about the nature of those subjects authorized to participate in the process and the kinds of claims they can reasonably put forth about their position in national, regional, and world classifications and hierarchies of places. The specificities of these subjects and claims contradict and misstate those of other place makers, even as they may form overlaps and links imaged as "flows." The channel-making activity of circulation, then, is always a contested and tentative formation of scales and landscapes. To avoid letting those who imagine themselves as winners call all of the terms, we need to attend to the missed encounters, clashes, misfires, and confusions that are as much part of global linkages as simple "flow."

Culture, specificity, and place making have conventionally been the domain of the discipline of anthropology, particularly as practiced in the United States. Because these kinds of issues are so often missing from discussions of the global, the stakes are particularly high in seeing their incorporation into global questions in anthropology. Yet it is not these issues that first chaperoned globalism into US anthropology. Instead, the charisma of the global was introduced to forward a disciplinary transition away from an overzealous and nonreflective localism. It is from the perspective of this trajectory that it is possible to examine the specific disciplinary practices through which globalist frameworks are being read by US anthropologists.

Readings in Anthropology

Social science globalisms take particular forms in relation to disciplinary reading and discussion practices. They gain their influence not only because they are adopted in the work of articulate practitioners but, equally importantly, because they enter local trajectories of disciplinary momentum. They are rebuilt to speak to disciplinary challenges as these, in turn, are understood in relation to specific social locations of scholarly practice. In the process, social science globalisms pick up regional and disciplinary frameworks and assumptions, even as they throw themselves as objections against others.

Anthropologists do not merely mimic the understandings of globalism of other experts, even as they are influenced by them. No anthropologist I know argues that the global future will be culturally homogeneous; even those anthropologists most wedded to the idea of a new global era imagine this era as characterized by "local" cultural diversity. Disciplinary concern with cultural diversity overrides the rhetoric of global cultural unification pervasive elsewhere, even though, for those in its sway, globalism still rules: diversity is generally imagined as forming a reaction or a backdrop to the singular and all-powerful "global forces" that create a new world. (Globalisms are not themselves regularly regarded as diverse.) Politically progressive anthropologists sometimes show how this kind of circumscribed, reactive, self-consciously "local" diversity is a form of resistance to the proliferation of globalist capitalism and hypermodernist governmentality; however, the possibility that capitalisms and governmentalities are themselves situated, contradictory, effervescent, or culturally circumscribed is much less explored. Anthropologists who have argued against simplistic models of "global culture" have also, then, naturalized globalist ideologies of the global.

In the United States, the excitement of this globalism for anthropologists draws from a rather "local" disciplinary heritage: a more than 25-year journey away from analyses of "cultures" as autonomous, self-generating, and bounded entities. In the 1960s and 1970s, US anthropologists criticized the discipline's complicity with colonial projects of conquest and administration. Historical, anticolonial, and world-systems frameworks moved to the discipline's center, ousting functionalism, and interpretive accounts of national and nationalist commitments replaced descriptions of isolated cultures. In the 1980s, ethnographic research and description were interrogated for their role in making cultures appear isolated, and US anthropologists recommitted themselves to more open, reflexive, and textually responsive ways of approaching the inequalities and interconnections among people and places. The recent turn to the global takes its alignment within this pathway of disciplinary self-criticism.

Globalism within this trajectory renews stereotypes of the anthropological past in order to confront them. The "old" anthropology imagined here describes cultures so grounded that they could not move out of place. This anthropology imprisons its objects in a cell; interconnection and movement in the form of "global flows" are thus experienced as a form of liberation. Furthermore, these flows fit most neatly inside the discipline when, in deference to past teachers and conventions, the boundedness of past cultures goes unchallenged; global flows can then take the discipline, and the world, into a freer future.

This "freeing up" variety of globalism is both exhilarating and problematic. On the one hand, it shows us new dreams and schemes of world making; on the other, as an aspect of its liberatory project, it also turns attention away from the quirky eccentricities of culture and history that have perhaps been US anthropology's most vital contribution to critical thought. In the process, too, anthropologists tend to endorse the globalist dreams of the people they study, and thus we lose the opportunity to address the located specificity of those globalist dreams.

The three features I have discussed as creating the charisma of social science globalisms are prominent in US anthropology. Each has been endorsed for good "local" reasons. Yet the very enthusiasm that each of these features has provoked has made it easier to erase specificities to create a misleading portrait of a single global future. It is hard not to universalize a globalist framework. But let me see if I can locate these globalisms – and in the process get them to do some very different work.

Futurism

US anthropologists come to an endorsement of a singular global future from their interest in the macroeconomic context of cultural diversity. An important part of the disciplinary trajectory away from the study of isolated cultures has been attention to the capitalist world system. Anthropologists have been able to show how even out-of-the-way and exotic cultures respond to capitalism's challenges. This is crucial work. At the same time, risks and dilemmas remain in this analysis: In turning one's gaze to the systemic features of world capitalism, it is easy to lose track of the specificity of particular capitalist niches. In coming to terms with the transnational scope of contemporary finance, marketing, and production, it is easy to endorse globalism as a predictive frame. Indeed, it is in this context that anthropologists most commonly imagine singular global futures. Even as critics, we are caught in the hyperboles imagined by advocates of neoliberalism, structural adjustment, and transnationalization.

Particularly in its critical versions, this global future forms part of a narrative of the evolution of capitalism. Furthermore, most anthropologists attracted by this narrative take their model from a single source: David Harvey's *The Condition of Postmodernity* (1989). Within much globalist anthropology, Harvey's book establishes the fact of epochal change, laying the ground for global futurism. Yet I find this a particular, peculiar reading of Harvey, and it is worth considering in its own right: For anthropologists, Harvey provides the evidence for a new era. As readers, they pick out "flexible specialization" and "time-space compression" as the characteristics of this new era.[16]

Yet, when I turn to Harvey's book, it seems to me that the central argument is that the "cultural aesthetic" of postmodernism is related to the economic logic of flexible accumulation. The first section of the book reviews modernism and postmodernism as trends in the arts and letters, including architecture and philosophy. This is "capital C" culture: a genealogy of great men and their ideas. The second section of the book turns to the economic "regimes of accumulation" of Fordism and post-Fordist "flexible accumulation." The book's original idea is to juxtapose these two bodies of literature and to argue that postmodernism mirrors post-Fordism. It takes a certain amount of economic determinism to make this argument, in which Culture acts as a mirror of economic realities.[17] But in this gap, space and time come in. For Harvey, the "experience" of space and time mediates between Culture and the (nonculturally organized) economy.

For me the space and time section is the least satisfying section of the book. Harvey describes categories for understanding human encounters with space and time, representations of space and time in the arts and letters (and, in one chapter, in two films), and anecdotes about space and time in the capitalist workplace. No ethnographic sources for understanding spatial and temporal texture or diversity are consulted. The concept of "experience" is never explained. Because the mirror relation between arts and letters and the economy has already been established, their mediation by experience is a formal requirement, needing no substantiation.

In this context, it is strange that anthropologists so often pick only "the acceleration of space-time compression" along with "flexible accumulation" out of this book. In the process of citation, too, the book's tone changes. Harvey's book is polemical. He ranges over a wide variety of scholarship to criticize postmodern aesthetics. This is not a science experiment but, rather, a book-length essay. Yet somehow Harvey's description of economic evolution comes to have the status of a fact when drawn into globalist anthropology. Harvey brings with him the ability to read economics, a skill few anthropologists have developed. It may be that anthropologists ignore the discussion of aesthetics, thinking they know more about culture than he does, and go for the accumulation strategy and associated space-time requirements because they feel like the macroeconomic facts that are outside of their knowledge base.

The result is that a selection of Harvey's terms is used to build a noncultural and nonsituated futurist framework, "beyond culture" (Gupta and Ferguson 1992). One set of problems derives from the attempt to make this future global; as anthropologist Michael Kearney admits, Harvey's thesis is "not dealing with globalization per se" (1995: 551). Indeed, Harvey has a distinct blindness for everything outside dominant Northern Cultures and economies; to make his story applicable to North–South articulations is not impossible, but it is a challenge. Another set of problems seems even more intractable. If we drop Harvey's discussion of aesthetics (as Culture) but still ignore the ethnographic sources through which anthropologists identify culture, just how do we know the shape of space and time? The pared-down Harvey readings preferred by anthropologists have lost even literary and filmic representations of temporal and spatial processes; we are left with economic facts. Without "Culture" or "culture," we must assume rapid circulation, fragmentation, compression, and globality; certainly, we cannot consult either popular or official representations, discourses, or cultural practices. Anthropological analysis, which could look at scale-making claims and representations in conjunction with the social processes that support and result from those claims and representations, becomes reduced to building starships on millennial fantasies.

Another way Harvey's work could be used is to scale back its epochal claims to look at some limited but powerful alliances between aesthetics and economics. Harvey's claim that postmodernism and flexible accumulation have something to do with each other could be pursued by locating patterns and players more specifically. This kind of project, however, diminishes the excitement of another globalist reading practice, which I have called "conflations". Let me examine how this practice both brings to life and impoverishes the anthropology of global interconnection.

Conflations

Not all anthropological globalism is engaged in understanding the systemics of capitalism; another significant sector attempts to hold onto "culture" as an anthropological object while showing its increased contemporary mobility and range. In this genre, anthropologists have done exciting work to specify modes of cultural interconnection that tie people in far-flung locales or travel with them across heterogeneous terrains. This work offers the possibility of attention to regionalisms and histories of place making within an appreciation of interconnection. However, to the extent that this work has been harnessed for the search for a singular anthropological globalism, it has blurred the differences among places and perspectives to emphasize the break from past localisms. This anthropological globalism renaturalizes global dreams instead of examining and locating them ethnographically. Moreover, it leads readers to assume that all globalisms are at base the same; thus, most readers read globalist anthropologists as an undifferentiated crowd.

Might a different kind of reading practice reestablish the potential for appreciating multiple, overlapping, and sometimes contradictory globalisms? Consider, for example, contrasts among the globalisms of Ulf Hannerz (1996), Michael Kearney (1996), and Arjun Appadurai (1996). I choose these authors because each has elaborated his ideas about globalism in a book-length exposition. Each sees his work as advancing the disciplinary trajectory of anthropology beyond the anthropology of separate, segregated cultures and societies. Each is concerned with migrants and travelers and the worlds they make and are made by; each argues that new analytic tools are necessary for new times.

Yet they conjure different global geographies. The globality of Hannerz, the "global ecumene" (1989), is a space of interaction among once-separate cultures now growing in dialogue and mutual acknowledgment. Its creolization is created by cultural flows – particularly flows from powerful centers to less powerful peripheries; it is carried and extended by cosmopolitans who, of necessity, acknowledge and extend European and North American cultural frameworks even as they incorporate and remake non-western cultures. Center–periphery relations thus organize world culture (Hannerz 1996).

In contrast, Kearney's postmodern globality is a critique of center–periphery frameworks, which Kearney identifies with the classificatory modernist era that has passed away as we have entered transnational hyperspace and nonteleological, postdevelopmental time. The key feature of the global era is the "implosion" of center and periphery, as distinctions between rural and urban as well as South and North disintegrate. Spatial and cultural discriminations become impossible in a world of global flows, as nonunitary migrant subjects are formed in the interstices of past classificatory principles. In the unruly "reticula" Kearney conjures, however, he retains a dialogue with Marxian political economy that gives his multiplicity of identities and geographies its shape. The organization of the transnational economy creates differences of class, power, and value that forge subaltern and dominant social niches of identity and agency.

In contrast again, Appadurai evokes a globality of contested "scapes" in which no single organizing principle rules. "Financescapes," which include capital flows, are only one of several imaginative geographies that compete to make the globe; Appadurai finds that "ethnoscapes" and "mediascapes" – the cultural worlds conjured by migrants and in movies, respectively – are more decisive features in the "rupture" of the global era, with its heightened dependence on the imagination. Like Kearney's, Appadurai's globalism refuses center–periphery frames, but, like Hannerz, he situates it squarely in modernity's worldwide cultural spread rather than postmodernism's epistemological disruptions. Appadurai's globalism refuses Kearney's sociology of migrants to foreground their cultural worlds; indeed, these kinds of cultural terrains, although ungrounded in space, are those criticized by Kearney as modernist classificatory tricks.

Different subjects are at the center of each of these understandings of the global. In the best spirit of anthropology, one might read each account, indeed, in relation to the author's ethnographic experience. Appadurai imagines global scapes from the perspective of his attention to the Indian diaspora and its cultural world. Kearney theorizes from his encounter with Mixtec "postpeasants": Mexican Indian farmers who have become migrants selling crafts in San Diego parking lots. Hannerz is concerned about cosmopolitans, world travelers, journalists, and city people everywhere; he returns often to his knowledge about Africa. These varied subjects assist the authors in evoking different globalisms. If, instead of assuming a single global trajectory, we attended to varied globalist claims and perspectives, what might we see?

Diasporas, almost by definition, conjure deterritorialized areas, worlds of meaning and "home" feeling detached from original territorial boundaries – like Appadurai's scapes. This kind of self-consciousness about the making of cultural worlds contrasts sharply with the cultural commitments of cosmopolitans and poor migrants, as these create focal knowledges for Hannerz and Kearney, respectively. Both cosmopolitans and poor migrants erase the specificity of their cultural tracks, although for different reasons: Poor migrants need to fit in the worlds of others; cosmopolitans want more of the world to be theirs. Cosmopolitans, like diasporas, promote projects of world making, but, as Hannerz stresses, the projects they endorse enlarge the hegemonies of Northern centers even as they incorporate peripheries. In contrast, neither the world-making projects of Southern diasporas nor those of poor migrants fit into a center–periphery frame. They limit, rather than spread, Northern hegemonies. In this spirit, Appadurai and Kearney implicitly criticize Hannerz's center–periphery approach. Yet it is also the case that Kearney's and Appadurai's actors diverge. Poor migrants, like those at the center of Kearney's globalism, are particularly aware of their need to survive – politically, economically, and culturally – in worlds that others have made; the imagination is never enough for them to create autonomy and self-determination. Thus, Kearney (1995: 553) refuses Appadurai's imagination-ruled scapes, while Appadurai and Hannerz, thinking through diasporas and cosmopolitans, respectively, stress the world-making power of imaginative perspectives.

The regional specificities of these focal knowledges may also be relevant to the globalisms imagined through them: I think of the strength of the culture and media industries of India and its diaspora, the self-consciousness about Northern cultural impositions of cosmopolitan Africans, and the centrality of transnational capitalism in Latin American studies. It also may be suggestive to compare all these knowledges with other angles for thinking about contemporary culture. Consider, for example, US minority groups who have demanded protection from the nation-state against discrimination; thinking through US minority culture provides a less fertile ground than diasporas, poor migrants, and cosmopolitans to imagine an inclusively postnational era.[18] These differences do not make these perspectives wrong; my point is to show that these are differences that matter theoretically. The next step for readers – and future researchers and writers – is to think about that world in which the respective focal knowledges on which they draw could *all* exist, whether in competition or alliance, in mutual acknowledgment or erasure, in misunderstanding or dialogue.

This task requires that we study folk understandings of the global, and the practices with which they are intertwined, rather than representing globalization as a transcultural historical process. With some modifications, each of the perspectives I have been describing can be used for this task. However, we would have to resituate the authors' theories in relation to histories of their respective knowledges of and experiences with specific people and events. We would have to abandon the search for a single global future.

Appadurai's stress on disjunction as well as on the importance of the imagination is well suited for thinking about the interplay of varied globalist perspectives. Yet imaginative landscapes come in many kinds, and this diversity is more useful to understanding disjunction than a division into functional domains of ethnicity, technology, finance, media, and ideology, for these posit a singular formula for "society." If, instead of hegemonic domain divisions, we turned to the social and cultural struggles through which imaginative visions come to count as "scapes" at all, we might be able to incorporate disjunction not only among domains but also among varied and contested kinds of imaginative landscape making in this framework. We might contrast the cultural world of the Indian diaspora with other globalist scapes. For example, Paulla Ebron (1998, 1999) has described the regional and global claims of African American history and memory landscapes; she traces these landscapes through many formats of discussion, which both enter and interrupt Appadurai's "mediascape" domain. Moving beyond a list of globally settled "scapes," we need to study how scales, geographies, eras, and other imaginative terrains are differentially and dialogically negotiated, refused, or erased.

Hannerz's attention to the cultural specificity of cosmopolitanisms is important to assess the power and limitations of claims about scale, era, and geography without subsuming one's own analysis under the truths these claims promote. Hannerz also usefully reminds us of the power of certain imaginative landscapes, especially those that "make people from western Europe and North America feel as much at home as possible" (1996: 107). Yet these powerful perspectives do not necessarily determine the cultural evolution of the whole world; the key is to *situate* them in relation to the political economies that make them possible and the struggles over meaning in which they participate.

In the process of putting global perspectives in situated dialogue, the political economy engaged (if not often endorsed) by Kearney is essential. Imaginative landscapes mobilize an audience through material and institutional resources. Yet, as discussed in the previous section, it is difficult to give full attention to such mobilizations with a theory of the singular evolution of a monolithic capitalism.[19] As J. K. Gibson-Graham (1996) argues, models that predict the stages of capitalism bow to the ideology of a single world-capitalist system rather than investigating its heterogeneous complexities. Instead, Kearney's concern with political economy, like that of Harvey, might point us toward an investigation of shifting cultural developments among surprisingly diverse capitalisms. The innovations of these approaches are not served well, however, by an overreliance on a vocabulary of "flows."

Circulation

Circulation has a deep genealogy in anthropology. I keep waiting to find an author who takes me through this legacy, perhaps tracing his or her thoughts from French structuralist "exchange" through global "flows." But I have not yet found that author. Instead, it has become easy for anthropologists to talk about global circulations as a sign of everything new and of future making.

Circulations are said to be what we are able to study as global. George Marcus is informative and clear about this in the introduction to the series of essays he edited as *Rereading Cultural Anthropology* (1992). Under the heading "Circulations," he says,

The other major related trend that concerns contemporary global transformations is a move out from local situations to understand how transcultural processes themselves are constituted in the world of the so-called "system" (modern interlocking institutions of media, markets, states, industries, universities – the worlds of elites and middle classes) that has encapsulated, transformed, and sometimes obliterated local cultures. This work examines the circulation of cultural meanings, objects, and identities in diffuse time-space. *It shows how the global arena is itself constituted by such circulations.* (1992: xiii, emphasis added)

Circulations define the newness of the global epoch. Kearney's review "The Local and the Global: The Anthropology of Globalization and Transnationalism" (1995) offers a useful statement of this. His field is the study of movement, both population movement and "the movement of information, symbols, capital, and commodities in global and transnational spaces.... Special attention is given to the significant contemporary increases in the volume and velocity of such flows for the dynamics of communities and for the identities of their members" (p. 547).

Newness is defined by increased flow. Because authors and readers focus on the excitement of this newness, there has been almost no discussion about the implied dichotomies here: circulation versus stagnation, new versus old. Does the newness and globality of movement mean that once-immobile "local" places have recently been transcended by "global" flow? If analysts must "move out of local situations" to find circulation, there must be some local folks who are still stuck inside them, being stagnant. These imagined stagnant locals are excluded from the new circulating globality, which leaves them outside, just as progress and modernity were imagined as leaving so many behind. Here we must consider which new Orientalisms will define who is in and who is out of circulation, just as frameworks of race, region, and religion defined those excluded from the idea of progress. Furthermore, if circulation is new, does that mean that the old order was static and segregated? Were there really, after all, isolated autonomous cultures out there until the circulations of the last few years? Each of these misleading dichotomies would encourage analysts to resurrect that very anthropology that has been criticized and reworked for the last twenty-five years: the anthropology that fixed and segregated cultures. But in each case, it would be resurrected only for special cases: the marginal, the past. A globalist anthropology of movement would reign at the center.[20] This will not do. To move beyond the contrast between past and local stability and present/future global flow, we need to examine different modes of regional-to-global interconnection.

The new attention to global circulation responds to real changes in the world – and in anthropology as practiced in the United States. Anthropologists once set out to study "communities"; they thought they could find society and culture within a relatively narrowly defined social sphere. For some years, it has seemed difficult to do anthropology without paying attention to much wider-ranging objects of study: national visions, elite networks, popular culture, social movements, state policies, histories of colonial thinking, and much more. One piece of the excitement of contemporary anthropology involves new ideas about how to do fieldwork on these complex objects. We rush into interdisciplinary social theory to find innovative, project-oriented suggestions. In this process, it is easy to endorse frameworks of globalization that transcend the limitations of site-oriented local research. Instead, I am arguing that we can study the landscape of circulation as well as the flow. How are people, cultures, and things remade as they travel?

Scale as an Object of Analysis

Understanding the institutional proliferation of particular globalization projects requires a sense of their cultural specificities as well as the travels and interactions through which these projects are reproduced and taken on in new places. In thinking about where one would begin a globally informed investigation of local and global processes that avoids the pitfalls I have been discussing, I might begin with two analytic principles. First, I would pay close attention to *ideologies* of scale, that is, cultural claims about locality, regionality, and globality; about stasis and circulation; and about networks and strategies of proliferation. I would track rhetorics of scale as well as contests over what will count as relevant scales. Second, I would break down the units of culture and political economy through which we make sense of events and social processes. Instead of looking for world-wrapping evolutionary stages, logics, and epistemes, I would begin by finding what I call "projects," that is, relatively coherent bundles of ideas and practices as realized in particular times and places. The choice of what counts as a project is to maintain a commitment to localization, even of the biggest world-making dreams and schemes. The various instantiations of capitalism can be regarded as projects; so can progressive social movements, everyday patterns of living, or university-based intellectual programs. Projects are to be traced in relation to particular historical travels from one place to another; they are caught up in local issues of translation and mobilization; although they may be very powerful, we cannot assume their ability to remake nature and society according to their visions. Projects may articulate with each other, creating moments of fabled stability and power (see Tsing 1999c, 2000). They may also rub up against each other awkwardly, creating messiness and new possibilities. Through joint attention to ideologies of scale and projects of scale making, it is possible to move into those cracks most neglected by unselfconscious reliance on global futurism, globalist conflation, and global circulation.

To illustrate such cracks, I turn to scholarship on the making of projects of environmental modernization. Although the rhetoric of globalization has much affected the reconstruction of cities, it is the rhetoric of modernization that continues to make rural hinterlands into the kinds of places that global capital and globalist planning can best use for their projects. Talk of national and international development still dominates the reshaping of the countryside; yet it is the complement of globalization talk. Global dreams require these rural modernization projects, and, thus, globalist strategies can be studied within them. Indeed, there are certain advantages of tracking the importance of globalism in an arena where this rhetoric does not amass a difficult-to-question hegemony.[21] It is easier to see the exotic particularities and the grounded travels of scale-making commitments where these are not the only goal of the scholarship. It is possible to read against the grain of analysis of modernism to make scale an object of analysis. I offer four examples of such starting points.

Scale making. Certainly, a key issue in assuming a critical perspective on global claims and processes is the making of scales – not just the global but also local and regional scales of all sorts. Through what social and material processes and cultural commitments do localities or globalities come, tentatively, into being? How are varied regional geographies made real? Globalism's automatic association of particular scales with particular eras makes it very difficult to notice the details and idiosyncrasies of scale making – thus, the more reason to foreground this issue. And, because the globe is a region made large, asking about the making of global scale brings forward questions of the various forms of region making that both facilitate and interrupt global claims.

Critical studies of environmental modernization offer a number of useful examples about how social scientists might approach the investigation of regional and global scale making. "Bioregions" have been a central feature of environmental policy; how are they made? I think of Warwick Anderson's (in press) research on the hygiene-oriented experiments that helped define "the tropics" as a zone of challenge for scientific modernism, or of Peter Haas's (1990) discussion of the transnational strategies of scientists in shaping the cross-border political treaties that made "the Mediterranean" a zone in which issues of water pollution could be addressed. And what of the making of the global superregion? Richard Grove's (1995) research on the construction of global environmental science is particularly exciting in thinking about the makings of globality. Grove shows how the imperial placement of scientists in botanical gardens and research stations across the European colonies inspired continent-crossing correspondence in the late eighteenth century. Through this correspondence, informed by widespread fears of climate change caused by colonial deforestation, colonial scientists formulated notions of a "global" climate. This commitment to planet-wide environmental process allowed further developments in imagining both science and policy on a global scale. Obviously, this is not the only global scale that matters. But in tracing its specificity, Grove offers a model for thinking about the many kinds of globality that have become important in the contemporary world.

Close encounters. Where circulation models have tended to focus only on message transmission, one might instead investigate interactions involving collaboration, misunderstanding, opposition, and dialogue. Attention to these processes provides an alternative to the conflation of varied scale-making claims, projects, and agents. One literature that has become unusually attentive to mixed encounters is the literature on transnational social movements, which require coalitions among extremely various kinds of people, with disparate goals and perceptions of the issues at hand (e.g., Keck and Sikkink 1998). Thus, for example, the coalitions that have been built for rain forest protection have brought together tribal leaders, union organizers, college professors, wildlife lovers, rural workers, cosmetic entrepreneurs, and activists for democratic reform, among others (see Brosius 1999, in press; Keck 1995; Tsing 1999a; Turner 1999).

To understand even momentary successes of this kind of motley coalition, analysts must attend to the changing definitions of *interests* and *identity* that both allow and result from collaborative activities. They must focus on the historical specificity of the events that resulted in alliance and the open-ended indeterminacy of the regional processes stimulated by that alliance (Tsing 1999b). These are useful reminders in rethinking transnational interactions.

It is not just in transient and defensive social movements, however, that it is important to look for social processes sparked by coalitions, dialogues, missed messages, and oppositional refusals. In considering developments in transnational capitalism, this kind of attention can offer an alternative to the blindfolded dedication to a singular unfolding economic logic that has characterized so much globalist analysis. If we investigate the series of historically specific collaborations that create distinctive cultural forms of capitalism, we might better appreciate global heterogeneity.

Peter Dauvergne (1997), for example, has shown how Japanese trading companies, requiring a mass scale of transactions, were able to form productive coalitions with national political leaders in Southeast Asia, who were seeking the support of powerful clients; together they created the distinctive features of the Southeast Asian timber industry, which has devastated regional rain forests for cheap plywood. The cultural and economic specificities of both Japanese trading companies and Southeast Asian national political regimes created a particular and peculiar capitalism that cannot be reduced to the playing out of a singular transnational capitalist logic. Instead, Dauvergne argues, it created economic and ecological "shadows" between Japan and Southeast Asia that redefined and reformulated their separate and combined regional agency. This kind of analysis should prove useful in understanding the many forms of capitalism that help to create regional and global scales.

Definitional struggles.   Circulation imagery can draw attention away from the transformation of actors, objects, goals, perspectives, and terrains that characterizes regional-to-global interaction. Instead, we might pay special attention to the roles of both cultural legacies and power inequalities in creating the institutional arenas and assumptions of world-making transitions. Every globalization project is shaped from somewhat unpredictable interactions among specific cultural legacies. Furthermore, the cultural frames and assumptions of globalization projects cannot be understood without attention to multiple levels of political negotiations, with their idiosyncratic and open-ended histories. "Definitional struggles" call attention to how these arenas are designed and the politics of their development. They can remind us that globalization both requires and exceeds the work of particularly positioned and repositioned globalizers.

Critical studies of environmental modernization can also provide illustrative guidance here. Consider, for example, how agribusiness came to power in the western United States. Donald Worster's (1985) study of the building of the great irrigation projects that stimulated the emergence of agribusiness offers a wealth of detail on the interacting cultural legacies that made the scale and design of these massive irrigation projects possible.[22] The wide streets of Mormon aesthetics inspired irrigation design, breaking it away from Hispanic community water control; the legal precedence of California gold rush mineral claims allowed the florescence of water law that privileged state–private coalitions; the opportunity for water engineers to tour the irrigation canals of British colonial India created a parallel vision for the western United States in which the landscape should properly be managed by alien experts. Compromises between populists and business advocates congealed center-oriented land allocation policies. These, and more, legacies shaped the design of the great water apparatus that transformed the US economy, bringing profitable farming from east to west and helping to build US imperial strength.

Not just definition but also struggle is at issue in the formation of projects of world transformation. Studies of the formation of the "frontier" in Amazonia, for example, could be told as the classic story of modernization, with its replacement of native traditional living spaces with cosmopolitan modern economies. But critical histories by scholars such as Hecht and Cockburn (1989) and Schmink and Wood (1992) have shown that the cultural assumptions of property and resource management that modernizers might want us to take for granted have been established unevenly, awkwardly, and tentatively, in the midst of passionate and unfinished struggles. Hecht and Cockburn stress the historically shifting wielders of power who have worked so hard, with varied success, for particular programs of frontier making. Schmink and Wood stress the uncanniness of the frontier, in which the best laid plans produce results opposite to their predictions. The works show varied histories at community, regional, and national scales; their components do not fit easily into a single story. Together, they highlight definitional struggles involved in making the frontier.

Concrete trajectories and engagements.   In contrast to the abstract globe conjured by social science globalism, the scholarship I am imagining would stress the concreteness of "movements" in both senses of the word: social mobilizations in which new identities and interests are formed, and travels from one place to another through which place-transcending interactions occur. These two senses of *movement* work together in remaking geographies and scales. Tracing them concretely offers more insight into planetary complexity than the endorsement of a heterogeneous globalism whose features ricochet helplessly between an imagined spreading global dynamism and its contained local Other.

How might this be done? A number of scholars have followed modern forestry, as developed in Europe, to examine its deployment in colonial regions. Here I am less interested in the metropole-to-colony transfer and more in the movement from one particular place to another, say of British forest science to India. Ramachandra Guha (1989), Ravi Rajan (1994), and K. Sivaramakrishnan (1996) have all done important research on this movement, as it made and transformed forestry experts, forest-dwelling human communities, and forests themselves. Each tells of the effects of this movement: the development of colonial authority relations, involving dissent and opposition as well as compliance, between forest experts and forest peasants; the importance of reaffirming cultural and scientific standards in empire-wide conferences; the incorporation of local knowledges into Indian forestry policy; and the changing practices of foresters as they learned the Indian landscape and its social and political conventions. The concrete sites of encounter and engagement among people as well as trees shape the trajectories of the forestry project. This kind of attention to particular "routes" of travel (Clifford 1997) is equally important in tracing contemporary social and cultural processes around the globe.

In globalization theories, we have confused what should be *questions* about the global ramifications of new technologies and social processes with *answers* about global change. Each of the starting points I have suggested offers an attempt to reverse this globalist thinking to turn concerns about the global back into researchable questions.

Release

Let me return for a moment to the parallels between modernization and globalization. Many anthropologists are able to look at the dreams and schemes of modernization with a critical distance. We need this critical distance, too, in studying globalization. Globalization is a set of projects that require us to imagine space and time in particular ways. These are curious, powerful projects. Anthropologists need not ignore them; we also need not renaturalize them by assuming that the terms they offer us are true.

At this point, some readers may say, "Why not throw out 'the global' completely, since it exists as a fantasy?" My answer is that even fantasies deserve serious engagement. The best legacies of ethnography allow us to take our objects of study seriously even as we examine them critically. To study ghosts ethnographically means to take issues of haunting seriously. If the analyst merely made fun of beliefs in ghosts, the study would be of little use. Several other steps would be needed: a description of ghost beliefs; an examination of the effects of ghost beliefs on social life; and, in the spirit of taking one's informants seriously, a close attention to the questions that ghosts raise, such as the presence of death and its eerie reminders of things gone. In the same spirit, an analyst of globalism cannot merely toss it out as a vacant deception. Instead, an ethnographic study of the global needs careful attention not only to global claims and their effects on social life but also to questions of interconnection, movement, and boundary crossing that globalist spokespeople have brought to the fore. To take globality as an object of study requires both distance and intimate engagement.

Other readers may object that it is important to reify globalization because of the terrible toll it promises to take on cultural diversity and human well-being. Their endorsement of a self-consciously paranoid vision of total transformation involves the choice to glimpse the terrors of the new world order it promises. Yet I would argue that by reproducing this totalizing framework of social change, critics bind themselves within the assumptions and fantasies of those they oppose. If we want to imagine emergent forms of resistance, new possibilities, and the messiness through which the best laid plans may not yet destroy all hope, we need to attune ourselves to the heterogeneity and open-endedness of the world.

This is not, however, an argument for "local" diversity; if anything, it is an argument for "global" diversity and the wrongheadedness of imagining diversity –

from an unquestioning globalist perspective – as a territorially circumscribed, "place-based," and antiglobalist phenomenon. (Since when are globalists not place based?) Unlike most anthropologists working on "global" issues, I have tried to examine some basic assumptions of globalism, using them to form a critical perspective rather than a negative or positive endorsement of projects for making a future imagined as global.

Most global anthropologists embrace the idea of diversity. Anthropologists have been critics of theories of global homogenization; at the same time, those who have joined the argument with globalization theorists have been influenced by the terms of debate to accept most of the premises of these theories in order to join the conversation. The debate about global cultural unification has encouraged anthropologists to agree that we are indeed entering an era properly called global, although that era, according to anthropologists, is characterized by local cultural divergences as much as unification. In the embrace of the argument, the cultural divergence we find must be part of the globalist phenomenon.[23]

This is not, I think, a useful place to be stuck. To get out of its grip, analysts need to give up several of the tools and frames we have found most easy to work with, perhaps because they resound so nicely with popular "common sense," at least in the United States. First, we might stop making a distinction between "global" *forces* and "local" *places*. This is a very seductive set of distinctions, promising as it does to give us both focused detail and the big picture, and I find myself slipping into this vocabulary all the time. But it draws us into globalist fantasies by obscuring the ways that the cultural processes of all "place" making and all "force" making are *both* local and global, that is, both socially and culturally particular and productive of widely spreading interactions. Through these terms, global "forces" gain the power to cause a total rupture that takes over the world.

Second, we might learn to investigate new developments without assuming either their universal extension or their fantastic ability to draw all world-making activities into their grasp. International finance, for example, has surely undergone striking and distinctive transformations [since the early 1970s]. Certainly this has effects everywhere, but what these effects are is unclear. It seems unlikely to me that a single logic of transformation is being produced – or a singular moment of rupture.[24]

Third, globalisms themselves need to be interrogated as an interconnected, but not homogeneous, set of projects – with their distinctive cultural commitments and their powerful but limited presence in the world. Critical studies of modernization projects provide some thought-provoking examples of analytic direction here.

Freed up in these ways, it might be possible to attend to global visions without imagining their world hegemony. Outside the thrall of globalization, a more nuanced and surprising appreciation of the making and remaking of geography might yet be possible.

NOTES

Acknowledgments: This essay began as a thought paper for the 1997 Histories of the Future Seminar at the University of California Humanities Research Institute. I thank the participants of that seminar for their suggestions and encouragement. It was resurrected for a University of California at Santa Cruz environmental politics study group in 1998; my thanks also go to the members of that group. I rewrote the essay for both the Institute of Advanced Study's volume on 25 years of social science and *Cultural Anthropology*. In that long process, I am particularly thankful for the comments of Arjun Appadurai, Kathryn Chetkovich, Timothy Choy, James Clifford, Paulla Ebron, Donna Haraway, Celia Lowe, Vicente Rafael, Annelise Riles, Lisa Rofel, Roger Rouse, Shiho Satsuka, Joan Scott, Dan Segal, Sylvia Yanagisako, and the anonymous reviewers of *Cultural Anthropology*. Their criticisms and suggestions have invigorated my writing even when I have not been able to fully incorporate them.

1 The image of sitting on top of the globe, either with one's body or one's technology, has become a mainstay of advertising. As I write this, for example, I have just received two telephone company advertisements: one, from a local telephone company (US West), features a woman sitting in an office chair on top of the globe while talking into the telephone and typing on her personal computer; the other, from a long-distance telephone company (MCI), shows a telephone receiver resting on top of the globe. This globe is a field to be mastered, managed, and controlled.

2 Garb (1990) argues that the image of the globe also brought with it political understandings about white male mastery and control; environmentalists have fought against these understandings in stressing the fragility of the earth but have also been influenced by them.

3 A fuller genealogy of the idea of globalization – whether in corporate policy, social commentary, or academic analysis – is beyond the scope of this essay. New books and articles appear on the subject every week. The inclusively imagined *Globalization Reader* (Lechner and Boli 2000) reprints a number of social science contributions to the conversation, offering a sense of its heterogeneity and breadth. Of the recent anthologies I have seen, I find *Globalisation and the Asia Pacific* (Olds et al. 1999) the most sensible and insightful.

4 Saskia Sassen nicely articulates this analytic choice, necessary to make globalization a significant field-defining process: "My approach entails...constructing 'the difference,' theoretically and empirically, so as to specify the current period" (1998: 85). She adds, frankly, "I do not deny the existence of many continuities, but my effort has been to understand the strategic discontinuities" (p. 101).

5 I take the notion of the building of a "bandwagon" effect from Joan Fujimura's (1988) work on cancer research.

6 For example, discussion of globalization has stimulated a rethinking of area studies scholarship in the United States; research and teaching programs are being revamped not only at many universities but also at many of the major research institutes and funding foundations. (See, for example, Abraham and Kassimir 1997 on the Social Science Research Council and Volkman 1998 on the Ford Foundation.) This rethinking allows promising new configurations of training and scholarship. At the same time, the national discussion about area studies illustrates the problems I refer to in describing the limitations of the dogma of global newness. Too many participants, asked to rethink areas in the light of globalization, jump to the conclusion that "areas" are archaic forms beset and overcome by newly emergent global forces. Scholarship, many conclude, should either position itself with the winners, studying global forces, or with the losers, attending to regional resistance. In this configuration of choice, no attention is paid to the continually shifting formation and negotiation of "areas," the consideration of which might have been the most exciting product of the rethinking of area studies.

7 Mintz (1998) argues in this spirit, reminding anthropologists that massive transcontinental migrations have occurred in past centuries. He suggests, provocatively, that scholars

find global migration new because large waves of people of color have recently turned up in the "big white societies" of Europe and its diaspora, where, in the nineteenth century, they were refused (p. 123).

8 In their first waves of enthusiasm about globalization, many scholars, social commentators, and policy makers argued that it was forcing nations to disappear. This remains perhaps the most popular argument (see, for example, Appadurai 1996; Miyoshi 1996). More recently, a number of scholars have argued that the nation-state takes new forms in the context of rapid international transfers of capital and labor (e.g., Ong 1997; Sassen 1998). Even the most rapidly mobile of corporations depends on the apparatus of the nation-state to guarantee its property and contracts; in this context, national deregulation reregulates the economic domain in the interest of global capital (Cerny 1993). Nation-states have also been instrumental in forging niches of ethnic and national privilege through which the new "global" entrepreneurs secure their advantage. For these kinds of arguments in particular, an appreciation of the shifting histories of the nation and of the hegemonies of particular nation-states – as I advocate here – seems essential.

9 This set of post-World War II nationalist commitments was brought to my attention in the insightful comments of Malaysian economist Jomo K. S. at the conference "Public Intellectuals in Southeast Asia," in Kuala Lumpur, May 1998. As an example, he pointed out that histories in which nationalism in Southeast Asia was stimulated by conversations with overseas Chinese (e.g., Pramoedya 1996) were suppressed by post-World War II Southeast Asian nations.

10 See also Lowe and Lloyd 1997 and Wilson and Dissanayake 1996a.

11 Why is globalization a new era (rather than, say, an object of reflection or an approach to appreciating culture) for these humanists? Some have come to their acceptance of cultural evolutionary stages from a slightly earlier exploration of "postmodernism" as the latest stage of cultural development; for them, globalization is a variation on postmodern culture. For some, too, the appeal of imagining globalization as a stage of cultural politics is drawn from Marxist evolutionary histories of capitalism; the cultural era is generated by the economic era as superstructure to base. For others, the main appeal seems to be the intervention into earlier civilization-bound humanities studies: the opportunity to draw together a diverse group of scholars who can talk to each other across lines of nation, language, and cultural background. Indeed, I see little evidence that most of the contributors to these volumes are themselves particularly invested in positing a singular global era; even the editors, in their separate articles, contribute to a much more nuanced approach. It seems there is something about introductory material that stimulates era making. There is also an admirable political goal in gathering a diverse group under a common banner: Perhaps a politically united front against unregulated corporate expansion can be formed. However, this political cause can only be aided by building an appreciation of the multiple and conflicting agendas of globalization.

12 Jameson and Miyoshi 1998 does not include an editors' introduction. In lieu of an introduction, the preface and the contributions by the two editors, however, offer the reader a sense of the editors' stakes and stand in that regard.

13 A number of the contributors, including the editors themselves, offer insightful descriptions of the coming together and coming apart of varied agendas of "globalization"; they describe the scope and the exclusions of varied transnational projects; they ask about the legacies and transformational possibilities of various global interconnections. But these kinds of insights are lost in those parts of the editors' introductions that condense this richness into the definitional homogeneity of a new era.

14 Riles's analysis is not a naive celebration of the possibilities of networks for global feminism. In fact, she emphasizes the strangeness of the object the women she studied called a "network." It did not, for example, include their ordinary collegial social

relationships; it was a formal design more suited for documents and diagrams than for everyday living. My goal in contrasting Riles's NGO networks and Rouse's corporate ones is not to show what Jameson would call the light and the dark side of globalization. Instead, from my perspective these are both curious ethnographic objects, and I am interested in how they are produced and maintained, separately and together, in the same world.

15 My comments are not meant as a criticism of the kind of analysis that shows how cosmopolitan ideas and institutions are translated and specified as they come to mean something in particular communities. To the contrary, I would like to see the extension of this kind of work to show the cultural specification of the cosmopolitan.

16 George Marcus makes Harvey's argument about accumulation the basis for his call for new research methods in anthropology:

For those across disciplines interested in placing their specific projects of research in the unfolding of new arrangements for which past historical narratives were not fully adequate, a firm sense of a world system framework was replaced by various accounts of dissolution, fragmentation, as well as new processes – captured in concepts like "post-Fordism" [Harvey], "time-space compression" [Harvey], "flexible specialization" [Harvey], "the end of organized capitalism" [Lash, Urry], and most recently "globalization" [Featherstone, Hannerz, Sklair] – none of which could be fully understood in terms of earlier macro-models of the capitalist world system. (1995: 98; I have substituted the names of authors for the numbered references included in the original.)

Michael Kearney brings up time and space:

The most cogent and comprehensive analysis of changing images of time and space associated with globalization is Harvey's [1989]. Although not dealing with globalization per se, Harvey's thesis is that a marked acceleration in a secular trend of time-space compression in capitalist political economy is central to current cultural change. (1995: 551)

Kearney usefully calls it a thesis; more often Harvey is mentioned to establish a fact.

17 There is also the suggestion that Culture can provide an aesthetic blueprint for the economy (e.g., Harvey 1989: 345).

18 Appadurai begins this comparison in his chapter "Patriotism and Its Futures" (1996: 168–72). However, he is interested in convergences between multicultural and postnational commitments. His goal is to mobilize a forward-looking form of postnationalism, not to assess the contrasts among groups with varied histories of dependence on and opposition to nation-states.

19 While Kearney appears to draw on a theory of capitalist stages in his review article (1995), in his book (1996), he refutes the centrality of capitalist accumulation strategies as producing historical stages. Yet his arguments are completely dependent on the eras he posits, which neatly join scholarly theory and world history. Because he rejects forms of economic, cultural, and historical logic that might generate these all-encompassing eras, I am not sure how they might appear in such a world-hegemonic form.

20 Some globalist anthropologists conflate the excitement of new postlocal approaches in anthropology and that of new developments in the world. But, thus, they weaken the case for each. Global interconnections are not just a new phenomenon, although they certainly have important new features and permutations. If older anthropological frameworks were unable to handle interconnection and mobility, this is a problem with the frame-

works and a reason for new ones but not the mirror of an evolutionary change in the world.

21 Environmental studies has generated its own local globalism. Unlike the globalisms I have been describing, it is not focused on the distinctive features of a future-making epoch. Instead, the most commonly promoted environmental globalism endorses a technical and moral "global" unit. The goal of this environmental globalism is to show the compatibility of all scales into the "global" across all time. (There has been some interest in the kinds of globalisms I have been describing here among environmental scholars, especially social scientists. But to trace the encounter between "globalization" and the technical-moral "global environment" is beyond the scope of this essay.) That "global" domain into which all other scales can be collapsed, across all time, is the domain of agency for global environmental science and activism. Social scientists and historians have been rather disruptive of this global domain, although not always self-consciously, when their descriptions establish the incompatibility of various socially defined spatial scales and historical periods, as nature is made and remade in diverse forms that evade simple conflations. The critical literature on environmental modernization, which I tap here, contributes a sense of the historical and spatial rupture of projects of making nature's modernity. Through this distinctive antiglobalism, it can perhaps offer possibilities for nonglobalist global analyses in a different scholarly conversation, in which we might begin to get around blinding endorsements of futurism, conflation, and circulation.

22 Worster's overriding theoretical interest in framing this book is the relationship of irrigation and state power. My discussion here turns instead to his fascinating account of irrigation history.

23 The power and dilemmas of arguing for diversity are illustrated in Albert Paolini's (1995) insightful review of the intersections between postcolonial literary studies and globalization in sociology. Paolini argues provocatively that the overhomogenization of the Third World in postcolonial studies has led to the ease with which globalist sociologists formulate unitary frameworks of modernist progress. But he cannot give up on these frameworks even as he argues against them – despite the fact that they turn Africa into a "nonplace." His alternative involves recognition of agency and ambiguity in African cultural formation. This seems right, but to avoid separate, segregated arguments for every neglected nonplace, we could demand, instead of worldwide modernist globalism, an examination of when, where, and how such frameworks hold sway.

24 In Tsing 2000, I explore one case of the specificity of international finance in relation to other "scale-making" claims.

REFERENCES

Abraham, Itty, and Ronald Kassimir
    1997   Internationalization of the Social Sciences and Humanities. *Items* 51(2–3): 23–30.
Anderson, Warwick
    In press   The Natures of Culture: Environment and Race in the Colonial Tropics. In *Imagination and Distress in Southern Environmental Projects*. Paul Greenough and Anna Tsing, eds.
Appadurai, Arjun
    1986   Introduction: Commodities and the Politics of Value. In *The Social Life of Things*. Arjun Appadurai, ed. Pp. 3–63. Cambridge: Cambridge University Press.
    1996   *Modernity at Large: Cultural Dimensions of Globalization*. Minneapolis: University of Minnesota.

Appiah, Kwame Anthony, and Henry Louis Gates, eds.
  1997   *The Dictionary of Global Culture*. New York: Knopf.
Baudrillard, Jean
  1975   *The Mirror of Production*. Mark Poster, trans. St. Louis: Telos Press.
Brosius, Peter
  1999   Green Dots, Pink Hearts: Displacing Politics from the Malaysian Rain Forest.
    American Anthropologist 101(1): 36–57.
  In press   The Forest and the Nation: Negotiating Citizenship in Sarawak, East Malaysia. In
    Cultural Citizenship in Southeast Asia. Renato Rosaldo, ed. Berkeley: University of
    California Press.
Cerny, Philip
  1993   The Deregulation and Re-Regulation of Financial Markets in a More Open World.
    In *Finance and World Politics*. Philip Cerny, ed. Pp. 51–85. Aldershot: Edward Elgar.
Chomsky, Noam
  1998   Free Trade and Free Market: Pretense and Practice. In *The Cultures of Globalization*.
    Frederic Jameson and Masao Miyoshi, eds. Pp. 356–70. Durham: Duke University Press.
Clifford, James
  1997   *Routes: Travel and Translation in the Late Twentieth Century*. Cambridge, MA:
    Harvard University Press.
Dauvergne, Peter
  1997   *Shadows in the Forest: Japan and the Politics of Timber in Southeast Asia*. Cam-
    bridge, MA: MIT Press.
Ebron, Paulla
  1998   Regional Differences in African American Culture. *American Anthropologist*
    100(1): 94–106.
  1999   Tourists as Pilgrims. *American Ethnologist* 26(4): 910–32.
Escobar, Arturo
  1995   *Encountering Development: The Making and Unmaking of the Third World*. Prin-
    ceton: Princeton University Press.
Ferguson, James
  1990   *The Anti-Politics Machine: "Development," Depoliticization, and Bureaucratic
    Power in Lesotho*. Cambridge: Cambridge University Press.
Fujimura, Joan
  1988   The Molecular Biological Bandwagon in Cancer Research: Where Social Worlds
    Meet. *Social Problems* 35(3): 261–84.
Garb, Yaakov
  1990   Perspective or Escape? Ecofeminist Musings on Contemporary Earth Imagery. In
    Reweaving the World: The Emergence of Ecofeminism. Irene Diamond and Gloria
    Orenstein, eds. Pp. 264–308. San Francisco: Sierra Club Books.
Gibson-Graham, J. K.
  1996   *The End of Capitalism (As We Knew It)*. Cambridge, MA: Blackwell Publishers.
Grove, Richard
  1995   *Green Imperialism*. Cambridge: Cambridge University Press.
Guha, Ramachandra
  1989   *The Unquiet Woods*. Berkeley: University of California Press.
Gupta, Akhil, and James Ferguson
  1992   Beyond "Culture": Space, Identity, and the Politics of Difference. *Cultural Anthro-
    pology* 7(1): 6–23.
Haas, Peter
  1990   *Saving the Mediterranean: The Politics of International Environmental Coopera-
    tion*. New York: Columbia University Press.

1992 Introduction: Epistemic Communities and International Policy Coordination. *International Organization* 46(1): 1–35.

Hannerz, Ulf
1989 Notes on the Global Ecumene. *Public Culture* 1(2): 66–75.
1996 *Transnational Connections*. New York: Routledge.

Harvey, David
1989 *The Condition of Postmodernity*. Cambridge, MA: Blackwell Publishers.

Hecht, Suzannah, and Alexander Cockburn
1989 *The Fate of the Forest: Developers, Destroyers, and Defenders of the Amazon*. New York: Verso.

Helleiner, Eric
1993 When Finance was the Servant: International Capital Movements in the Bretton Woods Order. In *Finance and World Politics*. Philip Cerny, ed. Pp. 20–48. Aldershot: Edward Elgar.

Jameson, Fredric
1998a Notes on Globalization as a Philosophical Issue. In *The Cultures of Globalization*. Frederic Jameson and Masao Miyoshi, eds. Pp. 54–77. Durham: Duke University Press.
1998b Preface. In *The Cultures of Globalization*. Frederic Jameson and Masao Miyoshi, eds. Pp. xi–xvii. Durham: Duke University Press.

Jameson, Fredric, and Masao Miyoshi, eds.
1998 *The Cultures of Globalization*. Durham: Duke University Press.

Kearney, Michael
1995 The Local and the Global: The Anthropology of Globalization and Transnationalism. *Annual Review of Anthropology* 24: 547–65.
1996 *Reconceptualizing the Peasantry: Anthropology in Global Perspective*. Boulder: Westview Press.

Keck, Margaret
1995 Social Equity and Environmental Politics in Brazil: Lessons from the Rubber Tappers of Acre. *Comparative Politics* 27(4): 409–25.

Keck, Margaret, and Kathryn Sikkink
1998 *Activists Beyond Borders*. Ithaca, NY: Cornell University Press.

Lechner, Frank, and John Boli, eds.
2000 *The Globalization Reader*. Oxford: Blackwell Publishers.

Lowe, Lisa, and David Lloyd, eds.
1997 *The Politics of Culture in the Shadow of Capital*. Durham: Duke University Press.

Marcus, George
1992 Introduction. In *Rereading Cultural Anthropology*. George Marcus, ed. Pp. vii–xiv. Durham: Duke University Press.
1995 Ethnography in/of the World System: The Emergence of Multi-Sited Ethnography. *Annual Review of Anthropology* 24: 95–117.

Mintz, Sidney
1998 The Localization of Anthropological Practice: From Area Studies to Transnationalism. *Critique of Anthropology* 18(2): 117–33.

Miyoshi, Masao
1996 A Borderless World? From Colonialism to Transnationalism and the Decline of the Nation-State. In *Global/Local: Cultural Production and the Transnational Imaginary*. Rob Wilson and Wimal Dissanayake, eds. Pp. 78–106. Durham: Duke University Press.

Olds, Kris, Peter Dicken, Philip Kelly, Lily Kong, and Henry Wai-Chung Yeung, eds.
1999 *Globalisation and the Asia Pacific*. London: Routledge.

Ong, Aihwa

  1997   Chinese Modernities: Narratives of National and of Capitalism. In *Ungrounded Empires: The Cultural Politics of Modern Chinese Transnationalism*. Aihwa Ong and Donald Nonini, eds. Pp. 171–202. New York: Routledge.

  1999   *Flexible Citizenship: The Cultural Logics of Transnationality*. Durham: Duke University Press.

Paolini, Albert

  1995   The Place of Africa in Discourses about the Postcolonial, the Global, and the Modern. *New Formations* 31 (summer): 83–106.

Peters, Pauline

  1994   *Dividing the Commons: Politics, Policy, and Culture in Botswana*. Charlottesville: University Press of Virginia.

Pigg, Stacey

  1992   Constructing Social Categories through Place: Social Representations and Development in Nepal. *Comparative Studies in Society and History* 34(3): 491–513.

Pramoedya Ananta Toer

  1996   *Child of All Nations*. Max Lane, trans. New York: Penguin.

Pred, Allan, and Michael Watts

  1992   *Reworking Modernity: Capitalism and Symbolic Discontent*. New Brunswick, NJ: Rutgers University Press.

Rajan, Ravi

  1994   Imperial Environmentalism. Ph.D. dissertation, University of Oxford.

Riles, Annelise

  1998a   Infinity within Brackets. *American Ethnologist* 25(3): 1–21.

  1998b   The Network Inside Out: Designs for a Global Reality. Paper presented at the Department of Anthropology, University of California at Santa Cruz.

Rouse, Roger

  1997   "There Will Be No More There": Globalization, Privatization, and the Family Form in the U.S. Corporate Imaginary. Unpublished MS, Department of Anthropology, University of California at Davis.

Sassen, Saskia

  1998   *Globalization and Its Discontents*. New York: The New Press.

Schiller, Nina Glick, Linda Basch, and Cristina Szanton Blanc, eds.

  1992   *Towards a Transnational Perspective on Migration: Race, Class, Ethnicity, and Nationalism Reconsidered*. New York: New York Academy of Sciences.

Schmink, Marianne, and Charles Wood

  1992   *Contested Frontiers in Amazonia*. New York: Columbia University Press.

Sivaramakrishnan, K.

  1996   Forest Politics and Governance in Bengal, 1794–1994. Ph.D. dissertation, Yale University.

Taylor, Peter, and Frederick Buttel

  1992   How Do We Know We Have Global Environmental Problems? Science and the Globalization of Environmental Discourse. *Geoforum* 23(3): 405–16.

Tsing, Anna

  1999a   Becoming a Tribal Elder, and Other Green Development Fantasies. In *Transforming the Indonesian Uplands*. Tania Li, ed. Pp. 159–202. London: Harwood Academic Press.

  1999b   Finding Our Differences Is the Beginning Not the End of Our Work. In *Culturally Conflicting Views of Nature*. Working Paper Series, Discussion Paper 3. Kent Redford, ed. Gainesville, FL: Conservation Development Forum.

1999c   *Notes on Culture and Natural Resource Management.* Berkeley Workshop on Environmental Politics, Working Paper WP99–4, Institute of International Studies, University of California at Berkeley.

2000   Inside the Economy of Appearances. *Public Culture* 12(1): 115–44.

Turner, Terrence

1999   Indigenous Rights, Indigenous Cultures, and Environmental Conservation: Convergence or Divergence? The Case of the Brazilian Kayapo. In *Earth, Air, Fire, Water.* Jill Conway, Kenneth Kenniston, and Leo Marx, eds. pp. 145–69. Amherst: University of Massachusetts Press.

Volkman, Toby

1998   *Crossing Borders: The Case for Area Studies.* Ford Foundation Report (winter): 28–9.

Wilson, Rob, and Wimal Dissanayake, eds.

1996a   *Global/Local: Cultural Production and the Transnational Imaginary.* Durham: Duke University Press.

1996b   Introduction: Tracking the Global/Local. In *Global/Local: Cultural Production and the Transnational Imaginary.* Rob Wilson and Wimal Dissanayake, eds. Pp. 1–18. Durham: Duke University Press.

Worster, Donald

1985   *Rivers of Empire.* New York: Oxford University Press.

Index